Now Read This III

Genreflecting Advisory Series

Diana Tixier Herald, Series Editor

Read the High Country: A Guide to Western Books and Films
John Mort

Graphic Novels: A Genre Guide to Comic Books, Manga, and More
Michael Pawuk

Genrefied Classics: A Guide to Reading Interests in Classic Literature
Tina Frolund

Encountering Enchantment: A Guide to Speculative Fiction for Teens
Susan Fichtelberg

Fluent in Fantasy: The Next Generation
Diana Tixier Herald and Bonnie Kunzel

Gay, Lesbian, Bisexual, and Transgendered Literature: A Genre Guide
Ellen Bosman and John Bradford; Edited by Robert B. Ridinger

Reality Rules!: A Guide to Teen Nonfiction Reading Interests
Elizabeth Fraser

Historical Fiction II: A Guide to the Genre
Sarah L. Johnson

Hooked on Horror III
Anthony J. Fonseca and June Michele Pulliam

Caught Up in Crime: A Reader's Guide to Crime Fiction and Nonfiction
Gary Warren Niebuhr

Latino Literature: A Guide to Reading Interests
Edited by Sara E. Martínez

Teen Chick Lit: A Guide to Reading Interests
Christine Meloni

Now Read This III

A Guide to Mainstream Fiction

Nancy Pearl and Sarah Statz Cords

Genreflecting Advisory Series

 LIBRARIES UNLIMITED

AN IMPRINT OF ABC-CLIO, LLC
Santa Barbara, California • Denver, Colorado • Oxford, England

Library of Congress Cataloging-in-Publication Data

Pearl, Nancy.
  Now read this III : a guide to mainstream fiction / Nancy Pearl and Sarah Statz Cords.
      p. cm. — (Genreflecting advisory series)
  Includes bibliographical references and index.
  ISBN 978-1-59158-570-1 (hardcover : acid-free paper) 1. Fiction—
20th century—Bibliography. 2. Fiction—20th century—Stories, plots, etc.—
Indexes. 3. Best books. I. Cords, Sarah Statz, 1974- II. Title. III. Title:
Now read this 3. IV. Title: Now read this three.
  Z5916.P43   2010
  [PN3503]
  016.80883'04—dc22   2009049898

ISBN: 978-1-59158-570-1

14 13 12 11 10   1 2 3 4 5

This book is also available on the World Wide Web as an eBook.
Visit www.abc-clio.com for details.

Libraries Unlimited
An Imprint of ABC-CLIO, LLC

ABC-CLIO, LLC
130 Cremona Drive, P.O. Box 1911
Santa Barbara, California 93116-1911

This book is printed on acid-free paper ∞™
Manufactured in the United States of America

Contents

Acknowledgments..vii

Introduction by Nancy Pearl ix
Introduction by Sarah Statz Cords xi

1—Setting 1

2—Story 47

3—Character 97

4—Language 193

Appendix A: Bridges to Genre Fiction.................................261
Appendix B: Book Awards 269
Appendix C: Resources 275
Appendix D: How to Create a Dynamic Book Club.............283

Author/Title Index..289
Subject Index...341

Acknowledgments

It has been such an honor to contribute to this volume. For this honor I owe my most heartfelt thanks to Nancy Pearl, on whose expertise and love of reading I relied, and who never failed to come up with great read-alike suggestions no matter how specific my desperate e-mails: "Can you suggest any novels with feisty teenage heroines, maybe some of which include flashbacks?"

The professionals and readers at Libraries Unlimited continue to astound me with their dedication to reading, readers, readers' advisors, and authors (particularly authors with more nebulous understandings of the term "deadline"). I would particularly like to thank Barbara Ittner for her title and read-alike suggestions and her editing prowess; Laura Calderone for her continuing dedication to the *Reader's Advisor Online* database; Diana Tixier Herald for her inspiration through the Genreflecting series; and Emma Bailey and Sharon DeJohn for their production and copyediting work.

It has also been my very great pleasure to work with and know such a wide variety of dedicated readers and readers' advisors, both inside libraries and outside of them. You know who you are—thank you. Come to town; we'll go to breakfast and talk books, my treat.

As always, thank you to my family, specifically to my parents, Roman and Jean Statz (readers both, and two of my favorite readers to foist books on—Dad, I'm still surprised you didn't like Ray Bradbury's *Something Wicked This Way Comes*, but I'll try to find something you like better). And, of course, thank you to Kevin, who is too unassuming to ever mention the countless things for which this author owes him her endless gratitude.

Introduction

Nancy Pearl

When I worked on the very first *Now Read This* (NRT) with Chris Higashi and Martha Knappe (now Martha Bayley) in the late 1990s, the world of readers' advisory was very different than it is today. For the most part, if they existed at all, online RA tools were in their infancy. The two iconic RA books—studied by librarians who wanted to help their library patrons find their next good book—were Joyce Saricks and Nancy Brown's *Reader's Advisory Service in the Public Library* (the first edition was published in 1997) and Betty Rosenberg and Diana Herald's *Genreflecting*. And that was pretty much that.

But then, little by little, RA became seen as being central to library services. (In the minds of many of us, of course, it always was central; we were all just swept away—against our will—in the tsunami of information access via computer technology.) In their groundbreaking book, Saricks and Brown came up with the appealing (couldn't resist that) notion of "appeal characteristics," defining them as those factors that drew a reader to a particular book. It occurred to me that it would be very interesting to see if we could somehow simplify the long list of possible appeal characteristics and classify nongenre, or, as we called it in the subtitle of *NRT*, "mainstream" fiction, according to what I think are the four major appeals: story, character, setting, and language.

In the introduction to *NRT*, I offered working definitions for each of these four appeals, and, reading over the definitions more than a decade later, I don't see much that I would change or amend. However, as a result of teaching RA classes at the University of Washington ISchool, as well as my obsessive (some might say) musings about books and reading—and putting someone together with his or her next "good" book—I have come to think in terms of "doorways," rather than in terms of "appeal characteristics." It seems to me to be an excellent, and intuitive, description of what happens when we read a book—we enter the world that the author has created through one of those four doorways. For me, it's always been less what the book is about, than what it is about the book that drew a reader to it, and I find "doorways" a comfortable and useful metaphor to use in doing RA work.

I am thrilled to be sharing the authorship of this book with Sarah Statz Cords, someone for whom I have enormous respect, both as a reader and as a writer. With young librarians like Sarah in our profession, writing, reading, and interacting with library patrons, I am confident that our understanding of why people enjoy the books they do—and how we can help them find those books—will only deepen.

Introduction

Sarah Statz Cords

In the opening of *Now Read This II*, Nancy Pearl speaks to the timeless allure of fiction, stating that "if you are a dedicated fiction reader, you already know that the pleasures and rewards of reading fiction are plentiful" (Pearl 2002, ix). Although the jury is still out on just how much reading is being done and why—the National Education Association thinks reading is at risk, whereas the Book Industry Study Group found that "total book sales rose 1.0% in 2008, to $40.3 billion" (Milliot 2009, 5) helped by sales of digital books—what an unmitigated pleasure it is to hear that reading should be, and is, above all else an activity that results in pleasures and rewards.

Increasingly, those who are tasked with helping readers find books they enjoy (readers' advisory librarians, collection developers, bookstore employees, circulation and other front-line service staff) are caught between two opposing forces: the huge number of books being published, even in the trying economic times at the end of the new millennium's first decade, and the increasingly compressed time available for advisors and staff at all levels to both help patrons and further their own knowledge and training. Very few people in the business of suggesting books have sufficient time, especially on the job, to study the books and genres that, to some extent, many patrons who approach them for help expect them to be experts on. Keeping up with authors who fit into popular and recognizable genres (Lee Child and his thriller series featuring Jack Reacher; Nora Roberts's romances; Stephen King's horror novels) can be difficult enough, but when we consider authors and titles that are more difficult to classify (does Jodi Picoult write women's fiction? Mainstream fiction? Commercial fiction?) and allow for the recent trend of genreblending (was Diana Gabaldon's *Outlander* pure romance? Historical fiction? Historical fantasy? Alternate world fantasy? Answers: yes, yes, yes, and yes.), becoming proficient in a wide variety of more mainstream fiction titles can be an intimidating proposition. And even if, as an advisor, you address all those issues, you're only halfway home: there's still the entire nonfiction half of the library!

But we are readers ourselves, and we are also professionals who always want to help people find books and reading they will enjoy. So we must continue to learn everything we can about fiction, and consider which authors will appeal to readers who like certain authors, and which books remind us of other books, and how we can start to make connections using all of that information and the reference sources available to us.

What Is Mainstream Fiction?

For our purposes, mainstream fiction comprises all those novels (and short story collections) that do not easily conform to any genre classifications. Generally, they are found in the "general fiction" or simply "fiction" sections of bookstores and libraries. Although some of the novels included in this volume could arguably be classified under different genre headings—most notably historical and women's fiction—these are primarily books that will appeal to readers through their character development, or prose styles, rather than for their conformity to genre conventions. (Another notable example of this conundrum is mainstream novels that have elements of romance in their plots; although some general fiction is undeniably romantic, readers of more stereotypical romance novels, which guarantee happy endings, might be surprised to find romantic fiction novels offer no such guarantee.)

The phrase "mainstream fiction" can also be a bit misleading; what is genre writer James Patterson if not "mainstream," in that he appeals to a broad cross-section of readers? However, the titles selected for this collection tend to hew a bit more closely to the troublesome "literary fiction" category. I say "troublesome" because "literary" is one of those loaded terms that immediately sidetracks readers from discussions of books and stories to discussions of the literary merits of those books. Readers often resist referring to authors they don't care for as "literary," preferring to save that label for authors they do love and who they feel conform to higher stylistic subjects.

Of course, some authors (e.g., John Updike, Philip Roth, Alice Munro) consistently receive acclaim in the most highly regarded of review sources and are largely agreed to be "literary" writers, but such distinctions become less clear-cut with authors whose styles or subjects leave the critics with more room for interpretation. Is Anne Tyler literary fiction? Is Alice Hoffman? Because it is not really our intent with this collection to start arguments or to become invested in arguing the literary merits of various authors, we use the heading "mainstream fiction" in part to give us a little bit of wiggle room on authors we included.

The Appeals Approach

Because mainstream fiction is generally more difficult than genre fiction to "categorize" and describe, this guide organizes titles according to their "appeal factors," which Joyce Saricks has described as those elements that "describe more accurately the 'feel' of a book" (Saricks 2005, 41). Although the types of appeal factors used by readers' advisors to help their patrons find books they might enjoy differ from practitioner to practitioner, and from theorist to theorist, the four appeal characteristics that Nancy Pearl settled on for her first two volumes of this book are **Setting**, **Story**, **Character**, and **Language**. (Saricks, by way of contrast, often uses the appeal factors pacing, characterization, story line, and frame to describe a book's essential "feel.") Readers and advisors often articulate their own ideas of what factors and characteristics of books appeal to readers; but largely for consistency with the previous two volumes (in the hope that all three can be used together), we have continued to use the four-appeal structure. Of course, this is only one way—of many—to approach the understanding and organization of mainstream novels.

A primary appeal characteristic has been chosen for each title, and that is the chapter in which it appears, although secondary characteristics have been chosen for many of the titles as well and are noted in the annotation. You may not always agree with us about where novels are categorized; in fact, we encourage that kind of questioning. I have always believed that discussing books and their attributes is the best way to get to know them, and if you feel strongly that Barbara Kingsolver's novel *Prodigal Summer* should be considered a character-centered read rather than one characterized by its setting, feel free to suggest it to fans of other character-centered novels that seem similar to you. In other words, this approach and categorization is only a starting point for thinking about novels, what they are about, and why they might (or might not) appeal to readers.

So why bother to categorize the books at all, you may ask, if we are going to encourage alternate categorizations? First of all, we categorize because it gives us a basis for starting to learn and compare mainstream fiction titles with a bit more nuance than simply referring to them as "mainstream," "literary," "popular," "general," "commercial," or even " 'good' versus 'bad.' " Second, even though subject matter may be a consideration for readers when choosing fiction (readers with an interest in British history, for instance, might consider a wide variety of novels, historical fiction, and even fantasy works set in Great Britain or making use of Celtic and other British mythologies), it is often not the main consideration for readers making their choices, and we need some form of alternative classification system. Last, but certainly not least, we have chosen to group books according to appeal factors because it has been long recognized that books sharing appeal factors can often serve as good "read-alikes" for one another, regardless of subject. It is true that, as Neil Hollands has suggested, "the language of appeal, when used correctly, attempts to describe the complex totality of a given reader's preference" (2007, 129). Thus, we would like to continue the tradition of using familiar vocabulary in the service of helping readers find books that are similar according to their emphasis on character, setting, language, or story.

Even as our RA focus moves from understanding and categorizing books to trying to better understand readers, continuing to study what it is about certain genres, titles, and authors that really appeals to readers continues to be of value to us—it helps us better develop our subject and book expertise. Nancy Pearl really said it best in her introduction to *Now Read This II*, when she stated that the purpose of these readers' guides is to "facilitate the process of finding something else to read and easily guide readers from one book to another along the meandering and ever-enlarging path of their own interests." (Pearl 2002, xi). Each of the four main appeal factors we have used to categorize books in this volume is described more fully at the beginning of the corresponding chapter, but brief descriptions are also included here:

- **Setting:** In books with Setting as their primary appeal factor, the place or time of the story is essential to understanding character, conflict, or theme. A novel that appeals to readers largely because of its setting or its author's skill in describing the setting is sometimes one in which the setting very nearly functions as a central character.

- **Story:** When Story is the primary doorway through which readers access a novel, the reader can be assured that the plot and the pacing dominate the reading experience. Descriptions of these books focus heavily on the events of the novel, with considerations of other attributes, such as character, often of secondary concern.

- **Character:** Books that are Character-driven feature three-dimensional characters who almost seem to step off the page. When readers describe these novels to us, they often start with the people in the novels—"I just felt really close to the characters," "I felt like I knew the characters," or other similar phrases might be used when advisors ask readers to articulate what they loved about certain books.

- **Language:** In books that appeal because of their authors' mastery of Language, the authors tell their stories and describe their characters and settings with writing that is noted for its skillful construction and style. The authors' use of language in these books can be evocative, unusual, thought-provoking, or poetic.

Now perhaps is a good a time to interject that none of this, even the professional jargon of "appeal factors," is set in stone. Even the terminology is up for debate; Nancy Pearl, for example, now refers to these factors (or characteristics, or aspects) as "doorways" into and between similar fiction (and even nonfiction!) titles. In her introduction she explains her reasoning for using the term "doorways." It is outside the scope of this guide to offer an in-depth discussion of the terminology used by both writers of professional library literature and front-line practitioners. However, plenty of other wonderful books and articles are available on that subject (and many are listed in appendix C).

Suffice it to say that engaging in those types of conversations or debates can only help our understanding of our own reading tastes—and those of our patrons—so although we will not embark on such a discussion here, we encourage you to do so in professional development trainings and meetings, as well as on library practice and readers' advisory Web sites and blogs. It bears repeating that the four primary appeal factors referred to in this guide are just a starting point for the deeper understanding and appreciation of mainstream fiction in all its legion forms and styles.

The Selection Process

As was done in *Now Read This II*, we have annotated slightly more than 500 general fiction titles available in English in this collection. These are all new titles, none of which were covered in the previous two editions, generally published between 2002 (when *Now Read This II* was published) and 2009 (when this collection is going to press). Short story collections are included as well as full-length novels.

Likewise, as in previous editions, the annual Notable Books lists produced by the American Library Association were the starting point; all of the books that received that honor for the years 2002–2009 are included. Joyce Saricks has noted that readers of literary fiction "always appreciate lists of award-winning titles and authors" (Saricks 2009, 184). Therefore, we have also included titles that were named New York Times Notable books, and the majority of those titles that have won the major awards, including the National Book Award, National Book Critics Circle Award, Pulitzer Prize, the Booker Prize, the IMPAC/Dublin Award, the Whitbread/Costa award, and a sampling of other international awards (such as the Sapir Prize, an Israeli prize, and the New South Wales (Australia) Premier Literary Awards.

We also strove to find and include books that were not prize winners, but that had garnered significant press and critical attention. Because multicultural issues and characters have become more popular subjects for novels, as have more far-flung locales, we have increased the number of books that were written in foreign languages and translated into English (such books have the tag "books in translation," which is also an entry in the subject index). We also made an effort to find and include "buzz" books, particularly those that have proven popular with book clubs. And finally, we included a number of books that may not have been prize winners or darlings of the literati press, but which we loved and wanted to share with you (e.g., P. F. Kluge's *Gone Tomorrow*, I'm looking at you.)

We have not included novels that align closely with more recognizable genres, feeling that genre guides are more useful for gathering such titles (more "traditional" works of historical fiction, for example, as opposed to "literary" historical fiction, can be found in Sarah Johnson's excellent guides *Historical Fiction: A Guide to the Genre* and *Historical Fiction II*). We have also not included very many graphic novels, as they have yet to make the large inroads into mainstream fiction market that they are charting into fantasy fiction, and even nonfiction, as Rick Geary's true crime graphic novels and David Small's graphic novel memoir *Stitches* prove. This collection showcases fiction; nonfiction titles are only included as read-alikes and related reads in the "Now Try" section of the annotations, and periodically in themed title lists designed to help readers and readers' advisors make connections between fiction and nonfiction books.

How to Use This Book

As noted previously, the mainstream titles in this collection have been grouped together according to their primary appeal characteristics of Setting, Story, Character, or Language. Books in each section are arranged alphabetically by the author's last name. Each annotation includes the title, author, bibliographic information, an annotation, and a list of numerous **Subjects** that we have assigned. Although many of these subjects roughly correspond with Dewey Decimal and Library of Congress Subject Headings (and describe straightforward attributes such as the geographic location in which a book is set, or the broad topic of the book), we have tried to make them reflect more informal and everyday language and terms. A number of them are also intended to give readers a better idea of the "feel" of the books in question, including such tags as "Quick Reads" and "Epic Reads" (applied to both books shorter than 250 pages and longer than 600 pages, also when a longer book is a "page-turner," or a shorter book is extremely lugubrious in its pacing or storytelling). Other subject tags that we have applied are "Classics" (books that we anticipate will continue to be read for many years to come), "YA" (books that may particularly appeal to younger adult and teen readers), and "Multicultural" (books in which themes of diversity and other world cultures are explored).

We have also sought to use the Subjects listings as a way to more fully describe the actual structure and attributes of books, including such terms as "First Person," "Multiple Viewpoints," "Men Writing as Women" (and vice versa; in which male authors write from a female character's point of view), "Black Humor" and "Humor," "British Authors" (and a wide variety of other nationalities), and "Flashbacks" (in which much of the narrative is told or revealed by characters relating events that have already happened).

Also included as Subjects are terms that indicate similarities to a wide variety of genres. For example, mainstream fiction titles that include elements of mystery are laneled "Mystery" (also keep an eye out for similar terms, such as Romance, Historical Fiction, Fantasy, Magic Realism, etc.) All of these Subjects are listed in the subject index, which can be used to locate books of possible interest or even to compile book lists of titles that share attributes.

Award-winning titles are identified by the icon 🏵 and include a list of the specific **Awards** after the Subjects section of the annotation. These are also listed in the subject index, so at a glance one can see lists of books that have won the major awards (such as the National Book Awards, the Booker Prize, the Pulitzer Prizes, and the National Book Critics Circle Awards), as well as those books that have been named ALA Notable and New York Times Notable books for the years since 2002.

Each annotation concludes with a **Now Try** section suggesting books that might also appeal to readers who enjoyed the annotated book. These suggestions include both read-alikes (in which books simply have a similar "feel" to the book being described, although they may be on widely divergent subjects) and related reads (in which books, particularly across the fiction/nonfiction divide, are suggested because they cover similar subjects, themes, or background). For example, for Glen David Gold's long-awaited novel *Sunnyside* (about early Hollywood and Charles Chaplin), our Now Try suggestions include read-alike titles by E. L. Doctorow—whose historical fiction titles are on subjects much different than Gold's, but offer a similar "feel" in their length, attention to historical detail, and even cameos by well-known historical figures—as well as related reads such as the nonfiction title *My Autobiography*, by Charles Chaplin himself. These Now Try sections include a wide array of nonfiction as well as fiction suggestions; not only because (I'll admit) I love and am addicted to nonfiction, but also because in the last decade there has been a proliferation of stylistically unique and narrative-driven nonfiction titles published, on a dizzying array of subjects.

The Now Try suggestions are offered in the spirit of getting advisors and readers started thinking about other books, authors, and subjects that might provide avenues for finding similar and other titles they might enjoy. Like this guide itself, they are emphatically not comprehensive (to list all the related reads and read-alikes that might appeal to readers of any given title in this book would make any collection of annotations prohibitively long!), but we did try to suggest several sound avenues for readers' advisors looking to help readers in their search for further reading.

In addition to the annotations and Now Try suggestions, we have provided lists of nonfiction titles under the heading "Now Consider Nonfiction . . ." that may particularly appeal to fiction readers. They are intended to provide more ways to help readers find both fiction and nonfiction titles they might enjoy. In fact, they often follow a title to which they are tangentially related. For example, in the Character chapter, a list of "Artists', Entertainers', and Writers' Biographies" follows the annotation for Slavenka Drakulic's biographical historical fiction novel *Frida's Bed*, based on the life of Frida Kahlo.

There are two indexes at the end of the book. You (and your readers) can use the author/title index to find specific authors and titles of interest. (Titles annotated in this volume, and the page numbers on which those annotations appear, are listed in **boldface** type). The subject index lists all of the Subject terms provided in the annotations; this provides you with access points to the titles by subject heading and the other intangible headings described previously.

The appendixes include a "Genre Bridges" list, in which mainstream titles that might particularly appeal to genre fans are provided; a list of some of the most well-known and popular fiction book awards; a list of suggested resources for learning more about mainstream and literary fiction; and a discussion of how to create a book club.

There are numerous ways to use this book. If you are interested in a certain author or subject, the first place to look is obviously the indexes. Likewise, if you are working with a patron who is looking for books similar to those by his or her favorite authors, not only can you search this book for an author and any annotations and Now Try suggestions we've made for that person, but you can also refer to the broader appeal factor categories surrounding the title. A reader who enjoys Anne Tyler, for example, whose many novels are often considered to have richly drawn characters, might also consider a wide variety of the authors included in our Character chapter. Likewise, if a reader indicates a preference for something a bit different from what he or she has been reading (this happens to me a lot; sometimes I'll read and love a ton of Language novels, but one day I'll just need something a little less stylized and perhaps with a faster pace—something more like a Story-driven read), you could always wander through sections that offer a contrast to what the reader typically chooses. Do you have a reader who normally likes Story-driven reads, but who is looking for something a little different? Some of the titles in the Character or Setting chapters might be suggested, particularly those that include the tag "Quick Reads," which might offer some sort of link to the reader's usual fare.

Likewise, readers who often browse the nonfiction aisles might sometimes be in the mood for fiction; always try to take a moment to discern what a reader liked about a nonfiction title, because it may provide clues for you about which mainstream fiction category to start with (readers of biographies, for example, which are about people's lives, might also consider a wide variety of Character-driven novels; fans of environmental writing classics by Bill McKibben or Wendell Berry might be interested in novels featuring well-described Settings—the possibilities are endless!).

Conclusion

For a long time I considered myself strictly a fiction reader. Then one day I stumbled across Matthew Hart's superlative investigative and natural science title *Diamond: Journey to the Heart of an Obsession*, and a nonfiction addict was born. After this awakening, I avoided the fiction side of the library like the plague, unless someone I knew made a particular recommendation I wanted to follow up on, or a book reviewed at Bookslut.com sounded particularly intriguing, or I was engaging in "comfort reading," re-reading novels I'd read years before. Just like my practical and realistic mother, I'd become a reader who was only interested in a story if it was "true."

But when the chance to work with Nancy Pearl, reader and readers' advisor extraordinaire, came around, I thought how nice it would be to become a fiction reader again. And so I did. And I found that fiction had changed in the years since I had last read it. Or perhaps I had become discerning and demanding enough to finally appreciate the joys of an evocatively described setting, a compellingly told story, a well-drawn character, and a nicely turned bit of prose. Whichever was the case, I found myself reading fiction with a renewed sense of interest and joy, and I hope the books annotated in this collection all bring you and the readers you help the same rewards and pleasures.

Sources

Hollands, Neil. 2007, Winter. "Back to the Future?: A Response to Dilevko and Magowan." *Reference and User Services Quarterly* 47, no. 2: 127–31.

Milliot, Jim. 2009, June. "BISG: Industry Grew 1% in 2008 to $40.3 Billion." *Publishers Weekly* 256, no. 22: 5.

Pearl, Nancy. 2002. *Now Read This II: A Guide to Mainstream Fiction, 1990–2001.* Englewood, CO: Libraries Unlimited.

Saricks, Joyce G. 2005. *Readers' Advisory Service in the Public Library.* 3rd ed. Chicago: ALA Editions.

Saricks, Joyce G. 2009. *The Readers' Advisory Guide to Genre Fiction.* 2nd ed. Chicago: ALA Editions.

Trends in Mainstream Fiction

In Pearl's *Now Read This II*, she discussed several trends in mainstream fiction publishing. I'm thinking of hitting her up for stock tips or even weather predictions, because for the most part the trends she identified then have become an accepted part of the publishing and reading landscape. Back in 2002, she referred to the state of the publishing world as "tumultuous," a word that is only more applicable today. Although the consolidation of smaller presses and imprints under the corporate umbrellas of fewer and fewer but ever-larger companies has very nearly run its course (simply because there are so few independent publishing concerns left to acquire), constant and shifting ownership (now through the selling off of properties or consolidations of imprints) continues to rock the marketplace.

Another publishing trend has affected the way novels (and books of all types) are discovered, reviewed, and discussed in the media. Recent years have seen a massive and disappointing collapse in the number of newspaper sections dedicated to book reviewing and book news. In the space of two years, several national newspaper stand-alone book review sections (e.g., *The Washington Post Book World* and *The Los Angeles Times Book Review*) have ceased publication, and coverage of books as a part of lifestyle and entertainment sections has shrunk. At the same time, the proliferation of lit blogs (blogs that primarily review books or report on book news) has produced, if not always high quality, at least large amounts of often very personal and typically very heartfelt reviews. Some have also developed into sites that pass muster with book critics and are recognized to be "venerable" and "critical organs," including Bookslut, N1BR, The Rumpus, The Elegant Variation, and Bookninja.

Thus, librarians and readers looking for books to read have more resources than ever before in which to read about books, but they must be willing to think outside the newspaper coverage box, and they must be aware that lit blogs vary widely in style, credibility, and just plain readability. (And sometimes, when blog authors run short on time or opinions, they simply cease to add new posts; a favorite blog one day can be a defunct blog the next.)

Nancy Pearl identified the trend of "near novels," or "books made up of a series of interconnected short stories," and this prediction too has proved to be prescient. (The winner of the 2008 Pulitzer Prize, Elizabeth Strout's novel *Olive Kitteridge*, is a fine example of this type of book.) She also noted that literature exploring other cultures and countries was becoming popular, and this trend too has accelerated. Many of the mainstream fiction novels finding their way to readers today are about exotic cultures, settings, and a variety of time periods. These books are not typical escapist literature; they often tackle themes of poverty, the new world order, terrorism, war, and the eternal travails of immigrants and refugees (Padma Viswanathan's *The Toss of a Lemon*, Jhumpa Lahiri's massively popular collection of short stories *Unaccustomed Earth*, and Nadeem Aslam's *The Wasted Vigils* are all examples of this type of book). An increasing number of these multiculturally themed books are by women authors, and many first-time novelists at that. They can be found in this volume by searching the subject index for the entry "multicultural."

But perhaps the prediction that packed the most punch was Nancy Pearl's recognition that the growth of book clubs—led by the largest of all, Oprah's Book Club—has been exponential. Book clubs and their participants' power to drive book sales have only become more influential over the intervening years, as publishers and authors have started to recognize the undeniable power of book groups, book circles, and online book clubs to drive positive word of mouth and sales. As reported recently in a *New York Times* article on the ubiquity and popularity of book groups, publishers have started to actively woo such groups and "have set up dedicated Web sites where reading group members can arrange phone chats with authors, download discussion guides and podcasts, and take part in live Web events" (Kaufman 2007, 5).

Adults are not the only readers getting in on the act, and the stereotypical picture of seven to ten women sitting around a suburban living room with books and glasses of wine is not always accurate. Increasingly adolescents are getting in on the act, and they are doing so using online and social networking tools. A February 2009 article in the *Journal of Adolescent and Adult Literacy* reports that not only are teens (and sometimes even preteens, as evidenced by the popularity of a wide variety of online Harry Potter book clubs) engaging in online book clubs, but "the most popular component to the clubs was the real-time chat where club members were all online at the same time" (Scharber 2009, 434). Clearly there's more than one way to hold a book group, and readers are finding new ways all the time.

If there is a variety of ways to hold or attend a book club, there is a dizzying variety of formats in which to read books. As technology continues to change the way we live, work, and recreate, it is impossible to believe that even the most venerated of cultural institutions, the book, will remain untouched. Not very long ago readers looking for different or more accessible formats had to rely on large-print books or audio books (on cassette only!). Now readers can find books, books on CD, audio books in formats that allow readers to download them directly onto computers and MP3 players, playaways, and a wide variety of e-books for a wider variety of e-book readers, including Amazon's Kindle and the Sony e-book reader. As technologies continue to improve and the Kindle makes its way through various incarnations, other methods for buying and reading will become ever more readily available; likewise, the increased popularity of audio books in such readily accessible formats may well change at least one way in which we talk with readers about books—as the narrator of a book becomes nearly as important to dedicated fans and listeners as the author who wrote the book in the first place.

Technology is also the driving force behind social networking sites, which have proliferated in the years since the 2002 edition of this book. These sites offer readers yet another outlet to discuss and compare their reading choices with their friends, acquaintances, and even thousands of strangers (although can two *readers* ever really be considered *strangers*?). Sites such as LibraryThing, Shelfari, and Goodreads offer individuals the chance to catalog and organize their own book collections, as well as to assign subject and other descriptive tags. They can also write reviews and show their libraries to anyone else who is a subscriber to or participant in the same network. As e-books proliferate and more and more information and cultural life can be found in the social computing "cloud" (the nebulous, online gathering of information that lives, not on each of our personal computers, but on networked server farms), we will likely see more readers not only using these tools to describe and discuss books, but also to find them, suggest them, and start to interact directly with them and their authors. Can we really be that far away from an environment in which readers go into online novels to add links of interest or to related texts and resources?

These sites will undoubtedly change the way we help and interact with readers and patrons. If anyone can join them and garner instant book recommendations and suggestions from other dedicated readers, what role will librarians and readers' advisors play in promoting not only reading in general, but also specific authors, titles, and genres? In what way can librarians use these new tools to reach out to patrons?

Although it may be tempting to throw up your hands in the belief that these sites will eventually make readers' advisors obsolete, it might be more productive to roll up our sleeves, reach into a variety of the sites, and figure out how to use them to better reach out to patrons, to not only develop, but also better promote our local collections. It's a brave new world indeed.

Of course, not all trends are technological in nature. At least four other book- and genre-related trends can currently be seen within the publishing world: the explosion of genreblending novels, the increasing popularity of "crossover" books (books that appeal to both adults and teens), the continued popularity of historical fiction, and the development of the women's fiction genre.

Recent years have found advisors questioning the validity of genre classifications. In the second edition of *Readers' Advisory Guide to Genre Fiction*, Joyce Saricks refers to genre classification as "antithetical" to readers' advisory work. True, authors have begun to take liberties (and what enjoyable, delicious liberties they are) in combining, subverting, and otherwise wreaking havoc with genre conventions. Authors like Suzanne Brockman blend romance and suspense; Dan Simmons combines historical fiction and thrillers; and then there are the really interesting cases, like Seth

Grahame-Smith's new novel *Pride and Prejudice and Zombies,* in which he combines a literary classic with elements of horror, humor, and satire. The popularity of these and many other genreblenders does not excuse us from our responsibility to understand how genres work and what readers love about their favorite genres, nor should it prevent us from classifying titles by genre and sharing those classifications professionally. If anything, it is more important that advisors understand genre characteristics and how they can be combined to appeal to new and different readers. Although this trend is more prevalent in straightforward genre novels than in mainstream fiction, there can be no doubt that genre elements are making inroads here as well. For example, Carlos Ruiz Zafón's novel *The Angel's Game* includes elements of suspense (perhaps its readers might consider other suspense novels and thrillers?), and Alice Hoffman's *Skylight Confessions* shares some similarities with contemporary romance.

In addition, "crossover books," or books that offer multigenerational appeal (and often refer to YA—young adult—books that adults might enjoy, or adult books that younger readers might love) are becoming increasingly popular. Also known variously as "adultescents," "twixters," and "kidults' " (Cart 2009, 74), these books offer the best of both worlds. The sharp dialogue and characterization, combined with briskly paced storytelling, which YA authors typically employ to appeal to a demanding youth audience, are often paired with more complex themes and dilemmas sufficient to challenge the most mature of readers.

The American Library Association has been at the forefront of recognizing the broad appeal of these titles. In 2000 it began to award the Michael L. Printz Award, which is given to young adult fiction novels of literary merit (past winners include John Green's novel *Looking for Alaska* and Angela Johnson's *The First Part Last*). Even if you never work with teen or adolescent readers, you might still want to keep an eye on new books published for that market, as many also appeal to the most demanding of adult fiction readers. Another award list to watch is the ALA's Alex Award, awarded since 1998. Alex winners are adult fiction and nonfiction books that have been deemed particularly appealing to younger readers. Because one of the primary criteria for Alex Award winners is that they be accessible enough to interest even reluctant readers, a readers' advisor can be secure in the knowledge that they will most likely be good suggestions for many adult readers as well.

Two genres that can look very similar to mainstream and general fiction are historical fiction and women's fiction. The continuing trend of genreblending and authors combining and expanding genre characteristics is at least partially responsible for the preponderance of literary and mainstream titles that could also be called historical fiction. In recent years more and more best sellers have been works of historical fiction (including Arthur Golden's *Memoirs of a Geisha* and Mary Ann Shaffer's *The Guernsey Literary and Potato Peel Pie Society*); these books are also making their presence known on award lists (including Edward P. Jones's National Book Critics Circle Award-winning title *The Known World* and Geraldine Brooks's *March,* which won the 2006 Pulitzer Prize). In an article on her blog *A World of Words,* Lucinda Byatt, an associate editor for the magazine *Solander* (a publication of the Historical Novel Society), noted that many of the novels long-listed for the 2009 Booker Prize featured historical themes, and added that she had been informed by one of the judges, Lucasta Miller, that almost half of all 132 novels submitted for consideration "had some historical element to them, so 'it's definitely something that's going on in fiction generally at the moment' " (Byatt 2009).

Sarah L. Johnson, author of the guides *Historical Fiction* and *Historical Fiction II*, has noted that the historical fiction books offering elements of other genres are those that have been gaining the most in popularity, stating that "literary historical fiction, which always existed to some degree, got a significant boost with Charles Frazier's 1997 novel *Cold Mountain* and continues to flourish" (Johnson 2005, 5). Whether you take "mainstream" fiction to be either popular or prize-winning or both, it is clear that many works of historical fiction will appeal to general fiction readers.

"Women's fiction" is a relatively new distinction, but it is definitely taking hold in both professional library literature and pop culture. A Google search for "women's fiction" and "definition" pulls up as many different definitions as any reader could want, but once again Joyce Saricks does a good job of synthesizing them, stating that women's fiction "consists of books written primarily by women for women, that feature female characters, and that address the issues women face in their professional and domestic lives" (Saricks 2003, 1144). Once again there is overlap, as many mainstream and literary novels meet those criteria, and since the runaway success of the chick lit title *Bridget Jones's Diary* by Helen Fielding, this type of novel only continues to grow in popularity. Because so many books, and particularly fiction, are bought by women, I think it is safe to say that stories written about their lives will only become more readily available on our bookstore and library shelves. According to research done by the Romance Writers of America, the category "chick lit, erotic romance, and women's fiction" constituted 2.9 percent of romance book titles in 2007, which seems like a small number—until you take into account that romance novels overall generated $1.375 *billion* in sales in 2007 (Romance Literature Statistics 2007). A quick glance at many of the authors in this collection shows how many are women, and it is only logical to suggest that many of those authors explore issues women (in particular) face.

The last trend I will discuss here is not related to the literature, but rather is a trend in the way readers' advisors provide services. Recent articles in the library literature suggest that "instead of focusing on *what* people read, we need to focus on *why* they read" (Beard and Thi-Beard 2008, 332). Instead of training themselves exclusively about types of books, genres, and authors, these theorists suggest, readers' advisors should also be learning more about their patrons as readers, and considering what motivates those people in their reading choices. For example, are they reading for escapism, relaxation, or instruction (to name just a few)? How readers' advisors learn about and approach readers is becoming as important as the books and resources we suggest. We must continually remind ourselves that people read for a wide variety of reasons, and that they are not always seeking something "just like" their favorite book or the novel or nonfiction title they just finished reading or listening to.

This trend demands that you increasingly go to where your readers are (through library book review blogs, for instance, or Facebook updates on new books and library book clubs and programs). We must maintain and grow our roles as trusted and knowledgeable contacts in our communities. Only then can we wow them with the breadth and depth of our mainstream fiction, genre fiction, and nonfiction knowledge and expertise.

Sources

Beard, David, and Kate Vo Thi-Beard. 2008, Summer. "Rethinking the Book: New Theories for Readers' Advisory." *Reference & User Services Quarterly* 47, no. 4: 331–35.

Byatt, Lucinda. 2009. "Historical Fiction on 2009 Booker Longlist." Available at http://textline.wordpress.com/2009/07/29/2009–booker-longlist/ (accessed September 10, 2009).

Cart, Michael. 2009, February 15. "Core Collection: Crossovers." *Booklist* 105, no. 12: 74–75.

Johnson, Sarah L. 2005. *Historical Fiction: A Guide to the Genre*. Westport, CT: Libraries Unlimited.

Kaufman, Joanne. 2007, November 19. "Publishers Seek to Mine Book Circles." *New York Times,* November 19, 5.

Pearl, Nancy. 2002. *Now Read This II: A Guide to Mainstream Fiction, 1990–2001.* Englewood, CO: Libraries Unlimited.

Romance Literature Statistics. 2007. Available at http://www.rwanational.org/cs/the_romance_genre/romance_literature_statistics (accessed August 17, 2009).

Saricks, Joyce G. 2003, March 1. "What Is Women's Fiction?" *Booklist* 99, no. 13: 1144.

Scharber, Cassandra. 2009, February. "Online Book Clubs: Bridges Between Old and New Literacies Practices." *Journal of Adolescent & Adult Literacy* 52, no. 5: 433–37.

Chapter 1

Setting

Books with **Setting** as their primary appeal factor are those in which the place or time of the story is essential to understanding character, conflict, or theme. Sometimes the setting itself very nearly functions as a central character. Readers and readers' advisors can often identify these books based solely on their jacket copy or well-written reviews; when a review opens with a description of where the novel is set (in some cases, the book's title even has a place-name in it—consider Annie Proulx's *Wyoming Stories* or Paul Gibbons-Kafka's *DuPont Circle*), chances are good that landscape and physical surroundings play a large part in the narrative. Be on the lookout for phrases like "descriptions of the landscape are vivid" and "the landscape itself becomes a character."

Setting can refer not only to *where* a book is set, but also *when* (aligning it more closely with what Joyce Saricks has defined as the appeal factor "frame"). Historical novels often appeal to readers because of the descriptions of their time periods and the physical surroundings in which the characters live and move—and often, the more detailed, the better. As a result, readers who enjoy **Setting** books might also consider other fiction genres in which physical surroundings and the "frame" of the story are of paramount importance, including many historical fiction, some fantasy and science fiction involving alternate or parallel worlds, and even some Westerns. These readers might also consider nonfiction, such as environmental writing, as well as history and travel titles in which landscapes and locations are of paramount importance.

Abbott, Shirley.

The Future of Love. **Algonquin Books of Chapel Hill, 2008. 306pp. ISBN 9781565125674.**

Abbott weaves together tales of the lives of eight New Yorkers, starting her narrative shortly before the terrorist attacks of September 11, 2001, and concluding it nearly a year later. From the elderly widow Antonia, striving simultaneously to save her daughter from a bad marriage and her friend Greg from the disease ravaging his body, to an older man in a loveless marriage who finds himself unexpectedly falling in love with Antonia, Abbott's characters and the city in which they live display a heartening resilience in the face of whatever events and sorrows cross their paths.

Second Appeal: Character

Subjects: 9/11; Adultery; Death and Dying; Family Relationships; First Novels; Friendships; Love Affairs; Marriage; Multiple Viewpoints; New York City; Women Authors; Women's Fiction

Now Try: This is Abbott's first novel, but she is also the author of the memoir *The Book-maker's Daughter*. Other books in which the events of 9/11 are part of the narrative are Jay McInerney's *The Good Life* and Joseph O'Neill's *Netherland*; other novels about neighbors in New York City might also appeal, such as Valerie Ann Leff's *Better Homes and Husbands*, Cheryl Mendelson's *Morningside Heights*, and Candace Bushnell's much more lighthearted (but still very New York-ish) *One Fifth Avenue*. Nonfiction about community life in New York City might also be suggested, such as Helene Hanff's classic *Letter from New York* and Pete Hamill's *Downtown: My Manhattan*.

Agee, Jonis.

The River Wife: A Novel. Random House, 2007. 393pp. ISBN 9781400065967.

The connections between family members living in different eras are made clear in this novel set in the Missouri Bootheel region. When Hedie Rails arrives there in the 1930s to marry Clement Ducharme, she eventually comes across the diaries of Annie Lark, a woman who lived a century earlier and was married to Ducharme's ancestor, Jacques. In addition to learning the stories of the women who came before her, including Annie, Jacques's second wife Laura, a freed female slave named Omah, and Laura's daughter Maddie, Hedie also learns the secrets behind her husband's family history and wealth.

Subjects: 19th Century; 1930s; American South; Diary; Family Relationships; Historical Fiction; Marriage; Missouri; Multigenerational Fiction; Women Authors

Now Try: Agee's earlier novels include *The Weight of Dreams* and *South of Resurrection*; she has also written several short story collections, including *Acts of Love on Indigo Road* and *Taking the Wall*. Another historical family saga set on the other side of the world is Kate Grenville's *The Secret River*; Wendell Berry's novels set in the fictional community of Port Royal, Kentucky, include *A Place on Earth*, *Nathan Coulter*, *A World Lost*, *Jayber Crow*, and *Hannah Coulter*. Michelle Slatalla's work of nonfiction history, biography, and speculation, *The Town on Beaver Creek: The Story of a Lost Kentucky Community*, also tells stories of the strong women in her family.

Ames, Greg.

Buffalo Lockjaw. Hyperion, 2009. 290pp. ISBN 9781401309800.

Although his friends in his hometown, Buffalo, New York, believe that James Fitz-roy is living a successful and sophisticated life in New York City, he knows that his life there is a sham, in reality made up of a poorly paying, unsatisfying job writing for a greeting-card company and drinking. When he goes back to Buffalo to visit his parents (his mother is in a nursing home with early onset Alzheimer's), he alternates between trying to make some sort of peace with his childhood and his surroundings, including listening to tapes he made years before as part of an oral history project about the area (the transcripts of which are interspersed between chapters), and ruminating on mortality and a person's right to die (which he is doing for a very simple and immediate reason).

Second Appeal: Character

Subjects: Alzheimer's Disease; Brothers and Sisters; Elderly; Family Relationships; Mothers and Sons; New York; Nursing Homes; Siblings; Young Men

Now Try: Although much less serious in subject matter, Kyle Beachy's novel *The Slide* also features a young male character who is drifting rather aimlessly through the summer after his college graduation. Other novels that may appeal to these readers are Sam Lipsyte's *Home Land* and *The Subject Steve*, Jonathan Ames's *The Extra Man* (as well as his memoir

I Love You More Than You Know), and Ian Samson's *The Impartial Recorder*. Another novel in which a young woman deals with a parent's illness is Lucinda Rosenfeld's *Why She Went Home*.

Anderson-Dargatz, Gail.

Turtle Valley. **Alfred A. Knopf Canada, 2007. 292pp. ISBN 9780676978858.**

When Kat returns to her family's homestead in the Turtle Valley of British Columbia, she arrives with her own overwhelming issue: her husband has suffered a stroke and has become more of an invalid burden than a partner, leaving her largely in charge of his care and that of their young son. When they arrive in Turtle Valley, her parents are also struggling with her father Gus's worsening health, as well as with nature's wrath in the form of massive wildfires that are threatening the entire area. Although Anderson-Dargatz portrays all the characters and their relationships, including Kat's reunion with her former lover, Jude, the real star of this story is the natural world (particularly the title valley) and its influence on Kat's and her family's lives.

Subjects: British Columbia, Canada; Canadian Authors; Disabilities; Elderly; Family Relationships; Family Secrets; First Person; Love Affairs; Marriage; Multigenerational Fiction; Natural Disasters; Strokes; Women Authors

Now Try: Anderson-Dargatz is also the author of the books *A Recipe for Bees* and *A Cure for Death by Lightning* (in which the story of Kat's mother Beth is told). Another novel in which the setting informs the story is Kim Barnes's *A Country Called Home*; Kate Jennings's *Moral Hazard* features a main character who has become the caregiver for her husband, who is suffering from early onset Alzheimer's disease.

Antunes, Antonio Lobo.

🏆 *The Inquisitors' Manual*. **Grove Press, 2003. 435pp. ISBN 9780802117328.**

Set in Portugal during the repressive regime of Antonio de Oliveira Salazar (who ruled for a good portion of the twentieth century, from 1932 to 1968), this novel follows the connected stories of the family of one of Salazar's government ministers. Joao, the son, is easily taken advantage of by his wife's much more clever family; his sister, Paula, is born illegitimate and is made to feel the stigma of that her entire life.

Subjects: 20th Century; Biographical Fiction; Books in Translation; Corruption; Dictators; Family Relationships; Historical Fiction; Oliveira Salazar, Antonio de; Political Fiction; Portugal; Portuguese Authors

Awards: ALA Notable; New York Times Notable

Now Try: Antunes's other novels include *What Can I Do When Everything's On Fire*, *Knowledge of Hell*, *The Return of the Caravels*, and *The Natural Order of Things*. Another Portuguese author, José Saramago, might appeal to these readers; his books include *Blindness*, *Seeing*, and *All the Names*. Other books with political themes might be suggested, such as Giles Foden's *The Last King of Scotland*, Ismail Kadare's *The Successor: A Novel*, Herta Müller's *The Land of Green Plums*, and Julia Alvarez's *In the Time of the Butterflies*.

Aridjis, Chloe.

Book of Clouds. **Black Cat, 2009. 209pp. ISBN 9780802170569.**

Tatiana, a young woman who is forging her own way in the world by frequently moving away from her family (as well as just plain moving, often once a year or so), finds her sojourn in the city of Berlin complicated by her freelance work for a historian named Doktor Weiss, a young man he introduces her to (Jonas Krantz), and a sudden rash of violent incidents in the city she has grown to love.

Subjects: Berlin; First Novels; First Person; Friendships; Germany; Love Affairs; Travel; Women Authors; Work Relationships; Young Women

Now Try: Aridjis's style is somewhat reminiscent of that of the popular and critically lauded Ian McEwan, whose novels *The Comfort of Strangers* and *Amsterdam* both contain undercurrents of violence and strong city settings. Other novels in which cities are described as lovingly as characters are Martin Millar's (much lighter in tone) *The Good Fairies of New York,* Joseph O'Neill's *Netherland,* Aleksandar Hemon's *The Lazarus Project,* and Anna Winger's *This Must Be the Place* (also about Berlin). Another novel in which a historian plays a central role is Askold Melnyczuk's *The House of Widows: An Oral History.* Nonfiction narratives in which authors describe their urban lives might also be suggested, such as Witold Rybczynski's *City Life: Urban Expectations in a New World,* Anna Quindlen's *Imagined London,* or Pete Hamill's *Downtown: My Manhattan.*

Now Consider Nonfiction . . . The Expatriate Life (Travel)

Expatriate travel narratives are less travel stories than they are lifestyle memoirs that happen to be set in other countries and exotic settings. These stories feature in-depth considerations of different environments, communities, landscapes, and interpersonal and cultural issues. Many of these titles showcase their authors' evocative use of language and are typically quite gentle in tone and plot.

De Blasi, Marlena. *A Thousand Days in Tuscany: A Bittersweet Adventure.*

Hessler, Peter. *Oracle Bones: A Journey Between China's Past and Present.*

Macdonald, Sarah. *Holy Cow: An Indian Adventure.*

Mayes, Frances. *Under the Tuscan Sun.*

Mayle, Peter. *A Year in Provence.*

Shah, Tahir. *The Caliph's House: A Year in Casablanca.*

Stewart, Chris. *Driving Over Lemons: An Optimist in Andalucia.*

Winter, Brian. *Long After Midnight at the Nino Bien: A Yanqui's Missteps in Argentina.*

Averill, Thomas Fox.

Ordinary Genius. **University of Nebraska Press, 2004. 148pp. ISBN 978-0803210684.**

Averill's twelve stories feature a wider variety of characters and situations than readers might initially believe can be found in Kansas, ranging from a high school basketball player's inner life, to a gay man's shopping trip with his father, to a stereotypical young couple expecting their stereotypical first baby who nonetheless witness something not at all stereotypical—or typical—in their backyard.

Subjects: American Midwest; Family Relationships; Kansas; Magic Realism; Quick Reads; Short Stories

Now Try: Averill is the author of two novels, *The Slow Air of Ewan McPherson* and *Secrets of the Tsil Café*, as well as an earlier story collection, *Seeing Mona Naked*. Another author who manages to make the mundane magical is Davy Rothbart, whose story collection *The Lone Surfer of Montana, Kansas*, shares both a setting and a tone with this collection (Rothbart's nonfiction compendium, *Found: The Best Lost, Tossed, and Forgotten Items from Around the World*, might also be suggested). This book is part of the University of Nebraska Press's <u>Flyover Fiction</u> series; other titles in that series include Pamela Carter Joern's *The Floor of the Sky*, Robert Vivian's *The Mover of Bones*, and Sherrie Flick's *Reconsidering Happiness*. Averill has won the O. Henry Award for his short story writing; other winners of the award might be suggested, such as Sherman Alexie (*The Toughest Indian in the World*), Kevin Brockmeier (*The View from the Seventh Layer* and *Things That Fall From the Sky*), and Raymond Carver (*Short Cuts* and *Call If You Need Me: The Uncollected Fiction and Other Prose*).

Baker, Kevin.

Strivers Row. HarperCollins, 2006. 550pp. ISBN 9780060195830.

The lives of Jonah Dove, a light-skinned black man who has "passed" for white during his college years, and Malcolm Little (destined to become Malcolm X) intersect in this sprawling historical epic set in 1940s Harlem. Telling his narrative from the different points of view of his characters, Baker weaves together different storylines masterfully in this third volume in his <u>City of Fire</u> trilogy.

Second Appeal: Story

Subjects: 1940s; American History; Biographical Fiction; Book Groups; Classics; Harlem; Historical Fiction; Malcolm X; Multiple Viewpoints; New York City; Poverty; Race Relations; Racism; Riots

Now Try: Kevin Baker is the author not only of the <u>City of Fire</u> trilogy (which began with *Dreamland* and *Paradise Alley*), but also of the novel *Sometimes You See It Coming* (about baseball). Other novelists who have set their stories in New York City might be offered, including E. L. Doctorow (*The Waterworks*), Mark Helprin (*Winter's Tale*), Pete Hamill (*Snow in August*), Oscar Hijuelos (*The Mambo Kings Play Songs of Love*), and Toni Morrison (*Jazz*). Mat Johnson's superlative graphic novel *Incognegro* also deals with issues of race, and readers might also consider nonfiction history and biographies like Taylor Branch's *Parting the Waters: America in the King Years, 1954–1963* or Alex Haley's and Malcolm X's *The Autobiography of Malcolm X.*

Barnes, Kim.

A Country Called Home. Knopf, 2008. 271pp. ISBN 9780307268952.

When newly graduated doctor Thomas Deracotte and his new bride, Helen, go to Idaho to live a simpler, back-to-the-land life, their new lifestyle turns out not to be the idyll they had pictured, particularly after Helen struggles through the difficult delivery of their twins, one of whom dies during childbirth. In the years after that, Helen struggles with loneliness and turns to the couple's hired hand, Manny, who had been in love with her from the moment of their introduction. (The town pharmacist, Manny's foster father of sorts and the town physician before Thomas's arrival, also has a large part to play in the narrative.) After Helen drowns in a nearby river the family, now consisting of Thomas, Manny, and Thomas and Helen's daughter Elise, remains on the land, but each family member struggles with his or her own battles—Elise's in particular, who goes from an obsession with a religious local family to a psychiatric facility before she is able to return to Thomas and Manny.

Second Appeal: Character

Subjects: Book Groups; Coming-of-age; Death and Dying; Family Relationships; Fathers and Daughters; Idaho; Marriage; Religion; Rural Life; Small-Town Life; Women Authors

Now Try: Barnes has written another novel, *Finding Caruso*, and is also the author of the superlative memoir of her own coming-of-age and experiences with extreme religiosity: *In the Wilderness: Coming of Age in an Unknown Country*. Other novels with strong regional descriptions and characterizations are Sheri Reynolds's *The Rapture of Canaan*, Mark Spragg's *An Unfinished Life*, and Kent Haruf's *Plainsong* and *The Tie That Binds*. Another novel set in Idaho is Melanie Rae Thon's *Iona Moon*; Pete Fromm's nonfiction account *Indian Creek Chronicles: A Winter Alone in the Wilderness* also showcases the state's landscape.

Now Consider Nonfiction ... Back to the Land Environmental Writing

Back to the land environmental narratives include stories of individuals seeking to live more sustainable lives by working in agriculture, but the majority are stories of individuals trying to find a way to feel connected to the world and landscapes in which they live.

Brox, Jane. *Here and Nowhere Else: Late Seasons of a Farm and Its Family.*

Fine, Doug. *Farewell, My Subaru: An Epic Adventure in Local Living.*

Kingsolver, Barbara. *Animal, Vegetable, Miracle: A Year of Food Life.*

LaBastille, Anne. *Woodswoman.*

Perry, Michael. *Coop: A Year of Poultry, Pigs, and Parenting.*

Proenneke, Richard, and Sam Keith. *One Man's Wilderness: An Alaskan Odyssey.*

Ward, Logan. *See You in a Hundred Years: Four Seasons in Forgotten America.*

Barthelme, Frederick.

Waveland. **Doubleday, 2009. 229pp. ISBN 9780385527293.**

Although the Mississippi Gulf Coast, shattered in the wake of Hurricane Katrina, provides the omnipresent and unsettled backdrop for this novel, Barthelme's sympathetically drawn characters give the setting a run for its money as the true appeal of this novel. Slightly past middle age and newly divorced from his wife Gail, Vaughn Williams finds himself aimlessly falling in love with Greta, a woman accused of shooting her former husband, and teaching classes at the local community college. When Gail, feeling threatened by her new boyfriend, asks Vaughn and Greta to move in with her, the trio get along but start to chafe under the weight of shared history (of Vaughn and Gail's marriage, as well as the suspicions, loudly voiced in the local newspapers, about Greta's involvement in her husband's murder five years before). The arrival of Vaughn's younger and pathologically successful brother Newton also adds a new dimension to their relationships. Sounds complicated? Not to worry; Barthelme's prose is brisk and simple and makes this a surprisingly coherent novel in the face of interpersonal and meteorological chaos.

Second Appeal: Character

Subjects: American South; Architects and Architecture; Humor; Hurricane Katrina; Marriage; Men's Lives; Mississippi; Quick Reads; Southern Authors

Now Try: Barthelme is also the author of story collections (*Moon Deluxe* and *The Law of Averages*) and the novels *Elroy Nights*, *Bob the Gambler*, and *Painted Desert* (as well as the memoir, *Double Down*, written with his brother Stephen). Michael Grant Jaffe's (rather lighter in tone) novel *Whirlwind* also features a male character not noted for his ambition (as well as a hurricane); Chang Rae Lee's novel *Aloft* features another middle-aged couple who continue to try to figure out their relationship. Tom Piazza's *City of Refuge* focuses on the city of New Orleans, post-Katrina; Nathan McCall's novel *Them* features a housing uproar in the shape of neighborhood gentrification. Nonfiction about making a place home might also be suggested, such as Dan Baum's *Nine Lives: Death and Life in New Orleans* or Judith Matloff's *Home Girl: Building a Dream House on a Lawless Block*.

Ben Jelloun, Tahar.

Leaving Tangier. **Penguin Books, 2009. 275pp. ISBN 9780143114659.**

Azel and Kenza, a brother and sister (respectively) who live in Tangier, Morocco, believe that a brighter future exists for both of them outside their native country. After Azel is severely beaten by the Moroccan police, he takes his chance to escape when a wealthy Spanish man (Miguel) proposes that Azel become his lover in exchange for a visa to Spain. Azel goes, and Kenza eventually follows, although both realize that happiness remains elusive, particularly as their situation becomes more complex when Kenza weds Miguel to get citizenship and then falls in love with another emigrant.

Second Appeal: Language

Subjects: Books in Translation; Brothers and Sisters; Expatriates; Explicit Sexuality; Family Relationships; French Authors; Gay Men; GLBTQ; Immigrants and Immigration; Islam; Morocco; Multiple Viewpoints; Siblings; Spain

Now Try: Ben Jelloun is also the author of the IMPAC-winning title *This Blinding Absence of Light*, as well as the novel *The Sand Child* and its sequel, *The Sacred Night*. Other novels about the moves people make around the globe for a variety of reasons are Trezza Azzopardi's *The Hiding Place*, Rose Tremain's *The Road Home*, and Lorraine Adams's *Harbor*. Ruth Knafo Setton's novel *The Road to Fez* is set in present-day Morocco; a language-driven novel about Islam (and the many ways in which it is practiced) is Michael Muhammad Knight's *The Taqwacores*. Although much more straightforward in narrative form, Tahir Shah's memoir *The Caliph's House: A Year in Casablanca* might also provide a read related by its setting and local color to Ben Jelloun's novel.

🌳 *This Blinding Absence of Light.* **New Press, 2002. 195pp. ISBN 9781565847231.**
Ben Jelloun offers a fictionalized story of the harshness and cruelties of life in the prison camps where King Hassan II of Moroco imprisoned his political enemies. The description of the desert camps and the atrocities perpetrated there may prove too much for some readers, but the author's focus on the human will to survive makes this a powerful novel of place and survival.

Subjects: 1970s; Books in Translation; First Person; Historical Fiction; Morocco; Prisons; Psychological Fiction; Survival

Awards: International IMPAC Dublin

Now Try: Ben Jelloun has written several other novels: *Leaving Tangier*, *The Sand Child*, and the latter's' sequel, *The Sacred Night*. Although set in modern-day Morocco, Laila Lalami's *Hope and Other Dangerous Pursuits* tells a story of individuals risking their lives to find better ones. Readers who could stand another horrific account of life in prison might consider Aleksandr Solzhenitsyn's nonfiction classic *The Gulag Archipelago* (or even his novel *One Day in the Life of Ivan Denisovich*).

Now Consider Nonfiction . . . Literary Travel

Literary travel narratives are characterized by their authors' use of language and prose styling and how they apply it, not only to landscape or character description, but also to rather more existential concerns, such as what it means to belong to or observe other cultures. These are reflective stories, not written to describe a place or tell the story of a journey, but rather to provoke thoughts about the nature of our places in the world, as well as our world's many unique geographies, cultures, and peoples.

Allende, Isabel. *My Invented Country: A Nostalgic Journey Through Chile.*

Frazier, Ian. *Great Plains.*

Iyer, Pico. *Sun After Dark: Flights into the Foreign.*

Newby, Eric. *Slowly Down the Ganges.*

Nicholson, Geoff. *The Lost Art of Walking: The History, Science, Philosophy, and Literature of Pedestrianism.*

Quindlen, Anna. *Imagined London: A Tour of the World's Greatest Fictional City.*

Thubron, Colin. *In Siberia.*

West, Rebecca. *Black Lamb and Grey Falcon: A Journey Through Yugoslavia.*

Winchester, Simon. *The River at the Center of the World: A Journey up the Yangtze, and Back in Chinese Time.*

Berlinski, Mischa.

Fieldwork: A Novel. **Farrar, Straus & Giroux, 2007. 320pp. ISBN 9780374299163.**
Berlinski tells a fictionalized but highly personal story of a young man (also named Mischa Berlinski) living in Thailand with his girlfriend, who becomes caught up in the story of Martiya van der Leun after another expatriate friend tells

him about her. Imprisoned in a Thai prison for murder, Martiya's story of how she came to be there is investigated by Berlinski, who eventually discovers her crime, her secrets, and the fateful love that changed the course of her life.

Second Appeal: Story

Subjects: Anthropology; Book Groups; Culture Clash; First Novels; First Person; Flashbacks; Love Affairs; Multicultural; Religion; Suspense; Thailand; Travel; Young Men

Now Try: Other novels in which well-described settings are combined with suspenseful stories might appeal, including Kira Salak's *The White Mary*, Zoë Ferraris's *Finding Nouf*, Kate Grenville's *The Secret River*, Barbara Kingsolver's *The Poisonwood Bible*, and Santiago Roncagliolo's *Red April*. A wide variety of adventurous nonfiction travel narratives might also appeal to these readers, including Redmond O'Hanlon's *Into the Heart of Borneo*, Bruce Chatwin's *The Songlines*, and Peter Matthiessen's *The Cloud Forest*.

Berry, Wendell.

Andy Catlett: Early Travels. Shoemaker & Hoard, 2006. 140pp. ISBN 9781593761363.

Berry's Port William (Kentucky) novels feature not only that recurring setting, but also recurring characters; Andy Catlett is no exception. In this story, the elderly Catlett looks back on his boyhood experiences in the 1940s, when he traveled among the homes and farms of his relatives. His memories range from the poignant, such as his grandmother's fine cooking, to complex, such as when he narrates his first awareness, gained from his aunt's behavior and beliefs, of racism and its effects.

Subjects: 1940s; Coming-of-age; Community Life; Domestic Fiction; Elderly; Family Relationships; Gentle Reads; Historical Fiction; Kentucky; Men's Lives; Quick Reads; Race Relations; Rural Life

Now Try: This is a later book in Berry's Port William series, which includes both story collections (*That Distant Land: The Collected Stories of Wendell Berry*) and novels (*A Place on Earth, Remembering*, and *A World Lost*—the latter two featuring Andy Catlett). Although set in North Carolina, Jan Karon's Mitford novels also feature a strong sense of place, interconnected characters, and a gentle reading experience; they include *At Home in Mitford, A Light in the Window*, and *These High, Green Hills*. Mary Lee Settle's Beaulah Quintet series, five historical novels set in West Virginia, also consider landscape and family ties together: they are *Prisons, O Beulah Land, Know Nothing, The Scapegoat*, and *The Killing Ground*. Another popular novel in which an elderly character looks back on his life is Sara Gruen's *Water for Elephants*.

Hannah Coulter. Shoemaker & Hoard, 2004. 190pp. ISBN 9781593760366.

When a novel is titled after its main character, chances are that the novel is character-driven, but in Berry's case his love for and description of the fictional community Port William, Kentucky, in which this book is set, informs the novel's events and its characters' motivations. Hannah, twice widowed and still living in Port William, relates the story of her life, including her work in town in the 1940s, both of her marriages, and how she perceives her children's life choices and the splintering and disintegration of her formerly cohesive rural community.

Second Appeal: Character

Subjects: 1940s; Community Life; Elderly; First Person; Gentle Reads; Kentucky; Men Writing as Women; Quick Reads; Rural Life; Widows

Now Try: Berry sets many of his novels in Port William; other books featuring that location include *Andy Catlett: Early Travels*, *Jayber Crow*, *The Memory of Old Jack*, and *A World Lost*. He has also written story collections set there: *That Distant Land*, *Watch With Me*, and *Fidelity*. He is also a prolific essayist and poet; his nonfiction collections include *The Long-Legged House* and *The Unsettling of America*. An imaginative nonfiction title about a real Kentucky community, Michelle Slatalla's *The Town on Beaver Creek: The Story of a Lost Kentucky Community*, might be suggested, as might Barbara Kingsolver's memoir of her family's return to her Appalachian roots, titled *Animal, Vegetable, Miracle*.

Boaz, Amy.

A Richer Dust. **Permanent Press, 2008. 215pp. ISBN 9781579621599.**

British painter and artist Doll follows a social philosopher, Abe Bronstone (with whom she is fascinated) and his wife to New Mexico in the 1920s; once there, she feels a strong connection to the land and decides to stay. The rest of her story is told from the vantage point of the 1960s, and the narrative also includes flashbacks to her youth in Victorian Great Britain. The novel is loosely based on the life of painter Dorothy Brett, who followed British novelist D. H. Lawrence and his wife to New Mexico in 1924.

Subjects: 1920s; 1960s; Art and Artists; Brett, Dorothy; First Novels; First Person; Friendships; Great Britain; Lawrence, D. H.; Love Affairs; New Mexico; Small Press; Victorian; Women Authors; Writers and Writing

Now Try: Two of Pat Barker's novels that deal with art (and love triangles) might be offered: *Life Class* and *Double Vision*. A more straightforward novelization of an artist's life is Slavenka Drakulic's *Frida's Bed* (about Frida Kahlo); another woman who went to New Mexico and was stunned by the landscape was Georgia O'Keeffe, and a biography of her might also appeal (such as Roxana Robinson's *Georgia O'Keeffe: A Life*). As this novel is loosely based on D. H. Lawrence, related nonfiction that might appeal includes Jeffrey Meyers's *D. H. Lawrence: A Biography* and Janet Byrne's *A Genius for Living: The Life of Frieda Lawrence*. Jude Morgan's novel of another set of famously charismatic men (Lord Byron, Percy Shelley, and John Keats) and the women who loved them, *Passion*, might also be a fun read-alike. Willa Cather's classic novel *Death Comes for the Archbishop* is also set in New Mexico.

Now Consider Nonfiction . . . Natural Places Environmental Writing

Natural places environmental narratives focus primarily on their authors' descriptions of certain landscapes and environmental life experiences.

Austin, Mary. *The Land of Little Rain.*

Ehrlich, Gretel. *The Solace of Open Spaces.*

Leopold, Aldo. *A Sand County Almanac.*

Lopez, Barry. *Arctic Dreams: Imagination and Desire in a Northern Landscape.*

Muir, John. *My First Summer in the Sierra.*

Ray, Janisse. *Pinhook: Finding Wholeness in a Fragmented Land.*

Shelton, Richard. *Going Back to Bisbee.*

Bushnell, Candace.

***One Fifth Avenue*. Voice, 2008. 433pp. ISBN 9781401301613.**

The lives of the residents of One Fifth Avenue all eventually intersect in Bushnell's narrative, firmly grounded in New York stories and sensibilities; the central question of the narrative is who will become the building's newest tenant in the newly vacated penthouse. Each apartment features its own unique inhabitant: art dealer Billy Litchfield, actress Schiffer Diamond, gossip columnist Enid Merle, her nephew Philip Oakland, old Mrs. Houghton (whose death creates the vacancy scrambled for by so many), and yuppie couple Mindy and James Gooch.

Second Appeal: Character

Subjects: Friendships; Homes; New York City; Social Class; Women Authors

Now Try: Bushnell is also the author of the infamous chick lit novels ***Sex and the City***, ***Four Blondes***, ***Trading Up***, and ***Lipstick Jungle***. Those readers more interested in the New York setting and the interplay of the characters might also consider Valerie Ann Leff's ***Better Homes and Husbands***, Cheryl Mendelson's ***Morningside Heights***, and Adam Langer's ***Ellington Boulevard***. Jane Stanton Hitchcock's smart mystery novels, also set among New York's high society, might also appeal; they are ***Social Crimes*** and ***One Dangerous Lady***.

Carlson, Ron.

***Five Skies*. Viking, 2007. 244pp. ISBN 9780670038503.**

The open skies and Rocky Mountain landscape of Idaho constitute a fourth character in this slim but thoughtful novel, which contains three distinct human characters: Darwin Gallegos, a man retreating from his previous life and responsibilities after the death of his wife; the giant and strong day laborer Arthur Key, who struggles with his own guilt and family issues; and young Ronnie Panelli, to whom both men eventually become attached despite his recklessness and aimlessness. The three men get to know one another when they work together on a construction project that was largely conceived of as a way to keep Gallegos's friend and former employer busy. A tragic event at the novel's end cements the bond between the three men and their surroundings.

Second Appeal: Character

Subjects: Death and Dying; Friendships; Idaho; Men's Lives; Mountains; Professions; Quick Reads; Work Relationships

Awards: ALA Notable

Now Try: Carlson's other novels (which also feature a clear sense of setting) are ***The Signal*** and ***Speed of Light***; he is also the author of the story collections ***A Kind of Flying***, ***The Hotel Eden***, and ***The News of the World***. Kim Barnes's novel ***A Country Called Home***, also set in Idaho, examines the connections characters have to each other through living arrangements and work; another (decidedly more surreal) novel in which characters are united by their work is Scottish author Magnus Mills's ***The Restraint of Beasts***. Carlson's style is similar to that of Rick Bass, whose novels ***Where the Sea Used to Be*** and ***The Sky, the Stars, the Wilderness*** might also be suggested. Nonfiction titles in which authors explore people's relations to landscapes, work, and life are Alexandra Fuller's ***The Legend of Colton H. Bryant*** (about a cowboy), Reg Theriault's ***How to Tell When You're Tired*** (about manual labor), and even Jon Krakauer's *Into the Wild* (about a young man who wanted to live and work on his own terms) might all be good read-alikes.

Casares, Oscar.

Brownsville: Stories. **Back Bay Books, 2003. 192pp. ISBN 9780316146807.**

Casares's collection of nine short stories set in and around the border community of Brownsville, Texas, feature a large cast of striving, sometimes down-on-their-luck, frankly drawn (and primarily) male characters who aren't always likable but who will certainly be familiar to anyone who has ever struggled to get along with the neighbors, been frustrated by adult children, or had life turn out not exactly as expected or hoped.

Subjects: Community Life; Humor; Immigrants and Immigration; Marriage; Men's Lives; Mexico; Short Stories; Social Class; Texas

Awards: ALA Notable

Now Try: Casares has also written a novel, *Amigoland*. Luis Alberto Urrea's *Into the Beautiful North* portrays similar characters with close bonds; Ana Castillo's novel *The Guardians* offers another look at lives divided by the border; and Luis Rodriguez's *The Republic of East L.A.: Stories* collection might also prove to be a good read-alike. Although it displays more of a sense of mysticism than Casares's grounded collection, Ray Gonzalez's *The Ghost of John Wayne, and Other Stories* also examines characters' lives in Texas, New Mexico, and Mexico. Joe Connelly's dark novel about a neighborhood farther north, but one in which neighbors still have their share of conflict, is Joe Connelly's *Crumbtown*. Nonfiction about the border regions and Mexican Americans' lives in America might be suggested, such as William Langewiesche's *Cutting for Sign*, Ruben Martinez's *Crossing Over*, or Paul Cuadros's *A Home on the Field: How One Championship Soccer Team Inspires Hope for the Revival of Small Town America*.

Choy, Wayson.

All That Matters. **Other Press, 2004. 425pp. ISBN 9781590512159.**

Kiam-Kim Chen is only three years old when he arrives in Vancouver with his father and his grandmother; soon his father remarries, and in addition to assimilating the culture of his Chinese family to that of his Canadian surroundings, Kiam-Kim must also adapt to a new stepfamily and friends.

Subjects: Canada; Canadian Authors; Culture Clash; Family Relationships; Historical Fiction; Immigrants and Immigration; Multicultural; Multigenerational Fiction; Stepfamilies; Vancouver; World War II

Now Try: Readers might also enjoy Choy's first novel, *The Jade Peony*, as well as his memoirs, *Paper Shadows* and *Not Yet*. Two other novels of culture clashes and characters' adaptations to them are Judy Fong Bates's *Midnight at the Dragon Café* and Janice Y. K. Lee's *The Piano Teacher*. This novel won the Trillium Book Award (awarded in Ontario, Canada); other winners of that award are Camilla Gibb's *Sweetness in the Belly*, Austin Clarke's *The Polished Hoe*, and Alistair MacLeod's *No Great Mischief*.

Cisneros, Sandra.

🌷 *Caramelo.* **Knopf, 2002. 443pp. ISBN 9780679435549.**

Celaya Rayes, known as Lala to her family, learns rather more than most children would want to know about her extended family as she listens to her parents tell stories about them on her family's drives back and forth to Mexico City. The youngest child in her family, she admits that her viewpoint can be unreliable as she relates tales of her grandmother and other relatives (known by such nicknames as Awful Grandmother, Uncle Fat-Face, etc.), their history, and their places in the communities of Mexico City, San Antonio, and Chicago.

Subjects: 20th Century; Book Groups; Classics; Family Relationships; Grandmothers; Historical Fiction; Mexico; Multigenerational Fiction; Unreliable Narrator; Women Authors; YA; Young Girls

Awards: ALA Notable, New York Times Notable

Now Try: Cisneros is also the author of the novel *The House on Mango Street* and the poetry collection *Loose Woman*. Other Latina novelists who tell family sagas and historical fiction stories are Julia Alvarez (*In the Time of the Butterflies* and *Saving the World*), Isabel Allende (*Ines of My Soul* and her Chilean series: *The House of the Spirits*, *Daughter of Fortune*, and *Portrait in Sepia*), and Kathleen Alcalá (*Treasures in Heaven* and *The Flower in the Skull*); a male author who writes similar stories, from the female perspective, is Luis Alberto Urrea (*The Hummingbird's Daughter* and the not-historical but still fantastic *Into the Beautiful North*).

Connelly, Joe.

Crumbtown. Knopf, 2003. 259pp. ISBN 9780375413643.

Connelly sheds light on the lives of the residents of Crumbtown (a run-down area of the fictional city Dodgeport), particularly Don Reedy, who started his criminal career by stealing and sabotaging the cars of affluent people and who eventually moved up to a bank heist (with his friends Tim and Tom), which went wrong, after which he threw all of the cash he had "liberated" to locals standing around in the area. The oppression of urban decay colors the novel, although Connelly is remarkably gentle in describing his characters, who not only make some questionable choices but also epitomize the saying that if it weren't for bad luck, they'd have no luck at all.

Second Appeal: Character

Subjects: Community Life; Crime; Dark Humor, Friendships; Men's Lives; Satire

Now Try: Connelly is also the author of the novel *Bringing Out the Dead*. A story collection about the border community of Brownsville, Texas, which also features a fair number of neighbor arguments and longstanding grudges, is Oscar Casares's *Brownsville*. Other novels about characters who would have no luck at all if it weren't for bad luck are Chuck Klosterman's *Downtown Owl* (about a small town in North Dakota), Tom Drury's *The Driftless Area* (set in Iowa), and Richard Russo's *Nobody's Fool*; Dermot McEvoy's political satire *Our Lady of Greenwich Village* might also be a good read-alike. Nonfiction titles like Mark Bowden's *Finders Keepers* (about a down-on-his-luck man who found several bags of currency dropped, accidentally, by armored truck drivers) or Jason Fagone's *Horsemen of the Esophagus* (about those seeking glory on the competitive eating circuit) might also appeal to these readers.

Crouch, Katie.

Girls in Trucks: Stories. Little, Brown, 2008. 241pp. ISBN 9780316002110.

Although each chapter in Crouch's debut novel could be considered its own narrative, they work together to tell the story of Sarah Walters's coming-of-age and debutante experiences in her hometown of Charleston,

South Carolina; her disillusion with that city and her desire to seek her fortune in New York City (where, ironically, she struggles with that city's differences from her more genteel upbringing); her struggle to find a meaningful love relationship (the search for which takes her to New York, then Peru, and eventually back to South Carolina); and a family crisis for which she must return home and reevaluate the power of the bonds between herself and her Southern friends (all part of the debutante organization called the Camellia Society).

Subjects: American South; Coming-of-age; Friendships; New York City; Women Authors; Women's Fiction; Young Women

Now Try: Another novel in which a woman sets out to find her fortune away from family is Melissa Bank's *The Wonder Spot*; Galt Niederhoffer's *The Romantics* showcases the activities of another group of friends who stay in contact past college (although they are decidedly less supportive of each other). Rebecca Wells's novels about family and friendship connections in a Southern community might also appeal; they include *Little Altars Everywhere* and *The Divine Secrets of the Ya-Ya Sisterhood*.

Davis, Claire.

Labors of the Heart: Stories. **St. Martin's Press, 2006. 228pp. ISBN 9780312332846.**

Davis's sympathetic but not particularly gentle collection of short stories focuses on characters who are misfits, unhappy for various reasons, or simply struggling with the challenges that face us all in daily life (infidelity, loneliness, frustration, etc.). Set primarily in small towns throughout the Western states of Montana, Idaho, and Washington, Davis provides not only very human stories, but also evocative landscapes.

Subjects: American West; Idaho; Montana; Quick Reads; Short Stories; Small-Town Life; Washington; Women Authors

Now Try: Davis is the author of two previous novels (also with a strong sense of place), *Season of the Snake* and *Winter Range*. Similar short story collections that might appeal to these readers are Bathsheba Monk's *Now You See It—Stories from Cokesville, PA*; Cathy Day's *The Circus in Winter*; E. Annie Proulx's Wyoming Stories series *Close Range*, *Bad Dirt*, and *Fine Just the Way It Is*; and Sherwood Anderson's classic *Winesburg, Ohio*. A short fiction anthology, *The Best of Montana's Short Fiction*, might also be suggested to these readers.

De Bernières, Louis.

🌾 *Birds without Wings.* **Knopf, 2004. 553pp. ISBN 9781400043415.**

The culture, landscape, and people of Turkey and the Ottoman Empire infuse this epic novel, told through chapters from different characters' points of view (including even chapters narrated by Mustafa Kemal, the "father of modern Turkey") and in different periods in history, from World War I to the Greek War of Independence and World War I. The reader is spoken to by Iskander the Potter, a beautiful young girl named Philothei, Iskander's son Karatavuk, and many other individuals, as they move through their lives and face sadness, joy, love, death, war, and the continuing realization that, as Iskander notes early on, "every birth entails a death."

Subjects: Book Groups; Epic Reads; Family Relationships; Historical Fiction; Multicultural; Multiple Viewpoints; Turkey; War

Awards: ALA Notable

Now Try: De Bernières's other novels include his 2008 title *A Partisan's Daughter*, as well as the popular title *Corelli's Mandolin* (which was made into a movie titled *Captain Corelli's Mandolin*), *The Troublesome Offspring of Cardinal Guzman*, and the short story collection (set in Australia) *Red Dog*. An author whose style is similar to De Bernières is Michael Ondaatje; his novels *The English Patient*, *Anil's Ghost*, and *Divisadero* might be suggested, as might historical fiction epics such as Sandra Cisneros's *Caramelo* or Alberto Luis Urrea's *The Hummingbird's Daughter*. Fiction and nonfiction titles by Orhan Pamuk set in Turkey might also be offered, including the novels *My Name Is Red* and *Snow*, as well as the memoir *Istanbul: Memories of the City*.

Dean, Debra.

The Madonnas of Leningrad. **William Morrow, 2006. 231pp. ISBN 978-0060825300.**

Marina narrates the story of meeting her husband during the World War II siege of Leningrad from the much later vantage point of her old age. Suffering from the early stages of Alzheimer's disease, she finds that the detail of the artworks it was her job to pack away for safety during the siege (she and her museum colleagues removed the paintings from the walls, but left the empty frames as a reminder that the art would be restored to its rightful place after the war) are much clearer in her mind than more recent events in the lives of her family members.

Second Appeal: Character

Subjects: Art and Artists; Book Groups; Elderly; First Novels; Historical Fiction; Immigrants and Immigration; Leningrad; Marriage; Quick Reads; Russia; Women Authors; World War II.

Now Try: Dean is the author of a subsequent collection of short stories, *Confessions of a Fallen Woman*. Other novels in which art and family histories intertwine are Sara Houghteling's *Pictures at an Exhibition*, Michael Pye's *The Pieces from Berlin*, and Dara Horn's *The World to Come*. Other novels about World War II events might appeal, such as Irene Nemirovsky's tragic *Suite Francaise* and *Fire in the Blood* or Mary Ann Shaffer's and Annie Barrows's decidedly lighter but still poignant novel *The Guernsey Literary and Potato Peel Pie Society*. Novels in which elderly women consider their own lives and pasts are Susan Minot's *Evening*, Harriet Scott Chessman's *Someone Not Really Her Mother*, and Sandra Birdsell's *The Russländer*.

Now Consider Nonfiction . . . The Settings of History

The settings of history narratives are told using a framework based on setting and the effects of certain locations on their residents. Authors of these titles are typically quite skilled in combining numerous details and anecdotes, garnered through extensive research, to create the bigger picture of each setting's overarching story.

Cahill, Thomas. *How the Irish Saved Civilization.*

Cahill, Thomas. *Sailing the Wine Dark Sea.*

Eliot, Marc. *Song of Brooklyn: An Oral History of America's Favorite Borough.*

English, T. J. *Havana Nocturne: How the Mob Owned Cuba—And Then Lost It to the Revolution.*

McPherson, James. *Hallowed Ground: A Walk at Gettysburg.*

Moorehead, Alan. *The Blue Nile.*

Moorehead, Alan. *The White Nile.*

Morris, Jan. *Hong Kong.*

Shorris, Earl. *The Life and Times of Mexico.*

Desai, Anita.

The Zigzag Way. **Houghton Mifflin, 2004. 159pp. ISBN 9780618042159.**

New England–born graduate student Eric finds himself out of his cultural and interpersonal depth when he follows his scientist girlfriend Em to Mexico on one of her research trips. Although he casts about for something to keep himself occupied during her long absences in the field, he is overwhelmed by his lush and rural surroundings (detailed in prose that critics have called equally lush), until he decides to learn more about his own family's past and his grandfather's experiences as a miner in the Sierra Madre, and comes into contact with a European woman, Doña Vera, who is as driven by her own past as Eric is passive about his.

Subjects: Coming-of-age; Culture Clash; Indian Authors; Love Affairs; Mexico; Quick Reads; Women Authors; Young Men

Now Try: Desai is a popular author whose novels are often in contention for the prestigious Booker Prize; three that were shortlisted for it were *Clear Light of Day*, *In Custody*, and *Fasting, Feasting*. A novel in which a young couple in love travels to Mexico and gets more than they bargained for is Joy Nicholson's *The Road to Esmerelda*. Another novel in which a young man's contentious relationship with his girlfriend leads him to resort to aimlessness and male friendships is Kyle Beachy's first novel, *The Slide*. A nonfiction history that gives an evocative account of the stories and appeal of Mexico is Earl Shorris's *The Life and Times of Mexico*. (Shorris's novel *In the Yucatan* might also be of some interest to these readers.)

Desarthes, Agnes.

Chez Moi. **Penguin, 2008. 272pp. ISBN 9780143113232.**

Forty-three-year old Myriam invests all she has (and takes out loans for more) in her intimate, twenty-five-person eatery tucked away on a small street in Paris. Both living and working in the restaurant, and allowing only glimpses of her past life to make it through to the reader of her first-person narrative, Myriam does not seek patrons or success and is astounded when both start to find her in this novel, which is also filled with evocative descriptions of Paris and Myriam's cooking.

Second Appeal: Language

Subjects: Books in Translation; First Person; Food; France; Friendships; Paris; Restaurants; Women Authors; Work Relationships

Now Try: Desarthes is also the author of the novels *Good Intentions* and *Five Photos of My Wife*; like this one they were all translated by Adriana Hunter. Although much more story-driven than Desarthes's narrative, both Laura Esquivel's *Like Water for Chocolate* and Joanne Harris's *Chocolat* (as well as its sequel, *The Girl with No Shadow*) are stories of the connections between women and men and food. Also of interest might be Josefina López's novel *Hungry Woman in Paris*. Another slim novel about a woman's determination to simultaneously serve others and keep to herself is Penelope Fitzgerald's *The Bookshop*. Self-discovery memoirs, particularly those involving food, such as Elizabeth Gilbert's *Eat, Pray, Love* or Kathleen Flinn's *The Sharper Your Knife the Less You Cry*, not to mention Ruth Reichl's classic *Tender at the Bone*, might all be good related reads for fans of this slim novel.

Doerr, Anthony.

🏆 *The Shell Collector: Stories.* Scribner, 2002. 219pp. ISBN 9780743212748.

There is less an exact setting in Doerr's short stories than an overall influence and feel of the natural world. In his eight stories, including "The Shell Collector," "The Hunter's Wife," and "So Many Chances," he describes his characters' careful interaction with and love for nature, including the man in the title story who makes a stunning medical discovery regarding snails native to where he lives, but who comes to regret the disrupting attention paid to his discovery.

Subjects: Biology; Environmental Writing; Family Relationships; Quick Reads; Short Stories

Awards: ALA Notable; New York Times Notable

Now Try: Doerr followed this story collection with a novel, *About Grace*. Other short story collections by similar authors might be suggested, including Rick Bass's *The Hermit's Story* and *The Lives of Rocks*, Charles Baxter's *Harmony of the World* and *Believers*, and Wendell Berry's *That Distant Land*. Nonfiction environmental narratives such as Annie Dillard's *Pilgrim at Tinker Creek*, Scott Russell Sanders's *Writing from the Center*, and William Least Heat Moon's *PrairyErth* might also be suggested.

Doig, Ivan.

🏆 *The Whistling Season.* Harcourt, 2006. 345pp. ISBN 9780151012374.

Doig's poignant historical novel starts in the 1950s, but most of the narrative (related by the main character) takes place in Montana in 1909. Nearing the end of his career as the state superintendent of Montana's schools, Paul Milliron laments the loss of his state's one-room schoolhouses (in the 1950s) and tells the story of his youth, when he and his brothers and father hired Rose Llewellyn, all the way from Minneapolis, to keep house for them, based solely on her advertisement for work, which stated "can't cook but doesn't bite." In addition to bringing her good nature and strong will to the Milliron household, Rose also brings her brother Morrie, who becomes the teacher in the town's one-room schoolhouse.

Subjects: 1900s; 1950s; Brothers and Sisters; Coming-of-age; Community Life; Education; Family Relationships; First Person; Gentle Reads; Historical Fiction; Men's Lives; Montana; Teachers; Westerns

Awards: ALA Notable; Alex Award

Now Try: Rick Bass reviewed this title for *Publishers Weekly* and compared it favorably to Wallace Stegner's *Crossing to Safety*; that novel, and others by Stegner might be offered (as might novels by Rick Bass himself, including *Where the Sea Used to Be* and *The Hermit's Story*). Other novels that might be suggested featuring a nostalgic tone and upright but interesting characters are Wendell Berry's *Jayber*

Crow, Kent Haruf's *Plainsong* and *The Tie That Binds*, and Elmer Kelton's *The Time It Never Rained*. Inspiring nonfiction about teachers, such as Mitch Albom's *Tuesdays with Morrie* or Sam Swope's *I Am a Pencil: A Teacher, His Kids, and Their World of Stories*, might also be offered.

Drayson, Nicholas.

A Guide to the Birds of East Africa. **Houghton Mifflin, 2008. 201pp. ISBN 9780547152585.**

Mr. Malik, an Indian widower living in Kenya, appears to be a dedicated bird-watcher, but in truth his real dedication is to his crush on Rose Mbikwa, who leads the bird-watching tours sponsored by his social club. His fondest hope is to escort Rose, herself a widow, to the Nairobi Hunt Club Ball, but his former classmate Harry Khan's arrival on the scene leads to both a love triangle and a bird-spotting competition.

Second Appeal: Character

Subjects: Africa; Animals; Birds; British Authors; Community Life; Family Relationships; Gentle Reads; Humor; Kenya; Love Affairs; Men's Lives; Quick Reads; Widowers; Widows

Now Try: Readers who enjoy Drayson's gentle storytelling and exotic locale might also consider Alexander McCall Smith's popular <u>Precious Ramotswe</u> and <u>Isabel Dalhousie</u> series; the former starts with *The No. 1 Ladies Detective Agency* and *Tears of the Giraffe*, the latter with the novels *The Sunday Philosophy Club* and *Friends, Lovers, Chocolate*. Other mature romances are Anne Tyler's *Back When We Were Grownups* and *Digging to America*, Robert Hellenga's *Philosophy Made Simple*, and Jeanne Ray's *Julie and Romeo* and *Julie and Romeo Get Lucky*. Gentle nonfiction reads about life in small communities might also be suggested to these authors, including Michael Perry's *Population 485: Meeting Your Neighbors One Siren at a Time* and Heather Lende's *If You Lived Here, I'd Know Your Name*. Jonathan Rosen's nonfiction memoir about birding, *The Life of the Skies: Birding at the End of Nature*, is a sobering but touching read about the joys of observing bird life; Mark Cocker's investigative nonfiction title *Birders: Tales of a Tribe* might also appeal.

Edgerton, Clyde.

The Bible Salesman. **Little, Brown, 2008. 241pp. ISBN 9780316117517.**

When Preston Clearwater, car thief, stops on the road to pick up the hitchhiking Henry Dampier, Bible salesman, he knows he's lucked onto the perfect patsy to unwittingly help with his grand theft auto plans. Convincing Dampier that he is a top-secret FBI agent, Clearwater leads him back and forth across North Carolina.

Second Appeal: Character

Subjects: 1950s; American South; Crime; Historical Fiction; Humor; Men's Lives; North Carolina; Religion; Road Novels; YA

Now Try: Edgerton's other novels, which often feature elderly characters, might nonetheless appeal to readers who enjoy his brand of understated humor; they include *Lunch at the Piccadilly*, *In Memory of Junior*, and *Walking Across Egypt*. Two other Southern authors who might appeal to Edgerton fans are Martin Clark (*The Many Aspects of Mobile Home Living* and *Plain Heathen Mischief*) and Larry Brown (*The Rabbit Factory*, *Fay: A Novel*, and *Joe*). Frank Abagnale Jr.'s autobiography about his own rather more successful days as a con artist, *Catch Me If You Can*, might also be a fun read-alike for this novel.

Enger, Lin.

Undiscovered Country. **Little, Brown, 2008. 308pp. ISBN 9780316006941.**

In this suspenseful and evocative novel set in Minnesota (during one of its frigid winters), Enger weaves a Hamlet-inspired tale, in which seventeen-year-old Jesse Matson struggles to understand his father's suicide ten years previously. Jesse struggles to accept the verdict of death by suicide (his father went hunting and was found dead of an apparent self-inflicted gunshot), which he eventually tries to prove false. Fueling his speculation is the reappearance of his father's brother Clay and Clay's too-sudden relationship with Jesse's mother; while he seeks to uncover the truth he must simultaneously cope with providing comfort for his younger brother and falling in love with a local girl, Christine Montez, who is wrestling with her own issues.

Subjects: Book Groups; Coming-of-age; Death and Dying; Family Relationships; First Novels; First Person; Literary Allusions; Minnesota; Murder; Shakespeare, William; Suspense; YA

Now Try: Another retelling of the Hamlet story (also set in the upper Midwest) is David Wroblewski's popular Oprah novel *The Story of Edgar Sawtelle*. Enger is the brother of author Leif Enger, whose novels share a style similar to Lin's and include *Peace Like a River* and *So Brave, Young and Handsome*. Larry Watson's style is similarly nostalgic (especially in his novels *Sundown, Yellow Moon*, and *Laura*). Joyce Maynard's YA novel *The Cloud Chamber* is another powerful coming-of-age narrative. Two other books set in northern climates are Mikael Niemi's *Popular Music from Vittula* and Per Petterson's *Out Stealing Horses*.

Ferraris, Zoë.

🏮 *Finding Nouf.* **Houghton Mifflin, 2008. 305pp. ISBN 9780618873883.**

When sixteen-year-old Nouf ash-Shrawi goes missing from her Saudi Arabian home and is later found dead in the desert, medical examiner Katya Hijazi and private investigator Nayir ash-Sharqi are charged with the duty of discovering how she got there, by whom she was pregnant, and what her family has to hide. Described as a "literary mystery," there is also skillful interplay here between Katya and Nayir, as Katya is a decidedly modern Saudi Arabian woman and Nayir is a more traditional Palestinian Muslim who nonetheless finds himself drawn to her intellect and confidence (so much so that he often has to remind himself that Katya is engaged to be married to his friend, and Nouf's adoptive brother, Othman). Ferraris, who lived in Saudi Arabia, evocatively describes the landscape and the culture.

Second Appeal: Story

Subjects: Family Relationships; Islam; Love Affairs; Multicultural; Murder; Psychological Fiction; Saudi Arabia; Suspense; Women Authors; YA

Awards: Alex Award

Now Try: This is Ferraris's first novel, but it included blurbs from many popular authors, including Diana Abu-Jaber (*Origin: A Novel*) and Anita Amirrezvani (*The Blood of Fathers*). This book won the ALA's Alex Award (awarded to adult books that are particularly accessible to young adults) for 2009; other award winners from that year are David Benioff's *City of Thieves* and Hannah Tinti's *The Good Thief*. Nonfiction titles about women's roles and lives in Middle Eastern countries might also be suggested; these include Azar Nafisi's *Reading Lolita in Tehran*, Åsne Seierstad's *The Bookseller of Kabul*, Greg Mortenson's *Three Cups of Tea: One Man's Mission to Fight Terrorism and Build Nations—One School at a Time*, and the memoirs *Persepolis* (by Marjane Satrapi) and *Journey from the Land of No* (by Roya Hakakian).

Frey, James.

Bright Shiny Morning. HarperCollins, 2008. 501pp. ISBN 9780061573132.

Frey's avant-garde novel tells a myriad of stories about the city of Los Angeles, weaving together the narratives of the city's history with the more personal narratives of such characters as Esperanza, a girl infamous for her oversized thighs; homeless Joe, who spends his days on the streets; young couple Dylan and Maddie, just seeking to make it through every day; and many others.

Subjects: American History; California; Family Relationships; First Novels; Interconnected Stories; Los Angeles; Love Affairs; Multiple Viewpoints

Now Try: Frey is no stranger to controversy; his Oprah-chosen memoir about drug abuse and recovery, *A Million Little Pieces*, was eventually found to be largely fabricated, which threw doubt on his second memoir, *My Friend Leonard*. The fact remains that his writing style stands out: his readers might also consider Charles Bock's debut novel *Beautiful Children* or Dave Eggers's novels *You Shall Know Our Velocity* and *What Is the What*. Joan Didion's memoir/nonfiction reflection on her home state of California, *Where I Was From*, might also make for good related reading.

Galloway, Steven.

The Cellist of Sarajevo. Riverhead Books, 2008. 235pp. ISBN 9781594489860.

Galloway tells the story of the siege of Sarajevo from the points of view of four very different characters: a cellist who decided to play in the street where numerous people were killed, as a tribute; the sniper assigned to protect him; a man simply trying to make it to and from his house with a week's supply of water; and another man who meets another old friend in the street and starts to regain a bit of the joy and humanity of his life that he thought had gone forever. Although most of the descriptions of the city focus on its destruction, the author also provides a real picture of the city as it must have been in its happier days.

Second Appeal: Language

Subjects: 1990s; Canadian Authors; Death and Dying; Historical Fiction; Multicultural; Multiple Viewpoints; Music and Musicians; Quick Reads; Sarajevo; War; Yugoslavia

Now Try: Galloway is also the author of the novels *Finnie Walsh* and *Ascension*. Other novels set in war-torn countries might be suggested to these readers, including Nadeem Aslam's *The Wasted Vigil*, Khaled Hosseini's *The Kite Runner*, Jeff Talarigo's *The Ginseng Hunter*, and Masha Hamilton's *The Distance Between Us*. Also of interest might be nonfiction narratives in which wars disrupt people's lives and living situations, such as Sandy Tolan's *The Lemon Tree: An Arab, a Jew, and the Heart of the Middle East*, Farah Ahmedi's *The Story of My Life: An Afghan Girl on the Other Side of the Sky*, and Ishmael Beah's *A Long Way Gone: Memoirs of a Boy Soldier*.

Goolrick, Robert.

A Reliable Wife. **Algonquin Books of Chapel Hill, 2009. 291pp. ISBN 9781565125964.**

When Ralph Truitt, of Truitt, Wisconsin, advertises for a "reliable wife," the woman who answers his ad, Catherine Land, turns out to be much, much more than the "simple honest woman" she proclaims herself to be in her introductory letter to him. Desperate to find the prodigal son who he drove out of his home many years previously, out of anger toward the son's unfaithful mother, Truitt sends Catherine (after marrying her) to St. Louis to find him. Set primarily in one of Wisconsin's frigid winters in the year 1907, the frozen landscape mirrors the soul of Catherine, whose ice-cold determination will make readers shiver almost as much as Goolrick's descriptions of ice and snow.

Second Appeal: Language

Subjects: 1900s; Book Groups; Explicit Sexuality; Family Relationships; Fathers and Sons; First Person; Historical Fiction; Love Affairs; Marriage; Men Writing as Women; Suspense; Unreliable Narrator; Wisconsin

Now Try: Goolrick is also the author of a memoir, *The End of the World As We Know It,* in which he describes his horrific 1950s childhood, his abusive father, and his Valium-addicted mother. Other novels in which the reader may not be entirely sure whose side to be on are Michael Faber's *The Crimson Petal and the White,* Gil Adamson's *The Outlander,* and David Wroblewski's *The Story of Edgar Sawtelle.* Amy Bloom's historical novel *Away* also features a strong woman protagonist. In his afterword, Goolrick also explains how his novel was inspired by Michael Lesy's nonfiction history title, *Wisconsin Death Trip,* which might appeal to these readers.

Grenville, Kate.

🏆 *The Secret River.* **Canongate, 2005. 334pp. ISBN 9781841957975.**

Sentenced to "transportation" for his theft, William Thornhill must begin life anew in Australia (specifically, New South Wales) with his wife Sal and their children. The year is 1806, and their lives in Australia are harsh, particularly as Thornhill must make his own way from being a convict to finally achieving his own land claim. When he does, however, he and his fellow immigrants begin to clash with the region's aboriginal peoples; although he differs with his neighbors on how to handle the conflict, he nevertheless finds himself drawn into the fray.

Second Appeal: Story

Subjects: 19th Century; Australia; Australian Authors; Book Groups; Culture Clash; Family Relationships; Historical Fiction; Immigrants and Immigration; New South Wales; Violence; Women Authors; Women Writing as Men

Awards: ALA Notable

Now Try: Grenville is also the author of *The Idea of Perfection* and *Albion's Story,* as well as the memoir *Searching for the Secret River.* Authors who have written similarly literary historical novels include fellow Aussie Peter Carey (*The True History of the Kelly Gang* and *Oscar and Lucinda*), Jane Urquhart (*Away: A Novel* and *The Stone Carvers*), and Matthew Kneale (*English Passengers*). Nonfiction history titles such as Carolly Erickson's rollicking *The Girl from Botany Bay* (about prisoners who were transported to Australia) or Bruce Chatwin's thoughtful travel classic *Songlines* might also appeal to these readers.

Harrison, Jim.

🖋 *The English Major*. Grove Press, 2008. 255pp. ISBN 9780802118639.

When sixty-year-old Cliff loses his inherited family farm and home through a shady real estate deal, he decides to take off on a tour of the fifty states (as guided by a childhood puzzle map of the country, a piece of which he tosses out every time he passes through a state). There's nothing to stop him; he's retired from his high school teaching career, his wife of thirty-eight years has been cheating on him, and his beloved dog is dead—so he hits the road, engaging in an affair of his own with a married former student and visiting his prosperous gay son Robert in San Francisco. But as his journey comes to an end, the question remains: Can you go home again, and should you even want to?

Subjects: Homes; Humor; Marriage; Men's Lives; Midlife Crisis; Quick Reads; Road Novels; Travel

Awards: New York Times Notable

Now Try: Harrison's others novels include *Returning to Earth, True North,* and *The Beast God Forgot to Invent*. This novel is rather more humorous than some of Harrison's earlier work; other authors who use humor in their narratives might be suggested, including John Irving (*A Prayer for Owen Meany* and *The World According to Garp*), Joe Coomer (*Apologizing to Dogs* and *The Loop*), and Richard Russo (*Nobody's Fool* and *Straight Man*). A nonfiction classic in which a man and his dog traveled throughout the United States is John Steinbeck's *Travels with Charley* (Charley being his dog); a fun nonfiction related read would be the essay collection *State by State*, to which a variety of popular authors contributed essays about each of the fifty states.

Helms, Beth.

Dervishes. Picador, 2008. 313pp. ISBN 9780312426194.

When a diplomatic family is posted to Ankara, Turkey, in the 1970s, the husband (Rand) views it largely as simply another job, but his wife Grace and his teenage daughter Canada are delighted with the city and landscape, and eventually venture farther afield than is really safe.

Subjects: 1970s; Culture Clash; Family Relationships; First Novels; First Person; Friendships; Marriage; Mothers and Daughters; Multicultural; Multiple Viewpoints; Teenage Girls; Travel; Turkey; Women Authors; Women's Fiction

Now Try: Other novels about families who travel together to foreign countries include Samantha Gillison's *The Undiscovered Country* and Barbara Kingsolver's *The Poisonwood Bible*; memoirs in which women recall their youths spent moving around the globe might also be of interest, such as Francine du Plessix Gray's *Them: A Memoir of Parents* and Moira Hodgson's *It Seemed Like a Good Idea at the Time*. Another memoir that may appeal is Alexandra Fuller's best seller about growing up in Rhodesia, *Don't Let's Go to the Dogs Tonight: An African Childhood*.

Holthe, Tess Uriza.

🖋 *The Five-Forty-Five to Cannes*. Crown, 2007. 274pp. ISBN 9780307351852.

The train to Cannes and the city itself provide the framework for these interconnected stories of love, loss, and reminiscence. When Chazz Jorgenson, suffering from a bipolar episode, becomes convinced that his beloved wife Claudette is going to leave him, he takes the train to Cannes, the last place he believes they were happy together. The tragedy that befalls him there, and its aftermath, draw together a disparate group of characters, including two men who had planned to rob him and his wife.

Second Appeal: Character

Subjects: Accidents; Bipolar Disease; Cannes; Death and Dying; France; Grief; Marriage; Mental Health; Short Stories; Travel; Women Authors

Awards: ALA Notable

Now Try: Holthe's earlier title is a novel set during World War II, *When the Elephants Dance*. Another novel in which travelers become involved in each others' lives is H. G. Mojtabai's *All That Road Going*; Anne Tyler's novel *Earthly Possessions* and Roland Merullo's *Breakfast with Buddha* also feature plots in which characters are traveling, and not particularly of their own accord. Another popular book of interconnected stories is Elizabeth Strout's Pulitzer Prize–winning *Olive Kitteridge*. Several nonfiction travel accounts might also appeal to these readers, including Paul Theroux's *The Old Patagonian Express: By Train Through the Americas* and Tahir Shah's *The Caliph's House: A Year in Casablanca*.

Hunt, Samantha.

The Invention of Everything Else. **Houghton Mifflin, 2008. 257pp. ISBN 9780618801121.**

An unlikely shared interest in and love for pigeons serves as the impetus for a friendship between New York City hotel chambermaid Louisa and one of the hotel's most infamous but eccentric residents, the inventor and engineer Nikola Tesla. As the new year of 1943 dawns, the friendship between Tesla and Louisa grows as they talk and Tesla opens up about his childhood in Croatia. The reclusive inventor is not the only eccentric to whom Louisa is close; her father knows a man who invented a time machine (which he very much wants to try), and the time machine is maintained by her beau Arthur, who may or may not be from the future himself.

Second Appeal: Character

Subjects: 1940s; Animals; Biographical Fiction; Birds; Historical Fiction; Love Affairs; New York City; Pigeons; Tesla, Nikola; Time Travel; Women Authors

Now Try: Hunt's first novel, *The Seas*, features a young girl who escapes her problems by indulging in the fantasy that she is a mermaid. Another quirky novel about time travel and human relationships is Audrey Niffenegger's popular *The Time Traveler's Wife*; Mark Helprin's sprawling historical epic *Winter's Tale* also provides a sense of old New York City and throws in a bit of magic realism to boot. Although much more stereotypically a chick lit novel, Toni Jordan's thoughtful *Addition* features a modern-day woman afflicted with obsessive compulsive disorder and a fascination for the work of Nikola Tesla. Marc Seifer's biography of Tesla, *Wizard: The Life and Times of Nikola Tesla* might also be suggested.

Jordan, Hillary.

🌳 *Mudbound: A Novel.* **Algonquin Books of Chapel Hill, 2008. 328pp. ISBN 9781565125698.**

The shock of moving from a more urban environment to an isolated farm in 1940s Mississippi proves overpowering for newlywed Laura, who leaves her teaching job and relatively cosmopolitan life in Memphis to join her husband on his home farm. Although they first face challenges to their marriage and livelihood with equanimity, their relationship starts to break down when her father-in-law moves in with them—and disturbs Laura with his deeply held and racist convictions—as well as when they are joined by her brother-in-law, newly returned from the war and appealingly worldly to a woman already struggling with loneliness.

Subjects: 1940s; Agriculture; Book Groups; Domestic Fiction; Family Relationships; First Novels; First Person; Historical Fiction; Marriage; Mississippi; Multiple Viewpoints; Race Relations; Rural Life; Women Authors; YA

Awards: Alex Award; Bellwether Prize for Fiction

Now Try: Another novel in which racism plays a part in family relationships is Deborah Johnson's *The Air Between Us*. Novels about women facing isolation and struggling in their relationships with their husbands are C. E. Morgan's *All the Living* (set in Appalachia), Wallace Stegner's classic *Angle of Repose* (set during the latter part of the nineteenth century), and A. Manette Ansay's *Vinegar Hill*. This novel won the Bellwether Prize for fiction (awarded "in support of a literature of social change") ; previous winners of this award include Heidi Durrow's *The Girl Who Fell from the Sky*, Marjorie Kowalski Cole's *Correcting the Landscape*, Gayle Brandeis's *The Book of Dead Birds*, and Donna Gershten's *Kissing the Virgin's Mouth*. Nonfiction titles about race relations might also be suggested, such as bell hooks's *Bone Black: Memories of Girlhood* and Paul Hendrickson's *Sons of Mississippi: A Story of Race and Its Legacy*.

Kafka-Gibbons, Paul.

DuPont Circle: A Novel. **Houghton Mifflin, 2001. 248pp. ISBN 9780395869321.**

Washington D.C.,'s liberal and genteel DuPont Circle neighborhood has been home to the Allard family for years; the patriarch, Judge Bailey Allard, is a prominent appeals court judge there, and his son, Jon, along with his partner Peter and their two children (adopted from Jon's sister), also lives in the area. At the same time that Jon arranges for a law student, Louisa, to board in widower Bailey's house, Bailey receives a case that may affect the legality of gay marriages nationwide.

Subjects: Book Groups; Family Relationships; Fathers and Sons; Gay Men; GLBTQ; Judges; Law and Lawyers; Marriage; Men's Lives; Washington, D.C.

Now Try: Kafka-Gibbons is also the author of the novel *Love <Enter>*. Also of interest might be books in which urban neighborhoods play a role, such as Adam Langer's *Crossing California* (Chicago) and *Ellington Boulevard* (New York), Stuart Dybek's *I Sailed with Magellan* (Chicago), and Pamela Holm's *The Night Garden* (San Francisco). Another political family can be found in Ward Just's *Echo House*, while other novels about troublesome legal cases and other professional quandaries might appeal, such as Gary Sernovitz's *The Contrarians*, Elizabeth Benedict's *The Practice of Deceit*, and Ken Wells's *Crawfish Mountain*. Kafka-Gibbons's style has also been compared to that of Stephen McCauley, whose novels *Alternatives to Sex*, *Making Love to the Minor Poets of Chicago*, and *The Object of My Affection* might be good read-alikes.

Kingsolver, Barbara.

Prodigal Summer. HarperCollins, 2000. 444pp. ISBN 9780060199654.

Three strong women and their relationships to their Appalachian surroundings and their loved ones are at the heart of this novel. Wildlife biologist Deanna Wolfe is torn between her desire to save a community of wolves and her growing love for a man who is a consummate hunter; Lusa Maluf Landowski feels out of place in the family she married into (even as she finds the insect life surrounding her new home fascinating); and seventy-something Nannie Land Rawley, an orchard owner, finds herself drawn into a feud (ripe with romantic overtones) with her equally crotchety widower neighbor, Garnett Walker.

Second Appeal: Character

Subjects: Animals; Appalachians; Biology; Book Groups; Classics; Family Relationships; Love Affairs; Multigenerational Fiction; Multiple Viewpoints; Women Authors; Women's Fiction

Now Try: Kingsolver's fiction is often informed by the settings she chooses, from the desert Southwest in *Animal Dreams, The Bean Trees,* and *Pigs in Heaven,* to Africa in her popular novel *The Poisonwood Bible.* She is also the author of a memoir about her native Appalachia, *Animal, Vegetable, Miracle.* Another novel featuring a strong woman character is Jeannette Walls's *Half Broke Horses;* strong characters and a distinct Southern setting can also be found in Olive Burns's classic *Cold Sassy Tree;* Stephanie Kallos's *Sing Them Home* also focuses on a variety of unique characters and a tightly knit community, and Anne Tyler's novels *Dinner at the Homesick Restaurant* and *If Morning Ever Comes* contain both well-described settings and love stories.

Kneale, Matthew.

🏆 *English Passengers.* Nan A. Talese, 2000. 446pp. ISBN 9780385497435.

Characters from all parts of the socioeconomic structure coexist in Kneale's historical novel about the founding of Tasmania: government bureaucrats, oceangoing adventurers and smugglers, and natives in the lands subject to the mighty British empire. Most of the novel's action revolves around two main storylines: the voyage of the ship *Sincerity,* captained by Quillian Kewley, to Tasmania; and, once the ship and its voyagers land, their journey to forge a new life in a new land, guided by an aboriginal named Peevay, who is not ready to surrender his way of life to the travelers.

Subjects: 19th Century; Adventure; Book Groups; British Authors; Colonialism; Exploration; Historical Fiction; Ocean; Tasmania; Travel

Awards: ALA Notable; Costa Novel Award; New York Times Notable

Now Try: Kneale's other novels are *When We Were Romans, Small Crimes in an Age of Abundance,* and *Whore Banquets.* Peter Carey's historical novel set in Australia, *The True History of the Kelly Gang,* is based on a true story. David Liss's literary historical novels might also be suggested (they include *A Conspiracy of Paper, The Coffee Trader,* and *The Whiskey Rebels*). Nonfiction titles about maritime adventures and travels might be suggested, such as Carolly Erickson's *The Girl from Botany Bay,* Robert Hughes's *The Fatal Shore: The Epic of Australia's Founding,* Sian Rees's *The Floating Brothel: The Extraordinary True Story of an Eighteenth-Century Ship and its Cargo of Female Convictions,* or Stephen Taylor's

Caliban's Shore. Adam Hochschild's shocking history of colonialism in Africa, *King Leopold's Ghost*, might be an interesting read-alike, as might Bruce Chatwin's classic travelogue about Australia, *The Songlines*.

Koënings, N. S.

Theft: Stories. **Little, Brown, 2008. 264pp. ISBN 9780316001861.**

A wide variety of characters and quandaries are on display in these five (near-novella length) stories; in them, characters struggle with the unintended consequences of their actions, their own prejudices and shortcomings, and just plain bad luck (as in the story "Setting Up Shop," where a young woman hopes to avoid an arranged marriage by demanding that her suitor give up his other wives—but he agrees to do so). The author also skillfully describes the landscape and feel of the African settings of his stories.

Second Appeal: Character

Subjects: Africa; Book Groups; Family Relationships; Multicultural; Short Stories; Women Authors

Now Try: Koëning's other book is a novel titled *The Blue Taxi*, which is set in East Africa. Other novels that feature exotic (but decidedly not posh) surroundings are Joan Silber's *The Size of the World*, Lucinda Roy's *The Hotel Alleluia*, and Kira Salak's *The White Mary*; the story collection *Say You're One of Them* by Uwem Akpan might also appeal.

Kushner, Rachel.

🌳 *Telex from Cuba: A Novel*. **Scribner, 2008. 322pp. ISBN 9781416561033.**

In this debut novel, Kushner relates a sprawling story of pre-revolutionary Cuba through the voices and viewpoints of multiple characters, including the children (Everly Lederer and K. C. Stites) of American and United Fruit Company business executives, cabaret dancers and agitators, and revolutionaries.

Subjects: Biographical Fiction; Book Groups; Castro, Fidel; Coming-of-age; Corporations; Cuba; First Novels; Historical Fiction; Multiple Viewpoints; Women Authors

Awards: New York Times Notable

Now Try: As a setting (for both residents and expatriates from the country), Cuba has been explored in numerous mainstream fiction titles that may appeal to these readers, including Daina Chaviano's *The Island of Eternal Love*; Reinaldo Arenas's *The Color of Summer*; Cristina Garcia's novels *A Handbook to Luck, Monkey Hunting, The Aguero Sisters*, and *Dreaming in Cuban*; Cecelia Samartin's *Broken Paradise*; Oscar Hijuelos's *A Simple Habana Melody: (From When the World Was Good)*; Ernesto Mestre-Reed's *The Second Death of Unica Aveyano*; and Ivonne Lamazares's *The Sugar Island*. Nonfiction titles that might appeal to these readers are Peter Chapman's *Bananas: How the United Fruit Company Changed the World* and T. J. English's *Havana Nocturne: How the Mob Owned Cuba . . . And Then Lost It to the Revolution*.

Langer, Adam.

Crossing California. **Riverhead Books, 2004. 432pp. ISBN 9781573222747.**

Teenagers Jill and Michelle Wasserstrom, Muley Wills (who is in love with Jill), and Larry Rovner (who aspires to both perfect Judaism and rock stardom) are the prime storytellers in this novel, set during the years 1979 through 1981 in

Chicago's West and East Rogers Park neighborhoods (separated by California Avenue into the upper-middle-class west side and the middle-class east side). The teenagers in this novel are not the only ones caught up in their own lives, relationships, and trials; their parents also struggle to find their equilibrium as the Iran hostage crisis first shocks the nation and then becomes a catalyst for national celebration and cohesion when Ronald Reagan is inaugurated into the presidency and the hostages are released.

Subjects: 1970s; 1980s; Book Groups; Chicago; Coming-of-age; Friendships; Iran Hostage Crisis; Jews and Judaism; Multiple Viewpoints; Social Class; Teenagers; YA

Now Try: Langer is also the author of two other novels that rely heavily on setting, *The Washington Story: A Novel in Five Spheres* (which is a sequel to this novel) and *Ellington Boulevard: A Novel in A-Flat*. Stuart Dybek's *I Sailed with Magellan*, also set in Chicago, might be offered, as might another coming-of-age book in which a teenager focuses on international events (in this case, the Falklands War): David Mitchell's *Black Swan Green*. Tom Perrotta's earlier novels, *Election* and *Joe College*, featuring characters close in age to Langer's, might also be good read-alikes.

Ellington Boulevard: A Novel in A-Flat. **Spiegel & Grau, 2008. 336pp. ISBN 9780385522052.**

When musician Ike Morphy and his dog Herbie Mann return to his apartment in the Roberto Clemente building after a short trip, Ike is surprised to find that it is being offered for sale by the son of the (recently deceased) landlord. Told over the transaction of the selling of the condo (the novel is separated into segments titled "An Offer is Accepted," "A Deal Is Closed," etc.) and from the viewpoints of Ike, his dog, the landlord's son Mark Masler, the buyer Rebecca Sugarman and her husband, and the broker Josh Dybnick (among others), this novel is alive with both fully drawn characters and a piece of New York City real estate that lives up to its importance to all of the novel's players.

Second Appeal: Character

Subjects: Animals; Book Groups; Dogs; Homes; Love Affairs; Men's Lives; Multiple Viewpoints; Music and Musicians; New York City

Now Try: Langer is also the author of the novels *The Washington Story* and *Crossing California*. Other novels that focus on characters' cities and their homes might be suggested, such as Cheryl Mendelson's *Morningside Heights* (also about New York City residents trying to keep their increasingly unaffordable homes) and *Love, Work, Children*, Anne Tyler's *Dinner at the Homesick Restaurant* and *Back When We Were Grownups*, and Paul Kafka-Gibbons's *DuPont Circle* (about Washington, D.C.). Nonfiction about making a home in New York might also be suggested, such as Judith Matloff's *Home Girl: Making a Life on a Lawless Block*, Colson Whitehead's *Colossus*, or even Pete Hamill's *Downtown: My Manhattan*.

Leshem, Ron.

Beaufort. **Delacorte Press, 2008. 360pp. ISBN 9780553806823.**

Twenty-one-year-old Liraz Liberti, a second lieutenant in the Israeli Defense Forces, is assigned to lead his much younger compatriots in their defense of Beaufort, a former Crusader fort in Lebanon. (The year is 1999, at the height of tensions between Israel and Hezbollah.) Tasked with keeping northern Israel safe from invasion, the soldiers at Beaufort suffer from a nearly constant barrage of weapons fire, and all the attendant psychological problems such incessant danger causes. Although Beaufort itself is a beautiful ancient fortress, and is beautifully described in Liberti's diary, its beauty is tragically overshadowed by the violence and death surrounding the soldiers.

Subjects: 1990s; Books in Translation; Coming-of-age; Diary; First Novels; First Person; Israel; Lebanon; Military; Terrorism; Violence; Young Men

Now Try: Fictional accounts of the psychological damage caused by war can be found in Tim O'Brien's *The Things They Carried* and *In the Lake of the Woods*, Denis Johnson's *Tree of Smoke*, and Erich Maria Remarque's classic *All Quiet on the Western Front*. Also of interest might be David Benioff's story of young men in wartime, *City of Thieves*. Nonfiction war accounts might also be suggested, such as Bing West's *No True Glory: A Frontline Account of the Battle for Fallujah*, Colby Buzzell's *My War: Killing Time in Iraq*, or Adam Harmon's *Lonely Soldier: The Memoir of an American Soldier in the Israeli Army*. Robert Fisk's history of Lebanon, *Pity the Nation*, might also be a good related read.

Logsdon, Gene.

The Last of the Husbandmen. Ohio University Press. 333pp. ISBN 9780821417850.

Two boyhood friends in rural Ohio, Ben Bump and Emmet Gowler, come from divergent social backgrounds (Ben is the son of immigrants; Emmet belongs to their community's "old money" contingent) but remain friends through school and their farming careers, which also diverge as Ben pursues organic and sustainable farming methods, while Emmet implements every technological advance and method that modern agribusiness had to offer through the latter half of the twentieth century. The effects of their differing approaches are described clearly; Logsdon's knowledge of and love for the land shines through his prose, regardless of which character's methods he is exploring.

Subjects: Agriculture; American Midwest; Coming-of-age; Community Life; Friendships; Men's Lives; Ohio; Rural Life; Small Press; Young Men

Now Try: Logsdon's other work of fiction is a novel titled *The Man Who Created Paradise*; he is also the author of several nonfiction classics, including *The Contrary Farmer*, *All Flesh Is Grass*, and *Living at Nature's Pace*. Another novel in which the traditional and modern methods of farming clash is Wendell Berry's *Jayber Crow* (Berry's nonfiction on the subject, including *The Unsettling of America*, might also be of interest). Other coming-of-age novels might also appeal, such as Larry Watson's *Sundown, Yellow Moon* and Tony Earley's *Jim the Boy* and *The Blue Star*.

Maillard, Keith.

The Clarinet Polka. St. Martin's Press, 2003. 406pp. ISBN 9780312308896.

When Jimmy Koprowski returns to his small West Virginia hometown (Raysburg) from the Vietnam War, he struggles to feel reconnected to his former life and neighbors and finds few other ways to cope besides drinking and gravitating toward disastrous love affairs. When his sister begins a polka band that will become a hit in the community, however, he finds his interest in the music helping to heal him in a way he would never have imagined.

Subjects: 1960s; Brothers and Sisters; Coming-of-age; Family Relationships; Men's Lives; Music and Musicians; Siblings; Small-Town Life; Vietnam War; West Virginia; Young Men

Now Try: Maillard is also the author of another coming-of-age novel, from a woman's point of view: *Gloria*; his four-volume series of novels set in West Virginia might also be suggested (*Running, Morgantown, Lyndon Johnson and the Majorettes,* and *Looking Good*). Another novel featuring a Vietnam veteran facing a tough challenge (in New Orleans, after Hurricane Katrina) is Tom Piazza's *City of Refuge*; Ivan Doig's novel *The Eleventh Man*, about a World War II veteran who loses several friends to the war, might also be a good read-alike. Danielle Trussoni's memoir of life with her father, a Vietnam veteran who returned to his hometown of LaCrosse, Wisconsin, *Falling through the Earth*, might be suggested, as might Tom Bissell's thoughtful *The Father of All Things: A Marine, His Son, and the Legacy of Vietnam.*

Marcom, Micheline Aharonian.

Draining the Sea. Riverhead Books, 2008. 335pp. ISBN 9781594489730.

Marcom's narrator, who remains unnamed throughout the novel, spends the majority of his time driving around his adopted city of Los Angeles and trying, unsuccessfully, to forget the crimes and atrocities (which he may or may not have participated in; the reader can never really be sure, as much of the book is told in image-rich but not chronological flashbacks) he witnessed during the Guatemalan civil war. The story hinges on the torture and murder of a young indigenous Guatemalan prostitute, which the protagonist cannot stop reliving, in between fixating on happier times spent with her in her native village. Marcom is not afraid of her subject, and readers should be aware that both sexual and violent encounters are described in very explicit language.

Subjects: Book Groups; California; Civil War; Explicit Sexuality; Flashbacks; Guatemala; Immigrants and Immigration; Los Angeles; Murder; Political Fiction; Prostitution; Torture; Violence; War; Women Authors; Women Writing as Men

Now Try: Marcom is also the author of the novels *Mirror in the Well, The Daydreaming Boy,* and *Three Apples Fell from Heaven.* Another novel in which a man struggles to understand memories he didn't know he had is J. Robert Lennon's *Castle.* Another somewhat existential novel set in Los Angeles is James Frey's *Bright Shiny Morning*; although different in setting and story, Charles Bock's *Beautiful Children*, set in the urban tangle of Las Vegas, might also prove to be a good stylistic read-alike.

Matthiessen, Peter.

🏵 *Shadow Country.* Modern Library, 2008. 892pp. ISBN 9780679640196.

Edited and combined into one volume, this novel contains the entire saga of the E. J. Watson story (which Matthiessen had previously told over the course of three novels). A Florida sugarcane farmer in nineteenth-century Florida, Watson was a hard man in a hard country, and was eventually murdered; in the latter part of this epic, his son Lucius returns home as a World War I veteran to piece together what really happened to his father, as well as to learn more about his own family and its secrets.

Second Appeal: Character

Subjects: 19th Century; Biographical Fiction; Classics; Epic Reads; Family Relationships; Family Secrets; Florida; Historical Fiction; Men's Lives; Murder

Awards: National Book Award

Now Try: Matthiessen has written other novels, including the popular *At Play in the Fields of the Lord* and *Far Tortuga,* as well as multiple setting-driven works of nonfiction, such as *The Snow Leopard* and *The Cloud Forest*. Another novel in which family secrets and the family business are entwined is Jane Smiley's *A Thousand Acres*; other historical sagas might be suggested to these readers, including Edna Ferber's *Giant*, Elmer Kelton's *Sons of Texas*, and Annie Dillard's *The Living*. Mark Arax's nonfiction histories of the frontier land of California might also be good read-alikes, particularly *In My Father's Name* (about his own father's murder), as well as *The King of California: J.G. Boswell and the Making of a Secret American Empire* and *West of the West: Dreamers, Believers, Builders, and Killers in the Golden State*.

McCall, Nathan.

Them: A Novel. Atria Books, 2007. 339pp. ISBN 9781416549154.

Forty-year-old Barlowe Reed is used to feeling that any progress he makes in life is in direct opposition to the efforts of "them"—the government bureaucrats, ex-girlfriends, and most particularly white people—who seek to keep hard workers and honest people poor. Through long hours working as a printer, he has nearly put together enough of a stake to buy the house he rents, along with his nephew Tyrone, in Atlanta, when the sudden and relentless arrival of white people set on gentrifying the neighborhood quickly drives house prices beyond his range. Bringing the conflict close to home, the new homeowners next to Barlowe are a white couple named Sandy and Sean; while Sandy makes friendly overtures toward him and the rest of the neighborhood, Sean and Barlowe perceive one another as natural enemies from the start.

Subjects: African American Authors; African Americans; Atlanta; Book Groups; Community Life; Friendships; Georgia; Homes; Men's Lives; Race Relations

Now Try: McCall is also the author of the essay collection *What's Going On: Personal Essays* and the memoir *Makes Me Wanna Holler: A Young Black Man in America*. A novel that considers gentrification in a slightly different neighborhood is Cheryl Mendelson's *Morningside Heights*; Judith Matloff's memoir *Home Girl: Building a Dream House on a Lawless Block* also looks at gentrification from a slightly different viewpoint. Those readers interested in other novels by African American men might also consider Eric Jerome Dickey's *Pleasure* and *Drive Me Crazy*, David Haynes's *Live at Five* and *The Full Matilda*, or even Charles Barkley's collection of conversations with black men about race, *Who's Afraid of a Large Black Man?*

McCann, Colum.

Let the Great World Spin. Random House, 2009. 349pp. ISBN 9781400063734.

Set in 1970s New York City, McCann's novel opens with Manhattan's residents watching, enthralled, as Philippe Petit walks between the towers of the World Trade Center on a tightrope. The large cast of characters includes two Irish brothers; a mother-and-daughter pair who work as prostitutes; the judge who sentences Petit for his stunt; and an artist and his wife, who cause an accident that will result in the fatalities of several of the characters (and will thus affect the lives of the others as well).

Second Appeal: Character

Subjects: 1970s; Biographical Fiction; Book Groups; Historical Fiction; Immigrants and Immigration; Irish Authors; New York City; Vietnam War

Now Try: McCann is the author of several other historical novels, including *Zoli*, *Dancer: A Novel* (based on the life of dancer Rudolf Nureyev), and *This Side of Brightness*. Other

"New York" novels might appeal to these readers, including Mark Helprin's classic *Winter's Tale*, Joseph O'Neill's *Netherland*, and Pete Hamill's *Forever* and *Snow in August*. A fascinating book about some of New York City's more eccentric residents (and the woman who photographed them best, Diane Arbus) is *Hubert's Freaks: The Rare-Book Dealer, The Times Square Talker, and the Lost Photos of Diane Arbus*, by Gregory Gibson.

McGraw, Erin.

The Seamstress of Hollywood Boulevard. **Houghton Mifflin, 2008. 373pp. ISBN 9780618386284.**

Kansas in the early part of the twentieth century is not a glamorous setting, a fact of which Nell Platt is all too well aware. Although she is married young (and disastrously) to a Kansas farmer whose two daughters she bears, she leaves her family behind to move to the new movie capital of the world, Hollywood, and reinvents herself as the skilled and sought after seamstress "Madame Annelle." She remarries and has another daughter, and seeks to leave her past behind, but the past—in the form of the two daughters she left behind—eventually finds her.

Second Appeal: Character

Subjects: 1900s; 1920s; California; Family Secrets; First Person; Historical Fiction; Hollywood; Kansas; Mothers and Daughters; Movies; Professions; Seamstresses; Women Authors; Women's Fiction

Now Try: McGraw is the author of a story collection titled *The Good Life*, as well as the novels *Lies of the Saints* and *The Baby Tree*. Another historical novel in which a woman makes the most of her sewing skills and intelligence is Amy Bloom's *Away*; other historical novels featuring strong women characters might also be suggested, including Joanna Herson's *The German Bride*, Lisa See's *Peony in Love*, and Janice Y. K. Lee's *The Piano Teacher*. A more modern novel in which a woman walks away from her family is Anne Tyler's lighter but still thoughtful *Ladder of Years*.

Mda, Zakes.

🌷 *The Madonna of Excelsior.* **Farrar, Straus & Giroux, 2002. 258pp. ISBN 9780374200084.**

Set in apartheid South Africa, Mda's novel examines that country's history of interracial relationships and laws regarding miscegenation. The reader first sees Niki, Mda's heroine, as she poses for a painting of the Madonna done by her white village priest; while that is as far as their relationship extends, Niki also garners interest from the white Afrikaner farmers and eventually bears a daughter, Popi, by one of them. Told over the course of thirty years and focusing on Niki's relationship with her children, including her activist son Viliki, this is a novel filled with both commentary and powerful visual imagery.

Subjects: Apartheid; Art and Artists; Biracial Characters; Family Relationships; Multicultural; Race Relations; South Africa; South African Authors

Awards: ALA Notable

Now Try: Mda is also the author of the novel *Ways of Dying*. Other historical novels that may appeal to Mda's readers are Tsitsi Dangarembga's *Nervous Conditions*, Alice Walker's *The Color Purple*, Toni Morrison's *The Bluest Eye*, Moses Isegawa's

Abyssinian Chronicles, and Sue Monk Kidd's *The Secret Life of Bees*, while modern novels set in South Africa might also work as related reads, including J. M. Coetzee's *Disgrace* and Nadine Gordimer's *Jump and Other Stories*, *My Son's Story*, and *July's People*. Nonfiction titles about race relations might also be suggested, such as Edward Balls's *Slaves in the Family* or Annette Gordon-Reed's *The Hemingses of Monticello: An American Family*.

Messud, Claire.

🌳 *The Emperor's Children: A Novel*. **Knopf, 2006. 431pp. ISBN 9780307264190.**

Danielle, Marina, and Julius, longtime friends and young professionals striving to make their way in their careers as they steadily approach their thirties, find there is little challenge to their friendships until Marina's cousin, Bootie Tub, arrives in New York City, determined to make his own way in journalism (and if he has to take down Murray Thwaite, Marina's father, and his uncle, to do so, he's okay with that). Much of the dialogue here is internal, as Messud strives to make clear the inner lives and motivations of her characters, but the events of 9/11 and her detailed description of New York City and its environs also make this a novel anchored in its place and time.

Second Appeal: Character

Subjects: 9/11; Family Relationships; Friendships; Gay Men; GLBTQ; Journalism; Love Affairs; Mass Media; New York City; Women Authors

Awards: New York Times Notable

Now Try: Messud has written two other novels, *The Last Life* and *When the World Was Steady*, as well as the collection of two novellas titled *The Hunters*. Other quintessential "New York novels" might be offered to these readers, including Joseph O'Neill's *Netherland*, Lynne Sharon Schwartz's *The Writing on the Wall*, Jonathan Safran Foer's *Extremely Loud and Incredibly Close*, and Jay McInerney's *The Good Life* (not to mention his classic novel *Bright Lights, Big City*). Authors with a similarly skillful prose style might appeal to her readers as well, including Jennifer Egan (*The Keep*) and Jonathan Franzen (*The Corrections* and the essay collection *The Discomfort Zone*).

Millar, Martin.

Suzy, Led Zeppelin, and Me. **Soft Skull Press, 2008. 222pp. ISBN 9781593762001.**

The appeal of this novel is truly a toss-up between setting and character, as Millar offers compelling descriptions of both. However, the novel is so steeped in its Glasgow location and time period (the early 1970s) that setting just edges out character. Millar's unnamed narrator describes his most transcendent experience from his 1972 high school year, his attendance at a Led Zeppelin concert, as well as his crush on neighbor Suzy, from his vantage point in the present, where he is trying to make sense of his friendship with Manx, an ex-girlfriend, and a grown-up life that seems to offer fewer and fewer such transcendent experiences.

Second Appeal: Character

Subjects: 1970s; British Authors; Coming-of-age; First Person; Friendships; Glasgow; Humor; Love Affairs; Music and Musicians; Quick Reads; Scotland; Scottish Authors; YA; Young Men

Now Try: Millar's books are wildly divergent in style and story; in addition to another fairly straightforward work of fiction, *Milk, Sulphate, and Alby Starvation*, his urban fantasies *The Good Fairies of New York* and *Lonely Werewolf Girl* might appeal to these readers, as might his fantasy series starting with the title *Thraxas* (which he wrote under the name Martin Scott). Other Scottish or British authors might appeal to these readers, particularly David Mitchell (*Black Swan Green*), Craig Ferguson (yes, the host of *The Late Late Show*; he's also written a novel titled *Between the Bridge and the River*), and Irvine Welsh (*Filth, Glue, Trainspotting*, and *The Bedroom Secrets of the Master Chefs*). In addition to providing a sense of setting (Glasgow in the 1970s), this is also a superlative coming-of-age novel; its readers might enjoy similarly skillful coming-of-age narratives by John Green (*Looking for Alaska, An Abundance of Katherines*, and *Paper Towns*).

Monaghan, Nicola.

The Killing Jar. **Scribner, 2006. 273pp. ISBN 9780743299688.**

Life is anything but idyllic or cozy in Monaghan's novel of life on a council estate (low-income housing in urban Great Britain; often compared to the "projects" found in American cities) in Nottingham. Kerrie-Ann Hill has been taking care of herself for as long as she can remember, and only rarely finds kind individuals with whom she can connect, including a kindly elderly neighbor who shows her how to collect and study butterflies, moths, and other insects (which the neighbor kills before dissection with the help of a chemical-filled "killing jar") , a teacher, and (at least in the beginning) her older and protective boyfriend Mark Scotland. In between taking care of her younger half-brother Jon, helping Mark with his drug-dealing business and watching him spiral downward in his heroin addiction, and falling prey herself to an ecstasy addiction, Kerrie-Ann somehow manages to keep her sense of self and self-preservation intact.

Second Appeal: Character

Subjects: British Authors; Brothers and Sisters; Coming-of-age; Drug Abuse; First Novels; First Person; Great Britain; Love Affairs; Siblings; Teenagers; Violence; Women Authors

Now Try: Monaghan's debut inevitably drew comparisons to Irvine Welsh's classic of urban youth and heroin addiction, *Trainspotting*; both books, although detailing decidedly ugly subjects, share the same tone of wonder at their protagonists' indomitable will to survive. Although not as bleak, two other British coming-of-age novels might be suggested to these readers: David Mitchell's *Black Swan Green* and Iain Banks's *The Crow Road*. Another British author who might appeal to Monaghan's readers is A. L. Kennedy; Anne Enright's novel *The Gathering* and Sebastian Barry's *Secret Scripture* also offer bleak tones but strong-willed characters.

Mones, Nicole.

The Last Chinese Chef. **Houghton Mifflin, 2007. 278pp. ISBN 978-0618619665.**

When food journalist Maggie McElroy's husband dies unexpectedly, she finds herself overwhelmed by grief, and then stunned by the revelation that her husband was having an affair (which she learns about when a paternity suit is brought against his estate). When she travels to Beijing (where the woman who made the claim lives), she also undertakes an assignment to do a profile on American-born Chinese chef Sam Liang, who is learning his craft and undertaking a translation of a cookbook used in the imperial court (which was written by his grandfather). As Sam begins to teach her about his personal and cultural history, primarily through his cooking, she gains a greater understanding of the culture in which she has become immersed, as well as of her own life and goals.

Subjects: Beijing; Book Groups; China; Death and Dying; Food; Love Affairs; Marriage; Quick Reads; Travel; Women Authors

Now Try: Mones's two other novels are also set in Beijing: *A Cup of Light* and *Lost in Translation*. Another novel that includes a historical backstory and centers on food is Monique Truong's *The Book of Salt*; although set in Hong Kong, Janice Y. K. Lee's novel *The Piano Teacher* might be a good read-alike. Travel nonfiction set in China might also be suggested, such as Polly Evans's *Fried Eggs with Chopsticks*, Peter Hessler's *River Town: Two Years on the Yangtze*, or Jen Lin-Liu's *Serve the People: A Stir-Fried Journey Through China*.

Mueenuddin, Daniyal.

In Other Rooms, Other Wonders. **Norton, 2009. 247pp. ISBN 9780393068009.**

The author's eight linked stories offer perfectly encapsulated vignettes of the lives of very different (but related) characters, from the rural electrician and jack of all trades, Nawab, whose livelihood and status depend on his motorbike, to the family and servants living in affluence (but not necessarily more accord) on the village's familial estate. Mueenuddin perfectly describes not only the characters and their community but also his native landscape (rural and urban) of Pakistan.

Second Appeal: Character

Subjects: First Novels; Interconnected Stories; Love Affairs; Men's Lives; Multicultural; Pakistan; Pakistani Authors; Quick Reads; Short Stories

Now Try: Another novel of linked stories that may appeal to these readers is A. G. Mojtabai's *All That Road Going* (although it is set in the United States). Set in India, Aravind Adiga's dark but brilliant novel *The White Tiger* might provide a similar reading experience, as might Kiran Desai's *The Inheritance of Loss*; also of interest might be Nadeem Aslam's *Maps for Lost Lovers* and Manil Suri's *The Death of Vishnu*.

Niemi, Mikael.

🌲 *Popular Music from Vittula.* **Seven Stories Press, 2003. 237pp. ISBN 9781583225233.**

The small town of Pajala, Sweden, during the 1960s, is a town north of the Arctic Circle populated primarily by lumberjacks and others who make their slim livings from the land. Told from the point of view of the eleven-year-old Matti, this coming-of-age novel lets the reader in on the particulars of a small-town boyhood, as well as the challenges and beauties of living in such an isolated location and punishing climate.

Subjects: 1960s; 1970s; Books in Translation; Community Life; Humor; Quick Reads; Short Stories; Small-Town Life; Sweden; Teenage Boys; Teenagers

Awards: ALA Notable

Now Try: Fans of this quick-reading novel might also consider Per Petterson's critically lauded novel *Out Stealing Horses*, which provides a similar Nordic setting and coming-of-age theme; other novels in which boys test their friendships might appeal, including Todd Tucker's *Over and Under*, Tim Winton's *Breath*, Nick Hornby's *About a Boy* (although one of the boys in that novel is a man in his thirties), or even Ray Bradbury's classic *Something Wicked This Way Comes*. Nonfiction memoirs in which men recall their childhoods or early friendships might also appeal to these readers, such as Jean Shepherd's dated but still very funny *In God We Trust, All Others Pay Cash*, J. R. Moehringer's *The Tender Bar*, David Benjamin's *The Life and Times of the Last Kid Picked*, or Homer Hickam's *Rocket Boys*.

Olmstead, Robert.

Far Bright Star: A Novel. **Algonquin Books of Chapel Hill, 2009. 207pp. ISBN 9781565125926.**

As part of the doomed 1916 mission to hunt down the Mexican folk hero Pancho Villa (whose daring and murderous raids on towns in New Mexico made him public enemy number one in the United States in the early twentieth century), cavalry officer Napoleon Childs soon finds he is in over his head. He must not only control a group of inexperienced horse soldiers with more enthusiasm for violence than sense or skill, but must also survive in the unforgiving desert landscape.

Second Appeal: Story

Subjects: 1910s; Historical Fiction; Mexico; New Mexico; Quick Reads; Villa, Pancho; Violence; War; Westerns

Now Try: Olmsted is the author of a number of other critically lauded novels, including *Coal Black Horse, America by Land*, and *A Trail of Heart's Blood Wherever We Go*, as well as the story collection *River Dogs* and the memoir *Stay Here with Me*. Olmstead's writing and skill at conjuring landscapes has been compared to that of Kent Haruf, whose novels *Plainsong* and *Eventide* might be suggested. Three other books set in the borderlands between Texas and Mexico might make good related reads: Rick Bass's *The Diezmo*, Elmer Kelton's *The Raiders: Sons of Texas*, and James Carlos Blake's *Borderlands: Short Fiction*.

O'Neill, Joseph.

🏵 *Netherland: A Novel.* **Pantheon, 2008. 256pp. ISBN 9780307377043.**

In post-9/11 New York City, Hans van den Broek has not only lost his actual residence (he and his family have been living in the Chelsea Hotel since their home was damaged in the terrorist attack), but is also casting about for metaphysical moorings, a feeling that is exacerbated by the decline of his marriage and his wife Rachel's departure, with their son Jake, for her native London. While she is gone, Hans meets the entrepreneurial, charming, yet highly secretive Chuck Ramkissoon, a native Trinidadian who dreams of setting up a cricket club in New York City but who is more gainfully and prosaically employed by the Russian mob.

Second Appeal: Language

Subjects: 9/11; Classics; Cricket; Family Relationships; First Person; Friendships; Immigrants and Immigration; Marriage; Men's Lives; New York City

Awards: PEN-Faulkner Award

Now Try: O'Neill is also the author of the novels *This Is the Life* and *The Breezes* and the nonfiction title *Blood-Dark Track*. Other post-9/11 novels set in New York City might be suggested, including *The Good Life* by Jay McInerney or *Extremely Loud and Incredibly Close* by Jonathan Safran Foer. Emily Perkins's *Novel About My Wife*, set in London and featuring a female character who is suffering after a traumatic event, might also appeal. This book has been compared by reviewers to a modern-day *The Great Gatsby*, which features similarly lost male characters who seemingly have it all, and might prove to be a good classic read-alike. Other novels that have won the prestigious PEN-Faulkner award might be suggested to these readers, including Kate Christensen's *The Great Man*, Ann Patchett's *Bel Canto*, and Michael Cunningham's *The Hours*.

Proulx, Annie.

🏵 *Fine Just the Way It Is: Wyoming Stories 3*. Scribner, 2008. 221pp. ISBN 9781416571667.

Proulx offers another collection of short stories set in Wyoming, rich with the landscape imagery and use of metaphors for which she has become famous. Many of these stories feature historical settings, in which the economic hard times of the first homesteaders in the nineteenth century, as well as later, during the Great Depression, serve as the merest of backdrops to stories in which stoic and hard-working individuals must struggle to eke out their livings in the beautiful but unforgiving West.

Subjects: American West; Quick Reads; Short Stories; Westerns; Women Authors; Wyoming

Awards: New York Times Notable

Now Try: Proulx's earlier story collections include the first two volumes in this Wyoming Stories series: *Close Range* (which included the novella *Brokeback Mountain*) and *Bad Dirt*; her novel *That Old Ace in the Hole* is also set in Texas and shares a similar feel to these stories. Although his books are much darker, Cormac McCarthy's border trilogy, also firmly grounded in the landscape of the American West, might be suggested: *All the Pretty Horses*, *The Crossing*, and *Cities of the Plain*. Elmer Kelton's modern Westerns might also appeal to these readers, including *Hard Trail to Follow*, *Brush Country*, and *The Time It Never Rained*.

Now Consider Nonfiction . . . Reflective Environmental Narratives

Reflective environmental narratives feature their authors' ability to both describe settings and landscapes as well as make masterful use of language to provoke thought. Authors in this subgenre urge their readers to ponder the nature of our interactions with the natural world, and although these narratives are not typically quickly paced, they are highly personal and evocative.

Dillard, Annie. *Pilgrim at Tinker Creek*.

Eiseley, Loren. *The Immense Journey*.

Heat Moon, William Least. *PrairyErth (A Deep Map)*.

Olson, Sigurd. *The Singing Wilderness*.

Sanders, Scott Russell. *Writing from the Center*.

Thoreau, Henry David. *Walden*.

Radulescu, Dominica.

Train to Trieste. Knopf, 2008. 305pp. ISBN 9780307268235.

In 1970s Romania, Nicolae Ceausescu's dictatorship and his liberal use of secret police to ferret out dissension is causing suspicion and distrust among neighbors, as well as among those who might be falling in love; when seventeen-year-old Mona meets and falls in love with Mihai in Brasov, where she spends her summers on vacation, she barely has time to make sense of her feelings before she finds herself suspecting that he might be one of Ceausescu's operatives. Fleeing her native country for Chicago, where she marries, has children, and strives to live a normal life, she nonetheless finds herself increasingly distracted by the past and her uncertainty about her former lover's actions. When she does return to Romania, she does so in the hope of learning the truth about Mihai.

Second Appeal: Character

Subjects: 1970s; Book Groups; Chicago; Communism; First Novels; Historical Fiction; Love Affairs; Multicultural; Romania; Women Authors

Now Try: Other historical novels about love and memory might appeal to these readers, including Debra Dean's *The Madonnas of Leningrad*, Amy Bloom's *Away*, James Buchan's *The Persian Bride*, and Arthur Golden's *Memoirs of a Geisha*. Present-day immigrant narratives might also be suggested, including Rose Tremain's *The Road Home* and Kiran Desai's *The Inheritance of Loss*.

Scott, Joanna Catherine.

The Road from Chapel Hill. Berkley Books, 2006. 340pp. ISBN 978-0425212523.

When Eugenia Spotswood's family falls on hard times, they must move from their North Carolina plantation home to a much smaller mining town, where Eugenia's father plans to make his fortune in gold. The reality of their lives, however, is hard work and drudgery, lightened only for Eugenia when her father buys another young slave, Tom; the two become close enough so that the entire community gossips about their relationship. As the war continues, the chaos in which it enveloped the entire Southern community is described with no flinching away from the details, including Eugenia's stint as a nurse to runaways and deserters from the war.

Second Appeal: Character

Subjects: 19th Century; Civil War; Domestic Fiction; Family Relationships; Historical Fiction; Love Affairs; North Carolina; Race Relations; Slavery; Women Authors

Now Try: Scott has written historical novels before; her earlier titles include *Charlie and the Children* and *Cassandra, Lost*. Another passionate recounting of the horrors of the Civil War can be found in Charles Frazier's *Cold Mountain*; also of interest might be Donald McCaig's imaginative telling of the life story of Rhett Butler (from the classic novel *Gone with the Wind*, by Margaret Mitchell) in *Rhett Butler's People*.

Shaffer, Mary Ann, and Annie Barrows.

The Guernsey Literary and Potato Peel Pie Society. Dial Press, 2008. 278pp. ISBN 9780385340991.

One of 2008's greatest crowd-pleasers, this novel told in letters is set directly after the conclusion of World War II in London and Guernsey, one of the Channel Islands. Juliet Ashton, writer of newspaper columns about life in London during the bombardment and user of the pen name Izzy Bickerstaff, one day receives a letter from a man named Dawsey Adams, who found her name and address in a book of essays by Charles Lamb. Adams, a resident of Guernsey, found and read the book during a meeting of that island's "Literary and Potato Peel Pie Society." Through the course of more letters from Adams and other inhabitants of the island, Juliet learns the story of the occupation by German forces, the power and camaraderie in a group of like-minded community members, and the singular person of Elizabeth McKenna, who cooked up the idea of the society as a way to divert suspicion. At turns lighthearted and humorous, then deathly serious, this novel also speaks to a love of reading and how it can bring people together.

Second Appeal: Character

Subjects: 1940s; Book Groups; Books and Reading; British History; Channel Islands; Classics; Community Life; Epistolary Fiction; Gentle Reads; Great Britain; Guernsey; Historical Fiction; Humor; Love Affairs; Quick Reads; Women Authors; World War II

Now Try: A wonderful subject and style read-alike for this novel is Helene Hanff's nonfiction classic *84, Charing Cross Road*, in which her correspondence with a British bookseller covers the course of twenty years in postwar Great Britain (readers might also want to consider the sequel, in which Hanff travels to London, *The Duchess of Bloomsbury*). Irene Nemirovksy's World War II novels *Suite Francaise* and *Fire in the Blood* might be suggested, as might the nonfiction classic *The Diary of Anne Frank*. Another nonfiction classic about the power of reading is Azar Nafisi's *Reading Lolita in Tehran*. Another decidedly quirky novel, which may appeal to Anglophile fans of this novel, is Alan Bennett's delightful *The Uncommon Reader*, about her majesty the Queen of England.

Silber, Joan.

The Size of the World. **Norton, 2008. 322pp. ISBN 9780393059090.**

A novel told through six interconnected stories, Silber's narrative ranges from time period to time period and setting to setting, including World War I Sicily, Mexico during the Vietnam War, and Bloomington, Indiana, post-9/11. Each story, told in the first person, reveals its characters' secrets and their connections to the other stories with measured pacing, and Silber's mastery of the details of time and place make this an almost journalistic work of fiction.

Subjects: Book Groups; Family Relationships; First Person; Historical Fiction; Interconnected Stories; Love Affairs; Multicultural; Travel; War; Women Authors

Now Try: Silber is also the author of *Ideas of Heaven*, which was nominated for a National Book Award. Graham Greene's classic novels *The Quiet American* and *The Power and the Glory*, the former set in Vietnam and the latter in Mexico, might be good stylistic read-alikes. This novel has also been described as being written "in the tradition of E. M. Forster"; novels by that author, including *A Passage to India* and *A Room with a View*, might also be suggested. Nonfiction titles that combine relationship stories with setting appeal might also be suggested, such as Neely Tucker's *Love in the Driest Season*, Doris Lessing's *Alfred and Emily*, Alexandra Fuller's *Don't Let's Go to the Dogs Tonight: An African Childhood*, and Tom Bissell's *The Father of All Things: A Marine, His Son, and the Legacy of Vietnam*.

Now Consider Nonfiction . . . Armchair Travel

Armchair travel nonfiction books focuses nearly exclusively on the setting of the travel author's destination(s), but also include a fair amount of detail about the traveler himself or herself. A large part of the appeal of these narratives is the chance they give readers to share the reactions of a tour guide they trust to an interesting or unique place. These books typically feature detailed and evocative descriptions of both landscape and the adventures undertaken by their authors.

Berendt, John. *The City of Falling Angels.*

Ehrlich, Gretel. *This Cold Heaven: Seven Seasons in Greenland.*

Elliot, Jason. *An Unexpected Light: Travels in Afghanistan.*

Greene, Graham. *Journey Without Maps.*

McCarthy, Pete. *McCarthy's Bar: A Journey of Discovery in the West of Ireland.*

Morris, Jan. *Coronation Everest.*

Yeadon, David. *The Back of Beyond: Travels to the Wild Places of the Earth.*

Soueif, Ahdaf.

I Think of You: Stories. Anchor, 2007. 182pp. ISBN 9780307277213.

Settings define the lives of the characters in Soueif's short stories in two ways; for the most part, they remain in their homelands (primarily Egypt) in spirit and in actions, but they must also adapt to and live in their adopted countries (in this case, Great Britain).

Subjects: Arab Authors; Culture Clash; Egypt; Middle East; Multicultural; Short Stories; Women Authors; Women's Fiction

Now Try: Soueif has also written several novels: *The Map of Love, Sandpiper, In the Eye of the Sun,* and *Aisha.* Other short story collections in which culture clashes play a part are Jhumpa Lahiri's *Unaccustomed Earth* and *Interpreter of Maladies,* Naama Goldstein's *The Place Will Comfort You,* Rishi Reddi's *Karma and Other Stories,* and Ha Jin's *The Bridegroom.* Short story authors who often take as their subject women's lives might also be suggested, such as Alice Munro (*The Love of a Good Woman* and *The View from Castle Rock*) and Antonya Nelson (*Female Trouble*).

St. John Mandel, Emily.

Last Night in Montreal. Unbridled Books, 2009. 247pp. ISBN 978-1932961683.

When twenty-seven-year-old graduate student Eli finally looks up after a day of his usual existential crises and working on a thesis that he's beginning to feel he may never finish, he notices that his girlfriend Lilia never returned to their apartment after she left in the morning to get a newspaper. With a history of leaving towns and lives with no real provocation (a trait she did inform Eli of early on, even if he missed the reference), Lilia appears to be a true free spirit, but her story (much of it, and the novel itself), told in flashbacks, offers clues to her rootlessness. When she leaves Brooklyn, Eli hears nothing more about her until a postcard from a woman named Michaela arrives, informing him that Lilia is in Montreal. When he journeys there and meets Michaela, he learns the story of Lilia's past, her connection to her father, and how both of them are connected to Michaela.

Subjects: Amnesia; Brooklyn; Canada; Canadian Authors; Family Relationships; Family Secrets; First Novels; Flashbacks; Kidnapping; Love Affairs; Montreal; Multiple Viewpoints; New York City; Quebec; Small Press; Women Authors

Now Try: Other novels in which young women seek to make their way in the world might be suggested, such as Julian Gough's coming-of-age novel about twins, *Juno and Juliet*; Robert Goolrick's rather darker historical novel *A Reliable Wife*; Amy Bloom's historical novel about an immigrant woman, *Away*; and Leah Stewart's *The Myth of You and Me*. Other complex relationships between men and women and their families are explored in Anne Tyler's novels *Searching for Caleb* and *Saint Maybe*.

Talarigo, Jeff.

🏵 *The Ginseng Hunter: A Novel.* **Doubleday, 2008. 177pp. ISBN 9780385517393.**

Talarigo's novel is as deeply rooted in the landscape of the Chinese mountain valley and village he describes as the ginseng root that his protagonist hunts is in the soil of his home forest. In short and lyrical chapters, we meet the ginseng hunter, who practices the livelihood taught him by his father and grandfather and periodically goes to his nearest village to visit a brothel, where he meets a North Korean girl who fled across the nearby river separating the two countries in search of food and survival. In alternating chapters we follow the hunter's story, including his growing love for the prostitute and his rescue of another young escapee from North Korea, as well as flashbacks from the prostitute's horrific former life with her mother in that country.

Second Appeal: Language

Subjects: Agriculture; Book Groups; China; Communism; First Person; Flashbacks; Love Affairs; Men's Lives; Multicultural; Multiple Viewpoints; North Korea; Quick Reads

Awards: ALA Notable

Now Try: Talarigo is the author of the similarly brief novel *The Pearl Diver*. Another novel in which a person somewhat unwillingly becomes involved in helping another is Christopher Bigsby's *Beautiful Dreamer* (set in the American South; Bigsby's main character, a white man, helps a black boy); Geoff Ryman's novel *Air*, although more of a science fiction novel, also features characters living in a small and insular Asian community. Although much different in subject matter and featuring a more modern story, Xiaolu Guo's *Twenty Fragments of a Ravenous Youth* might also serve as a stylistic read-alike for Talarigo's beautifully written story.

Tóibín, Colm.

Brooklyn: A Novel. **Scribner, 2009. 262pp. ISBN 9781439138311.**

After World War II, immigrant Ellis Lacey journeys from her native Ireland to New York (specifically Brooklyn), where she falls in love with an Italian man and finds work in a department store. When her sister dies, however, she returns to Ireland to mourn her and finds that home, too, is offering its young people new opportunities and joys. She must choose: Will she try to make her way in a changing Ireland, or return to the new life she had begun forging in America?

Subjects: 1950s; Brooklyn; Classics; Death and Dying; Historical Fiction; Immigrants and Immigration; Ireland; Irish Authors; Love Affairs; Men Writing as Women; New York City; Sisters

Now Try: Tóibín's other historical novels include *The Master* (a fictionalization of the life of Henry James) and *The South*; another of his novels, *The Heather Blazing*, is set in Ireland. Other historical novels in which immigrants seek to make their way in America might appeal, such as Amy Bloom's *Away* and Marge Piercy's *Sex Wars*. A novel set in modern-day Brooklyn, also rich in family relationships, is Alice Mattison's *Nothing Is Quite Forgotten in Brooklyn*. Nonfiction immigrant narratives might also be suggested, such as Frank McCourt's *Angela's Ashes* and *'Tis* (as well as his latest, *Teacher Man*); memoirs about women's experiences of self discovery might also make good read-alikes, such as Elizabeth Gilbert's *Eat, Pray, Love* and Lori Tharps's *Kinky Gazpacho: Life, Love & Spain*.

Tuck, Lily.

The News from Paraguay. HarperCollins, 2004. 248pp. ISBN 978-0066209449.

Tuck's historical novel relates the story of two real people from history, Paraguay's nineteenth-century dictator Francisco Solano Lopez and his mistress, Ella Lynch, a woman of Irish descent who is divorced and living with a Russian count in Paris when Franco first sees her. Although the two flee to and strive to make Paraguay their own version of paradise, a costly war with Argentina and Brazil leaves the country crushed and Ella questioning her devotion to her dictator.

Subjects: 19th Century; Biographical Fiction; Dictators; Historical Fiction; Lopez, Francisco Solano; Love Affairs; Lynch, Ella; Multiple Viewpoints; Paraguay; Political Fiction; Women Authors

Awards: National Book Award

Now Try: Tuck is also the author of the novel *The Woman Who Walked on Water* and the story collection *Limbo, and Other Places I Have Lived*. Other novels in which women's lives and love affairs are affected by political events are Ceridwen Dovey's *Blood Kin* and Jaime Manrique's *Our Lives Are the Rivers*; also of interest might be Antonio Lobo Antunes's *The Inquistors' Manual*.

Unsworth, Barry.

Land of Marvels. Doubleday, 2009. 287pp. ISBN 9780385520072.

The year is 1914, and in Mesopotamia, British archaeologist John Somerville feels that he is close to a breakthrough discovery after years of fruitless excavations in the desert. Obstacles stand in his way, however: his excavation is threatened by business interests who want to build a railway through the site, an overly smooth American geologist with plans for the land of his own, and his own deteriorating relationship with his wife, Edith. Part archaeological thriller, part measured character study, and throughout informed by descriptions of the surrounding landscape and its physical and political attributes, this is historical fiction at its most literary.

Second Appeal: Character

Subjects: 1910s; Archaeology; British Authors; Colonialism; Historical Fiction; Marriage; Mesopotamia; Suspense

Now Try: Many of Unsworth's historical fiction titles are set much more distantly in time from our own era, including *The Ruby in Her Navel* (twelfth century), *The Songs of the Kings* (ancient Greece history), and *Sacred Hunger* (his Man Booker

Prize winner; set in the eighteenth century). A more classical mystery set in Mesopotamia is Agatha Christie's *Murder in Mesopotamia*. Historical fiction from such literary authors as Andrea Barrett (*The Voyage of the Narwhal* and *The Air We Breathe*) and Peter Ackroyd (*First Light* and *The Fall of Troy* both offer archaeological plots) might also appeal. Georgina Howell's rollicking biography of a singular adventurer, *Gertrude Bell: Queen of the Desert, Shaper of Nations*, is also set during roughly the same era.

Urrea, Luis Alberto.

🏵 *The Hummingbird's Daughter*. Little, Brown, 2005. 499pp. ISBN 978-0316745468.

Based on the life of the author's great-aunt, known as Saint Teresa of Cabora, this sprawling historical novel is infused with the spirit, landscape, and language of Mexico. Following Teresita's life from her birth through her discovery of her parentage; her training in the arts of healing by Huila, the midwife who helped birth her; and the growth of her faith and the revolutionary events of the late nineteenth century, Urrea tells a story of a singular woman in unstable times and the beauty and turbulence of the region along Mexico's border with the Southwestern United States.

Second Appeal: Story

Subjects: 19th Century; Biographical Fiction; Classics; Family Relationships; Friendships; Health Issues; Historical Fiction; Men Writing as Women; Mexican Authors; Mexico; Religion

Awards: ALA Notable

Now Try: Urrea is also the author of a nonfiction trilogy about the lives of Mexicans and Mexican immigrants: *Across the Wire: Life and Hard Times on the Mexican Border*, *By the Lake of Sleeping Children: The Secret Life of the Mexican Border*, and *Nobody's Son: Notes from an American Life*. Novels by other Latino authors, particularly family sagas, might also appeal, including titles by Isabel Allende (*The House of the Spirits*), Sandra Cisneros (*Caramelo*), Julia Alvarez (*In the Time of the Butterflies*), and Laura Esquivel (*Malinche* and *Swift as Desire*). Louise Erdrich's novels of families and their historical roots might also be good stylistic read-alikes; they include *The Porcupine Year*, *The Master Butchers' Singing Club*, and *The Last Report on the Miracles at Little No Horse*.

Into the Beautiful North. Little, Brown, 2009. 342pp. ISBN 9780316025270.

When teenager Nayeli looks around her Mexican hometown of Tres Camarones and realizes that there are no men left there, she becomes increasingly worried about the influence of drug-smuggling and other bandidos who will soon figure out there's no one to keep them from taking what they want from, and ruling, the town. She decides to make the trip north herself, perhaps to find and return with her father, but also in the hopes of finding other men who will return to the town with her.

Subjects: Book Groups; Fathers and Daughters; Friendships; Gay Men; GLBTQ; Illinois; Men Writing as Women; Mexican Authors; Mexico; Smuggling; Teenage Girls; Teenagers; YA

Now Try: Urrea's other novels are *The Hummingbird's Daughter* and *In Search of Snow*. Other stories of the lives of Mexican American immigrants are Oscar Casares's short story collection *Brownsville*, Susan Straight's *Highwire Moon*, and Ana Castillo's *The Guardians*. Reyna Grande's novel *Across a Hundred Mountains* features another driven young girl in much the same situation as Urrea's protagonist. Another novel, although it is more a work of magic realism, in which fathers seemingly disappear is Dean Bakopoulos's *Please*

Don't Come Back from the Moon. This novel, with its feisty young female protagonist, might also appeal to many young adult readers; other YA novels that feature strong female characters are Libba Bray's <u>Gemma Doyle</u> trilogy (*A Great and Terrible Beauty, Rebel Angels,* and *The Sweet Far Thing*), Joan Bauer's *Rules of the Road,* and even Charlotte Brontë's classic novel *Jane Eyre*.

Now Consider Nonfiction . . . Immigrant Experience Memoirs

Immigrant experience memoirs are narratives relating personal experiences with immigration, including the challenge of leaving one's family and culture and relocating to an often completely different and new environment. They often offer vivid landscape and cultural descriptions, as well as stories of personal perseverance and survival in an unfamiliar place.

Abu-Jaber, Diana. *The Language of Baklava.*

Arana, Marie. *American Chica: Two Worlds, One Childhood.*

Bernstein, Harry. *The Dream: A Memoir.*

Eire, Carlos. *Waiting for Snow in Havana: Confessions of a Cuban Boy.*

Hakakian, Roya. *Journey from the Land of No: A Girlhood Caught in Revolutionary Iran.*

Hoffman, Eva. *Lost in Translation: A Life in a New Language.*

Minatoya, Lydia. *Talking to High Monks in the Snow: An Asian American Odyssey.*

Watson, Larry.

Sundown, Yellow Moon. **Random House, 2007. 309pp. ISBN 978-0375507229.**

One day North Dakota teenager Gene Stoddard returns home to find his father Raymond sitting in the kitchen (an unsettling event, in 1960s Midwestern America, to find your father home in the middle of the day); later he will have the misfortune of discovering Raymond after he kills himself, and after the family learns that Raymond is also responsible for the fatal shooting of state Senator Monty Burnham earlier that same day. Much of the story is told in flashback and from the point of view of Gene's boyhood friend (now an author) as he tries, forty years later, to understand what really happened that day, as well as to come to terms with his own obsession with Gene's family.

Second Appeal: Story

Subjects: 1960s; Coming-of-age; Family Relationships; Fathers and Sons; First Person; Friendships; Historical Fiction; Love Affairs; Men's Lives; Murder; Mystery; North Dakota; Teenage Boys; Teenagers; Unreliable Narrator

Now Try: Watson's novels are often described as "elegiac"; they might appeal to readers of this novel and include *Orchard, Laura,* and *White Crosses.* Another novel set in North Dakota (although it is a bit more modern in tone) is Chuck Klosterman's *Downtown Owl;* Tony Earley's historical novels (which also feel somewhat "elegiac") *Jim the Boy* and *Blue Star* might also be suggested. Kent

Haruf's novels also combine a haunting sense of place with sometimes unhappy stories; they are *The Tie That Binds*, *Where You Once Belonged*, *Plainsong*, and *Eventide*.

Wells, Ken.

Crawfish Mountain: A Novel. **Random House, 2007. 364pp. ISBN 9780375508769.**

After inheriting a piece of his trapper and hunter grandfather's bayou land in Louisiana, Justin Pitre remains true to his grandfather's charge to keep and care for the land. What he did not bargain for, however, was the single-minded drive of oilman Tom Huff's plan to build a pipeline through the land, either after buying it or obtaining it through more questionable means. Together with his wife, Grace, Justin fights the encroaching big business; eventually the matter comes to the attention of both Louisiana's playboy governor, Joe T. Evangeline, and an environmental activist, Julie Galjour (much as those two come to the sometimes contentious attention of one another). Although this story-driven novel hinges on political and business deals, Wells's evocative descriptions of the Louisiana bayou are what give the book its flavor.

Second Appeal: Story

Subjects: American South; Corruption; Environmental Writing; Family Relationships; Government; Louisiana; Love Affairs; Men's Lives; Oil; Political Fiction

Now Try: Wells's other novels, *Logan's Storm, Junior's Leg,* and *Meely LeBauve,* are set in the South as well. Other Southern authors who provided blurbs for Wells's quickly paced book are Carl Hiaasen (whose books are often set in Florida, including *Nature Girl, Skinny Dip,* and *Sick Puppy*) and Robert Olen Butler (*Had a Good Time* and *A Good Scent from a Strange Mountain*). Frederick Barthelme's *Waveland,* although not as story-driven, also strongly grounds its characters in the power of its Southern landscape, and James Lee Burke's Dave Robicheaux novels, set in New Orleans, might also appeal (the series starts with *Neon Rain, Heaven's Prisoners,* and *Black Cherry Blues*). Although they are both about New Orleans (rather than about Louisiana's rural areas and bayous), Dan Baum's *Nine Lives: Death and Life in New Orleans* and Roy Blount Jr.'s *Feet on the Street: Rambles around New Orleans* also provide a flavor of the region. The story of another environmental battle is told in Erik Reece's *Lost Mountain*.

Winton, Tim.

🌱 *The Turning: New Stories.* **Scribner, 2004. 321pp. ISBN 9780743276931.**

Winton's collection of interconnected short stories, all set in a small fishing town on Australia's west coast, features a cast of characters who strive, sometimes against long odds caused by others' violence, abuse, and problems, to make sense of and find happiness in their lives.

Subjects: Abuse; Australia; Australian Authors; Family Relationships; Interconnected Stories; Marriage; Short Stories; Teenage Boys; Teenagers

Awards: Christina Stead Prize for Fiction

Now Try: Winton has written another story collection, *Minimum of Two,* as well as several novels (all set in Australia), including *Breath, Cloudstreet,* and *Dirt Music.* Other winners of the Christina Stead Prize for Fiction might be good read-alikes for this novel; they include Michelle De Kretser's *The Lost Dog,* Peter Carey's *Theft,* and Kate Grenville's historical novel *The Secret River.* Louis De Bernières's story collection *Red Dog* is also set in Australia; another popular novel of interconnected stories in a small community is Elizabeth Strout's Pulitzer Prize–winning collection *Olive Kitteridge*.

Woodward, Gerard.

August. **Norton, 2008. 308pp. ISBN 9780393332711.**

Aldous Jones tumbles over his bicycle handlebars on a Welsh road in 1955, outside a lonely farm where, over the course of the next fifteen years, he takes his family for camping vacations. The loveliness of the countryside provides a backdrop against which the Jones family grows up and engages in the complications and sadnesses that often befall families (the Evans family, who own the farm, also have issues of their own). Even on vacation, the reader learns from these families, there is no escaping reality.

Subjects: 1950s; 1960s; British Authors; Domestic Fiction; Family Relationships; First Novels; Great Britain; Rural Life; Wales

Now Try: This is the first book in Woodward's trilogy about the Jones family; the subsequent two novels are *I'll Go to Bed at Noon* and *A Curious Earth*. Other British authors whose novels might appeal to fans of this novel are Tessa Hadley (*The Master Bedroom, Everything Will Be All Right*, and *Accidents in the Home*), Iain M. Banks (*The Crow Road* and *The Steep Approach to Garbadale*), and A. L. Kennedy (*Day, Paradise*, and *Indelible Acts*).

Chapter 2

Story

When **Story** is the primary doorway through which readers access a novel, the reader can be assured that the plot and the pacing dominate the reading experience. Readers eagerly turn the pages of these books to find out what happens next; often these readers read as though driven, on the "edge of their seats," keen to follow the story's complexities and the many plot twists authors of these types of books often employ. Descriptions of these books focus heavily on the events, with considerations of other attributes, such as character, often of secondary concern. For example, in Josh Bazell's *Beat the Reaper*, Bazell's doctor character finds himself careening from one bad situation to another, from being mugged to being forced to treat a mob boss for whom he once worked. Annotations of story-driven novels tend to include such descriptors and phrases as "quickly paced," "page-turner," "breakneck pace," "thrilling conclusion," and "plot twists abound." Although the majority of these books feature quickly paced storytelling, in mainstream fiction stories may also stand out for being compelling or for being built slowly but persistently throughout the narrative arc. Often story-driven books are recognizable for their adherence to standard formulas, such as characters who embark on quests, seek to unravel puzzles, or find themselves involved in love affairs or other inexorable events.

These novels, particularly those that feature fast pacing, are closely related to other genres that Joyce Saricks has referred to as "adrenaline" reads—adventure, thriller, and suspense novels. However, those who read story-driven novels to unravel puzzles or to lose themselves in quests, literary retellings, or unexpected events might also consider a wide variety of mystery novels; true crime titles, in which the focus is on the good guys trying to apprehend the bad guys; true adventure titles, in which heroes take on survival and other challenges; and a wide variety of history nonfiction titles, which tell those stories that have taken on the feel of legends and epic tales.

Adiga, Aravind.

🏵 *The White Tiger.* **Free Press, 2008. 276pp. ISBN 9781416562597.**
The protagonist of Adiga's fast-paced epistolary novel (a novel in which the story is told through a series of letters), Balram Halwai, also known as the "White Tiger," writes a series of letters to Chinese premier Wen Jiabao on the occasion of Wen's visit to India, expressly to describe the vehemence of Indian entrepreneurship. Halwai recounts the story of his youth, his rise to the prestigious work of driving a wealthy patron, and his own single-minded dedication to achieving his

goals and the actions he is prepared to take (and has taken) to do so. The backdrop to Adiga's sometimes shocking but never dull tale is the throbbing, teeming land- and people-scape of India in the twenty-first century. "I'll say it was all worth-while to know, just for a day, just for an hour, just for a *minute*, what it means not to be a servant."

Second Appeal: Setting

Subjects: Business; Crime; Dark Humor; Epistolary Fiction; Family Relationships; First Novels; First Person; India; Indian Authors; Multicultural; Murder; Quick Reads; Unreli-able Narrator

Awards: Man Booker Prize

Now Try: Gary Shteyngart's novel *The Russian Debutante's Handbook* is very similar in its reliance on bleak humor. Other novels with mesmerizing but decidedly unreliable nar-rators might be suggested, including Michael Cox's *The Meaning of Night*, Patrick McGrath's *Spider* and *Poet Mungo*, and even Junot Díaz's *The Brief Wondrous Life of Os-car Wao*. Those readers who are enthralled with the setting and culture of India might also consider Suketu Mehta's memoir of his family's move to Bombay in *Maximum City: Bombay Lost and Found*.

Alameddine, Rabih.

🐦 *The Hakawati: A Story.* **Knopf, 2008. 513pp. ISBN 9780307266798.**

When Osama al-Kharrat returns to Beirut to visit his father in the hospital, he finds the war-beaten and bombed city a shadow of the place where he grew up. In the tradition of his grandfather, a "hakawati," or storyteller, Osama relates his own childhood and family story, while coming to terms with his father's approaching death. Interspersed in his narrative are tales from Middle Eastern history, includ-ing such religious and historical figures as Abraham and Isaac, Ishmael, and Fatima (among many others).

Subjects: Beirut; Book Groups; Death and Dying; Epic Reads; Family Relationships; Leba-non; Magic Realism; Middle East; Multicultural

Awards: ALA Notable

Now Try: Alameddine's earlier novels, also featuring Lebanese characters and settings, are *I, the Divine: A Novel in First Chapters* and *Koolaids: The Art of War*. Other epic fam-ily stories may appeal to these readers, such as Abraham Verghese's *Cutting for Stone*, Preeta Samarasan's *Evening is the Whole Day*, Padma Viswanathan's *The Toss of a Lemon*, and Amy Tan's *The Bonesetter's Daughter*. (Another novel in which a son visits his father's deathbed, and in which stories play a large part, is Daniel Wallace's more light-hearted *Big Fish*.) Those readers interested in nonfiction might consider a Middle Eastern saga of shifting borders and homes, which change ownership from generation to genera-tion: Sandy Tolan's *The Lemon Tree: An Arab, a Jew, and the Heart of the Middle East*, Thomas Friedman's *From Beirut to Jerusalem*, or Robert Fisk's definitive history of war in Lebanon, *Pity the Nation: The Abduction of Lebanon*.

Ali, Monica.

In the Kitchen. **Simon & Schuster, 2009. 436pp. ISBN 9781416571681.**

Previously heralded as a young, up-and-coming chef in Great Britain's culinary circles, chef Gabriel Lightfoot lost his first restaurant through bad choices and drug addiction. Twenty years later, given another chance to prove himself in a busy London hotel kitchen, he finds his world unraveling once again as his own demons resurface, an employee is found murdered in the hotel kitchen, and he becomes entangled in a relationship with a woman from Belarus who has a dangerous and unhappy past.

Subjects: British Authors; Food; Great Britain; Immigrants and Immigration; London; Love Affairs; Murder; Restaurants; Unreliable Narrator; Women Authors; Women Writing as Men; Work Relationships

Now Try: Monica Ali is the author of the popular novel *Brick Lane*, also set in Great Britain, and of a collection of short stories titled *Alentejo Blue*. Another novel with a subplot of an immigrant working in busy restaurant kitchens is Kiran Desai's *The Inheritance of Loss*; Rose Tremain's *The Road Home* is also set in Great Britain and features a male protagonist who is from an eastern bloc nation. Those readers particularly interested in the restaurant and food aspects of this novel might also consider Hannah McCouch's *Girl Cook* (set in New York City), or nonfiction memoirs like Anthony Bourdain's *Kitchen Confidential* (or any of Bourdain's food-related novels) and Patricia Volk's *Stuffed: Adventures of a Restaurant Family*.

Amidon, Stephen.

Security: A Novel. Farrar, Straus & Giroux, 2009. 276pp. ISBN 978-0374257118.

Sleepy on its surface, the small, quiet college town of Stoneleigh, Massachusetts, is a hotbed of secrets, unsavory events, and residents who struggle with their interpersonal relationships, as well as their roles in the community. When a late-night alarm sounds from the wealthy Doyle Cutler's home, Edward Inman, the owner of the private security firm Stoneleigh Sentinel, decides to check it out personally. Although Cutler assures him it's a false alarm, the situation becomes tense when Mary Steckl, a local student, later comes forward to claim that she was sexually assaulted at the house that night. As Edward investigates further, he learns that his old flame Kathryn's son may be the only one who knows the truth about what happened that night, and that it is sometimes too easy to assign guilt to the troubled and poor while ignoring the possible culpability of the more socially acceptable and affluent.

Second Appeal: Character

Subjects: Community Life; Crime; Family Relationships; Massachusetts; Multiple Viewpoints; Psychological Fiction; Satire; Small-Town Life

Now Try: Amidon's other plot-driven novels are *Human Capital*, *The New City*, *The Primitive*, and *Thirst*. Another novel featuring a confusing crime is Brock Clarke's *An Arsonist's Guide to Writers' Homes in New England*; Tom Perrotta's *Little Children* and *The Abstinence Teacher* both explore events in communities where residents seek to blame the "other" for their fears and problems. Lewis Robinson's novel *Water Dogs* also centers on a crime and the suspicion it casts on two brothers. In the true crime narrative *A Death in Belmont*, Sebastian Junger questions whether a man convicted of a crime in the Belmont, Massachusetts, neighborhood in 1963 was convicted largely for racial reasons.

Auster, Paul.

Man in the Dark. Henry Holt, 2008. 180pp. ISBN 9780805088397.

August Brill, mentally hiding from the reality that his granddaughter Katya's boyfriend Titus has been killed in the Iraq War, retreats into a world of his own creation (including a protagonist to be his stand-in, named Owen Brick), where the events of 9/11 never happened and the disputed election of 2000 led to a bloody and brutal civil war.

Second Appeal: Language

Subjects: 9/11; Alternate Realities; Death and Dying; Elderly; Family Relationships; First Person; Iraq War (2003); Magic Realism; Quick Reads; Satire; Science Fiction; Vermont; War

Now Try: Auster's earlier novels (which are also rich with magic realism) include *Travels in the Scriptorium*, *Oracle Night*, *The Book of Illusions*, and *Timbuktu*. Another author who may appeal to these readers is Don DeLillo, whose novels *Falling Man*, *The Body Artist*, and *White Noise* might be suggested. Also of interest might be other literary parallel worlds titles from the science fiction genre, such as Philip K. Dick's *Flow My Tears, the Policeman Said* or Ronald Wright's *A Scientific Romance*.

Baruth, Philip.

The Brothers Boswell. **Soho Press, 2009. 329pp. ISBN 9781569475591.**

In this combination literary thriller and historical novel, the narrator is John Boswell, the decidedly unbalanced but fiendishly clever brother of James Boswell, better known as the biographer who wrote *The Life of Samuel Johnson*, about one of the eighteenth century's most famous British personages. Following his brother James as he forges his new friendship with Johnson, John watches the two, lays plans to murder them both, and shares with the reader his own earlier encounter with Johnson, as well as the jealousy and difficulties of his relationship with his brother James.

Second Appeal: Setting

Subjects: 18th Century; Biographical Fiction; Book Groups; Boswell, James; Great Britain; Historical Fiction; Johnson, Samuel; Literary Lives; London; Mental Health; Psychological Fiction; Suspense; Unreliable Narrator; Writers and Writing

Now Try: Baruth has also written a science fiction thriller, *The X President: A Novel of the Cigarette Wars*, as well as the story collection *The Dream of the White Village: A Novel in Stories*. Other imaginative novels based on real people are Richard Liebmann-Smith's *The James Boys: A Novel Account of William, Henry, Frank and Jesse*; Susan Sellers's *Vanessa and Virginia*; and Douglas A. Martin's *Branwell: A Novel of the Brontë Brother*. A novel set slightly later in time but also featuring an unreliable narrator is Michael Cox's *The Meaning of Night*. Another author of literary and thrilling historical novels, David Liss (*The Whiskey Rebels*, *The Coffee Trader*, *A Conspiracy of Paper*), might also be a good read-alike. Of course, readers interested in either James Boswell or Samuel Johnson might consider Boswell's classic biography *The Life of Samuel Johnson*, or the decidedly more modern *Boswell's Presumptuous Task: The Making of the Life of Dr. Johnson*, by Adam Sisman.

Bates, Judy Fong.

🐾 *Midnight at the Dragon Café.* **Counterpoint, 2004. 317pp. ISBN 9781582431895.**

Su-Jen Chou is only six when she and her mother Jing emigrate from China to join Jing's much older husband in the small town of Irvine, Ontario, where he has settled and opened a family restaurant. As more family members arrive, including her older half-brother, Su-Jen (now known as Annie) knows there are many secrets being held and long-held grudges festering under the surface of their placid relationships. Eventually learning to speak English and assimilating better than her parents, Annie nonetheless continues to feel the deep and primal tug of family loyalties and love.

Subjects: 1950s; Canada; Canadian Authors; Classics; Culture Clash; Domestic Fiction; Family Relationships; Family Secrets; First Novels; First Person; Historical Fiction; Immigrants and Immigration; Restaurants; Small-Town Life

Awards: ALA Notable; Alex Award

Now Try: Bates has also written a short story collection titled *China Dog and Other Tales from a Chinese Laundry*. Other novels about arranged marriages, family relationships, and immigration are Saher Alam's *The Groom to Have Been*, Wayson Choy's *All That Matters* (both also feature Canadian settings and characters—although not about arranged marriages, Choy's novel *The Jade Peony* might also appeal), and Lisa See's *Shanghai Girls*. Nonfiction titles about the challenges of the immigrant life might also be suggested, including Iris Chang's *The Chinese in America: A Narrative History* and Lydia Minatoya's *Talking to High Monks in the Snow: An Asian American Odyssey*.

Bausch, Richard.

🐾 *Peace: A Novel.* Knopf, 2008. 171pp. ISBN 9780307268334.

Wet, tired, and under tremendous pressure, three soldiers stationed in Italy during World War II (in the winter of 1944, to be exact) set off under orders to complete a reconnaissance mission to the top of a nearby mountain. Along the way they are guided by Angelo, an elderly Italian man whose loyalties are unclear not only to the reader but also to the three soldiers. Surrounded by death, and disheartened by the loss of men under his command, Corporal Robert Marson nonetheless strives to remain true to his own humanity.

Subjects: Book Groups; Espionage; Friendships; Historical Fiction; Italy; Profanity; Psychological Fiction; Quick Reads; Violence; World War II

Awards: ALA Notable

Now Try: Bausch has written several other novels that feature taut plotting; they are *Thanksgiving Night, In the Night Season,* and *Violence* (as well as the story collections *Wives and Lovers* and *The Stories of Richard Bausch*). Other psychological novels of war, such as Tim O'Brien's *Going after Cacciato* or Robert Stone's *A Flag for Sunrise* or *Damascus Gate*, might be suggested, as might nonfiction titles about the ambiguous nature of wartime experiences, such as Michael Herr's *Dispatches*, John Burnett's *Uncivilized Beasts and Shameless Hellions*, or Andrew Mueller's *I Wouldn't Start from Here: The 21st Century and Where It All Went Wrong* (although John Hersey's World War II–era title *Into the Valley: Marines at Guadalcanal* might provide more context).

Bazell, Josh.

Beat the Reaper. Little, Brown, 2009. 310pp. ISBN 9780316032223.

Twists and turns abound in this literary thriller, which unfolds over the course of one action-packed day in Dr. Peter Brown's medical practice at the city's worst hospital, Manhattan Catholic. But there's more to the story than Brown's horrific day treating patients while himself ingesting an unhealthy amount of drugs (obtained freely from pharmaceutical sales reps, of course); half of the story is the telling of events from his former life as mob hit man Pietro "Bearclaw" Brnwa and the murders of his grandparents, the investigation of which led to his becoming a contract killer. His two lives collide in the form of a patient, Eddy Squillante, who is dying of cancer but recognizes Brown as Brwna and threatens to blow his cover as a doctor if anything goes wrong with his medical care. What's really criminal about this fast-paced and bitterly funny novel is that it is Bazell's first.

Subjects: Dark Humor; Day in the Life; Doctors; First Novels; First Person; Friendships; Jews and Judaism; Love Affairs; Medicine; New York City; Organized Crime; Quick Reads; Suspense; Unreliable Narrator

Now Try: Although not as dark as this novel, British actor and author Hugh Laurie's satirical novel *The Gun Seller* also provides a fast and bitterly funny read. Another novel in which events quickly spiral out of control for a rather unassuming protagonist is Charlie Huston's *The Mystic Arts of Erasing All Signs of Death*; Jimmy Breslin's classic novel about an inept mob family, *The Gang That Couldn't Shoot Straight*, might also be a fun read-alike. Other very dark nonfiction tales about the modern medical and pharmaceutical industries might be suggested, including Jim Knipfel's memoir of his many health challenges, *Slackjaw*, Peter Rost's *The Whistleblower: Confessions of a Healthcare Hitman*, and Jamie Reidy's memoir *Hard Sell: The Evolution of a Viagra Salesman*.

Beckett, Bernard.

Genesis: A Novel. **Houghton Mifflin Harcourt, 2009. 150pp. ISBN 9780547225494.**

Although not typically what a reader might imagine as a good "story-driven" read, Beckett's slim and literary science fiction novel tells a story within a story—and finishes both with twists—set in the futuristic society known as The Republic in the year 2075. The form of the novel is a spoken examination of a young scholar named Anaximander, who is hoping to get into her society's rarefied center of learning, The Academy, by relating her research about Adam Forde, a man famous in this future society for his infamous dissent and his eventual debates with a machine about what constitutes "consciousness."

Second Appeal: Language

Subjects: Artificial Intelligence; Dystopia; Men Writing as Women; Philosophical Fiction; Quick Reads; Science; Science Fiction; Technology; YA

Now Try: Beckett is also the author of a YA novel, *Malcolm and Juliet*. The sole blurb on the back of this novel is by Jonathan Stroud, whose imaginative <u>Bartimaeus</u> fantasy series (*The Amulet of Samarkand, The Golem's Eye*, and *Ptolemy's Gate*) might also appeal to these readers. Another YA series that is surprisingly literary and thought-provoking is Phillip Pullman's <u>His Dark Materials</u> (*The Golden Compass, The Subtle Knife*, and *The Amber Spyglass*). Other books that combine philosophy and futurism are Aldous Huxley's classic *Brave New World*, Margaret Atwood's *The Handmaid's Tale* and *Oryx and Crake*, Kazuo Ishiguro's *Never Let Me Go*, and Cormac McCarthy's *The Road*. Matt Ruff's short and chilling *Bad Monkeys*, with some very interesting plot twists of its own, might also appeal. Other novels in which the educational settings are not what they seem to be are Richard Powers's *Galatea 2.2* and James Morrow's *The Philosopher's Apprentice*.

Now Consider Nonfiction . . . Adventures in Science

Science news stories are typically exciting because they herald new discoveries or describe human leaps in scientific understanding; these "adventures in science" stories detail those exciting discoveries, leaps, and explorations (of everything from microscopic materials to outer space). They feature compelling stories and descriptive writing.

Alibek, Ken. *Biohazard: The Chilling True Story of the Largest Covert Biological Weapons Program in the World.*

Alvarez, Walter. *T. Rex and the Crater of Doom.*

Barry, Susan. *Fixing My Gaze: A Scientist's Journey Into Seeing In Three Dimensions.*

Chaikin, Andrew. *A Man on the Moon: The Voyages of the Apollo Astronauts.*

Jones, Chris. *Too Far from Home: A Story of Life and Death in Space.*

Preston, Richard. *The Hot Zone: A Terrifying True Story.*

Benioff, David.

🏆 *City of Thieves.* **Viking, 2008. 258pp. ISBN 9780670018703.**

Benioff's tale, set during the siege of Leningrad and World War II, alternates bleak events and characters with surprising bursts of humor and humanity; it is loosely based on his grandfather's experiences during the war. When seventeen-year-old Lev is caught looting a German paratrooper's corpse, he is imprisoned alongside a more brash youth, Kolya, who eventually becomes his partner in a quest to find a dozen eggs for the Russian army colonel who has imprisoned them (who needs the eggs for his daughter's wedding cake).

Subjects: 1940s; Classics; Coming-of-age; First Person; Friendships; Historical Fiction; Leningrad, Russia, Teenage Boys; Teenagers; World War II; YA

Awards: ALA Notable, Alex Award

Now Try: Benioff is also the author of the novel *The 25th Hour* (which was made into a film of the same name) and the story collection *When the Nines Roll Over, and Other Stories*. Joseph Heller's classic novel *Catch-22* might be a fun read-alike (it also highlights the frequent absurdities in wartime), as might Kurt Vonnegut's satirical *Mother Night*. Another historical novel featuring a wager is Glen David Gold's *Carter Beats the Devil*. Another, perhaps more serious, novel of history, family relationships and secrets, and a young boy's coming-of-age is Robert Alexander's *The Kitchen Boy*.

Bennett, Alan.

The Uncommon Reader. **Farrar, Straus & Giroux, 2007. 120pp. ISBN 978-0374280963.**

Her majesty, Queen of England, Elizabeth II, is a very busy woman, and her time is rarely her own. So when she stops in to visit the palace bookmobile (a conscientious monarch and consummate hostess, she wants everyone on the grounds to feel part of the majesty of Britannia) and starts finding more and more books she wants to read, her palace staff are justly concerned that she might shirk her royal duties in order to read. Aided and abetted by a young kitchen staff member, Norman, who she soon relies upon as her own personal librarian, her majesty soon discovers there's nothing better than rushing through one's professional duties to get back to reading.

Subjects: Book Groups; Books and Reading; British Authors; Classics; Elizabeth II; Gay Men; GLBTQ; Great Britain; Humor; London; Quick Reads; Royalty

Now Try: Bennett's other subtly humorous novel, *The Clothes They Stood Up In*, might be suggested, as might his story collection *The Laying on of Hands*. Anglophiles who also love books and reading might consider Helene Hanff's classic nonfiction collection of letters she wrote to a British bookstore, *84, Charing Cross Road* (don't forget to mention the sequel, Hanff's *The Duchess of Bloomsbury*). Of course, this book is more about reading than it is about Queen Elizabeth II, but also of interest might be the beautifully photographed and wonderfully informative nonfiction title *A Year with the Queen*, by Robert Hardman.

Bennett, Ronan.

Zugzwang: A Novel. **Bloomsbury, 2007. 273pp. ISBN 9781596912533.**

Set amid the chaos of early twentieth-century St. Petersburg, Russia, Bennett's historical thriller starts with the murder of one of the city's prominent newsmen, editor O. V. Gulko. When a second slaying occurs, psychoanalyst Otto Spethmann becomes a prime suspect (suspicion of them has more than a little to do with rampant anti-Semitism in the city) and must use his own not inconsiderable analytical skills to help the police detective in charge of the case, Mintimer Lychev, discover the true culprit.

Subjects: 1910s; Chess; Historical Fiction; Irish Authors; Jews and Judaism; Murder; Political Fiction; Psychological Fiction; Russia; Suspense

Now Try: Bennett is also the author of the historical novel *Havoc, in Its Third Year* and the literary novel *The Catastrophist*. Other literary and smart thrillers might also be suggested, such as Alan Furst's *The Spies of Warsaw*, *The Foreign Correspondent*, and *Blood of Victory*; Arturo Perez-Reverte's *The Flanders Panel*, *The Club Dumas*, and *The Fencing Master*; or David Hewson's Nic Costa mysteries, starting with *A Season for the Dead* and *The Villa of Mysteries*. Also of interest might be Jed Rubenfeld's historical mystery *The Interpretation of Murder*.

Now Consider Nonfiction . . . Intrigue and Espionage (True Adventure)

Intrigue and espionage true adventure narratives tell fast-paced stories of espionage, spy activities, interrogations, and political intrigue. They can be set in a wide variety of foreign (and often exotic) locales, although the majority take place during World War II and the Cold War era. They feature intriguing storytelling and complex heroes and antiheroes.

Conant, Jennet. *The Irregulars: Roald Dahl and the British Spy Ring in Wartime Washington.*

Deschamps, Héléne. *Spyglass: An Autobiography.*

Earley, Pete. *Family of Spies: The John Walker Spy Ring.*

Hollington, Kris. *Wolves, Jackals, and Foxes: The Assassins Who Changed History.*

Lindsey, Robert. *The Falcon and the Snowman: A True Story of Friendship and Espionage.*

O'Donnell, Patrick K. *Operatives, Spies, and Saboteurs: The Unknown Story of the Men and Women of WWII's OSS.*

Berg, Elizabeth.

We Are All Welcome Here. **Random House, 2006. 187pp. ISBN 978-1400061617.**

In 1960s Tupelo, Mississippi, thirteen-year-old Diana Dunn, always a help to her mother Paige, a victim of severe polio, and her mother's African American nurse Peacie, takes on ever more responsibilities for her care. Understandably chafing under her heavy responsibilities, Diana often finds herself at odds with Peacie, until Peacie's boyfriend finds himself in trouble over trying to register African American voters, and Paige Dunn's support of the couple opens Diana's eyes to the possibilities of courage and love. The novel is based on a true story.

Subjects: 1960s; African Americans; Coming-of-age; Family Relationships; Health Issues; Mississippi; Mothers and Daughters; Polio; Race Relations; Women Authors

Now Try: Berg has tried her hand at another historical era, World War II, in her 2007 novel *Dream When You're Feeling Blue*; she is also the author of the novels *The Year of Pleasures, The Art of Mending,* and *Say When.* Those readers interested in the coming-of-age aspect of the story might enjoy other novels featuring unique young female protagonists, including Kathryn Stockett's *The Help,* Sue Monk Kidd's *The Secret Life of Bees,* Harper Lee's classic *To Kill a Mockingbird,* and Kaye Gibbons's *Ellen Foster.* An inspiring nonfiction account of another African American woman's struggle to achieve voting rights is Kay Mills's *This Little Light of Mine: The Life of Fannie Lou Hamer.*

Bohjalian, Chris.

Trans-sister Radio. **Harmony Books, 2000. 344pp. ISBN 9780609604076.**

When long-divorced schoolteacher Allison Banks falls in love with the younger, appealing Dana Stevens, a man she meets while attending a film class he's teaching, the last thing she expects is to have to come to terms with his confession to her that he has always thought of himself as female and will soon be undergoing a long-planned sex change operation. Allison tries to continue the relationship after Dana's operation, in the face of community cruelties and snubs and despite her ex-husband Will's overt opposition to it, but her own undeniable feelings eventually make themselves known. Told in alternating first-person voices, the novel is patterned on an NPR broadcast in which the story's participants each tell their sides through interviews.

Subjects: Book Groups; Community Life; First Person; Love Affairs; Men Writing as Women; Multiple Viewpoints; Sexuality; Vermont

Now Try: Bohjalian's other popular novels, including the Oprah book *Midwives,* as well as *The Double Bind, Before You Know Kindness,* and *The Law of Similars,* might all be offered to his fans. Another novel about gender issues, Jeffrey Eugenides's popular *Middlesex,* might appeal, as might a wide variety of memoirs and nonfiction works on sexuality, including Jennifer Finney Boylan's *She's Not There: A Life in Two Genders* or *I'm Looking Through You: Growing Up Haunted,* as well as John Colapinto's *As Nature Made Him: The Boy Who Was Raised as a Girl.*

Brooks, Geraldine.

People of the Book. Viking, 2008. 372pp. ISBN 9780670018215.

Brooks's novel is an epic that sprawls across global locations and time periods, but it reads "faster" than most epics because of its intense storylines and the author's literary skill. Told in the voices of multiple characters, the story follows the life of the *Sarajevo Haggadah*, a book that surfaces not only in the present day, to be studied by restoration expert Hanna Heath (who discovers much about the book due to tiny artifacts left in its binding and pages), but also in 1940 Sarajevo, 1894 Vienna, 1609 Venice, 1492 Tarragona, and 1480 Seville. In addition to rich historical detail and characterization, a great secret about the book itself is eventually revealed.

Subjects: Barcelona; Book Groups; Books and Reading; Bosnia; Classics; Historical Fiction; Inquisition; Jews and Judaism; Multiple Viewpoints; Seville; Venice; Vienna; Women Authors

Now Try: Brooks is also the author of the popular historical novels *Year of Wonders* and *March*, as well as the investigative nonfiction title *Nine Parts of Desire: The Hidden World of Islamic Women.* (She is also married to writer Tony Horwitz, author of the nonfiction travel titles *Baghdad without a Map, Blue Latitudes,* and *Confederates in the Attic.*) Another novel in which a historical story and a book play a central role is A. S. Byatt's *Possession*; Ray Bradbury's classic about book-burning, *Fahrenheit 451,* might also hold some appeal; and a blurb is provided on this book by novelist Karen Joy Fowler, whose book *The Jane Austen Book Club* might also appeal. Michael Ondaatje's *Anil's Ghost* also features a young woman traveling and following her career, as does Amitav Ghosh's *The Hungry Tide*. Nonfiction titles about long-lost books and their discoveries might also be of interest, such as David Damrosch's *The Buried Book: The Loss and Rediscovery of the Great Epic of Gilgamesh* or Herbert Krosney's *The Lost Gospel: The Quest for the Gospel of Judas Iscariot.*

Buckley, Christopher.

Supreme Courtship. Twelve, 2008. 285pp. ISBN 9780446579827.

Donald Vanderkamp, president of the United States of America, is tired of nominating justices for the Supreme Court who keep getting rejected by the Senate (after their backgrounds are tirelessly combed for imbroglios and scandals by the president's many enemies). He decides to outwit the politicos at their own game by nominating a hugely popular but controversial choice: Pepper Cartwright, known more for her pop culture status as a television judge than for her legal experience. Hijinks, hilarity, and a topsy-turvy election featuring Vanderkamp squaring off against his sworn enemy, former Senator Dexter Mitchell, ensue in this political satire.

Subjects: Government; Humor; Judges; Law and Lawyers; Political Fiction; Quick Reads; Satire; Washington, D.C.

Now Try: Buckley has written numerous satirical novels about political and legal issues; his other novels that may appeal are *Boomsday, No Way to Treat a First Lady, Little Green Men,* and *Thank You for Smoking* (his memoir about his parents, Pat and William F. Buckley Jr., might also appeal; it is titled *Losing Mum and Pup*). Another modern satirist, Tom Wolfe, might be suggested; his novels include *I Am Charlotte Simmons* and *The Bonfire of the Vanities*. Although much gentler in tone, the humorous mystery series of Alexander McCall Smith might also appeal, including the Precious Ramotswe series (starting with *The No. 1 Ladies Detective Agency*) and the Isabel Dalhousie series (starting with *The*

Sunday Philosophy Club). Political nonfiction like Jeffrey Toobin's *The Nine: Inside the Secret World of the Supreme Court* might be a good related read, as might political and cultural humor books by conservative humorist P. J. O'Rourke.

Bull, Emma.

Territory. **Tor, 2007. 318pp. ISBN 9780312857356.**

Bull's mythic reality fantasy novel is a genreblender extraordinaire, including elements of literary fiction, fantasy writing, and a Western setting and sensibility. Mildred Benjamin, a quiet widow who earns her keep setting type in the infamous town of Tombstone, Arizona, during the 1880s, learns more than she's telling about all the principal characters involved in the shoot-out at the OK Corral. The story goes well beyond that legend, however, incorporating elements of mystery, suspense, and even dark magic in its multiple storylines of personal reinvention in the American West, the battle of good versus evil, and the inevitable conflict between larger-than-life personalities.

Subjects: 19th Century; American West; Arizona; Biographical Fiction; Dark Magic; Earp, Wyatt; Fantasy; Historical Fiction; Holliday, Doc; Love Affairs; Westerns; Women Authors

Now Try: Bull's other imaginative novels include *War for the Oaks* and *Finder: A Novel of the Borderlands*. Other novels that blend elements of fantasy and history might appeal, including Jo Graham's *Black Ships*, Susanna Clarke's *Jonathan Strange and Mrs. Norrell* and *The Ladies of Grace Adieu and Other Stories*, and Andrew Sean Greer's *The Confessions of Max Tivoli*.

Burke, Shannon.

Black Flies. **Soft Skull Press, 2008. 185pp. ISBN 9781593761912.**

After failing to do well enough on his MCATs to attend the medical school of his choice, Ollie Cross goes to work as a paramedic in one of the most embattled neighborhoods in Harlem (in 1990s New York City). Over the course of his first year, he works with jaded colleagues; becomes frustrated by demanding and ungrateful patients; and becomes involved in an incident with his partner Rutkovsky, a good but beyond burnt-out medic, that leaves him questioning both his own altruistic desires and the power of healing, which can also lead people to forget the distinctions between good and evil.

Subjects: 1990s; Book Groups; Friendships; Harlem; Medicine; New York City; Quick Reads; Small Press; Violence; Work Relationships

Awards: New York Times Notable

Now Try: Burke is also the author of the novel *Safelight*. A similarly dark and urban story is Joe Connelly's *Bringing out the Dead*. Dark modern thrillers by Sean Dolittle might also appeal (*Safer, The Cleanup, Burn*, and *Dirt*). Although much lighter in tone, Michael Perry's memoir *Population 485: Meeting Your Neighbors One Siren at a Time* or Jane Stern's *Ambulance Girl* might also provide valuable glimpses into medics' worlds and duties. This slim novel was published by Soft Skull; other novels from that press might appeal, such as Cristy Road's *Bad Habits: A Love Story*, Jonathan Evison's *All About Lulu*, Lydia Millett's *Everyone's Pretty*, and Thomas Kelly's *Sandhogs*.

Carey, Jacqueline.

It's a Crime. **Ballantine Books, 2008. 274pp. ISBN 9780345459923.**

> Financial fraud meets quirky restitution in this story. When landscape architect Pat Foy's husband is indicted for fraud at his company, LinkAge, Pat sets out to try to repay the victims of the company's fraudulent practices. Along the way she meets up with her former lover and best friend (respectively), Lemuel Samuel and Ginny Howley, who have both been hurt by their investment in Pat's husband's company. The story is told through multiple viewpoints and combines aspects of both mystery and satirical writing.

> **Subjects:** Book Groups; Business; Corruption; Family Relationships; Fraud; Humor; Multiple Viewpoints; Mystery; Quick Reads; Satire; Women Authors

> **Now Try:** Jacqueline Carey is the author of two other literary novels, *The Crossley Baby* and *The Other Family*, but she is best known for her fantasy series, Kushiel's Legacy (starting with *Kushiel's Dart* and *Kushiel's Chosen*), featuring Phedre, a young female character who is trained as a courtesan. Stanley Bing's *You Look Nice Today* throws a spotlight on other crimes that can be alleged in business; Jane Smiley's *Ten Days in the Hills* is another novel that combines domestic fiction with satire.

Carey, Peter.

🌟 *The True History of the Kelly Gang.* **Knopf, 2000. 349pp. ISBN 9780375410840.**

> Historical fiction is rarely this rip-roarin', but it makes sense here, as the narrator of Carey's story-driven novel is the leader of the Kelly gang himself, Ned Kelly. By the time Ned is relating the story of his life, times, and crimes (in the hopes that his baby daughter will get to know him from his stories), the reader knows how things have ended (not well) for the infamous Australian outlaw, whose name was synonymous with "Robin Hood" to his fellow Australians but denoted only brutal criminality to the English and their colonial laws.

> **Subjects:** 19th Century; Australia; Australian Authors; Biographical Fiction; Classics; Crime; First Person; Flashbacks; Historical Fiction; Kelly, Ned; Murder

> **Awards:** ALA Notable; Man Booker Prize; Commonwealth Writers' Prize

> **Now Try:** Although this novel is a bit more overt about its main characters' criminality, many of Carey's novels feature characters who dance just on the wrong side of the law, including *Oscar and Lucinda, Theft: A Love Story*, and *His Illegal Self.* Another novel based on real criminals is Liza Ward's *Outside Valentine.* Other fast-paced true crime narratives might also be suggested to these readers, especially those on historical topics, including E. R. Milner's *The Lives and Times of Bonnie & Clyde*, Erik Larson's *The Devil in the White City*, and Matthew Hart's *The Irish Game: A True Story of Crime and Art.*

Carrell, Jennifer Lee.

Interred with Their Bones. **Dutton, 2007. 416pp. ISBN 9780525949701.**

> While working in her new capacity as director of the production of Shakespeare's plays at London's rebuilt Globe Theatre, Kate Shelton is shocked when her former mentor, Roz, shows up with a mysterious gift that she promises will lead to a lost Shakespeare manuscript. Kate accepts the gift, but it is not until Roz is found murdered that she earnestly tries to decipher the meaning the gift (a small Victorian mourning brooch) and discover where the manuscript might be hidden.

Subjects: Book Groups; First Novels; Great Britain; London; Murder; Shakespeare, William; Suspense; Theater; Travel; Women Authors

Now Try: This is Carrell's first novel; she has also written the nonfiction history *The Speckled Monster: A Historical Tale of Battling Smallpox*. The obvious comparison for this novel is Dan Brown's extremely popular cipher thrillers, including *The Da Vinci Code* and *Angels and Demons*; other literary thrillers might be suggested as well, including Ian Caldwell's *The Rule of Four*, Jed Rubenfeld's *The Interpretation of Murder*, and Iain Pears's *An Instance of the Fingerpost*. Some quirky nonfiction titles about William Shakespeare might also appeal, such as Charles Nicholls's *The Lodger Shakespeare: His Life on Silver Street* and John Michell's *Who Wrote Shakespeare?* (as well as the more traditional biography, *Will in the World*, by Stephen Greenblatt).

Now Consider Nonfiction . . . Micro-Histories

Micro-histories are stories in which authors examine very specific people, places, or things and relate their stories as a new way in which to view the grand sweep of history. They have been referred to by Nancy Pearl, the co-author of this guide, as "one-word wonders" (because many of their titles consist of one word), and their authors provide accessible stories about everyday objects and ideas. They are story-driven narratives, and their authors often present a vast amount of historical detail more informally or even humorously than do their more scholarly counterparts.

> Brooks, Robin. *The Portland Vase: The Extraordinary Odyssey of a Mysterious Roman Treasure.*
>
> Huler, Scott. *Defining the Wind: How a 19th Century Admiral Turned Science into Poetry.*
>
> Kurlansky, Mark. *Salt: A World History.*
>
> Perrottet, Tony. *The Naked Olympics: The True Story of the Ancient Games.*
>
> Petroski, Henry. *The Toothpick: Technology and Culture.*
>
> Sullivan, Robert. *Rats: Observations on the History and Habitat of the City's Most Unwanted Inhabitants.*

Carson, Ciaran.

The Tain: A New Translation of the Tain bo Cuailnge. **Viking, 2007. 223pp. ISBN 9780670018680.**

The legend of the "Cattle Raid of the Tooley," originally part of the eighth-century "Ulster Cycle" of Irish tales and mythology, centers on the plan of Queen Medb of Connacht, whose jealousy of her husband, King Alill's, prize bull prompts her to invade a neighboring kingdom to obtain a bull owned by the king of Ulster, and thence to become more wealthy and powerful than her husband.

Subjects: 8th Century; Animals; Books in Translation; Ireland; Irish Authors; Legends; Mythology; War

Now Try: Carson is also the author of the modern fantasy novel (which also includes elements of Irish legend) *Shamrock Tea*. Other new translations of ancient classics might also appeal to these readers, including Seamus Heaney's *Beowulf: A New Verse Translation*, Simon Armitage's *Sir Gawain and the Green Knight*, and Ted Hughes's more challenging but still hypnotizing *The Oresteia of Aeschylus*; Stephen Lawhead's Pendragon cycle, starting with *Taliesin*, might also appeal, as might fantasy legend novels such as J. R. R. Tolkien's *The Legend of Sigurd and Gudrun* and *Tales from the Perilous Realm*. More modern takes on legends might be fun related reads, including John Gardner's *Grendel* and Steven Sherrill's *The Minotaur Takes a Cigarette Break*.

Castillo, Ana.

The Guardians: A Novel. **Random House, 2007. 211pp. ISBN 9781400065004.**

In her fifties, widowed and raising the teenage son of her brother Rafa, Regina lives a less tenuous life than many immigrants, as she has a job (albeit a poorly paid one) and resident status, thanks to her marriage to a man who was killed in the Vietnam War. Life is hard but acceptable, until her brother, who lives in Mexico but repeatedly crosses into the United States for work, goes missing, leading Regina to join forces with a younger male colleague, Miguel Betancourt, to discover the truth of what has happened to him.

Second Appeal: Language

Subjects: Family Relationships; First Person; Friendships; Immigrants and Immigration; Mexico; Multiple Viewpoints; Teenage Boys; Teenagers; Women Authors

Now Try: Castillo's other novels include *Peel My Love Like an Onion* and *So Far from God*; she is also the author of the essay collection *Massacre of the Dreamers* and the poetry book *I Ask the Impossible*. Other Latina and Latino writers who are similar in style to Castillo are Cristina García (*Dreaming in Cuban* and *The Aguero Sisters*), Julia Alvarez (*How the Garcia Girls Lost Their Accent* and *Yo!*), and Oscar Hijuelos (*The Mambo Kings Play Songs of Love*). A wide variety of nonfiction titles on the lives of immigrants and border crossings are also available, including William Langewiesche's *Cutting for Sign* and Ruben Martinez's *Crossing Over: A Mexican Family on the Migrant Trail*. Teresa Rodriguez's unsettling true crime narrative, *The Daughters of Juarez: A True Story of Serial Murder South of the Border*, also explores the dangers of the border regions.

Charyn, Jerome.

Johnny One-Eye: A Tale of the American Revolution. **Norton, 2008. 479pp. ISBN 9780393064971.**

In this imaginative, humorous, and yet soberingly detailed chronicle of the American Revolution as it was fought in New York City, Charyn throws historically accurate and quickly paced battle and war scenes together with a truly breathtaking range of real characters, including Alexander Hamilton and George Washington; his fictional characters, including a spy named John Stocking and a brothel madam named Gertrude Jennings, face a wide variety of near escapes and political machinations with aplomb and camaraderie.

Subjects: 18th Century; American Revolution; Biographical Fiction; Book Groups; First Person; Historical Fiction; Humor; Love Affairs; New York City; Prostitution; War; YA

Now Try: Charyn is a master at writing in a number of different genre forms, but his other historical novels might particularly appeal to these readers, including *Captain Kidd* and *The Green Lantern*; also of interest might be his New York mystery series featuring Isaac Sidel, which started with the title *Blue Eyes*. Reviewers have compared this novel to E. L.

Doctorow's classic *Ragtime*. John Barth's *The Sot-Weed Factor* offers another take on this era, and M. T. Anderson's fantastic YA novel *The Astonishing Life of Octavian Nothing, Traitor to the Nation* is another American Revolution–era story.

Choi, Susan.

A Person of Interest. **Viking, 2008. 356pp. ISBN 9780670018468.**

When Korean American professor of mathematics Wen Ho Lee becomes a "person of interest" in the FBI investigation of a bomb explosion that injured one of his popular young departmental colleagues, he slowly loses his grasp on reality under the suspicion and his increasing thoughts and regrets about his past marriages and other rocky personal and professional relationships.

Subjects: Academia; Adultery; Fathers and Daughters; Korean Americans; Mathematics; Murder; Serial Killers; Suspense; Violence; Women Authors

Now Try: Choi is also the author of the novels *The Foreign Student* and *American Woman*. Two other novels in which individuals are forced to hide revolutionary crimes might prove interesting read-alikes: Hari Kunzru's *My Revolutions* and Janis Hallowell's *She Was*. Other novels of psychological suspense, including Ruth Rendell's *The Water's Lovely* or *13 Steps Down*, might be of interest, as might Daphne du Maurier's classics, such as *My Cousin Rachel* or *Rebecca*.

Chupack, Edward.

Silver: My Own Tale as Written by Me with a Goodly Amount of Murder. **Thomas Dunne Books, 2008. 275pp. ISBN 9780312373658.**

Long John Silver, the infamous pirate from Robert Stevenson's classic *Treasure Island*, tells his own story in this swashbuckling, first-person account of his violent and bloody rise to power, pirate exploits, and gathering and hiding of vast amounts of treasure.

Subjects: 19th Century; Adventure; First Novels; First Person; Historical Fiction; Literary Allusions; Ocean; Pirates; Quick Reads; Silver, Long John; Travel; Unreliable Narrator; YA

Now Try: Readers who enjoy this novel will definitely want to check out the source material, Robert Louis Stevenson's classic *Treasure Island* (if they haven't already). Other novels of pirate and nautical adventures may be of interest, including Neal Stephenson's *The Confusion* (part of his <u>Baroque Cycle</u> series), D. M. Cornish's fantasy/pirate novel *The Foundling*, or any number of classics by Rafael Sabatini.

Clarke, Brock.

🎣 *An Arsonist's Guide to Writers' Homes in New England.* **Algonquin Books of Chapel Hill, 2007. 303pp. ISBN 9781565125513.**

When Sam Pulsifer gets out of prison after serving time for setting fire to the Emily Dickinson house (arson wasn't his only crime; he didn't know that two people were in the house at the time), he sets out to reconstruct his life, marrying and having a family. However, when other long-dead authors' homes start going up in flames, suspicion focuses on him once again. Because he knows he's innocent, he sets out to find out who is setting the fires—and is shocked when the answer is uncomfortably close to home.

Subjects: Arson; Family Relationships; First Person; Humor; Literary Lives; Men's Lives; Murder; Psychological Fiction

Awards: ALA Notable

Now Try: Clarke is also the author of the novels *Carrying the Torch* and *The Ordinary White Boy*, as well as the story collection *What We Won't Do*. Other quickly paced novels about characters with, shall we say, questionable pasts, are Josh Bazell's *Beat the Reaper* and Clyde Edgerton's *The Bible Salesman*; Martin Millar's quirky novel *Milk, Sulphate, and Alby Starvation* also features a male character somewhat on the lam (but for a much different reason). Sam Lipsyte's literary style is similar to Clarke's; his novels *Home Land* and *The Subject Steve* might also be suggested.

Collins, David.

Maxxed Out. HarperCollins, 2009. 310pp. ISBN 9780061456190.

When David Collins, a down-on-his-luck writer in the middle of a messy marital separation and a decided downturn in his literary fortunes, is offered the chance to ghostwrite a best seller for business magnate and general celebrity Robert Maxx, he is less than enthused, but he agrees, largely because of the money involved. As he insinuates himself into Maxx's life to write his gutsy life story, he finds himself both attracted to and repelled by the charismatic but unscrupulous man—as well as a prime suspect in his murder.

Subjects: Business; Finance; First Person; Journalism; Literary Lives; Marriage; Men's Lives; Murder; New York City; Satire; Suspense; Writers and Writing

Now Try: The author is a journalist, ghostwriter, and sometime investor in real estate, so he knows of what he speaks; other novels in which finance and business play a large role might be offered, such as Stanley Bing's *Lloyd: What Happened* and *You Look Nice Today*, Brad Meltzer's suspenseful *The Millionaires*, and Joseph Finder's *Power Play*. This novel is supposedly based on the story of another well-known New York City real estate mogul, whose popular business book *Trump: The Art of the Deal*, might be a fun related read. Another story-driven novel about one man trying to figure out another is Eli Gottlieb's *Now You See Him*.

Crace, Jim.

🎖 *The Pesthouse: A Novel.* Nan A. Talese, 2007. 255pp. ISBN 9780385520751.

Left for dead in her community's "pesthouse" while she suffers from the flux, Margaret has given up hope for survival in postapocalyptic America, where society and government have collapsed. When a traveler named Franklin arrives and must stay in town to help his brother Jackson, the two come to an understanding and decide to travel to the coast, where residents embark on ships to try to reach safety in Europe. Along the way Franklin is captured by slave traders, and Margaret falls in with a severe religious sect, but they continue to seek one another and a new life even while separated.

Second Appeal: Language

Subjects: Apocalypse; Book Groups; Community Life; Death and Dying; Dystopia; Health Issues; Love Affairs; Psychological Fiction; Suspense

Awards: ALA Notable; National Book Critics Circle Award

Now Try: Crace is also the author of the novels *A Birth of Stones*, *Being Dead*, and *Quarantine*. Fans of this eerie novel might consider Cormac McCarthy's similarly themed novel

The Road or Howard James Kunstler's postapocalyptic *World Made by Hand* as well; Matthew Sharpe's *Jamestown* and David Mitchell's *The Cloud Atlas* might also be good read-alikes. A similarly themed novel is José Saramago's *Blindness*.

Dovey, Ceridwen.

Blood Kin: A Novel. **Viking, 2007. 183pp. ISBN 9780670018567.**

A small nation about to experience a coup d'état is the setting for Dovey's novel in three parts. The first tells the story of three men (a barber, a portraitist, and a chef) who must switch their allegiance and assistance to the deposed president to the new leader, known only as the Commander; in the second, three women linked in various ways to the men provide their viewpoints on the events. In the third and concluding section, the transitory nature of power and loyalty is displayed as another coup threatens.

Subjects: Coups; First Person; Hostages; Marriage; Multiple Viewpoints; Political Fiction; Psychological Fiction; Quick Reads; Suspense; Women Authors

Now Try: Although much more languidly paced, Ann Patchett's *Bel Canto* is another study of political power and individual motives; Imre Kertesz's slim *Detective Story* also displays the intoxication of promised power and to what depths humans will sink to achieve it. George Saunders's *The Brief and Frightening Reign of Phil*, although much more lighthearted in tone, is also a serious satire about the dangers of political extremism.

Durcan, Liam.

Garcia's Heart. **Thomas Dunne Books, 2007. 296pp. ISBN 9780312367084.**

Patrick Lazerenko struggles with his mixed feelings for his former mentor and friend, Hernan Garcia de la Cruz, a store owner and leader in the immigrant community in Montreal (who was once a practicing doctor in his native Honduras and often dispensed medical advice and care in the back of his store). All of that is in the past, however; when the reader joins the story, Patrick is traveling to The Hague to witness Garcia's war trial and try to reconcile his knowledge of the man who inspired him to become a physician with the war criminal being charged for his long-ago complicity in torture and other crimes in Honduras.

Subjects: Brain; Canada; Canadian Authors; Doctors; First Novels; Friendships; Honduras; Montreal; Neurology; Political Fiction; Suspense; Torture; War

Now Try: Other smart political thrillers might be suggested to these readers, including Michael Palmer's *The First Patient* (which includes a medical mystery), Stephen Frey's *The Successor*, and David Baldacci's *Simple Genius*. Slavenka Drakulic's fascinating nonfiction study of those on trial at The Hague, *They Would Never Hurt a Fly*, might also appeal; other nonfiction titles about torture and the history of torture might also be considered, such as Dominic Streatfeild's *Brainwash: The Secret History of Mind Control* and Jon Ronson's thoroughly creepy *The Men Who Stare at Goats*.

Ford, Jeffrey.

The Shadow Year. **William Morrow, 2008. 289pp. ISBN 9780061231520.**

In Ford's unnervingly creepy novel about the world kids inhabit and their understanding of the adults around them (including the stalking and dangerous figure Mr. White, whose long white car is often seen in the vicinity of accidents and mayhem), his unnamed narrator joins forces with his older brother Jim and his younger sister Mary to try to unravel the evil behind disappearances and crimes in their 1960s Long Island neighborhood. Based on the author's earlier short story, "Botch Town," the novel also features the children building a replica of their town in their basement (which they call "Botch Town") and their little sister's eerie predictions when she starts to place figures representing the town's inhabitants around the town in unexpected locations, prefiguring events that happen to them.

Subjects: 1960s; Alcoholism; Community Life; Family Relationships; First Person; Long Island; Murder; Psychological Fiction; Serial Killers; Siblings; Suspense

Now Try: Ford is also the author of the Well-Built City fantasy trilogy, including the titles *The Physiogomy, Memoranda*, and *The Beyond*; the Edgar Award–winning novel *The Girl in the Glass*; and the story collections *The Empire of Ice Cream* and *The Fantasy Writer's Assistant*. Ford's book has been compared to Ray Bradbury's classics *Dandelion Wine* and *Something Wicked This Way Comes*; other thrillers such as *The Church of Dead Girls* might also appeal. Neil Gaiman's entirely creepy books from children's points of view, *Coraline* and *The Graveyard Book*, might also be shivery read-alikes.

Fowler, Karen Joy.

Wit's End. **Putnam, 2008. 324pp. ISBN 9780399154751.**

Reeling from the death of her father, twenty-nine-year-old Rima Lanisell travels to California to visit her godmother—who happens to be Addison Early, the enormously popular author and creator of a series of mysteries fronted by her detective character, Maxwell Lane. It has become a habit with Addison to be as secretive as possible, to preserve both the integrity of her forthcoming mysteries and her own privacy, but the barriers between her and her fans (as well as between her and Rima, who slowly starts to piece together the true nature of Addison's former relationship with Rima's father) start to crumble as those fans speculate and blog ever more insistently about both the plotlines of Addison's forthcoming books and her private life.

Subjects: Books and Reading; California; Family Secrets; Friendships; Godmothers; Humor; Literary Lives; Mystery; Women Authors; Writers and Writing

Now Try: Fowler has explored the theme of readers' connections to books in her earlier novel *The Jane Austen Book Club*. Another author character who is trying to reconcile his literary output and reputation with his personal life can be found in P. F. Kluge's thoughtful novel *Gone Tomorrow*. Although more fantastic in nature, Jasper Fforde's Tuesday Next series (set in an alternate 1985 world, where literary matters are of all-consuming importance), starting with *The Eyre Affair* and *Lost in a Good Book*, might also appeal to these readers.

Gibson, Tanya Egan.

How to Buy a Love of Reading. **Dutton, 2009. 392pp. ISBN 9780525951148.**

Although not as fast paced as some of the other titles listed here, Gibson's novel nonetheless merits inclusion because of its "story within a story" framework. Deciding that their money can fix their daughter's abhorrence for all things bookish and literary, prep school student Carley Wells's parents decide to buy her an author, who will write a book just for her, tailored to her specific desires. Although she goes along with the plan partly as a way to gain the attention of an older boy, her friend Hunter Cay (who himself has no problem loving books but who loves drinking and prescription drugs more), Carley eventually finds herself caught up in both the story being created for her and the story she is living with Hunter.

Second Appeal: Character

Subjects: Books and Reading; Coming-of-age; Drug Abuse; Education; First Novels; Friendships; Literary Lives; Teenage Girls; Teenagers; Women Authors; YA

Now Try: Other novels in which young girls are the main (but not always the most likable) characters might appeal, such as Curtis Sittenfeld's *Prep*, Zoey Dean's *How to Teach Filthy Rich Girls*, Galt Niederhoffer's *A Taxonomy of Barnacles* and *The Romantics*, Nancy Lieberman's *Admissions*, and Elinor Lipman's *My Latest Grievance*.

Ginsberg, Debra.

The Grift: A Novel. **Shaye Areheart Books, 2008. 337pp. ISBN 978-0307382726.**

Marina Marks, daughter of an alcoholic and inattentive mother, learned early on how to read people; as an adult, she uses this ability while she masquerades as a psychic and makes her living finding individuals who will come to depend on the fortunes she tells. After going too far in taking advantage of an elderly woman client in Florida, Marks relocates to California, where she is disconcerted to find that she has truly developed the ability to read the future and that her future is a complex and scary one, including a man named Gideon, who is following her because of her past, and violent confrontations with family members of her current clients.

Subjects: California; Florida; Fortune Telling; Fraud; Love Affairs; Psychics; Women Authors

Now Try: Ginsberg is the author of a previous novel, *Blind Submission*, as well as the superlative memoirs *Waiting*, *Raising Blaze*, and *About My Sisters*. Brunonia Barry's novel *The Lace Reader* also features female characters with unique abilities; Anne Tyler's novel *Searching for Caleb* also features a main character who reads tarot cards and finds herself in complex relationships with her family, friends, and husband. Readers who enjoy this novel of secrets and relationships might also consider Kate Atkinson's popular Jackson Brodie series, consisting (so far) of *Case Histories*, *One Good Turn*, and *When Will There Be Good News?*

Gottlieb, Eli.

Now You See Him. **William Morrow, 2008. 261pp. ISBN 9780061284649.**

Gottlieb's psychological novel focuses on the relationship between Nick Framingham, a responsible family man and member of society, and his friend Rob Castor, who, as the novel opens, has committed suicide after being charged with the murder of his girlfriend. As Nick thinks back on their childhood and school friendship, he not only rediscovers secrets and forgotten truths about each of their pasts and personalities, he also finds his present life changing in unforeseeable ways.

Second Appeal: Story

Subjects: Book Groups; Family Secrets; First Person; Flashbacks; Friendships; Love Affairs; Marriage; Men's Lives; Murder; Suburbia; Suicide; Suspense

Now Try: Gottlieb's earlier novel is titled *The Boy Who Went Away*. Other books in which mysterious circumstances are slowly revealed are Audrey Niffeneggers's *The Time Traveler's Wife*, Emily Perkins's *Novel About My Wife*, Emily St. John Mandel's *Last Night in Montreal*, and Larry Watson's *Sundown, Yellow Moon*. John Knowles's classic novel *A Separate Peace* also explores the strong friendship between two boys, as does John Green's YA novel *Looking for Alaska*. Other novels about writers are Joshua Henkin's *Matrimony* and Joey Goebel's *Torture the Artist*.

Hall, Sarah.

Daughters of the North. **Harper Perennial, 2007. 209pp. ISBN 9780061430367.**

Great Britain of the near future, a land in which massive flooding has led to the breakdown of society, is the setting for this novel. In response to the flooding and widespread destruction of land and property, an authoritarian quasi-governmental agency known, appropriately, as the Authority, has ruled that all women must undergo enforced sterilization and has enacted a number of other dictatorial controls. The narrator of this tale, known only as Sister, escapes from her home to journey to a feminine commune in the north of the country, run by the charismatic Jackie Nixon; when she arrives, however, she finds that she has largely traded one cruel master for another.

Second Appeal: Setting

Subjects: Agriculture; Bleak Future; British Authors; Dystopia; Feminism; Great Britain; Natural Disasters; Science Fiction; Society; Women Authors; YA

Now Try: Hall is also the author of two other novels, *The Electric Michelangelo* and *Haweswater* (which is more similar in plot to this novel, although it is a work of historical fiction). Also of interest might be other novels in which individuals in futuristic societies don't get much say about personal rights and civil liberties, including Margaret Atwood's *The Handmaid's Tale, Cat's Eye*, and *Oryx and Crake* and Aldous Huxley's classic *Brave New World*; also of interest might be other works of dystopian fiction, like Kurt Vonnegut's *Welcome to the Monkey House*, James Howard Kunstler's *World Made By Hand*, and James Crace's *The Pesthouse*. This novel also won the James Tiptree Jr. fantasy award; other winners of that award include Denise Shawl's *Filter House*, Shelley Jackson's *Half Life*, and Geoff Ryman's *Air*.

Harris, Joanne.

Gentlemen and Players. **William Morrow, 2006. 422pp. ISBN 9780060559144.**

At a sleepy boys' boarding school in Great Britain (St. Oswald's Grammar School for Boys), longtime educator Roy Straitley is preparing to retire. Before he can, however, he must face an unknown adversary who is bent on destroying the school. Harris's novel is a fast and suspenseful read, but it does switch between two narrators, both of whom use the first person, and the book demands that the reader pay attention to follow the voice and plot twists.

Subjects: British Authors; Education; First Person; Great Britain; Multiple Viewpoints; Mystery; Psychological Fiction; Suspense; Women Authors; Women Writing as Men

Now Try: Harris is also the author of the popular novels *Chocolat* and its sequel, *The Girl with No Shadow*, as well as the more mysterious *Five Quarters of the Orange, Coastliners*, and *Runemarks*. Other mysteries featuring diabolical planners include Patricia Highsmith's *The Talented Mr. Ripley*, Donna Tartt's *The Secret History*, and Michael Cox's *The Meaning of Night*. This novel is much more of a thriller than Harris typically writes; its fans might consider other popular thriller authors such as Peter Robinson (*Gallows View* and *A Dedicated Man*) or Barbara Vine,aka Ruth Rendell (*The Birthday Present*, *The Minotaur: A Novel*, or *The Blood Doctor*). Roald Dahl's memoir *Boy*, about his youth and experiences in British boarding schools, might provide an interesting related and coming-of-age read.

Hein, Christoph.

Settlement: A Novel. **Metropolitan Books, 2008. 323pp. ISBN 9780805077681.**

When Bernhard Haber and his family are sent as refugees to live in the small provincial town of Guldenberg in Germany, they suffer not only from their father's severe injury, which makes it difficult for him to earn a living, but also from being the target of the numerous petty crimes and vindictive actions taken against them by the town's residents, who are weary of refugees joining their communities. Haber undertakes to exact his revenge on the town, and the story of his machinations to seek retribution by becoming one of the town's most successful residents unfolds over fifty years, through the voices of five of the town's residents.

Subjects: Books in Translation, Community Life; Germany; Multicultural; Multiple Viewpoints; Refugees; Suspense; Unreliable Narrator; World War II

Now Try: Hein's other novels are *Willenbrock, The Tango Player*, and *The Distant Lover*. Tom Bissell's book of short stories, *God Lives in St. Petersburg*, offers a similar reading experience. Although much longer, Jonathan Littell's favorably reviewed novel *The Kindly Ones* also provides a character portrait of a man who changed his identity to try to escape the crimes he committed. Frederick Reuss's novel *Mohr*, based on the life of a German-Jewish doctor who was exiled from Germany in 1934, might also be of interest. Joseph Berger's memoir *Displaced Persons: Growing Up American after the Holocaust*, also examines the lives of immigrant refugees.

Hill, Lawrence.

🎋 *Someone Knows My Name*. **Norton, 2007. 486pp. ISBN 9780393065787.**

Aminata Diallo, captured in Africa in 1745 (at the age of eleven) and transported to South Carolina, becomes the slave of an indigo farmer. During the course of her work there, a manager on the farm notes her intelligence and secretly teaches her to read. This skill becomes useful when she is traded to a Jewish bureaucrat in Manhattan; while working for him she helps to keep lists of African American loyalists who escape slavery and emigrate to Nova Scotia and Sierra Leone. Although her own journey is fraught with dangers and she very rarely gets to experience any normal family life with her husband and two children, she nonetheless succeeds in her desire to become, and remain, a free woman.

Subjects: African Americans; American Revolution; Book Groups; Canadian Authors; Historical Fiction; Men Writing as Women; Nova Scotia; Sierra Leone; Slavery; South Carolina

Awards: Commonwealth Writers' Prize

Now Try: Hill's other novels are *Any Known Blood* and *Some Great Thing*; he also coauthored the poignant memoir *The Deserter*, with Joshua Key, about Key's experiences fighting in the Iraq War and his decision to go AWOL rather than return to duty in Iraq. Another popular, prize-winning historical novel about slavery is Edward P. Jones's *The Known World*; Toni Morrison's *A Mercy* offers a similarly strong female character, as does Breena Clarke's *Stand the Storm*. Other winners of the Commonwealth Prize might also appeal, such as Lloyd Jones's *Mister Pip*, Kate Grenville's *The Secret River*, and Austin Clarke's *The Polished Hoe*.

Horn, Dara.

🏵 *The World To Come*. **Norton, 2006. 314pp. ISBN 9780393051070.**

Benjamin Ziskind, knowing that his family has a special connection to Marc Chagall's sketch *Over Vitebsk*, being displayed in a New York museum, steals it (and then enlists the help of his sister Sara to help keep him from being apprehended for the crime). In addition to the modern-day heist story, Horn tells the interconnected stories of Chagall's life and the creation of his art, as well as Ziskind's family's emigration from Eastern Europe to the United States.

Subjects: Art and Artists; Biographical Fiction; Brothers and Sisters; Chagall, Marc; Crime; Family Relationships; Historical Fiction; Jewish American Authors; Siblings; Women Authors

Awards: National Jewish Book Award

Now Try: Horn is also the author of a novel titled *In the Image*, and a historical novel titled *All Other Nights*. Other novels in which the protagonists feel strong connections to artworks might be suggested, including Sara Houghteling's *Pictures at an Exhibition*, Debra Dean's *The Madonnas of Leningrad*, and Justin Cartwright's *The Promise of Happiness*. Nonfiction titles about art theft, particularly that which took place during World War II, might also be offered, including Lynn Nicholas's *The Rape of Europa* and Catherine Scott-Clark and Adrian Levy's *The Amber Room: The Fate of the World's Greatest Lost Treasure*.

Houghteling, Sara.

Pictures at an Exhibition. **Knopf, 2009. 243pp. ISBN 9780307266859.**

Max Berenzon, son of a prominent art dealer and a musician, grows up in Paris loving and surrounded by art, but is precluded from taking over his father's business because his father maintains he has no true talent for it. As he becomes more convinced that that cannot be the real reason for his father's intractable decision, he simultaneously falls in love with his father's gallery assistant, Rose Clément, and learns more about his family's (and Rose's) secrets, both within their own relationships and in the larger art world. (The novel is based on the true story of Rose Valland, the former curator of the Jeu de Paume.)

Subjects: Art and Artists; Biographical Fiction; First Novels; First Person; Historical Fiction; Jews and Judaism; Love Affairs; Paris; Women Writing as Men; World War II

Now Try: Other novels in which characters' connections to art are explored are Dara Horn's *The World to Come*, Kate Christensen's *A Great Man*, and Debra Dean's *The Madonnas of Leningrad*. Nonfiction titles on art theft and the Nazis might be suggested, such as Lynn Nicholas's *The Rape of Europa* and Catherine Scott-Clark and Adrian Levy's *The Amber Room: The Fate of the World's Greatest Lost Treasure*. Those readers fascinated by the world of art dealing might also consider the biography of one of history's most infamous dealers, Joseph Duveen, titled *Duveen: A Life in Art*, by Meryle Secrest; also of interest might be Sarah Thornton's investigative title *Seven Days in the Art World*.

Iagnemma, Karl.

The Expeditions: A Novel. **Dial Press, 2008. 322pp. ISBN 9780385335959.**

The year is 1844, and Elisha Stone has journeyed to Michigan's Upper Peninsula as part of an exploratory and scientific expedition. After he writes a letter to his mother in New England to inform her of his whereabouts, his ailing father sets out on an expedition of his own to find his son; the narrative shifts between Elisha's exploits and his father's journey and reflections.

Subjects: 19th Century; Coming-of-age; Family Relationships; Fathers and Sons; Historical Fiction; Michigan; Multiple Viewpoints; New England

Now Try: Iagnemma has also written a story collection titled *On the Nature of Human Romantic Interaction*. Another story-driven historical narrative in which a young woman flees her former husband's family is Gil Adamson's *The Outlander*; Jane Urquhart's historical novel *The Stone Carvers* also features a family whose relationships are close but troubled. Iagnemma works as a research scientist at the Massachusetts Institute of Technology; another scientist who writes skillful prose is Liam Durcan, whose thoughtful and suspenseful novel *Garcia's Heart* might also be suggested. Another novel that shares this novel's setting of the Upper Peninsula (although in a more contemporary time) is Jim Harrison's *True North*; Per Petterson's *Out Stealing Horses*, though set on another continent, shares a theme of reflecting on the past and a similar northern setting and climate.

Jaffe, Michael Grant.

Whirlwind: A Novel. **Norton, 2004. 287pp. ISBN 9780393059618.**

Lucas Prouty is a decidedly forgettable meteorologist, until a hurricane sweeps through his region of the North Carolina coastline and, in the course of reporting live on the storm, he is swept away by it; he is found days later. Although his career had previously been in the doldrums, his newfound fame leads to new job offers and opportunities—but will they be worth giving up his chance at new love with Kiki, a local no-nonsense bartender who's not nearly as impressed with his ordeal as everyone else is?

Second Appeal: Character

Subjects: First Person; Humor; Hurricanes; Love Affairs; Mass Media; Men's Lives; Meteorology; North Carolina; Satire; Television

Now Try: Jaffe is also the author of the novels *Skateaway* and *Dance Real Slow*. Frederick Barthelme's novel *Waveland* also features a likable male protagonist and a natural disaster; John Irving's novels, particularly those noted for their humor (*A Prayer for Owen Meany* and *A Son of the Circus*), might also be suggested. Although a much harsher satire of the mass media, Joyce Maynard's classic novel *To Die For* might also be a fun related read.

Johnson, Denis.

Nobody Move. **Farrar, Straus & Giroux, 2009. 196pp. ISBN 9780374222901.**

Quentin Tarantino meets literature in this short, action-packed narrative of individuals all on the take in Bakersfield, California: down-on-his-luck gambler Jimmy Luntz, who only postpones the inevitable when he shoots the man sent to collect his debts; Anita Desilvera, the wife of a prominent attorney who is being framed for a $2.3 million heist; and Ernest Gambol, the man shot by Jimmy, who, with the love of a good woman who can sew up a gunshot wound, fully intends to get both his revenge and the cash he's owed.

Subjects: California; Gamblers and Gambling; Love Affairs; Noir; Quick Reads; Violence

Now Try: Johnson is also the author of the National Book Award–winning novel *Tree of Smoke*, as well as *Angels, Fiskadoro*, and *Already Dead: A California Gothic*. Richard Price's novels also feature complex ties between characters and violent plots, particularly *Lush Life* and *Samaritan*. Johnson's quickly paced style is similar to that of Elmore Leonard, whose novels *Road Dogs, Mr. Paradise*, and *Get Shorty* might all be good read-alikes. Thomas Pynchon, another well-regarded literary fiction author, has recently written a novel with elements of suspense, titled *Inherent Vice*.

Jones, Edward P.

🌳 *The Known World.* **Amistad, 2003. 388pp. ISBN 9780060557546.**

Jones provides a twist on the typical slavery novel by offering as his main character a man named Henry Townsend, a black man who is purchased and freed by his own father, but who turns to his former owner for lessons in running a plantation; eventually, he buys slaves of his own. After his death at a young age, his widow, Caldonia, more conflicted about the ownership of slaves than her husband was, allows lax discipline; eventually the plantation falls into chaos as she loses control of her workers. Jones's narrative moves back and forth in time to relate the stories of both Henry and his father, Augustus; he also provides context through other characters, most notably a Virginia county sheriff (John Skiffington) who is given a slave as a wedding present and rebels against treating her as property.

Subjects: 18th Century; 19th Century; African American Authors; American South; Book Groups; Civil War; Classics; Historical Fiction; Race Relations; Slavery; Virginia

Awards: ALA Notable; International IMPAC Dublin Literary Award; National Book Award; National Book Critics Circle Award; Pulitzer Prize

Now Try: Jones has also written two story collections, *Lost in the City* and *All Aunt Hagar's Children*. Other unique slave narratives might be offered to these readers, including Lawrence Hill's *Someone Knows My Name* and William Styron's classic *The Confessions of Nat Turner*; other related historical novels such as Geraldine Brooks's *March* might also be suggested. Edward Ball's nonfiction about families' relationships with their slaves might also appeal, including *Slaves in the Family* and *The Sweet Hell Inside*.

Jones, Lloyd.

🌳 *Mister Pip.* **Dial Press, 2006. 256pp. ISBN 9780385341066.**

When Bougainville Island, located off the coast of Papua New Guinea, is torn apart by the violence of locals and invaders seeking to exploit the land's copper resources, all of the teachers at Matilda Laimo's school desert their posts. Matilda and the other children are left to be taught by the single eccentric white man (who is married to one of the local residents) who stays, Mr. Watts. Left to his own devices, Mr. Watts decides simply to read to the children, and chooses his favorite book, Charles Dickens's *Great Expectations*. Although the children are at first stymied by the story and its vocabulary, they soon begin to see the parallels in their coming-of-age experiences and those of Dickens's main character, young Pip.

Subjects: 1990s; Book Groups; Books and Reading; Colonialism; Coming-of-age; Education; First Person; Literary Allusions; Men Writing as Women; New Zealand Authors; Teenagers; Violence; War; YA

Awards: ALA Notable; Alex Award; Commonwealth Writers' Prize; Kiriyama Pacific Rim Book Prize

Now Try: Jones's other novels include *Here at the End of the World We Learn to Dance, Napoleon and the Chicken Farmer,* and *The Book of Fame.* Those readers whose curiosity is engaged by Mr. Watts's allegiance to Charles Dickens's classic might also want to try *Great Expectations.* Other novels that explore the importance of books and reading to characters are Masha Hamilton's *The Camel Bookmobile,* Janice Kulyk Keefer's *The Ladies' Lending Library,* and Kate Morton's *The Forgotten Garden.* The memoir *Reading Lolita in Tehran,* by Azar Nafisi, might also be a good related read.

Kent, Kathleen.

The Heretic's Daughter. **Little, Brown, 2008. 332pp. ISBN 9780316024488.**

Sarah Carrier Chapman writes a long letter to her granddaughter, explaining the Salem witchcraft trials of her youth, while also setting the record straight regarding the conviction of her mother, Martha. Based on Kent's real family history, this is a powerful first novel describing mass hysteria, family feuds that spiral out of control, and the actions of an unbending woman who is ahead of her time in her refusal to bow to community demands.

Subjects: 17th Century; Biographical Fiction; Diary; Epistolary Fiction; Family Relationships; First Novels; Historical Fiction; Massachusetts; Salem; Trials; Witchcraft; Women Authors; YA

Now Try: Other novels based on the Salem witchcraft trials might appeal to these readers, such as the very dark *Dorcas Good: The Diary of a Salem Witch* by Rose Earhart, *The Last Witchfinder* by James Morrow, or Megan Chance's *Susannah Morrow;* Brunonia Barry's *The Lace Reader,* although set in the present day, also features a character struggling with her heritage and the community of Salem. Other books written in a similarly personal style are Jim Crace's *The Pesthouse* and Sarah Hall's *Daughters of the North.*

Kertész, Imre.

Detective Story. **Knopf, 2008. 112pp. ISBN 9780307266446.**

Although Kertész's slim novel is not what a reader might typically think of as "story-driven," it is sometimes classified as a mystery and has a definite air of suspense and anticipation to its first-person narration. It is the account of Antonio Martens, who is being sentenced to die for the murders of Federigo and Enrique Salinas; they were prominent society members who questioned the regime for which Martens worked as a torturer, and who therefore opened themselves up to violence and retaliation.

Subjects: Books in Translation; First Person; Hungarian Authors; Latin America; Murder; Political Fiction; Quick Reads; Social Class; Torture; War

Now Try: Kertész is the author of several previous novels, all translated from his native Hungarian: *The Pathseeker, Fatelessness, Liquidation,* and *Kaddish for a Child Not Yet Born.* Liam Durcan's *Garcia's Heart* offers another story of a war criminal (on trial at The Hague); Elie Wiesel's *The Town Beyond the Wall* features a character trying to survive torture; and Canadian author Giles Blunt's literary thriller *Breaking Lorca*, about the use of torture in El Salvador in the 1970s, might also be suggested. Nonfiction on the subject, although very distressing to read, might also make for good related reading; such titles include Philip Gourevitch's and Errol Morris's *Standard Operating Procedure* and Dominic Streatfeild's *Brainwash: The Secret History of Mind Control*.

Khadra, Yasmina.

🐦 *The Attack*. **Doubleday, 2005. 257pp. ISBN 9780385517485.**

When the Tel Aviv hospital where Dr. Amin Jaafari works is the target of a terrorist attack, he works for hours to help the victims survive. After doing what he can to ameliorate the effects of the attack, he is surprised to return home and find his wife Sihem absent—and even more surprised when he receives a phone call shortly thereafter telling him that the main suspect in the bombing is his wife. Is it possible, he wonders, to live with and love someone, and be so unaware of her deepest thoughts and plans?

Subjects: Arab–Israeli Conflict; Book Groups; Books in Translation; Doctors; Flashbacks; Israel; Marriage; Middle East; Multicultural; Palestinians; Psychological Fiction; Quick Reads; Terrorism

Awards: ALA Notable

Now Try: Khadra has just started to receive the attention due him; he has written many other novels, including *The Sirens of Baghdad*, *The Swallows of Kabul*, *Wolf Dreams*, and *In the Name of God* (he is also the author of the <u>Inspector Llob</u> mysteries, which start with *Morituri*). Another story-driven novel of life in the Middle East is *Finding Nouf*, by Zoë Ferraris; although the setting is very different, Larry McMurtry's *Yellow Moon Dog* also features a protagonist trying to understand a violent crime. The coming-of-age memoir *Tasting the Sky: A Palestinian Childhood*, by Ibtisam Barakat, might also provide context for the Middle East region and situation between Israel and Palestine.

Kogan, Deborah Copaken.

Between Here and April. **Algonquin Books of Chapel Hill, 2008. 280pp. ISBN 9781565125629.**

While attending a performance of the play *Medea* with her husband, mother of two and former photojournalist Elizabeth Burns Steiger is stricken by such a flood of memories and unanswered questions from her childhood that she faints. Thereafter she undertakes to discover the truth of what really happened to her friend April, who disappeared from their first-grade class with no explanation. Using her journalistic training to return to her home town and interview anyone who might have known what happened to April and her mother, Adele Cassidy, she also finds herself dealing with a horrific experience that befell her while she was on a war reporting assignment many years previously.

Second Appeal: Character

Subjects: Death and Dying; Family Relationships; Feminism; First Novels; Marriage; Mothers and Daughters; Parenting; Suicide; Suspense; Women Authors; Women's Fiction

Now Try: Kogan is also the author of the superlative memoir of her photography career, *Shutterbabe*. Other novels about the vagaries of memory might be suggested, such as Diana Spechler's *Who by Fire* and Heidi Julavits's *The Uses of Enchantment*; more straightforward books in which teenagers and children go missing are Stewart O'Nan's *Songs for* *the Missing* and Andre Dubus's *The Garden of Last Days*. Memoirs in which women examine the difficulties and challenges inherent in marriage and motherhood might also be suggested, such as Rachel Cusk's *A Life's Work: On Becoming a Mother* or Lynn Darling's *Necessary Sins*; Alice Sebold's very visceral *Lucky*, in which she examines the aftermath of her rape, might also be considered.

Krol, Torsten.

Callisto: A Novel. HarperPerennial, 2009. 437pp. ISBN 9780061672941.

Odell Deefus is on his way to a military recruiting center in Callisto, Kansas, when his car breaks down. When he is picked up by Dean Mowry, a man with a lawn-mowing business who turns out to have other businesses (and an interest in Islam on the side), Odell finds himself becoming ever more deeply involved in Dean's life (which is awkward, considering that shortly after meeting him, Odell accidentally killed Dean). Although his only hope at the beginning of the novel was to get to a military recruiting station, and despite his professed love for Condoleezza Rice, the FBI is soon investigating him for his (or Dean's) supposed role in a terrorist sleeper cell.

Subjects: Bush, George W.; Crime; Dark Humor; First Person; Kansas; Military; Murder; Satire

Now Try: Other novels in which events spiral rapidly out of the control of the protagonists are Magnus Mills's *The Restraint of Beasts*, Scott Smith's *A Simple Plan*, and even John Kennedy Toole's classic *A Confederacy of Dunces*. Joseph Heller's satirical classics *Catch-22* and *Closing Time* might be suggested, as might Kurt Vonnegut's *Breakfast of Champions* and *God Bless You, Dr. Kevorkian*. Both Josh Bazell's *Beat the Reaper* and Denis Johnson's *Nobody Move* also pack suspenseful punches.

Kunzru, Hari.

 My Revolutions: A Novel. Dutton, 2007. 280pp. ISBN 9780525949329.

British former revolutionary and violent protestor of the Vietnam War Chris Carver has been living for many years as a family man and upstanding member of society known as "Michael Frame." However, when a former friend and conspirator finds him and blackmails him for ideology rather than cash (his associate wants Carver/Frame to give false evidence against another friend of theirs, rising through the political ranks as a member of the Labour Party), he must confront and make peace with his past.

Subjects: British Authors; Family Relationships; Great Britain; Men's Lives; Political Fiction; Suspense; Terrorism; Vietnam War

Awards: New York Times Notable

Now Try: Kunzru has also written the novels *Transmission* and *The Impressionist*. Janis Hallowell's *She Was* also offers a main character running from her protesting past. Another novel in which individuals must reconcile their passionate and political pasts with their more mundane present circumstances is Ha Jin's *Waiting*; in V. S. Naipaul's novel *Magic Seeds* an older man joins an underground movement in India, only to spend many subsequent years in jail; and Peter Carey's *His Illegal Self* explores the life of a much younger fugitive.

Laird, Nick.

Glover's Mistake. **Penguin, 2009. 247pp. ISBN 9780670020973.**

David Pinner, blog author and developing misanthrope, seeks to reconnect with an older American artist, Ruth Marks, who was once his college teacher. As they become friends, his more romantic imaginings about their relationship grow, until she meets his younger flatmate, James Glover, and the two of them begin a passionate love affair. Set against the backdrop of the London art scene, the love triangle at the heart of the story—and David's growing determination to do something, anything, about the relationship he covets—leads to the destruction of friendships and passions.

Subjects: Art and Artists; Great Britain; Irish Authors; London; Love Affairs; Men's Lives; Unreliable Narrator

Now Try: Laird is the author of a previous novel, *Utterly Monkey*, and two collections of poetry, *To a Fault* and *On Purpose*. Another novel in which the art world and its effect on relationships is explored is Kate Christensen's *The Great Man*. Two other novels about young people and their complex love affairs are Julian Gough's charming *Juno and Juliet* (set in Ireland) and David Nicholls's *A Question of Attraction* (set in a British university); a more disturbing look at obsessed roommates can be found in Danzy Senna's psychological thriller *Symptomatic*.

Lakhani, Anisha.

Schooled. **Hyperion, 2008. 345pp. ISBN 9781401322878.**

Bright, idealistic new teacher Anna Taggert arrives at a well-respected Manhattan private school ready to impart wisdom to her receptive students, but finds that reality is more about her work as an after-school tutor (which is the only way she can make real money); her students' desire to coast through their education with an eye only to getting into the appropriate college; and the parents of her students, willing to pay any price to get them into those appropriate colleges. As her first year passes and Anna finds herself spiraling downward into the belief that money can buy anything, she nonetheless starts to see the ways in which some teachers and students strive to stay above the fray.

Subjects: Corruption; Education; First Novels; Humor; New York City; Teenagers; Women Authors

Now Try: Fans of this sometimes bleak comic novel might consider other titles set in schools, such as Curtis Sittenfeld's novel *Prep* or Wade Rouse's forthright memoir *Confessions of a Prep School Mommy Handler*. Jean Hanff Korelitz's novel *Admission*, about an admissions counselor at Princeton, is more serious in tone but also offers an inside look at education as a business. The popular novel *The Nanny Diaries*, by Emma Laughlin and Nicola Krauss, might also appeal; Lauren Weisberger's sharp fashion and big city novels *The Devil Wears Prada*, *Everyone Worth Knowing*, and *Chasing Harry Winston* might be good escapist read-alikes.

Le, Nam.

🌸 *The Boat.* **Knopf, 2008. 272pp. ISBN 9780307268082.**

In this collection of seven short stories, Le opens with a story about a young Vietnamese man's writer's block as he struggles with his father's near death in the massacre at My Lai, their subsequent experiences as "boat people," and his own quest to do fulfilling work writing (rather than as a practicing attorney) while still trying to make his father proud of him. In the book's title story, "The Boat," Le tells a more harrowing and immediate tale of a woman's struggle to survive her refugee experiences. In other stories he tells narratives of a dying father trying to connect with his long-estranged daughter; a hit man moving through the streets of Cartagena, Colombia; and a boy's struggle with his mother's approaching death.

Subjects: Australian Authors; Family Relationships; Multicultural; Refugees; Short Stories; Vietnam War

Awards: New York Times Notable

Now Try: Other short story authors who provided blurbs for Le's popular book included Mary Gaitskill (*Don't Cry* and *Because They Wanted To*) and Adam Haslett (*You Are Not a Stranger Here*). The New York Times Notable Book list for 2008 contained a fair number of story collections; others selected for that honor included Chris Adrian's *A Better Angel*, Steven Millhauser's *Dangerous Laughter*, Jhumpa Lahiri's *Unaccustomed Earth*, and Tobias Wolff's *Our Story Begins*. Andrew Pham's memoir of his return to his parents' homeland of Vietnam, *Catfish and Mandala*, might also be suggested to these readers.

Lee, Janice Y. K.

The Piano Teacher. **Viking Penguin, 2008. 328pp. ISBN 9780670020485.**

When Brit Claire Pendleton accompanies her new husband Martin to Hong Kong in the aftermath of World War II, she uses her musical skills to teach piano lessons to the young daughter of wealthy Hong Kong residents, Locket Chen. Over time she gets to know Chen's family's enigmatic British chauffeur, Will Truesdale, as well as the full story of his life and the lives of other British citizens who lived in Hong Kong while the Japanese occupied the region.

Second Appeal: Setting

Subjects: 1940s; 1950s; Culture Clash; First Novels; Flashbacks; Historical Fiction; Hong Kong; Love Affairs; Marriage; Multicultural; Music and Musicians; War; Women Authors; World War II

Now Try: Other atmospheric novels that combine love affairs and culture clashes are David Guterson's *Snow Falling on Cedars*, Michael Ondaatje's *The English Patient*, Kazuo Ishiguro's *When We Were Orphans*, and Jeff Talarigo's *The Ginseng Hunter*. Other historical novels that may interest these readers are Lisa See's *Peony in Love* and *Shanghai Girls* and Wayson Choy's *The Jade Peony*. Hampton Sides's historical nonfiction title *Ghost Soldiers: The Forgotten Epic Story of World War II's Most Dramatic Mission*, although not set in Hong Kong, also tells a story about the Japanese treatment of war prisoners.

Lennon, J. Robert.

Castle: A Novel. **Graywolf Press, 2009. 229pp. ISBN 9781555975227.**

The suspense builds throughout Lennon's slim novel about a man seeking to start over in the very place where he was set upon his life's trajectory. When Eric Loesch returns to his hometown of Gerrysburg, New York, and buys 600 acres, complete with a small home in need of renovation, he finds himself increasingly drawn to a small parcel of land that his deed records indicate are not part of the property he owns. As he begins to remember events in his own past, various aspects of his personality and his reasons for wanting to start over become clearer to the reader.

Second Appeal: Setting

Subjects: Abuse; Family Relationships; First Person; Men's Lives; Military; New York; Psychological Fiction; Small Press; Suspense; War

Now Try: Lennon is also the author of the imaginative titles *The Funnies*, *The Light of Falling Stars*, *On the Night Plain*, and *Mailman*. Dirk Wittenborn's novel *Pharmakon* also examines its protagonists' mental states; unsettling nonfiction titles such as Theodore Nadelson's *Trained to Kill*, Dave Grossman's *On Killing: The Psychological Cost of Learning to Kill in War and Society*, and Evan Wright's *Generation Kill* might be suggested as related reads.

Liebmann-Smith, Richard.

The James Boys: A Novel Account of Four Desperate Brothers. **Random House, 2008. 261pp. ISBN 9780345470782.**

How weird would it have been if the erudite, East Coast brothers William and Henry James (a philosopher and a novelist—and a hypochondriac novelist at that—respectively) had found that the Wild West James brothers, Jesse and Frank, were there long-lost older brothers, presumed killed in the Civil War? This is exactly the story Liebman-Smith sets out to tell, in this completely unique historical/literary fiction mash-up, peopled with eccentric characters who cross the James brothers' paths, and drawing on real historical events to flesh out a rollicking story.

Second Appeal: Character

Subjects: 19th Century; American West; Biographical Fiction; Book Groups; Historical Fiction; James, Frank; James, Henry; James, Jesse; James, William; Literary Allusions; Westerns

Now Try: Other imaginative novels based on the lives of authors and other historical characters might be offered to these readers, including Philip Baruth's *The Brothers Boswell: A Novel*, Susan Sellers's *Vanessa and Virginia*, and Darin Strauss's *Chang and Eng* or *The Real McCoy*. Nonfiction titles about any or all of the "James boys" might also be suggested, such as R. W. B. Lewis's *The Jameses: A Family Narrative*, Fred Kaplan's *Henry James: The Imagination of Genius*, Linda Simon's *Genuine Reality: A Life of William James*, or T. J. Stiles's *Jesse James: Last Rebel of the Civil War*.

Lustig, Arnost.

🐦 *Lovely Green Eyes*. **Arcade, 2002. 248pp. ISBN 9781559706292.**

After she witnesses the deaths of all her family members, fifteen-year-old Hanka Kaudersová is faced with her own horrific choice: death, or work as a prostitute in a brothel for German soldiers. She chooses the latter, and is sustained through her brutal experiences by her hatred of the soldiers and her desire to live at all costs.

Subjects: Atrocities; Book Groups; Books in Translation; Czech Authors; Death and Dying; Explicit Sexuality; Germany; Historical Fiction; Holocaust; Prostitution; Teenage Girls; Teenagers; World War II

Awards: ALA Notable

Now Try: Lustig has written other novels about the Holocaust, including *Night and Hope*, *Darkness Casts No Shadows*, and *Diamonds of the Night*. Also of interest to these readers might be William Styron's classic novel *Sophie's Choice*, as well as the anonymous wartime memoir *A Woman in Berlin*. Another novel featuring a teenage character facing more than his fair share of misfortune is Sylvain Trudel's *Mercury Under My Tongue*. Although it was marketed as a YA novel, Markus Zusak's novel about the Holocaust, *The Book Thief*, might also be suggested.

Martin, Clancy.

How to Sell. **Farrar, Straus & Giroux, 2009. 296pp. ISBN 9780374173357.**

Shortly after Jim Clark leaves Canada to make his fortune in the jewelry business in Fort Worth, Texas, his sixteen-year-old brother, Bobby, drops out of school and follows him. While learning the ropes of the (largely illicit) jewelry trade, Bobby also engages in an affair with Jim's mistress Lisa, and develops some costly drug addictions. Although the jewelry store for which they work is shut down because of its sketchy business practices, Jim and Bobby strike out on their own and continue with their goals to make as much money as possible, do as many drugs as possible, and yet still somehow help Lisa, whose job eventually morphs from sales into a different (and much older) profession.

Subjects: 1980s; Book Groups; Brothers; Business; Canada; Coming-of-age; Drug Abuse; Family Relationships; First Person; Love Affairs; Men's Lives; Retail; Satire; Siblings; Texas; Young Men

Now Try: Another novel in which a character struggles with twin desires to make money and be decent is Gary Shteyngart's *The Russian Debutante's Handbook*. Other novels in which men pursue material success are Glenn Gaslin's *Beemer: A Novel*, William Sutcliffe's *Whatever Makes You Happy*, and Augusten Burroughs's satirical novel *Sellevision*. Nonfiction titles about gamesmanship in sales and making money might also appeal, such as Michael Lewis's classic insider's look at Wall Street, *Liar's Poker*; Nick Leeson's *Rogue Trader*; or Ben Mezrich's *Bringing Down the House: The Inside Story of Six MIT Students Who Took Vegas for Millions*. David Collins's satirical finance novel, *Maxxed Out* (based on the life of a certain business mogul with big hair, a television show to hire his apprentices, and an office building named after him in Manhattan) might also be a good read-alike.

Martin, Valerie.

Trespass: A Novel. **Doubleday, 2007. 288pp. ISBN 9780385515450.**

When Toby Dale brings home his new girlfriend, a Croatian immigrant named Salome Drago, to meet his parents, Chloe and Brendan, they are less than ecstatic with his choice. Exotic and evidently hypnotizing to Toby, Salome nonetheless leaves both his parents with the distinct impression that she is more interested in Toby's family's affluence and upper-middle-class background than she is in him; when the pair hastily marry (after Salome becomes pregnant) and move to Europe to seek out Salome's mother, previously believed dead, Chloe sends Brendan after them to bring Toby back home—which proves to be a grave miscalculation.

Subjects: Family Relationships; Immigrants and Immigration; Italy; Love Affairs; Marriage; New York; Suspense; Women Authors; Women Writing as Men; Young Men

Now Try: Martin is known for her literary thrillers, including *Italian Fever* and the historical novel *Mary Reilly*. Also of interest to these readers might be other novels in which cultural and socioeconomic clashes play a large role in the narrative, including Andre Dubus's *House of Sand and Fog*, Antonya Nelson's *Nothing Right: Short Stories*, and Chris Cleave's *Little Bee*. Mary McGarry Morris's *The Last Secret* might also appeal to fans of this fast-paced domestic novel.

Martínez, Guillermo.

The Book of Murder. Viking, 2008. 215pp. ISBN 9780670019946.

In Martínez's literary thriller, a young (and frustrated) author narrates a tale of paranoia and suspicion. While he goes about his career, trying to break into a mystery market dominated by best-selling author and cultural force "Kloster," he is approached by a young woman named Luciana, who is convinced that Kloster is stalking her and killing members of her family (and using the crimes as a basis for his novels). Set in Buenos Aires, this fast-paced novel of psychological suspense will leave the reader with one question: Which came first, the book or the murder?

Subjects: Argentinean Authors; Books in Translation; Buenos Aires; First Person; Literary Lives; Psychological Fiction; Quick Reads; Suspense; Unreliable Narrator; YA

Now Try: Martínez is also the author of the thriller *The Oxford Murders*. Other literary thrillers that might appeal to these readers are *2666* by Roberto Bolaño (which is a good stylistic read-alike, although 700 pages longer) and *The Girl with the Dragon Tattoo* by Stieg Larsson, as well as Arturo Perez-Reverte's *The Flanders Panel* or *The King's Gold*. Another author who might appeal to Martínez's fans is Iain Pears; consider suggesting his *Stone's Fall*, *The Raphael Affair*, and *The Portrait*. Also of interest may be the small mystery/horror novel *The Man in the Picture*, by Susan Hill. Carlos Ruiz Zafón's literary thriller about a Barcelona novelist, *The Angel's Game*, might also appeal to these readers.

Mastras, George.

Fidali's Way. Scribner, 2009. 388pp. ISBN 9781416556183.

After spending months backpacking through South Asia, part of the time in the company of a beautiful woman named Yvette DePomeroy, Nicholas Sunder wakes up in Pakistan, ready to make his return trip to India that same day. The Pakistani police who show up to arrest him for the murder of Yvette, however, have other plans for him, including torture and interrogation. Although he manages to escape from them, he follows a path through the mountains of Kashmir, where the elements and warring factions nearly combine to kill him, until he is found and helped by a Kashmiri smuggler named Fidali. With Fidali's help, he makes it to Kashmir, where he meets Aysha, a woman whose tender ministering to the region's sick and suffering makes Sunder wonder about the differences between East and West.

Subjects: Adventure; Crime; Culture Clash; First Novels; Friendships; India; Kashmir; Love Affairs; Men's Lives; Murder; Pakistan; Survival; Travel; Violence; War

Now Try: Although it features a protagonist who is choosing to examine his own conscience in solitude, Tim Parks's novel *Cleaver* might provide a similarly suspenseful reading experience. Nonfiction accounts of daring prison escapes might also be suggested, such as Billy Hayes's classic *Midnight Express* or David McMillan's *Escape: The True Story of the Only Westerner Ever to Break Out of Thailand's Bangkok Hilton*. Other travel and true adventure narratives might also be suggested to these readers, such as Joel Hafvenstein's *Opium Season: A Year on the Afghan Frontier*, Tom Hart Dyke's and Paul Winder's *The Cloud Garden: A True Story of Adventure, Survival, and Extreme Horticulture*, and Garry Leech's *Beyond Bogotá: Diary of a Drug War Journalist in Colombia*. Readers fascinated with the Pakistani setting of this novel might also consider Greg

Mortenson's and David Oliver Relin's travelogue about building schools in the area, *Three Cups of Tea: One Man's Mission to Promote Peace . . . One School at a Time*.

McEvoy, Dermot.

Our Lady of Greenwich Village. Skyhorse, 2008. 326pp. ISBN 978-1602393516.

McEvoy's novel of divine politics offers the story of corrupt Republican congressman Jackie Swift, who suddenly faces a challenge for his seat in the form of former campaign manager and staunch Irish Catholic Wolfe Tone O'Rourke, who decides to run (with the slogan "No More Bullshit") after the Virgin Mary appears to him in a dream. This political satire is rich with duplicitous characters as well as drenched in atmospheric details of New York City, Irish immigrant heritage, and dirty politics (not necessarily in that order).

Subjects: Catholic Church; Corruption; First Novels; Men's Lives; New York City; Political Fiction; Religion; Satire

Now Try: Roland Merullo's political satire *American Savior: A Novel of Divine Politics* might appeal, as might *Primary Colors* and any number of satirical political novels by Christopher Buckley, including *Supreme Courtship*. The Virgin Mary not only appears to the main character in Diane Schoemperlen's novel *Our Lady of the Lost and Found*, she stays with her for a few days' vacation. Those readers interested in political machinations might also consider the nonfiction title *Confessions of a Political Hitman* by Stephen Marks. This novel was also blurbed by Frank McCourt, whose memoirs of life in Ireland and New York, *Angela's Ashes* and *'Tis*, might also appeal (although readers should be made aware that they are fairly harsh family stories). Thomas Fleming's memoir *Mysteries of My Father* blends Irish family stories and participation in a political machine (and similar Jersey City surroundings) in one title.

Merullo, Roland.

American Savior: A Novel of Divine Politics. Algonquin Books of Chapel Hill, 2008. 312pp. ISBN 9781565126077.

What would Jesus do if he returned to live among us? Why, run for president, of course—or so posits Merullo in his novel of political satire. When Jesus returns and chooses a cynical reporter, Russ Thomas, to work with him and lead his Jesus for America campaign, the question is: Will this candidate and his mother (whom he chooses for his running mate) really resonate with American voters?

Subjects: Humor; Jesus; Journalism; Mass Media; Political Fiction; Religion; Satire

Now Try: Other novels of Merullo's that may appeal to fans of this title are *Breakfast with Buddha* and *Golfing with God*. Another book about divine intervention and politics is Dermot McEvoy's *Our Lady of Greenwich Village*. Satirical and humorous novels by Christopher Moore might also be suggested; they include *Lamb: The Mystical Gospel According to Biff, Christ's Childhood Pal*, *The Stupidest Angel*, or *Fool*. Another somewhat cynical take on American politics is the novel *Primary Colors*, whose author was first listed as "Anonymous," but was eventually revealed to be political operative Joe Klein.

Morris, Mary McGarry.

The Last Secret. **Shaye Areheart Books, 2009. 274pp. ISBN 9780307451279.**

Wealthy, respected mother of two and loving wife Nora Hammond seems to have the perfect life—and does—until her husband reveals that he has been sleeping with his best friend's wife for several years. Add to this crushing blow the return of a dangerous man from Nora's past, and you have a psychological and quickly paced "domestic thriller."

Subjects: Adultery; Crime; Family Secrets; Psychological Fiction; Suspense; Women Authors

Now Try: Morris is the author of several books, including the ALA Notable book *A Dangerous Woman* and its sequel, *Fiona Range*, as well as the stand-alone title *Songs in Ordinary Time*. Another suspenseful novel of a marriage gone wrong (although all the warning signs were in place from the start) is Robert Goolrick's *A Reliable Wife*; Janet Fitch's novels *White Oleander* and *Paint It Black*, Valerie Martin's *Trespass*, and Darin Strauss's *More Than It Hurts You* could also be described as "domestic thrillers."

Morrow, James.

The Philosopher's Apprentice. **William Morrow, 2008. 411pp. ISBN 978-0061351440.**

When Mason Ambrose takes a job tutoring Londa Sabacthani, a young girl whose traumatic brain injury has wiped her memory and cognitive knowledge to a blank slate, he soon learns there is more going on than meets the eye at her home (and the home of her mother, Edwina, a famed molecular geneticist with plans of her own for Londa and the others who live with them).

Subjects: Book Groups; Cloning; Dystopia; First Person; Humor; Philosophical Fiction; Science Fiction; YA; Young Men

Now Try: Morrow's other imaginative novels include *Shambling Towards Hiroshima*, *The Last Witchfinder*, and the <u>Godhead Trilogy</u>, which began with the novel *Towing Jehovah*. Bernard Beckett's bleak future novel *Genesis*, which also comes with a heavy dose of philosophy, might also appeal to these readers. Other literary science fiction novels, particularly those concerned with biological advances and issues, might also appeal, such as Ursula K. Le Guin's classic *The Left Hand of Darkness* or Margaret Atwood's *The Handmaid's Tale* or *Oryx and Crake*.

Morton, Kate.

The Forgotten Garden. **Atria Books, 2009. 552pp. ISBN 9781416550549.**

Mysteries abound in Morton's novel, which weaves together parallel story lines from different eras and continents. As ninety-five-year-old Nell Andrews lies dying in an Australian hospital in 2005, she still dreams of discovering the truth of her birth and parentage. She has been struggling with unanswered questions about herself since her adoptive father told her, when she turned twenty-one, that he and his wife took her home when she had seemingly been abandoned. Also part of the story is her granddaughter Cassandra, whom she'd largely raised, and who undertakes the search for Nell's mother herself, traveling from Australia to England, where she learns the truth about what really happened in 1913 (as well as in 1976, when Nell took the same trip to England to try to discover the truth), how Nell was connected to the author of a book of fairy tales that was her only real possession, and how the troubled Mountrachet family kept secrets at Blackhurst Manor, their Cornish estate.

Subjects: Australia; Australian Authors; Cornwall; Epic Reads; Fairy Tales; Family Secrets; Great Britain; Historical Fiction; Mothers and Daughters; Multigenerational Fiction; Multiple Viewpoints; Women Authors

Now Try: Morton's first novel was titled *A House at Riverton*. Another Australian author's novel of family secrets is Kate Grenville's *The Secret River*; other multigenerational novels include Isabel Allende's *The House of the Spirits*, Charlotte Bacon's *Lost Geography*, Kaye Gibbons's *Charms for the Easy Life*, and Zadie Smith's *White Teeth*.

Mosley, Walter.

Diablerie: A Novel. **Bloomsbury, 2008. 180pp. ISBN 9781596913974.**

Mosley's protagonist, Ben Dibbuk, works as a computer programmer, and is in a satisfactory if not titillating marriage. When his wife takes him to a launch party for a new crime-writing magazine called *Diablerie*, however, he is introduced to a woman who knows more about his past and crimes he may or may not have committed than anyone else.

Second Appeal: Character

Subjects: Adultery; African American Authors; Alcoholism; Crime; Explicit Sexuality; New York City; Suspense

Now Try: Mosley has become a prolific author, with several mystery series, all of which feature compelling characterizations and atmospheric surroundings, to his credit, including the Easy Rawlins mysteries (starting with *Devil in a Blue Dress*), the Fearless Jones mysteries (starting with *Fearless Jones*), and his more philosophical Socrates Fortlow novels (starting with *Always Outnumbered, Always Outgunned*); another stand-alone title, his "sexistentialist novel" *Killing Johnny Fry*, might also appeal to these readers. Don DeLillo's novel *The Body Artist* also features a character who knows more about the protagonist than seems possible, while Chuck Palahniuk's *Fight Club* also addresses exploring one's darker proclivities.

Oates, Joyce Carol.

Dear Husband: Stories. **Ecco Press, 2009. 326pp. ISBN 9780061704314.**

Prolific author Oates presents fourteen stories of what seem to be straightforward family narratives, focusing primarily on relationships between parents and their children, but that typically end with decidedly dark and unsettling plot twists or revelations.

Second Appeal: Language

Subjects: Family Relationships; Quick Reads; Short Stories; Society; Violence; Women Authors

Now Try: Oates's literary output is truly outstanding and runs the gamut from short story collections to horror novels to historical fiction to literary fiction; her story collections include *Wild Nights*, *The Museum of Dr. Moses*, and *The Female of the Species*; her most recent novels are *Little Bird of Heaven*, the historical novel *Mysteries of Winterthurn*, *The Gravedigger's Daughter*, and *Black Girl, White Girl*. Other story collections that might appeal to these readers are Antonya Nelson's *Female Trouble*, Alice Munro's *Hateship, Friendship, Courtship, Loveship, Marriage*, Chris Adrian's *A Better Angel*, and Dan Chaon's *Among the Missing*.

O'Connor, John.

🎗 *Star of the Sea.* Harcourt, 2002. 386pp. ISBN 9780151009084.

The year is 1847, and the setting is the ship *Star of the Sea*, making the crossing to America from famine- and poverty-wracked Ireland, in this taut novel of suspense. The story is narrated by one of the ship's passengers, G. Grantley Dixon, who is engaged in an affair with the wife of a fellow passenger. Such connections are common; many of the characters know one another for various and nefarious reasons. In a situation in which tensions would already be high, the author ups the stakes by hinting that one of the ship's passengers is determined to murder one of their fellow travelers before the ship reaches its destination.

Second Appeal: Character

Subjects: 19th Century; Book Groups; Historical Fiction; Immigrants and Immigration; Ireland; Irish Authors; Murder; Ocean; Suspense; Violence

Awards: ALA Notable; New York Times Notable

Now Try: O'Connor's other novels include *Redemption Falls: A Novel* and *The Salesman*. Two other historical thrillers might be suggested: Philip Baruth's *The Brothers Boswell* and Michael Cox's *The Glass of Time*. Nonfiction accounts of other perilous maritime journeys include Carolly Erickson's *The Girl from Botany Bay*, Stephen Taylor's *Caliban's Shore: The Wreck of the Grosvenor and the Strange Fate of Her Survivors*, and Jonathan Miles's *The Wreck of the Medusa: The Most Famous Sea Disaster of the Nineteenth Century*.

Palahniuk, Chuck.

Snuff. Doubleday, 2008. 197pp. ISBN 9780385517881.

The reader might not think there'd be lots of room for secrets on a movie set, where porn star Cassie Wright is trying to set a world record for having sex with 600 men in one porn shoot (and all 600 have to wait around naked), but secrets abound, about Wright's reason for doing the shoot, the identities of some of the men waiting to do their bit, and the identity and actions of the woman Wright hired to assist in keeping the shoot moving smoothly. Told from the various viewpoints of Mrs. 72, 137, and 600, as well as the assistant Sheila, this is a wickedly dark novel and definitely not for the faint of heart.

Subjects: Actors and Acting; Explicit Sexuality; Movies; Multiple Viewpoints; Pornography; Quick Reads

Now Try: Palahniuk's other darker books include *Choke, Lullaby, Haunted*, and *Fight Club*. Other dark, dark, dark novels by such authors as Bret Easton Ellis (*American Psycho* and *Glamorama*), Anthony Burgess (*A Clockwork Orange*), Alex Garland (*The Beach*), Irvine Welsh (*Porno* and *Trainspotting*), and Scott Spencer (*Willing*) might be suggested. Another satirical novel of the adult film industry is Terry Southern's *Blue Movie*. A surprisingly comprehensive oral history of the industry is available in Leggs McNeil's and Jennifer Osborne's *The Other Hollywood: The Uncensored Oral History of the Porn Film Industry*; Jenna Jameson's fast-paced memoir *How to Make Love Like a Porn Star* is also a surprisingly empathetic (toward porn industry workers) read but is definitely for mature adults only.

Pamuk, Orhan.

🎖 *My Name Is Red.* Knopf, 2001. 417pp. ISBN 9780375406959.

In sixteenth-century Islamic Istanbul, the practice of portraying human figures in art is forbidden. When the Sultan commissions artists and miniaturists to illuminate a book telling the story of his life using such figurative techniques, one of the painters (named Elegant) is killed. Enishte, Elegant's employer, is understandably interested in learning who took justice into his or her own hands; one of his employees, Black, is interested in solving the mystery to impress his employer and win the hand of his daughter in marriage.

Subjects: 16th Century; Art and Artists; Book Groups; Books in Translation; Classics; Historical Fiction; Islam; Love Affairs; Multiple Viewpoints; Ottoman Empire; Turkey

Awards: International IMPAC Dublin Literary Award

Now Try: This book has been described as a follow-up to Pamuk's 1997 novel *The New Life*; his other titles include the novels *The Black Book* and *Snow*, as well as the memoir *Istanbul: Memories and the City*. Other literary mysteries that may appeal to these readers are Vikram Chandra's *Sacred Games*, David Liss's *The Coffee Trader*, Matthew Pearl's *The Dante Club*, Arturo Perez-Reverte's *The Fencing Master* and *The King's Gold*, and Umberto Eco's classic *The Name of the Rose*. Richard Zimler's historical thriller *The Last Kabbalist of Lisbon* is also set during the sixteenth century, but in Portugal; Tariq Ali's *The Book of Saladin*, a literary historical novel about the Crusades, might also be a good read-alike for Pamuk's fans.

Parks, Tim.

Rapids: A Novel. Arcade, 2005. 245pp. ISBN 9781559708111.

Six adults and nine teenagers vacation in the Italian Alps, facing the physical and mental challenges of rafting the region's wild rivers. As the difficulties of the trip mount, so do the tensions within the group—particularly as nobody has much confidence in their alpha male leader, Clive, or his unnervingly quiet girlfriend, Michela.

Subjects: Adventure; British Authors; Friendships; Men's Lives; Midlife Crisis; Rivers; Survival; Suspense; Teenagers; Travel

Now Try: Parks is the author of other tautly plotted novels, including *Cleaver*, *Mimi's Ghost, Destiny*, and *Europa*. Other adventure-driven literary novels, such as George Mastras's *Fidali's Way*, James McManus's *Going to the Sun*, or Barbara Hodgson's *Hippolyte's Island*, might be suggested, as might nonfiction travel adventures such as Colin Angus's *Amazon Extreme* and *Lost in Mongolia*, Ewan McGregor's *Long Way Round*, or Kevin Patterson's *The Water in Between: A Journey at Sea*.

Now Consider Nonfiction . . . Survival and Disaster Stories (True Adventure)

Survival and disaster true adventure stories can feature either natural disasters that humans couldn't have avoided, or disasters that result from daring or poor choices made by sporting participants or individuals who are simply in the wrong place at the wrong time. They are suspenseful stories and often feature characters for whom readers feel empathy.

Junger, Sebastian. *The Perfect Storm.*

Krakauer, Jon. *Into the Wild.*

Krakauer, Jon. *Into Thin Air.*

Lewan, Todd. *The Last Run: A True Story of Rescue and Redemption on the Alaskan Seas.*

Maclean, Norman. *Young Men and Fire.*

Ralston, Aron. *Between a Rock and a Hard Place.*

Read, Piers Paul. *Alive: The Story of the Andes Survivors.*

Perrotta, Tom.

🌲 *The Abstinence Teacher.* **St. Martin's Press, 2007. 358pp. ISBN 9780312358334.**

Tempers flare in a suburban high school and community when the health and human sexuality teacher, Ruth Ramsey, teaches the course by emphasizing pleasure and healthy sexual practices rather than abstinence at all costs. This stance puts her at odds with a local Christian evangelical church, most particularly with another teacher at the school, Tim Mason. Ruth herself is not without her own harsh opinions about Tim's faith, particularly after he leads a team he coaches in a spontaneous prayer after a victory. All the characters, of course, are motivated by past experiences and struggles, which come to light over the course of the story, and Perrotta describes all of them with a surprisingly evenhanded empathy.

Subjects: Community Life; Education; Friendships; Marriage; Men's Lives; Parenting; Religion; Suburbia; Teachers

Awards: New York Times Notable

Now Try: Perrotta has plumbed the dearth of suburbia before, in his earlier novels *Election* and *Little Children.* Other novels in which characters' carefully constructed suburban lives are crumbling away from under them are Marisa de los Santos's *Belong to Me*, Amy Koppelman's *I Smile Back*, and Richard Ford's Frank Bascombe trilogy, starting with *The Sportswriter.* Another author who has made a career out of exploring male angst is John Updike, whose classic novel *Rabbit, Run* might appeal to these readers (as well as his more recent books, such as *The Terrorist* and *My Father's Tears and Other Stories*).

Pierre, D. B. C.

🌲 *Vernon God Little.* **Canongate, 2003. 279pp. ISBN 9781841954608.**

In this satirical novel that gives new meaning to the phrase "dark humor," Vernon God Little becomes the prime suspect in the school shooting of sixteen students at a high school in Texas. But his life isn't disrupted nearly as much as one might expect; friends and neighbors deliver quantities of barbeque to help the family; and Vernon spends much of his time hoping for a celebrity defense attorney, or at least an actor who could play one.

Second Appeal: Language

Subjects: Australian Authors; Coming-of-age; Dark Humor; Education; First Novels; First Person; Profanity; Satire; Teenage Boys; Teenagers; Texas

Awards: Costa First Novel Award; Man Booker Prize; New York Times Notable

Now Try: Pierre has written a subsequent novel titled *Ludmila's Broken English*. Other dark novels and satires that might appeal to these readers are Joyce Maynard's *To Die For*, Chuck Palahniuk's *Pygmy*, Dennis Cooper's story collection *Ugly Man*, George Pendle's *Death: A Life*, and George Saunders's story collections *Pastoralia*, *In Persuasion Nation*, and *CivilWarLand in Bad Decline*. Critics have also compared this darkly humorous satire to John Kennedy Toole's novel *A Confederacy of Dunces*.

Price, Richard.

🏆 *Lush Life.* Farrar, Straus & Giroux, 2008. 455pp. ISBN 9780374299255.

When three colleagues and friends go bar-hopping on Manhattan's lower East Side after their hard night of restaurant work, one ends up shot and the other two a target of the police investigation into the crime. Although witnesses say otherwise, thirty-five-year-old Eric Cash and his other friend maintain that they and their murdered friend Ike Marcus were mugged and accosted by teenagers; the police are left to shift through conflicting accounts and a stable of suspects, including Cash and several local teens, who are all harboring their own secrets.

Subjects: Crime; Friendships; Law Enforcement; Murder; New York City; Noir; Social Class; Suspense; Teenagers; Young Men

Awards: New York Times Notable

Now Try: Price is well known as a master of urban crime fiction; his earlier novels include *Samaritan*, *Freedomland*, and *Clockers*. Another contemporary suspense/thriller author who might appeal to these readers is George Pelecanos; his smart urban mysteries *Drama City*, *The Turnaround*, and *The Night Gardener* might appeal, as might classics by an earlier master of urban street fiction, Donald Goines (*Whoreson*, *Street Players*, and *Never Die Alone*). Two other "noir" authors who might appeal to Price's fans are Walter Mosley (whose Easy Rawlins series began with *Devil in the Blue Dress*) and Jim Thompson (*The Transgressors*, *The Grifters*, and his autobiographical *Bad Boy*).

Rash, Ron.

Serena: A Novel. Ecco, 2008. 371pp. ISBN 9780061470851.

By all accounts a singular young woman, Serena Pemberton accepts all the challenges of moving from civilized Boston to her new husband George's logging camp in rugged South Carolina, where she is fueled by her "unchecked ambition" to succeed in both business and her more domestic duties (which are considerable, considering that the novel is set in the rough-and-tumble 1920s). Upon her arrival at her new home, however, she is greeted by the one thing she can't control: George already has a young son by Rachel Harman, a young woman he met before his marriage. As Serena's failure to have a child of her own turns into mania, she turns her tremendous energy to trying to destroy both mother and child, whom she suspects George of protecting from her wrath at every turn.

Second Appeal: Setting

Subjects: 1920s; Book Groups; Family Secrets; Historical Fiction; Love Affairs; Marriage; Men Writing as Women; Psychological Fiction; Revenge; South Carolina; Suspense

Now Try: Rash's other novels, which combine powerful stories with well-described land-scapes, are *The World Made Straight*, *Saints at the River*, and *One Foot in Eden*; he has also written a story collection titled *Chemistry and Other Stories*. Other novels featuring strong characters and roiling undercurrents of barely contained violence include David Wroblewski's *The Story of Edgar Sawtelle*, Jeffrey Lent's *Lost Nation* and *In the Fall*, and Gil Adamson's *The Outlander*. Wallace Stegner's classic *Angle of Repose* also features a singular married couple; Kent Haruf's *The Tie That Binds* also showcases a female character of iron strength. Similarly epic family sagas are Luis Alberto Urrea's *The Humming-bird's Daughter* and *Into the Beautiful North*.

Robinson, Lewis.

Water Dogs. Random House, 2009. 244pp. ISBN 9781400062171.

When Bennie, a twenty-seven-year-old college dropout and animal shelter employee, and his brother Littlefield go out into a winter storm to finish up an intense game of paintball they'd started with some friends earlier, neither could predict that the end of the day would find Bennie in the hospital after falling into a ravine, another young member of their party missing in a brutal Maine snowstorm, and Littlefield the prime suspect in his disappearance. As both brothers deal with the suspicion surrounding them, Bennie finds himself struggling to understand and make a connection with his increasingly emotionally distant brother at the same time that he is falling in love with Helen, a local waitress, and becoming closer to his twin sister, Gwen.

Second Appeal: Character

Subjects: Animals; Book Groups; Brothers; Family Relationships; Maine; Psychological Fiction; Quick Reads; Suspense; Young Men

Now Try: Robinson is also the author of the story collection *Officer Friendly and Other Stories*. Other novels in which suspicion and violence interfere with personal relationships might be suggested, including Scott Smith's *A Simple Plan* and Leif Enger's *Peace Like a River*. A blizzard also plays a pivotal role in Chuck Klosterman's *Downtown Owl*, a novel of life in 1980s North Dakota; Tom Drury's *The Driftless Area* also features a male protagonist of the same age and trouble-attracting proclivity. Two powerful memoirs of men's relationships might also be suggested: Nick Flynn's straightforward *Another Bullshit Night in Suck City* and J. R. Moehringer's *The Tender Bar*.

Roncagliolo, Santiago.

Red April. Pantheon Books, 2009. 271pp. ISBN 9780375425448.

It is Holy Week in Peru (in March 2000), and the only pageantry more involved than that of the Catholic Church is the political and social unrest in the nation's capital, Lima. When police inspector Félix Chacaltana Saldívar is assigned to a homicide investigation, he finds himself overwhelmed by the case (which may have connections to Peru's guerrilla fighters, known as the Shining Path) and increasingly troubled by his own past and memories—which will turn out to be shockingly relevant to his investigation.

Subjects: Books in Translation; Family Relationships; Latin America; Mothers and Sons; Murder; Mystery; Peru; Political Fiction; Psychological Fiction

Now Try: Two other books in translation that offer numerous plot twists are Guillermo Martinez's *Book of Murder* and Roberto Bolaño's *2666*. Robert Wilson's <u>Javier Falcón Seville</u> series of books might offer a similarly suspenseful and political read; they are *The Blind Man of Seville*, *The Vanished Hands*, *The Hidden Assassins*, and *The Ignorance of*

Blood. Another political and true crime nonfiction account that may appeal to these readers is Francisco Goldman's *The Art of Political Murder: Who Killed the Bishop*? This title won the 2006 Alfaguara Prize; another winner of that award that might be suggested to these readers is Eliseo Alberto's *Caracol Beach*.

Roth, Philip.

🏅 *The Plot Against America*. **Houghton Mifflin, 2004. 391pp. ISBN 978-0618509287.**

Roth asks, and answers, what would have happened to America if Franklin D. Roosevelt had not become the American president in 1940. What if, instead, the popular Charles Lindbergh had run and won? Roth writes his novel from the perspective of a young Jewish boy growing up in New Jersey, and suggests ways in which the American experience might have been very different under more fascist and anti-Semitic policies and politics.

Subjects: 1940s; Alternate Histories; Anti-Semitism; Biographical Fiction; Book Groups; Classics; Historical Fiction; Jewish American Authors; Lindbergh, Charles; New Jersey; Political Fiction; Quick Reads; World War II

Awards: ALA Notable; New York Times Notable

Now Try: Roth is a popular and prolific author. Many of his other novels might appeal, including his Nathan Zuckerman series (starting with *The Ghost Writer*), as well as his stand-alone titles *Indignation*, *The Great American Novel*; his classic *Portnoy's Complaint* might also be suggested. Also of interest might be several other World War II "alternate histories": Philip K. Dick's *The Man in the High Castle*, Robert Harris's *Fatherland*, and Owen Sheers's *Resistance*.

Ruiz Zafón, Carlos.

The Angel's Game. **Doubleday, 2009. 531pp. ISBN 9780385528702.**

In 1920s Barcelona, writer David Martin is taken under the wing of a prominent publisher and man-about-town, Pedro Vidal, who eventually helps him turn a lowly job at a local newspaper into a serial crime-writing gig. Eventually Martin becomes a pulp fiction novelist, who works at such a frenetic pace that he is able to produce works under his own name and Vidal's—but his success comes with a price, including his loss to Vidal of the woman he loves, and increasingly shady deals with another publisher who wants to make the most of Martin's talent.

Second Appeal: Setting

Subjects: 1920s; Barcelona; Book Groups; Books and Reading; Books in Translation; Crime; Literary Lives; Love Affairs; Magic Realism; Spain; Suspense; Unreliable Narrator; Writers and Writing; YA

Now Try: Ruiz Zafón's earlier novel, *The Shadow of the Wind*, was also about books, writing, and reading. Other literary (literally) thrillers that may appeal to these readers include Guillermo Martinez's *The Book of Murder*, Umberto Eco's *The Name of the Rose*, Jennifer Lee Carrell's *Interred with Their Bones*, and Arturo Perez-Reverte's *The Club Dumas*. Another author who might appeal to these readers is David Liss; his historical thrillers, including *A Conspiracy of Paper* and *The Coffee Trader*, also combine suspenseful stories with historical detail.

Salak, Kira.

The White Mary. **Henry Holt, 2008. 351pp. ISBN 9780805088472.**

Marika Vecera has made a career out of going to the scariest places the world has to offer to get her story, so when she learns that her journalism mentor, Pulitzer Prize winner Robert Lewis, has gone missing in the interior of Papua New Guinea, she has few qualms about going there to seek him out. When she finds him, led by her spirit guide and Papua New Guinea native Tobo (who often has his own agenda), she finds a man battling for his sanity and unable to sufficiently banish his memories to leave and rejoin his former world. For Marika, who before leaving to find Lewis had been forming a new relationship with Seb, a man with secrets of his own, must decide if she, too, has the strength to leave the darkly seductive country.

Second Appeal: Setting

Subjects: Journalism; Love Affairs; Multicultural; Papua New Guinea; Psychological Fiction; Travel; Violence; Women Authors

Now Try: Salak knows of what she writes; she has also written the nonfiction travel accounts *Four Corners: A Journey into the Heart of Papua New Guinea* and *Cruelest Journey: Six Hundred Miles to Timbuktu.* Other novels in which characters journey into unfamiliar surroundings are Deborah Copaken Kogan's *Between Here and April,* Barbara Kingsolver's *The Poisonwood Bible,* Masha Hamilton's *The Distance Between Us,* Amitav Ghosh's *The Hungry Tide,* and Lara Santoro's *Mercy: A Novel;* Philip Caputo's *Exiles* and *Act of Faith,* as well as his nonfiction *Means of Escape* and *In the Shadows of the Morning,* might also be good read-alikes.

Now Consider Nonfiction . . . Journey Narratives

Journey narratives are travel stories in which authors describe both the settings of their destinations, as well as the interesting and humorous details of the actual travel process. In addition to describing the how of travel by illuminating the mechanical details of travel movement (e.g., by plane, train, or automobile), these stories often also provide the why; many of the titles in this subgenre include healthy doses of autobiographical and explanatory information from their authors, who frequently write in the first person and a more personal style.

Evans, Polly. *Fried Eggs with Chopsticks.*

Gelman, Rita Golden. *Tales of a Female Nomad.*

Honigsbaum, Mark. *The Fever Trail: In Search of the Cure for Malaria.*

Jenkins, Peter. *A Walk Across America.*

Matthiessen, Peter. *The Cloud Forest: A Chronicle of the South American Wildness.*

Shah, Tahir. *In Search of King Solomon's Mines.*

Schwartz, David.

Superpowers. **Three Rivers Press, 2008. 377pp. ISBN 9780307394408.**

Schwartz's rollicking, quasi-fantastic story, set in the college town of Madison, Wisconsin, follows the exploits of five friends who wake up after a night of partying with one another, only to find they have each gained a different superpower.

Banding together to become a ragtag band of superhero good Samaritans, they find their powers bring not only satisfaction but also challenges and specialized hardships of their own.

Subjects: Friendships; Humor; Multiple Viewpoints; Quick Reads; Superheroes; Wisconsin; YA; Young Men; Young Women

Now Try: Other fun, superhero-related books might be suggested to these readers, including Tom De Haven's *It's Superman!*, Austin Grossman's *Soon I Will Be Invincible*, and even Michael Chabon's *The Amazing Adventures of Kavalier and Clay*, the comic book series **The Amazing Adventures of the Escapist**, and the graphic novel *Nobody Gets the Girl* by James Maxey.

Schwartz, Leslie.

Angels Crest. **Doubleday, 2004. 303pp. ISBN 9780385511858.**

When Ethan Denton pulls his car to the side of the road in northern California and leaves his three-year-old son Nate there for just a few minutes (the two were on a drive to enjoy nature; Ethan spots a couple of bucks and wants to follow them a bit deeper into the woods), he returns to find him missing. A desperate hunt and the cooperation of several residents of Angels Crest (all with their own concerns and troubles) lead to the discovery of Nate's body; then Ethan and his ex-wife Cindy must cope with the fallout from the event and their own uncontrollable feelings of guilt.

Subjects: Alcoholism; California; Fathers and Sons; GLBTQ; Kidnapping; Lesbians; Parenting; Psychological Fiction; Storms; Suspense; Weather; Women Authors; Women Writing as Men

Now Try: Schwartz's first novel was *Jumping the Green*. Other novels that feature missing persons and suspenseful tones are Lewis Robinson's *Water Dogs*, Stewart O'Nan's *Songs for the Missing*, and Andre Dubus's *The Garden of Last Days*; other melodramatic family tales include Kim Edwards's *The Memory Keeper's Daughter* and Christina Schwarz's *Drowning Ruth*.

Self, Will.

The Butt: An Exit Strategy. **Bloomsbury, 2008. 355pp. ISBN 9781596915558.**

When Tom Brodzinski decides to give up smoking, he is on holiday with his family in an unnamed country in the near future (postcolonial Feltham Islands). His conclusion to kick his habit might not have been such a big deal, but when he flips his last spent cigarette butt over his hotel room balcony, it lands on an older gentleman and causes a burn. Even this might have gone unpunished, but when elderly Reggie Lincoln dies during the night, Tom finds himself dragged into police custody and charged with murder—a charge made all the more serious because the deceased's much younger wife is a native tribeswoman with protected rights that also apply to her husband. Sent into tribal lands to pay restitution with another transgressor, Brian Prentice, Tom finds himself on a nightmare journey instigated at the request of Bigger Brother.

Subjects: Book Groups; British Authors; Dark Humor; Family Relationships; Law and Lawyers; Murder; Satire; Trials

Now Try: Self's fiction is imaginative and is consistently inconsistent in his choice of subjects; some of his most recent novels are *The Book of Dave, Dorian: An Imitation, How the Dead Live*, and *Great Apes*. Another satirical novel about smoking is Christopher Buckley's *Thank You for Smoking* (which was made into a movie of the same name); another satirical novel in which land disputes play a role is George Saunders's *The Brief and Frightening Reign of Phil*. Another British author who might appeal to Self's fans is Martin Amis, whose popular novels *The Information* and *London Fields* might be suitable read-alikes for this title.

Now Consider Nonfiction . . . Investigative Exposés

Investigative exposés are fact-heavy stories that reveal the details behind shocking stories, government cover-ups, appalling incidences of incompetence or evil design, or widespread and pervasive conspiracies. Exposé authors use their considerable narrative skills to tell compelling stories, and often offer suggestions or opinions about change.

Bowe, John. *Nobodies: Modern American Slave Labor and the Dark Side of the New Global Economy.*

Coll, Steve. *Ghost Wars: The Secret History of the CIA, Afghanistan, and Bin Laden, from the Soviet Invasion to September 10, 2001.*

Drakulic, Slavenka. *They Would Never Hurt a Fly: War Criminals on Trial in The Hague.*

Fainaru-Wada, Mark, and Lance Williams. *Game of Shadows: Barry Bonds, BALCO, and the Steroids Scandal That Rocked Professional Sports.*

Harr, Jonathan. *A Civil Action.*

Kozol, Jonathan. *The Shame of the Nation: The Restoration of Apartheid Schooling in America.*

Mayer, Jane. *The Dark Side: The Inside Story of How the War on Terror Turned into a War on American Ideals.*

Scahill, Jeremy. *Blackwater: The Rise of the World's Most Powerful Mercenary Army.*

Schlosser, Eric. *Fast Food Nation: The Dark Side of the All-American Meal.*

Senna, Danzy.

Symptomatic. **Riverhead Books, 2004. 213pp. ISBN 9781573222754.**

Senna's unnamed narrator, a biracial woman who moves from Berkeley to New York to further her career, is reeling from the psychological blow of the racist comments made by the friends of her boyfriend (with whom she is living) when she decides to find another living situation as soon as possible. What she finds is an apartment to share with an older woman named Greta Hicks, in Brooklyn; she is also in the process of finding love with an up-and-coming artist when her living situation starts to take a turn for the worse, with Greta becoming ever more controlling and demanding.

Subjects: Biracial Characters; First Person; Friendships; Interracial Relationships; New York City; Psychological Fiction; Suspense; Women Authors

Now Try: Senna is also the author of the coming-of-age novel *Caucasia,* which also dealt with interracial relationships and was favored by critics and reviewers, and the memoir *Where Did You Sleep Last Night? A Personal History*. Another tale of friendship gone wrong is Zoë Heller's *What Was She Thinking: Notes on a Scandal;* Sarah Hall's futuristic *Daughters of the North* explores a community run by women who do not tolerate dissent. Although not a thriller or suspenseful read, Z. Z. Packer's literary collection of stories, *Drinking Coffee Elsewhere,* also features a variety of women trying to make their way in the world while dealing with issues of race and belonging.

Shalev, Meir.

🎗 *A Pigeon and a Boy.* Schocken Books, 2007. 311pp. ISBN 9780805242515.

A story that unfolds over decades starts with the legend, overheard by Yair Mendelsohn, that a young pigeon handler during World War II sent out one last message of love, via pigeon, to his one true love. The stories of the pigeon handler and Mendelsohn are woven together in this character-rich but story-driven narrative of love, memory, and the sustaining power of legends and love affairs.

Second Appeal: Character

Subjects: 1940s; Animals; Birds; Books in Translation; Historical Fiction; Israel; Love Affairs; War

Awards: National Jewish Book Award

Now Try: Shalev has also written the novels *The Loves of Judith, Esau,* and *The Blue Mountain*. Other love stories that transcend time might be considered, such as Michael Ondaatje's *The English Patient,* Barry Callaghan's *Beside Still Waters,* Tony Earley's *The Blue Star,* Sara Gruen's *Water for Elephants,* Irene Nemirovsky's *Suite Francaise,* and Jane Urquhart's *The Stone Carvers*. Nonfiction memoirs of love across barriers might also be suggested, such as Harry Bernstein's *The Invisible Wall: A Love Story That Broke Barriers,* Betty Schimmel's *To See You Again: A True Story of Love in a Time of War,* and even Rob Sheffield's more contemporary *Love Is a Mix Tape*.

Shreve, Susan Richards.

A Student of Living Things. Viking, 2006. 246pp. ISBN 9780670037582.

Set in the near future, in a Washington, D.C., rocked by nearly continual and violent terrorist attacks, the Frayn family must deal with their own family tragedy when their son Steven Frayn is shot on the steps of one of the city's libraries. What makes the incident all the more shocking is that Steven's sister, Claire, is next to him when he is shot, and spends the rest of the narrative trying to unravel her brother's murder and the possible conspiracy behind it.

Subjects: Brothers and Sisters; Death and Dying; Family Relationships; First Person; Political Fiction; Siblings; Suspense; Terrorism; Washington, D.C.; Women Authors

Now Try: Shreve is the author of numerous other books for adults and children, but her suspenseful novels *The Visiting Physician, The Train Home,* and *Queen of Hearts* might particularly appeal to these readers. Although it is more obviously dystopian than Shreve's novel, Sarah Hall's futuristic tale of a woman fighting for her rights, *Daughters of the North*, might also appeal. Another novel that shares the setting of Washington, D.C., and also involves political issues is Paul Kafka-Gibbons's *DuPont Circle*.

Terrell, Heather.

The Map Thief. Ballantine Books, 2008. 251pp. ISBN 9780345494689.

When art expert and investigator Mara Coyne is hired by political power broker Richard Tobias to retrieve a centuries-old map that has been stolen from an archaeological dig in China that he is sponsoring, she soon realizes there's more about the map he's not telling her. Terrell takes the reader from time period to time period, and location to location (including 1421 China and 1496 Portugal), but it is the modern-day story of Coyne's investigations that will enthrall readers.

Subjects: 15th Century; Art and Artists; Historical Fiction; Quick Reads; Suspense; Women Authors

Now Try: This is the second novel featuring Mara Coyne; the first was *The Chrysalis*. Literary and intelligent thrillers from such authors as Javier Sierra (*The Secret Supper* and *The Lady in Blue*), Steve Berry (*The Amber Room*, *The Third Secret*, and *The Templar Legacy* —which is the first of his Cotton Malone novels), and Arturo Perez-Reverte (*The Club Dumas*, *The Fencing Master*, *The Seville Communion*, and *Captain Alatriste*) might be suggested, as might Geraldine Brooks's slower paced but still fascinating novel *People of the Book*.

Thornton, Lawrence.

Sailors on the Inward Sea. Free Press, 2004. 268pp. ISBN 9780743260077.

The relationship between author Joseph Conrad and his friend Jack Malone (who Thornton imagines as the inspiration for Conrad's character Marlow in *Heart of Darkness*) is at the heart of this psychological adventure novel. Written as the memoir of Malone, it describes the action during a sea battle between a British minesweeper and a German submarine during World War I.

Second Appeal: Character

Subjects: 19th Century; 20th Century; Adventure; Biographical Fiction; Conrad, Joseph; Historical Fiction; Literary Lives; Ocean; Psychological Fiction; World War I; Writers and Writing

Now Try: Thornton is also the author of the political trio of novels *Imagining Argentina*, *Tales from the Blue Archives*, and *Naming the Spirits*. Although readers interested in this novel may already have read some of Conrad's classics, it never hurts to make the suggestion; they include *Heart of Darkness*, *Lord Jim*, and *The Secret Agent*. Another book based on nautical adventures and literary characters is Edward Chupack's rather more violent *Silver: My Own Tale as Written by Me with a Goodly Amount of Murder* (based on the character Long John Silver in Robert Louis Stevenson's *Treasure Island*).

Now Consider Nonfiction . . . Travel Adventures

Travel adventure narratives, often referred to as "extreme travel adventures," offer not only setting descriptions, but also the vivid storytelling skills of their authors, who have typically undertaken an atypically challenging travel experience. Although setting is part of their appeal, these quickly paced narratives do not usually include details of the writers' journeys or cultural surroundings, but rather provide more linear stories of unique challenges overcome by intrepid author-adventurers.

Angus, Colin. *Lost in Mongolia: Rafting the World's Last Unchallenged River.*

Birkett, Dea. *Serpent in Paradise.*

Bissell, Tom. *Chasing the Sea: Lost Among the Ghosts of Empire in Central Asia.*

Elliot, Jason. *An Unexpected Light: Travels in Afghanistan.*

Nichols, Peter. *Sea Change: Alone Across the Atlantic in a Wooden Boat.*

Yeadon, David. *The Back of Beyond: Travels to the Wild Places of the Earth.*

Waldman, Ayelet.

Love and Other Impossible Pursuits. **Doubleday, 2006. 340pp. ISBN 9780385515306.**

Emilia Greenleaf fell in love with the man of her dreams at first sight, but their romance was complicated by the fact that Jack Woolf was already married and had a son. Although this story begins after they have married, Emilia continues to struggle in her relationship with Jack's son William, a lactose-intolerant, precocious child whom she feels is anything but cute. Their relationship, as well as her new marriage to Jack, is also not helped by the death of their baby, Isabel, for which Emilia feels responsible, or by her unresolved anger toward her own father, whose adulterous affairs led to the breakup of his marriage to her mother.

Second Appeal: Character

Subjects: Adultery; Death and Dying; Domestic Fiction; Family Relationships; First Person; Marriage; Parenting; Stepfamilies; Women Authors; Women's Fiction

Now Try: Waldman is also the author of the Mommy Track mystery series (*Nursery Crimes, The Big Nap,* and *A Playdate with Death*) and the nonfiction book *Bad Mother: A Chronicle of Maternal Crimes, Minor Calamities, and Occasional Moments of Grace.* Other novels in which women endure initially rocky relationships with children are Marisa de los Santos's *Love Walked In* and Carrie Adams's *The Stepmother;* Rachel Cusk's forthright memoir of motherhood, *A Life's Work: On Becoming a Mother* might be interesting to these readers, as might Adam Gopnik's memoir of raising children in New York City (and introducing them to Central Park), *Through the Children's Gate: A Home in New York.*

Wallace, Daniel.

Mr. Sebastian and the Negro Magician. **Bantam, 2007. 257pp. ISBN 978-0385521093.**

After the disappearance in 1954 of Henry Walker, the "Negro magician" employed by Jeremiah Musgrove's Chinese Circus, several of his friends from the circus and other acquaintances relate what they knew about Walker and the stories he had told them, including how he received the gift of illusion from the devil (but lost something infinitely precious in return), fell in love with his assistant—who had unique abilities of her own—and made his way across America (and Europe, during World War II) performing magic and illusions, with the biggest illusion being his very identity.

Subjects: 1950s; American South; Book Groups; Circus; Devil; Family Relationships; Friendships; Magic and Magicians; Multiple Viewpoints; Quick Reads

Now Try: Daniel Wallace's other novels include *The Watermelon King*, *Ray in Reverse*, and *Big Fish* (which was made into a motion picture). Another novel in which a circus figures prominently and the story is told from a slightly different vantage point is Sara Gruen's *Water for Elephants*; also of interest might be Christopher Priest's *The Prestige*, another twisty-turny tale of magicians. Audrey Niffeneggers's debut novel *The Time Traveler's Wife* is also a story about love across time. Another author who writes powerful family and friendship sagas set in the American South, Fannie Flagg, might appeal (she also provided a blurb for this book); her novels include *Fried Green Tomatoes at the Whistle Stop Café*, *Standing in the Rainbow*, and *Can't Wait to Get to Heaven*.

Waters, Sarah.

The Little Stranger. **Penguin, 2009. 466pp. ISBN 9781594488801.**

One of Great Britain's grand Georgian homes, Hundreds Hall, is the setting for this atmospheric and almost gothic haunted house story. The Ayres family, owners of Hundreds Hall, have fallen on hard times, as postwar rationing and other shortages have made it almost impossible to maintain their stately home. Roderick, the son, is suffering from war injuries and stress; Caroline, the daughter, is edging toward unhappy spinsterhood and is trying (largely unsuccessfully) to maintain the home herself, while their mother largely laments the long-ago loss of her first child Susan and happier times when the family was more affluent. As Dr. Faraday, a professional man with a chip on his shoulder due to his lower class upbringing, becomes close to the family, he is increasingly drawn into their stories and experiences of strange noises, violent accidents, and an overall feeling of evil exuded by the home itself.

Subjects: 1940s; Doctors; Family Relationships; Ghosts; Great Britain; Haunted Houses; Health Issues; Historical Fiction; Horror; Love Affairs; Psychological Fiction

Now Try: Waters is also the author of the acclaimed historical novels *Fingersmith*, *The Night Watch*, *Tipping the Velvet*, and *Affinity* (all of which feature what has been described as "lesbian Victoriana" plotlines). Other novels that feature brooding tales of formless evil are Jennifer Egan's *The Keep*, John Fowles's *The Magus*, and Donna Tartt's rather more straightforward (but still unsettling) novel *The Secret History*. Other novels in which hauntings cannot be determined to be real or psychological are Henry James's classic *The Turn of the Screw* (a bit shorter than this novel), Dan Simmons's *Drood* (a bit longer than this novel, and set in Victorian times), and Susan Hill's *The Man in the Picture: A Ghost Story*.

Welsh, Irvine.

Crime. **Norton, 2008. 344pp. ISBN 9780393068191.**

Ray Lennox and his fiancée Trudi are on vacation in Florida when Ray, an Edinburgh police officer whose vacation was suggested by his superiors as a way to recover from a work-related breakdown, finds himself embroiled in as sordid a situation as the crimes he was trying to leave behind. After going to a bar alone in search of alcohol and cocaine, he goes home with a woman and meets her ten-year-old daughter Tianna, who is the target of a pedophilia ring operated by her mother's sometime boyfriend. Dealing with his own demons, Ray nonetheless tries to rescue Tianna and put an end to her abuse at the hands of the many men involved.

Subjects: Abuse; Book Groups; Drug Abuse; Explicit Sexuality; Florida; Friendships; Law Enforcement; Pedophilia; Scottish Authors; Suspense

Now Try: Irvine's other novels include *Trainspotting*, *Glue*, and *Ecstasy: Three Tales of Chemical Romance*. Thrillers by British author Minette Walters might be good read-alikes (Walters is always very empathetic toward her victims); they include *Fox Evil*, *Acid Row*, and *The Shape of Snakes*. Another Scottish author, whose crime series featuring Inspector John Rebus might appeal, is Ian Rankin; the first books in that series are *Knots and Crosses*, *Hide and Seek*, and *Tooth and Nail*.

Winterson, Jeannette.

The Stone Gods. Harcourt, 2007. 206pp. ISBN 9780151014910.

Winterson's intrepid heroine, Billie Crusoe, headlines all three of these interconnected stories about the colonization and destruction of the earth. In the first, space travelers (having destroyed their own home planet of Orbus) seek a new planet, and when they find Planet Blue (known to us more familiarly as Earth), they make it suitable for habitation by firing an asteroid at it to encourage the extinction of the dinosaurs. In the second and third scenarios, the settlers continue their destructive ways while actually living on the planet. In all three stories Billie changes form slightly, as does her romantic counterpart, a "robo sapiens" known most often as Spike.

Subjects: Bleak Future; British Authors; Explicit Sexuality; Feminism; GLBTQ; Quick Reads; Science Fiction; Women Authors

Now Try: Winterson's other novels, *Sexing the Cherry* and *The PowerBook*, might also be suggested to these readers, as might her story collections *Art & Lies* and *The World and Other Places*. Another novel in which time and space travel are woven into a greater social narrative is Kurt Vonnegut's *Slaughterhouse-5*; other challenging science fiction novels such as Margaret Atwood's *Oryx & Crake* and *The Handmaid's Tale*, Sarah Hall's *Daughters of the North*, or Octavia Butler's *Dawn* might be offered.

Wittenborn, Dirk.

Pharmakon. Viking, 2008. 406pp. ISBN 9780670019427.

The dawn of the pharmaceutical era, in the 1950s, is the backdrop for this psychological (in subject and tone) drama. Dr. William Friedrich is a workaday psychologist and researcher at Yale when he begins to work with a colleague, Dr. Bunny Winton, on a revolutionary treatment: a drug that will make people feel happy. The results are promising until one of their subjects, a suicidal young man named Casper Gedsic, engages in acts of violence that will forever make Dr. Friedrich question his chemical breakthrough; by the time his son narrates the story of his later life, in the 1990s, he is struggling with the legacy of his career and his frustration with his children's decisions to pursue careers that are more creative than financially lucrative.

Subjects: 1950s; Family Relationships; Fathers and Sons; Health Issues; Medicine; Mental Health; Pharmacology; Psychological Fiction; Suicide

Now Try: Wittenborn's first novel was *Fierce People*. Chip Kidd's novel *The Learners* also centers on a disturbing psychology experiment; another novel in which medical staff clash with a family is Darin Strauss's *More Than It Hurts You*. Nonfiction narratives about the psychopharmacology industry might prove interesting reads—these include Elizabeth Wurtzel's memoir *Prozac Nation* and Charles Barber's *Comfortably Numb: How Psychiatry Is Medicating a Nation*; also of interest might be psychology histories, such as Lauren Slater's *Opening Skinner's Box*.

Chapter 3

Character

Perhaps the easiest appeal factor to spot in fiction is **Character**; this category is certainly the largest in this book, simply because so many of the most popular and best-selling novels published today are distinguished by their authors' descriptions of characters with whom the reader identifies (or doesn't, in some notable cases). Books that are character-driven feature three-dimensional characters who almost seem to step off the page. When readers describe these novels to us, they often start by describing the people in the novels—"I just felt really close to the characters," "I felt like I knew the characters"—or other similar phrases might be used when advisors ask readers to articulate what they loved about certain books.

Although it is not always this straightforward, a lot of these titles actually include the characters' names in their titles, for example, Elisa Albert's *The Book of Dahlia* (about a woman named Dahlia), Charles Baxter's *Saul and Patsy*, and Saul Bellow's classic *The Adventures of Augie March*. (And when they don't include a proper name, the titles still often allude to the characters by their characteristics or attributes; examples here include Saher Alam's *The Groom to Have Been*, Tiffany Baker's *The Little Giant of Aberdeen County*, and Ivan Doig's *The Eleventh Man*.) What sets these novels apart is that as readers we are more interested in the people who populate them than in what they are doing or where they are doing it. Although many of these books, like a lot of good-quality mainstream fiction titles, could be considered literary, the author's mastery of language is primarily used in painting vivid and detailed portraits of characters.

Readers who enjoy novels with strong **Character** appeal often enjoy a wide variety of other mainstream fiction titles as well, particularly those titles mentioned in the other chapters of this book that feature character as a secondary appeal—novels in which Story is the primary appeal, but that feature sharp and well-written dialogue, spoken by unique characters, might be particularly interesting to these readers. A wide variety of other character-driven genres might also appeal, such as some romance titles, women's fiction, and any genre title you can think of in which the characters really make the book. These readers might also be open to suggestions about character-driven works of nonfiction, particularly the very personal nonfiction genres that revolve around "life stories"—biographies, memoirs, and relationships nonfiction (in which communities, friendships, and love stories are described).

Agarwal, Shilpa.

Haunting Bombay. **Soho Press, 2009. 362pp. ISBN 9781569475584.**

Taken in by her grandmother Maji when her mother died, Pinky Mittal is forced to navigate a family situation in which her grandmother lovingly cares for her, but she is largely resented by everyone else in the house, including her uncle Jaginder, her spiteful aunt Savita, and Savita's three sons. When thirteen-year-old Pinky succumbs to curiosity and unlocks the door to a room that the superstitious family had previously locked every night, she unleashes angry ghosts upon her adoptive family.

Second Appeal: Setting

Subjects: 1960s; Bombay; Book Groups; Family Relationships; Family Secrets; First Novels; Ghosts; Grandmothers; Historical Fiction; India; Indian Authors; Magic Realism; Multicultural; Psychological Fiction; Women Authors; Women's Fiction

Now Try: Other books set in India in which family secrets play a role include Padma Viswanathan's *The Toss of a Lemon*, Salman Rushdie's *Midnight's Children*, Amitav Ghosh's *The Hungry Tide*, and Chitra Banerjee Divakaruni's *Sister of My Heart*. Other modern ghost stories might also be suggested, such as Beth Gutcheon's *More Than You Know*, Sean Stewart's *A Perfect Circle*, or Abby Frucht's *Polly's Ghost*. Sarah Waters's *The Little Stranger*, set in 1940s Great Britain, might also appeal. Magic realism novels, particularly from a woman's point of view, such as Isabel Allende's *House of the Spirits*, Kiran Desai's *Hullabaloo in the Guava Orchard*, and Sarah Addison Allen's *Garden Spells*, might also be offered.

Alam, Saher.

The Groom to Have Been. **Spiegel & Grau, 2008. 399pp. ISBN 9780385524605.**

Although Nasr allows his traditionally minded mother to arrange his marriage to Farah, a woman she deems proper and worthy, he finds himself falling in love with his childhood friend Jameela, whose independence and argumentative nature both excites and unnerves him. Although told partially in flashbacks, the majority of the story takes place during Nasr's engagement party to Farah; the terrorist attacks of September 11, 2001, also have an impact on the narrative (although his family lives in Canada, Nasr has been living and working in New York City). Alam evocatively details the struggle to find a livable balance between tradition and modernity, particularly within immigrant communities; he also states that his story was inspired by Edith Wharton's classic novel *The Age of Innocence.*

Subjects: 9/11; Arranged Marriages; Asian Canadian Authors; Book Groups; Canada; Culture Clash; Family Relationships; First Novels; Flashbacks; Immigrants and Immigration; Islam; Literary Allusions; Love Affairs; Marriage; Men's Lives; Multicultural; New York City

Now Try: Readers enthralled with Alam's novel might also be interested in reading Edith Wharton's classic novel of manners, marriage, and society, *The Age of Innocence*. Other books in which immigrants (particularly from India) learn to navigate their new cultures and marriage customs include Monica Ali's *Brick Lane*, Jhumpa Lahiri's *The Namesake* and her story collection *Unaccustomed Earth*, Anne Cherian's *A Good Indian Wife*, and Zadie Smith's *White Teeth*.

Albert, Elisa.

The Book of Dahlia. **Free Press, 2008. 276pp. ISBN 9780743291293.**

Twenty-nine-year-old Dahlia Finger is forced to reevaluate what she has done with her life when she is diagnosed with terminal brain cancer. Alternatively wry, sarcastic, and angry in the face of her curtailed future, she particularly reexamines her relationships with her easygoing father, her eccentric mother, and her sometimes cruel brother. She also examines, often while undergoing radiation and therapy sessions, her Jewish religion, her lack of professional ambition, and her ambivalent relationships with men; although the broad picture is one of a "wasted" life, the depths of Dahlia's feelings and her often bleak but unexpected and smart humor rather proves that there is no such thing.

Subjects: Book Groups; California; Cancer; Death and Dying; Family Relationships; First Novels; Flashbacks; Health Issues; Jewish American Authors; Jews and Judaism; Profanity; Women Authors

Now Try: Albert is also the author of a collection of short stories, *How This Night Is Different*. Other novels in which characters face their own mortality at much too young an age include Sylvain Trudel's *Mercury Under My Tongue*, Christine Schutt's *All Souls*, and Elizabeth Berg's *Talk Before Sleep*. Nonfiction memoirs in which feisty women face their health challenges with bravery and wit include two graphic novels: Marisa Acocella Marchetto's *Cancer Vixen: A True Story*, and Brian Fies's *Mom's Cancer*; also of interest might be Lucy Grealy's *Autobiography of a Face* and Amy Silverstein's *Sick Girl*.

Ali, Monica.

🏅 *Brick Lane.* **Scribner, 2003. 369pp. ISBN 9780743243308.**

Nanzeen, a young Bangladeshi woman, moves to London for an arranged marriage to an older man and gradually sheds her docility amid the clash of different cultures.

Subjects: Adultery; Arranged Marriages; Book Groups; Classics; Culture Clash; Domestic Fiction; Great Britain; Immigrants and Immigration; Marriage; Multicultural; Pakistan; Women Authors; Women's Fiction

Awards: ALA Notable

Now Try: Nadeem Aslam's *Maps for Lost Lovers* is another novel about Pakistani immigrants in England. The role of Muslim women in an immigrant community is explored in *Minaret* by Leila Aboulela; Jhumpa Lahiri's *The Namesake* and Kavita Daswani's *For Matrimonial Purposes* also look at conflicting cultures and arranged marriages among immigrants. Two other novels are noteworthy for their examinations of the immigrant experience: Khaled Hosseini's *The Kite Runner* (as well as that author's first novel) and Chitra Banerjee Divakaruni's *The Vine of Desire*. An unusual setting provides the background for Bapsi Sidhwa's *The Pakistani Bride*. The lives of women in Pakistan are explored in many of the novels by Kamila Shamsie, including *Burnt Shadows* and *Broken Verses*.

Alvarez, Julia.

Saving the World. **Algonquin Books of Chapel Hill, 2006. 368pp. ISBN 9781565125100.**

Alvarez tells the parallel stories of the writer Alma Huebner, whose husband travels to the Dominican Republic to combat the spread of AIDS in the population, and of Doña Isabel Sendales y Gómez (a real woman in history), who traveled to Central America from Spain in 1906 with a number of orphans who had been vaccinated with cowpox. When both humanitarian missions fail, each woman is left to help the man in her life understand and accept the difficulty of changing the world, as well as to accept the fact that such missions cannot always provide the salvation they promise.

Second Appeal: Setting

Subjects: 19th Century; AIDS; Balmis, Francisco Xavier de; Biographical Fiction; Central America; Culture Clash; Dominican Authors; Dominican Republic; Historical Fiction; Latino Authors; Literary Lives; Medicine; Multiple Viewpoints; Sendales y Gómez, Doña Isabel; Vermont; Women Authors; Writers and Writing

Now Try: Several of Alvarez's earlier novels also tell historical stories, including *In the Time of the Butterflies* and *Before We Were Free*. Other novels in which individuals experience culture clashes might be suggested; these include Paul Theroux's *The Mosquito Coast*, Barbara Kingsolver's *The Poisonwood Bible*, Mario Vargas Llosa's novel *The Feast of the Goat*, and *Fieldwork* by Mischa Berlinski. Edwidge Danticat's novel *The Farming of Bones*, also set in the Dominican Republic, might also appeal.

Anam, Tahmima.

🏵 *A Golden Age*. HarperCollins, 2007. 276pp. ISBN 9780061478741.

The war for independence fought between Bangladesh and Pakistan in the early 1970s provides the backdrop for this family drama. The widow Rehana, fiercely devoted to both her teenage son Soheil and daughter Maya, discovers that her devotion and her willingness to aid her children in both their personal and political decisions will come with a steep price.

Second Appeal: Setting

Subjects: 1970s; Bangladesh; Bangladeshi Authors; Book Groups; Brothers and Sisters; Family Relationships; First Novels; Historical Fiction; Multicultural; Siblings; South Asia; Violence; War; Widows; Women Authors

Awards: Commonwealth Writer's Prize

Now Try: Other novels about the impact of war on family and other relationships might be suggested, including Kamila Shamsie's *Burnt Shadows*, Nadeem Aslam's *The Wasted Vigil*, Steven Galloway's *The Cellist of Sarajevo*, James Buchan's *The Persian Bride*, and Khaled Hosseini's *The Kite Runner*. Tasalima Nasarina's *Shame: A Novel*, and Amitav Ghosh's *The Hungry Tide* are also set in Bangladesh; Steve Coll's nonfiction travelogue of his journeys through India, Bangladesh, and South Asia, *On the Grand Trunk Road*, might also appeal to these readers.

Aslam, Nadeem.

🏵 *The Wasted Vigil*. Knopf, 2008. 319pp. ISBN 9780307268426.

Disparate lives intersect in this novel set in post-9/11 Afghanistan. There is Lara, a Russian woman searching for news of her brother, lost during his military service in the Soviet invasion of the country; Marcus, the elderly English doctor with whom she stays, whose wife was murdered by the Taliban and whose daughter disappeared in the wake of false accusations made against her; David, an American whose love for Marcus's daughter has kept him in the country and linked to Marcus as they search for the son they know she had; Casa, a young man blinded by his hatred for the West; and his polar opposite, Special Forces soldier James, whose own zealotry for clearly delineated ideas of right and wrong make him as dangerous as the Taliban.

Second Appeal: Setting

Subjects: 9/11; Afghanistan; Book Groups; Family Relationships; Grief; Islam; Love Affairs; Multicultural; Multiple Viewpoints; Pakistani Authors; Taliban; War

Awards: ALA Notable

Now Try: Aslam is also the author of the novels *Season of the Rainbirds* and *Maps for Lost Lovers* (a New York Times Notable Book). Other character-driven novels set in Afghanistan might be suggested, including Khaled Hosseini's *The Kite Runner* and *A Thousand Splendid Suns* and Yasmina Khadra's *The Swallows of Kabul*. Nonfiction about conflict and religious culture in Afghanistan might also be offered, including Ted Rall's graphic novel *To Afghanistan and Back*, Åsne Seierstad's investigative title *The Bookseller of Kabul*, Jason Elliot's travelogue *An Unexpected Light: Travels in Afghanistan*, or the graphic novel *The Photographer* (illustrated by Emmanuel Guibert; written by Didier Lefevre and Frederic Lemercier). Another novel about life in a war-torn region, Steven Galloway's *The Cellist of Sarajevo*, might also be suggested.

Attenberg, Jami.

The Kept Man. **Riverhead Books, 2007. 294pp. ISBN 9781594489525.**

For six years Brooklynite Jarvis Miller's husband, the artist Martin Miller, has been living in a nonresponsive coma and is being cared for in a nearby nursing home. Although she primarily leaves the apartment only to visit him, she eventually finds herself partaking more in community life and friendships, particularly with a group of neighborhood men who frequent her local laundromat, as well as her husband's art dealers and friends. When her life, already on hold, is further derailed by a secret she learns about her husband, she must decide what it means for both their futures and their marriage.

Subjects: Art and Artists; Brooklyn; Coma Patients; Family Secrets; First Novels; First Person; Friendships; Health Issues; Marriage; New York City; Women Authors

Now Try: Attenberg is also the author of a collection of short stories titled *Instant Love*. Other novels about spouses and partners dealing with a loved one's debilitating health issues might prove good read-alikes; these include Elizabeth Berg's *Range of Motion* and Rosellen Brown's *Tender Mercies*. In Pat Barker's novel *Double Vision*, the death of her photojournalist husband leaves Kate Frobisher bereft as she tries to make her way through life without him. Both Zoë Heller's novel *The Believers* and Kate Christensen's *The Great Man* are stories about the secrets kept in families and the effect of a strong patriarch on family relationships. A memoir about a woman discovering some devastating secrets about her husband is Julie Metz's *Perfection: A Memoir of Betrayal and Trust*.

Bacon, Charlotte.

Split Estate. **Farrar, Straus & Giroux, 2008. 290pp. ISBN 9780374281830.**

When Laura King commits suicide, she leaves behind her grieving husband Arthur and two teenage children, daughters Celia and Cam, who sleepwalk through the months following her death. Eventually Arthur decides to move his family to his mother Lucy's ranch in Wyoming for the summer;

while there, they become embroiled in his mother's attempts to halt exploration and drilling for minerals on and around her land, as well as in their own romantic entanglements.

Subjects: Death and Dying; Domestic Fiction; Dysfunctional Families; Family Relationships; Multiple Viewpoints; New York City; Suicide; Teenage Girls; Teenagers; Women Authors; Wyoming

Now Try: Bacon is also the author of the novels *Lost Geography* and *There Is Room for You*. Other novels in which characters strive to understand a loved one's suicide might be suggested, including Stacey D'Erasmo's *Tea*, Zoë Heller's *Everything You Know*, and Ann Packer's *Songs Without Words*; also of interest might be Joan Wickersham's memoir about her father's death, *The Suicide Index: Putting My Father's Death in Order*. Novels in which family members react to grief in their own ways might also appeal, such as Kim Barnes's *A Country Called Home* and Anne Tyler's *The Accidental Tourist*.

There Is Room for You. **Farrar, Straus & Giroux, 2004. 276pp. ISBN 978-0374281854.**

Two events propel Anna Singer to take an epic journey alone to India: the death of her father, with whom she had a close relationship, and the collapse of her marriage. Upon learning of her daughter's trip, Anna's mother Rose gives her the memoir about her own childhood—as the daughter of an English family in India—that she has been writing for Anna. The narrative is told partially in flashbacks to Rose's difficult youth, as prompted by the memoir, and partly in '1992 as Anna travels through India.

Second Appeal: Setting

Subjects: 1990s; Book Groups; Culture Clash; Death and Dying; Family Relationships; Family Secrets; First Person; Flashbacks; India; Marriage; Mothers and Daughters; Multigenerational Fiction; Travel; Women Authors; Women's Fiction

Now Try: Bacon is also the author of the novels *Split Estate* and *Lost Geography* and the short story collection *A Private State*. Jhumpa Lahiri's short story collection, *Unaccustomed Earth*, offers many narratives about the dynamics between parents and children. Although Nicole Krauss's novel *A History of Love* is a bit more complex than this novel in its narrative structure, it is similar in its plotline of past loves and family connections. A memoir in which the daughter of a British Foreign Services agent describes her childhood and travels, Moira Hodgson's *It Seemed Like a Good Idea at the Time*, might be suggested; another memoir of life in India, during World War I, is Jon Godden's *Two Under the Indian Sun*. Also consider travel narratives about India, such as Eric Newby's *Slowly Down the Ganges* or Suketu Mehta's *Maximum City: Bombay Lost and Found*.

Baker, Tiffany.

The Little Giant of Aberdeen County. **Grand Central, 2009. 341pp. ISBN 978-0446194204.**

Truly Plaice has never felt truly comfortable in her own skin; the residents of Aberdeen county all know her as the oversized baby whose mother died during her traumatic birth, the sister who couldn't compare to the tiny and doll-like perfection of her sister Serena Jane, and eventually the large woman who moves in with her sister's husband to look after her child when Serena Jane deserts her family. Her sister's husband, Robert Morgan, one in a long line of Robert Morgans who has doctored the community over several generations, keeps a secret from Truly, but Truly has secrets of her own, including how she unlocks the pattern of a quilt sewn by Tabitha Dyerson (the wife of the town's original Dr. Morgan), whose recipes for folk remedies Truly uses for both kindness and vengeance. Interlocking and complex relationships abound among the characters of this gothic-feeling novel.

Subjects: 1960s; 1970s; Book Groups; Community Life; Death and Dying; Doctors; Domestic Fiction; Family Relationships; First Novels; First Person; Friendships; Obesity; Siblings; Sisters; Small-town Life; Women Authors; Women's Fiction

Now Try: Other novels featuring inordinately strong (even if they don't know it) women characters are Stephanie Kallos's *Sing Them Home*, Anne Tyler's *If Morning Ever Comes*, Jeannette Walls's *Half Broke Horses*, and Fannie Flagg's *Fried Green Tomatoes at the Whistle Stop Café*. Other novels in which a character is ostracized for his or her unusual physical characteristics are Elizabeth McCracken's *The Giant's House: A Romance* and John Irving's *A Prayer for Owen Meany*; Judith Moore's heartbreaking memoir *Fat Girl* also illuminates the stigma of looking and always feeling different.

Banks, Russell.

The Darling. HarperCollins, 2004. 391pp. ISBN 9780060197353.

Banks's novel opens with Hannah Musgrave's description of the farm she owns in upstate New York and the local women she has employed to help her run it; however, the bulk of the story is told in flashbacks to the 1970s and 1980s as she recounts her membership in the revolutionary group Weather Underground, her emigration to Liberia, her marriage to one of that country's cabinet members, her relationships with Liberians Samuel Doe and Charles Taylor, and her decision to leave her sons in that country when she had to flee during its civil war.

Second Appeal: Setting

Subjects: 1970s; 1980s; Africa; Biographical Fiction; Corruption; Elderly; First Person; Friendships; Historical Fiction; Liberia; Men Writing as Women; Political Fiction; Race Relations; Taylor, Charles; Unreliable Narrator

Now Try: Banks has tackled a wide variety of subjects and time periods in his novels, including his historical fiction *The Reserve* and *Cloudsplitter*; in other novels, such as *The Sweet Hereafter*, *Affliction*, and *Continental Drift*, he explores the plight of the working classes. Doris Lessing's part novel, part memoir *Alfred and Emily* might also appeal, as might Helene Cooper's memoir of her childhood in Liberia, *The House at Sugar Beach: In Search of a Lost African Childhood*. Other political fiction might be suggested, such as J. M. Coetzee's *The Age of Iron*, Julia Alvarez's *In the Time of the Butterflies*, and Graham Greene's classics *The Heart of the Matter* and *The Quiet American*. Two other novels about going underground in the 1960s and 1970s are Marge Piercy's *Vida* and Susan Choi's *American Woman*.

Barbery, Muriel.

The Elegance of the Hedgehog. Europa Editions, 2008. 325pp. ISBN 978-1933372600.

In her fifties and working as a combination super/jack of all trades in a small apartment building in France, Renée Michel is not the type of woman who gets many second looks, and she's fine with that. One of the tenants in her building, twelve-year-old Paloma, has likewise decided that she's had enough of seeing the world and plans her own suicide. Between the two of them, however, and with the help of a new tenant, a Japanese man named

Kakuro Ozu, they will come to learn that each has much more to offer the world (and each other) than either had previously believed.

Subjects: Book Groups; Books in Translation; Coming-of-age; France; Friendships; Hotels; Humor; Social Class; Teenage Girls; Teenagers; Women Authors; YA

Now Try: Reviewers have compared this novel to the works of Alexander McCall Smith, a prolific author whose multiple series include the Precious Ramotswe mysteries (starting with *The No. 1 Ladies Detective Agency*) and Isabel Dalhousie series (starting with *The Sunday Philosophy Club*). Other books in which surprising relationships provide sustenance for the friends involved include Yoko Ogawa's *The Professor and the Housekeeper*, John Irving's *A Prayer for Owen Meany* and *The Cider House Rules*, and Catherine O'Flynn's *What Was Lost*. Other books with strong and intelligent teenage heroines are Alan Bradley's *The Sweetness at the Bottom of the Pie*, Joan Bauer's *The Rules of the Road*, Marisha Pessl's *Special Topics in Calamity Physics*, and the YA novels *Vegan Virgin Valentine* (by Carolyn Mackler) and *Naomi and Ely's No Kiss List* (by Rachel Cohn and David Levithan), which also features an apartment building full of unique neighbors.

Barker, Pat.

Double Vision. **Farrar, Straus & Giroux, 2003. 258pp. ISBN 9780374209056.**

In Barker's slim psychological drama, friends Stephen Sharkey and Ben Frobisher, fellow creative workers in New York City (the former a writer, the latter a photographer) part ways after the terrorist attacks of September 11, 2001, and follow very different paths. Stephen discovers his wife's affair and leaves the country and his job, while Ben travels to Afghanistan to document the war there and is killed. It is typical of Barker that such a complex story is largely the backstory to this novel, in which Stephen, Ben's widow Kate, Kate's clergyman friend Alec and his daughter Justine, and Kate's young assistant (he is helping her complete a large commissioned sculpture) become entwined with one another. All is also not as it seems with Peter (Kate's assistant), lending a suspenseful air to the narrative.

Second Appeal: Story

Subjects: 9/11; Art and Artists; Book Groups; British Authors; Friendships; Great Britain; Love Affairs; Marriage; Psychological Fiction; Quick Reads; Suspense; Violence; War; Women Authors

Now Try: Barker is a master of psychological drama, and this novel harks back to her first novel, *Union Street*, and her unflinching portrayals of prostitutes in England's industrial North. Her dark and classic series about war and its aftermath, the Regeneration Trilogy, might also appeal (it comprises the novels *Regeneration*, *The Eye in the Door*, and *Ghost Road*). Although the subjects she deals with are often more domestic in nature, another British author, Tessa Hadley, has a style similar to Barker's, and her novels *Accidents in the Home* and *Master Bedroom* might also appeal. Nonfiction books in which authors struggle to make sense of war, might also be suggested; these include Tom Bissell's memoir *The Father of All Things: A Marine, His Son, and the Legacy of Vietnam* and *Shutterbabe*, a memoir of war, love, and photography by Deborah Copaken Kogan. The graphic novel *The Photographer: Into War-Torn Afghanistan with Doctors Without Borders*, written by Didier Lefevre and Frederic Lemercier and illustrated by Emmanuel Guibert, might also be suggested.

🌳 *Life Class.* **Doubleday, 2007. 311pp. ISBN 9780385524353.**

Four friends who attend the same art class (one as a model, the others as students) find their lives irrevocably changed when the men (Paul Tarrant and Kit Neville) leave Great Britain in 1914 to volunteer as Red Cross workers in Europe prior to the outbreak of the Great War. The lives of the women (Elinor Brooke and Teresa

Halliday) are no less changed as they too witness the effects of the world war on those they know and love.

Subjects: 1910s; Art and Artists; Book Groups; British Authors; Friendships; Great Britain; Historical Fiction; Love Affairs; War; Women Authors; World War I

Awards: New York Times Notable

Now Try: Barker is best known for her World War I <u>Regeneration Trilogy</u> (*Regeneration*, *The Eye in the Door*, and *Ghost Road*). Other novels about World War I and the effect of wars on personal relationships might be suggested, including Erich Maria Remarque's classic *All Quiet on the Western Front* and Kate Morton's *The House at Riverton*; Doris Lessing's part-fiction, part-memoir *Alfred and Emily* might also appeal. The World War I wartime memoir of well-known British pacifist Vera Brittain, *Testament of Youth*, might be suggested, as might *Letters from a Lost Generation*, the collection of her letters to her brother, who died in the conflict.

Barnes, Julian.

Arthur & George. **Knopf, 2005. 385pp. ISBN 9780307263100.**

Based in large part on actual events and documentation, Barnes's novel includes elements of historical fiction, mystery, and history. Using the varying viewpoints of the main characters (with each story helpfully labeled as either "Arthur" or "George") , Barnes weaves a tale of false accusations and racism against George Edalji, a part-Indian vicar's son accused of writing obscene letters and mutilating farm animals, and of Arthur Conan Doyle, who sets out to prove his friend George could not have committed the crimes (while dealing with his own literary fame, the popularity of his character Sherlock Holmes, and his desperate but chaste love for a woman who was not his wife).

Subjects: Biographical Fiction; British Authors; Culture Clash; Doyle, Arthur Conan; Friendships; Great Britain; Historical Fiction; Literary Allusions; Multiple Viewpoints; Mystery; Racism; Victorian

Now Try: Barnes is a prolific author; his novels include *Metroland, Flaubert's Parrot, Cross Channel*, and *England, England*; he has also written nonfiction (*The Pedant in the Kitchen* and *Nothing to Be Frightened Of*, his exploration of his atheism in the face of aging), as well as the story collection *The Lemon Table*. Other literary historical novels might appeal to these readers, such as Michael Cox's *The Meaning of Night*, Charles Finch's *A Beautiful Blue Death*, or Philip Baruth's *The Brothers Boswell* (also based on real people); also of interest might be Laurie King's erudite <u>Mary Russell and Sherlock Holmes</u> mystery series (starting with *The Beekeeper's Apprentice* and *A Monstrous Regiment of Women*), as well as a wide variety of Arthur Conan Doyle's own mystery novels featuring Sherlock Holmes. Other biographical novels include *The Master* by Colm Tóibín, *The Fall of Frost* by Brian Hall, and *Vanessa and Virginia* by Susan Sellers.

Barry, Brunonia.

The Lace Reader. **William Morrow, 2008. 390pp. ISBN 9780061624766.**

Towner Whitney returns to her hometown of Salem, Massachusetts, to deal with her great-aunt Eva's mysterious death, and finds that the secrets and complexities of her childhood are all still in place. Her relationship with her mother May, who runs a shelter for abused women, is precarious; her father, Cal Boynton, is being heralded as a community spiritual leader; and her memories of her twin sister, Lyndley, who died at birth, are intruding ever more often on her thoughts. Throughout the story, which takes several darker turns (particularly with a revelation of past events at the novel's end), Towner also struggles with her inherited ability to "read lace" (a way of telling the future that runs in her family and in the community's tradition) and her growing attraction to John Rafferty, a local police officer.

Second Appeal: Story

Subjects: Abuse; Book Groups; Clairvoyance; Dysfunctional Families; Family Relationships; Family Secrets; First Novels; Massachusetts; Mothers and Daughters; Psychological Fiction; Salem; Suspense; Unreliable Narrator; Women Authors; Women's Fiction

Now Try: Fans of the psychological angles of Barry's novel might also consider Matt Ruff's (somewhat darker) novel *Set This House in Order* or Dennis Lehane's psychological thriller *Shutter Island*. Other novels in which family secrets are revealed might also appeal, including Kim Edwards's *The Memory Keeper's Daughter*, David Wroblewski's *The Story of Edgar Sawtelle*, Kathleen Kent's historical novel *The Heretic's Daughter*, Christina Sunley's *The Tricking of Freya*, Ann-Marie MacDonald's *Fall on Your Knees*, and Annie Proulx's *The Shipping News*.

Baxter, Charles.

Saul and Patsy. **Pantheon, 2003. 317pp. ISBN 9780375410291.**

Strangely protected by their unshakable love for each other, Saul and Patsy Bernstein leave the boundaries of their former experiences and urban lives and move to a small town in Michigan, where Saul becomes a high school teacher and Patsy a bank teller. In the midst of vague rumblings of anti-Semitism and starting their own family, a struggling student of Saul's, Gordy Himmelman, commits suicide, further inciting the town's ire against Saul. Although reviewers have faulted Baxter for the languid pacing of this quiet novel, his dialogue crackles and his characters, particularly Saul and Patsy, are so realistically drawn in their foibles and their relationship that the reader feels they might know them as well as their own neighbors.

Subjects: American Midwest; Community Life; Domestic Fiction; Education; Humor; Jews and Judaism; Marriage; Michigan; Small-Town Life; Suicide; Teachers

Now Try: Baxter's other novels, including *Harmony of the World, Believers, Through the Safety Net*, and *The Feast of Love*, are all relatively slow-paced novels but nevertheless feature sparkling dialogue. Other novels in which the dynamics of marriage are explored are Laurie Colwin's *Family Happiness*, Robb Forman Dew's *Dale Loves Sophie to Death*, Richard Russo's *Straight Man* (which is also set in the world of academia), and Anne Tyler's *Breathing Lessons*. Another novel of community life and the heated tempers that can accompany school controversies is Tom Perrotta's *The Abstinence Teacher*. Although both are told from the viewpoint of a spouse who has lost a partner, the memoirs *The Year of Magical Thinking* by Joan Didion and *About Alice* by Calvin Trillin also paint portraits of strong marriages.

The Soul Thief. **Pantheon, 2008. 210pp. ISBN 9780375422522.**

Nathaniel Mason spends much of his time as a graduate student trying to figure out who he is and with whom he is in love (he is intrigued by, and sleeps with, two very different women, Theresa and Jamie, in the first half of the novel); this identity crisis is exacerbated when Theresa's boyfriend, Jerome Coolberg, becomes obsessed with Nathaniel and starts to adopt his mannerisms and tell Nathaniel's stories as his own. The novel's second half revisits all the characters and reveals secrets about Nathaniel and Jerome and the arcs their lives have followed since graduate school.

Second Appeal: Language

Subjects: 1970s; Academia; Book Groups; College Life; First Person; Friendships; Love Affairs; Mental Health; Psychological Fiction; Rape; Suspense

Now Try: Baxter excels at telling quietly dramatic tales; fans of this book might also consider his novels *Saul and Patsy*, *A Relative Stranger*, and *The Feast of Love*. Similarly unsettling stories about secrets, relationships, and obsession might also be suggested, including Donna Tartt's *The Secret History*, Haven Kimmel's *Iodine*, Monica Ferrell's *The Answer Is Always Yes*, and Ian McEwan's *The Comfort of Strangers*. Obsessive relationships are also at the heart of Nick Laird's novel *Glover's Mistake*. Peter Cameron's novel *The City of Your Final Destination* also features a graduate student trying to finish an arduous writing project.

Beachy, Kyle.

The Slide. Dial Press, 2009. 287pp. ISBN 9780385341851.

Crushed by his girlfriend Audrey's sudden decision to travel around Europe with her friend Carmel (whose bisexuality is the attribute most worried about and mentioned by the narrator), recent college graduate Potter Mays returns home to live with his parents and try to figure out what Audrey is trying to tell him about their relationship. While his mother spoils him and his father not-so-subtly suggests he find gainful employment, Potter finds himself spending most of his time with his best friend Stuart, who is also living with his parents (in their beach house) and justifying his residence there because he is starting a business as an "Independent Thought Contractor."

Subjects: American Midwest; Coming-of-age; Family Relationships; First Novels; First Person; Friendships; Humor; Men's Lives; Missouri; Young Men

Now Try: Potter is the latest in a long line of appealing but confused young male protagonists in fiction; also of interest to these readers might be J. D. Salinger's classic *The Catcher in the Rye*, British author David Nicholls's *A Question of Attraction*, Greg Ames's *Buffalo Lockjaw*, Anne Tyler's *Saint Maybe*, Walker Percy's classic *The Moviegoer*, and Nick Hornby's *High Fidelity*. Humorous and coming-of-age memoirs by young male authors might also appeal, including Sam MacDonald's *The Urban Hermit: A Memoir*, J. R. Moehringer's *The Tender Bar*, and Chuck Klosterman's *Fargo Rock City*.

Berg, Elizabeth.

Home Safe. Random House, 2009. 260pp. ISBN 9781400065110.

In the aftermath of her husband Dan's death, novelist Helen Ames finds that not only were certain friends correct in their charges that she let him handle all the details of their life together (or, to put it more succinctly, that she infantilized herself), but that she misses infantilizing herself. Early attempts to secure a part-time job while she struggles with writer's block become more serious when she learns that, shortly before his death, Dan spent a large chunk of their retirement money; ever more desperate to come up with something to write about, she decides to pour her energy into managing the life of her daughter Tessa (who neither particularly needs nor cares for her mother's interference). Helen's transformation from an unformed to a surprisingly feisty woman throughout Berg's text is a pleasure to watch.

Subjects: Book Groups; Death and Dying; Domestic Fiction; Family Relationships; Family Secrets; Friendships; Illinois; Literary Lives; Marriage; Mothers and Daughters; Quick Reads; Widows; Women Authors; Women's Fiction; Writers and Writing

Now Try: Strong women characters who learn more about themselves than they ever thought possible are a trademark of Berg's novels, which include *The Art of Mending*, *Open House*, *Talk Before Sleep*, and *Durable Goods*. Another novel in which a woman learns a secret about her husband's life as he nears death is Zoë Heller's *The Believers*; Charlotte Bacon's novel *Split Estate* also features a family struggling to live normally in the aftermath of a spouse's death. Joan Didion, a novelist and author, wrote a memoir of her grieving process after her husband, author John Gregory Dunne, died; it is titled *The Year of Magical Thinking*.

Berne, Suzanne.

A Ghost at the Table. **Algonquin Books of Chapel Hill, 2006. 292pp. ISBN 978-1565123342.**

Suspicion about their father's role in their mother's death twenty-five years earlier is only one of the reasons sisters Cynthia and Frances have spent most of their adult lives widely separated from one another. When Frances plans a Thanksgiving family get-together and invites her sister, plans spiral out of control when they are also forced to bring their father to stay at Frances's house until a spot can open up for him in a nursing home. Under the same roof, and with the additional complications of Frances's faltering marriage, rebellious teenage daughters, and the resurgence of their own complex feelings about one another and their father, the sisters find that no matter how much family members love one another, it is not always possible to live together.

Subjects: Book Groups; Dysfunctional Families; Family Relationships; Family Secrets; Fathers and Daughters; First Person; Marriage; Multigenerational Fiction; Parkinson's Disease; Psychological Fiction; Teenage Girls; Teenagers; Women Authors; Writers and Writing

Now Try: Berne is also the author of the novels *A Crime in the Neighborhood* and *A Perfect Arrangement*. Another novel in which a parent suffers from a debilitating disease and family secrets abound is Stephanie Kallos's *Sing Them Home*; other novels in which family reunions don't go as planned include Elizabeth Berg's *The Art of Mending*, Tawni O'Dell's *Sister Mine*, and Kathryn Harrison's *Envy: A Novel*. Another novel featuring a lifelong and rocky relationship between two sisters is Julia Glass's *I See You Everywhere*; the nonfiction title *The Sisters Antipodes*, by Jane Alison, also focuses on sibling relationships and family secrets. Other nonfiction memoirs in which family relationships are explored might also be suggested, such as Meg Federico's *Welcome to the Departure Lounge: Adventures in Mothering Mother* and A. M. Homes's *The Mistress's Daughter*.

Bingham, Sallie.

Red Car: Stories. **Sarabande Books, 2008. 181pp. ISBN 9781932511598.**

The former director of the National Book Critics Circle offers twelve modern and surprisingly upbeat stories about characters who have made sometimes eccentric decisions and choices, but who nonetheless manage to put together fairly happy lives, including stories about a woman who marries four times but remains sanguine about marriage and parenthood; a family living in France at the close of

World War II; and a writer living an isolated life in Colorado, who discovers that helping others can be a transformative experience.

Subjects: France; Love Affairs; Quick Reads; Short Stories; Southern Authors; Women Authors

Now Try: Bingham is also the author of the story collection *Transgressions* and the memoir *Passion and Prejudice: A Family Memoir*, about her wealthy family's newspaper empire. Other skillfully written short story collections might appeal to these readers, including Lorrie Moore's *Birds of America*, Antonya Nelson's *Nothing Right*, Dan Chaon's *Among the Missing*, Elizabeth McCracken's *Here's Your Hat, What's Your Hurry*, Carol Windley's *Home Schooling: Stories*, and Amy Bloom's *A Blind Man Can See How Much I Love You*.

Bloom, Amy.

🌱 *Away: A Novel*. **Random House, 2007. 240pp. ISBN 9781400063567.**

Bloom's lyrically written novel relates the experiences of Lillian Leyb, a woman whose will to survive and chart her own course takes her from Russia (where her family and daughter Sophie are killed in a pogrom) to New York City in the 1920s, then Seattle, and eventually Alaska, and from relationships of convenience with her New York employer (and his father) to one of true partnership. Nothing is certain in this novel, not even Lillian's understanding of what happened in Russia after she sent her daughter running to escape their attackers, except her resourcefulness and her ability to find joy in a life not characterized by stability.

Second Appeal: Language

Subjects: 1920s; Alaska; Anti-Semitism; Book Groups; Classics; Historical Fiction; Immigrants and Immigration; Jews and Judaism; Love Affairs; New York City; Russia; Seattle; Women Authors; Women's Fiction

Awards: ALA Notable

Now Try: Bloom is also the author of the novels *Come to Me* (a National Book Award finalist), *A Blind Man Can See How Much I Love You*, and *Love Invents Us*; she has also written a slim but informative and sympathetic nonfiction book, *Normal: Transsexual CEOs, Crossdressing Cops, and Hermaphrodites with Attitudes*. Two other historical fiction titles featuring strong women characters (set in the early twentieth century) are Erin McGraw's *The Seamstress of Hollywood Boulevard* and Robert Goolrick's *A Reliable Wife*; other historical novels about the immigrant experience might appeal, such as Katie Singer's *The Wholeness of a Broken Heart* or Amy Tan's *The Bonesetter's Daughter*. (Another novel, *Away*, by Jane Urquhart, also features strong women characters and the theme of immigration.) Nonfiction narratives about the immigrant experience might also be suggested, including Eva Hoffman's *After Such Knowledge* and *Lost in Translation*, Helen Fremont's *After Long Silence*, and Valerie Steiker's *The Leopard Hat: A Daughter's Story*. Another novel in which a character endures hardships and danger is Audrey Schulman's *The Cage*.

Boyd, William.

Any Human Heart. **Knopf, 2002. 498pp. ISBN 9780375414930.**

Written in diary form, this story of the twentieth-century life of Logan Mountstuart starts when Logan is seventeen years old (in 1923) and continues through his education, his making his way in the world, his love affairs with singular women, World War II, and the other experiences of, in his own description, a "man of the world," until his death in 1991. In addition to Logan's strong and personal voice, this novel offers vicarious thrills in the form of the many historical personages who wander through its pages, including James Joyce, Pablo Picasso, the Duke and Duchess of Windsor, Virginia Woolf, and many, many more (the "novel" even includes an index listing these famous people and places). Mountstuart's tale is truly that of the twentieth century.

Subjects: 20th Century; Aging; Art and Artists; Biographical Fiction; Book Groups; British Authors; Diary; Epic Reads; First Person; Love Affairs; Men's Lives; Satire; Travel; World History; Writers and Writing

Now Try: *New Confessions* is another "fictional biography" by Boyd; his other novels, such as *Brazzaville Beach, An Ice Cream War,* and *Armadillo,* explore human interactions. In Mark Helprin's *Memoir from an Antproof Case* an old man writes about his life for his young son; the protagonist of Jonathan Hull's *Losing Julia* ruminates on his longtime love for the wife of his best friend. Experience the tumult of an artist's life in *Burnt Umber,* by Sheldon Green, or Jane Urquhart's *The Underpainter.*

Boyle, T. Coraghessan

Talk Talk. **Viking, 2006. 340pp. ISBN 9780670037704.**

When Dana Halter is unceremoniously booked into jail for the weekend after a routine traffic stop revealed outstanding warrants for her arrest, she has a difficult time making her jailers understand that they must be looking for some other Dana Halter. Chief among her difficulties is the fact that she is deaf and can't seem to get anyone to understand her speech; when she finally is allowed to call her boyfriend, Bridger Martin, he doesn't have much more success convincing the authorities that she can't possibly be the felon they're looking for. Eventually exonerated as a victim of identity theft, Halter decides to track down her alter ego, taking Bridger along for a trip that will prove more dangerous than either imagined. Although told primarily from Dana's point of view, the man who stole her identity, William "Peck" Wilson, is also allowed to tell his part of the story, meaning that Boyle's readers get a surprising look inside the characters of both protagonist and antagonist.

Second Appeal: Story

Subjects: Book Groups; California; Deafness; Disabilities; Fraud; Identity Theft; Multiple Viewpoints; Suspense; Theft; Travel

Now Try: Boyle writes in many different styles, but his books of short stories might particularly appeal to these readers, including *Tooth and Claw* and *After the Plague;* his novel *The Tortilla Curtain* also features multiple viewpoints. Other books in which couples join in the struggle against malevolent outside forces include Matt Ruff's *Set This House in Order* and James Hynes's decidedly more surreal *Kings of Infinite Space;* Patrick Somerville's *The Cradle* is also about a couple's search for a woman's sense of identity (as embodied in the cradle her mother owned).

The Women: A Novel. **Viking, 2009. 451pp. ISBN 9780670020416.**

In his time, infamous architect Frank Lloyd Wright was a favorite subject of the press, not only for his professional exploits and successes but also for his complex personal life. In this sprawling historical novel, Boyle tells Wright's story by relating the stories of the four very different women who loved him most: Kitty Tobin, Mamah Cheney, Maude Miriam Noel, and Olgivanna Milanoff. The novel is narrated by a (fictional) apprentice of Wright's and proceeds backward in time through Wright's tumultuous love affairs, devoting plenty of attention to not only his quirks, but also the personalities of the women.

Subjects: 20th Century; Adultery; Architects and Architecture; Biographical Fiction; Book Groups; Historical Fiction; Love Affairs; Marriage; Men Writing as Women; Multiple Viewpoints; Society; Wisconsin; Wright, Frank Lloyd

Now Try: Fans of this historical novel might consider Boyle's other historical novels, including *The Road to Wellville*, *Riven Rock*, *World's End*, and *Drop City* (about life on a 1970s commune). Another part of Wright's life is told in Nancy Horan's novel *Loving Frank*; those readers really fascinated by the subject might want to consider a biography of the architect such as Meryle Secrest's *Frank Lloyd Wright: A Biography*. Other fictional biographies, or novels with historical characters, might also appeal, such as Michael Cunningham's *The Hours*, Jody Shields's *The Fig Eater*, Paulette Jiles's *The Color of Lightning,* or E. L. Doctorow's *Ragtime*.

Brinkman, Kiara.

Up High in the Trees. **Grove Press, 2007. 328pp. ISBN 9780802118479.**

Eight-year-old Sebby is devastated by the sudden death of his mother, who was struck by a car on one of her habitual late-night jogs, and doesn't receive much in the way of comfort from his father, who is also bereft. When the pair move to their summer vacation house in the countryside, Sebby finds two real friends in the neighbor children, Jackson and Shelly, who don't seem put off by his sadness or his Asperger's syndrome, and whose single mother arguably lets them run too wild but also provides a sympathetic ear for both Sebby and his father.

Subjects: Asperger's Syndrome; Child's Point of View; Death and Dying; Family Relationships; Fathers and Sons; First Novels; First Person; Friendships; Grief; Marriage; Massachusetts; Women Authors

Now Try: Another novel that features a sympathetic main character with autism is Mark Haddon's *The Curious Incident of the Dog in the Night-Time*. Anne Tyler's *The Tin-Can Tree*, Charlotte Bacon's *Split Estate*, and Mary Lawson's *Crow Lake* all examine how grief affects family life. In Alison Smith's memoir *Name All the Animals*, the author describes the death of her eighteen year old brother and how that event changed her family forever; although he was older than the protagonist in Brinkman's novel when he lost both his parents, Dave Eggers provides a poignant first-person account of his reaction to their deaths and his subsequent raising of his younger brother in *A Heartbreaking Work of Staggering Genius*.

Brookner, Anita.

Leaving Home. **Random House, 2005. 212pp. ISBN 9781400064144.**

At the age of twenty-six, Emma Roberts knows the time has come to leave home, but has difficulty formulating a plan about where she will go and why. Eventually, determining that she would like to study classical garden design, she moves to a small apartment in Paris, where she is befriended by the ebullient and flamboyant Françoise Desnoyers, whose own relationship with her controlling mother is as tempestuous as Roberts's relationship with her shy mother was quiet.

Subjects: 1970s; British Authors; Family Relationships; France; Friendships; Gardening; Mothers and Daughters; Paris; Women Authors

Now Try: Brookner is a prolific author, and many of her novels share this one's deceptively quiet storytelling and slow pacing; fans of this title might also enjoy *The Rules of Engagement*, *The Bay of Angels*, *Undue Influence*, *Falling Slowly*, and *Hotel du Lac*. Another author whose books include quiet portrayals of women and the choices they make is Anne Tyler; her novels *Searching for Caleb*, *The Clock Winder*, *Back When We Were Grownups*, *The Amateur Marriage*, and *Ladder of Years* might be suggested. The quietly fascinating biography of gardener and writer Elizabeth Lawrence, *No One Gardens Alone: A Life of Elizabeth Lawrence*, by Emily Herring Wilson, might also prove an interesting read-alike.

Brooks, Geraldine.

🌹 *March.* **Viking, 2005. 280pp. ISBN 9780670033355.**

Brooks tells the story of the patriarch of the March family portrayed in Louisa May Alcott's classic novel *Little Women*, describing his experiences fighting in the Civil War, the changes he undergoes in some of his most fervently held beliefs and principles, and his desire to return to his family.

Subjects: Australian Authors; Civil War; Classics; Fathers and Daughters; First Person; Historical Fiction; Literary Allusions; Men's Lives; Race Relations; War; Women Authors; Women Writing as Men

Awards: Pulitzer Prize

Now Try: Brooks is also the author of the literary historical novels *Year of Wonders* and *People of the Book*. Other literary retellings that might appeal to these readers include the classic *Wide Sargasso Sea* by Jean Rhys (a reimagining of Charlotte Brontë's *Jane Eyre*), Jon Clinch's *Finn*, and Colm Tóibín's *The Master*. Readers might enjoy Brooks's source material, the novel *Little Women*, while those interested in the Civil War might consider Charles Frazier's classic novel *Cold Mountain*. John Matteson's fascinating biography of the real-life relationship between Alcott and her father Bronson, *Eden's Outcasts: The Story of Louisa May Alcott and Her Father*, might also be a fun related read.

Brown, Carrie.

The Rope Walk. **Pantheon, 2007. 321pp. ISBN 9780375424632.**

The summer Alice turns ten years old, two individuals who will have a great impact on her life move to her small Vermont community: Theo, a biracial boy who quickly becomes her best friend and confidante, and Kenneth Fitzgerald, an older man suffering from AIDS, who is coming home to live with and be cared for by his sister. As the months unfold, the unlikely trio of Alice, Theo, and Kenneth bond over a shared love of books and adventure (particularly adventures found in the journals of Lewis and Clark, which are read with Kenneth and then acted out by the children). After building a "rope walk" (a planned path with rope for a guide) for Kenneth, a tragic event occurs that leads to the adults in their lives separating Alice and Theo, a state of affairs that seems to them unjust at best and needlessly cruel at worst.

Subjects: AIDS; Biracial Characters; Book Groups; Books and Reading; Coming-of-age; Death and Dying; Family Relationships; Fathers and Daughters; Friendships; Siblings; Small-Town Life; Vermont; Women Authors

Now Try: Brown is also the author of the enduringly popular romance novel *Lamb in Love*, as well as the novels *Rose's Garden* and *Confinement*. Books in which the power of reading and learning are described might appeal; these include Masha Hamilton's *The Camel Bookmobile* and Brian Hall's *The Saskiad*. Brown's novels almost read like classics from an earlier age; her readers might consider other readable classics such as Harper Lee's *To Kill a Mockingbird* or Ernest J. Gaines's *A Lesson Before Dying*.

Byatt, A. S.

🏵 *The Biographer's Tale.* Knopf, 2000. 305pp. ISBN 9780375411144.

Phineas G. Nanson abruptly decides, in the middle of his studies, to get out of the field of postmodern literary criticism and into the earthier, more fact-bound world of biography writing. He takes as his subject a biographer named Scholes Destry-Scholes, whose many subjects included Carl Linneaus, Sir Francis Galton, and Henrik Ibsen. His fascination with life stories nicely morphs into a fascination for life, particularly when he meets Vera, the charming and lovely niece of Destry-Scholes.

Subjects: 1990s; Biographical Fiction; British Authors; Satire; Women Authors; Writers and Writing; Young Men

Awards: New York Times Notable

Now Try: Byatt herself is a scholar and a lover of literature, both of which attributes come through in her earlier novels, *Possession* and *The Virgin in the Garden* (the first in a series of three that concludes with *Still Life* and *Babel Tower*). Carol Shields's novel *Swann*, a literary mystery about the fictional poet Mary Swann and her untimely death, might appeal to these readers; another novel about the relationship between a biographer and his subject is Sheila Heti's *Ticknor*. One of history's most famous biographers, James Boswell (author of *The Life of Samuel Johnson*), is the subject of the suspense novel *The Brothers Boswell* by Philip Baruth

Carey, Peter.

🏵 *His Illegal Self.* Knopf, 2008. 271pp. ISBN 9780307263728.

Seven-year-old Che is being raised in relative luxury in 1970s New York City by his affluent grandmother, when a woman claiming to be his mother shows up and whisks him off to Australia. Although originally excited to be reunited with his mother (the woman, named Dial, turns out to be not his mother after all, but rather a messenger from her) and hopeful that he would also soon meet his father, the reality of the commune to which the woman takes him is infighting and a daily struggle to survive.

Subjects: 1960s; 1970s; Australia; Australian Authors; Family Relationships; Fugitives; Grandmothers; Kidnapping; New York City; Psychological Fiction; Suspense; Young Boys

Awards: New York Times Notable

Now Try: Carey has written other novels about precarious interpersonal relationships, including *Theft* and *Oscar and Lucinda*; in his historical novel *The True History of the Kelly Gang* he describes another band of outlaws. The life of a fugitive is excellently described in Janis Hallowell's novel *She Was*; T. C. Boyle's novel *Drop City* also features a commune, while his novel *Talk Talk* features a pair of characters on the move, following the thieves who have stolen one of their identities. Tim Winton's *Breath* is also an unnerving coming-of-age boy's tale set in Australia.

Cartwright, Justin.

🏵 *The Promise of Happiness.* St. Martin's Press, 2006. 308pp. ISBN 978-0312348809.

The members of the Judd family have their hands full with their own problems: Charles, the patriarch, is struggling with the demise of his professional career; his wife Daphne has turned to cooking as an outlet for her frustrations; and their three children, Sophie, Charlie, and Juliet, are struggling with their careers and relationships. Juliet's career as an art historian has the most bearing on the story, as when the novel opens she is being released from jail for her part in the trafficking of stolen Tiffany windows. As the family members make their separate ways toward one another and a reunion in Great Britain, they also find themselves learning once again the power of family ties and the connections forged to the people who may not know you the best, but have known you the longest.

Subjects: Art and Artists; British Authors; Family Relationships; Family Secrets; Marriage; Prisons; Siblings

Awards: Hawthornden Prize

Now Try: Cartwright is also the author of the Costa Award–winning novel *Leading the Cheers*, as well as the historical novel *The Song Before It Is Sung*. Other winners of the Hawthornden Prize (a British award) might appeal to these readers, including Nicola Barker's *Darkmans*, Helen Simpson's story collection *Getting a Life*, and John Lanchester's *The Debt to Pleasure*. Other novels about sibling relationships include Antonya Nelson's *Living to Tell*, Anne Tyler's *Dinner at the Homesick Restaurant*, and Julia Glass's *I See You Everywhere*. Another novel about family relationships and art is Dara Horn's *The World to Come*; Sarah Thornton's book-length journalistic investigation of the art world and those involved in it, *Seven Days in the Art World*, might also be a fun related read.

Chamberlain, Marisha.

The Rose Variations. Soho Press, 2009. 341pp. ISBN 9781569475386.

The year is 1975, and Rose MacGregor is teaching at a small college in St. Paul, Minnesota, where she finds that obtaining tenure is the least of the problems facing a young independent woman who is trying to balance a career in writing and teaching music with finding true love (as well as trying to navigate complex friendships with Alan, a closeted colleague in the department, and Frances, the department's secretary and former mistress of another of Rose's colleagues).

Subjects: 1970s; Academia; Book Groups; First Novels; Friendships; GLBTQ; Love Affairs; Minnesota; Music and Musicians; Women Authors

Now Try: Other books featuring women who work in academia include Jean Hanff Korelitz's *Admission* and A. S. Byatt's *Possession*. This novel, though set in the 1970s, has a timeless feel to it; classics such as Virginia Woolf's *Mrs. Dalloway* and Edith Wharton's *The House of Mirth* might also be suggested.

Christensen, Lars Saabye.

🏵 *The Half Brother.* Arcade, 2004. 682pp. ISBN 9781559707152.

This epic novel of one Norwegian family's history over the course of fifty years hinges on the relationship between the narrator, Barnum, and his half-brother, Fred. The older brother, Fred, was conceived when their mother Vera was raped in the waning days of World War II; angry, tough, and prone to mood swings, he serves as the protector of his younger half-brother Barnum throughout much of the narrative. As unpredictable as his brother can be, when he leaves the family to make his way in the world, Barnum feels set adrift and continues to feel that way throughout much of his adult life; he finds success as a screenwriter but finds it difficult to maintain long-lasting relationships with either friends or his wife,

Vivian, whose infidelity is proven when she becomes pregnant (which preys on Barnum's mind, as he knows he is infertile).

Subjects: Books in Translation; Brothers; Epic Reads; European History; Family Relationships; First Novels; Historical Fiction; Norway; Norwegian Authors; Rape; Siblings; World War II

Awards: ALA Notable

Now Try: Other books featuring complex family dynamics might also be suggested, such as Jeremy Page's *Salt*, Junot Díaz's *The Brief Wondrous Life of Oscar Wao*, Jayne Anne Phillips's *Lark and Termite*, and Per Petterson's *In the Wake* and *Out Stealing Horses*. Another wonderful novel set in Holland during the Nazi era is Harry Mulisch's *The Assault*. Two fascinating nonfiction accounts of World War II experiences in the Scandinavian countries might also appeal: David Howarth's *We Die Alone: A World War II Epic of Escape and Endurance*, and Odd Nansen's classic diary *From Day to Day*.

Clarke, Breena.

Stand the Storm. **Little, Brown, 2008. 321pp. ISBN 9780316007047.**

"Sewing Annie" Coats, the matriarch in this multigenerational tale set in Georgetown just before, during, and after the Civil War, takes care to teach her children her valuable sewing and quilting skills, knowing that slaves who display unique talents are more valuable to their owners and thus less likely to be sold and separated. That emphasis on family is woven throughout the story, as Annie's son Gabriel is apprenticed to a town tailor who secretly disapproves of slavery; eventually he will work to buy himself into quasi-freedom and join the Union Army, acting under the belief that he must fight to protect his and his family's tenuous liberty.

Second Appeal: Story

Subjects: 19th Century; African American Authors; African Americans; Book Groups; Civil War; Family Relationships; Historical Fiction; Mothers and Sons; Quilting; Race Relations; Sewing; Slavery; Washington, D.C.; Women Authors

Now Try: Clarke is also the author of the popular Oprah book *River, Cross My Heart*. Other historical novels in which the Civil War and slavery are key issues are Lawrence Hill's *Someone Knows My Name* and *Any Known Blood*, Edward P. Jones's *The Known World*, James McBride's *Song Yet Sung,* and Paulette Jiles's *Enemy Women* and *The Color of Lightning*. Novels in which sewing and quilting play an important role might also be suggested, such as Jennifer Chiaverini's *The Runaway Quilt* (all of Chiaverini's Elm Creek Quilts novels might appeal) or Tiffany Baker's *The Little Giant of Aberdeen County*. Novels featuring strong African American women might also appeal, such as Sue Monk Kidd's *The Secret Life of Bees*, April Reynolds's *Knee Deep in Wonder*, Lalita Tademy's *Cane River*, and the novels of Pearl Cleage (especially *What Looks Like Crazy on an Ordinary Day*), or even the nonfiction account *Having Our Say: The Delany Sisters' First 100 Years* by Sarah Delany and Elizabeth Delany.

Cleave, Chris.

Little Bee. **Simon & Schuster, 2009. 271pp. ISBN 9781416589631.**

Although the jacket copy implores those who have read this novel not to tell their friends the story (because "the magic is in how the story unfolds"), what can be divulged is that it is the story of two women, from different parts of the globe, whose lives collide once, violently, on a beach in Africa, and then come together a second time as a result of that first meeting. The narrative follows the exploits of Little Bee, a young woman from Nigeria, who makes her way to Great Britain, and through no little amount of ingenuity, ends up on the doorstep of Sarah O'Rourke (and her family, although Sarah's husband Andrew commits suicide—seemingly just days before Little Bee's arrival).

Subjects: Africa; Book Groups; British Authors; Family Relationships; First Person; Great Britain; Immigrants and Immigration; Marriage; Men Writing as Women; Multicultural; Multiple Viewpoints; Parenting; Quick Reads

Now Try: Cleave has written another novel centering on current political events, *Incendiary*. Critics have compared this novel to Khaled Hosseini's *The Kite Runner* (primarily for its moving characters and plot, which make it a solid book club choice); other novels about moral choices and unforeseeable events might also be offered to these readers, including William Styron's classic *Sophie's Choice* and Anne Tyler's somewhat lighter but still thoughtful *Saint Maybe*. Abraham Verghese's novel *Cutting for Stone* also follows a character from one continent to another; another formidable female character can be found in Monica Ali's *Brick Lane*. Also of interest might be nonfiction titles from Africa, particularly Ishmael Beah's memoir of his time as a child soldier, *A Long Way Gone*, or Helene Cooper's *The House at Sugar Beach: In Search of a Lost African Childhood*, about her youth in Liberia and how she had to flee the country during its civil war (leaving behind an adopted sister).

Clinch, Jon.

🐾 *Finn: A Novel.* **Random House, 2007. 287pp. ISBN 9781400065912.**

In this literary reimagining of Mark Twain's novel *The Adventures of Huckleberry Finn*, Clinch tells a story of racism, hatred, and seething resentments and bad blood, centering on Huck Finn's father, Pap Finn. The book opens with the discovery of an African American woman's corpse in the river, and the narrative really doesn't become any gentler after that, as Finn's complex attitude toward African Americans is revealed, along with his terrible relationship with his domineering father the Judge, and his propensity for drunkenness and violence.

Second Appeal: Story

Subjects: American South; Book Groups; Coming-of-age; Family Relationships; Fathers and Sons; First Novels; Literary Allusions; Mississippi; Murder; Race Relations; Twain, Mark

Awards: ALA Notable

Now Try: Readers fascinated by this novel might already have read them, but consider suggesting Mark Twain's classics *The Adventures of Huckleberry Finn* and *Tom Sawyer*. Also of interest might be other novels that offer new perspectives on literary classics, including Nancy Rawles's *My Jim*, Geraldine Brooks's *March*, or Alice Randall's *The Wind Done Gone*; more straightforward literary historical fiction like Robert Hicks's *The Widow of the South* or Christopher Bigsby's *Beautiful Dreamer* might also be offered. Nonfiction history accounts that might appeal to these readers include Annette Gordon-Reed's *The Hemingses of Monticello* and Anthony Gerzina's *Mr. and Mrs. Prince: How an Extraordinary Eighteenth-Century Family Moved out of Slavery and into Legend*; Mat Johnson's graphic novel *Incognegro* might also be a good read-alike.

Coomer, Joe.

🏵 *One Vacant Chair.* **Graywolf Press, 2003. 273pp. ISBN 9781555973858.**

When Sarah learns that her grandmother' dying wish was for her ashes to be scattered in Scotland, she suddenly finds herself traveling there with her Aunt Edna, an artist who paints portraits of empty chairs and harbors a surprising number of secrets, including her love for a blind neighbor and the small but decidedly illegal method of pilfering that will pay for their trip to Scotland.

Subjects: Art and Artists; Death and Dying; Elderly; Family Relationships; Gentle Reads; Humor; Men Writing as Women; Obesity; Scotland; Small Press; Texas; Travel

Awards: S. Mariella Gable Prize

Now Try: Coomer's other novels, which blend humor and vivid characterization, include *Pocketful of Names, Apologizing to Dogs, The Loop,* and *Beachcombing for a Shipwrecked God.* Several other male writers with offbeat senses of humor are Clyde Edgerton (*The Bible Salesman, Lunch at the Piccadilly,* and *Walking Across Egypt*), Michael Malone (*Handling Sin* and *Foolscap*), Timothy Schaffert (*The Phantom Limbs of the Rollow Sisters* and *The Singing and Dancing Daughters of God*), Chang-Rae Lee (*Aloft*), and John Irving (*The World According to Garp* and *A Prayer for Owen Meany*).

Crandell, Doug.

Hairdos of the Mildly Depressed. **Virgin Books, 2008. 273pp. ISBN 978-0753513781.**

Brad Orville has a lot on his mind: he's caring for his brother Compton, who is recovering from a brain trauma injury; he's still dealing with an earlier deception perpetrated on him by that same brother; and Compton and his disabled wife Peaches are expecting a baby. As stressful as all those problems are, Brad thinks he could handle them, . . . if only he wasn't going bald as well. Humor and absurdity abound in this strangely gentle novel of finding happiness in the midst of nonstop challenges.

Subjects: American South; Brain; Brothers; Disabilities; Dysfunctional Families; Family Relationships; Georgia; Health Issues; Humor; Men's Lives; Quick Reads

Now Try: This is the second novel in a series (<u>Beauty Knows No Pain</u>) by Crandell, whose earlier novel *The Flawless Skin of Ugly People* might appeal to his readers, as might his darkly humorous memoir *Pig Boy's Wicked Bird.* Gently eccentric male characters also populate the novels of Richard Russo (*Nobody's Fool* and *Straight Man*); Jim Knipfel's hilariously bitter nonfiction memoirs might also appeal, including *Slackjaw* and *Ruining It for Everybody.*

Cusk, Rachel.

Arlington Park. **Farrar, Straus & Giroux, 2006. 248pp. ISBN 9780374100803.**

The residents of the London suburb of Arlington Park are experiencing various levels of contentment (and in some cases, discontent) in their lives; in this novel, told over the course of one day in the neighborhood, the lives of Juliet Randall, Amanda Clapp, Maisie Carrington, and Christine Lanham intersect as they go to their jobs, talk among themselves, host dinner parties, and even give birth. Readers should note that the label "domestic fiction" applied to this story does not imply coziness; Cusk's tone often veers closer to biting social commentary than to sentimentality.

Subjects: British Authors; Dark Humor; Day in the Life; Domestic Fiction; Great Britain; Marriage; Multiple Viewpoints; Parenting; Suburbia; Women Authors

Now Try: Cusk's first novel, *Saving Agnes*, won the 1993 Whitbread Prize for Best Novel; since then she has written prolifically, producing the novels *The Country Life*, *The Temporary*, *The Lucky Ones*, and *In the Fold*, as well as the nonfiction titles *A Life's Work: On Becoming a Mother* and *The Last Supper: A Summer in Italy*. Of particular interest to these readers might be other domestic novels that are anything but sentimental, such as Anne Tyler's *The Accidental Tourist* and *Saint Maybe*, Tom Perrotta's *Little Children*, or Cheryl Mendelson's *Morningside Heights*; nonfiction narratives about the challenges of parenthood might also appeal, including Michael Lewis's *Home Game*, Neal Pollack's *Alternadad*, or Heather Armstrong's *It Sucked and Then I Cried: How I Had a Baby, a Breakdown, and a Much Needed Margarita*.

In the Fold. **Little, Brown, 2005. 262pp. ISBN 9780316058278.**

The grass is always greener on the other side of the fence, and nowhere more so than in Cusk's novel of relationships and manners, in which Michael is introduced to his friend Adam Hanbury's country estate and home, known as "Egypt," during college. Enthralled by the country surroundings and the surface gentility of Adam's family, Michael retains Egypt in his memory as an idyll, and when he is invited back, years later, to help with seasonal work (specifically, with the lambing), he is eager to go. Also high on his list of reasons for going is his increasingly difficult and unhappy marriage to Rebecca and his failure to understand the sometimes strange behavior of his four-year-old son Hamish; but it doesn't take long for him to realize that other families, no matter how tranquil they seem on the surface, all have their own histories, resentments, and challenges.

Subjects: Agriculture; Animals; British Authors; Coming-of-age; Domestic Fiction; Family Relationships; Family Secrets; First Person; Friendships; Great Britain; Humor; Marriage; Men's Lives; Rural Life; Women Authors; Women Writing as Men

Now Try: Cusk is also the author of the novels *Arlington Park*, *The Country Life*, and *The Lucky Ones*. Other books in which individuals fall in love with families that are not their own are Evelyn Waugh's classic novel *Brideshead Revisited*, Alan Hollinghurst's *The Line of Beauty*, Anita Brookner's *Leaving Home*, Benjamin Taylor's *The Book of Getting Even*, and even Richard Russo's *Nobody's Fool*. Cusk's very British writing style is somewhat similar to Joanna Trollope's; her novels *Second Honeymoon* and *Brother and Sister* might also be suggested.

Desai, Kiran.

🎗 *The Inheritance of Loss*. **Atlantic Monthly Press, 2006. 324pp. ISBN 978-0871139290.**

With civil unrest running high and their resources running low, the Judge, his granddaughter Sai, and their Cook find the safe haven of their home frequently invaded by soldiers and young men taking advantage of the politically unsettled times (the novel is set in India during the 1980s). In addition to Sai's tale, the Judge's earlier life and his unhappy marriage provide context for his relationship with his granddaughter, and the Cook's son, working a variety of low-wage restaurant jobs as an illegal immigrant in America, also narrates part of the story.

Second Appeal: Setting

Subjects: 1980s; Book Groups; Classics; Family Relationships; Grandfathers; Immigrants and Immigration; India; Indian Authors; Multicultural; Multigenerational Fiction; New York City; Political Fiction; Restaurants; Women Authors

Awards: ALA Notable; Man Booker Prize; National Book Critics Circle Award; New York Times Notable

Now Try: Desai is also the author of the novel *Hullabaloo in the Guava Orchard*. Other Booker prize-winning novels set in India might be suggested to these readers, including *The God of Small Things* by Arundhati Roy, *The White Tiger* by Aravind Adiga, and the classic *Heat and Dust* by Ruth Prawer Jhabvala. Bapsi Sidhwa's multigenerational novel *Cracking India* might also be a good read-alike for this title. Novels featuring South Asian and immigration themes might also appeal, such as Monica Ali's *Brick Lane*, Anne Cheria's *A Good Indian Wife*, Tania James's *Atlas of Unknowns*, Saher Alam's *The Groom to Have Been*, Chitra Banerjee Divakaruni's *Sister of My Heart* and *The Vine of Desire*, and Preeta Samarasan's *Evening Is the Whole Day*.

Divakaruni, Chitra.

The Vine of Desire. **Doubleday, 2002. 373pp. ISBN 9780385497299.**

In this sequel to *Sister of My Heart*, Divakaruni continues the life stories of cousins Sudha and Anju as they leave India and resettle in the Bay area of California. Although close, their jealousy of each other's lives (each focusing her desire on what her cousin has that she doesn't) eventually tears them apart.

Subjects: Book Groups; California; Domestic Fiction; Family Relationships; Immigrants and Immigration; Indian Authors; Marriage; Women Authors; Women's Fiction

Now Try: Divakaruni is also the author of *Sister of My Heart*, which tells the first part of Sudha's and Anju's story, as well as the novels *The Mistress of Spices*, *The Unknown Errors of Our Lives*, *Arranged Marriage*, and the fantasy novel *The Palace of Illusions*. Another novel that follows the lives of sisters who share a complex relationship is Lisa See's historical novel *Shanghai Girls*. Also of interest might be Jhumpa Lahiri's story collection *Unaccustomed Earth* or her novel *The Namesake*, Tania James's *Atlas of Unknowns*, or Anita Desai's *Fasting, Feasting*.

Doig, Ivan.

The Eleventh Man. **Harcourt, 2008. 406pp. ISBN 9780151012435.**

After leading their Montana college football team to a championship, all eleven teammates make one last play in tandem: they volunteer for service during World War II. They are dispersed to different battle locations around the globe. Although he enters pilot training, an accident grounds Ben Reinking, who is soon given the assignment of tracking down and writing about his former teammates for a publication run by the combined armed forces. Bad luck seems to follow his friends as, one after another, they are killed; meanwhile Ben, being flown to his interviews by the wife of another serviceman, struggles with their mutual attraction.

Subjects: 1940s; Death and Dying; Friendships; Gentle Reads; Historical Fiction; Love Affairs; Men's Lives; Montana; Sports; World War II

Now Try: Doig's other novels include *The Whistling Season* and the McCaskill Family series (starting with *English Creek*); he has also written two memoirs, *This*

House of Sky and *Heart Earth*. Other books set during the era might appeal, such as Anne Tyler's *The Amateur Marriage*, Homer Hickam's *The Far Reaches*, Marge Piercy's *Gone to Soldiers*, and Tony Earley's *The Blue Star*; also consider Tom Brokaw's nonfiction titles *The Greatest Generation* and *The Greatest Generation Speaks* or Bob Greene's *Once Upon a Town: The Miracle of the North Platte Canteen*.

Donoghue, Emma.

Landing: A Novel. **Harcourt, 2007. 324pp. ISBN 9780151012978.**

Twenty-five year old Jude Turner, afraid of flying and tied to her independent life in a small town in Canada, meets older and more worldly Sile O'Shaughnessy while on a flight to Ireland to visit her ailing mother. Although a strong connection is formed between the two women immediately and is followed up on in subsequent passionate e-mails and letters, both continue to respond to former relationships, at the expense of forming a new one with each another.

Subjects: Canada; Epistolary Fiction; Friendships; GLBTQ; Humor; Ireland; Irish Authors; Lesbians; Love Affairs; Women Authors

Now Try: Donoghue is also the author of another novel about lesbian women's relationships, *Hood*, as well as the historical novels *Slammerkin* and *Life Mask*. Other novels that feature women falling in love are Jeanette Winterson's *Oranges Are Not the Only Fruit* and Carol Anshaw's *Lucky in the Corner*. Alison Bechdel's graphic novel memoir *Fun Home* is really more of a coming-of-age tale than a love story, but she does include some vignettes about falling in love wither other women. Carol Shields's novel *A Celibate Season* and Mark Dunn's *Ella Minnow Pea* are also both epistolary novels. Novels featuring offbeat relationships between men and women are Mameve Medwed's *Mail* and *Of Men and Their Mothers* and Anne Tyler's *Celestial Navigation* and *The Clock Winder.*

Doyle, Roddy.

Paula Spencer. **Viking, 2006. 281pp. ISBN 9780670038169.**

Doyle continues the story of Paula Spencer, whom he introduced (along with her abusive husband) in an earlier novel, *The Woman Who Walked into Doors*. This novel, which finds Spencer widowed and tenaciously clinging to sobriety, also finds her struggling in her relationships with her sons—John Paul, who has both a heroin addiction and two young children of his own,and her youngest, Jack, who is good-natured but doesn't really rely upon her as a parent—and her daughters, Nicola and Leanne (the former is too controlling; the latter, Paula worries, will follow her path of addiction and unhappiness).

Subjects: Alcoholism; Dark Humor; Domestic Fiction; Drug Abuse; Dysfunctional Families; Family Relationships; Humor; Ireland; Irish Authors; Men Writing as Women; Social Class; Widows

Now Try: Doyle's best-known novels (which make up the <u>Barrytown Trilogy</u>) about working-class individuals with both affection for and frustration with one another, *The Commitments*, *The Snapper*, and *The Van*, might appeal, as might his Booker Prize–winning novel *Paddy Clarke Ha Ha Ha*. Another novel about social class (by a British author) is David Nicholls's coming-of-age novel *A Question of Attraction*. Nick Hornby's novel *How to Be Good* features a more affluent family, but still highlights the difficulty of family relationships. Memoirs in which mothers struggle to raise their kids and make a living include Beverly Donofrio's *Riding in Cars with Boys*, Joyce Maynard's *At Home in the World*, and Debra Gwartney's *Live Through This*.

Drakulic, Slavenka.

Frida's Bed. **Penguin, 2008. 162pp. ISBN 9780143114154.**

In this novelization of artist Frida Kahlo's life, Drakulic provides the inner monologue of the singular woman and iconic artist who lived with nearly constant pain (after a childhood spent suffering from polio and surviving a horrific accident in her later teen years) but with vigor, marking out her territory as an artist, being a partner in a complex marriage that withstood multiple infidelities, and engaging in passionate love affairs of her own.

Subjects: 20th Century; Accidents; Art and Artists; Biographical Fiction; Book Groups; Books in Translation; Croatian Authors; Family Relationships; Health Issues; Kahlo, Frida; Love Affairs; Marriage; Mexico; Quick Reads; Women Authors

Now Try: Drakulic is also the author of *S: A Novel about the Balkans,* as well as nonfiction titles, including the ALA Notable book *The Balkan Express: Fragments from the Other Side of War* and *They Would Never Hurt a Fly: War Criminals on Trial in the Hague.* Novelizations of other artists' lives might also appeal, including Tracy Chevalier's *Girl with a Pearl Earring,* Susan Vreeland's *Girl in Hyacinth Blue* and *Luncheon of the Boating Party,* Harriet Scott Chessman's *Lydia Cassatt Reading the Morning Paper,* and Alexandra Lapierre's *Artemisia: A Novel.* Also of interest to these readers might be biographies of Frida Kahlo and Diego Rivera, such as Hayden Herrera's *Frida: The Biography of Frida Kahlo,* Martha Zamora's *Frida Kahlo: The Brush of Anguish,* or Diego Rivera's autobiography *My Art, My Life.*

Now Consider Nonfiction . . . Biographies of Artists, Entertainers, and Writers

These biographies take as their subject artists, entertainers, writers, and other creative trailblazers who dedicated their lives to creating great or legendary works of art or performances. Lives lived creatively are not always easy, and many of these narratives explore not only their subjects' artistic genius, but also their corresponding trials and tribulations.

Ackroyd, Peter. *Poe: A Life Cut Short.*

Bailey, Blake. *Cheever: A Life.*

Gooch, Brad. *Flannery: A Life of Flannery O'Connor.*

Gordon, Robert. *Can't Be Satisfied: The Life and Times of Muddy Waters.*

Lee, Hermione. *Edith Wharton.*

Polito, Robert. *Savage Art: A Biography of Jim Thompson.*

Solomon, Deborah. *Utopia Parkway: The Life and Work of Joseph Cornell.*

Weller, Sheila. *Girls Like Us: Carole King, Joni Mitchell, and Carly Simon —and the Journey of a Generation.*

Drury, Tom.

The Driftless Area. **Atlantic Monthly Press, 2006. 215pp. ISBN 978-0871139436.**

Pierre Hunter is meandering through his life after losing his parents— bartending at a local supper club, hunting with his good friend Roland, and generally endeavoring to walk lightly on the earth—when he goes ice skating late one night and falls through the ice. When he is rescued by a local woman, Stella Rosmarin, who is recovering from an injury of her own, he falls irretrievably in love, setting in motion a chain of events that will include a hitchhiking journey, his stealing $77,000 from a man who was trying to steal from him, and several deaths (which will not be as final as they sound).

Subjects: American Midwest, Book Groups, Coming-of-age, Dark Humor, Death and Dying, Friendships, Iowa, Love Affairs, Men's Lives, Quick Reads, Young Men

Now Try: Drury's other quietly and darkly humorous novels might appeal: *Hunts in Dreams*, *The End of Vandalism*, and *Black Brook*. Another novel that turns on an ice-skating incident and offers a likable young male protagonist is David Mitchell's *Black Swan Green*. Charles Baxter's somewhat dark but still humorous novels of the Midwest might be suggested, including *Saul and Patsy* and *The Feast of Love*; as might Jonathan Carroll's *The Ghost in Love* and Peter Hedges's *An Ocean in Iowa*. Nonfiction titles about Iowa might also prove to be fun read-alikes, particularly Peter Feldstein and Stephen Bloom's wonderful photography and text collaboration, *The Oxford Project*, and Danny Wilcox Frazier's photography book *Driftless: Photographs from Iowa*.

D'Souza, Tony.

Konkans. **Harcourt, 2008. 308pp. ISBN 9780151015191.**

Francisco D'Sai narrates his life story, describing particularly his parents' meeting and relationship (his mother, Denise, is a white woman who traveled to India with the Peace Corps, where she met his father, Lawrence, a member of the Konkan group of South Asians, who were once Hindus but were converted to Catholicism in the sixteenth century). When Denise and Lawrence return to America, Lawrence does everything he can to assimilate, climb the corporate ladder, and achieve social status, while his brother Sam, who joins them in Chicago, retains more of a sense of Konkan culture and traditions.

Subjects: 1970s; Alcoholism; Biracial Characters; Book Groups; Catholic Church; Chicago; Culture Clash; Family Relationships; First Person; Immigrants and Immigration; India; Marriage; Men's Lives; Multicultural; Race Relations; Religion; Social Class

Now Try: D'Souza is also the author of the critically well-received novel *Whiteman*. Other novels that feature characters experiencing culture clashes are Amitav Ghosh's *The Hungry Tide*, Charlotte Bacon's *There Is Room for You*, and Andre Dubus III's *The House of Sand and Fog*. Readers enthralled with this book of family and race might consider another famous memoir, Barack Obama's *Dreams from My Father*. Danzy Senna's novel *Caucasia* features biracial sisters.

Dubus, Andre.

The Garden of Last Days. **Norton, 2008. 537pp. ISBN 9780393041651.**

When April's babysitter cancels at the last minute, April has no choice but to take her three-year-old daughter Franny to work with her at a strip club, where she leaves her in the charge of the club's manager. She is soon distracted by the possibilities inherent in the wanton spending of money by an Arabic man named Bassam. When Franny disappears from the club, April's life becomes a shambles as she is maligned as an unfit parent, and another of the club's customers, A. J., is accused of kidnapping Franny. Tragedy abounds in the basic story line, but is further deepened by the awareness that the story is based on the rumors that, in the days before they perpetrated the 9/11 terror attacks, the Islamic terrorists spent money freely in the pursuit of profligate living.

Subjects: 9/11; Family Relationships; Florida; Kidnapping; Men Writing as Women; Parenting; Suspense; Terrorism

Now Try: Dubus is also the author of the Oprah book club selection *The House of Sand and Fog*, the novel *Bluesman*, and the story collection *The Cage Keeper and Other Stories*. Barbara Gowdy's *Helpless* is another unsettling novel in which a young girl disappears; other novels with connections to the events of 9/11 include Moshin Hamid's *The Young Fundamentalist*, Helen Schulman's *A Day at the Beach*, Julia Glass's *The Whole World Over*, Richard Flanagan's *The Unknown Terrorist*, and Jay McInerney's *The Good Life*.

Dybek, Stuart.

🎗 *I Sailed with Magellan*. **Farrar, Straus & Giroux, 2003. 307pp. ISBN 9780374174071.**

In this collection of eleven linked short stories, Chicago South Side native Perry Katzek moves through his life with a mixture of pragmatism and big dreams, finding joy in such experiences as his uncle's making the round of local taverns with him in tow, singing for tips, and spying on the neighbors.

Second Appeal: Setting

Subjects: Chicago; Coming-of-age; Family Relationships; First Person; Interconnected Stories; Short Stories

Awards: ALA Notable

Now Try: Dybek is also the author of the story collections *Childhood and Other Neighborhoods* and *The Coast of Chicago*, as well as the poetry collection *Brass Knuckles*. He has been compared to Nelson Algren, whose classic urban novels *The Man with the Golden Arm* and *A Walk on the Wild Side* might appeal; also of interest might by the gritty modern novels *Knockemstiff* by Donald Ray Pollock or *Crumbtown* by Joe Connelly. Other collections of linked short stories include Elizabeth Strout's *Olive Kitteridge* and several of the stories in Amanda Eyre Ward's *Love Stories in This Town*. A memoir in which an uncle and a nephew make a tavern their home away from home is J. R. Moehringer's *The Tender Bar*.

Earley, Tony.

🎗 *The Blue Star*. **Little, Brown, 2008. 286pp. ISBN 9780316199070.**

World War II has come to every small town in America, including Aliceville in North Carolina, where Jim Glass is starting his final year of high school. Growing up is complicated enough, but Jim has unwittingly made matters even more challenging by falling in love with Chrissie Steppe, whose boyfriend Bucky Bucklaw has already enlisted, and whose family views Chrissie as both his intended and a girl who can be made to work for them for free. All is not as it seems, however, between Chrissie and Bucky, between Chrissie and her mother, and between Chrissie's family and Jim's family (which consists of his uncles Zeno, Al, and Coran, and Jim's mother).

Subjects: 1940s; American Indians; American South; Biracial Characters; Book Groups; Coming-of-age; Family Relationships; Friendships; Gentle Reads; Love Affairs; Men's Lives; World War II; Young Men

Awards: New York Times Notable

Now Try: This is the sequel to Earley's novel *Jim the Boy*; he is also the author of the story collection *Here We Are in Paradise* and the part-fiction, part-memoir title *Somehow Form a Family*. Other classic coming-of-age tales might appeal to these readers, such as Harper Lee's *To Kill a Mockingbird* or Willa Cather's *My Antonia*; also of interest might be Jim Lynch's *The Highest Tide* or Ed McClanahan's *O the Clear Moment*. Novels featuring "men's stories" from World War II might also appeal, such as Wendell Berry's *A Place on Earth*, Ivan Doig's *The Eleventh Man*, and Graham Swift's *Last Orders*, while coming-of-age memoirs might also appeal, including Sterling North's classic *Rascal*, Robert Newton Peck's fictionalized memoir *A Day No Pigs Would Die*, or Willie Morris's *My Dog Skip*.

Now Consider Nonfiction . . . Coming-of-age Memoirs

Coming-of-age memoirs tell the stories of their authors' growth from childhood or adolescence into adulthood, and often include descriptions of transforming experiences that aided in that transition.

Arenas, Reinaldo. *Before Night Falls.*

Bryson, Bill. *The Life and Times of the Thunderbolt Kid.*

Conway, Jill Ker. *The Road from Coorain.*

Hickam, Homer. *Rocket Boys.*

Kimmel, Haven. *A Girl Named Zippy.*

McCarthy, Mary. *Memories of a Catholic Girlhood.*

Morris, Willie. *My Dog Skip.*

Obama, Barack. *Dreams from My Father: A Story of Race and Inheritance.*

Sessums, Kevin. *Mississippi Sissy.*

Walls, Jeannette. *The Glass Castle.*

Wolff, Tobias. *This Boy's Life.*

Enger, Leif.

🎗 *Peace Like a River.* **Atlantic Monthly Press, 2001. 313pp. ISBN 9780871137951.**

Love and violence intersect in this author's first novel, set in Minnesota. After Tommy Basca and Israel Finch (neighborhood bullies who seem intent on ratcheting their low-level menace into more serious violence) attempt to rape Davy Land's girlfriend and Davy foils that plan, they threaten his sister Swede, so Davy shoots them both when they show up at his home. After being captured by police, Davy escapes from jail and embarks on a fugitive life; for the majority of the novel, the reader follows his eleven-year-old brother Reuben and their father's attempts to find Davy.

Subjects: 1960s; Brothers; Child's Point of View; Classics; Coming-of-age; Family Relationships; First Novels; First Person; Minnesota; Siblings; YA

Awards: Alex Award

Now Try: Enger's follow-up novel to this title is *So Brave, Young and Handsome*. Other classics about crime and its effects on families and communities are Harper Lee's *To Kill a Mockingbird*, Kent Haruf's *The Tie That Binds*, David Wroblewski's *The Story of Edgar Sawtelle*, and Todd Tucker's *Over and Under*. Enger's brother, Lin Enger, has written a similarly haunting novel, *Undiscovered Country* (a literary reimagining of Hamlet). Other novels from a child's point of view include Reif Larsen's *The Collected Works of T.S. Spivet* and Victor Lodato's *Mathilda Savitch: A Novel*.

Englander, Nathan.

🌻 *The Ministry of Special Cases.* **Knopf, 2007. 339pp. ISBN 9780375404931.**
Englander's novel follows the exploits of Kaddish Poznan, an Argentine Jew who makes his living toiling in the Jewish cemetery at night, paid by individuals to chisel their family's Jewish names and family connections off gravestones. When his son Pato is seized by the authorities, Kaddish must face the literal erasing of a human being (as opposed to the figurative erasings he performs at night) and endeavor, partially through his appeal to the Ministry of Special Cases, to find out what has happened to his son during Argentina's "dirty war."

Second Appeal: Language

Subjects: 1970s; Argentina; Book Groups; Buenos Aires; Family Relationships; Fathers and Sons; Immigrants and Immigration; Jewish American Authors; Jews and Judaism; Multicultural; War

Awards: ALA Notable

Now Try: Englander is also the author of the critically acclaimed short story collection *For the Relief of Unbearable Urges*. Two other novels that combine strong character portraits and skillful prose are Michael Chabon's *The Adventures of Kavalier and Clay* and *The Yiddish Policemen's Union* (which also feature Jewish characters); Junot Díaz's *The Brief Wondrous Life of Oscar Wao* is another critically well-received novel about a young man's life and experiences, while the surreal nature of Rivka Galchen's novel *Atmospheric Disturbances* also features an Argentine character. Lawrence Thornton's novel *Imagining Argentina* shares a setting with Englander's book, as does Marcelo Birmajer's *Three Musketeers*.

Erdrich, Louise.

🌻 *The Plague of Doves.* **HarperCollins, 2008. 313pp. ISBN 9780060515126.**
Shifting back and forth in time and character viewpoint, this novel tells the stories of the residents of Pluto, North Dakota, particularly the Peace and Harp families, and all the residents who are still troubled by an unsolved mystery in their collective past: the murder of a farm family and the subsequent lynching of three wrongfully accused Native Americans. Most vividly drawn are Evelina Harp, a young part Ojibwe, part white girl who hears the town's stories from her grandfather, Seraph Milk ("Mooshum"), and Judge Antone Bazil Coutts, whose quiet and enduring love story spans much of the community's history.

Subjects: Biracial Characters; Book Groups; Classics; Coming-of-age; Family Relationships; Grandfathers; Historical Fiction; Multicultural; Multigenerational Fiction; Multiple Viewpoints; Native American Authors; Native Americans; North Dakota; Ojibwas; Women Authors

Awards: ALA Notable

Now Try: Erdrich is a master of writing novels in which characters strive to understand and own their racial heritages; some of her other titles that may appeal to these readers are *The Antelope Wife*, *The Beet Queen*, and *Love Medicine*. Other books in which incidents far in the past haunt individuals and communities include Leif Enger's *Peace Like a River*, Per Petterson's *Out Stealing Horses*, Debra Magpie Earling's *Perma Red*, and Terri Jentz's nonfiction memoir *Strange Piece of Paradise*.

Evison, Jonathan.

All about Lulu. **Soft Skull Press, 2008. 340pp. ISBN 9781593761967.**

Will Miller has a typical relationship with his father (a bodybuilder), his brothers Doug and Ross (following in their father's bodybuilding footsteps), and his stepmother, but his relationship with his stepsister Lulu is anything but typical: enthralled by her from the first moment he meets her, he spends the next twenty years of his life (the novel opens in the late 1970s) recording his observations of and thoughts about her. Although Will's first-person narrative puts him on display for the reader, the title character, Lulu, is always as elusive and unfathomable to the reader as she is to Will, until the secret she has kept from him for so many years is revealed. Although some of the novel's themes and situations will not appeal to all readers, this is nonetheless a darkly fascinating and strangely gentle exploration of the intangible and sometimes impossible nature of love.

Subjects: 1980s; 1990s; Coming-of-age; Dark Humor; Dysfunctional Families; Family Relationships; First Novels; First Person; Love Affairs; Small Press; Teenage Boys; Teenage Girls; Teenagers; YA

Now Try: A lyrical prose treatment of a forbidden relationship can also be found in Vladimir Nabokov's classic novel *Lolita*; other novels in which characters engage in love affairs that may not be right for them include Tim Winton's *Breath*, Daniel Handler's *Watch Your Mouth*, and Zoë Heller's *What Was She Thinking? Notes on a Scandal*. Yet another novel in which a young male narrator is obsessed with unknowable but unforgettable females is Jeffrey Eugenides's *The Virgin Suicides*; in Matthew Sharpe's *Sleeping Father* another family must work their way through complex relationships with one another. Two other novels about difficult relationships are Tess Callahan's *April & Oliver* and Barbara Gowdy's *The Romantic*.

Ferrell, Monica.

The Answer Is Always Yes. **Dial Press, 2008. 382pp. ISBN 9780385339292.**

Matthew Acciaccatura, of Teaneck, New Jersey, wants nothing more than to forget his former obesity problem and his high school years, in his pursuit of coolness during his first year at NYU. Although early efforts at successfully mingling with his peers achieve less than desired results, soon he becomes known as "Magic Matt," an infamous music promoter in the hottest clubs of 1990s New York—although his new career will bring with it some unsettling events and consequences. Equally unsettling are the interludes in the book when Matt's trajectory is charted by a professor named Hans Mannheim, whose fixation makes this novel equal parts dark psychological study and coming-of-age story.

Second Appeal: Language

Subjects: 1990s; Book Groups; Coming-of-age; Drug Abuse; First Novels; Friendships; Music and Musicians; New York City; Psychological Fiction; Teenage Boys; Teenagers; Women Authors; Women Writing as Men; YA; Young Men

Now Try: Jonathan Safran Foer's novels also feature simultaneously precocious and eccentric narrators; they are *Everything Is Illuminated* and *Extremely Loud and Incredibly Close*. Charles Baxter's quasi-thriller *The Soul Thief*, also about a close-knit group of college students, might appeal, as might Donna Tartt's classic *The Secret History*. Joseph O'Neill's *Netherland* is similar to Ferrell's novel in both its New York setting and its avant-garde style; Nick Flynn's memoir *Another Bullshit Night in Suck City* is also a painfully honest look at a young man's attempt to navigate an often very harsh world.

Franzen, Jonathan.

The Corrections. **Farrar, Straus & Giroux, 2001. 567pp. ISBN 978-0374129989.**

Enid, the mother of a quintessentially dysfunctional Midwestern family, struggles to reunite her three adult children with their ailing father for "one last Christmas," in this darkly funny postmodern novel.

Subjects: American Midwest; Book Groups; Brothers and Sisters; Classics; Dark Humor; Domestic Fiction; Dysfunctional Families; Epic Reads; Family Relationships; Parkinson's Disease; Siblings

Awards: ALA Notable; National Book Award

Now Try: Franzen is the author of two other novels, *The Twenty-Seventh City* and *Strong Motion*, and a book of essays, *How to Be Alone*. Two other postmodern novels with interesting characters are Don DeLillo's *White Noise* and Tom Drury's *Hunts in Dreams* (another family story set in the Midwest). Anne Tyler's novels *Dinner at the Homesick Restaurant* and *Back When We Were Grownups* also include richly drawn characters and dysfunctional families, although Tyler's are a bit more quirky than Franzen's. Another novel that includes an aging parent dealing with Parkinson's disease is *The Distinguished Guest* by Sue Miller.

Now Consider Nonfiction . . . Challenging Family Stories

Challenging family stories are nonfiction family relationship narratives that explore dysfunctional or otherwise unhappy or challenging family situations, particularly those involving abuse, the deaths of parents or siblings, or other conflicts. Many are fast paced, and they can be graphic in both descriptive detail and subject matter.

Burroughs, Augusten. *Running with Scissors.*

Cooper, Bernard. *The Bill from My Father.*

Eggers, Dave. *A Heartbreaking Work of Staggering Genius.*

Fuller, Alexandra. *Don't Let's Go to the Dogs Tonight: An African Childhood.*

Karr, Mary. *The Liar's Club.*

Sheff, David. *Beautiful Boy: A Father's Journey Through His Son's Meth Addiction.*

Genova, Alice.

Still Alice. **Pocket Books, 2007. 293pp. ISBN 9781439102817.**

Psychologist Alice Howland is enjoying a successful professional career and a fulfilling personal life when a series of disconcerting but not (so she thinks) overly serious memory lapses lead her to visit her doctor, where she receives the devastating diagnosis of early onset Alzheimer's disease. Better acquainted than most with neurological processes and issues of identity, she documents her own descent into disorientation and the erosion of what she views as the essence of her "self" and personality with heartbreaking exactness.

Subjects: Alzheimer's Disease; Book Groups; Brain; Family Relationships; First Novels; Health Issues; Medicine; Neuroscience; Psychological Fiction; Women Authors; Women's Fiction

Now Try: Another novel in which a couple struggles with this horrific disease is Kate Jennings's *Moral Hazard*. In Richard Powers's *The Echo Maker* a young man also struggles with a neurological condition that leaves him unable to recognize those close to him; the same disease manifests itself in Rivka Galchen's *Atmospheric Disturbances*. Novels in which characters face terminal prognoses might also be suggested, such as Sylvain Trudel's thoughtful *Mercury Under My Tongue*, Sam Lipsyte's *The Subject Steve*, Elisa Albert's *The Book of Dahlia*, and Roland Merullo's *A Little Love Story*. Nonfiction accounts in which authors struggle with debilitating illnesses might also appeal, including Jill Bolte Taylor's *My Stroke of Insight*, Robert McCrum's *My Year Off*, and Jill Price's *The Woman Who Can't Forget*.

Gessen, Keith.

All the Sad Young Literary Men. **Viking, 2008. 242pp. ISBN 9780670018550.**

Three very different young men struggle to find their place in the world after drifting through college. Sam dreams of producing the next great Zionist novel, but a trip to Israel and the occupied territories fails to provide any inspiration; Mark, the scholar, endlessly toils on his dissertation, but finds himself unable to concentrate after the breakup of his marriage; and (the semiautobiographical) Keith, a Russian immigrant, finds it difficult to keep his political proselytizing out of his writing. All three are indeed sad, young, and literary men, although Gessen tries to set them on the path to a bit more maturity and understanding of the world around them as the novel progresses.

Subjects: Coming-of-age; First Novels; Friendships; Immigrants and Immigration; Jews and Judaism; Marriage; Men's Lives; Writers and Writing; Young Men

Now Try: Kyle Beachy's *The Slide*, Greg Ames's *Buffalo Lockjaw*, and Benjamin Kunkel's *Indecision* also feature young male characters who are rather uncertain of what steps to take next in their adulthood. Gessen is the founder of the literary journal *n+1*; another literary publisher/blogger is Mark Sarvas, whose novel *Harry, Revised* might also appeal to these readers.

Ghosh, Amitav.

🏵 *The Hungry Tide.* **Houghton Mifflin, 2005. 333pp. ISBN 9780618329977.**

Marine biologist Piyali Roy, born in India but raised in America, returns to her home country and the Sundarban islands to study the region's rare Irawaddy river dolphins. While there, she nearly dies when she falls into the river whose inhabitants she is studying, but is saved by Fokir, an illiterate fisherman who becomes her guide. Rounding out a trio of complex characters, Roy also contracts with Kanai Dutt, an interpreter, who is struggling with the history of the region (and the 1979 siege of Morichjhapi in particular) as learned from his uncle Nirmal's journals. Although the interplay among the characters is masterfully written, Ghosh also provides a wealth of setting and historical details, including the danger and fear invoked when the characters face a dangerous tornado near the conclusion of the story.

Second Appeal: Setting

Subjects: Animals; Biology; Book Groups; Culture Clash; Environmental Writing; India; Indian Authors; Love Affairs; Men Writing as Women; Multicultural; Science; Social Class; Travel

Awards: ALA Notable

Now Try: Ghosh is also the author of the novels *Sea of Poppies* and *The Glass Palace*. Other novels featuring strongly drawn characters and an Indian setting are Aravind Adiga's Booker Prize–winning novel *The White Tiger*, Chitra Divakaruni's *The Palace of Illusions*, and Tahmima Anam's *A Golden Age*. Another novel in which a woman sets out on a quest fraught with peril is Kira Salak's *The White Mary*; Rosemary Mahoney's nonfiction travel title *Down the Nile: Alone in a Fisherman's Skiff* might also appeal.

Glass, Julia.

I See You Everywhere. **Pantheon, 2008. 287pp. ISBN 9780375422751.**

Told in the alternating voices of the sisters Clem and Louisa, Glass's novel encompasses twenty-five years in their lives, during which they pursue very different lifestyles. The elder sister by four years, Louisa moves through life more sedately and with a steadier hope for true love and a stable home life, while the younger sister Clem lives at a more mercurial pace, dispensing with jobs, lifestyles, and men with equal aplomb.

Subjects: Art and Artists; Book Groups; Death and Dying; Family Relationships; Multiple Viewpoints; Siblings; Sisters; Suicide; Vermont; Women Authors; Women's Fiction

Now Try: Glass is also the author of the novels *The Whole World Over* and the National Book Award–winning *Three Junes*. Other books in which sisters, siblings, and close friends share sometimes tempestuous relationships are Lori Lansens's *The Girls*, Audrey Niffeneggers's *Her Fearful Symmetry*, Rebecca Wells's *Divine Secrets of the Ya-Ya Sisterhood*, Anne Tyler's *Dinner at the Homesick Restaurant* (as well as *If Morning Ever Comes* and *Saint Maybe*), Tawni O'Dell's *Sister Mine*, Anita Shreve's *Body Surfing*, and Diane Johnson's *Le Divorce*.

🌳 *Three Junes.* **Pantheon, 2002. 353pp. ISBN 9780375421440.**

Three interconnected stories set in Greece, Scotland, and New York explore the complex lives and loves of different generations of the McLeod family during June 1989, 1995, and 1999.

Subjects: Book Groups; Brothers; Family Relationships; Fathers and Sons; Interconnected Stories; Gay Men; GLBTQ; Greece; Marriage; Multigenerational Fiction; New York City; Scotland; Women Authors; Women's Fiction

Awards: National Book Award

Now Try: Glass's other novels are *The Whole World Over* and *I See You Everywhere*. Michael Cunningham's *The Hours* also consists of three interrelated but separate stories involving characters who ruminate on the paths they've chosen. Ian McEwan's *Atonement* is another novel that deftly explores family relationships over time and includes believable, nuanced characters. Also of interest might be Elizabeth Strout's Pulitzer Prize–winning novel *Olive Kitteridge*, which also contains multiple story lines about the same characters.

Goldman, Francisco.

The Divine Husband. **Atlantic Monthly Press, 2004. ISBN 9780871139153.**

Goldman tells a tale based on the life of poet José Martí, inventing a fictional mistress named Paquita who may have borne him an illegitimate child. In addition to the love story, this novel also follows the childhood friendship of Paquita and María de las Nieves Moran, who enter a convent together largely to discourage the advances of an older revolutionary toward the twelve-year-old Paquita. When the revolutionary eventually seizes power in the country, Paquita not only becomes his mistress, but also embarks on a life of experiences and loves with many others.

Subjects: 19th Century; Biographical Fiction; Guatemala; Historical Fiction; Latin America; Love Affairs; Magic Realism; New York City; Political Fiction

Now Try: Goldman is also the author of the novels *The Long Night of White Chickens* and *The Ordinary Seaman*, as well as the nonfiction title *The Art of Political Murder: Who Killed the Bishop?* Other novels based on real people, particularly from South and Latin America, might also be suggested, including Julia Alvarez's *In the Time of the Butterflies*, Slavenka Drakulic's *Frida's Bed* (about Frida Kahlo), and Luis Alberto Urrea's *The Hummingbird's Daughter*. These readers might also consider books by Roberto Bolaño, such as *2666, By Night in Chile*, and *The Savage Detectives*.

Goodman, Matthew Aaron.

Hold Love Strong. **Simon & Schuster, 2009. 358pp. ISBN 9781416562030.**

Abraham Singleton comes into the world with very few advantages: born to a thirteen-year-old in the bathroom in her and her mother's apartment in the projects, he will have to navigate his way through close and multiple family connections and relationships (which provide sustaining love but can also feel claustrophobic to a young boy), poverty, and rampant drug use and crime.

Subjects: African Americans; AIDS; Coming-of-age; Death and Dying; Family Relationships; First Novels; Grandmothers; Multigenerational Fiction; New York City; Poverty; Young Men

Now Try: Goodman's immediate and affecting novel is very similar to the nonfiction narratives *Random Family: Love, Drugs, Trouble, and Coming-of-age in the Bronx* by Adrian Nicole LeBlanc and *Rosa Lee* by Leon Dash. asha bandele is another author who has experienced what she writes about, both in fiction (*Daughter: A Novel*) and nonfiction (*The Prisoner's Wife* and *Something Like Beautiful*). Although it is a YA novel, Angela Johnson's *The First Part Last* is a powerful urban coming-of-age narrative as well.

Gowdy, Barbara.

🎗 *Helpless: A Novel.* **Metropolitan Books, 2007. 307pp. ISBN 9780805082883.**

Single mom Celia Fox has her hands full, working two jobs and caring for her nine-year-old daughter Rachel, who often accompanies her to her job as a lounge singer in a neighborhood bar, and whose luminous and precocious beauty regularly attracts the attention of model and talent scouts. Unfortunately, scouts are not the only ones drawn to Rachel; when a middle-aged man named Ron sees her on her school playground, he immediately "falls in love" and makes plans to abduct her from (he feels) her neglectful mother. Convincing his girlfriend that he loves the girl like a daughter, he treats her kindly, but the temptation to push the boundaries of that love grows in him even as Celia and her friends frantically search for her.

Subjects: Biracial Characters; Canada; Canadian Authors; Kidnapping; Multiple Viewpoints; Pedophilia; Single Mothers; Suspense; Toronto; Women Authors

Awards: Trillium Book Award

Now Try: Several of Gowdy's other novels also focus on obsession; they are *The Romantic* and her story collection *We So Seldom Look on Love*. Although much more straightforward and descriptive in their focus on pedophiles, Vladimir Nabokov's classic novel *Lolita* and Irvine Welsh's crime thriller *Crime* also offer suspenseful and unsettling reading experiences. Andre Dubus's novel *The Garden of Last Days* offers an eerily similar plotline in which a young girl disappears from her mother's place of employment. Although the young heroine in Elizabeth Strout's novel *Amy and Isabelle* is older than the one in this novel, her portrait of the single mother struggling to raise her teenage daughter may provide a similar reading experience. Other dark novels by female Canadian authors might prove similar reads, such as Carol Shields's *Unless* and Ann-Marie MacDonald's *Fall on Your Knees*.

Groff, Lauren.

The Monsters of Templeton. **Hyperion, 2008. 364pp. ISBN 9781401322250.**
When Willie Upton returns to her hometown of Templeton, New York, in the wake of a failed love affair with one of her professors, her mother sees fit to tell her that her father (whom she never knew) was not, in fact, a nameless hippie lover, but rather a man from Templeton. While Willie goes about trying to unearth both the secrets of her own parentage and, by extension, of the town, a somewhat more tangible mystery surfaces in the form of a lake monster.

Second Appeal: Story

Subjects: Book Groups; Dysfunctional Families; Family Secrets; Fantasy; First Novels; Monsters; New York; Suspense; Women Authors; Young Women

Now Try: Groff is also the author of a collection of nine short stories, *Delicate Edible Birds*. Other novels in which authors blend elements of the supernatural and the suspenseful with strongly drawn characters might appeal to these readers, such as Diane Setterfield's *The Thirteenth Tale*, Jennifer Egan's *The Keep*, James Hynes's *The Kings of Infinite Space*, and Jonathan Barnes's *The Somnambulist*.

Haddon, Mark.

🎗 *The Curious Incident of the Dog in the Night-Time.* **Doubleday, 2003. 226pp. ISBN 9780385509459.**
An autistic teenager decides to discover the murderer of a neighbor's dog while coping with the loss of his mother and the parental shortcomings of his father.

Subjects: Autism; British Authors; Classics; Coming-of-age; Family Relationships; Family Secrets; Fathers and Sons; Great Britain; Humor; Quick Reads; Teenage Boys; Teenagers; YA

Awards: ALA Notable; Whitbread Award

Now Try: Haddon followed this spectacular novel with a strong second novel, *A Spot of Bother*. In *The Speed of Dark* by Elizabeth Moon, multiple autistic characters are asked to undergo an experimental cure for autism in order to retain their jobs. The fictional *When I Was Five I Killed Myself* by Howard Buten is another poignant tale from the perspective of a child labeled autistic. *The Pleasure of My Company* by Steve Martin is an impressive novella about a man with dysfunctional neuroses; a slightly more feminine take on growing up in Great Britain is Kate Long's bleakly humorous *The Bad Mother's Handbook*. Nonfiction accounts of living with autism and Asperger's syndrome might also be suggested; these include John Elder Robison's *Look Me in the Eye: My Life with Asperger's* and Daniel Tammet's *Born on a Blue Day*. Nonfiction titles by Temple Grandin about her life spent helping animals and coping with her autism might also be good read-alikes for this title; they include *Animals in Translation*, *Thinking in Pictures*, and *Animals Make Us Human*. Another book by a British author (and, weirdly enough, featuring a similar orange book cover, complete with the image of a dog on it) is Matt Haig's *The Labrador Pact*.

Hadley, Tessa.

The Master Bedroom. Henry Holt, 2007. 339pp. ISBN 9780805080766.

Forty-three-year-old Kate Flynn, feeling unsettled in her London life, moves to Wales to move in with and care for her aging mother Billie. When she arrives she finds that her former friend Carol's younger brother David, who had a crush on her in their youth, still lives there and is struggling in his own marriage. Although David never quite finds the courage to try to form a relationship with Kate, his son Jamie—a teenager—does.

Subjects: Book Groups; British Authors; Dark Humor; Elderly; Family Relationships; Great Britain; Love Affairs; Midlife Crisis; Mothers and Daughters; Teenage Boys; Teenagers; Wales; Women Authors

Now Try: Tessa Hadley's other novels are similar in style; they are *Accidents in the Home* and *Everything Will Be All Right*. Another British author, Kate Long, tells a story of several generations of women living under the same roof in *The Bad Mother's Handbook*; another woman character seeking comfort through her sexuality can be found in Lisa Zeidner's *Layover*. Nonfiction accounts in which women examine their relationships with their mothers might also appeal, such as Mary Gordon's *Circling My Mother*, Meg Federico's *Welcome to the Departure Lounge: Adventures in Mothering Mother*, and Vivian Gornick's *Fierce Attachments*.

Haig, Matt.

The Labrador Pact. Viking, 2004. 341pp. ISBN 9780670018529.

It's not often that the "character" in a "character-driven novel" is a dog, but that is the case in Haig's story, in which loyal Labrador Prince narrates the story of his life with his British family, whom he tries to keep on the straight and narrow. (Adam Hunter, his owner, is going through a midlife crisis, his wife Kate is attracted to another man, and their children have all sorts of issues.) Although he has varying degrees of success with his machinations, Prince strives to live up to the training of his own mentor, a police dog named Henry, as he tries to encourage his owners (through the only means available to him, of course: tail-wagging, barking, and sniffing) to do what is best for their family, as well as unravel a series of disappearances in their neighborhood.

Subjects: Animals; Book Groups; British Authors; Death and Dying; Dogs; Family Relationships; Great Britain; Mystery

Now Try: Haig is also the author of the novel *The Dead Fathers Club*. Other books narrated (in full or in part) by dogs might appeal to these readers, including Garth Stein's *The Art of Racing in the Rain*, Peter Mayle's *A Dog's Life*, David Wroblewski's *The Story of Edgar Sawtelle*, and Merrill Markoe's *Walking in Circles Before Lying Down*. Memoirs in which dogs play a large role might also appeal, such as John Grogan's best-selling *Marley & Me* and Ted Kerasote's *Merle's Door*. Other books featuring dogs and their relationships with their humans might also appeal, such as Jon Katz's memoirs *A Good Dog: The Story of Orson, Who Changed My Life*, *The Dogs of Bedlam Farm*, and *A Dog Year: Twelve Months, Four Dogs, and Me* or Farley Mowat's *The Dog Who Wouldn't Be*. Another book narrated by an animal is Layne Maheu's *Song of the Crow* (featuring a crow as the main character). Another book by a British author (and, weirdly enough, featuring a similar orange book cover, complete with the image of a dog on it) is Mark Haddon's *The Curious Incident of the Dog in the Night-Time*.

Now Consider Nonfiction . . . Animal Stories

Animal stories, a subgenre of nonfiction environmental writing, can be extremely personal stories of friendship, not only between human beings but also between humans and animals.

Adamson, Joy. *Born Free: A Lioness of Two Worlds.*

Bourke, Anthony. *A Lion Called Christian.*

Herriot, James. *All Creatures Great and Small.*

Mowat, Farley. *Never Cry Wolf.*

Myron, Vicki. *Dewey: The Small-Town Library Cat Who Changed the World.*

North, Sterling. *Rascal.*

Haigh, Jennifer.

The Condition: A Novel. **Harper, 2008. 390pp. ISBN 9780060755782.**

Until the McKotch family vacationed with their friends at Cape Cod and noticed how diminutive their thirteen-year-old daughter Gwen is when compared with her young cousin, their marriage and family life had been much like any other suburban family's. However, in the aftermath of Gwen's diagnosis of Turner's syndrome (which keeps her from maturing at a normal rate), her parents Paulette and Frank find themselves growing increasingly distant from one another, particularly in light of their different approaches to Gwen's treatment (Paulette nears outright denial in her understated response, while Frank, a doctor, is much more active in seeking alternative treatments and therapies). Told from the varying viewpoints of Paulette, Frank, Gwen, and her brother Scott, this family story encompasses tragedies but refuses to allow them to conquer the narrative.

Subjects: 1970s; Book Groups; Domestic Fiction; Family Relationships; Health Issues; Love Affairs; Marriage; Medicine; Multiple Viewpoints; Siblings; Women Authors; Women's Fiction

Now Try: Haigh is also the author of the novel *Mrs. Kimble* and the historical fiction title *Baker Towers*. Another author who often explores the stresses put upon marriage when children become ill is Jodi Picoult—especially in her novels *My Sister's Keeper* and *Handle with Care*. Other authors who may appeal to Haigh's readers are Wally Lamb (*I Know This Much Is True* and *The Hour I First Believed*) and Anita Shreve (*The Pilot's Wife* and *Body Surfing*). Anne Fadiman's nonfiction classic about a family struggling with the dictates of modern medicine, *The Spirit Catches You and You Fall Down*, might also be suggested.

Haji, Nafisa.

The Writing on My Forehead. **William Morrow, 2009. 308pp. ISBN 978-0061493850.**

Saira Qader, an independent journalist who has spent a lifetime rebelling against her Muslim Indo-Pakistani family's expectations and belief systems, finds her world turned upside down when her sister Ameena's family is destroyed by a senseless tragedy. In taking over the care of Ameena's daughter Sakina, Saira must come to terms with secrets in her own and Ameena's past, give in to the love she feels for Sakina, and come to a greater understanding of her family's reliance on religion and tradition.

Subjects: California; Family Relationships; Family Secrets; First Novels; First Person; Immigrants and Immigration; Islam; Los Angeles; Mothers and Daughters; Multicultural; Pakistan; Parenting; Siblings; Sisters; Women Authors

Now Try: Jhumpa Lahiri's fiction titles also explore issues of immigrants' experiences and family relationships; they include the story collection *Unaccustomed Earth* and the novel *The Namesake*. Other novels in which family relationships among women are explored are Kamila Shamsie's *Broken Verses*, Khaled Hosseini's *A Thousand Splendid Suns*, and Chitra Banerjee Divakaruni's *Sister of My Heart*. Also of interest might be other novels in which family secrets are slowly revealed, including Brunonia Barry's *The Lace Reader*, Christina Sunley's *The Tricking of Freya*, Jean Hanff Korelitz's *Admission*, and Abraham Verghese's *Cutting for Stone*.

Hallowell, Janis.

She Was. **William Morrow, 2008. 322pp. ISBN 9780061243257.**

Doreen Woods, successful dentist, loving wife and mother, and devoted helper of her brother, disabled Vietnam veteran Adam MacFadden, has been living a lie for thirty-five years. Or was the lie her briefer lifetime as Lucy Johansson, the political activist and love-blinded member of Fishbone, an organization that was responsible for bombing a campus building, undertaken as a war protest, but in which an innocent janitor lost his life? In this complex but not particularly story-driven narrative, told in flashbacks and from the points of view of various characters, Hallowell tells a haunting story that touches on issues of justice, identity, and love.

Subjects: 1970s; Book Groups; Colorado; Denver; Family Relationships; Family Secrets; Flashbacks; Friendships; Gay Men; GLBTQ; Historical Fiction; Multiple Viewpoints; Political Fiction; Suspense; Vietnam War; Women Authors

Now Try: Hallowell is also the author of *The Annunciation of Francesca Dunn*. Another book in which undercurrents of the Vietnam War can be found in a family story is Tim O'Brien's suspenseful *In the Lake of the Woods*; a nonfiction account of family life with a Vietnam veteran is Tom Bissell's transcendent memoir *The Father of All Things*. Other novels by women with political themes include Marge Piercy's *Vida: A Novel*, and Susan Choi's *American Woman* (her novel *A Person of Interest* might also appeal). Hallowell also suggests nonfiction titles about the Vietnam War, including Michael Herr's immersion journalism classic *Dispatches* and David Halberstam's history *The Best and the Brightest*.

Hamilton, Jane.

Laura Rider's Masterpiece. **Grand Central, 2009. 214pp. ISBN 9780446538954.**

After twelve years of enjoying what she refers to as her husband Charlie's "one superb talent" of lovemaking, Laura Rider decides she's simply done with sex for the time being and promptly stops sleeping with her husband. What she really wants to do, she decides, is write a book, but she could also use some romantic inspiration, so she encourages Charlie to flirt and engage in an affair with Jenna, a local radio talk show personality.

Subjects: American Midwest; Book Groups; Explicit Sexuality; Humor; Love Affairs; Marriage; Midlife Crisis; Quick Reads; Satire; Wisconsin; Women Authors; Writers and Writing

Now Try: Hamilton is not known for her use of humor, but her earlier novels all include good character development and may appeal to these readers; they are the Oprah book club choices *A Map of the World* and *The Book of Ruth*, as well as the novel *The Short History of a Prince*. Another sharp chronicler of women's lives and marriage is Meg Wolitzer (*The Position* and *The Wife*); Anne Tyler's novel *Breathing Lessons* also combines humor with the demands of marriage. Pagan Kennedy's fascinating collection of essays *The Dangerous Joy of Dr. Sex and Other True Stories* features a long character profile of Dr. Alex Comfort, the earnest author of the classic *The Joy of Sex*.

Harris, Joanne.

The Girl with No Shadow. **William Morrow, 2007. 444pp. ISBN 9780061431623.**

In this long-anticipated sequel to Harris's best-selling novel (and popular movie of the same name) *Chocolat*, Vianne Rocher opens a new chocolaterie in Paris and, in her typical indomitable fashion, endeavors to bring joy to others, in the form of chocolates and other delicacies, while she keeps her own secrets. When a former friend threatens to destroy everything she has once again built, she finds she must act to preserve her new business and life.

Second Appeal: Setting

Subjects: British Authors; Chocolate; Food; France; Mothers and Daughters; Paris; Women Authors; Women's Fiction

Now Try: Harris is also the author of the novel *Chocolat*, of course, as well as the titles *Blackberry Wine, Gentlemen and Players, Holy Fools,* and *Five Quarters of the Orange*. She has also written a nonfiction book of recipes, *My French Kitchen: A Book of 120 Treasured Recipes*; other nonfiction and expatriate travel tales about France might also be suggested to these readers, including Kathleen Flinn's *The Sharper Your Knife, The Less You Cry*, Julia Child's *My Year in France*, and Betsy Draine's and Michael Hinden's *A Castle in the Backyard: The Dream of a House in France*. Those readers up for the challenge of a novel in translation might also consider Agnes Desarthes's very evocative novel *Chez Moi*, also about a woman who opens a restaurant.

Harrison, Kathryn.

🏆 *Envy: A Novel.* **Random House, 2005. 301pp. ISBN 9781400063468.**

Forty-seven-year-old psychoanalyst William Moreland arguably has more personal and psychological crises in his own life than he has patients: since his son's death three years previously his wife Carole has become increasingly distant; his father is having an affair; he lives in his successful and estranged brother's shadow; and he has to face both his mid-life crisis and a former girlfriend with secrets about their shared past at his twenty-five-year college reunion. Harrison is noted for the sensational and descriptive nature of her prose, and this novel is no exception.

Subjects: Adultery; Explicit Sexuality; Family Relationships; Family Secrets; Marriage; Men's Lives; Midlife Crisis; Psychological Fiction; Siblings; Women Authors; Women Writing as Men

Awards: New York Times Notable

Now Try: Harrison has written other novels, including *Thicker Than Water, Poison, Exposure,* and *The Seal Wife,* but she is perhaps best known for her unflinching memoirs, including *The Kiss* (an account of her incestuous and quasi-consensual relationship with her father), *The Mother Knot,* and *Seeking Rapture.* Another novel in which the family patriarch's life work of psychology impacts his family is Dirk Wittenborn's *Pharmakon.* Harrison's style has been compared by critics to such iconic male authors as John Updike (*Rabbit Run, The Witches of Eastwick,* and *Couples*), John Cheever (*The Wapshot Chronicle*), and Robert Olen Butler (*Fair Warning* and *Intercourse: Stories*). Harrison is married to another writer, novelist Colin Harrison; in his books (particularly *The Finder, The Havana Room,* and *Manhattan Nocturne*), he also pays attention to the sometimes seamy undersides of our relationships.

Haruf, Kent.

Eventide. **Knopf, 2004. 299pp. ISBN 9780375411588.**

In this sequel to Haruf's best seller *Plainsong,* he continues the story of the bachelor brothers Harold and Raymond McPheron, as well as their "adopted" daughter Victoria and her daughter Katie. Maggie Jones and Tom Guthrie also return, while unexpected events conspire to allow Haruf to introduce new characters and community members of Holt, Colorado, including social worker Rose Tyler, a disabled couple in her care, and an orphan boy named D. J. Kephart, who befriends the two young daughters of Mary Wells, whose husband has abandoned their family.

Second Appeal: Setting

Subjects: American West; Colorado; Coming-of-age; Community Life; Domestic Fiction; Family Relationships; Friendships; Men's Lives; Mothers and Daughters; Multigenerational Fiction; Small-Town Life

Now Try: Haruf is also the author of the quietly glorious novels *The Tie That Binds* and *Where You Once Belonged,* as well as the prequel to this novel, *Plainsong.* In Kiara Brinkman's *Up High in the Trees,* a young boy also befriends the neighbors, including a young brother-and-sister pair, who help him deal with his mother's sudden death. Larry Watson's novels are also character-driven and often set in landscapes described as richly as Haruf's; they include *Sundown, Yellow Moon; Laura; White Crosses;* and *Montana 1948.* Another author whose novels are strongly rooted in both community and character is

Wendell Berry (*Jayber Crow*, *Nathan Coulter*, and *A Place on Earth*). Michael Perry writes memoirs rich with details of small-town life and the importance of looking out for one's neighbors and friends; they are *Population: 485*, *Truck: A Love Story*, and *Coop: A Year of Poultry, Pigs, and Parenting*.

Heller, Zoë.

The Believers. HarperCollins, 2008. 335pp. ISBN 9780061430206.

When lawyer Joel Litvinoff suffers a stroke while trying a case in court, his family, including his wife Audrey and his children Karla, Rosa, and Lenny, gather at the hospital. Over the next few days and weeks, as he remains in a vegetative state, events continue to unfold around him: his wife learns a secret about another of his relationships; Lenny struggles with his addiction problems; Karla falls in love with a man who is not her husband (while concurrently trying desperately to get pregnant or adopt a child with her husband Mike); and Rosa continues her search for fulfillment in Judaism.

Subjects: Adultery; Book Groups; British Authors; Death and Dying; Family Relationships; Family Secrets; Jews and Judaism; Law and Lawyers; Love Affairs; Marriage; New York City; Siblings; Women Authors

Now Try: Heller is not a prolific author, but she is a virtuoso at exploring human relationships; her earlier novels are *What Was She Thinking? Notes on a Scandal* (which was made into a movie starring Cate Blanchett and Judi Dench) and *Everything You Know*. Novels of modern family life by Zadie Smith (*White Teeth* and *On Beauty: A Novel*), Ayelet Waldman (*Love and Other Impossible Pursuits*), and Elizabeth Kelly (*Apologize, Apologize!*) might be suggested, as might another novel of a family dealing with death and family secrets, Anne Enright's Man Booker Prize–winning *The Gathering*. The conjunctions between family relationships and grief are also explored at great lengthy in Anne Tyler's *The Tin Can Tree* and Nellie Hermann's *The Cure for Grief*.

What Was She Thinking? Notes On a Scandal. Holt, 2003. 258pp. ISBN 978-0805073331.

Sheba Hart, a popular teacher in her early forties, seemingly has it all—career, a happy marriage, two kids—until she puts it all in jeopardy by having a sexual affair with high school student Steven Connolly. The third person in the novel's tragic love triangle, however, is not Sheba's husband, but rather Barbara Covett, an older teacher and Hart's friend and confidante.

Subjects: British Authors; Education; Explicit Sexuality; First Person; Friendships; Quick Reads; Teachers; Teenage Boys; Teenagers; Unreliable Narrator; Women Authors

Now Try: Heller is also the author of the novels *Everything You Know* and *The Believers*. Other tales of obsession and diabolical planning in school settings that might appeal to these readers are Joanne Harris's *Gentlemen and Players* and Curtis Sittenfeld's *Prep*. Tom Perrotta's novels *Little Children, Joe College,* and *The Abstinence Teacher*, though steeped in suburbia, also explore a seamy underside of the perfect characters in his books; Amy Koppelman's *I Smile Back* also features a female protagonist who is losing the fight against her own personal demons.

Hendricks, Judith Ryan.

The Laws of Harmony. **Harper, 2009. 480pp. ISBN 9780061687365.**

Growing up on a commune in New Mexico, Sunny Cooper loathed the lack of privacy and disliked much of her childhood, which ended tragically the day she witnessed the accidental death of her younger sister. Years later, and in a relationship with a man she can't quite bring herself to commit to (for fear of tempting fate), she is crushed not only when she learns of his fatal accident when he is traveling for work, but also about the many secrets he was keeping from her. Distraught, she moves to the community of Harmony, on San Miguel Island (off the coast of Washington State), where she finally learns both how to truly take care of herself, as well as to find peace with her past.

Subjects: Book Groups; Communes; Community Life; Death and Dying; Family Relationships; First Person; Mothers and Daughters; New Mexico; Women Authors; Women's Fiction

Now Try: Hendricks is also the author of the novels *The Baker's Apprentice, Isabel's Daughter,* and *Bread Alone.* Two other novels about the keeping of secrets and how their revelation can change characters' lives are Anita Shreve's *The Pilot's Wife* and Nicole Mones's *The Last Chinese Chef.* Another quietly elegiac book about communal living is Nancy Peacock's *Life Without Water.* Hendricks has been compared by critics to Barbara Kingsolver; Kingsolver's novels *The Bean Trees, Pigs in Heaven,* and *The Poisonwood Bible* might all be suggested.

Hill, Roccie.

Three Minutes on Love. **Permanent Press, 2008. 272pp. ISBN 9781579621698.**

When Rosie Kettle leaves her small hometown in California to make her way to San Francisco in the 1960s, she embarks upon a career in which she will become a well-known music and rock photographer, and which will also lead to a complex friendship with an illegal Hungarian immigrant named Peter, who runs a music newspaper and to whom she sells photographs. Her job also propels her into a love affair with blues guitarist David Wilderspin, whose own complex relationship with his estranged father will eventually have horrifying consequences for Rosie, David, and their son Sam.

Subjects: 1960s; California; Coming-of-age; Family Relationships; Fathers and Sons; First Novels; First Person; Love Affairs; Music and Musicians; Photography; San Francisco; Small Press; Women Authors

Now Try: Fans of this coming-of-age story might also consider photographer Deborah Copaken Kogan's memoir *Shutterbabe: Adventures in Love and War,* or even her novel *Between Here and April.* Other novels of young women making their way in love and life might appeal, such as Mary Gaitskill's *Veronica* and Haven Kimmel's *The Used World.* Also of interest might be women's memoirs of self-discovery, including Paule Marshall's *Triangular Road,* Sara Paretsky's *Writing in an Age of Silence,* and Wendy Werris's *An Alphabetical Life: Living It Up in the World of Books* (set in Los Angeles, California).

Hoffman, Alice.

Skylight Confessions. **Little, Brown, 2007. 262pp. ISBN 9780316058780.**

What does it mean to depend on fate? Hoffman answers that question with the story of a marriage that Arlyn Singer pursues with single-minded intensity after she pledges, shortly after her father's funeral, to marry the next man she sees. That man is John Moody, an architecture student who stops and asks her for directions shortly after she makes her pledge. Although they do marry, and have a son, the marriage is not a success, and Arlyn engages in a passionate affair with another man (by whom she bears a daughter) before she succumbs to cancer. Using multiple voices, Hoffman explores the dynamics of Arlyn's unhappiness in her marriage, her son Sam's loneliness and difficulty with interpersonal relationships after she dies, and her daughter Blanca's struggle to find her own place in the world.

Subjects: Adultery; Architects and Architecture; Brothers and Sisters; Connecticut; Death and Dying; Dysfunctional Families; Family Relationships; Love Affairs; Marriage; Multiple Viewpoints; New York City; Quick Reads; Women Authors; Women's Fiction

Now Try: Hoffman is a prolific and popular novelist; other titles in which she explores family dynamics might appeal, including *Fortune's Daughter*, *Second Nature*, *Here on Earth*, and *Blue Diary*. Other novels in which fate plays a role are Debra Ginsberg's *The Grift*, Peter Carey's *Oscar and Lucinda* (which, like this novel, features a building largely made of glass), and Anita Shreve's *The Pilot's Wife*.

The Story Sisters. **Shaye Areheart Books, 2009. 325pp. ISBN 9780307393869.**

The Story sisters (Elv, Megan, and Claire) have always been close and have had much practice in creating an imaginative world of their own, but a string of tragedies and bad luck (including sexual abuse) slowly wears at Elv's ability to weave stories to help herself and her sisters cope with the unrelenting harshness of their worlds.

Subjects: Family Relationships; Family Secrets; Magic Realism; Mothers and Daughters; Multiple Viewpoints; Psychological Fiction; Sexual Abuse; Siblings; Sisters; Women Authors; Women's Fiction

Now Try: Hoffman's other books featuring family relationships among women might particularly appeal to these readers, including *Practical Magic*, *The Probable Future*, and *The Third Angel*. Other novels in which family secrets come to light are Brunonia Barry's *The Lace Reader*, Matt Ruff's *Set This House in Order*, and Jodi Picoult's *Keeping Faith* and *Perfect Match*.

Hollinghurst, Alan.

🏵 *The Line of Beauty*. **Bloomsbury, 2004. 438pp. ISBN 9781582345086.**

Twenty-one-year old Nick Guest is friends with both the daughter (Catherine) and the son (Toby) of the prominent British political family the Feddens, who invite him to stay at their posh home while he looks for a place of his own and to make his own way in London during the 1980s. As he ventures tentatively into his first sexual relationships with other men, he also finds himself becoming seduced by the power, influence, and quiet affluence of his host family during the prosperous (for some) Thatcher years of the 1980s.

Subjects: 1980s; Book Groups; British Authors; Coming-of-age; Explicit Sexuality; Family Relationships; Friendships; Gay Men; GLBTQ; Men's Lives; Political Fiction; Social Class; Young Men

Awards: Man Booker Prize; New York Times Notable

Now Try: Hollinghurst's earlier novels are *The Spell*, *The Folding Star*, and *The Swimming-Pool Library*. Other novels in which individuals become closely attached to families that aren't technically their own are Rachel Cusk's *In the Fold* and Evelyn Waugh's classic *Brideshead Revisited*. In Paul Kafka-Gibbons's novel *DuPont Circle*, set in Washington, D.C., the personal and political are also connected. Other novels in which characters explore their sexuality might be offered, such as Geoff Dyer's *Paris Trance: A Romance*, Peter Cameron's *Leap Year* and *Someday This Pain Will Be Useful to You*, and Jim Grimsley's *Comfort and Joy*.

Hornby, Nick.

A Long Way Down. Riverhead Books, 2005. 333pp. ISBN 9781573223010.

When four attendees at a New Year's Eve party in Great Britain find themselves on the roof together, they're even more surprised to find that they're all there for the same purpose: to commit suicide. However, as they become involved in speaking with one another and attempting to solve one another's problems (which Hornby is astute enough to know always seem easier to solve than one's own), the night progresses with fewer and fewer thoughts of actually going through with the act.

Subjects: British Authors; Dark Humor; Day in the Life; Friendships; Great Britain; Multiple Viewpoints; Suicide; Teenagers

Now Try: Fans of Hornby's unique humor and simple style might enjoy both his other novels (including *About a Boy*, *High Fidelity*, and *How to Be Good*) as well as his nonfiction essay collections, such as *The Polysyllabic Spree* and *Housekeeping vs. The Dirt*. Other British and Irish authors with similar writing styles to Hornby's might appeal, including Mark Haddon (*The Curious Incident of the Dog in the Night-Time* and *A Spot of Bother*), Roddy Doyle (*The Commitments*, *Paddy Clarke Ha Ha Ha*, and *The Deportees*), and David Mitchell (*Ghostwritten* and *Black Swan Green*). Although they are considered YA novels, John Green's *Looking for Alaska* and *Paper Towns* and Rachel Cohn and David Levithan's coauthored *Nick and Norah's Infinite Playlist* might also appeal to readers who enjoy strong ensemble casts of characters.

Hosseini, Khaled.

🏵 *The Kite Runner*. Riverhead Books, 2003. 324pp. ISBN 9781573222457.

As an adult, Amir, the son of a wealthy Kabul businessman, returns to war-torn Afghanistan from America to find forgiveness for a childhood act of cruelty.

Subjects: 1970s; Afghanistan; Book Groups; Classics; Coming-of-age; Culture Clash; Fathers and Sons; First Novels; First Person; Friendships; Men's Lives; Multicultural; War

Awards: ALA Notable; Alex Award

Now Try: Hosseini's subsequent novel, *A Thousand Splendid Suns*, might also appeal to these readers. His fans might enjoy other literary novels featuring similar characters and "culture clash" plots, such as Monica Ali's *Brick Lane* or Leila Aboulela's *Minaret* (which feature Bangladeshi and Sudanese characters, respectively, although both are set in London); Jhumpa Lahiri's *The Namesake* (which focuses on a family from Calcutta in America); or even Marsha Mehran's *Pomegranate Soup* (in which Iranian sisters emigrate to Ireland). Novels featuring male characters and relationships might also appeal: *Little America* by Henry Bromell, *The Paperboy* by Pete Dexter, *The Umbrella Country* by Bino Realuyo, or *The Weight of Dreams* by Jonis Agee. Those readers particularly interested in the setting of Hosseini's novel might also consider Yasmina Khadra's novel *The Swallows of Kabul* (about life in Afghanistan under the Taliban); nonfiction travel narratives set in the region, such as Jason Elliot's *An Unexpected Light: Travels in Afghanistan* or Asne

Seierstad's *The Bookseller of Kabul*; and Tom Bissell's *Chasing the Sea: Lost Among the Ghosts of Empire in Central Asia* (which is set in Uzbekistan but has a similarly earnest tone).

A Thousand Splendid Suns. **Riverhead Books, 2007. 372pp. ISBN 9781594489501.**

The friendship and love that grow between two women is at the heart of Hosseini's second novel. Mariam and Laila are both the wives of Rasheed, with Mariam being the elder and Laila the younger (and more heralded for her beauty) wife; both suffer from systematic abuse and cruelty perpetrated against them by Rasheed. As the two of them learn to live together and with Rasheed, they find their relationship a growing source of strength in both their abusive marriage and dealing with the privations of their war-torn country (Afghanistan).

Subjects: 20th Century; Abuse; Afghanistan; Arranged Marriages; Book Groups; Friendships; Marriage; Men Writing as Women; War; Women's Fiction

Now Try: Fans of this novel will also want to read Hosseini's first, the critically acclaimed, best-selling *The Kite Runner*. Novels and nonfiction sharing the setting of Afghanistan might be offered; the former include Nadeem Aslam's *The Wasted Vigil*, Francesca Marciano's *The End of Manners*, and Yasmina Khadra's *The Attack*; the latter include *The Bookseller of Kabul* by Åsne Seierstad, *Kabul Beauty School* by Deborah Rodriguez, and *Nine Parts of Desire: The Hidden World of Islamic Women* by Geraldine Brooks. Another popular nonfiction title, Greg Mortenson's and David Relin's *Three Cups of Tea: One Man's Mission to Promote Peace . . . One School at a Time*, might also appeal because of its similar setting and its emphasis on educating boys AND girls in Pakistan and Afghanistan.

Hustvedt, Siri.

The Sorrows of an American. **Holt, 2008. 306pp. ISBN 9780805079081.**

Erik Davidsen and his sister Inga are already reeling from a series of deaths (including that of their father, as well as of Inga's husband Max) when they find a note in their father Lars's papers indicating that he may have been involved in another person's death. In addition to trying to decipher the mystery at the heart of the note and in their father's diary, both Erik and Inga have enough stressors in their own lives; Erik, a newly divorced psychoanalyst, is hopelessly in love with a woman who is also a tenant of his, while Inga and her daughter are being pursued by a woman threatening to publish letters that implicate Inga's husband in an affair.

Subjects: Book Groups; Brothers and Sisters; Death and Dying; Family Relationships; Family Secrets; Grief; Love Affairs; Minnesota; Psychological Fiction; Women Authors

Now Try: Hustvedt's critically popular earlier novels include *What I Loved* and *The Enchantment of Lily Dahl*. Another novel of a family gathering after a family member's death is Anne Enright's *The Gathering*; in Zoë Heller's novel *The Believers*, a patriarch's wife and children gather around his sickbed. Per Petterson's *Out Stealing Horses* also features a story line in which past events intrude upon the present-day narrative.

Irving, John.

Last Night in Twisted River. **Random House, 2009. 554pp. ISBN 978 1400063840.**

The year is 1954, and Dominic Baciagalupo and his twelve-year-old son Danny work and live in a New Hampshire logging camp. When a violent accident forces Dominic and Danny to flee the camp, they are joined by a former logger and river driver, who accompanies them on their fugitive journeys through Boston, Vermont, and even Toronto—all places to which they must flee to avoid the lawman who has been tracking them since New Hampshire. As the years pass Danny finds his own work as a novelist, but their unfortunate pasts compel the trio to continue moving and living restlessly throughout twentieth-century America.

Subjects: 1950s; 20th Century; Accidents; Boston; Canada; Fathers and Sons; Friendships; Historical Fiction; Men's Lives; New Hampshire; Toronto; Vermont ; Writers and Writing

Now Try: Critics have compared this historical novel to Irving's earlier best seller, *The World According to Garp*; other novels of his that might appeal include *A Prayer for Owen Meany* and *The Cider House Rules*. Another historical novel about the relationship between a father and son is Karl Iagnemma's *The Expeditions*; Per Petterson's novel *Out Stealing Horses* also examines the effects of past mistakes on the current lives of its characters.

Until I Find You. **Random House, 2005. 824pp. ISBN 9781400063833.**

Jack Burns's entire troubled childhood is a series of journeys: with his mother, Alice, while they travel throughout northern Europe in search of his father; through a variety of boarding schools (first an all-girls' school, then an all-boys' school), in which he survives more than his fair share of sexual exploitation and molestation at the hands of older girls and women; and then alone, once again through Europe, on his own quest to find his father.

Subjects: Actors and Acting; Dark Humor; Epic Reads; Explicit Sexuality; Family Relationships; Men's Lives; Mothers and Sons; New England; Travel

Now Try: Although critics were not kind to this novel, Irving's fans are notably loyal; his other novels include *The World According to Garp*, *A Prayer for Owen Meany*, *The Hotel New Hampshire*, *The Cider House Rules*, and *The Fourth Hand*. Tom Wolfe's *I Am Charlotte Simmons* features a female protagonist but is also a coming-of-age tale; Philip Roth's novels, which typically feature healthy doses of sexual experimentation, might also be suggested, including *The Dying Animal*, *Sabbath's Theater*, and *The Ghost Writer* (the first title in his Nathan Zuckerman series).

James, Tania.

Atlas of Unknowns. **Knopf, 2009. 319pp. ISBN 9780307268907.**

Brought up together in Kerala, India, by their father, Linno and Anju (the former the older sister) share a relationship similar to that of most sisters: close at times, distant at others. The sharpest blow to their friendship comes when Anju passes off her sister's artworks as her own to win a prestigious scholarship to an American art school; when her lack of talent is discovered, she runs away to work in a beauty salon in Queens. Linno, meanwhile, manages to escape an arranged marriage (having lost a hand in a childhood accident, she is not viewed favorably on the marriage market) and, after achieving success of her own, sets out to find her younger sister in America and bring her home.

Subjects: Art and Artists; Family Relationships; First Novels; India; Multicultural; New York City; Siblings; Sisters; Women Authors

Now Try: Authors who provided blurbs for James's first novel include Chitra Banerjee Divakaruni (*Queen of Dreams, Sister of My Heart,* and *The Vine of Desire*) and Nathan Englander (*For the Relief of Unbearable Urges* and *The Ministry of Special Cases*). Another novel of sisters with a complex relationship is Lisa See's historical work *Shanghai Girls*; Khaled Hosseini's *A Thousand Splendid Suns* might also appeal.

Janowitz, Tama.

Peyton Amberg. **St. Martin's Press, 2003. 335pp. ISBN 9780312318444.**

Peyton Amberg is married young, and securely, to a Long Island dentist with solid career prospects. What he does not offer is much in the way of sexual excitement, which, as a travel agent, Peyton seeks to correct as she travels abroad for her career and engages in a series of progressively more violent and degrading sexual affairs. Filled with personal (and interpersonal) ennui, this novel has been billed as a modern *Madame Bovary*.

Subjects: Adultery; Explicit Sexuality; Flashbacks; Literary Allusions; Marriage; Satire; Travel; Women Authors

Now Try: Janowitz is the author of several other books, although she is best known for the novel *A Certain Age* and the story collection *Slaves of New York*. Other novels in which women seek out something that is missing in their marriage might be offered, such as Amy Koppelman's *I Smile Back*, Lisa Zeidner's *Layover*, or Tom Perrotta's *Little Children*. Of course, these readers might also consider the classic to which this book has been compared, Gustave Flaubert's *Madame Bovary*.

Jordan, Toni.

Addition: A Novel. **William Morrow, 2009. 260pp. ISBN 9780061582578.**

Aussie Grace Lisa Vandenburg lives a life governed by counting and numbers: the nineteen letters in her name; the various numbers she counts as she moves through her day, including the numbers of steps she takes to and from various locations; her age, thirty-five. Her obsession has led to dismissal from her teaching job and is steadily encroaching on all areas of her life until she meets Seamus Joseph O'Reilly (whose name, like hers, also consists of nineteen letters), who challenges her to seek help to overcome what he views as her problem, but which she feels almost unable to part with as an integral (really; no pun intended) part of her personality.

Subjects: Australia; Australian Authors; First Novels; First Person; Love Affairs; Mathematics; Mental Health; Quick Reads; Romance; Tesla, Nikola; Women Authors; Women's Fiction

Now Try: Jordan's novel is a thoughtful combination of chick lit and empathetic characterization; similar novels featuring strong female characters who nonetheless have their own sets of struggles are Melissa Bank's *The Wonder Spot*, Jean Hanff Korelitz's *Admission*, and Jennifer Weiner's *Good in Bed*. Grace is also fascinated by Nikola Tesla, and Jordan suggests several works about him that her readers might enjoy, including *Tesla: Man Out of Time* and Marc J. Seiffer's *Wizard: The Life and Times of Nikola Tesla*. Honest and affecting memoirs of people living with OCD might also appeal, such as Jennifer Traig's *The Devil in the Details* and Amy

Wilensky's *Passing for Normal: A Memoir of Compulsion*. Tesla has also appeared in more than his fair share of fiction titles, including Paul Auster's *Moon Palace*, Samantha Hunt's *The Invention of Everything Else*, and Spider Robinson's <u>Callahan Place</u> science fiction series (which starts with *Callahan's Crosstime Saloon* and *Time Travelers Strictly Cash*).

Kallos, Stephanie.

Sing Them Home. **Atlantic Monthly Press, 2009. 542pp. ISBN 9780871139634.**

The death of Llewellyn Jones, mayor of the small town of Emlyn Springs, Nebraska, triggers several reunions of his children, daughters Larken and Bonnie and son Gaelen, together with his longtime mistress and then common-law wife Viney Closs. At the heart of the story is the tornado that ripped through their lives nearly twenty years previously, in which Bonnie was seriously injured (and was found in such a way as to provide the townsfolk with a legend they'd retell for years) and their mother, Hope Jones, who was wheelchair-bound and suffering from multiple sclerosis, was lost and presumed dead. Secrets abound, but so do numerous human kindnesses and redemptions, in this sprawling novel, which is also rich with details about community life (particularly the community's Welsh roots and their practice of "singing the dead home" at funerals).

Second Appeal: Story

Subjects: Adultery; Book Groups; Brothers and Sisters; Community Life; Family Relationships; Natural Disasters; Nebraska; Siblings; Small-Town Life; Tornadoes; Weather; Women Authors; Women's Fiction

Now Try: Kallos is also the author of the novel *Broken for You*. Readers who enjoy her masterful descriptions of (not always gentle) small-town life and family secrets might also consider Tiffany Baker's *The Little Giant of Aberdeen County*, David Wroblewski's *The Story of Edgar Sawtelle*, or A. Manette Ansay's *Vinegar Hill*. Mysterious disappearances are also at the heart of Deborah Copaken Kogan's *Between Here and April*.

Kavenna, Joanna.

Inglorious. **Metropolitan Books, 2007. 286pp. ISBN 9780805081893.**

Rosa Lane is a thirty-five-year-old woman living in London who, after losing her mother, her boyfriend, and her job, spends most of her time writing letters she'll never send and making to-do lists she'll never revisit, while staying with friends and endeavoring to stay unemployed. Described as "darkly comic," this novel surprises with unexpected plot twists, and Rosa is a character who will resonate with anyone who has ever found herself forced to send cover letters and resumés but would really rather write the letter she finds herself writing: "Dear sir, I would like a job. Actually that's not true. Without wanting to trouble you with my ambivalence, a job is what I need."

Subjects: British Authors; Dark Humor; Epistolary Fiction; First Novels; Friendships; Great Britain; London; Love Affairs; Women Authors; Work Relationships

Now Try: Kavenna is also the author of the fascinating nonfiction travel/investigative title *The Ice Museum: In Search of the Lost Land of Thule*. Fans of Kavenna's novel might also consider thoughtful (and sometimes sharply comic) fiction by other British authors, including Rachel Cusk (*The Country Life* and *Arlington Park*) and Margaret Drabble (*The Middle Ground, The Millstone, and The Seven Sisters*), as well as American authors Mameve Medwed (*How Elizabeth Barrett Browning Saved My Life* and *Mail*), Matthew

Quick (*The Silver Linings Playbook*), and James Collins (*Beginner's Greek*). "Dark" in tone nonfiction titles by Brit Anneli Rufus (*Stuck: Why We Can't (or Won't) Move On* and *Party of One: The Loner's Manifesto*) might appeal, as might memoirs by the always forthright Jim Knipfel (*Slackjaw* and *Ruining It for Everybody*) and Hollis Gillespie (*Bleachy Haired Honky Bitch* and *Trailer Trashed*).

Kelly, Elizabeth.

Apologize, Apologize! **Twelve, 2009. 324pp. ISBN 9780446406147.**

Growing up on Martha's Vineyard and struggling with a mix of feelings of entitlement and the battling nature of the underdog (imbibed from his mother's moneyed background and liberal politics and his father's Irish heritage and struggles with alcoholism and adultery), Collie Flanagan and his brother Bingo rely heavily on one another for companionship and love in their household. Throughout their childhood and young adulthood, both boys struggle to find their place in the world and to navigate the relationships and histories of their parents, their father's brother (their Uncle Tom, who lives with the family and looks after the boys), and their grandfather Peregrine Lowell, whom they dub "the Falcon" for his fierce visage.

Subjects: Brothers; Coming-of-age; Death and Dying; Dysfunctional Families; El Salvador; Family Relationships; First Novels; Martha's Vineyard; Siblings; Women Authors; Women Writing as Men

Now Try: This novel has been described as being about the "dysfunctionally rich"; other affluent families with complex relationships can be found in Anita Shreve's novel *Body Surfing*, Zoë Heller's *The Believers*, Terry Gamble's *Good Family*, and Matthew Rothschild's memoir *Dumbfounded: Big Money, Big Hair, Big Problems, or Why Having It All Isn't for Sissies*. Also of interest might be J. R. Moehringer's coming-of-age memoir *The Tender Bar*, as he also had a close relationship with his uncle while growing up.

Khadra, Yasmina.

🎋 *The Swallows of Kabul.* **Doubleday, 2004. 195pp. ISBN 9780385510011.**

Amid the decaying landscape of Kabul, Afghanistan, two very different men and their wives struggle for survival and redemption under the oppressive regime of the Taliban.

Subjects: Afghanistan; Book Groups; Islam; Men's Lives; Middle East; Multicultural; Political Fiction; Quick Reads; Religion; Taliban

Awards: ALA Notable

Now Try: Khadra is also the author of the more story-driven narrative *The Attack*. Two other excellent novels set in Afghanistan are *The Kite Runner* by Khaled Hosseini and the historical fiction title *The Mulberry Empire* (by Philip Hensher). Nonfiction books about life in contemporary Afghanistan include *Kabul* by M. E. Hirsh, *The Bookseller of Kabul* by Åsne Seierstad and Ingrid Christopherson, and *The Sewing Circles of Herat: A Personal Voyage Through Afghanistan* by Christina Lamb. For a different look at women living under the precepts of Islamic law, try Nadeem Aslam's *Maps for Lost Lovers*. Another city is destroyed by war in Steven Galloway's *The Cellist of Sarajevo*.

Kim, Eugenia.

The Calligrapher's Daughter. **Henry Holt, 2009. 400pp. ISBN 978 0805089127.**

When the Japanese occupied Korea in the beginning of the twentieth century, they undertook a systematic and effective policy of denying and destroying Korean culture. Caught in this tumultuous time, a young woman named Najin (a nickname only; her father refused to name her as she was born shortly after the Japanese invaded) is sent by her parents to the court of the Korean royal family to try to better her fortunes; while there, she receives an education and strives to make her own way in a world continually rocked by invasions, occupations, war, and cultural expectations. Throughout a life fraught with relationships stressed by separation and hardship, her relationship with her mother in particular remains strong.

Second Appeal: Setting

Subjects: 20th Century; Book Groups; Family Relationships; First Novels; First Person; Historical Fiction; Korea; Love Affairs; Mothers and Daughters; Multicultural; Women Authors; World War II

Now Try: Other historical fiction titles set in Asian countries and featuring strong women characters might also appeal to these readers, such as Lisa See's *Snow Flower and the Secret Fan* and *Shanghai Girls*, Padma Viswanathan's *The Toss of a Lemon*, and Amy Tan's *The Bonesetter's Daughter*; another novel in which political tension (this time between Korea and China) plays a part is Jeff Talarigo's *The Ginseng Hunter*. Memoirs about women's struggles to find their places in the world might also be suggested, such as Maxine Hong Kingston's *Woman Warrior: Memoirs of a Girlhood Among Ghosts*, Marie Arana's *American Chica: Two Worlds, One Childhood*, and Roya Hakakian's *Journey from the Land of No: A Girlhood Caught in Revolutionary Iran*.

Kimmel, Haven.

Iodine: A Novel. **Free Press, 2008. 223pp. ISBN 9781416572848.**

Trace Pennington, a senior at a small college in Indiana, spends most of her time alone in the abandoned house where she lives with her dog Weeds, alternating between complete lucidity (she's at the top of her college class) and delusions and unsettling dreams attributable to her mental illness. Writing in her journal and allowing the reader brief and horrific glances into a childhood filled with abuse, Trace has been referred to by reviewers as the "ultimate unreliable narrator," but she is nonetheless a compelling character whose plight will draw in Kimmel's readers.

Subjects: American West; Animals; Book Groups; Dogs; Indiana; Love Affairs; Mental Health; Psychological Fiction; Quick Reads; Suspense; Unreliable Narrator; Women Authors

Now Try: Kimmel's memoirs *A Girl Named Zippy* and *She Got up off the Couch* are considerably lighter in tone than is this novel, but her other novels might particularly appeal to fans of this book: *The Used World, The Solace of Leaving Early*, and *Something Rising (Light and Swift)*. Mary Gaitskill's slim and sobering novel *Veronica* might also be suggested, as might Kim Barnes's *A Country Called Home*, or even Julian Gough's *Juno and Juliet* (which features college-aged twins, one of whom has an affair with one of her professors). Memoirs in which women struggle with their own and others' health issues are Jennifer Traig's *The Devil in the Details*, Laura Flynn's *Swallow the Ocean*, and Barbara Robinette Moss's *Fierce*.

Kingsolver, Barbara.

The Lacuna. HarperCollins, 2009. 507pp. ISBN 9780060852573.

Kingsolver's protagonist in this ambitious and literary historical novel is Harrison William Shepherd, a writer who was born in the United States but raised largely in Mexico, whose restless spirit as he comes of age and searches for his true place in this world leads him to encounters with artists Diego Rivera and Frida Kahlo and communist revolutionary Leon Trotsky. Later he experiences an America deep in the patriotic throes of involvement in World War II—and again finds himself making difficult choices in his continuing search for his own true identity.

Subjects: 20th Century; Art and Artists; Biographical Fiction; Book Groups; Coming-of-Age, Historical Fiction; Kahlo, Frida; Mexico; Rivera, Diego; Trotsky, Leon; Women Authors; Women Writing as Men; World War II; Writers and Writing

Now Try: Kingsolver is the popular and acclaimed author of the novels *The Bean Trees, Animal Dreams, The Poisonwood Bible,* and *Prodigal Summer* (among others), as well as the memoir *Animal, Vegetable, Miracle: A Year of Food Life.* Those readers interested in artists Rivera and Kahlo might also consider the historical novel *Frida's Bed* (about Kahlo) by Slavenka Drakulic; another ambitious historical novel about Mexico is Luis Alberto Urrea's *The Hummingbird's Daughter.* Earl Shorris's nonfiction *The Life and Times of Mexico* might also prove to be a good related read. Fans of Kingsolver's writing style might also consider works by Louise Erdrich and Ann Patchett.

Klosterman, Chuck.

Downtown Owl. Scribner, 2008. 275pp. ISBN 9781416544180.

Klosterman's first novel follows the exploits of the residents of the town of Owl, North Dakota, during the winter before a massive blizzard that will bring tragedy to the community. The story is told from the varying viewpoints of high schooler Mitch Hrlicka, new teacher Julia Rabia, and longtime town resident Horace Jones. Klosterman (born in Minnesota and raised in North Dakota himself), perfectly describes both the claustrophobia and the comforting cohesion of Midwestern small-town life in the 1980s.

Subjects: 1980s; American Midwest; Blizzards; Book Groups; Community Life; Family Relationships; First Novels; Friendships; Humor; Multiple Viewpoints; North Dakota; Small-Town Life; Teenage Boys; Teenagers; Weather; Young Men

Now Try: Fans of Klosterman's novel might also consider his memoirs, *Fargo Rock City* and *Killing Yourself to Live,* as well as his essay collections *Sex, Drugs, and Cocoa Puffs: A Low Culture Manifesto* and *Chuck Klosterman IV.* Tom Drury's novel of the Midwest (specifically, Iowa), *The Driftless Area,* might appeal, as might Kyle Beachy's novel about a young man searching for his moorings, *The Slide.* Other decidedly unsentimental takes on small-town life can be found in Richard Russo's novels *Empire Falls* and *Nobody's Fool,* as well as Michael Perry's memoir *Population: 485.*

Now Consider Nonfiction . . . Character Profiles

Character profiles provide researched and comprehensive investigative stories, but add the dimension of detailed (and often empathetic) character development. Although not all of these stories end happily, they all feature unique and nuanced individual stories.

Gilbert, Elizabeth. *The Last American Man.*

Greene, Melissa Faye. *There Is No Me Without You.*

LeBlanc, Adrian Nicole. *Random Family: Love, Drugs, Trouble, and Coming-of-age in the Bronx.*

Mishler, William. *A Measure of Endurance: The Unlikely Triumph of Steven Sharpe.*

Orlean, Susan. *The Orchid Thief.*

Singer, Mark. *Character Studies: Encounters with the Curiously Obsessed.*

Koppelman, Amy.

I Smile Back. **Two Dollar Radio, 2008. 188pp. ISBN 9780976389590.**

Laney Brooks appears to be living the epitome of the American dream—a successful and loving husband, two kids, and a nice house in suburban New Jersey—but underneath her stylish and carefully maintained exterior, a roiling unhappiness seethes and eventually forces action in the form of numerous affairs (explicitly described) and drug abuse. Short chapters and frank language make this a fast-paced novel, told in three parts, starting on Labor Day 2002, moving through a short stint of Laney's enforced rehab stay, and concluding five weeks later.

Second Appeal: Language

Subjects: Adultery; Drug Abuse; Explicit Sexuality; Fathers and Daughters; Marriage; Midlife Crisis; Quick Reads; Small Press; Suburbia; Women Authors

Now Try: Koppelman is also the author of the novel *A Mouthful of Air*. Other novels in which the protagonists struggle with the soullessness of suburban life are Richard Yates's classic *Revolutionary Road*, Tom Perrotta's *Little Children* and *The Abstinence Teacher*, James Boice's *NoVA: A Novel*, and Rachel Cusk's *Arlington Park*. In Lisa Zeidner's novel *Layover*, the protagonist also seeks to lessen her pain (in her case, grief over the death of her child) through sexual encounters with strangers.

Korelitz, Jean Hanff.

Admission: A Novel. **Grand Central, 2009. 452pp. ISBN 9780446540704.**

Thirty-eight-year-old Portia Nathan is the epitome of the successful and totally self-assured professional; as an admissions officer for Princeton University, she travels to find students who will best contribute to the university and will be well-served by it, and feels pride and fulfillment in her work. She lives with a colleague, Mark, in such harmony that they often feel superior to married and less harmonious couples. But under her veneer of self-control and placidity, Portia is hiding a secret about her own college years, one that will come crashing to the fore when she visits a new high school to find applicants and is reintroduced to John Halsey, a man who knew her when they both attended Dartmouth.

Subjects: Academia; Book Groups; Coming-of-age; Education; Flashbacks; Friendships; Love Affairs; Mothers and Daughters; New England; New Jersey; Women Authors

Now Try: Korelitz is also the author of the novels *The White Rose*, *The Sabbathday River*, and *A Jury of Her Peers*. Other works set in academic surroundings might appeal, including Richard Russo's *Straight Man*, Julian Gough's *Juno and Juliet*, P. F. Kluge's *Gone To-*

morrow, and Jane Smiley's *Moo*. Korelitz also suggests books about Princeton that might be fun to track down: Rebecca Goldstein's *The Mind-Body Problem* and Eileen Simpson's *Poets in Their Youth*. The nonfiction investigative writing title *The Gatekeepers: Inside the Admissions Process of a Premier College*, by Jacques Steinberg, might also prove an interesting related read.

Krauss, Nicole.

The History of Love. Norton, 2005. 252pp. ISBN 9780393060348.

Retired locksmith and Jewish immigrant Leo Gursky lives a lonely life in New York City, but his complex personal history of escaping Poland, authoring a book titled *The History of Love* (which later turns up published under another's name), and fathering a son who doesn't know him is about to come to the surface. In a parallel story line, a teenage girl named Alma tries to find a suitor for her widowed mother and keep her younger brother (who believes he might be a messiah) out of trouble. The conclusion of the novel features taut plotting that shows how all these characters' lives intersect.

Second Appeal: Language

Subjects: Book Groups; Books and Reading; Classics; Fathers and Sons; First Person; Immigrants and Immigration; Jews and Judaism; Multigenerational Fiction; Multiple Viewpoints; New York City; Refugees; Teenage Girls; Teenagers; Writers and Writing

Now Try: Krauss's first novel was *Man Walks into a Room*. The quest for family history, as well as post-Holocaust Eastern European Jewish issues, will resonate with fans of *Everything Is Illuminated* by Jonathan Safran Foer. The concept of the *Lamed vavniks* (thirty-six "Just Men") who bear the burdens of the world on their shoulders, and from whom is born a messiah every generation, is described in *The Last of the Just* by André Schwartz-Bart. The magic realism of Krauss's novel evokes *Love in the Time of Cholera* by Gabriel García Márquez and Isabel Allende's *Eva Luna*. The book-within-a-book resembles the language of *Invisible Cities* by Italo Calvino and the work of Jorge Luis Borges; the plot of Peter Carey's *My Life as a Fake* also centers around a book's authorship and the reactions of its readers.

Lahiri, Jhumpa.

Unaccustomed Earth. Knopf, 2008. 333pp. ISBN 9780307265739.

In this collection of eight short stories, Lahiri examines family relationships, individuals striving to reconcile two very different cultures (particularly the divide between American "modernism" and Indian "traditionalism" and family expectations), and marriages. The final three stories are linked and titled, as a group, "Hema and Kaushik," and in those stories Lahiri explores the coming-of-age of two young characters, whose relationship changes from their meeting as children through chance meetings when they are adults with a shared history.

Subjects: Book Groups; Classics; Coming-of-age; Culture Clash; Domestic Fiction; Family Relationships; Immigrants and Immigration; India; Interconnected Stories; Marriage; Multicultural; Short Stories; Women Authors

Awards: ALA Notable; New York Times Notable

Now Try: Lahiri is the author of an earlier story collection, *Interpreter of Maladies*, and the novel *The Namesake*. Another Iranian family is featured in Anne Tyler's

Digging to America; other short story collections such as *The Unknown Errors of Our Lives* by Chitra Banerjee Divakaruni and *Sari of the Gods* by G. S. Chandra might also appeal. Another prize-winning collection of linked short stories, Elizabeth Strout's *Olive Kitteridge*, might also be a good read-alike for this story collection.

Lamb, Wally.

The Hour I First Believed. HarperCollins, 2008. 740pp. ISBN 9780060393496.

Bad luck and tragic events coincide in Lamb's sprawling domestic novel. Caelum Quirk, middle-aged and still recovering from the near-death of his marriage due to his wife Maureen's infidelity, flies across country from Colorado to Connecticut to visit his aunt, Lolly, who has suffered a stroke. While he is away, on April 20, 1999, Maureen (a school nurse) is trapped in Columbine High School during the school shootings there; shortly thereafter, his aunt dies. Deciding to make a fresh start, Caelum and Maureen move to Connecticut, but Maureen is unable to recover from her post-traumatic stress disorder and eventually develops a prescription drug addiction, which will have severe consequences in her life. Caelum, meanwhile, discovers a trove of letters and newspaper clippings that throw into confusion all he thought he knew about his aunt, his parents, and his family.

Subjects: Colorado; Columbine High School; Connecticut; Domestic Fiction; Epic Reads; Family Secrets; First Person; Marriage; Men's Lives; Prisons; School Shootings

Now Try: Lamb is also the author of the best-selling books (which were also Oprah club selections) *She's Come Undone* and *I Know This Much Is True*. Because he covers so many subjects so well, there are many avenues to follow for read-alikes. Readers drawn by his understandings of school shootings might also consider Jodi Picoult's novel *Nineteen Minutes*, Lionel Shriver's *We Need to Talk About Kevin*, or Dave Cullen's nonfiction account *Columbine*. Prisons also play a large part in this narrative, so novels like Janet Fitch's *White Oleander*, Jane Hamilton's *A Map of the World*, or Ralph Blumenthal's enlightening nonfiction account *Miracle at Sing Sing* might appeal. Likewise, numerous novels in which family secrets are revealed might also be offered, such as Brunonia Barry's *The Lace Reader*, Judy Fong Bates's *Midnight at the Dragon Café*, Robert Goolrick's *A Reliable Wife*, David Wroblewski's *The Story of Edgar Sawtelle*, or Ann-Marie MacDonald's *Fall on Your Knees*.

Lansens, Lori.

🌳 *The Girls: A Novel.* Little, Brown, 2006. 345pp. ISBN 9780316069038.

Although joined at the head, craniophagus conjoined twins Ruby and Rose Darlen are nonetheless very different girls. When she learns, in their late twenties, that they are dying, the stronger and more "dominant" twin, Rose, sets about writing their life story ; she also persuades Ruby to write down her viewpoint, which appears as shorter chapters throughout Rose's narrative. Raised in a small town in Ontario by their adoptive parents, Aunt Lovey and Uncle Stash, the girls suffer a variety of ailments and frustration over their physical status, but nonetheless experience and are thankful for the love shown them by their adoptive parents and one another.

Subjects: Adoption; Book Groups; Canada; Family Relationships; First Person; Health Issues; Ontario; Siamese Twins; Siblings; Sisters; Twins; Women Authors

Awards: ALA Notable

Now Try: Lansens is also the author of a previous novel titled *Rush Home Road*. Stories told from the perspective of characters nearing the ends of their lives might also be offered; these include Alice Sebold's *The Lovely Bones* (in which the narrator has already died), Sara Gruen's *Water for Elephants*, Susan Minot's *Evening*, Penelope Lively's *Moon Tiger*, Abby Frucht's *Life Before Death*, and Elizabeth Subercaseaux's *A Week in October*. Another novel about twins who share a close (if not a physical) bond is Audrey Niffeneggers's *Her Fearful Symmetry*. Memoirs about the relationships between sisters and siblings could also be suggested, such as Debra Ginsberg's heartfelt *About My Sisters* or Jeannette Walls's *The Glass Castle*.

Lee, Chang-Rae.

Aloft. **Riverhead Books, 2004. 343pp. ISBN 9781573222631.**

Fifty-nine-year-old Jerry Battle finds that when he escapes the ground in his small airplane, he can almost convince himself that all of his problems are too far below him to matter. And he does have problems: his longtime girlfriend Rita has finally tired of his noncommittal approach to their relationship and left him, his son is running the family business into the ground, his father is unhappily housed in an assisted living facility, and his newly pregnant and very secretive daughter is keeping a devastating secret about her own health from him.

Subjects: Asian American Authors; Domestic Fiction; Family Relationships; First Person; Flying; Humor; Long Island; Men's Lives; Widowers

Now Try: Lee is also the author of the critically acclaimed novels *A Gesture Life* and *Native Speaker*. Other novels focusing on men's lives might appeal to these readers, including Richard Russo's *Nobody's Fool* and *Straight Man*, Tim O'Brien's *Tomcat in Love*, Richard Ford's Frank Bascombe series (starting with *The Sportswriter*), John Irving's *The Water-Method Man*, and John Updike's Rabbit Angstrom series (starting with the classic *Rabbit, Run*). Eric Kraft's omnibus of three novels about a man and the summer he spent flying across the country, *Flying*, might also have a certain offbeat appeal for these readers; a particularly beautiful nonfiction treatise on the glory of flight is William Langewiesche's *Inside the Sky: Meditations on Flight*

Lesley, Craig.

Storm Riders. **Picador, 2000. 339pp. ISBN 9780312245542.**

The last thing Clark and Payette Woods are expecting to challenge their new marriage is their adoption of Payette's young cousin, a boy named Wade, who may suffer from fetal alcohol syndrome (the doctors can't agree on a diagnosis) and whose behavioral problems soon drive a wedge between the pair. After Payette leaves, Clark, a professor at a college in Oregon, is left to struggle with Wade's care on his own, and fiercely defends him from the community's charges about Wade's involvement in various accidents and incidents.

Subjects: Abuse; Adoption; American Indians; Family Relationships; Fathers and Sons; Marriage; Men's Lives; Mental Health; Oregon; Pacific Northwest

Now Try: Lesley is also the author of the novels *Winterkill*, *River Song*, and *The Sky Fisherman*. Other books in which authors struggle to provide care and love for adopted and foster children might also appeal to these readers, including Barbara

Kingsolver's *Pigs in Heaven*, Michael Dorris's *The Yellow Raft*, Catherine Hyde's *Love in the Present Tense*, and Kaye Gibbons's *Ellen Foster*. Michael Dorris's nonfiction account of his adoption of a child who suffered from fetal alcohol syndrome, *The Broken Cord*, might also be a suitable related read.

Lipman, Elinor.

The Family Man. Houghton Mifflin Harcourt, 2009. 305pp. ISBN 9780618644667.

Henry Archer, twenty-five years after being divorced from his wife Denise (he was closeted during their marriage, but after Denise left him for another man, he came out), learns that her husband has died and calls her to offer his condolences, setting in motion a chain of events including his reconnection with his former stepdaughter Thalia. After offering her a place to live in his townhouse and reconnecting as a friend with Denise, he also finds himself falling in love with a man named Todd (introduced to him by Denise) and becoming, for really the first time in his life, a consummate family man.

Subjects: Family Relationships; Fathers and Daughters; Gay Men; GLBTQ; Humor; Love Affairs; Marriage; New York City; Women Authors

Now Try: This is Lipman's tenth novel; her earlier novels, including *My Latest Grievance*, *The Pursuit of Alice Thrift*, *The Ladies' Man*, and *The Inn at Lake Devine*, might all appeal. Other novels about father and daughter relationships might be suggested, including Benjamin Markovits's *Fathers and Daughters: A Novel* and Adrienne Miller's *The Coast of Akron*. Lighthearted but still literary relationship novels such as Mameve Medwed's *Mail* and *How Elizabeth Barrett Browning Saved My Life*, James Collins's *Beginner's Greek*, Stephen McCauley's *The Easy Way Out*, and Matthew Quick's *The Silver Linings Playbook*, might also be enjoyable read-alikes for Lipman fans.

My Latest Grievance. Houghton Mifflin, 2006. 243pp. ISBN 9780618644650.

Growing up on the campus of a small liberal arts college, where she has lived in a residential hall with her residential hall–director and professor parents, Frederica Hatch has long been the college's unofficial mascot and resident precocious child. She has also been the recipient of an almost unbearable amount of parental love and concern, so when she learns her grandmother is still in contact with her father's first wife, Laura Lee (a wife she never knew he had), she can't help but shake things up by contriving to start a friendship with Laura Lee.

Subjects: 1970s; Academia; Adultery; Boston; Family Relationships; First Person; Humor; Multigenerational Fiction; Parenting; Quick Reads; Teenage Girls; Teenagers; Women Authors

Now Try: Several of Lipman's other novels about family relationships might also be offered, including *The Family Man*, *The Dearly Departed*, and *Then She Found Me*. Catherine O'Flynn's novel *What Was Lost* also features a precocious but likable main character, as does E. Lockhart's *The Disreputable History of Frankie Landau-Banks*. Binnie Kirshenbaum's *An Almost Perfect Moment* also tells the story of a young girl growing up with close and loving but still sometimes stifling adults.

Lively, Penelope.

Consequences: A Novel. Viking, 2007. 258pp. ISBN 9780670038565.

Lively tells the intertwined stories of three different women in three different time periods: Lorna (and her husband Matt) during World War II; their daughter

Molly, and Molly's daughter Ruth, whose personal journey of discovery leads her back to her grandmother's story in 1941.

Subjects: 1940s; British Authors; Great Britain; Historical Fiction; Interconnected Stories; London; Multigenerational Fiction; Women Authors; World War II

Now Try: Several of Lively's other novels may appeal to these readers, including her semiautobiographical *Making It Up*, *Perfect Happiness*, *Passing On*, and the Man Booker Prize–winning *Moon Tiger*. Also of interest might be novels about other women connected through time, such as Michael Cunningham's *The Hours*, Margot Livesey's *The House on Fortune Street*, and Ian McEwan's *Atonement*; Lionel Shriver's novel *The Post-Birthday World* explores one woman's different destinies. Lively's style has also been compared to that of Anita Brookner (*Falling Slowly* and *The Rules of Engagement*) and Barbara Pym (*Excellent Women* and *A Few Green Leaves*). Other historical novels set during World War II might appeal, such as *The Guernsey Literary and Potato Peel Pie Society* (by Mary Ann Shaffer and Annie Barrows), Elizabeth Berg's *Dream When You're Feeling Blue*, and Anne Tyler's *The Amateur Marriage*.

Lodge, David.

Deaf Sentence. **Viking, 2008. 294pp. ISBN 9780670019922.**

Professor Desmond Bates, facing retirement from teaching linguistics and his encroaching deafness with something less like resignation than regret (particularly as his wife, Winifred, has an interior decorating business that is growing more prosperous by the day), suddenly finds a bit more interest in life when he is pursued by a young and enigmatic graduate student. Although in the beginning of this novel, told in the form of the professor's stately paced diary, he is flattered by Alex Loom's attention, before long he becomes unnerved by her skill in manipulating him and others.

Subjects: Academia; British Authors; Deafness; Diary; Elderly; Humor; Linguistics; Marriage; Men's Lives

Now Try: This is Lodge's thirteenth novel; his earlier books might appeal, particularly *Thinks*, *Home Truths*, and *Therapy*. Two other books in which humorous male authors poke some fun at academia are Richard Russo's *Straight Man* and P. F. Kluge's *Gone Tomorrow*; those with a taste for more serious fiction but also featuring an aging professor might consider J. M. Coetzee's *Disgrace*. T. C. Boyle's frenetic *Talk Talk*, with a feisty deaf protagonist, might also be suggested. Leah Hager Cohen's nonfiction title about students and teachers at the Lexington School for the Deaf, *Train Go Sorry*, might provide a good related read as well.

Long, Kate.

The Bad Mother's Handbook. **Ballantine Books, 2004. 351pp. ISBN 978-0345479655.**

Three stories intersect in this novel of working-class Britain: seventeen-year-old Charlotte's, her mother Karen's, and her grandmother Nan's. Each of the three relates her story in her own unique voice. Charlotte's tale of woe, including an unplanned pregnancy, strikes the right note of teen uncertainty; Karen's frustration about trying to care for the two generations she's sandwiched between and never having time for herself is understandable; and Nan's nostalgia and clearer grip on events decades in the past than on those in the present is told in her "working-class lilt." The story is anything but beautiful, but the strength and humor of the three women, as well as their connections to each other, make it a beautiful novel nonetheless.

Subjects: British Authors; Elderly; Family Relationships; Great Britain; Humor; Mothers and Daughters; Multigenerational Fiction; Multiple Viewpoints; Parenting; Teenage Girls; Teenagers; Women Authors

Now Try: Fans of Long's likable characters might consider other (particularly British) novels, which focus on the connections between family members, including David Mitchell's *Black Swan Green* (from a teen boy's point of view), Philip Hensher's *Northern Clemency*, Mark Haddon's *A Spot of Bother*, and Jonathan Coe's Birmingham (England) novels *The Rotters' Club* and *The Closed Circle*. Beverly Donofrio wrote about her experience as a teen mother in the simultaneously humorous and poignant memoir *Riding in Cars with Boys*. Although not all readers will agree with her very opinionated (but always feisty and personable) take on the subject of motherhood, Ayelet Waldman's essay collection *Bad Mother: A Chronicle of Maternal Crimes, Minor Calamities, and Occasional Moments of Grace* might also be suggested to fans of this novel.

Macy, Caitlin.

Spoiled: Stories. **Random House, 2009. 220pp. ISBN 9781400061990.**

In Macy's nine stories, primarily about upper-class women in their thirties who live in New York City, just having money and supposedly more fulfilling lives than their mothers had is often not enough to guarantee happiness.

Subjects: Friendships; New York City; Quick Reads; Short Stories; Social Class; Women Authors; Women's Fiction

Now Try: Macy is also the author of the novel *The Fundamentals of Play*, which includes a similar circle of characters (but who are younger, in their twenties). Susan Minot's short story collection *Lust* might appeal to these readers, as might other novels about social class and personal lives set in New York City, including Cheryl Mendelson's *Morningside Heights* and *Love, Work, Children*, Valerie Leff's *Better Homes and Husbands*, and Candace Bushnell's *Lipstick Jungle* and *One Fifth Avenue*. Curtis Sittenfeld's novel *Prep*, about a young girl who enrolls in an exclusive private school in Massachusetts, might also be suggested. Nonfiction about women's choices and lifestyles might also be suggested, such as Leslie Bennetts's passionately argued *The Feminine Mistake: Are We Giving up Too Much?* and its polar opposite, Caitlin Flanagan's collection of essays titled *To Hell with All That: Loving and Loathing Our Inner Housewife*.

Malone, Michael.

The Four Corners of the Sky. **Sourcebooks Landmark, 2009. 544pp. ISBN 978-1570717444.**

Left behind to live with her aunt Sam and Sam's boyfriend Clark when she was seven years old, Annie Peregrine Goode has never quite lost the wanderlust instilled in her by her father, Jack, who, up until he left her with Sam, had taken her along on his travels and the working of elaborate cons. After Annie has grown up and met her need for speed by becoming a navy fighter pilot, she receives a message from her father that he needs her help on one big last job—to which she agrees, but only after striking the bargain that he will then reveal the identity of her mother.

Subjects: Adventure; American South; Con Artists; Family Relationships; Fathers and Daughters; Humor; Men Writing as Women; Pilots

Now Try: This is Malone's tenth novel; his earlier titles include *Foolscap, Handling Sin, The Last Noel*, and the story collection *Red Clay, Blue Cadillac*. A quickly paced fiction title featuring a con artist is Clyde Edgerton's *The Bible Salesman*; the nonfiction classic *Catch Me If You Can* by Frank Abagnale might also appeal. Another author whose early novels in particular might appeal to Malone's readers is Richard Russo; consider suggesting his titles *The Risk Pool* and *Nobody's Fool*.

Manseau, Peter.

🎗 *Songs for the Butcher's Daughter*. **Free Press, 2008. 370pp. ISBN 978-1416538707.**

The Yiddish poet Itzik Malpesh, ninety years old and living in Baltimore, decides to employ a young Yiddish scholar to translate his memoirs, most of which have been recorded in a series of notebooks, into English. As the older man clarifies the stories told in his notebook, he relieves his youth in Russia and Poland, his arrival in the United States, and particularly the legend that he was saved from certain death as a baby during the pogroms when the four-year-old butcher's daughter, Sasha, chased the killers away from him. Eventually even the truth of that legend is revealed when Sasha herself arrives in America in the 1930s and Malpesh tracks her down, believing it is their romantic fate to be together.

Subjects. 20th Century; Baltimore; Books and Reading; Diary; Elderly; First Person; Historical Fiction; Immigrants and Immigration; Jews and Judaism; Men's Lives; Poland; Religion; Young Men

Awards: National Jewish Book Award

Now Try: Manseau is also the author of the superlative memoir *Vows: The Story of a Priest, a Nun, and Their Son* and the travel book *Rag and Bone: A Journey Among the World's Holy Dead*. Other novels in which the importance of past stories are paramount are Geraldine Brooks's *The People of the Book*, Amy Bloom's *Away*, Debra Dean's *The Madonnas of Leningrad*, Nicole Krauss's *The History of Love*, and Lillian Nattel's *The River Midnight*. Another story of survival in the face of war is David Benioff's *City of Thieves*, and Robert Alexander's historical novel *The Kitchen Boy* also depends on a personal diary. A nonfiction account of a man who strove to save Yiddish books from destruction is Aaron Lansky's *Outwitting History: The Amazing Adventures of a Man Who Rescued a Million Yiddish Books*; Daniel Mendelsohn's personal and evocative memoir *The Lost: Searching for Six of Six Million* might also appeal.

Mapson, Jo-Ann.

The Owl & Moon Café. **Simon & Schuster, 2006. 356pp. ISBN 9780743266413.**

Four generations of Moon women, including college professor Mariah Moon and her twelve-year-old daughter Lindsay, Mariah's mother Allegra, and Allegra's mother Bess, find themselves living and working together in the restaurant Allegra owns in Pacific Grove, California. Health, love, and other life challenges face all these women, but as able and creative in facing adversity as they are individually (Lindsay, for one, uses her science knowledge to start a less than legal agricultural project to help alleviate her grandmother's financial woes), they are even stronger together.

Subjects: Book Groups; California; Cancer; Domestic Fiction; Family Relationships; Health Issues; Mothers and Daughters; Multigenerational Fiction; Multiple Viewpoints; Restaurants; Women Authors; Women's Fiction

Now Try: Mapson is also the author of the <u>Bad Girl Creek</u> trilogy, comprising *Bad Girl Creek, Along Came Mary*, and *Goodbye, Earl*. Alice Hoffman's novel about close sisters (who share magical abilities to boot) is *Practical Magic*. Other novels featuring strong female characters are Rebecca Wells's *Divine Secrets of the Ya-Ya Sisterhood*; Sue Monk Kidd's *The Secret Life of Bees*; Kristin Hannah's *On Mystic Lake, The Things We Do for Love*, and *Magic Hour*; and Barbara Kingsolver's *The Bean Trees* and *Pigs in Heaven*. The restaurant setting plays an important role in this novel; other titles set in and around restaurants might also be suggested, such as Judith Ryan Hendricks's *Bread Alone* and *The Baker's Apprentice*, Karen Hubert Allison's *How I Gave My Heart to the Restaurant Business*, or even Fannie Flagg's *Fried Green Tomatoes at the Whistle Stop Cafe*.

Mattison, Alice.

Nothing Is Quite Forgotten in Brooklyn. HarperCollins, 2008. 290pp. ISBN 9780061430558.

Mattison tells two stories, set in the same location and featuring the same characters, but in two different time periods. In the first story, set in 1989, Constance (Con) Tepper is apartment-sitting for her mother Gert, in Brooklyn, while the older woman is visiting a friend, Marlene Silverman, of whom Con has always been slightly in awe. Over the course of a week, the apartment is broken into and her own purse stolen; while making calls to deal with that, she learns a number of things about her mother and her husband that set her life on a very different course. The second story, set in 2003, finds Constance living and working in the city, but still dealing with the repercussions of that singular week in 1989, especially in regard to her relationships with her mother and her mother's friend Marlene (as well as with her own daughter, Joanna).

Subjects: 1980s; Book Groups; Brooklyn; Family Relationships; Family Secrets; Friendships; Mothers and Daughters; New York City; Women Authors; Women's Fiction

Now Try: Mattison is also the author of the novels *Field of Stars, Hilda and Pearl*, and *The Book Borrower* (as well as the story collections *In Case We're Separated* and *Men Giving Money, Women Yelling*). Her fiction writing style has been compared to that of Grace Paley, whose omnibus *The Collected Stories* might appeal (another popular author whose subjects often center on women's lives is Carol Shields; her story collections *Dressing up for the Carnival* and *Collected Stories* might also be suggested, as might Lydia Davis's *Break It Down* and *Varieties of Disturbance*). Julia Glass's novels, also set at least partially in New York, might appeal (they include *Three Junes* and *The Whole World Over*). Those readers enthralled with the Brooklyn setting of the novel might also consider Colm Tóibín's *Brooklyn: A Novel* or Marc Eliot's oral history of the borough, *Song of Brooklyn*.

McGahern, John.

🎀 *By the Lake.* Knopf, 2002. 335pp. ISBN 9780679419143.

McGahern's large cast of characters, including the local IRA chapter's leader, Jimmy Joe McKiernan, womanizer John Quinn, expatriates from London the Ruttledges, and the richest man in the village, known only as "the Shah," work and live together in their community in a series of related vignettes told over the course of a year.

Second Appeal: Setting

Subjects: Community Life; Friendships; Interconnected Stories; Ireland; Irish Authors; Men's Lives; Small-town Life

Awards: ALA Notable; New York Times Notable

Now Try: McGahern's other books include *The Barracks, The Dark, Amongst Women*, and *The Pornographer*. Although somewhat grittier in tone and language, Roddy Doyle's humorous <u>Barrytown Trilogy</u> also offers a look at Irish society and friendships; those three titles are *The Commitments, The Snapper*, and *The Van*. Other works in which communities of characters interact with one another are Wendell Berry's *Jayber Crow*, Oscar Casares's *Brownsville*, and Joe Connelly's somewhat bleaker *Crumbtown*. Another Irish author who might appeal to McGahern's readers is William Trevor; his novels include *Felicia's Journey*, and his short story collections *Cheating at Canasta* and *The Hill Bachelors* might be of particular interest.

McGhee, Alison.

Falling Boy. Picador, 2007. 194pp. ISBN 9780312425920.

When sixteen-year-old Joseph is in an accident and loses the use of his legs, he moves to stay with his father in Minneapolis, Minnesota, and becomes the nucleus of an oddly cohesive group of teens: Zap, his coworker at a bakery; Mai, who conceals a growing crush on Joseph; her brother Cha, who largely exists in a world of his own, and a younger neighborhood girl, Enzo, who seems to badly need to believe Zap's cover story for Joseph (that Joseph was a superhero injured in the line of flying and other superhero duties).

Subjects: Accidents; Coming-of-age; Disabilities; Friendships; Minnesota; Quick Reads; Superheroes; Teenagers; Women Authors; YA

Now Try: McGhee is also the author of other YA-friendly novels for adults, including *Shadow Baby, All Rivers Flow to the Sea, Rainlight*, and *Was It Beautiful?* Other books featuring strong children protagonists include Kaye Gibbons's *Ellen Foster*, Kiara Brinkman's *Up High in the Trees*; Catherine O'Flynn's *What Was Lost*, and the more language-driven but still fascinating *Mercury Under My Tongue* by Sylvain Trudel. Two other authors who are marketed to the YA audience but whose books might appeal to adults are John Green (*Looking for Alaska, An Abundance of Katherines*, and *Paper Towns*) and the writing team Rachel Cohn and David Levithan (*Nick and Norah's Infinite Playlist* and *Naomi and Ely's No-Kiss List*). Craig Thompson's coming-of-age graphic novel *Blankets* might also be suggested to these readers.

McLain, Paula.

A Ticket to Ride: A Novel. Ecco, 2008. 254pp. ISBN 9780061340512.

It's the summer of 1973, and fifteen-year-old Jamie Lynn, who has spent most of her life being cared for by her grandparents in California, has been sent to live with her uncle Raymond in Illinois. Her life there is one of quiet boredom, until her cousin, sixteen-year-old Fawn, comes to stay with them for the summer. Almost immediately consumed by her fascination with and desire for Fawn to like her, Jamie starts engaging in willful behavior like her cousin's, and the pair eventually end up in a bad situation in Chicago (which will get much worse, not for them, but for another innocent friend they convinced to drive them there). Although primarily told in the first person by Jamie, the stories of Raymond's attempts to save his sister Suzette

(Jamie's mother, who left Jamie with her own parents) from various entanglements and problems periodically interrupt Jamie's narration.

Subjects: 1970s; American Midwest; Coming-of-age; Family Relationships; First Novels; First Person; Friendships; Illinois; Multiple Viewpoints; Teenage Girls; Teenagers; Women Authors

Now Try: McLain has also written a memoir, *Like Family: Growing up in Other People's Houses*. Other books about the connections between girls and young women might be suggested, such as Leah Stewart's *The Myth of You and Me* or Jennifer Paddock's *A Secret Word*; novels about missing children might be interesting read-alikes, such as *Songs for the Missing* by Stewart O'Nan or *Who by Fire* by Diana Spechler. Women's coming-of-age memoirs, such as Nicole Lea Helget's *The Summer of Ordinary Ways*, Mary Karr's *The Liar's Club*, or Danielle Trussoni's *Falling Through the Earth* (about being raised by her father, who was a Vietnam veteran), might also appeal.

Meek, James.

We Are Now Beginning Our Descent. **Canongate, 2008. 295pp. ISBN 978-1847671769.**

Welsh journalist Adam Kellas is only covering wars long enough to write a thriller novel and make his millions, until the events of 9/11 happen and steal what he had mapped out as a fictional plot. On the edge of a midlife crisis, out of a failed marriage, and with a thriller idea he can no longer market, he agrees to cover the war in Afghanistan for a London paper. There he meets Astrid Walsh, an American reporter, with whom he shares conversation, a profession, and one passionate night before their lives diverge. As Kellas continues thereafter to move through his life without much direction, he eventually finds himself reunited with Astrid in a small American town, where they struggle once again to connect.

Subjects: Afghanistan; Expatriates; Great Britain; Journalism; London; Love Affairs; Men's Lives; Midlife Crisis; Travel; War

Now Try: James Meek's first novel, *The People's Act of Love*, also received good reviews and might appeal to these readers. Fiction about expatriates and wartime experiences includes Pat Barker's novel *Double Vision*, Mary Lee Settle's *Celebration*, and Francesca Marciano's *Rules of the Wild* and *The End of Manners*. Other novels in which men and women engage in nontraditional love affairs might be offered, such as Andrew Sean Greer's *The Story of a Marriage*, Joseph O'Neill's *Netherland*, Tom Perrotta's *Little Children*, Deborah Copaken Kogan's *Between Here and April*, and Frederick Barthelme's *Second Marriage*. Other novels and nonfiction with international settings might also be suggested, including Paul Theroux's novel *The Mosquito Coast*, Alex Garland's novel *The Beach*, or even Åsne Seierstad's nonfiction *The Bookseller of Kabul*.

Millar, Martin.

The Good Fairies of New York. **Soft Skull Press, 2006. 242pp. ISBN 978-1933368368.**

New York city residents and neighbors Dinnie and Kerry find their lives invaded by two small Scottish fairies, Heather and Morag, on the lam from their native Scotland and still hoping to go home someday to form their Celtic thrash band. Invisible to all but a few select New Yorkers, the fairies are shocked to find they're not the only fairies in the city—and they just might need all the help they can get, as Tala, the Cornish king of the fairies, wants to hunt down his escaped children Petal and Tulip, who are also hiding in New York. Also on hand is a homeless woman who is busily leading her troops into battle as Xenophon—and then things get weird.

Subjects: Fairies; Fantasy; Humor; Music and Musicians; New York City; Quick Reads; Scottish Authors; Small Press; YA

Now Try: Millar's other quick-reading novels include the coming-of-age story *Suzy, Led Zeppelin, and Me* and *Milk, Sulphate, and Alby Starvation*, as well as a fantasy series (under the name Martin Scott) that started with the title *Thraxas*. Neil Gaiman wrote the introduction to this Soft Skull edition of Millar's book; Gaiman's series of graphic novels, starting with *The Sandman: Preludes and Nocturnes*, might be suggested, as might his novels *Neverwhere* and *Stardust*. Although it is a YA series, Eoin Colfer's Artemis Fowl books, featuring relationships between the human and faerie worlds, might also be suggested; that series starts with *Artemis Fowl*. Although his books can't really be categorized as fantasy, Magnus Mills's enjoyably weird and culturally similar (Millar and Mills share a Scottish background) novels *The Restraint of Beasts* and *The Scheme for Full Employment* might be enjoyable read-alikes.

Miller, Sue.

Lost in the Forest. Knopf, 2005. 247pp. ISBN 9781400042265.

When Eva's second husband John is killed in a car accident, the abrupt shattering of her family—which includes two daughters by her first husband, Mark, and a young son, Theo, with John—mires Eva in shock and grief, and sends her middle daughter, fifteen-year-old Daisy, searching for love and comfort in the form of an inappropriate and sexual affair with the much older husband of one of her mother's friends.

Subjects: Adultery; Book Groups; California; Death and Dying; Domestic Fiction; Family Relationships; Grief; Multiple Viewpoints; Sexuality; Single Mothers; Teenage Girls; Teenagers; Widows; Women Authors; Women's Fiction

Now Try: Miller's earlier novels, including *While I Was Gone* and *The Good Mother*, might be suggested to these readers. Other novels in which the death of a parent sends children reeling include David Rhodes's *Rock Island Line*, Willam Maxwell's *They Came Like Swallows* and *So Long, See You Tomorrow*, Eliza Minot's *The Tiny One*, Stephanie Kallos's *Sing Them Home*, and Nicole Krauss's *The History of Love*. In Veronica Chater's memoir *Waiting for the Apocalypse: A Memoir of Faith and Family*, the author discusses her relationship with her uber-Catholic father and the effect it had on her future relationships; Jennifer Lauck's *Blackbird: A Childhood Lost and Found*, about the deaths of both her parents, might also be suggested.

The Senator's Wife. Knopf, 2008. 305pp. ISBN 9780307264206.

Meri Fowler and Delia Naughton, both at very different places in their lives and marriages, nonetheless share geography in the form of a New England townhouse, in which they live in separate but adjoining quarters with their respective husbands. Delia, having long ago accepted her senator husband's philandering ways, and Meri, adrift in new motherhood and coming to grips with uncomfortable aspects of her own childhood, grow close as friends, but such closeness also leads to events that will destroy their friendship.

Subjects: Academia; Adultery; Book Groups; Domestic Fiction; Friendships; Marriage; Parenting; Political Fiction; Women Authors; Women's Fiction

Now Try: Miller is also the author of the novels *Lost in the Forest*, *The Distinguished Guest*, and *The World Below*. Although the political story line in Miller's novel is not the focal point, other novels in which women are involved in politics might appeal, including Curtis Sittenfeld's *American Wife*, Marge Piercy's *The Third Child*, and Ann Patchett's *Run*. Another author who might appeal to Sue Miller fans is Jacquelyn Mitchard; consider suggesting her novels *Twelve Times Blessed* and *The Breakdown Lane*.

Mitchell, David.

🌳 *Black Swan Green*. **Random House, 2006. 294pp. ISBN 9781400063796.**

Thirteen-year-old Jason Taylor, coming of age in the British suburban village Black Swan Green in 1982, lets the reader in on his atypical typical life: trying to conquer his stutter (or, at the very least, keep it hidden from his classmates), trying to look away during his parents' increasingly frequent fights, and trying to figure out how one obtains a girlfriend to "snog and be seen snogging." Mitchell's storytelling is fluid and full of imagery, but Jason's extreme likeability and decency are what ground this novel.

Subjects: 1980s; British Authors; Coming-of-age; Family Relationships; First Person; Great Britain; Humor; Teenage Boys; Teenagers; YA

Awards: ALA Notable; Alex Award; New York Times Notable

Now Try: Mitchell is also the author of the less narratively straightforward but still interesting novels *Ghostwritten*, *Number9Dream*, and *The Cloud Atlas*. Novels by other British (and Scottish) male authors may appeal, including those by Mark Haddon (*The Curious Incident of the Dog in the Night-Time*), Nick Hornby (*About a Boy*, *High Fidelity*, and the YA novel *Slam*), Iain Banks (*Crow Road*), Martin Millar (*Suzy, Led Zeppelin, and Me*), Philip Hensher (*The Northern Clemency*), and William Sutcliffe (*Whatever Makes You Happy*). The quintessential male coming-of-age novel *The Catcher in the Rye*, by J. D. Salinger, might also appeal to these readers. A number of humorous memoirs in which boys try to make their way in the world while still being themselves might appeal, including Mark Barrowcliff's *The Elfish Gene: Dungeons, Dragons, and Growing up Strange*, Paul Feig's *Kick Me: Adventures in Adolescence* and *Superstud: Or, How I Became a 24-Year-Old Virgin*, and Benjamin Nugent's *American Nerd: The Story of My People*.

Mootoo, Shani.

He Drown She in the Sea. **Grove Press, 2005. 321pp. ISBN 9780802117984.**

On the (fictional) Caribbean island Guanagaspar, childhood friends Rose Sangha and Harry St. George are able to ignore their differences in class, until an incident in which they are caught together (innocently enough) prompts the adults who catch them to demand their separation. Harry does eventually leave the island for Vancouver, Canada, but is never really able to get over Rose; she remains on the island and marries a prestigious man, with whom she is not really happy. Eventually, however, Rose's visit to her daughter, who also lives in Vancouver, will change the trajectory of both their lives forever.

Second Appeal: Setting

Subjects: Canada; Canadian Authors; Caribbean; Flashbacks; Friendships; Love Affairs; Marriage; Multicultural; Racism; Social Class; Women Authors

Now Try: Guanagaspar was also the setting for Mootoo's first novel, *Cereus Blooms at Night*. Sara Gruen's *Water for Elephants* focuses on an unforgettable love affair, as does Beth Gutcheon's *More Than You Know*. Jhumpa Lahiri's story collection *Unaccustomed Earth*, with its focus on relationships, might also be a good read-alike for this novel. Several nonfiction accounts of unforgettable love affairs are Harry Bernstein's *Invisible Wall: A Love Story That Broke Barriers*, Med Vehta's *Red Letters*, and Rob Sheffield's *Love Is a Mix Tape*. Kiran Desai's *The Inheritance of Loss*, another novel that deals with themes of loves lost and family connections broken, as well as of immigration and immigrant lives, might also appeal to these readers. Rafael Yglesias's novel *A Happy Marriage*, about a couple who were able to act on their love for one another and marry, is also told in flashbacks and deals with separation of a different sort.

Mura, David.

Famous Suicides of the Japanese Empire. **Coffee House Press, 2008. 269pp. ISBN 9781566892155.**

In this moving novel, told largely in flashback, Chicago academic and teacher Ben Ohara, the sole remaining member of his family, relives his childhood in Chicago, spent largely trying to understand his younger and bizarrely brilliant brother Tommy, who disappeared as an adult after a trip to the Mojave Desert. In addition to telling the story of his current life, teaching and raising a family, and his childhood memories, Ohara also shares snippets from a book he is writing (titled, of course, *Famous Suicides of the Japanese Empire*) and intersperses details of his parents' lives and their internment in camps for Japanese Americans during World War II.

Subjects: Academia; Asian Americans; Chicago; Coming-of-age; Family Relationships; Family Secrets; Fathers and Sons; First Novels; First Person; Flashbacks; Internment Camps; Japanese American Authors; Japanese Americans; Men's Lives; Small Press; Suicide; World War II

Now Try: Mura is also the author of the memoirs *Turning Japanese* and *Where the Body Meets Memory*, as well as three books of poetry. Other novels in which political and historical events influence their characters might be suggested, such as Ha Jin's *Waiting* and *A Free Life*, Gish Jen's *The Love Wife*, and David Guterson's *Snow Falling on Cedars*. Scott Lasser's *The Year That Follows* also features a family coming to terms with tragedy.

Nahai, Gina.

Caspian Rain. **MacAdam Cage, 2007. 298pp. ISBN 9781596922518.**

Set in the decade prior to the Islamic Revolution in Iran, Nahai's novel focuses on the Iranian Jewish family of Omid Arbab, his wife Bahar (whose upbringing in the Jewish slums she tries to forget and keep secret), and their daughter Yaas, a sensitive girl who is going deaf and worries that she continually falls short of her mother's expectations.

Subjects: Book Groups; Deafness; Disabilities; Family Relationships; Iran; Islamic Revolution; Jews and Judaism; Mothers and Daughters; Multicultural; Women Authors

Now Try: Nahai is also the author of the novels *Sunday's Silence*, *Moonlight on the Avenue of Faith*, and *Cry of the Peacock*. Another view of the Islamic Revolution can be found in Marjane Satrapi's graphic novels *Persepolis* and *Persepolis II*. Dalia Sofer's *The Septembers of Shiraz* and Khaled Hosseini's *A Thousand Splendid Suns* also feature the effect of religion and politics on family life. Azadeh Moaveni's *Lipstick Jihad: A Memoir of Growing up Iranian in America and American in Iran* and *Honeymoon in Tehran: Two Years of Love and Danger in Iran*, Said Sayrafiezadah's

When Skateboards Will Be Free: A Memoir of a Political Childhood, and Farideh Goldin's *Wedding Song: Memoirs of an Iranian Jewish Woman* are all nonfiction titles that might appeal to these readers.

Nelson, Antonya.

Nothing Right: Short Stories. **Bloomsbury, 2009. 296pp. ISBN 9781596915749.**

Nelson's collection of eleven short stories opens with the briskly paced and still sobering title short story, in which Hannah learns about her teenage son's girlfriend and about the girl's pregnancy while she and the girl's father share community service duties (the punishment for various transgressions of their children). Coming at a moment when Hannah is stymied by how to care for her own son, the timing is difficult, to say the least. And the stories don't get any easier from there, examining issues of parenting, family relationships, and the special sort of spiraling out of control that only a personal life can undergo.

Subjects: Dysfunctional Families; Family Relationships; Parenting; Short Stories; Society; Women Authors

Now Try: Nelson is a critically acclaimed short story writer; her other unflinching collections, titled *Female Trouble* and *The Expendables,* might be offered, as might her novel *Nobody's Girl.* Other short story collections that may appeal to these readers include Ali Smith's *The First Person and Other Stories,* Maxim Biller's *Love Today: Stories,* Mary Gaitskill's *Don't Cry: Stories,* and Miranda July's *No One Belongs Here More Than You: Stories.*

Nicholls, David.

A Question of Attraction. **Villard Books, 2003. 338pp. ISBN 9781400061815.**

The year is 1985, and Brian Jackson is moving from the small house he shares with his mother on England's eastern coast to a university, where he hopes to embark upon a quest for knowledge, make his dad (who died when he was little) proud of him, and fall in love (not necessarily in that order). When he tries out for *University Challenge,* a trivia game show that pits university teams against one another, and meets the beautiful Alice Harbinson, he thinks all his dreams are finally coming true, if he can just contain his often misunderstood sense of humor (not to mention his acne). Although everything he wants is seemingly within his grasp, fate intervenes in the form of a nonconformist named Rebecca and an appearance on the game show that emphatically does not go as planned.

Subjects: 1980s; Academia; British Authors; Coming-of-age; First Novels; First Person; Friendships; Great Britain; Humor; Love Affairs; Men's Lives; Young Men

Now Try: *A Question of Attraction* was the basis for the film *Starter for 10*; Nicholls is also the author of the novel *The Understudy.* Other male coming-of-age stories that might appeal to these readers include David Mitchell's *Black Swan Green,* Kyle Beachy's *The Slide,* and Roddy Doyle's *The Commitments.* David Lodge's *Small World: An Academic Romance* is also set on college campuses and displays a similar understated style of humor.

Niederhoffer, Galt.

The Romantics. **St. Martin's Press, 2008. 277pp. ISBN 9780312373375.**

Niederhoffer's "Romantics" are a group of former Yale classmates and friends who are now moving through their mid- and late twenties. Gathered together once again six years after graduation, for the Maine wedding of two of their members, Tom McDevon and Lila Hayes, the friends will rekindle old alliances, jealousies, and disputes, particularly the long-standing rivalry between Lila and Tom's first girlfriend, Laura (who was always an uneasy member of the group, particularly because of her ethnic background and Judaism).

Subjects: Academia; Friendships; Jews and Judaism; Love Affairs; Maine; Romance; Women Authors

Now Try: Niederhoffer's first novel was titled *A Taxonomy of Barnacles*. Other novels in which women have difficulty getting over their first loves are Leah Stewart's *The Myth of You and Me*, Jean Hanff Korelitz's *Admission*, Anne Tyler's *Back When We Were Grownups*, and Mary Guterson's *We Are All Fine Here*. A more suspenseful novel about a group of college friends is Donna Tartt's *The Secret History*; other college friendships are explored in Joanna Rakoff Smith's *A Fortunate Age* and Mary McCarthy's classic *The Group*; Curtis Sittenfeld's novel *Prep* is set among a slightly younger set of prep school students.

Niffenegger, Audrey.

Her Fearful Symmetry. Scribner, 2009. 406pp. ISBN 9781439165393.

When Elspeth Noblin dies, she leaves her London flat and her entire estate to her nieces, identical twins Julia and Valentina Poole, who at age twenty-one are still living with their parents in a Chicago suburb. There is one stipulation, however; they must agree to live together in the flat for one year before selling it, and their parents (including their mother Edie, Elspeth's identical twin sister) are not allowed to enter the flat if they visit. The more dominant of the pair, Julia, decides the flat is just the thing they have been waiting for, and they travels to London and move in. They discover that their downstairs neighbor is their aunt Elspeth's boyfriend Robert, and their upstairs neighbor is a man suffering from OCD. They are not the only residents of the house; Elspeth, too, makes her residence there (as a ghost, who "works out" so that she can contact the living through various means), with plans of her own.

Subjects: Death and Dying; Family Relationships; Family Secrets; Ghosts; Great Britain; London; Love Affairs; Multiple Viewpoints; Siblings; Sisters; Twins; Women Authors

Now Try: Niffenegger is also the author of the novel *The Time Traveler's Wife*, as well as the graphic novels *The Three Incestuous Sisters* and *The Adventuress*. Two other novels in which twins and sisters share a special relationship are Lori Lansens's *The Girls* and Edward Carey's *Alva & Irva: The Twins Who Saved a City*. Another novel set in Great Britain and informed by a female character who has died before her time is Catherine O'Flynn's *What Was Lost*; Kate Christensen's skill in telling a story using multiple voices in *The Great Man* might also make that novel a good read-alike.

O'Dell, Tawni.

Sister Mine. Shaye Areheart Books, 2007. 405pp. ISBN 9780307351265.

Shae-Lynn Penrose returns to her hometown of Jolly Mount, Pennsylvania, hoping that she can put the memories of her harsh childhood behind her and start fresh with a new job (and one for her twenty-four-year-old son Clay as well). Her hopes that the past will not intrude on her future are dashed when a lawyer shows up looking for her sister, who Shae-Lynn had believed was murdered eighteen years previously. When her sister Shannon herself shows up, heavily pregnant, Shae-Lynn must come to terms with her childhood, her relationship with her sister, and what it really means to go home again.

Subjects: Book Groups; Family Relationships; Family Secrets; First Person; Pennsylvania; Siblings; Sisters; Women Authors; Women's Fiction

Now Try: O'Dell is also the author of the Oprah Book Club choice *Back Roads* and the novel *Coal Run*. In this novel Shae-Lynn's boyfriend is the survivor of a coal-mining accident; the short nonfiction book *The Scotia Widows*, also about a mine accident, might appeal. Other works that have been selected by Oprah for her book club might appeal to O'Dell's readers, including Lalita Tademy's *Cane River*, Christina Schwarz's *Drowning Ruth*, A. Manette Ansay's *Vinegar Hill*, and Bret Lott's *Jewel*.

O'Flynn, Catherine.

🏆 *What Was Lost.* Holt, 2008. 246pp. ISBN 9780805088335.

In 1984 in Birmingham, Great Britain, ten-year-old Kate Meaney has a fledgling detective agency and a propensity to wander about her town's shopping complex on the lookout for suspicious behavior. When she disappears, suspicion is immediately focused on her neighbor, twenty-two-year-old Adrian, who works in his father's shop and, along with being Kate's friend, was the last person to see her alive. Fast forward twenty years, and the narrative shifts to the story of Kurt and Lisa (Adrian's younger sister), who are brought together when Kurt is the only one who can see what appears to be a lost young girl on the mall's security cameras. The final effect is haunting, with O'Flynn's intricate piecing together of events and characters only resolved in the last few pages.

Subjects: British Authors; Coming-of-age; Family Relationships; First Novels; Friendships; Great Britain; Kidnapping; Love Affairs; Multiple Viewpoints; Retail; Women Authors

Awards: Costa First Novel Award

Now Try: David Mitchell's novel *Black Swan Green*, set during the same time period in Great Britain, might also appeal to these readers, as might Martin Millar's surprisingly gentle novel of love and music, *Suzy, Led Zeppelin, and Me*. A classic novel with an outstanding female protagonist is Harper Lee's *To Kill a Mockingbird*; Alice Sebold's *The Lovely Bones*, though more shocking in subject matter, also involves the disappearance of a young girl. Other novels that focus on missing children might be suggested, such as Donna Tartt's *The Little Friend*, Tana French's *In the Woods*, Diana Spechler's *Who by Fire*, Stewart O'Nan's *Songs for the Missing*, and Keith Donohue's *The Stolen Child*.

O'Nan, Stewart.

Last Night at the Lobster. Viking, 2007. 146pp. ISBN 9780670018277.

The order has come down from corporate, and the Red Lobster restaurant that Manny DeLeon manages will be closed down. In this chronicle of his and his staff's last day and night at the Lobster, Manny finds himself at the mercy of mutinous staff members who weren't all that motivated to begin with; tortured by his continuing feelings for Jacquie, a waitress with whom he had an affair but who has left him because of her desire to stay with her boyfriend and because Manny's girlfriend is pregnant; and facing a bevy of typically difficult customers, all in the middle of a terrible snowstorm, and still wondering what to get his girlfriend for the perfect Christmas gift. Looking for a perfect last day at the restaurant, he gets anything but . . . which turns out to be oddly appropriate anyhow.

Subjects: Book Groups; Connecticut; Friendships; Humor; Love Affairs; Men's Lives; New England; Quick Reads; Restaurants; Retail; Work Relationships

Now Try: O'Nan's other novels, including *In the Walled City, Snow Angels*, and *The Names of the Dead*, might also appeal. Two other novels of workplace dynamics are Joshua Ferris's well-reviewed *Then We Came to the End* and Douglas Coupland's *Microserfs*. A wide variety of nonfiction memoirs and investigative writing about restaurants and service jobs might be suggested, such as Debra Ginsberg's *Waiting: The True Confessions of a Waitress, Waiter Rant* (by an author known only as "the waiter"), Phoebe Damrosch's *Service Included: Four-Star Secrets of an Eavesdropping Waiter*, Iain Levison's *A Working Stiff's Manifesto* (as well as his novel *Since the Layoffs*), and Barbara Ehrenreich's classic *Nickel and Dimed: On (Not) Getting by in America*.

Songs for the Missing. **Viking, 2008. 287pp. ISBN 9780670020324.**

The disappearance of their daughter, sibling, friend, and girlfriend, Kim, affects her parents Ed and Fran, her sister Lindsay, her friends, and her boyfriend in different ways—thereby illuminating the reality of how many different personalities and functions even one person can exhibit. Told from the multiple viewpoints of all the people whom Kim's disappearance has affected, and years after the fact, O'Nan's quietly elegiac novel explores the havoc that loss can wreak on family relationships, and highlights the difficulties all people have in dealing with uncertainty (particularly the horrid uncertainty of not knowing the whereabouts of your own child).

Subjects: Book Groups; Family Relationships; Kidnapping; Multiple Viewpoints; Ohio; Parents; Siblings; Sisters; Teenage Girls; Teenagers

Now Try: O'Nan's other novels include the historical fiction title *A Prayer for the Dying*, as well as *The Names of the Dead, Snow Angels*, and *Wish You Were Here*. Other novels about missing children are Catherine O'Flynn's *What Was Lost*, Deborah Copaken Kogan's *Between Here and April*, *Unless* by Carol Shields, and *Beautiful Children* by Charles Bock (although this latter novel might be a bit free-flowing for those who enjoy a more straightforward narrative). Paula McLain's *A Ticket to Ride* also examines family dynamics and teenage girls' rebellious streaks. The heartbreaking true crime titles *Fall* by Ron Franscell, *Strange Piece of Paradise* by Terri Jentz, and *A Rip in Heaven: A Memoir of Murder and Its Aftermath* by Jeanine Cummins also illustrate how devastating crimes can be to families.

Packer, Z. Z.

Drinking Coffee Elsewhere. **Riverhead Books, 2003. 238pp. ISBN 9781573222341.**

Packer's debut collection, consisting of eight stories, features diverse settings (from Washington, D.C., to Baltimore to Japan) but strongly and consistently drawn characters, most of whom are African American women at different stages in their lives, but all of whom are facing issues of race, religion, and sexuality.

Subjects: African American Authors; African Americans; Coming-of-age; Race Relations; Racism; Religion; Short Stories; Women Authors

Awards: ALA Notable; Alex Award; New York Times Notable

Now Try: Another short story collection that was a New York Times Notable and features a similar focus on race is Edward P. Jones's *All Aunt Hagar's Children: Stories*. Gayl Jones's classic *White Rat: Short Stories*, first published in 1977, might also be suggested, as might Anika Nailah's *Free: And Other Stories*. Other novels written by African American women might appeal, such as Bebe Moore Campbell's *Brothers and Sisters*, Benilde Little's *The Itch*, and Valerie Wilson Wesley's *Ain't Nobody's Business If I Do*. Although Jacqueline Woodson is known primarily as a YA author, her adult novel *Autobiography of a Family Photo* might also be a good read-alike for Packer's fans.

Parks, Tim.

Cleaver: A Novel. **Arcade, 2006. 316pp. ISBN 9781559708555.**

Harold Cleaver is at the peak of his journalism career: having just obliterated the sitting American president (so broadly drawn as to be a caricature of George W. Bush) in a widely publicized television interview, he is much in demand professionally. Personally, however, he is facing numerous challenges: his son is publishing a memoir about his childhood that does not reflect kindly on Harold (or his string of extramarital affairs with much younger women), and he has never really recovered from the death of his daughter Andrea. To sequester himself and deal with his personal issues, he isolates himself in a remote cabin in Germany, where he struggles to survive against both a challenging environment and the harshness of his memories.

Second Appeal: Language

Subjects: Adultery; Adventure; British Authors; Family Relationships; Fathers and Sons; Journalism; Men's Lives; Midlife Crisis; Psychological Fiction; Satire

Now Try: Parks's other novels include *Rapids, Judge Savage, Destiny*, and *Europa*; he has also written *Italian Neighbors* and *An Italian Education* (nonfiction travel narratives). Other suspenseful novels about men's personal journeys are J. Robert Lennon's *Castle*, Ian McEwan's *Amsterdam*, and Jim Harrison's *True North*. Nonfiction titles in which men retreat to the wilderness to depend upon themselves might also appeal, such as Edward Abbey's *Desert Solitaire: A Season in the Wilderness* and Jon Krakauer's *Into the Wild*.

Patchett, Ann.

Run: A Novel. **Harper, 2007. 295pp. ISBN 9780061340635.**

Bernard Doyle (referred to simply as "Doyle" throughout the novel) lost his wife Bernadette to cancer more than ten years prior to the opening of this novel, which finds him struggling to relate to his sons: Sullivan, the eldest, and two adopted African American sons, Tip and Teddy, who are in their early twenties. Himself the former mayor of Boston, Doyle's fondest wish is that any of his boys will follow into political careers, but none shows a particular interest in the field. However, events that follow Doyle's and his two adopted sons' attendance at a political rally will set them on a course where they at least learn to understand one another better.

Subjects: Adoption; Book Groups; Boston; Death and Dying; Family Relationships; Fathers and Sons; Interracial Families; Massachusetts; Parenting; Political Fiction; Women Authors; Women Writing as Men

Now Try: Patchett is also the author of the critically acclaimed novels *The Patron Saint of Liars, The Magician's Assistant*, and *Bel Canto*. Other political novels are Curtis Sittenfeld's *American Wife*, Sue Miller's *The Senator's Wife*, Marge Piercy's *The Third Child*, Paul Kafka-Gibbons's *DuPont Circle*, and Alan Hollinghurst's *The Line of Beauty*. Other novels featuring interracial families are Zadie Smith's *White Teeth* and *On Beauty* and Danzy Senna's *Caucasia*.

Peacock, Nancy.

Life Without Water. **Longstreet Press. 1996. 182pp. ISBN 9781563523373.**

When Sara finds Sol during the summer of love (1968), she finds herself so in love that she doesn't mind moving, with him, into a ramshackle house with no running water and floorboards painted in various colors by their many like-minded friends (many of whom are also purchasing their marijuana from Sol). After giving birth to their daughter, Cedar, however, Sara decides to leave Sol to take an extended road trip, during which she falls in love with Daniel. Eventually Sara, Cedar, and Daniel return to Sol's house and, although he has gone, in his place are a couple named Woody and Elaine. The two couples and their children then function rather as a commune—until an outsider moves in with them and upsets their tenuous harmony, leading Sara to once again leave, this time to flee to a life of respectability with a new husband. Throughout the narrative Cedar offers a clear-eyed assessment of both her mother's wandering and her relationships, and in the end, through a bundle of letters she finds in the house, comes more fully to understand her mother's restlessness.

Subjects: 1960s; Book Groups; Communes; Dysfunctional Families; Family Relationships; Love Affairs; Marriage; Mothers and Daughters; Quick Reads; Vietnam War; Women Authors

Now Try: Peacock is the author of another novel, *Home Across the Road,* as well as the nonfiction writing guide *A Broom of One's Own: Words on Writing, Housecleaning, and Life.* At the heart of this novel, Peacock has hidden a brother and sister story; a similar such story exists at the heart of Janis Hallowell's Vietnam War–era novel *She Was.* Other books about the counterculture might be offered to these readers, including T. C. Boyle's novel *Drop City,* Maxine Swann's *Flower Children,* and Kim Barnes's *A Country Called Home,* as well as nonfiction titles like Mark Kurlansky's *1968,* Tom Brokaw's *Boom! Voices of the Sixties,* and Robert Stone's *Prime Green: Remembering the Sixties.*

Perrotta, Tom.

🌳 *Little Children.* **St. Martin's Press, 2004. 355pp. ISBN 9780312315719.**

Living in the suburbs and staying at home to take care of her daughter Lucy, Sarah is feeling both boredom and a sense that she has been untrue to her feminist ideals, when she meets Todd, a stay-at-home dad who is known around the neighborhood as the "Prom King" for his good looks. Feeling unstimulated and unappreciated by their respective spouses, Sarah and Todd fall into an uneasy affair with one another. Complicating matters is the uproar caused in the neighborhood when a convicted sex offender named Ronnie moves in.

Subjects: Adultery; Classics; Community Life; Family Relationships; Marriage; Men Writing as Women; Parenting; Sex Offenders; Suburbia

Awards: ALA Notable; New York Times Notable

Now Try: Perrotta is also the author of the novels *The Wishbones, Election, Joe College,* and *The Abstinence Teacher.* Another novel in which characters chafe at the bounds of suburban life is Richard Yates's classic *Revolutionary Road;* Amy Koppelman's novel *I Smile Back* offers an even darker look at a woman's struggle to achieve happiness even though she already possesses what many would consider the American dream. Nonfiction titles in which parents try to raise their children and retain their own senses of individuality include Neal Pollack's *Alternadad*, Heather Armstrong's *It Sucked and Then I Cried*, and Rebecca Woolf's *Rockabye: From Wild to Child*.

Phillips, Jayne Anne.

Lark and Termite. **Knopf, 2009. 254pp. ISBN 9780375401954.**

The destructive power of war on families—even families who live half a world away from where the war is being fought—is the subject of Phillips's quiet but compelling novel. The story is told by several of the principal characters: Robert Leavitt, a soldier posted to Korea; his wife Lola; and their children, Lark and her younger brother, known by the nickname Termite. The family faces a terrible loss, but Lark and her brother, in particular, draw strength from their relationship.

Subjects: 1950s; Brothers and Sisters; Coming-of-age; Disabilities; Family Relationships; First Person; Historical Fiction; Korean War; Multiple Viewpoints; Siblings; West Virginia; Women Authors; Women's Fiction

Now Try: Phillips is also the author of the novels *Machine Dreams, Shelter, MotherKind*, and the story collection *Fast Lane*. Other novels set during the 1950s and primarily about family relationships might also be suggested, including Rita Mae Brown's *The Sand Castle*, Jane Hamilton's *When Madeline Was Young*, and Elizabeth Strout's *Abide with Me*. Tom Bissell's memoir of the effects of war on survivors is *The Father of All Things: A Marine, His Son, and the Legacy of Vietnam*.

Pupek, Jayne.

Tomato Girl. **Algonquin Books of Chapel Hill, 2008. 298pp. ISBN 978-1565124721.**

Eleven-year-old Ellie's life is upended when her father, stymied by her mother's mental instabilities, falls in love with and installs the teenage girl who raises and sells produce at his store as his lover and an informal caretaker for Ellie and her mother. Overcome by shock at her father's disloyalty and her hatred for Tess, the teen "tomato girl," Ellie retreats into a fantasy world of her own making, where her mother is well, her father is happy and satisfied, and Tess is gone forever.

Subjects: Adultery; American South; Book Groups; Family Relationships; Fathers and Daughters; First Novels; First Person; Mental Health; Women Authors

Now Try: Other novels in which complex family dynamics play a role are David Wroblewski's *The Story of Edgar Sawtelle*, Tiffany Baker's *The Little Giant of Aberdeen County*, Stephanie Kallos's *Sing Them Home*, Kim Barnes's *A Country Called Home*, and Elizabeth Strout's collection of interconnected stories, *Olive Kitteridge*. Memoirs in which children try to make sense of their parents' mental health issues include David Lozell Martin's *Losing Everything*, Augusten Burroughs's *Running with Scissors*, Laura Flynn's *Swallow the Ocean*, and Nick Flynn's *Another Bullshit Night in Suck City*.

Reuss, Frederick.

Mohr: A Novel. **Unbridled Books, 2006. 312pp. ISBN 9781932961171.**

Based on the real-life story of Max Mohr, a Jewish playwright and doctor and relative of the author, this is Mohr's story of leaving his homeland of Germany, as well as his wife and daughter, to work among the Chinese as they fought the early and horrific battles of World War II against Japan. In addition to this character portrait of a complex individual, Reuss also uses a unique writing style to make readers feel that they themselves are living Mohr's life as it unfolds.

Subjects: 1930s; Biographical Fiction; China; Doctors; Family Relationships; Germany; Historical Fiction; Japan; Jews and Judaism; Mohr, Max; Small Press; World War II

Now Try: Reuss's other stylized but still character-driven books include *Henry of Atlantic City* (which also features a father who leaves his family), *The Wasties*, and *Horace Afoot*. A horrific account of the hostilities between China and Japan during this era can be found in Iris Chang's classic *The Rape of Nanking*; a nonfiction account by another German in Nanking who tried to help the city's residents is John Rabe's *The Good Man of Nanking: The Diaries of John Rabe*. Other biographical fiction titles might be suggested, such as John Pipkin's *Woodsburner* (based on the life of Henry David Thoreau) or Colm Tóibín's *The Master* (about Henry James).

Reynolds, Sheri.

The Sweet In-Between. **Shaye Areheart Books, 2008. 208pp. ISBN 978-0307393890.**

Nearly eighteen-year-old Kendra ("Kenny") Lugo has not had an easy life, by any standard: her mother died of cancer, her father is in jail, and she must live with her father's girlfriend, Aunt Glo, who has problems of her own, including a painkiller addiction and unruly children. Add in Kenny's gender confusion (in the beginning of the novel she cuts off her hair and binds her breasts to appear more masculine), which is not something that is easily accepted in her small Virginia town, and her fixation on their alcoholic next-door neighbor and a crime he commits, and the result is a novel that although narrated by Kenny in rather matter-of-fact tones, roils with underlying tension and secrets.

Subjects: American South; Book Groups; Coming-of-age; Dysfunctional Families; Family Relationships; First Person; Sexuality; Southern Authors; Teenage Girls; Teenagers; Virginia; Women Authors

Now Try: Reynolds is also the author of the best-selling novel *The Rapture of Canaan*, about religious fanaticism and its effects on another young girl's life (as well as the titles *A Gracious Plenty* and *Firefly Cloak*). Other novels about young girls making their way in a cruel world are Kaye Gibbons's *Ellen Foster* and Tiffany Baker's *The Little Giant of Aberdeen County*. Memoirs in which authors struggle in their own lives with personal identity issues or indifferent parenting might also appeal, such as Kevin Sessums's *Mississippi Sissy* (a male coming-of-age narrative that also includes a crime) or Mary Karr's *The Liar's Club*.

Roth, Philip.

🖈 *Exit Ghost.* **Houghton Mifflin, 2007. 292pp. ISBN 9780618915477.**

In the ninth novel in Roth's iconic Nathan Zuckerman series, Zuckerman returns to New York City in the wake of the 9/11 terrorist attacks. Although he is over seventy years old and in the city to see a doctor about prostate problems, he nonetheless finds time to meet Amy Bellette, the former lover of Zuckerman's literary hero S. I. Lonoff, and to take a rather prurient interest in the wife of a young writing colleague.

Subjects: 9/11; Classics; First Person; Health Issues; Jewish American Authors; Literary Lives; Love Affairs; Men's Lives; New York City; Writers and Writing

Awards: New York Times Notable

Now Try: Roth's Zuckerman series began in 1979 with the publication of *The Ghostwriter*; in addition to this series, he is a prolific author of stand-alone books, which include the classics *Portnoy's Complaint, Everyman, Sabbath's Theater,* and *The Plot Against America*. Telling the story of twentieth-century America from a decidedly more WASP-ish point of view is John Updike, whose own iconic series featuring a man named Rabbit Angstrom, which started with *Rabbit, Run,* might also appeal to these readers, as might Jewish American author Phillip Lopate's novella *Two Marriages,* as well as his essay collections *Getting Personal* and *Against Joie de Vivre*.

🎗 *Indignation.* **Houghton Mifflin, 2008. 233pp. ISBN 9780547054841.**

Marcus Messner, desperate to get away from his kindly but overbearing parents and their butcher-shop livelihood, decides to attend college in the place and culture farthest away from his own that he can find: Winesburg, Ohio. Although his education proceeds apace for a while (complete with dates with popular and mature Olivia Hutton), he eventually is expelled from the school because of his refusal to attend chapel. The eventual consequences of that action and his expulsion are revealed by Roth both on the first and last pages of this slim novel.

Subjects: Academia; American Midwest; Classics; Coming-of-age; Family Relationships; First Person; Jewish American Authors; Jews and Judaism; Korean War; Ohio; Quick Reads; Teenage Boys; Young Men

Awards: New York Times Notable

Now Try: Roth is an iconic and prolific author; his character-driven Zuckerman novels (starting with the story collection *My Life as a Man* and *The Ghost Writer*) might appeal, as might stand-alone titles such as *Portnoy's Complaint* and *Everyman*. Another novel set in a college in Ohio is P. F. Kluge's *Gone Tomorrow*; authors similar in style to Roth include Saul Bellow (*The Adventures of Augie March, Herzog,* and *Ravelstein*), Nathan Englander (*For the Relief of Unbearable Urges* and *The Ministry of Special Cases*), and Cynthia Ozick (*Dictation: A Quartet* and *The Puttermesser Papers*). Another fun related read might be Sherwood Anderson's classic collection of short stories, *Winesburg, Ohio*.

Russo, Richard.

🎗 *Bridge of Sighs.* **Knopf, 2007. 527pp. ISBN 9780375414954.**

Louis Charles Lynch (known as "Lucy" to his childhood friends, with whom he largely still associates) has lived in the town of Thomaston, New York, all his life. Forty years after marrying another childhood friend, Sarah Berg, and after achieving enough success to live in the most affluent neighborhood the town has to offer, the pair decide to visit another childhood friend, Bobby Marconi, who is living an expatriate artist's life in Venice, and with whom many of their childhood secrets and stories are shared. Told partially in flashbacks that paint a picture of troubled family relationships and small-town claustrophobia, Russo slowly unfolds his epic of community life and shared ties.

Subjects: Book Groups; Expatriates; Family Relationships; Flashbacks; Friendships; First Person; Humor; Italy; Marriage; Men's Lives; Midlife Crisis; Multiple Viewpoints; New York; Small-Town Life

Awards: New York Times Notable

Now Try: Russo is often referred to as the "bard of Main Street," and earlier novels of his that may particularly appeal to these readers are *Mohawk, Empire Falls*, and *Nobody's Fool*. Another author who may prove popular with Russo's readers is John Irving, whose novels *The World According to Garp* and *A Prayer for Owen Meany* might also be suggested. Another fiction series told from a man's point of view is Richard Ford's <u>Frank Bascombe</u> series: *The Sportswriter, Independence Day*, and *The Lay of the Land*.

That Old Cape Magic. **Knopf, 2009. 261pp. ISBN 9780375414961.**

Although Jack Griffin doesn't admit it, the marriage that most affects his life and weighs in his thoughts is not his own, to his wife Joy, but rather the unhappy but unforgettable one between his mother and father. Unsatisfied academics, his parents really only enjoyed one another's company when they vacationed on Cape Cod every summer while Jack was growing up. Jack, now an academic himself, must reconcile his complicated feelings for his parents while simultaneously coping with his own midlife crisis, failing marriage, and sadness at "losing" his daughter, who has left the nest and is getting married.

Second Appeal: Setting

Subjects: Academia; Cape Cod; Family Relationships; Humor; Marriage; Massachusetts; Men's Lives; Midlife Crisis; Quick Reads

Now Try: Russo is also the author of the novels *Straight Man* (also about a man who works in academia) and *Bridge of Sighs*. Another novel about an academic mired in a midlife crisis is Tim O'Brien's *Tomcat in Love*; another author who makes relationships between men and women come alive through dialogue is Frederick Barthelme, whose novel *Waveland* is informed by both characters and setting.

Savage, Sam.

Firmin: Adventures of a Metropolitan Lowlife. **Coffee House Press, 2006. 151pp. ISBN 9781566891813.**

Born in a Boston bookstore to a distracted mother with more than enough other rat children to keep her occupied, Firmin the rat starts eating the pages of old books for physical sustenance and finds that they provide food for his soul as well. Although an early fascination with the owner of Pembroke Books, Norman Shine, is repaid with unkindness, Firmin does eventually find a human kindred spirit in the author Jerry Magoon as he takes to exploring the store's neighborhood, in this singular coming-of-age and literary tale (he may be a rat, but Firmin is one of the more likable and thoughtful characters to be found in modern literary fiction).

Subjects: 1960s; Animals; Book Groups; Books and Reading; Boston; Fantasy; First Novels; Humor; Magic Realism; Quick Reads; Rats; Small Press

Awards: ALA Notable

Now Try: Although Firmin's life intersects with humans much more than do the lives of the rabbits in the novel *Watership Down*, by Richard Adams, that novel might also appeal to animal lovers. Another book-loving protagonist can be found in Junot Díaz's *The Brief Wondrous Life of Oscar Wao*; memoirs set in bookshops might also appeal, including Lewis Buzbee's *The Yellow-Lighted Bookshop*, Paul Collins's *Sixpence House*, and Larry McMurtry's *Books: A Memoir*. Another charming novel about creatures you wouldn't expect to find in the big city is Martin Millar's *The Good Fairies of New York*.

Schmais, Libby.

The Essential Charlotte. **Thomas Dunne Books, 2003. 242pp. ISBN 9780312311643.**

Thirty-three-year-old medical researcher Charlotte is still struggling to cope with the death of her mother, a free-spirited New Yorker, when she learns that her mother's will included an unusual condition: in order to inherit her mother's loft in the city, she must live there for a year with her father. This comes as rather a surprise to Charlotte—she had thought he was also dead.

Subjects: Death and Dying; Family Relationships; Fathers and Daughters; Love Affairs; New York City; Quick Reads; Romance; Women Authors; Women's Fiction; Young Women

Now Try: Schmais is also the author of the romantic comedy *The Perfect Elizabeth: A Tale of Two Sisters*. Other novels in which fathers and daughters get to know one another are Elinor Lipman's *The Family Man*, Michael Malone's *The Four Corners of the Sky*, Ruth Ozeki's *All Over Creation*, and Benjamin Markovits's aptly titled *Fathers and Daughters*.

Schwartz, Lynne Sharon.

The Writing on the Wall. **Counterpoint, 2005. 295pp. ISBN 9781582432991.**

Thirty-four-year-old Renata is satisfied with her life as a librarian and independent woman who very rarely indulges in intimacies of any kind, with friends or lovers. When she meets Jack, however, she finds herself more interested in getting to know a man—and letting a man know her—than she's ever been. Then one day she walks to work along the Brooklyn Bridge and witnesses the destruction of the Twin Towers on 9/11—and her carefully constructed world (in which she made no room to remember the deaths of her twin sister and other loved ones) begins to crumble as well.

Subjects: 9/11; Book Groups; Death and Dying; Family Secrets; Grief; Love Affairs; New York City; Parenting; Siblings; Sisters; Women Authors; Women's Fiction

Now Try: Schwartz is also the author of the story collection *Referred Pain*, as well as the novels *In the Family Way* and *Disturbances in the Field*. Another novel in which a strong-minded woman has repressed certain memories and events is Jean Hanff Korelitz's *Admission*. Other novels about 9/11 might be offered (Shirley Abbott's *The Future of Love*, Joseph O'Neill's *Netherland*, Jay McInerney's *The Good Life*, and Helen Schulman's *A Day at the Beach*), as might nonfiction memoirs about the events of that day (Kristen Breitweiser's *Wake-Up Call: The Political Education of a 9/11 Widow*, Art Spiegelman's graphic novel *In the Shadow of No Towers*, or Marian Fontana's *A Widow's Walk: A Memoir of 9/11*).

Scott, Joanna.

Follow Me. **Little, Brown, 2009. 420pp. ISBN 9780316051651.**

As a teenager in Pennsylvania in the 1940s, Sally Werner becomes pregnant after an encounter with her cousin that started as seduction but eventually more resembled a rape; after having the baby, she abandoned it, and then embarked on a life of moving through a series of different communities and reinventing herself as she went. The story is also told in the present day by her granddaughter and namesake, Sally, who has become her grandmother's confidante.

Subjects: 1940s; Book Groups; Elderly; Family Relationships; Family Secrets; Grandmothers; Historical Fiction; Love Affairs; Multigenerational Fiction; Multiple Viewpoints; Pennsylvania; Women Authors

Now Try: Scott is also the author of the novels *Tourmaline, Liberation*, and *Make Believe*, as well as the story collection *Everybody Loves Somebody*. Novels in which elderly people look back on their lives are *Gilead* by Marilynne Robinson, *Water for Elephants* by Sara Gruen, and *Evening* by Susan Minot. Although gentler in tone, Anne Tyler's novel *Ladder of Years* also features a woman who, quite suddenly one summer, walks away from her marriage and life to start fresh in a different small community. Thomas Hardy's classics *Tess of the D'urbevilles* and *Far from the Madding Crowd* both feature strong women heroines who suffer through unhappy relationships. Meredith Hall's memoir *Without a Map*, about the difficulty of giving up one's child for adoption, might also appeal to these readers.

See, Lisa.

Shanghai Girls. **Random House, 2009. 314pp. ISBN 9781400067114.**

Sisters Pearl and May find that their great beauty brings more sorrow than joy, as it is used by their father to arrange their marriages to Chinese men living in America (a lucrative deal for him, which enables him to settle his own gambling debts). Throughout lifetimes that include more than their fair shares of abuse and hardship, as well as betrayals and misunderstandings, the sisters struggle to maintain their loyalty and attachment to one another.

Subjects: 1930s; Book Groups; Family Secrets; Historical Fiction; Immigrants and Immigration; Los Angeles; Multicultural; Siblings; Sisters; Women Authors; Women's Fiction

Now Try: Lisa See is a popular fiction author and book group pick; her other novels are *Snow Flower and the Secret Fan* and *Peony in Love*. Another novel of sisters and immigration, although set in the present day, is Tania James's *Atlas of Unknowns*; *The Seamstress of Hollywood Boulevard* is another historical novel set in Los Angeles (albeit one in which the female character exercises more control over her destiny). Family relationships and immigrant pressures also play a part in Judy Fong Bates's *Midnight at the Dragon Café*.

Semple, Maria.

This One Is Mine. **Little, Brown, 2008. 289pp. ISBN 9780316031165.**

Misunderstandings and missed connections abound in Semple's novel, which is domestic in story line but decidedly Los Angeles professional and urban in tone. Violet Parry, feeling dissatisfied in her marriage to her music producer husband David and unfulfilled by new motherhood, finds herself embroiled in a seamy love affair with guitarist Teddy Reyes; David's sister Sally, meanwhile, is doing her damnedest to achieve everything she thinks her sister-in-law Violet has by setting her marriage sights on Jeremy, a sportswriter.

Subjects: Adultery; Domestic Fiction; Family Relationships; First Novels; Humor; Los Angeles; Love Affairs; Marriage; Music and Musicians; Satire; Siblings; Women Authors

Now Try: Other novels about Los Angeles, including Steve Martin's *Shopgirl* and Deirdre Shaw's *Love or Something Like It*, might appeal to these readers. Other authors who explore the more challenging aspects of domestic life include Tom Perrota (*Little Children* and *The Abstinence Teacher*), Marisa de Los Santos (*Belong to Me*), Mary McGarry Morris (*The Last Secret*), and Sue Miller (*The Senator's Wife*).

Shriver, Lionel.

The Post-Birthday World. HarperCollins, 2007. 517pp. ISBN 9780061187841.

How would our lives be different if we made different choices? If we loved different people? These are the questions Shriver answers in her novel about Irina McGovern, a children's book illustrator living a contented life with her scholarly partner, Lawrence Trainer, in Great Britain. The narrative proceeds in straightforward style until Irina joins a friend of the couple, professional snooker player Ramsey Acton, for his birthday supper, and acts on a strange feeling of connection by kissing him, at which point the story is told in parallel to describe what her life would be like if she stayed with Lawrence and what it would be like if she left him for Ramsey instead.

Second Appeal: Language

Subjects: Art and Artists; British Authors; Great Britain; London; Love Affairs; Marriage; Sports; Women Authors

Now Try: Shriver is also the author of the Orange Prize–winning novel *We Need to Talk about Kevin*, as well as *Double Fault* and *The Female of the Species*. Shriver's writing is sensuous without being overly explicit; authors who write in a similar way include Ian McEwan (*The Comfort of Strangers, Amsterdam*, and *Atonement*) and Milan Kundera (*The Unbearable Lightness of Being* and *Slowness*). Two other authors who may appeal to Shriver's fans are Audrey Niffenegger (*The Time Traveler's Wife*), Marge Piercy (*Three Women* and *The Longings of Women*), and Amy Bloom (*Love Invents Us* and *Away*).

Sittenfeld, Curtis.

🐾 *American Wife.* Random House, 2008. 558pp. ISBN 9781400064755.

In this fictional take on the life of an American first lady (specifically Laura Bush), Sittenfeld tells the life story of Alice Lindgren, from her small-town upbringing in Wisconsin and her complex relationship with her grandmother, through the automobile accident in which she collided with and killed the teenage boy with whom she was falling in love; later chapters detail her single life in Madison, meeting the wild, charming, and family-moneyed Charlie Blackwell, and their unexpected ascendancy to the White House (as well as her reaction to the fame and scrutiny of both her public role and her opinions of her husband's policies).

Subjects: 20th Century; Book Groups; Domestic Fiction; First Person; Marriage; Political Fiction; Presidents; Small-Town Life; Wisconsin; Women Authors; Women's Fiction

Awards: New York Times Notable

Now Try: Sittenfeld is also the author of the novels *The Man of My Dreams* and *Prep*. Other recent novels in which wives question their lives and marriage choices are Sue Miller's *The Senator's Wife*, Anita Shreve's *The Pilot's Wife*, Zoë Heller's *The Believers*, and Kate Christensen's *Trouble*. Also of interest might be Sittenfeld's source materials, including Ann Gerhart's *The Perfect Wife: The Life and Choices of Laura Bush*, Frank Bruni's *Ambling into History: The Unlikely Odyssey of George W. Bush*, and Sally Bedell Smith's *For Love of Politics: Inside the Clinton White House*.

Smiley, Jane.

Ten Days in the Hills. Knopf, 2007. 449pp. ISBN 9781400040612.

In a novel based loosely on the story and format of a classical work of literature, Boccaccio's *Decameron*, Smiley tells the story of a group of family members and

Hollywood insiders who, while sequestered in their Los Angeles mansion, debate the issues surrounding the start of the 2003 invasion of Iraq and fall into and out of sexual and other relationships with one another. At the heart of the story is the middle-aged director Max and his girlfriend Elena; also partaking in the arguments are their respective children, Max's agent Stoney, and Max's friend Charlie (who is ecstatic to have traded his suburban existence for a hedonistic stay as Max's house guest, even if it is only temporary).

Subjects: Book Groups; California; Explicit Sexuality; Hollywood; Iraq War (2003); Los Angeles; Love Affairs; Marriage; Movies; Satire; Women Authors; Women's Fiction

Now Try: Smiley is also the author of the novels *Good Faith*, *Horse Heaven*, *A Thousand Acres*, and the Pulitzer Prize–winning *Moo*. Other novels set among families also living in Los Angeles might appeal, including Maria Semple's *This One Is Mine* and Deirdre Shaw's *Love or Something Like It*. Other novels combining elements of domestic fiction and satire might be suggested, such as Charles Webb's *Home School* and Jacqueline Carey's *It's a Crime*.

Somerville, Patrick.

The Cradle: A Novel. **Little, Brown, 2009. 203 pages. ISBN 9780316036122.**

In her eighth month of pregnancy, Marissa Bishop abruptly decides that she needs a cradle for her baby, and not just any cradle—she wants the cradle she once slept in, which was owned by her mother, who deserted her when she was just a baby. Convinced that her mother still has the cradle, and that her husband Matthew can track her down and obtain it, Marissa asks him to undertake the journey. Along the way he will come to terms with his own birth parents (he himself was an orphan) and will bring back something to Marissa that will change their (growing) family's lives forever.

Subjects: Adoption; Childbirth; Family Relationships; Family Secrets; Mothers and Daughters; Multiple Viewpoints; Parenting; Quick Reads; Travel; Wisconsin

Now Try: Somerville has also published a collection of stories, *Trouble*. Other novels involving family secrets might be suggested, such as Mary Guterson's *We Are All Fine Here*, Robert Goolrick's historical fiction title *A Reliable Wife*, Nancy Peacock's *Life Without Water*, and Leah Hager Cohen's *House Lights*. Another slim first novel noted for its author's powerful prose is C. E. Morgan's *All the Living: A Novel*.

Spechler, Diana.

Who by Fire. **HarperPerennial, 2008. 343pp. ISBN 9780061572937.**

In the aftermath of the disappearance of their baby sister Alena, siblings Bits and Ash Kellerman, along with their mother, Ellie, struggle to continue on with their lives. In this narrative, told from the varying viewpoints of each character years later, we learn how the three have each dealt with the tragedy. Bits seeks comfort in frequent sexual liaisons, Ash has turned to Orthodox Judaism and life on a yeshiva, and Ellie seeks to understand and help her two remaining children. Likewise, when Alena's remains are found, each family member reacts differently, and slowly a long-held secret one of them is keeping is revealed.

Subjects: Book Groups; Brothers and Sisters; Domestic Fiction; Family Relationships; Family Secrets; First Novels; Jews and Judaism; Kidnapping; Multiple Viewpoints; Women Authors

Now Try: Another family's secrets are explored in Deborah Copaken Kogan's novel *Between Here and April*; the disappearance of a young girl is also central to the novels *What Was Lost* (by Catherine O'Flynn), *Songs for the Missing* (Stewart O'Nan), and *Case Histories* (Kate Atkinson). Other novels similar in style to Spechler's are Tatiana de Rosnay's *Sarah's Key* and Kathryn Stockett's *The Help*.

Spencer, Scott.

Willing: A Novel. Ecco, 2008. 244pp. ISBN 9780060760151.

Thirty-seven-year-old Avery Jankowsky's a bit young for a midlife crisis, but with his current girlfriend, Deirdre, cheating on him, his professional life at a standstill, and his inability to afford any place to live in New York City other than the apartment he shares with Deirdre, he nonetheless feels he's hit rock-bottom. When his Uncle Ezra offers him a way out by sending him on a high-end "sex tour" (through such freer-thinking European cities as Reykjavik and Oslo), Jankowsky further decides to cash in on the experience by proposing to a literary agent that he write a memoir about the experience.

Subjects: Explicit Sexuality; Humor; Iceland; Men's Lives; Midlife Crisis; Norway; Oslo; Prostitution; Reykjavik; Satire; Travel; Writers and Writing

Now Try: Spencer is also the author of the novels *Waking the Dead*, *Men in Black*, *Endless Love*, and *The Rich Man's Table*. Other novels in which main characters' journeys through somewhat unsettling subcultures are explored might appeal, including Chuck Palahniuk's *Fight Club* and *Snuff*, Bret Easton Ellis's *American Psycho*, Stephen Elliott's *"My Girlfriend Comes to the City and Beats Me Up"*, and Walter Mosley's *Killing Johnny Fry: A Sexistentialist Novel*; Hunter Thompson's classics of nonfiction participation journalism, *Hell's Angels* and *Fear and Loathing in Las Vegas*, might also be suggested.

Now Consider Nonfiction . . . Immersion Journalism

Immersion journalism is what writers engage in when they go beyond the bounds of objectively researching a story and instead step directly into it, living whatever experience they're writing about and periodically injecting their own reactions and thoughts into their narrative. They are firsthand accounts and rely heavily for their appeal on their authors' skill in storytelling and use of language.

Buford, Bill. *Heat: An Amateur's Adventures as Kitchen Slave, Line Cook, Pasta Maker, and Apprentice to a Dante-Quoting Butcher in Tuscany.*

Conover, Ted. *Newjack: Guarding Sing Sing.*

Ehrenreich, Barbara. *Nickel and Dimed: On (Not) Getting by in America.*

Fatsis, Stefan. *Word Freak: Heartbreak, Triumph, Genius, and Obsession in the World of Competitive Scrabble Players.*

Huler, Scott. *No Man's Lands: One Man's Odyssey Through the Odyssey.*

Jacobs, A. J. *The Year of Living Biblically: One Man's Humble Quest to Follow the Bible as Literally as Possible.*

Preston, Richard. *The Wild Trees: A Story of Passion and Daring.*

Stockett, Kathryn.

The Help: A Novel. **Penguin, 2009. 451pp. ISBN 9780399155345.**

When Eugenia "Skeeter" Phelan returns to her hometown of Jackson, Mississippi, she does so with vague plans to become a writer, but, as the novel is set in the 1960s, her struggle to get a foothold on a career path is not easy, and she has few examples because many of her former friends and classmates are married and consumed with the business of running their households. The running of those households typically also includes the supervision of black maids and helpers, who do most of the work, including raising the children, but who are never considered part of the family or on a remotely equal footing with their employers. When Skeeter finally gets a job on a local newspaper writing a household hints column, she has to turn to a friend's maid, Aibileen, who not only shares her wealth of household knowledge, but also helps Skeeter understand the lives of the women and workers that she and the rest of her white contemporaries have spent a lifetime not seeing.

Subjects: 1960s; African Americans; American South; Civil Rights; Domestic Fiction; First Novels; First Persons; Friendships; Historical Fiction; Journalism; Mississippi; Race Relations; Women Authors; Women's Fiction

Now Try: Other books about race relations and friendships, particularly between women, might also be suggested to these readers, including Sue Monk Kidd's *The Secret Life of Bees*, Kaye Gibbons's *Ellen Foster*, and Bebe Moore Campbell's *Brothers and Sisters*. Other (sometimes unlikely) friendships are explored in the novels *The Guernsey Literary and Potato Peel Society* by Mary Ann Shaffer and Annie Barrows and *The Elegance of the Hedgehog* by Muriel Barbery. Character-driven nonfiction titles about the civil rights movement might also work as related reads; consider suggesting Kay Mills's *This Little Light of Mine: The Life of Fannie Lou Hamer* or Melba Pattillo Beals's *Warriors Don't Cry: A Searing Memoir of the Battle to Integrate Little Rock's Central High*.

Strout, Elizabeth.

🌳 *Olive Kitteridge.* **Random House, 2008. 270pp. ISBN 9781400062089.**

In thirteen distinct chapters, Strout weaves community and individual tales of residents of a small Maine town, all of whom have some connection to Olive Kitteridge, a junior high teacher in town. Told in multiple voices, including those of Kitteridge's husband and son, these are stories of everyday struggles with depression, unhappiness, human connections, and love, but are surprisingly luminous when taken as a whole (particularly considering their sometimes dark subject matter).

Second Appeal: Language

Subjects: Book Groups; Classics; Community Life; Domestic Fiction; Family Relationships; Interconnected Stories; Maine; Multiple Viewpoints; New England; Women Authors; Women's Fiction

Awards: ALA Notable; Pulitzer Prize

Now Try: Strout is also the author of the popular novels *Amy and Isabelle* and *Abide with Me*. Other story collections in which the stories are connected by characters and events include Tess Holthe's decidedly more exotically set *The Five-Forty-Five to Cannes*, Margaret Atwood's *Moral Disorder*, and Alice Hoffman's

Local Girls. Another novel in which related characters tell family stories is Anne Tyler's *Dinner at the Homesick Restaurant.*

Sullivan, Faith.

Gardenias: A Novel. **Milkweed Editions, 2005. 381pp. ISBN 9781571310453.**

Lark Ann Erhardt travels with her mother Arlene and her aunt Betty to California, along with multitudes of other families made (at least) temporarily fatherless by World War II. Searching for work in the region's factories, the two older women and nine-year-old Lark struggle to make new lives and friends for themselves, far from the small Minnesota town they left to start fresh.

Subjects: 1940s; California; Family Relationships; Historical Fiction; Mothers and Daughters; Multigenerational Fiction; Small Press; Women Authors; Women's Fiction; World War II

Now Try: This is the follow-up novel to Sullivan's *The Cape Ann,* which featured Lark as a six-year-old girl. Other novels in which families struggle to make their way in the world and stay connected to one another are Jayne Anne Phillips's *Lark and Termite* (which also features a character named Lark, but which is set during the Korean War) and the historical fiction title *The Guernsey Literary and Potato Peel Pie Society* by Mary Ann Shaffer and Annie Barrows. Other novels about the war experience stateside are Ella Leffland's *Rumors of Peace* and Steve Amick's *Nothing But a Smile*; Kaye Gibbons's multigenerational novel, *Charms for the Easy Life*, might also be suggested.

Suri, Manil.

The Age of Shiva. **Norton, 2007. 455pp. ISBN 9780393065695.**

Meera Sawhney, unhappy in her early marriage to singer Dev Arora, has to contend with both his alcoholism and her family's (particularly her father's) assertions that she has disgraced their family by her marriage to the lower-class Arora. Not until she gives birth to a son, Ashvin, does she feel that her life has meaning; as he grows, she will struggle to balance her love and need for him with her growing realization that he must live his own life.

Subjects: 1960s; Alcoholism; Bombay; Book Groups; Family Relationships; First Person; Hindus; Historical Fiction; India; Indian Authors; Indian American Authors; Marriage; Men Writing as Women; Mothers and Sons; Multicultural; Parenting; Political Fiction

Now Try: Suri's first novel was *The Death of Vishnu*; although this novel is not really a sequel, it has been suggested that it is the second volume in what will be a loosely connected trilogy. Novels by authors Bharti Kirchner (*Darjeeling, Sharmila's Book*, and *Shiva Dancing*) and Chitra Banerjee Divakaruni (*Queen of Dreams* and *Sister of My Heart* and its sequel *The Vine of Desire*) might also appeal to these readers.

Sutcliffe, William.

Whatever Makes You Happy. **Bloomsbury USA, 2008. 292pp. ISBN 978-1596914506.**

Three friends decide that it is once again time for them to get to know their respective sons and give them some motherly pushes toward happiness and the production of grandchildren; they decide to achieve this by going to visit each of their sons for a week. Within the three pairings, Carol finds herself frustrated by her son Matt's obviously successful but strangely empty "laddish" lifestyle (he loves his video games and he works for a magazine called *Balls*), Helen learns what she really knew all along when she meets her son Paul's boyfriend, and Gillian pushes Daniel to not only find a girl but find a suitable girl who's not opposed to motherhood.

Subjects: British Authors; Family Relationships; Gay Men; GLBTQ; Great Britain; Humor; Love Affairs; Mothers and Sons; Multiple Viewpoints; Quick Reads; Young Men

Now Try: Sutcliffe's other novels are *Are You Experienced?* and *The Love Hexagon*. Other novels about the sometimes frustrating, sometimes fulfilling, and never-dull relationships between mothers and their sons might be suggested, such as Mameve Medwed's *Of Men and Their Mothers*, Colm Tóibín's story collection *Mothers and Sons*, John Kennedy Toole's classic *A Confederacy of Dunces*, Paul Rudnick's *I'll Take It*, and Kate Saunders's *Bachelor Boys*. Memoirs about sons and their mothers might also appeal; consider Tobias Wolff's *This Boy's Life* and Rick Bragg's *All Over but the Shoutin'*.

Swift, Graham.

Tomorrow. Knopf, 2007. 255pp. ISBN 9780307266903.

The year is 1995, but Paula Hook is lying awake and thinking about the events of 1966, when she and her husband Mike met at a university during the height of the sexual revolution. Keeping her awake is her anticipation of the family secret that she and Mike have decided to tell their twins, Nick and Kate, in the morning; although it must be left to the reader to discover that secret, the author suggests that Paula's anxiety is just as much about the pace, demands, and obligations of modern life as it is about her family's personal secrets.

Subjects: 1960s; 1990s; British Authors; Day in the Life; Family Secrets; First Person; Marriage; Men Writing as Women; Mothers and Sons; Parenting; Teenagers

Now Try: This title was not as critically lauded as were several of Swift's earlier novels, including *Last Orders*, *Waterland*, and *The Light of Day*. It has been noted, however, that he very skillfully portrayed a woman's point of view; two other male authors who can do that are Wally Lamb (*She's Come Undone*) and Joe Coomer (*One Vacant Chair*). These readers might also consider novels by Ian McEwan that focus on single events, including *Saturday* and *On Chesil Beach*.

Taylor, Benjamin.

The Book of Getting Even. Steerforth Press, 2008. 166pp. ISBN 978-1586421434.

Gabriel Geismar, son of a New Orleans rabbi, seeks to put as much distance between himself and his father's expectations and lifestyle as possible by going to college at Swarthmore, in Pennsylvania, where he meets the twins Danny and Marghie Hundert. Over the course of the next few years, Gabriel immerses himself in their family's lives, only to find that all families, even those we adopt on our own, have secrets and conflicts.

Subjects: 1970s; Family Relationships; Gay Men; GLBTQ; Jews and Judaism; Mathematics; New Orleans; Quick Reads; Small Press; Young Men

Now Try: Taylor is also the author of the novel *Tales Out of School* and was the editor of *The Letters of Saul Bellow*. Other novels featuring college-aged (and just out of college) men might also be suggested, including Monica Ferrell's *The Answer Is*

Always Yes, Rachel Cusk's *In the Fold*, Philip Roth's *Indignation*, and Alan Hollinghurst's *The Line of Beauty*.

Taylor, Billy.

Based on the Movie. **Atria Books, 2008. 310pp. ISBN 9781416548775.**

Dolly grip Bobby Conlon has been left by his wife and is becoming worn down by both the physical demands of his job (lining up camera shots and building the tracks for the cameras to move along) and the networking requirements of Hollywood, when he decides to take on one last big job (and with it, a chance to direct his own movie) in—of all places—Texas. The author, himself a longtime worker in the film industry, offers just the right mix of technical knowledge about a job not often fictionalized, as well as compelling portraits of film workers and their industry camaraderie.

Subjects: California; First Novels; Humor; Marriage; Men's Lives; Movies; Professions; Texas; Work Relationships

Now Try: Taylor's novel is gently funny; other novels combining humor and a similar film industry setting are Larry McMurtry's *Loop Group*, Geoff Nicholson's *The Hollywood Dodo*, and Elmore Leonard's *Get Shorty*. Debra Ginsberg's novel about publishing, *Blind Submission*, offers a similar "inside look" at an industry, as might nonfiction "working life" memoirs such as Anthony Bourdain's *Kitchen Confidential*, Toby Cecchini's *Cosmopolitan: A Bartender's Life*, Edward Conlon's *Blue Blood*, or Steve Martin's *Born Standing Up*.

Now Consider Nonfiction . . . Working Life Memoirs

Work memoirs address a huge part of their authors' (and everybody's) lives: what it is they do for a living all day long. These authors provide the "inside look" at a variety of professions; many include elements of humor and relationship stories, and they are typically quite personal and informal narratives.

Anonymous. *The Secret Diary of a Call Girl.*

Bourdain, Anthony. *Kitchen Confidential: Adventures in the Culinary Underbelly.*

Gawande, Atul. *Complications: A Surgeon's Notes on an Imperfect Science.*

Ginsberg, Debra. *Waiting: The True Confessions of a Waitress.*

McCourt, Frank. *Teacher Man: A Memoir.*

Yancey, Richard. *Confessions of a Tax Collector: One Man's Tour of Duty Inside the IRS.*

Thompson, Jean.

Do Not Deny Me: Stories. **Simon & Schuster, 2009. 292pp. ISBN 9781416595632.**

Thompson's character-driven, dark, and somehow simultaneously bitter and touching short stories focus on entirely typical characters: a burnt-out literature professor, an office worker, and a divorced suburban wife wading back into dating (online). Through a combination of entirely accessible slices of life, dialogue, and sympathetic characterization, Thompson creates stories that will have you silently pulling for her characters to succeed, change, find happiness, or simply make it through another day unscathed.

Subjects: Family Relationships; Humor; Marriage; Quick Reads; Short Stories; Women Authors

Now Try: Thompson is also the author of the story collections *Throw Like a Girl* and *Who Do You Love*, as well as the novels *City Boy* and *Wild Blue Yonder*. She has been called the "American Alice Munro," by critics, and her readers might like to try some of Munro's collections (three of them are *Runaway*, *The Love of a Good Woman*, and *Hateship, Friendship, Courtship, Loveship, Marriage*); Carol Shields's *Collected Stories* and Antonya Nelson's *Female Trouble* might also be suggested. This collection also features a blurb from David Sedaris, whose humorous (sometimes bleakly so) memoirs, such as *Dress Your Family in Corduroy and Denim* and *When You Are Engulfed in Flames*, might also appeal. Another female nonfiction writer whose memoirs might be good read-alikes for Thompson's stories is Hollis Gillespie (*Bleachy Haired Honky Bitch* and *Trailer Trashed*).

Tóibín, Colm.

Mothers and Sons: Stories. Scribner, 2007. 271pp. ISBN 9781416534655.

The nine short stories in this volume all highlight very disparate relationships between mothers and sons, including a son whose mother's pub drinking habits and penchant for gossip nearly expose his criminal activities, the mother of a priest being charged with sexual abuse, and a musician whose pub crawl with his friends ends up in the same pub as his mother.

Subjects: Alcoholism; Family Relationships; Ireland; Irish Authors; Men's Lives; Mothers and Sons; Music and Musicians; Short Stories

Now Try: Tóibín is also the author of the historical novels *The Master* and *Brooklyn: A Novel*. He is also a previous winner of the International IMPAC Dublin award and a critically lauded Irish author; other Irish authors who may appeal to his readers are William Trevor (*Felicia's Journey*, *The Hill Bachelors*, and *Cheating at Canasta: Stories*), Sebastian Barry (*The Whereabouts of Eneas McNulty* and *The Secret Scripture*), and Anne Enright (*The Gathering* and *Yesterday's Weather: Stories*). Novels in which relationships between mothers and their sons are explored might also be suggested, including Anne Tyler's *Dinner at the Homesick Restaurant* and John Kennedy Toole's classic *A Confederacy of Dunces*; nonfiction like Tobias Wolff's classic *This Boy's Life*, Rick Bragg's *All Over But the Shoutin'*, and Bernard Cooper's *The Bill from My Father* might also appeal to these readers.

Tower, Wells.

Everything Ravaged, Everything Burned. Farrar, Straus & Giroux, 2009. 238pp. ISBN 9780374292195.

In nine disparate stories, wildly varying in landscape and characters, Tower explores the lives we are all stuck living with one another—whether it is the brother who only wanted what the other had; the down-on-his-luck contractor whose wife decides, faced with evidence of his infidelity, that he should live in his uncle's beach house (in a different state) for a while; or the teenage girls caught up in vicious competition with each another. Reviewers have referred to these stories as "well-crafted"; another descriptive phrase might be "deceptively simple" or "compulsively readable."

Subjects: Family Relationships; Humor; Quick Reads; Short Stories; Teenage Girls; Teenagers

Now Try: Other story collections that might appeal to these readers are Jay McInerney's *How It Ended*, Richard Ford's *A Multitude of Sins*, David Gates's *The Wonders of the Invisible World*, and Miranda July's *No One Belongs Here More Than You* (which also, interestingly enough, features a bright yellow cover).

Tremain, Rose.

🏵 *The Road Home*. Little, Brown, 2007. 417pp. ISBN 9780316002615.

Lev Olev, forty-two years old and seeking a new beginning outside the eastern bloc homeland where he has left his wife and child, makes his way to London to find work and a new life. Once there, however, he suffers from both homesickness and a nebulous hostility to immigrants displayed by the Britons. Not everyone is unfriendly, however, and among the surprisingly kindred souls Lev finds are Lydia (a fellow immigrant), his landlord, Christy, and even Gregory, the boss at the restaurant where he finds work.

Second Appeal: Setting

Subjects: Book Groups; British Authors; Eastern Europe; Friendships; Great Britain; Immigrants and Immigration; Multicultural; Women Authors; Women Writing as Men

Awards: New York Times Notable; Orange Prize

Now Try: Tremain is the author of many other novels, including *Sacred Country* and *The Way I Found Her*, as well as the historical novels *Restoration*, *Music and Silence*, and *The Colour*. Kiran Desai's novel *The Inheritance of Loss* also features an immigrant from India in America struggling with homesickness; Lara Vapnyar's story collection *Broccoli and Other Tales of Food and Love* also features tales of lonely immigrants and their desire both to assimilate to their new surroundings and still feel some connections to their old ones.

Trollope, Joanna.

Brother and Sister. Bloomsbury, 2004. 311pp. ISBN 9781582344003.

Although content for many years not to seek out information about her birth parents, Nathalie Dexter has decided that she would like to find her birth mother, and she wants her brother David (who was also adopted by their parents, Lynne and Ralph) to help her search for both her biological parents and his. Although she does not intend to cause family discord, her search nonetheless disrupts her relationship with her brother (and his wife and three kids) as well as with her partner Steve and their daughter Polly.

Subjects: Adoption; Book Groups; British Authors; Brothers and Sisters; Domestic Fiction; Family Relationships; Great Britain; Marriage; Parenting; Siblings; Women Authors; Women's Fiction

Now Try: Trollope is also the author of the novels *The Men and the Girls*, *A Passionate Man*, *Next of Kin*, *Second Honeymoon*, and *Friday Nights*. Other novels featuring adopted characters are George Hagen's *The Laments*, Elizabeth Brundage's *Somebody Else's Daughter*, and Caroline Leavitt's *Girls in Trouble*. Trollope has also been compared to fellow British author Marcia Willett, whose novels *The Way We Were*, *The Children's Hour*, and *Echoes of the Dance* might be suitable read-alikes. Memoirs about adoption might also be suggested; consider A. M. Homes's *The Mistress's Daughter*, Meredith Hall's *Without a Map*, and Ann Fessler's investigative title *The Girls Who Went Away: The Hidden History of Women Who Surrendered Children for Adoption in the Decades Before Roe v. Wade*.

Tucker, Lisa.

The Promised World. **Atria Books, 2009. 336pp. ISBN 9781416575382.**

Billy Cole and his fraternal twin sister Lila have always been closer than most siblings, but after Billy commits suicide (ostensibly because of the termination of his visitation rights to his children), his twin starts to experience a breakdown in her own memories and understanding of reality. After learning from Billy's widow that the twins' parents, who he had previously believed were deceased, are alive, Lila's husband Patrick contacts them and begins to learn secrets about the twins' pasts and their relationship.

Subjects: Book Groups; Brothers and Sisters; Family Relationships; Family Secrets; Multiple Viewpoints; Siblings; Suicide; Women Authors; Women's Fiction

Now Try: This is Tucker's fifth novel; her earlier titles are *The Song Reader, Shout Down the Moon, Once Upon a Day,* and *The Cure for Modern Life.* Another novel in which a brother and sister have a complex relationship (one that their significant others would like to understand) is Joanna Trollope's *Brother and Sister;* a pair of conjoined twins tell their story in Lori Lansens's *The Girls.* Another series in which characters are often strongly influenced by past experiences is Kate Atkinson's Jackson Brodie series, starting with *Case Histories* and *One Good Turn* (her novel *Behind the Scenes at the Museum* also centers on family secrets).

Tucker, Todd.

🎗 *Over and Under.* **St. Martin's Press, 2008. 275pp. ISBN 9780312379902.**

Best friends Tom Kruer and Andy Gray spend the summer before they go to high school doing what they've always done: staying outside from dawn to dark and exploring. Things change, however, when a labor dispute at their town's major employer, the Borden Casket Company, starts to intrude upon their friendship, as does Andy's awareness of girls, particularly a quiet neighbor girl whose home life is anything but ideal. When a man is killed in an explosion at the plant, the boys start to fall into the roles adopted by their respective parents, and eventually play a key role in the discovery of those who sabotaged the plant, in this moving and thoughtful coming-of-age narrative.

Subjects: 1970s; Abuse; American Midwest; Book Groups; Coming-of-age; First Novels; Friendships; Indiana; Labor History; Teenage Boys; Teenagers; Unions; YA

Awards: Alex Award

Now Try: Tucker is also the author of several volumes of nonfiction history, including *Atomic America* and *The Great Starvation Experiment.* In reviews, this novel was referred to as "reminiscent of Harper Lee's classic *To Kill a Mockingbird*"; other novels about boys growing up together might appeal, including Jonathan Coe's *The Rotters' Club* (also set during the 1970s, but in Great Britain), Alison McGhee's *Falling Boy,* and John Knowles's classic *A Separate Peace.* Male coming-of-age memoirs might also be fun read-alikes, particularly those by Jean Shepherd (which are also set in Indiana), *In God We Trust, All Others Pay Cash,* and *Wanda Hickey's Night of Golden Memories;* as well as J. R. Moehringer's *The Tender Bar,* Homer Hickam's *Rocket Boys,* and David Benjamin's *The Life and Times of the Last Kid Picked.* Two other titles about the battle between corporate profits and worker safety (in coal mines) are Denise Giardina's historical novels *Storming Heaven* and *The Unquiet Earth.*

Tyler, Anne.

🏵 *Digging to America*. Knopf, 2006. 277pp. ISBN 9780307263940.

Two very different families are bound together forever when they meet one another in the same Baltimore airport, on the same day, to welcome the baby daughters they're each adopting from Korea. Although their daughters share an arrival date, each family pursues different ideals in their childrearing: the Yazdans (husband Sami, wife Ziba, and Sami's mother Maryam), one generation removed from Iran and still somewhat unsteady in their own assimilation, name their daughter Susan; whereas Brad and Bitsy Donaldson loudly proclaim their intention to teach their daughter Jin-Ho everything they can about her Korean culture. The families get together annually to celebrate their daughters' arrival in the United States; it is through these events that Sami's mother, Maryam, gets to know Bitsy's father Dave (a new widower), and the two feel a rapport and attachment despite the differences in their lives and the lives of their children.

Subjects: Adoption; Baltimore; Book Groups; Classics; Domestic Fiction; Family Relationships; Friendships; Immigrants and Immigration; Iranian Americans; Maryland; Widowers; Widows; Women Authors; Women's Fiction

Awards: New York Times Notable

Now Try: Tyler is a perpetual favorite with readers; her other novels include *Back When We Were Grownups*, *Ladder of Years*, *Breathing Lessons*, *Searching for Caleb*, and *Saint Maybe*. Other writers whose style may appeal to Tyler's readers include Christine Schutt (*Florida* and *All Souls*), Elizabeth Strout (*Olive Kitteridge* and *Amy and Isabelle*), and Stephanie Kallos (*Broken for You* and *Sing Them Home*).

Now Consider Nonfiction . . . Gentle Family Reads

Gentle family reads are character-driven nonfiction family relationship narratives that explore positive or inspiring relationships among family members and relatives. They are feel-good reads and are typically quite fast paced, and their authors often exhibit a sense of wonder or gratitude for their family situations.

Briggs, Raymond. *Ethel and Ernest: A True Story*.

Gopnik, Adam. *Through the Children's Gate: At Home in New York*.

Kalish, Mildred Armstrong. *Little Heathens: Hard Times and High Spirits on an Iowa Farm During the Great Depression*.

Sparks, Nicholas. *Three Weeks with My Brother*.

Tucker, Neely. *Love in the Driest Season: A Family Memoir*.

Urquhart, Jane.

A Map of Glass. MacAdam/Cage, 2006. 371pp. ISBN 9781596921702.

The body of Andrew Woodman is discovered, frozen, on an island in Lake Ontario, by an artist named Jerome McNaughton. The mystery of the man's death (as well as his life) is eventually made clearer to Jerome when a woman named Sylvia Bradley shows up on his Toronto doorstep to tell him of the longtime love affair she had with Woodman before he began to suffer from Alzheimer's disease.

Through the sharing of her stories, Jerome and his girlfriend Mira come to understand more about his fear of relationships, as instilled in him by his abusive and alcoholic father. Much of the story is told in flashbacks, but Urquhart is a master at weaving historical stories into current narratives and illustrating how people struggling with all sorts of damage can start to heal.

Subjects: Alzheimer's Disease; Art and Artists; Book Groups; Canada; Canadian Authors; Death and Dying; Flashbacks; Psychological Fiction; Weather; Women Authors

Now Try: Urquhart is also the author of the novel *The Underpainter*, in which an elderly man reflects on his life and artwork, as well as the historical novels *The Stone Carvers* and *Away*. Pat Barker also explores how people recover (or don't) from psychological and physical maladies in her novels, including *Life Class*, *Double Vision*, and the Regeneration Trilogy (starting with the novel *Regeneration*). Another Canadian author whose style might appeal to Urquhart's readers is Carol Shields; of particular interest might be her historical fiction title *The Stone Diaries*.

Vargas Llosa, Mario.

🏆 *The Bad Girl*. Farrar, Straus & Giroux, 2007. 276pp. ISBN 9780374182434.

Free spirit Lily (the "bad girl" of Vargas Llosa's title), always traveling the globe to participate in revolutions and marriages with equal abandon, is the object of affection and near obsession of native Peruvian Ricardo Somocurcio, who meets her and falls irreparably in love when both are young and living in Lima. Although he becomes a translator with UNESCO and himself travels the globe, whenever he and Lily cross paths he continues to be cast in the role of the "good boy," with whom she can enjoy (sensually written) sexual encounters but whom she never seriously considers as a true partner or possible long-term love interest.

Subjects: 1950s; 20th Century; Books in Translation; Historical Fiction; Love Affairs; Peru; Peruvian Authors; Travel

Awards: New York Times Notable

Now Try: Vargas Llosa's other novels might also be suggested to these readers, including *The Way to Paradise* and *The Feast of the Goat*, as well as his essay collection *Wellsprings*. Other novels that feature strong-minded female characters are James Meek's *We Are Now Beginning Our Descent*, Slavenka Drakulic's *Frida's Bed*, and even Charles Dickens's classic *Great Expectations*. Edith Grossman, who translated this book, has also translated two other books that might appeal to these readers: the rather more sexually explicit novel *Loves That Bind* (by Julian Rios), and *Red April* (also set in Peru) by Santiago Roncagliolo.

Viswanathan, Padma.

The Toss of a Lemon. Harcourt, 2008. 619pp. ISBN 9780151015337.

In her extended family epic (based on her own grandmother's life), Viswanathan tells the stories of Sivakami, married at ten years old to astrologer Hanumarathnam; their "golden daughter" Thangan, who has ten children of her own; and their son Vairum, in the course of whose stars his father foresees his own early death. In addition to the complexities of these family's lives, the author also weaves in stories of India's history and the simultaneously simple and complex rigidities of the caste system.

Subjects: Astrology; Book Groups; Canadian Authors; Epic Reads; Family Relationships; First Novels; India; Indian Authors; Multicultural; Multigenerational Fiction; Women Authors; Women's Fiction

Now Try: Another novel in which the events hinge on the caste system (and Indian politics) is Rohinton Mistry's *A Fine Balance*. A number of other multicultural titles set in India (and written by women authors) might also appeal to these readers, including Kiran Desai's *The Inheritance of Loss*, Chitra Banerjee Divakaruni's *The Mistress of Spices*, Anita Desai's *Fasting, Feasting* and *Clear Light of Day*, and Indira Ganesan's *Inheritance*. Another novel set in a southern Indian state, which garnered good reviews, is Moncy Pothen's *Beneath the Clouds and Coconut Leaves*. John Speed's historical novels of India, *The Temple Dancer* and *Tiger Claw*, might be suggested; and a good readable history of India is Michael Wood's *India*, which combines historical writing with first-person accounts and travel writing.

Walbert, Kate.

A Short History of Women. Scribner, 2009. 239pp. ISBN 9781416594987.

The stories of several generations of strong-willed women are told in Walbert's character-driven historical fiction. The first woman to relate her story is Dorothy Townsend, a suffragette in turn-of-the-century Great Britain, who dies for her cause; then her daughter Evelyn travels to America after World War I to further her professional career; finally, her niece (also named Dorothy) is imprisoned in 2003 for taking photographs of a top-secret military installation. Numerous other stories are told in this sprawling novel of the twentieth century, and Walbert never forgets to explore the human cost of her characters' sometimes extreme beliefs and actions.

Subjects: Great Britain; Historical Fiction; Immigrants and Immigration; Interconnected Stories; Multigenerational Fiction; Multiple Viewpoints; Women Authors; Women's Fiction

Now Try: Walbert is also the author of the story collection *Where She Went*, as well as the novels *The Gardens of Kyoto* and *Our Kind* (which was nominated for a National Book Award). Other novels told across multiple time periods and from multiple viewpoints might appeal to these readers, including Geraldine Brooks's *People of the Book* or Kirsten Menger-Anderson's *Doctor Olaf von Schuler's Brain*; those readers more interested in women's lives and romance (combined with time travels) might consider the popular and readable classics *The Time Traveler's Wife* (by Audrey Niffenegger) and *Outlander* (by Diana Gabaldon). Another novelist who writes about women characters and the cultures in which they find themselves is Meg Wolitzer (*The Wife*, *The Ten-Year Nap*, and *The Position*).

Walls, Jeannette.

Half Broke Horses: A True-Life Novel. Scribner, 2009. 288pp. ISBN 9781416586289.

Lily Casey Smith, the author's real-life grandmother, may not have had an easy life, but she certainly had a story-worthy one. In this "true life novel," Walls details Smith's life, from her hardscrabble upbringing and sporadic education, which was more off than on due to her family's poverty; her marriage to a bigamist; her moves through several states, including Illinois, Arizona, and New Mexico; and her second marriage to a rancher, with whom she has two children and more than her fair share of adventures (including booze-running during Prohibition and work breaking horses).

Subjects: American West; Book Groups; Family Relationships; Historical Fiction; Marriage; Poverty; Women Authors

Now Try: Walls is also the author of the hugely popular memoir *The Glass Castle*, in which she detailed her own decidedly untraditional upbringing by her two independent and often very poor parents. Memoirs like Rick Bragg's *All Over but the Shoutin'* and James McBride's *The Color of Water* are also tributes to those authors' mothers; Michelle Slatalla's part-history, part-novel *The Town on Beaver Creek*, about her strong-minded female ancestors, might also appeal. Wallace Stegner's classic novel *Angle of Repose*, which also features a woman trying to navigate her marriage and the wild nature of the American West, might be suggested, as might Ron Rash's darker novel *Serena*, about one woman's driving ambition and obsession.

Weber, Katharine.

Triangle. **Farrar, Straus & Giroux, 2006. 242pp. ISBN 9780374281427.**

When Esther Gottesfeld, 106 years old and the sole remaining survivor of the horrific Triangle Shirtwaist Factory fire in 1911 New York City, dies, her granddaughter Rebecca sets out to learn her grandmother's story through the papers she left in a safe deposit box. Although centered on a historical event, this novel is emphatically set in the present, where Rebecca is in a comfortable relationship with composer George Botkin, but whose comfort will be shattered by her grandmother's recorded memories (especially of the death of her sister) and the incessant questioning of Ruth Zion, a feminist scholar determined to find at least one version of the truth regarding the fire.

Subjects: 1910s; Book Groups; Death and Dying; Elderly; Family Relationships; Family Secrets; Historical Fiction; Jews and Judaism; Labor History; Love Affairs; New York City; Women Authors

Now Try: Weber is also the author of a retelling of the classic *Little Women*, titled *The Little Women*, as well as the novels *Objects in Mirror Are Closer Than They Appear* and *Music Lesson*. Another book in which a longtime mystery is slowly revealed in the present is A. S. Byatt's *Possession*; in both Diane Setterfield's *The Thirteenth Tale* and Joanna Scott's *Follow Me* the secrets of older women are revealed to younger women. These readers might also consider David Von Drehle's masterful nonfiction account of the Triangle fire, *Triangle: The Fire That Changed America*.

Whitehead, Colson.

Sag Harbor: A Novel. **Doubleday, 2009. 273pp. ISBN 9780385527651.**

New York in the 1980s is the setting for Whitehead's self-described autobiographical fourth novel. Each summer, brothers Reggie and Benji stay with their family in the east end of the community of Sag Harbor, which is primarily African American and populated largely by the sons and daughters of black professionals who work in the city the rest of the year. Each summer is a revelation for Benji, who never quite feels like he fits in at his decidedly preppie (and white) Manhattan school, but his fifteenth summer in particular is rich with typical but memorable teen experiences of trying to find cars for various road trips and first encounters with girls.

Subjects: 1980s; African American Authors; African Americans; Book Groups; Brothers; Coming-of-age; Community Life; Education; First Person; New York; New York City; Race Relations; Siblings; Teenage Boys; Teenagers

Now Try: Whitehead's fiction varies widely, but readers might enjoy his other novels, *The Intuitionist*, *John Henry Days*, and *Apex Hides the Hurt*, as well as his nonfiction title about New York City, *Colossus*. Another novel about an outsider trying to fit in at his prep school is Tobias Wolff's *Old School*; nonfiction titles about education and race relations might also be considered, such as Ron Suskind's *A Hope in the Unseen: An American Odyssey from the Inner City to the Ivy League* and Alex Kotlowitz's *There Are No Children Here*.

Wideman, John Edgar.

🎗 *Fanon: A Novel*. **Houghton Mifflin, 2008. 229pp. ISBN 9780618942633.**

Wideman combines fiction, biography, and history in this novel about Frantz Fanon, a political activist who fought against France for Algeria's independence. To add another layer of autobiography to this work, Wideman structures his novel as though it were the memoir of an African American author (named Thomas) who is struggling to write a book about Fanon.

Second Appeal: Language

Subjects: African American Authors; Algeria; Biographical Fiction; Fanon, Frantz; France; Martinique; Political Fiction; Race Relations; War

Awards: New York Times Notable

Now Try: Those readers fascinated by Fanon as a character might also consider the nonfiction *Frantz Fanon: A Biography* by David Macey, or even Fanon's own books *Black Skin, White Masks* and *The Wretched of the Earth*. Wideman's other novels, all of which are rather stylistically complex, include *Brothers and Keepers*, *Damballah*, and *Two Cities*; he is also the author of the nonfiction titles *The Island, Martinique*, and *Every Tongue Got to Confess: Negro Folk-Tales from the Gulf States*. Two other authors who might appeal to Wideman's fans are Zora Neale Hurston, who also blends fiction and autobiography in *Their Eyes Were Watching God*; and Lawrence Hill, a Canadian author who also tells complex historical stories in his novels *Any Known Blood* and *Someone Knows My Name*.

Now Consider Nonfiction . . . Change-Makers and Activists Biographies

Change-maker and activist biographies take as their subject individuals who seek to right wrongs or correct injustices through feats of great personal risk-taking, bravery, or perseverance. They offer inspiring stories of individuals taking heroic stands and are appealing due to their often stark depiction of the right versus the wrong sides of various issues.

Chadha, Yogesh. *Gandhi: A Life.*

Haley, Alex, and Malcolm X. *The Autobiography of Malcolm X.*

Iyer, Pico. *Open Road: The Global Journey of the Fourteenth Dalai Lama.*

Mills, Kay. *This Little Light of Mine: The Life of Fannie Lou Hamer.*

Oates, Stephen B. *Let the Trumpet Sound: A Life of Martin Luther King, Jr.*

Wildgen, Michelle.

You're Not You. **Thomas Dunne Books, 2006. 274pp. ISBN 9780312352295.**

Young college student Bec is moving aimlessly through her college life and classes, and although she is engaging in an affair with a married professor, seems not to be allowing any experiences to have an undue effect on her. Until, that is, she takes a summer job caring for another young woman, Kate, with Lou Gehrig's disease, whose caustic wit and acceptance of her own mortality, as well as her determination not to despair when she finds out her husband Evan is cheating on her, inspires Bec to give more of herself in the care of another person than she had ever thought possible.

Subjects: Academia; Adultery; American Midwest; Coming-of-age; Disabilities; First Novels; First Person; Friendships; Health Issues; Marriage; Wisconsin; Women Authors; Women's Fiction; Young Women

Now Try: Other novels in which women's experiences as caregivers strongly affect them might appeal to these readers, including Anne Tyler's *The Clock Winder* and *Searching for Caleb*, as well as Leah Stewart's *The Myth of You and Me*. Ann Patchett's novel *The Dive from Clausen's Pier* is also set in a Wisconsin college town (and also explores debilitating health issues). Authors who provided blurbs for this title included Margot Livesey (*The Missing World* and *The House on Fortune Street*) and Whitney Otto (*How To Make an American Quilt* and *A Collection of Beauties at the Height of Their Popularity*); their novels might appeal to these readers as well.

Willis, Sarah.

The Sound of Us. Berkley Books, 2005. 324pp. ISBN 9780425203026.

Alice Marlowe, who works as an interpreter for the deaf in Cleveland, Ohio, has in her late forties largely made peace with her single life, although she does sometimes struggle with loneliness. When she interprets on a phone call for a young girl named Larissa Benton, however, and tries to help the terrified young girl (who is reporting that her mother has abandoned her), she finds herself applying to become Larissa's foster mother for reasons she doesn't entirely understand.

Subjects: Abuse; American Midwest; Book Groups; Cleveland; Deafness; Disabilities; First Person; Foster Children; Grief; Mothers and Daughters; Ohio; Women Authors

Now Try: Willis is also the author of the novels *Some Things That Stay* and *The Rehearsal*. Other books in which adults find themselves drawn into caring for children, sometimes against long odds, are Barbara Kingsolver's novels *The Bean Trees* and *Pigs in Heaven*, as well as Kaye Gibbons's *Ellen Foster* (which is told from the child's point of view). Another novel in which no easy answers are suggested for sometimes difficult family relationships and complex home lives is Matthew Goodman's *Hold Love Strong*. A slightly different novel, in which a woman strives not to let her deafness define her, is T. Coraghessan Boyle's novel *Talk Talk*.

Winton, Tim.

🏵 *Breath: A Novel.* Farrar, Straus & Giroux, 2008. 217pp. ISBN 978-0374116347.

When middle-aged paramedic Bruce is called to the scene of a teenager's death that looks like suicide, he recognizes it as an accident more so than a planned event, largely due to his own experiences as a teenager many years before. The bulk of this slim novel follows the exploits of Bruce when he was a young teen and his best friend Loonie, and the challenges their friendship faced when they fell in with a surfing couple whose unsteady marriage had far-reaching consequences for the two boys.

Subjects: 1970s; Australia; Australian Authors; Book Groups; Coming-of-age; Death and Dying; Explicit Sexuality; Friendships; Love Affairs; Marriage; Quick Reads; Surfing; Teenage Boys; Teenagers

Awards: New York Times Notable

Now Try: Winton is a hugely popular, award-winning Australian author whose other titles include *Cloudstreet*, *Dirt Music*, and the story collection *The Turning*. James Boice's *NoVA*, like this novel, also opens with the death of a teenager. Two other tales of a young man's sexual awakening through his love for an older woman are Rose Tremain's *The Way I Found Her* and Bernhard Schlink's *The Reader*. Graham Swift's haunting novel *Waterland* might also be suggested to these readers.

Wolff, Tobias.

🐾 *Old School*. Knopf, 2003. 195pp. ISBN 9780375401466.

The narrator, entrenched in a series of literary competitions, looks back on his outsider experiences at a New England prep school and his efforts to win one of the coveted private visits with a literary giant of the 1960s.

Subjects: 1960s; Coming-of-age; Education; First Person; New England; Prep Schools; Quick Reads; Teenage Boys; Teenagers; Writers and Writing

Awards: ALA Notable

Now Try: This is Wolff's first novel, but his other works include numerous short stories (*Our Story Begins: New and Selected Stories*) and a memoir, *This Boy's Life*. Other books about young boys who feel like outsiders might appeal to these readers, including the classics *The Catcher in the Rye* (by J. D. Salinger) and *A Separate Peace* (by John Knowles); more recent titles that might appeal include Martin Millar's coming-of-age novel set in Glasgow, *Suzy, Led Zeppelin, and Me*, John Green's YA novel *Looking for Alaska*, and Robert Cormier's YA classic *The Chocolate War*. Another novel about the conjunction between literary ambition and education is Muriel Spark's *The Finishing School*.

Yarbrough, Steve.

The End of California. Knopf, 2006. 303pp. ISBN 9781400044382.

Can you go home again? That is the question Dr. Pete Barrington is going to have to answer when he is forced out of his successful medical practice in California (due to his involvement in a sexual scandal) and decides to move, with his wife Angela and their teenage daughter, back to his hometown of Loring, Mississippi. He may have left the scandal behind, but what Pete finds upon his return to his hometown is that some grudges, particularly the one held against him by a former friend (whose mother Pete had a dalliance with in high school), are impossible to run away from.

Subjects: Adultery; American South; California; Community Life; Doctors; Explicit Sexuality; Family Relationships; Marriage; Mississippi; Small-Town Life; Suspense

Now Try: Yarbrough has written two other (historical) novels set in Loring: *Visible Spirits* and *Prisoner of War*, as well as *The Oxygen Man*. Violence hides just under the surface in many of Ian McEwan's novels, including *The Comfort of Strangers* and *Amsterdam*. Also of interest might be Pete Dexter's novels, which often feature characters with secrets of their own; these include *The Paperboy*, *Brotherly Love*, and *Spooner*.

Yglesias, Rafael.

A Happy Marriage. Scribner, 2009. 371pp. ISBN 9781439102305.

Yglesias offers a fictionalized memoir of his thirty-year marriage to Margaret (although fiction, the main characters share the names of the author and his wife, who really did die from cancer in 2004), told in alternating chapters of flashbacks to their first meetings, courtship, and early years of their marriage, interspersed with chapters in which the author and the character chart the ravages of the disease as it takes over his wife's body. Rarely do readers get to see characters at all stages of their development, from first love to death (and afterward), making this a unique tale of love, marriage, and frailty.

Subjects: Cancer; Death and Dying; Family Relationships; Flashbacks; Love Affairs; Marriage; Men's Lives

Now Try: Yglesias is the author of several other novels, including *Dr. Neruda's Cure for Evil* and *Fearless.* Zoë Heller's novel *The Believers* features a female character looking back on her marriage to a complex man (who, throughout the narrative, is in the hospital after suffering a stroke); in Kate Christensen's novel *The Great Man* the lives of the very different women who loved the same man and painter (the "great man") are explored. Another novel in which a man looks back on his wife's life and their marriage is John Banville's Booker Award–winning *The Sea.* This novel also hews very closely to memoir, memoirs in which authors have dealt with the sicknesses and deaths of their spouses might provide similar reading experiences, including Joan Didion's *The Year of Magical Thinking*, C. S. Lewis's *A Grief Observed*, and Rob Sheffield's *Love Is a Mix Tape.*

Yoshikawa, Mako.

Once Removed. Bantam Books, 2003. 289pp. ISBN 9780553801552.

Although they were stepsisters and once the closest of friends, Claudia Klein and Rei Watanabe find that, after seventeen years of separation (largely encouraged by their respective parents—when Claudia's father Henry married Rei's mother, Claudia's birth mother resented her immediate connection with her stepsister Rei), it is harder than they might have originally believed to reconcile their childhood memories and reforge their previous bonds, regardless of how much they both want to rekindle their friendship.

Subjects: Asian American Authors; Asian Americans; Family Relationships; Family Secrets; Japanese American Authors; Japanese Americans; Jews and Judaism; Marriage; Siblings; Stepfamilies; Women Authors

Now Try: Yoshikawa is also the author of the novel *One Hundred and One Ways.* Another novel of family life that might appeal to these readers is David Mura's *Famous Suicides of the Japanese Empire*; also of interest might be Ruth Ozeki's *My Year of Meats*, Susan Choi's *American Woman*, and Julie Shigekuni's *A Bridge Between Us.* A nonfiction account of women who became stepsisters in two unconventional blended families is Jane Alison's *The Sisters Antipodes.*

Chapter 4

Language

In books that appeal because of their authors' mastery of **Language**, the authors tell their stories and describe their characters and settings with writing that is noted for its skillful construction and style. The authors' use of language in these books can be evocative, unusual, thought-provoking, or poetic; when words like "lyrical," "evocative," "stylized," "thoughtful," "elegiac," "ambitious," and "imaginative" start popping up in book reviews, you can guess that the book in question strongly appeals because of its author's use of language. Books that feature Language as a primary appeal can also be avant-garde or experimental in their structure; a book like Jonathan Safran Foer's *Extremely Loud and Incredibly Close* features both high quality prose and a structure that includes shifting points of view, photographs, and pages with just a few words of text. These books are not typically narrative-driven and are not often quick reads; rather, they are meant to be read slowly and savored, encouraging their readers to take the time necessary to appreciate the care that was given to word choice and literary style.

Readers who enjoy **Language** titles are often the most dedicated, not only enjoying a wide variety of fiction (and often nonfiction as well), but also aware of book awards, "buzz" books and authors, and book news. Although demanding and discerning readers, they can also be the most adventurous and ready to follow where an advisor feels inspired enough to lead, so don't be afraid to take some chances in your suggestions. As long as a book features a distinctive or experimental prose style, or its author is critically lauded (or has won an award or is noted as a particularly "buzzworthy" author), readers of **Language** books will largely be happy. They might consider a wide variety of all mainstream fiction titles, regardless of appeal factor characteristics, as well as the more complex mysteries and literary thrillers of all types (think more Arturo Perez-Reverte and Umberto Eco and less Dan Brown). Likewise, smart and stylish historical fiction, science fiction, and even some fantasy (think Charles De Lint, Emma Bull, or Haruki Murakami) titles might also appeal to these readers. They might also be open to a wide variety of nonfiction titles, particularly lyrical or reflective environmental writing; history titles in which authors focus more on evocative descriptions rather than just chronology; and a wide variety of titles in which authors seek to "make sense" of the world around them (by such authors as Malcolm Gladwell, Alain de Botton, or Witold Rybczynski). Literary science titles by authors such as Diane Ackerman might also have some appeal.

Adamson, Gil.

The Outlander: A Novel. Ecco, 2007. 389pp. ISBN 9780061491252.

Although Adamson's main character is primarily identified as "the widow," readers will nonetheless become immediately involved with her harrowing flight across the Canadian West in 1903, away from the crime she had committed (the one that made her both a widow and a murderer) and the ruthless dogging of her trail by her former brothers-in-law, a pair of red-haired, menacing twins.

Second Appeal: Setting

Subjects: 1900s; Canada; Canadian Authors; Crime; Environmental Writing; Family Relationships; First Novels; Historical Fiction; Murder; Widows; Wilderness; Women Authors

Now Try: Adamson is better known as a poet; her poetry collection *Ashland* might also appeal to her readers. Her novel, set in the often bleakly cold and overwhelming Canadian wilderness, has been compared to Cormac McCarthy's novels *No Country for Old Men* and *The Road*, as well as to Charles Frazier's *Cold Mountain*. Another novel featuring a determined female main character is Jim Crace's equally atmospheric *The Pesthouse*; smart historical fiction imbued with a sense of place might also be suggested, such as Ron Rash's *Serena* or Tim Gautreaux's *The Clearing*.

Adrian, Chris.

🌳 *A Better Angel: Stories.* Farrar, Straus & Giroux, 2008. 227pp. ISBN 978-0374289904.

Pediatrician and author Adrian offers nine stories in which his characters experience numerous types of suffering—grief, ill health, loneliness, missed human connections—but continue struggling on in their lives (well, with the exception of Bernice, in the story "The Sum of Our Parts," who is simply waiting out her own body). Adrian does not shy away from either bleak humor or unnervingly detailed descriptions of hospital (and other less sterile and more criminal) procedures and routines, although the stories themselves have a distinctly ethereal feel.

Subjects: Child's Point of View; Dark Humor; Death and Dying; Grief; Health Issues; Hospitals; Short Stories

Awards: New York Times Notable

Now Try: Adrian is also the author of the novels *Gob's Grief* and *The Children's Hospital*. Jim Crace's novel *Being Dead*, which features in-depth prose descriptions of the breakdown of the human body after death, might be considered, as might a number of other short story collections in which authors do not sugarcoat uncomfortable plotlines, such as Antonya Nelson's *Living to Tell*, Mary Gaitskill's *Don't Cry*, and J. C. Hallman's *The Hospital for Dead Poets*. Those readers interested in how Adrian uses his medical knowledge in his fiction might also consider medical professionals' memoirs, such as Paul Austin's *Something for the Pain: One Doctor's Account of Life and Death in the ER*, Atul Gawande's *Complications: A Surgeon's Notes on an Imperfect Science*, or Jerome Groopman's *How Doctors Think*.

Now Consider Nonfiction . . . Making Sense: Of Ourselves and Each Other

In nonfiction books considered part of the "Making Sense: Of Ourselves and Each Other" stylistic genre, authors strive to make sense of people and their interactions with one another; they typically focus on subject areas such as psychology and sociology. They are synthesizing works that offer a variety of research or facts about human behavior and interaction (and showcase their authors' writing skills in pulling research together).

Gladwell, Malcom. *Blink: The Power of Thinking Without Thinking.*

Gladwell, Malcom. *The Tipping Point.*

Hallinan, Joseph T. *Why We Make Mistakes.*

Jamison, Kay Redfield. *Exuberance: The Passion for Life.*

Lehrer, Jonah. *How We Decide.*

Martin, Russell. *Out of Silence: A Journey into Language.*

Anderson, Scott.

Moonlight Hotel. **Doubleday, 2006. 371pp. ISBN 9780385515566.**

Previously having enjoyed his rather stress-free life as a diplomat to the (fictional) Middle Eastern country Kutar, David Richards is unprepared for the civil war and violence that result from conflict among the country's ethnic tribes, which is made worse by the involvement of America's and other country's military forces. As he and the British ambassador hole up in the Moonlight Hotel to try to encourage a diplomatic resolution, he is also troubled by memories of his brother's service in Vietnam and worries about the outcome for the country if all outside powers depart.

Subjects: Culture Clash; Diplomats and Diplomacy; Men's Lives; Middle East; Political Fiction; Satire; War

Now Try: Anderson is also the author of an earlier novel, titled *Triage*, and a biography about relief worker Fred Cuny, *The Man Who Tried to Save the World: The Dangerous Life and Mysterious Disappearance of an American Hero*. Another novel that examines the lingering effects of the Vietnam War (although it is set while the war is taking place) is Denis Johnson's National Book Award–winning novel *Tree of Smoke*. Other novels in which characters become involved (and are often out of their depth) in political situations are Graham Greene's classic *The Quiet American*, Giles Foden's *The Last King of Scotland*, and Frederick Forsyth's *The Dogs of War*. Political memoirs and histories might also appeal to these readers, including Craig Murray's memoir, *Dirty Diplomacy: The Rough-and-Tumble Adventures of a Scotch-Drinking, Skirt-Chasing, Dictator-Busting, and Thoroughly Unrepentant Ambassador Stuck on the Frontline of the War Against Terror* and Adam Roberts's *The Wonga Coup: Guns, Thugs, and a Ruthless Determination to Create Mayhem in an Oil-Rich Corner of Africa*.

Auster, Paul.

🎗 *The Book of Illusions.* **Henry Holt, 2002. 321pp. ISBN 9780805054088.**

Auster employs a "book within a book" motif to relate the story of David Zimmer, a professor who has recently lost his wife and sons in a plane crash and has retreated to his Vermont home, where he is helpless in his grief. When he watches a movie starring the silent film star Hector Mann, however, he feels both beholden to Mann (for providing his first laugh in months) and interested enough in him to try to track down what happened to the actor after he left the film industry. After writing a book about Mann,

Zimmer receives an enigmatic note asking if he'd like to learn more about the man and his work.

Subjects: 1920s; Death and Dying; Grief; Love Affairs; Men's Lives; Movies; Psychological Fiction; Vermont

Awards: ALA Notable; New York Times Notable

Now Try: Auster is the author of the popular New York Trilogy, comprising *City of Glass*, *Ghosts*, and *The Locked Room*. Another novel in which a man retreats to solitude to work through emotional duress is Tim Parks's *Cleaver*; a novel about a real Hollywood star, Charlie Chaplin, Glen David Gold's *Sunnyside*, might also be an enjoyable related read.

Banville, John.

🌳 *The Sea*. Knopf, 2005. 195pp. ISBN 9780307263117.

Searching for comfort or perhaps just a way to indulge in memories that are not of his wife (who has recently died of cancer), Max Morden returns to the Irish seaside town and the boarding house (the Cedars) where he often stayed as a child with his family. Interspersed with descriptions of the beach and seaside as he experiences them now are his memories of his life with Anna; he also relates earlier memories of the enigmatic and decidedly glamorous Graces family, who also vacationed in the small Irish town.

Subjects: Cancer; Death and Dying; Family Relationships; First Person; Flashbacks; Ireland; Irish Authors; Marriage; Widowers

Awards: Man Booker Prize; New York Times Notable

Now Try: Banville has written several other novels, including *Shroud*, *Eclipse*, *Mefisto*, *The Untouchable*, and *Doctor Copernicus*. Although set in Wales, another novel about the importance of place and memory is Gerard Woodward's *August*. Another slim novel that highlights its author's skill with prose is Ian McEwan's *On Chesil Beach*; other books about mourning a spouse might also be suggested, such as Rafael Yglesias's *A Happy Marriage*, John Bayley's *Elegy for Iris*, and Joan Didion's *The Year of Magical Thinking*.

Barker, Nicola.

🌳 *Darkmans*. HarperPerennial, 2007. 838pp. ISBN 9780061575211.

A conflicted father-and-son duo are at the heart of Barker's novel, set in Ashford (a British city near the Channel Tunnel); Beede works in a hospital laundry, while his son son Kane deals prescription drugs (illegally). Although prickly with each other on the surface, the men are more alike than not, and each has his own caring side, which Barker displays slowly over the course of her 800+ page narrative. Also involved in the story are Isidore, Elen, and their five-year-old son Fleet (Elen is a podiatrist who has treated both Beede and Kane), as well as a third family, the Broads, known in the neighborhood for their decidedly lower-class lifestyle. Also stalking through the novel is a spirit known as "Darkmans," who periodically inhabits various characters and induces them to commit various and sundry pranks and misdeeds. Barker employs numerous stylistic hijinks herself—including such stage directions for her characters as "pause" and "silence." Although this prose and the magic realism won't be for everyone, readers who go along for the ride and notice Barker's overall theme of how the past can control us even when we're not aware of it, will totally love it.

Subjects: British Authors; Dark Humor; Drug Abuse; Epic Reads; Family Relationships; Fantasy; Fathers and Sons; Friendships; Magic Realism; Women Authors

Awards: Hawthornden Prize

Now Try: Barker is also the author of the earlier novels *Clear*, *Behindlings*, and *Wide Open*, and was named one of Granta's Best British Novelists in 2003. Other epic books that will demand attention and inspire love in readers are David Foster Wallace's *Infinite Jest*, Roberto Bolaño's *2666*, and Junot Díaz's *The Brief Wondrous Life of Oscar Wao*. Other winners of the Hawthornden Prize (a British award noted for its approval of "imaginative literature") might also appeal, including M. J. Hyland's *Carry Me Down*, Alexander Masters's *Stuart*, and Justin Cartwright's *The Promise of Happiness*. Another novel that involves possession is *All Shall Be Well and All Shall Be Well and All Manner of Things Shall Be Well*.

Barnes, Julian.

🎖 *The Lemon Table: Stories.* **Knopf, 2004. 241pp. ISBN 9781400042142.**

British author Barnes offers eleven very different short stories about, variously, a nineteenth-century love affair that is never consummated nor even acknowledged; a man whose visits to his longtime mistress are revealed to be something different than they first appeared; and a recounting of a man's barber shop experiences. Although deceptively little happens in these stories, Barnes is a master at making the most ordinary of events seem loaded with meaning.

Subjects: British Authors; Family Relationships; Great Britain; Quick Reads; Short Stories

Awards: ALA Notable

Now Try: Barnes is also the author of another story collection, *Cross Channel*, as well as the recent novels *Arthur & George*, *Love, Etc.*, and *England, England*. (He has also written a memoir about his thoughts on mortality, *Nothing to Be Frightened Of*.) Readers who enjoy his skill with prose might also consider such authors as Ian McEwan (*Atonement*, *On Chesil Beach*, *Saturday*), Richard Ford (*The Sportswriter* and the story collection *A Multitude of Sins*), or Jonathan Coe (*The Rotters' Club* and *The House of Sleep*).

Barrico, Alessandro.

Without Blood. **Knopf, 2004. 97pp. ISBN 9781400041459.**

Italian novelist Barrico's both spare and lyrical prose tells a story set in an unspecified country, in the aftermath of a violent civil war. When a small group of men decide to exact vengeance for their own suffering from war by murdering a farmer and his son, the farmer's daughter, Nina, hides from the massacre but is discovered and allowed to live by Tito, one of the band of murderers. Years later Nina, now an old woman, and Tito cross paths once again, and Nina challenges Tito to answer for his crimes.

Subjects: Books in Translation; Crime; Death and Dying; Elderly; Italian Authors; Murder; Quick Reads; Violence; War

Now Try: Barrico's other novels include *Silk*, *Open Sea*, and *City*, as well as a translation of the classical work *An Iliad*. Other novels in which themes of violence and vengeance are explored are Ian McEwan's *The Comfort of Strangers* and *Amsterdam*; Cormac McCarthy's *Blood Meridian*, and Santiago Roncagliolo's *Red April*

(another book in translation). Although they make for difficult reading, Jean Hatzfeld's investigative series of books about the Rwandan genocide and its aftermath might be suggested: *Machete Season* (from the points of view of the Hutu killers), *Life Laid Bare* (from the points of view of the Tutsi survivors), and *The Antelope's Strategy: Living in Rwanda after the Genocide*.

Barry, Sebastian.

🏆 *The Secret Scripture*. **Viking, 2008. 300pp. ISBN 9780670019403.**

When Dr. Grene, the ranking doctor at the Roscommon mental hospital, is charged with determining which patients will go where when it closes, to fulfill his duties he begins in-depth interviews with many patients he hardly knows. One such patient is Roseanne McNulty, a woman whose admission to the facility is so far in the past that no one really remembers when or why she came; as he tries to draw her out in conversations, she remains enigmatic, but is secretly confessing her story (which will have a greater personal impact on Dr. Grene than he realizes) to a diary she will leave behind.

Subjects: Catholic Church; Doctors; Family Relationships; Family Secrets; Historical Fiction; Ireland; Irish Authors; Love Affairs; Men Writing as Women; Mental Health; Priests

Awards: Costa Book of the Year Award; Costa Novel Award

Now Try: Barry is best known as a playwright, but he has written several other novels, including *The Whereabouts of Eneas McNulty* (this book is a sequel of sorts to that one), *A Long Long Way*, and *Annie Dunne*. Other Irish authors who explore family dynamics in their novels might appeal, including Anne Enright (*The Gathering*), John McGahern (*The Dark*, *Amongst Women*, and *By the Lake*), and John Banville (*The Sea*). Another novel about family secrets is Kate Morton's *The Forgotten Garden*. Another book in which the Catholic Church is a direct participant in a pair's love affair is Graham Greene's classic *The End of the Affair*; Deirdre Madden's novel *One by One in the Darkness* also explores violent episodes between Catholic and Protestant factions in Northern Ireland.

Bender, Aimee.

Willful Creatures: Stories. **Doubleday, 2005. 208pp. ISBN 9780385501132.**

Bender's stories are as willful (and as whimsical) as the creatures who populate them; over the course of fifteen stories, she relates the tales of a Big Man who keeps a Little Man as a pet; ten men who receive fatal prognoses from their doctors and how they each react; and a boy born with keys for fingers who spends his life looking for the doors his hands will fit and open; among many others.

Subjects: Fantasy; Humor; Quick Reads; Satire; Short Stories; Women Authors

Now Try: Bender is also the author of the novel *An Invisible Sign of My Own* and another story collection, *The Girl in the Flammable Skirt*. Other unique (some might say "strange," but we'll stick with "unique") story collections might appeal to these readers, including Kelly Link's *Magic for Beginners* and *Stranger Things Happen*, John Kessel's *The Baum Plan for Financial Independence*, and Etgar Keret's *The Girl on the Fridge* and *The Nimrod Flipout*. Dan Chaon's story collection, *Among the Missing*, although gentler than the rest of these titles, also packs a punch and will leave its readers thinking long after they're done reading it.

Bigsby, Christopher.

🎗 *Beautiful Dreamer.* Thomas Dunne Books, 2006. 183pp. ISBN 978-0312355838.

Told in the first person from the viewpoints of a number of different characters, this slim but weighty novel tells the horrific story of a white man (Jake Benchley) who provides shelter to a black boy whose father has been lynched (the boy himself looks after Benchley, who has been beaten and branded by the lynchers), earning the epithet "nigger lover" from those men still seeking to track down the child. Also telling his story is the sheriff, who is trying to head off violence among all the parties without really becoming involved in the fray. For all the characters, however, it becomes clear that seeking to avoid the problems of hate crimes and violence is a futile endeavor.

Subjects: American South; First Person; Law Enforcement; Multiple Viewpoints; Quick Reads; Racism; Suspense; Tennessee; Violence

Awards: ALA Notable

Now Try: Bigsby has written two other historical novels, *Hester: A Novel* and *Pearl*. Two other short (sometimes violent) novels in which older characters look after younger ones are Cormac McCarthy's *The Road* and Jeff Talarigo's *The Ginseng Hunter*. Also of interest might be related nonfiction titles about race relations, including Mat Johnson's graphic novel *Incognegro*, Kevin Boyle's *Arc of Justice: A Saga of Race, Civil Rights, and Murder in the Jazz Age*, and Paul Hendrickson's *Sons of Mississippi: A Story of Race and Its Legacy*; these nonfiction histories feature compelling stories and skillful writing.

Bock, Charles.

🎗 *Beautiful Children.* Random House, 2008. 417pp. ISBN 9781400066506.

The lives of various residents of Las Vegas, Nevada, intersect in this story about the disappearance of twelve-year-old Newell Ewing. As his parents search for him and his case is treated as an abduction, eventually the circumstances of his disappearance come to light through the varying narratives of not only Newell and his parents, but also Newell's friend Kenny, a jaded comic-book writer named Bing, a stripper named Cheri, and numerous other runaway teens and kids who have created their own street societies and families.

Subjects: Book Groups; Comic Books; Dysfunctional Families; Epic Reads; First Novels; Friendships; Kidnapping; Las Vegas; Marriage; Parenting; Runaways; Suburbia; Teenage Boys; Teenagers

Awards: New York Times Notable

Now Try: Two other novels in which teenage boys struggle to find their places in life are Monica Ferrell's *The Answer Is Always Yes* and James Boice's *NoVA: A Novel*; Junot Díaz's coming-of-age narrative *The Brief Wondrous Life of Oscar Wao* might also appeal, as might Irvine Welsh's classic novel about drug abuse and urban life, *Trainspotting*. Rene Denfeld's nonfiction (and somewhat frightening) title about street kids might also be suggested: *All God's Children: Inside the Dark and Violent World of Street Families*.

Boice, James.

NoVA: A Novel. Scribner, 2009. 314pp. ISBN 9781416575429.

Boice tells a stylistically disjointed tale of the residents of a suburb in northern Virginia in 1998: Grayson Donald, the teen whose suicide opens the book; his parents, whose marriage is strained by his mother Vicki's religiosity and his father's porn addiction; and Amy Gauthier, the marijuana-smoking gym teacher at the high school where Vicki teaches.

Subjects: Dysfunctional Families; Family Relationships; Flashbacks; Multiple Viewpoints; Profanity; Suburbia; Suicide; Teenagers; Virginia

Now Try: Boice's earlier novel, *MVP*, is also a challenging read in subject matter (a popular high school athlete commits rape and murder). Other novels that feature sobering stories about the lives of teenagers and the disjointedness of modern communities are Charles Bock's *Beautiful Children*, Tom Perrotta's *Little Children* and *The Abstinence Teacher*, Tim Winton's *Breath*, Sherman Alexie's *The Toughest Indian in the World*, and Daniel Clay's *Broken*.

Bolaño, Roberto.

🎗 *2666.* Farrar, Straus & Giroux, 2008. 898pp. ISBN 9780374100148.

Bolaño's massive novel in five parts opens with a story recounting the relationships of five scholars, all fascinated with the same obscure German author, Benno von Archimboldi. It proceeds into three different and related stories of a Spanish professor who moves to Santa Teresa, Mexico, with his daughter Rosa; an African American journalist who is sent to cover a prize fight in the area and ends up saving Rosa; and the horrific rapes and murders of young girls that are taking place around the area. A final chapter, "The Part about Archimboldi," wraps up the author's multiple story lines and provides closure (of sorts) for the crime. The author's skill is not only in his plotting and foreshadowing, but also in his use of language (and part of the kudos must go to the translator of this novel as well) and the quiet beauty of such passages as "In February María de la Luz Romero died. She was fourteen, and five foot three, with long hair down to her waist, although she planned to cut it someday soon, as she had revealed to one of her sisters" (p. 450).

Subjects: Books and Reading; Books in Translation; Classics; Death and Dying; Epic Reads; Juarez; Literary Lives; Mexico; Psychological Fiction

Awards: National Book Critics Circle Award; New York Times Notable

Now Try: Although Bolaño died in 2003, he wrote several books prior to this one: *By Night in Chile, Last Evenings on Earth, Amulet, The Savage Detectives*, and *Nazi Literature in the Americas*. Similarly big, audacious, and challenging novels that might appeal to these readers include Nicola Barker's *Darkmans*, Jonathan Littell's *The Kindly Ones*, Javier Calvo's *Wonderful World*, Gabriel García Márquez's *One Hundred Years of Solitude*, and James Joyce's classics *Ulysses* or *Portrait of the Artist as a Young Man*. Other Chilean authors might appeal to Bolaño's readers as well, particularly Isabel Allende (*The House of the Spirits, Daughter of Fortune*, and *Portrait in Sepia*) and poet Pablo Neruda (*The Poetry of Pablo Neruda*).

Brockmeier, Kevin.

The View from the Seventh Layer. **Pantheon, 2008. 267pp. ISBN 978-0375425301.**

Brockmeier offers thirteen stories that combine the fantastic and the mundane in his own blend of magic realism. They include a story written in the style of a "Choose Your Own Adventure" book, an opening story about a mute man who collected birds to do his singing for him, and a preacher who learns that the person paying the most attention to his sermons is a ghost.

Subjects: Book Groups; Books and Reading; Magic Realism; Quick Reads; Short Stories

Now Try: Brockmeier authored an earlier collection of short stories, *Things That Fall from the Sky*, as well as the novels *The Truth about Celia* and *The Brief History of the Dead*. Other avant-garde story and literary stylists whom Brockmeier's fans might enjoy are Aimee Bender (*The Girl in the Flammable Skirt, An Invisible Sign of My Own*, and *Willful Creatures*), Lydia Davis (*Samuel Johnson Is Indignant* and *Varieties of Disturbance*), Dan Chaon (*You Remind Me of Me* and *Among the Missing*), and John Kessel (*The Baum Plan for Financial Independence*). Another literary stylist who writes novels, Lydia Millet, might also appeal to these readers (consider starting with *How the Dead Dream* and *Oh Pure and Radiant Heart*).

Busch, Frederick.

🎗 *Don't Tell Anyone: Fiction.* **Norton, 2000. 309pp. ISBN 9780393049732.**

In this collection of seventeen short stories, Busch uses all his powers of stylistic writing and characterization to tell fully formed (there is little ambiguity in the conclusions of Busch's tales) stories of love, betrayal, complex family relationships, and our connectedness to one another. In one story a teenager learns his mother is having an affair with his mentor; in another, a married couple questions their understanding of an earlier conversation, and, by extension, their understanding of one another; in a third (and the title story), the son of Holocaust survivors struggles with the politics of academia and his love for a married woman.

Subjects: Domestic Fiction; Family Relationships; Love Affairs; Marriage; Short Stories; Society

Awards: ALA Notable; New York Times Notable

Now Try: Busch is also the author of the story collections *Rescue Missions* and *Domestic Particulars*, as well as the novels *Girls* (and its follow-up, *North*), *Harry and Catherine*, *War Babies*, and *Rounds*. Other short story collections written by men about various features of American life and turn-of-the-century culture are Ward Just's *Twenty-One: Selected Stories* (Just's novels might also appeal, including *Exiles in the Garden* and *An Unfinished Season*), Frederick Barthelme's *The Law of Averages* and *Chroma*, and Richard Ford's *A Multitude of Sins*.

Butler, Robert Olen.

Intercourse: Stories. **Chronicle Books, 2008. 216pp. ISBN 9780811863575.**

In this unique narrative, Butler imagines numerous sexual couplings throughout history, from both participants' points of view; each partner gets one page for his or her inner monologue. The stories start with Adam and Eve (Eve: "He is flailing around and proud of his own little snake.") , Zeus and Leda, Helen and Paris, moving all the way through history to Pablo Picasso and Fernande Olivier, Robert F. Kennedy and Marilyn Monroe, and George and Laura Bush (among many others).

Subjects: Erotica; Explicit Sexuality; Historical Fiction; Literary Allusions; Love Affairs; Marriage; Satire; Short Stories

Now Try: Butler is a Pulitzer Prize–winning author of fiction; his other novels might appeal (particularly *Fair Warning* and *They Whisper*), as might his similar collection *Severance*. A blurb for this title came from Susie Bright, who edits **The Best American Erotica** series; other literary retellings such as Steven Millhauser's *The King in the Tree* (with the title novella being a retelling of the love story of Tristan and Isolde), or Alexandra Lapierre's *Artemisia: A Novel* (or Susan Vreeland's *The Passion of Artemisia*) might appeal as well. Susan Minot's novel *Rapture* also focuses on the act of intercourse; while Barbara Gowdy's thought-provoking story collection *We So Seldom Look on Love* and Yan Lianke's decidedly racy and satirical *Serve the People!* might also appeal to these readers.

Calvo, Javier.

Wonderful World. Harper, 2009. 470pp. ISBN 9780061557682.

Calvo's sprawling narrative offers a cast of characters as varied as his story lines. Lucas Giraut, a Barcelona antiques dealer, starts down a shady path when he tries to find who in the city's crime organization was responsible for his father's imprisonment; meanwhile, he tries simultaneously to get along with his eccentric mother and a twelve-year-old girl who lives in his apartment building, Valentina Parini. Valentina has an obsession very nearly as driving as Lucas's—she is a rabid fan of Stephen King's fiction—and Calvo pays homage to that writer by concluding several of his book's thematic sections with chapters from a work supposedly written by King, titled *Wonderful World.*

Second Appeal: Story

Subjects: Barcelona; Books in Translation; Epic Reads; Family Relationships; Friendships; Organized Crime; Pop Culture; Psychological Fiction; Spain; Spanish Authors

Now Try: This is the first of Calvo's works to be translated into English, but more will most likely arrive soon. Readers who glory in Calvo's big, audacious plots and literary experimentation might also enjoy Robert Bolano's *2666* or Jonathan Littell's *The Kindly Ones*. Other literary thrillers that may appeal to these readers are Stieg Larsson's *The Girl with the Dragon Tattoo*, Charlie Huston's *The Mystic Arts of Erasing All Signs of Death*, and Josh Bazell's *Beat the Reaper* (which also features an organized crime subplot). Another more character-driven novel in which a younger girl befriends an older man is Catherine O'Flynn's *What Was Lost.*

Carey, Edward.

Alva & Irva: The Twins Who Saved a City. Harcourt, 2003. 207pp. ISBN 978-0151007820.

Literary fiction meets magic realism and fantasy in this imaginative novel, in which identical twins Alva and Irva navigate the sometimes rocky paths of their relationships to each other and the world. Alva, the novel's narrator, is also the more adventurous twin, who ventures out into the world to work and travel, whereas Irva, the quieter twin, remains at home. Eventually the two share a hobby of making a scale model of the (fictional) city in which they live, Entralla; after a devastating earthquake hits the city, the model plays a fundamental role in the rebirth of the city and its reconstruction.

Subjects: British Authors; Family Relationships; Fantasy; First Person; Magic Realism; Siblings; Sisters

Awards: ALA Notable

Now Try: Carey's first novel, *Observatory Mansions*, is also peopled with eccentric characters. Another novel in which a pair of twins (conjoined, in this novel) look back on their lives together is Lori Lansens's *The Girls*; Audrey Niffeneggers's novel *Her Fearful Symmetry* also centers on a pair of twins who share a fantastic experience (that of being haunted by their deceased aunt). In Paul Lisicky's delightful memoir *Famous Builder*, he recounts his childhood dream of becoming an architect and "famous builder." Steven Millhauser's collection *Dangerous Laughter* also includes a story in which a city and its construction are the focus of the narrative.

Chabon, Michael.

🎗 *The Final Solution: A Story of Detection*. **Fourth Estate, 2004. 131pp. ISBN 9780060763404.**

Critically revered author Chabon tries his hand at a historical mystery (or mysterious historical novel, however you want to look at it), set in 1940s Great Britain. When a man is murdered near a small English town, a reclusive but reputedly brilliant retired detective (known only as "the old man," though readers may have some ideas about who the sleuth is by novel's end) gets back into the business of detection by trying to decipher the connection that Linus Steinman, a mute Jewish refugee boy from Germany, and his pet, a numbers- and clue-spouting parrot named Bruno, have to the crime.

Second Appeal: Story

Subjects: 1940s; Great Britain; Historical Fiction; Holocaust; Jewish American Authors; Jews and Judaism; Literary Allusions; Mystery; Quick Reads

Awards: National Jewish Book Award

Now Try: Chabon is a master of genreblending, and fans of this slim novel might enjoy his other imaginative novels, including the historical adventure tale *Gentlemen of the Road*, as well as the historical novels *The Yiddish Policemen's Union* and *The Amazing Adventures of Kavalier and Clay*. Reviewers have noted that aspects of this book mirror the structure and style classic mystery authors such as Agatha Christie, Dorothy Sayers, and Margery Allingham; another popular mystery series that may be offered to these readers is Laurie King's <u>Mary Russell</u> novels, starting with *The Beekeeper's Apprentice*.

The Yiddish Policeman's Union. **HarperCollins, 2007. 414pp. ISBN 978 0007149827.**

Chabon, a master of genreblending, weaves a complex story of alternate history, in which the "Frozen Chosen," two million Jews, try to make lives for themselves in Sitka, Alaska, the temporary homeland assigned them after the conclusion of World War II. In addition to the historical story line, Chabon also offers another in a long line of complex characters, rogue cop Meyer Landsman, who has to battle both personal demons and the unsolved case of the murder of one of his neighbors.

Second Appeal: Story

Subjects: Alaska; Alternate Histories; Book Groups; Classics; Jewish American Authors; Jews and Judaism; Law Enforcement; Men's Lives; Murder; Mystery; Work Relationships

Now Try: Those readers particularly enthralled with Chabon's weaving of Jewish themes and histories into his fiction might consider his earlier titles, including *The Amazing Adventures of Kavalier and Clay*, the mystery *The Final Solution*, and the adventure title *Gentlemen of the Road* (which Chabon originally wanted to call "Jews with Swords") . Philip Roth's alternate history *The Plot Against America* might also appeal, as might Robert Harris's *Fatherland*. This novel was reviewed for *Publishers Weekly* by Jess Walter, whose novels *The Zero* and *Citizen Vince* might also be suggested.

Christensen, Kate.

🐾 *The Great Man.* **Doubleday, 2007. 305pp. ISBN 9780385518451.**

Oscar Feldman, the "Great Man" of Christensen's title, is the central figure of this novel, even though the book opens with his obituary, and the story of his life is told by the three women who knew him best: his wife Abigail, his longtime mistress Claire (nicknamed Teddy), and his sister Maxine (an artist in her own right). Each woman had her own complex relationship with Oscar, whose status as a "great man" of either art or interpersonal relationships is strongly called into question by the three very different portraits of him painted (in words) by these three very different women.

Second Appeal: Character

Subjects: Art and Artists; Elderly; Family Relationships; Friendships; Love Affairs; Marriage; Multiple Viewpoints; Women Authors

Awards: PEN-Faulkner Award

Now Try: Christensen's other novels include *In the Drink, Jeremy Thane, The Epicure's Lament,* and *Trouble.* Other novels about art and artists might appeal to these readers, including Slavenka Drakulic's *Frida's Bed*, Justin Cartwright's *The Promise of Happiness*, and Pat Barker's *Double Vision.* Other novels in which characters look back on loved ones who have either died or are dying might provide a similar reading experience, including Emily Perkins's *Novel About My Wife* or Zoë Heller's *The Believers.*

Clay, Daniel.

Broken: A Novel. **HarperPerennial, 2008. 306pp. ISBN 9780061561047.**

In the suburban south of England, a placid-on-the-surface neighborhood teems with violence and unrest. When one of Bob Oswald's five daughters accuses their quiet teen neighbor Rick Buckley of rape, Oswald cannot rest until he punishes Buckley physically. Although the charges are dropped, the damage to Buckley's psyche is done; he first retreats to his home, but eventually emerges from it intent on doing his own damage. Watching all of these events is eleven-year-old Skunk Cunningham, who lives with her father and an au pair and who struggles to make sense of the violent events unfolding around her.

Subjects: British Authors; Coming-of-age; Community Life; Dark Humor; Family Relationships; Fathers and Daughters; First Novels; Great Britain; Literary Allusions; Siblings; Sisters; Suburbia; Teenage Girls; Teenagers; Violence

Now Try: This novel, Clay's first, is advertised as "inspired by Harper Lee's classic *To Kill a Mockingbird*"; readers might consider that classic novel as well. Another novel in which a large family of daughters struggles with school and family relationships is Jeffrey Eugenides's *The Virgin Suicides*; James Boice's *NoVA* also explores the difficulties of teenagers' lives even in suburbia. Although much harsher in tone and setting, György Dragoman's *The White King: A Novel*, set in a fictional Eastern bloc country during the 1980s, might also appeal to Clay's readers.

Coetzee, J. M.

🎗 *Diary of a Bad Year.* **Viking, 2007. 231pp. ISBN 9780670018758.**

Critics have speculated about how much of this novel's main character, a writer edging his way toward his later years and known only as Señor C, is based on Coetzee himself. In a daring three-way narrative split, the story is told (on each page) through Señor C's political and cultural diatribes, his quieter diary entries, and the story of his much younger and more attractive neighbor, Anya, who agrees to work as his typist.

Subjects: Australia; Autobiographical Fiction; Culture Clash; Diary; Friendships; Men's Lives; Quick Reads; South African Authors

Awards: New York Times Notable

Now Try: This is Coetzee's nineteenth book; fans of this title might also enjoy his novels *Disgrace, Elizabeth Costello*, and *Slow Man*. Another novel in which an older professional man engages in an unlikely May–December romance is Paul Kafka-Gibbons's *Dupont Circle*; while another stylistically daring take on love and marriage can be found in Phillip Lopate's *Two Marriages*, a novel in two novellas. Philip Roth's somewhat self-aware fiction might also appeal, particularly his Nathan Zuckerman novels, the most recent of which is *Exit Ghost* (the first in that series is *The Ghost Writer*).

Davis, Kathryn.

The Thin Place. **Little, Brown, 2006. 277pp. ISBN 9780316735049.**

Davis's fictional town of Varennes is an example of a "thin place," a location where the distance between the concrete life and the supernatural is said to be thin, and her characters seem to take all the gentle oddities of lives lived in such a place in stride. When three young girls find a dead man on the beach, one of them revives him with ease; the same girl can communicate with dogs, and various other fantastic events occur involving the residents of Varennes with surprising regularity.

Second Appeal: Setting

Subjects: Animals; Community Life; Dogs; Elderly; Friendships; Magic Realism; Multiple Viewpoints; Quick Reads; Small-Town Life

Now Try: Davis is also the author of *The Girl Who Trod on a Loaf, Hell, The Walking Tour*, and *Versailles*. Other novels in which authors employ contemporary magic realism are Kevin Brockmeier's *The Brief History of the Dead*, Ray Bradbury's classics *Something Wicked This Way Comes* and *Dandelion Wine*, James Hynes's *The Kings of Infinite Space*, and Lydia Millet's *Oh Pure and Radiant Heart*.

Davis, Lydia.

🌳 *Samuel Johnson Is Indignant: Stories.* McSweeney's Books, 2001. 201pp. ISBN 9780970335593.

Davis's fifty-six stories range in length from a paragraph to several pages, as well as across topics from work relationships to interpersonal relationships to child-bearing; from the problem of boring friends to linguistic puzzles such as how funeral homes get away with using the word "cremains." The only thing to be expected throughout this collection, really, is the unexpected.

Subjects: Humor; Satire; Short Stories; Small Press; Women Authors

Awards: ALA Notable

Now Try: Davis is the author of three other books of stories, *Varieties of Disturbance, Almost No Memory*, and *Break It Down*, as well as the novel *The End of the Story*. Aimee Bender's decidedly surreal short story collection *Willful Creatures* might appeal to these readers, as might Etgar Keret's *The Nimrod Flipout*. This book was published by McSweeney's, a small publisher associated with the Web site McSweeney's Internet Tendency; other books associated with the press are *The McSweeney's Book of Poets Picking Poets, The McSweeney's Joke Book of Book Jokes*, and Lawrence Weschler's nonfiction title of essays and photography, *Everything That Rises: A Book of Convergences*.

🌳 *Varieties of Disturbance: Stories.* Farrar, Straus & Giroux, 2007. 219pp. ISBN 9780374281731.

Davis is nothing if not a daring short story stylist, and many of the stories here are short, stream-of-consciousness pieces that work in concert with their titles. (Consider the story titled "Idea for a Short Documentary Film"; the entire story is "Representatives of different food products manufacturers try to open their own packaging.")

Subjects: Humor; Satire; Short Stories; Women Authors

Awards: New York Times Notable

Now Try: Davis is also the author of the novels *Almost No Memory* and *The End of the Story*. Other modern short story stylists might appeal to her readers, including Etgar Keret (*The Nimrod Flipout*); Miranda July (*No One Belongs Here More Than You*); and George Saunders, whose short satirical novel *The Brief and Frightening Reign of Phil*, might be enjoyed as much as his *Pastoralia: Stories*. The collection of short, short stories titled *Flash Fiction Forward: 80 Very Short Stories*, published by Norton, might appeal, as might the decidedly existential short, short memoir collection *Not Quite What I Was Planning: Six-Word Memoirs by Writers Famous and Obscure*.

De Kretser, Michelle.

🌳 *The Lost Dog.* Little, Brown, 2007. 326pp. ISBN 9780316001830.

Retired professor Tom Loxley, living in Australia and ostensibly writing a scholarly biography of Henry James, really spends much of his time pursuing his own thoughts and frittering away hours in the consideration of self-concerned interests (including trying to describe his own smell). When his dog goes missing in the Australian bush, much of his "scholarly work" is neglected as he searches for the dog, and he enlists the help of his artist neighbor Nelly Zhang. His interest in Nelly eventually leads him to investigate her somewhat suspicious past.

Subjects: Academia; Animals; Australia; Australian Authors; Dogs; Love Affairs; Mothers and Sons; Women Authors

Awards: Christina Stead Prize for Fiction

Now Try: De Kretser is also the author of the novels *The Hamilton Case* and *The Rose Grower*. Although it is told from the dog's point of view, Matt Haig's novel *The Labrador Pact* might also appeal to these readers. Other books about men who work in or who have retired from academia might also be suggested, including Tim O'Brien's *Tomcat in Love*, J. M. Coetzee's *Disgrace*, David Lodge's *Deaf Sentence*, or Richard Russo's decidedly more lighthearted *Straight Man*. Another novel in which a man falls in love with a woman with a questionable past is Frederick Barthelme's *Waveland*.

DeLillo, Don.

Falling Man. Scribner, 2007. 246pp. ISBN 9781416546023.

Lawyer Keith Neudecker stumbles, alive, from the World Trade Center shortly before its collapse during the terrorist attack of September 11, 2001, trying to make his way to the apartment of his ex-wife and son. Over the course of DeLillo's emotionally described but never sentimental novel, each of the characters (Keith, his ex-wife, and their son) finds the events of that day affecting his or her everyday activities, interests, and relationships.

Subjects: 9/11; Adultery; Classics; Family Relationships; Marriage; Men's Lives; New York City; Terrorism

Now Try: DeLillo is a well-known author whose smooth and skillful prose is always appreciated by reviewers; his earlier novels include *Cosmopolis*, *The Body Artist*, *Underworld*, and *White Noise*. Other novels that offer unique portraits of the unsettled state of American culture after 9/11 might be suggested, including Jess Walter's *The Zero*, Jay McInerney's *The Good Life*, and Joseph O'Neill's *Netherland*. Another critically popular author who might appeal to DeLillo's readers is Richard Powers, whose novels *The Time of Our Singing* and *The Echo Maker* might be suggested.

D'Erasmo, Stacey.

The Sky Below. Houghton Mifflin Harcourt, 2009. 271pp. ISBN 978-0618439256.

Gabriel Callahan, an obituary writer for a dying New York City newspaper and the collector of various bits and pieces of effluvia from the lives and environment around him (his collection functions for him as a way to relive his life's experiences and memories, and may remind the reader of artist Joseph Cornell's modernist "memory boxes"), moves through his life searching for the proper mix of independence and commitment. Although his lover, Janos, wants Gabriel to move in with him, Gabriel resists, even when faced with a portentous health prognosis, after which he journeys to Mexico to attempt, one last time, to reconcile his spirituality with his troubled youth and relationship struggles.

Second Appeal: Character

Subjects: Art and Artists; Cancer; Coming-of-age; Family Relationships; First Person; Gay Men; GLBTQ; Health Issues; Love Affairs; Magic Realism; Mexico; Mothers and Sons; New York City; Women Authors

Now Try: D'Erasmo's other novels, including *A Seashore Year* and *Salt*, might also appeal to these readers. Another novel in which an artist struggles with his interpersonal relationships is Anne Tyler's *Celestial Navigation*. Deborah Solomon's biography *Utopia Parkway: The Life and Work of Joseph Cornell* features a real-life artist who pioneered the art of shadow boxes. Another novel in which friends and protagonists struggle to reconcile their personal lives with their work is Mary Gaitskill's *Veronica*. Although not about art, Reinaldo Arenas's coming-of-age tale about his homosexuality and immigration, *Before Night Falls*, might also be suggested.

Díaz, Junot.

🎖 *The Brief Wondrous Life of Oscar Wao.* **Riverhead Books, 2007. 339pp. ISBN 9781594489587.**

Although a life characterized by its owner's obesity and twin desires to rid himself of his virginity and become a fantasy author might be considered, at first glance, to be anything but wondrous, Díaz nonetheless spins a marvelous tale around his protagonist through flashbacks and multiple viewpoints. Rich with imagery and description of the culture of Wao's ancestral home, the Dominican Republic, as well as descriptions of numerous eccentric family members (who are afflicted by a longtime curse, a "fukú") and friends, not to mention literary allusions too numerous to mention, this is a sprawling but richly evocative multigenerational story. Diaz also plays fast and loose with the language and structure of his writing, including many footnotes and offering fast and punchy dialogue, sometimes in the Spanish language.

Subjects: Book Groups; Classics; Dominican American Authors; Dominican Republic; Family Relationships; Footnotes; Literary Allusions; Multiple Viewpoints; YA; Young Men

Awards: National Book Critics Circle Award; New York Times Notable; Pulitzer Prize

Now Try: Díaz is also the author of the short story collection *Drown*. Other authors who write big, sprawling, somewhat avant-garde novels might also appeal, including Roberto Bolaño (*2666* and *The Savage Detectives*), Javier Calvo (*Wonderful World*), David Foster Wallace (*Infinite Jest*), Denis Johnson (*Tree of Smoke*), Matthew Sharpe (*Jamestown: A Novel*), and Michael Chabon (*The Amazing Adventures of Cavalier and Klay*). Other novels set in the Dominican Republic might also appeal, such as Julia Alvarez's *Before We Were Free* (also about the dictator Trujillo) and *In the Time of the Butterflies* (about the infamous Mirabel sisters and their place in Dominican history, which is also alluded to by Díaz), Nelly Rosario's *Song of the Water Saints*, and Edwidge Danticat's *The Farming of Bones*. Other readers will need to look no further for related reads than the text, in which Díaz frequently references such authors as Ayn Rand, as well as fantasy authors like Margaret Weis and J. R. R. Tolkien.

Now Consider Nonfiction . . . Making Sense: Of Our Culture and Society

Nonfiction titles in the "Making Sense: Of Our Culture and Society" stylistic genre are often classified as "cultural studies" or "pop culture" works. They are synthesizing works that offer a variety of research about our culture and societies, as well as their authors' theories about why and how we engage with our cultural and community surroundings.

De Botton, Alain. *Status Anxiety.*

Denby, David. *Snark: A Polemic in Seven Fits.*

Frankfurt, Harry G. *On Bullshit.*

Jacoby, Susan. *The Age of American Unreason.*

Johnson, Steven. *Everything Bad Is Good for You.*

Manguel, Alberto. *A History of Reading.*

Taleb, Nassim Nicholas. *The Black Swan: The Impact of the Highly Improbable.*

Doctorow, E. L.

🎗 *The March: A Novel.* **Random House, 2005. 363pp. ISBN 9780375506710.**

Known for the fluidity of his prose and mastery of the historical events he portrays in his fiction, Doctorow here uses all his skills to tell the story of Union general William Tecumseh Sherman's march through Georgia and the Carolinas in his triumphant military return to the north during the Civil War. Although Sherman appears as a character here, Doctorow gives equal time to the fictional characters through whose viewpoints and lives he relates the horrendous cost exacted on the American South (and by extension, on the entire nation) by the war.

Second Appeal: Story

Subjects: 19th Century; American South; Biographical Fiction; Book Groups; Civil War; Historical Fiction; Military; Sherman, William Tecumseh

Awards: National Book Critics Circle Award; New York Times Notable; PEN-Faulkner Award

Now Try: Doctorow is a master of literary historical fiction, and his other novels that might appeal to these readers are *Ragtime, Billy Bathgate,* and *The Waterworks.* Other novelists with similar skill at rendering story- and character-rich historical fiction (primarily through their prose skills) are Paulette Jiles (*Enemy Women* and *The Color of Lightning*), Jeffrey Lent (*In the Fall*), Charles Frazier (*Cold Mountain*), and Mark Helprin (*Winter's Tale* and *A Soldier of the Great War,* as well as the lively but not really historical *Freddy and Fredericka*).

Doyle, Roddy.

The Deportees and Other Stories. **Viking, 2007. 242pp. ISBN 9780670018451.**

Doyle explores the experiences of present-day immigrants to Ireland in this collection of eight short stories, many of which offer likable characters, even if they are put in situations involving class tension and race relations that don't always bring out the best in everyone.

Subjects: Dark Humor; Immigrants and Immigration; Ireland; Irish Authors; Race Relations; Short Stories

Now Try: Doyle is the author of the novels *Paddy Clarke Ha Ha Ha, The Woman Who Walked into Doors,* and *Paula Spencer,* as well as the Barrytown Trilogy (*The Commitments, The Snapper,* and *The Van*). Other short story collections in which authors explore characters' immigrant lifestyles are Jhumpa Lahiri's *Unaccustomed Earth,* Ellen Litman's *The Last Chicken in America,* and Rose Tremain's *The Road Home* (which is a novel, not a story collection, but also focuses on immigration in the United Kingdom).

Dragoman, György.

The White King. **Houghton Mifflin, 2007. 263pp. ISBN 9780618945177.**

Eleven-year-old Djata is largely left to fend for himself in a country ravaged by dictatorship and suspicion (modeled strongly on 1980s Romania), after his father is dragged away, charged with political dissidence by officials acting under orders of the totalitarian regime. This is a child's-eye-view of his harsh surroundings, a world populated by teachers who threaten violence and bullies who are seemingly in training to become political heavies and thugs.

Subjects: 1980s; Books in Translation; Child's Point of View; Coming-of-age; First Novels; Political Fiction; Romania; Violence

Now Try: Although less brutal in tone, Roddy Doyle's novel *Paddy Clarke Ha Ha Ha* also shows how mean little kids can be to one another; other unsettling coming-of-age novels are Jeffrey Eugenides's *The Virgin Suicides*, Robert Cormier's (YA) classic *The Chocolate War*, Daniel Clay's *Broken*, and Morgan Llywelyn's historical novel *1972: A Novel of Ireland's Unfinished Revolution.* Another tale of a child facing brutality when orphaned in wartime is Arnost Lustig's *Lovely Green Eyes*.

Du Boucheron, Bernard.

The Voyage of the Short Serpent. **Overlook Press, 2008. 206pp. ISBN 978-1585679201.**

The setting is fifteenth-century Iceland; the task at hand for the Catholic bishop Einar Sokkason is to investigate a far northern village, which has reportedly turned pagan and is engaging in atrocities, including cannibalism. Translated from the French and including descriptions of blood and gore that are not for the faint of heart, this novel nonetheless also considers what it means to be civilized and civilizing.

Subjects: 15th Century; Adventure; Books in Translation; Cannibalism; Catholic Church; Dark Humor; French Authors; Historical Fiction; Iceland; Religion; Violence

Now Try: Critics have referred to this stark novel as a "frostbitten version of Conrad's *Heart of Darkness.*" Other novels in which the driving need to survive dictates the story include Gil Adamson's *The Outlander*, Cormac McCarthy's *The Road* and *Blood Meridian*, Jim Crace's *The Pesthouse*, James Howard Kunstler's *World Made by Hand*, and Max Brooks's *World War Z*.

DuCornet, Rikki.

The One Marvelous Thing. **Dalkey Archive Press, 2008. 161pp. ISBN 978-1564785190.**

DuCornet offers a completely unique (some have termed it "postmodern") reading experience in this collection of short prose pieces, many illustrated by artist Tom Motley. (Although we have tagged this as a "graphic novel," it is more of a prose piece with line illustrations.) Her favorite subjects include the ironies of modern living (one of her characters, a poet, accepts sponsorship money from the Fossil Fuel Foundation and titles the sponsored poetry collection "The Greenhouse Gas Chamber") and the indignities and inequalities sometimes inherent in relationships and marriages.

Subjects: Family Relationships; Graphic Novels; Humor; Magic Realism; Marriage; Quick Reads; Satire; Short Stories; Women Authors

Now Try: DuCornet's other imaginative works include the historical novels *The Stain* and *Gazelle*, as well as the story collection *The Word "Desire"*. This book is also part of the Dalkey Archive Press's new <u>American Literature</u> series; another title in that series is Damion Searls's *What We Were Doing and Where We Were Going*. Another imaginative collection of stories is John Kessel's *The Baum Plan for Financial Independence*; Rivka Galchen's language-driven novel *Atmospheric Disturbances* also examines a marriage undergoing a challenge of a slightly metaphysical sort, and might appeal to these readers. Another author of slightly surreal but also engaging short stories and novels is Aimee Bender; consider suggesting her story collections *Willful Creatures* and *The Girl in the Flammable Skirt* or her novel *An Invisible Sign of My Own*.

Enright, Anne.

🦋 *The Gathering.* Black Cat, 2007. 260pp. ISBN 9780802170392.

After the suicide of her brother Liam, Veronica joins nine other members of her immediate family (the Hegarty clan originally consisted of fourteen family members) for his wake and funeral. While there she remembers their harsh childhoods and the sexual abuse that she believes poisoned Liam's entire future.

Second Appeal: Character

Subjects: Abuse; Alcoholism; Book Groups; Death and Dying; Family Relationships; First Person; Flashbacks; Ireland; Irish Authors; Sexual Abuse; Siblings; Suicide; Women Authors

Awards: Man Booker Prize; New York Times Notable

Now Try: Enright's earlier novels include *The Pleasure of Eliza Lynch* and *What Are You Like?*, as well as the story collection *Yesterday's Weather*. Another book in which an Irish author examines past events that shaped a person's life is Sebastian Barry's *The Secret Scripture*; the characters in Annie Proulx's *The Shipping News* also keep secrets from one another. Frank McCourt's best-selling memoir *Angela's Ashes* also explores family dynamics and privation, as does his brother Malachy McCourt's memoir *A Monk Swimming*.

🦋 *Yesterday's Weather: Stories.* Grove Press, 2008. 308pp. ISBN 978-0802118745.

Irish author Enright offers thirty-one stories, primarily about the everyday business of human existence, including domestic life, marriage, friendships, pregnancy, and many other relationships both healthy and not so healthy. All the stories, though about the most commonplace of subjects, nonetheless display a subtle darkness of tone, and many offer surprising twists and revelations.

Subjects: Domestic Fiction; Family Relationships; Irish Authors; Marriage; Short Stories; Women Authors

Awards: New York Times Notable

Now Try: Enright is also the author of the Booker Prize–winning novel *The Gathering*, and a historical novel titled *The Pleasure of Eliza Lynch*. Also of interest might be short story collections by fellow Irish authors William Trevor (*The Hill Bachelors*, *A Bit on the Side*, *Cheating at Canasta*), Roddy Doyle (*The Deportees*), Colm Tóibín (*Mothers and Sons*), as well as novels by popular Irish American author Alice McDermott (*At Weddings and Wakes* and *Charming Billy*). Irish author Nuala

O'Faolain's novel, *My Dream of You*, might be offered as a read-alike, as might her memoir, *Are You Somebody? The Accidental Memoir of a Dublin Woman*.

Eugenides, Jeffrey.

🎗 *Middlesex*. **Farrar, Straus & Giroux, 2002. 529pp. ISBN 9780374199692.**

Eugenides's protagonist Calliope is born a girl in the 1960s, but upon discovering that she is a hermaphrodite during her teen years, she elects to undergo surgery to become a boy ("Cal"). Not content to tell only that story, the author also relates the experiences of Cal's grandparents, who emigrated to the United States from Greece in the 1920s, with secrets of their own.

Subjects: 1920s; 1970s; Book Groups; Brothers and Sisters; Classics; First Person; Hermaphrodites; Historical Fiction; Immigrants and Immigration; Incest; Men Writing as Women; Michigan; Teenage Girls; Teenagers

Awards: Pulitzer Prize

Now Try: Eugenides's earlier novel, *The Virgin Suicides*, was also a critically acclaimed best seller. A nonfiction account of another person born a woman who indefatigably pursued what she felt was her true male gender is Pagan Kennedy's *The First Man-Made Man*. Two other authors who might appeal to Eugenides's readers are the skilled prose practitioners Michael Chabon (*The Amazing Adventures of Kavalier and Clay* and *The Yiddish Policemen's Union*) and Jonathan Franzen (*The Corrections*).

Faber, Michael.

Vanilla Bright Like Eminem: Stories. **Harcourt, 2005. 246pp. ISBN 9780151013142.**

Faber masterfully blends the surreal and the surrealistic in this collection of sixteen short stories. His characters range from a man who recovers suddenly from some unnamed mental malady and is sent home with his less-than-enthusiastic spouse to a parent and child on their state-supervised visit. Although the stories are evocative flashes of situations more than fully fleshed out narratives, Faber's unique writing style imbues even the plainest of circumstances with underlying meaning and tension.

Subjects: Dark Humor; Fantasy; Psychological Fiction; Short Stories; Society

Now Try: Michel Faber is also the author of the historical fiction cult favorite *The Crimson Petal and the White*, as well as the dystopian fantasy *Under the Skin* (and another short story collection, *Some Rain Must Fall*). Readers who enjoy his dark but always compelling narratives and imagery might enjoy other genrebending authors such as Matt Ruff (*Bad Monkeys* and *Set This House in Order*) or George Saunders (*The Brief and Frightening Reign of Phil* or the essay collection *The Braindead Megaphone*). Other authors who might appeal include the Scot Magnus Mills (*The Restraint of Beasts* and *All Quiet on the Orient Express*), Denis Johnson (*Tree of Smoke*), and Junot Díaz (*The Brief and Wondrous Life of Oscar Wao*).

Foer, Jonathan Safran.

🎗 *Everything Is Illuminated*. **Houghton Mifflin, 2002. 276pp. ISBN 978-0618173877.**

Foer's story within a story (within a story) is about a young writer named Jonathan Safran Foer, who travels to the Ukraine to find Augustine, the woman who saved his ancestor from the Nazis, with the help of his translator Alexi (as well as

Alexi's grandfather and dog); interspersed with that narrative is the historical story of Trachimbrod, a Polish *shtetl* where the fictional Foer's ancestors settled in the nineteenth century.

Subjects: 19th Century; Book Groups; Classics; Elderly; Flashbacks; Grandfathers; Grandmothers; Holocaust; Jewish American Authors; Jews and Judaism; Magic Realism; Multigenerational Fiction; Multiple Viewpoints

Awards: National Jewish Book Award

Now Try: Foer is also the author of a well-reviewed second novel, *Extremely Loud and Incredibly Close*. Other imaginative works of fiction about the Holocaust are Jonathan Littell's epic *The Kindly Ones*, Marcus Zusak's *The Book Thief*, and Thane Rosenbaum's *The Golems of Gotham*. Josh Bazell's literary thriller *Beat the Reaper* also offers a Holocaust subplot. Another novel of family secrets and with Ukrainian characters is Marina Lewycka's *A Short History of Tractors in Ukrainian*.

Extremely Loud and Incredibly Close. **Houghton Mifflin, 2005. 326pp. ISBN 9780618329700.**

Parallel family stories and tragedies frame Foer's narrative, largely told from nine-year-old Oskar Schell's point of view. Oskar's father, a unique man who often set up "mysteries" and clues for his precocious son to unravel, is killed in the events of 9/11, after which Oskar finds a key in his closet and becomes convinced that it is one final clue his father left for him to follow. He lives with his mother and is also close to his feisty grandmother, who herself has a complex history of marriage and relationships and lost a beloved sister, Anna, in the Holocaust. Foer is known for his unique styles, and this book includes photographs and shifting points of view.

Second Appeal: Character

Subjects: 9/11; Book Groups; Child's Point of View; Classics; Death and Dying; Experimental Fiction; Family Relationships; First Person; Grandmothers; Grief; Holocaust; Jewish American Authors; New York City

Now Try: These readers might also enjoy Foer's first novel, *Everything Is Illuminated*, as well as his nonfiction polemic *Eating Animals*. Books featuring young and endearingly precocious narrators might also appeal to these readers, including Mark Haddon's *The Curious Incident of the Dog in the Night-Time*, Kiara Brinkman's *Up High in the Trees*, or Catherine O'Flynn's *What Was Lost* (in which the young protagonist is not the narrator but is a very unique young character nonetheless). Fans of Foer's brand of imaginative fiction might also enjoy Nicole Krauss (*The History of Love*), Michael Chabon (*The Yiddish Policemen's Union* and *The Amazing Adventures of Kavalier and Clay*), Cynthia Ozick (*The Messiah of Stockholm* or *Heir to the Glimmering World*), or Salman Rushdie (*Midnight's Children* and *The Satanic Verses*).

Fonseca, Rubem.

The Taker: And Other Stories. **Open Letter, 2008. 166pp. ISBN 9781934824023.**

Brazilian author Fonseca offers a collection of fifteen short (sometimes very short, one- to three-page) stories that immediately grab the reader with their dark subject matter and descriptions, offered in seemingly banal tones and settings. Opening with stories in which a suburban man punctuates his nightly relaxation drives with the running down of innocent pedestrians and a murderer finds the perfect girlfriend who supports and helps plan his crime, the collection is sure to grab the instant attention of many readers.

Subjects: Books in Translation; Brazil; Brazilian Authors; Dark Humor; Murder; Quick Reads; Society; South America; Violence

Now Try: Fonseca is also the author of the novels *Bufo &Spallanzani, High Art*, and *Vast Emotions and Imperfect Thoughts*. Other somewhat dark, surrealistic, or spare collections of short fiction might be enjoyed by these readers, including Roald Dahl's classic *Kiss, Kiss*, Michael Faber's *Vanilla Bright Like Eminem*, and James Salter's *Dusk and Other Stories*.

Ford, Richard.

A Multitude of Sins. **Random House, 2001. 286pp. ISBN 9780375412127.**

No one is better than Ford at exploring the many ways in which love doesn't fulfill us but rather leads to an ever more complex series of decisions, justifications, and resignations. In this collection of nine stories and a short novella, he primarily explores how the acts, revelations, and outright discoveries of infidelities affect the lives of both those engaging in trysts and those wronged by them.

Subjects: Adultery; Family Relationships; Humor; Love Affairs; Marriage; Short Stories

Now Try: Ford is also the author of the popular Frank Bascombe trilogy, comprising the titles *The Sportswriter, Independence Day* (which won the Pulitzer Prize), and *The Lay of the Land*. Susan Minot's collection of stories, *Lust*, might also appeal to these readers, as might the poignant memoir *Losing Everything* by David Lozell Martin, in which he also plumbs the depths of adultery's effects on relationships.

Gaitskill, Mary.

🕭 *Veronica: A Novel.* **Pantheon Books, 2005. 227pp. ISBN 9780375421457.**

From her vantage point as a middle-aged woman suffering from hepatitis and in an unromantic career as a cleaning woman, Alison looks back on her tempestuous youth, her beauty and modeling career, her experiences in San Francisco and among like-minded artists and bohemians, and most particularly her friendship with Veronica, an older woman who contracted AIDS from a lover. Gaitskill's skill with prose, stylized but disjointed, makes readers feel as though they are experiencing youth and heartbreak along with Alison.

Subjects: AIDS; Book Groups; Death and Dying; Explicit Sexuality; Family Relationships; First Person; Friendships; Health Issues; New York City; San Francisco; Teenage Girls; Teenagers; Women Authors

Awards: ALA Notable; National Book Award

Now Try: Gaitskill's writing skill is clearly on display in her other novels, including *Bad Behavior* and *Two Girls, Fat and Thin*, as well as her story collections *Because They Wanted To* and *Don't Cry*. Two other novels about complex friendships (and obsession) are Ann Beattie's *My Life, Starring Dara Falcon* and Charles Baxter's *The Soul Thief;* also of interest might be Ann Patchett's memoir of her intense friendship with Lucy Grealy, *Truty & Beauty: A Friendship*. Other novels in which characters look back over their lives and decisions might also be suggested, such as Susan Minot's *Evening* or Virginia Woolf's classic *Mrs. Dalloway*. Memoirs in which young women strive to make their way in an often cruel and unfair world might also appeal, including Wendy Werris's *An Alphabetical Life: Living It Up in the World of Books*, Mary Karr's *The Liar's Club*, and A. M. Homes's *The Mistress's Daughter*.

Galchen, Rivka.

🏵 *Atmospheric Disturbances.* **Farrar, Straus & Giroux, 2008. 240pp. ISBN 9780374200114.**

What would you do if your spouse came home one day and you didn't believe it was actually your spouse? This is what Leo Liebenstein, himself a psychiatrist, believes when one day his wife Rema comes home, and he becomes convinced it's not really her (but is instead a "simulacrum" of her, or her doppelganger). While trying to figure out who the stranger now sharing his life is and continuing to work with one of his patients, Harvey, Leo becomes increasingly delusional and dependent on the enigmatic meteorologist Dr. Tzvi Gal-Chen.

Subjects: Book Groups; Canadian Authors; First Novels; First Person; Marriage; Psychological Fiction; Unreliable Narrator; Women Authors

Awards: ALA Notable; New York Times Notable

Now Try: Reviewers have compared this book to Thomas Pynchon's classic novel, *The Crying of Lot 49*; Pynchon's other decidedly surreal novels might also appeal, including *Against the Day*, *V*, and *Gravity's Rainbow*. Other novels in which the boundaries of reality are decidedly fluid are Emily Perkins's *Novel about My Wife*, James Hynes's *The Kings of Infinite Space*, and Magnus Mills's *All Quiet on the Orient Express* and *Three to See the King*. Those readers fascinated by the more physical processes that are sometimes behind our motivations, actions, and brain chemistry might also consider Oliver Sacks's popular nonfiction title *The Man Who Mistook His Wife for a Hat*.

Ghosh, Amitav.

Sea of Poppies. **Farrar, Straus & Giroux, 2008. 515pp. ISBN 9780374174224.**

Set in nineteenth-century Calcutta, Ghosh's literary historical fiction novel features a disparate cast of characters, from a widowed opium farmer to an American sailor, making their way across the Bay of Bengal on the *Ibis*, a ship transporting opium (during the Opium Wars). Although setting and story play an important part in the narrative, the richly descriptive language steals the show: "The Ganga seemed to be flowing between twin glaciers, both its banks being blanketed by thick drifts of white-petalled flowers."

Second Appeal: Setting

Subjects: 19th Century; Book Groups; Calcutta; Historical Fiction; India; Indian Authors; Multicultural; Ocean; Opium

Now Try: Ghosh is also the author of the novels *The Glass Palace*, *The Shadow Lines*, and *The Hungry Tide*, as well as the nonfiction title *In an Antique Land: History in the Guise of a Traveler's Tale*. Other literary historical novels that might appeal to these readers are Philip Hensher's *The Mulberry Empire*, Hari Kunzru's *The Impressionist*, Peter Carey's *Oscar and Lucinda*, and Salman Rushdie's *The Enchantress of Florence*.

Gold, Glen David.

Sunnyside. **Knopf, 2009. 559pp. ISBN 9780307270689.**

Gold's sprawling historical novel, set in 1916, follows the fortunes of silent film star Charlie Chaplin; a man named Leland Wheeler, who's desperate to become a star in Hollywood but is drafted into war in Europe instead, still managing to parlay a tender moment caring for two puppies on the front line into a film career; and Hugo Black, a man who volunteers to fight in World War I and finds himself in the thick of the action in Russia.

Subjects: 1910s; Biographical Fiction; Book Groups; California; Chaplin, Charlie; Historical Fiction; Hollywood; Men's Lives; Movies; Multiple Viewpoints; World War I

Now Try: Gold is also the author of the cult classic historical fiction title *Carter Beats the Devil*. He has also been compared to another popular literary historical novelist, E. L. Doctorow (*Billy Bathgate, The Waterworks, Ragtime*, and *The March*); other literary novelists who have tried their hands at historical fiction might be suggested, including Michael Chabon (*The Yiddish Policemen's Union*), Russell Banks (*The Reserve*), Kevin Baker (*Strivers Row* and *Paradise Alley*), and William P. Kennedy (*Roscoe* and *Legs*, which is the first title in Kennedy's <u>Albany Cycle</u>). Biographies of Charlie Chaplin might also be enjoyable related reads for fans of this novel; consider *My Autobiography* by Charles Chaplin and David Robinson or Kenneth Schuyler Lynn's *Charlie Chaplin and His Times*.

Gordimer, Nadine.

Beethoven Was One-Sixteenth Black: And Other Stories. **Farrar, Straus & Giroux, 2007. 177pp. ISBN 9780374109820.**

South African author Gordimer tells thirteen stories in which narrators seek to better understand their origins and their identities (racial and otherwise). Not all of the narrators are run-of-the-mill characters; one story is told from the viewpoint of a tapeworm, and another relates a conversation between the ghosts of Edward Said and Susan Sontag (moderated by the sleeper who is dreaming the encounter).

Second Appeal: Setting

Subjects: Identity; Political Fiction; Race Relations; Short Stories; South Africa; South African Authors; Women Authors

Now Try: Gordimer is a prolific (and prize-winning) novelist and short story writer; her other story collections might appeal to these readers, including *Loot, and Other Stories, Jump and Other Stories*, and *Something Out There: Stories*. Other Nobel Prize–winning authors who might be suggested to Gordimer's readers are Doris Lessing (*The Golden Notebook, The Fifth Child*, and *Alfred and Emily*), fellow South African writer J. M. Coetzee (*Disgrace* and *Diary of a Bad Year*), and Toni Morrison (*The Bluest Eye, Song of Solomon*, and *Beloved*). Gordimer's having some fun here playing with the idea of how we relate to literature; John Kessel's story collection *The Baum Plan for Financial Independence* also blurs the lines between writer and reader, and P. F. Kluge's novel *Gone Tomorrow* details a narrator's lifelong relationship with his unwritten book.

Guo, Xiaolu.

Twenty Fragments of a Ravenous Youth. **Doubleday, 2008. 167pp. ISBN 978-0385525923.**

Twenty-one-year-old Fenfang Wang leaves her peasant village in China to make her way in the film industry in Beijing. In twenty disparate vignettes she relates the story of her work, her memories of her village and farm and her desire to escape both, and her relationships with two very different men (one Chinese, one English).

Second Appeal: Setting

Subjects: Beijing; Book Groups; Books in Translation; China; Chinese Authors; Coming-of-age; Love Affairs; Movies; Multicultural; Professions; Quick Reads; Society; Women Authors

Now Try: Guo is also the author of *A Concise Chinese-English Dictionary for Lovers*. Another novel featuring a young woman making her way in the Chinese society of the twenty-first century that might appeal is Annie Wang's *The People's Republic of Desire*; the collection *Chairman Mao Would Not Be Amused* offers stories by twenty young Chinese authors. Ma Jian's novel about a Tiananmen Square protestor awakening from a coma to a changed society, *Beijing Coma*, might also provide a similar reading experience. Two nonfiction titles may also be of interest to these readers: Lijia Zhang's memoir *"Socialism Is Great!": A Worker's Memoir of the New China* and Leslie T. Chang's investigative title *Factory Girls: From Village to City in a Changing China*.

Guterson, David.

The Other. Knopf, 2008. 255pp. ISBN 9780307263155.

The paths of childhood friends John William Barry and Neil Countryman diverge as they grow older; although they spent the majority of their youth together in the wilds of their native state of Washington, after graduating from college Neil follows the more traditional path of building his career and marrying, while John William, increasingly convinced of the evils of modern life, returns to live more fully in the rural backcountry. Their lives converge once again when John William asks Neil for help concealing his whereabouts from his family.

Second Appeal: Setting

Subjects: 1970s; Environmental Writing; Flashbacks; Friendships; Men's Lives; Suspense; Washington

Now Try: Guterson is not a prolific author, but his books are all thoughtful treatises on difficult choices and interpersonal relationships; many are set in the Pacific Northwest, including *Snow Falling on Cedars*, *East of the Mountains*, and *Our Lady of the Forest*. Other novels in which boys' friendships will affect their adults lives include Per Petterson's superlative (also featuring a strongly drawn setting) *Out Stealing Horses*, Eli Gottlieb's *Now You See Him*, and Todd Tucker's *Over and Under*. Readers interested in similar nonfiction titles might enjoy Jon Krakauer's investigative adventure title *Into the Wild* (about a young man who also wanted to live on his own terms) and Elizabeth Gilbert's profile of Eustace Conway, another man seeking a more authentic life, *The Last American Man*.

Hacker, Katharina.

The Have-Nots. Europa, 2007. 341pp. ISBN 9781933372419.

In this novel about 9/11 and modern urban life, three stories intersect in London: those of Jakob and Isabelle, thirty-something newlyweds starting a new life in the city and trying to make sense of a relationship forged during the intensity of post-9/11 world events and now foundering; their neighbor Sara, a young girl with abusive parents; and Jim, a drug dealer with a fascination for Isabelle. This novel won the German Book Prize.

Subjects: 9/11; Abuse; Books in Translation; German Authors; Interconnected Stories; London; Marriage; Violence

Now Try: Hacker has written another novel, *The Lifeguard*, as well as a story collection, *Morpheus*. Joseph O'Neill's novel *Netherland* also looks at the effect of the events of 9/11 on a marriage (and is also set at least partially in London). Another novel in translation, Muriel Barbery's *The Elegance of the Hedgehog*, set in France and featuring a complex main character and her relationships with other tenants in her building, might also appeal to these readers.

Harding, Paul.

Tinkers. Bellevue Literary Press, 2009. 191pp. ISBN 9781934137123.

In Harding's slim and atmospheric novel, the elderly George Washington Crosby lies dying in his home, surrounded by his children and grandchildren and hallucinating his way back through his memories and life. In addition to dreaming of his own life's work of fixing and maintaining clocks, George also relives as dreams the work and story of his father, Howard Aaron Crosby, who worked as a traveling salesman (in the days when people still drove wagons) and tinker.

Subjects: Book Groups; Death and Dying; Elderly; Epilepsy; Family Relationships; Fathers and Sons; First Novels; Historical Fiction; New England; Psychological Fiction; Quick Reads; Small Press

Now Try: Other novels in which the ethereal feel of individuals working backward through their lives might appeal include Marilynne Robinson's novels *Gilead* and *Home*, Susan Minot's novel *Evening*, Jonathan Coe's *The Rain Before It Falls*, Sebastian Barry's *The Secret Scripture*, Daniel Wallace's *Big Fish*, and Gabriel García Márquez's *Memories of My Melancholy Whores*. James Howard Kunstler's *World Made by Hand*, at 256 pages, is also a relatively slim novel about nostalgia for a world that wasn't perfect; Wallace Stegner's classic *Angle of Repose* (though much longer than *Tinkers*) also offers a story of complex family dynamics and a strong sense of place.

Haskell, John.

Out of My Skin. Farrar, Straus & Giroux, 2009. 211pp. ISBN 9780374299095.

Haskell's unnamed narrator, who moved from New York to Los Angeles to write and review movies, gets to know a Steve Martin impersonator and decides to appropriate the role for himself—not so much as a Martin look-alike but as one who has his unique way of moving through the world. "Being" Steve starts to pay off immediately, as the writer falls in love, but the role becomes problematic when he finds himself increasingly unwilling to abandon the persona.

Subjects: California; First Person; Humor; Literary Lives; Los Angeles; Love Affairs; Martin, Steve; Men's Lives; Quick Reads

Now Try: Haskell's other novels, *American Purgatorio* and *I Am Not Jackson Pollock*, are equally imaginative works of fiction. Those readers interested in the rather ironic fact that Steve Martin's a novelist in his own right might enjoy his novellas *The Pleasure of My Company* and *Shopgirl*, as well as his nonfiction humor collection *Cruel Shoes* or his memoir *Born Standing Up: A Comic's Life*. Wells Tower's critically lauded collection of short fiction, *Everything Ravaged, Everything Burned*, offers some equally mind-bending fiction, as do Benjamin Kunkel's novel *Indecision: A Novel* and Denis Johnson's ode to noir fiction, *Nobody Move*.

Hemon, Aleksandar.

The Lazarus Project. **Riverhead Books, 2008. 294pp. ISBN 978-1594489884.**

In 1908 in Chicago, Jewish immigrant Lazarus Averbuch was shot and killed by police chief George Shippy after Averbuch was admitted into Shippy's home with a delivery. A century later, Vladimir Brik (himself a Bosnian American) gets a grant to study the incident (Was the shooting justified? Was Averbuch an anarchist, as Shippy claimed?) and travels to Eastern Europe with Rora, a fellow Bosnian and war photographer, to try to piece together the true story of not only the shooting, but also Averbuch's life before that day.

Second Appeal: Setting

Subjects: Anarchists; Book Groups; Chicago; Eastern Europe; Immigrants and Immigration; Jews and Judaism; Literary Lives; Murder

Awards: New York Times Notable

Now Try: Hemon has written another novel, *Nowhere Man*, as well as two short story collections, *The Question of Bruno* and *Love and Obstacles*. Another novel in which a young man travels to find the truth of a historical legend is Jonathan Safran Foer's *Everything Is Illuminated*. The immigrant narrative received a postmodern twist in Gary Shteyngart's *The Russian Debutante's Handbook*. This novel is infused with character details about the city of Chicago; other novels in which the city is important to the narrative are Saul Bellow's classic *The Adventures of Augie March* and Nelson Algren's classic *The Man with the Golden Arm* (not to mention his nonfiction title, *Chicago: City on the Make*).

Now Consider Nonfiction . . . Making Sense: Of Our Histories

In nonfiction titles in the "Making Sense: Of Our Histories" stylistic genre authors provide historical details about specific events, in addition to examining the effects of such events on our human and societal development. They are synthesizing works that offer a variety of historical stories and anecdotes and often feature their authors' speculation about how certain historical happenings affected the course of history.

Diamond, Jared. *Collapse: How Societies Choose to Fail or Succeed.*

Diamond, Jared. *Guns, Germs, and Steel.*

Greider, William. *Who Will Tell the People: The Betrayal of American Democracy.*

Hoffman, Eva. *After Such Knowledge: Memory, History, and the Legacy of the Holocaust.*

Menand, Louis. *The Metaphysical Club: A Story of Ideas in America.*

Stille, Alexander. *The Future of the Past.*

Hemon, Aleksandar.

Love and Obstacles: Stories. Riverhead Books, 2009. 209pp. ISBN 9781594488641.

Hemon's eight stories are notable for both his talent in writing prose in English (made all the more remarkable by the fact that it is not his first language) and their subject matter; although the story "Stairway to Heaven" is a fairly standard story of coming-of-age rebellion, and the other stories deal with love affairs and other typical plots, they are all informed by Hemon's dark undertones and his settings and context (he himself was unable to return from America to his home country, Sarajevo) in bleak situations and surroundings.

Subjects: Chicago; Dark Humor; Immigrants and Immigration; Quick Reads; Short Stories

Now Try: Hemon's other story collections, *Nowhere Man* and *The Question of Bruno*, might be suggested to these readers, as might his critically lauded novel *The Lazarus Project*. Hemon's style somehow gives the reader a sense of his more international background; other authors who might appeal to his readers include Milan Kundera (*The Unbearable Lightness of Being* and *Ignorance*), Vladimir Nabokov (*Lolita* and *The Stories of Vladimir Nabokov*), Lara Vapnyar (*Broccoli and Other Tales of Food and Love*), and Gary Shteyngart (*The Russian Debutante's Handbook* and *Absurdistan*). Other story collections and novels set in Chicago might appeal to these readers, such as Stuart Dybek's *I Sailed with Magellan: Stories* or Nelson Algren's classics *The Man with the Golden Arm* and *A Walk on the Wild Side*.

Hogan, Linda.

Power. Norton. 1998. 235pp. ISBN 9780393046366.

Sixteen-year-old Omishto (her name translates as "One Who Watches") grows up in a culture that is barely avoiding extinction; as a member of Florida's Taiga people, the encroachment of developers and other players on her people's lands and wilderness provides the backdrop to her youth. When Ama, an older woman in her community whom Omishto has known as a friend and mentor, must stand trial for killing a panther (an endangered and protected animal under Florida law), Omishto must try to decipher Ama's motives and come to terms with her own involvement in the incident.

Second Appeal: Story

Subjects: Animals; Coming-of-age; Culture Clash; Environmental Writing; Florida; Friendships; Law and Lawyers; Law Enforcement; Native American Authors; Native Americans; Quick Reads; Teenage Girls; Teenagers; Trials; Women Authors; YA

Now Try: Hogan has explored other Native American stories in her novels *Mean Spirit*, *Solar Storms*, and *People of the Whale*; she has also written a memoir, *The Woman Who Watches Over the World*, and a collection of poetry (*The Book of Medicines*). Louise Erdrich's writing, which is similar both in style and subject to Hogan's, might also appeal, particularly her novels *Tracks*, *The Antelope Wife*, and *The Plague of Doves*. Susan Power's novel *The Grass Dancer* and Leslie Marmon Silko's classic novel *Ceremony* also tell similar stories (and feature their authors' powerful and skillful writing skills as well). Another novel in which a younger woman tries to decipher the secrets and stories of an older woman is Diane Setterfield's *The Thirteenth Tale*.

Hynes, James.

Kings of Infinite Space. **St. Martin's Press, 2004. 341pp. ISBN 978-0312456450.**

Paul Trilby really has enough to be worried about, what with the angry ghost of his former girlfriend's cat Charlotte haunting him (Paul was responsible for Charlotte's death, after all), without having to figure out both the office politics and the vaguely unsettling post-work activities of his new workplace. Eventually, with the help of Callie, a woman with whom he falls in love, he starts to unravel the sinister mysteries of the office—although he must figure out the mysteries of the cat ghost on his own.

Subjects: Animals; Cannibalism; Cats; Dark Humor; Ghosts; Professions; Psychological Fiction; Science Fiction; Work Relationships

Now Try: Hynes's other decidedly surreal works include *Publish or Perish: Three Tales of Tenure and Terror* and *The Lecturer's Tale*. Joshua Ferris's novel *Then We Came to the End* doesn't feature a supernatural plot, but rivals Hynes's book in describing the monotony of working in a cubicle; Iain Levison has discussed work both in fiction (*Since the Layoffs*) and memoir (*A Working Stiff's Manifesto*) form. Authors who rival Hynes's ability to tell vaguely unsettling stories are Magnus Mills (*The Restraint of Beasts* and *Explorers of the New Century*), Tom McCarthy (*Remainder*), and Michael Faber (*Under the Skin*).

Ishiguro, Kazuo.

🌸 *Never Let Me Go.* **Knopf, 2005. 288pp. ISBN 9781400043392.**

Kathy H., a thirty-one-year-old "carer," narrates the story of her childhood and upbringing at the British school of Hailsham. Although her tale is a common enough one of friendships, falling in love, and other first-time experiences, what makes it uncommon is her growing realization that she and the rest of her classmates (and eventually colleagues) are not being trained for lives of their own, but rather for a larger purpose, revealed only gradually throughout Ishiguro's carefully paced and eerie novel.

Second Appeal: Story

Subjects: British Authors; Coming-of-age; First Person; Friendships; Genetics; Health Issues; Japanese Authors; Medicine; Men Writing as Women; Psychological Fiction; Science Fiction; YA

Awards: ALA Notable; Alex Award; New York Times Notable

Now Try: Ishiguro's other novels are also masterpieces of subtle characterization and storytelling; they include *A Pale View of the Hills*, *An Artist of the Floating World*, *The Unconsoled*, *The Remains of the Day*, and *When We Were Orphans*. Other literary science fiction novels might appeal to these readers, including Margaret Atwood's *The Handmaid's Tale* and *Oryx and Crake*, P. D. James's *Children of Men*, Ray Bradbury's *Fahrenheit 451*, and Philip K. Dick's *Minority Report*.

Iweala, Uzodinma.

🌸 *Beasts of No Nation.* **HarperCollins, 2005. 142pp. ISBN 9780719567520.**

Iweala drops the reader directly into the first-person and stream-of-consciousness narrative of Agu, a child soldier in an unnamed West African nation. After his father is killed, Agu is forced into violent paramilitary duty;

through the use of evocative imagery the reader feels the discomfort, suffering, and anguish of the boy killer ("It is starting like this. I am feeling itch like insect is crawling on my skin, and then my head is just starting to tingle right between my eye . . . .")

Subjects: Africa; Child Soldiers; Child's Point of View; Psychological Fiction; Quick Reads; Violence; War

Awards: ALA Notable; New York Times Notable

Now Try: Dave Eggers's novel *What Is the What* is similar to this one in subject and style, although it is set in Sudan. Three authors who might appeal to Iweala's readers are Chinua Achebe (*Things Fall Apart*, *No Longer at Ease*, and *Anthills of the Savannah*), whose novels often focus on the corrupting nature of power; Uwem Akpan (*Say You're One of Them*); and Ben Okri, whose Booker Prize–winning novel *The Famished Road* might be a good read-alike. It is noted in this book that the author was advised by fellow author Jamaica Kincaid, whose lyrically written novels *Mr. Potter* and *The Autobiography of My Mother* might prove to be good read-alikes. Ishmael Beah's memoir of his experiences as a child soldier, *A Long Way Gone: Memoirs of a Boy Soldier*, might be suggested, as might Jean Hatzfeld's powerful oral histories of the genocide in Rwanda, *Machete Season* and *Life Laid Bare*.

Jin, Ha.

🌑 *War Trash*. **Pantheon, 2004. 352pp. ISBN 9780375422768.**

In the middle is not often an easy place to be, particularly during wartime. The year is 1951, and when Chinese officer Yu Yuan is captured during the war in Korea, he is pressed into service as a translator between Korean captors and Chinese captives, which means both sides distrust him.

Subjects: 1950s; Chinese American Authors; Chinese Authors; Communism; First Person; Historical Fiction; Korea; Korean War; Prisoners of War; Prisons

Awards: New York Times Notable; PEN-Faulkner Award

Now Try: Jin is a popular and critically revered author; his other novels, including *A Free Life*, *Crazed*, and *Waiting*, might also be enjoyed by these readers. Another book in which a man is faced with a plethora of dangerous choices during wartime is Jeff Talarigo's *The Ginseng Hunter*; other war stories written with spare prose similar to Jin's include Erich Maria Remarque's classic *All Quiet on the Western Front* and William Styron's *The Long March and in the Clap Shack*. Although more of a satirical novel, which was banned in China, Yan Lianke's *Serve the People!*, about life at the height of China's Cultural Revolution, might also appeal to these readers.

Johnson, Denis.

🌑 *Tree of Smoke*. **Farrar, Straus & Giroux, 2007. 614pp. ISBN 9780374279127.**

Johnson's magnum opus (to date; who knows what he'll write next?) tells the story of the Vietnam War through the viewpoints of multiple characters, all with their own histories and politics; among them are "Skip" Sands, the CIA operative recruited to work in Indochina by his uncle, Francis X; a North Vietnamese spy named Trung; the brothers Bill and James Houston, from Arizona, as American as their last name and caught up in the war's fighting; and a Canadian nurse, who provides the epilogue to the story. Viewpoints and story lines shift as the complexity of all the story's moving parts mirror the complexity of war, but the story is organized chronologically, starting in 1963 and proceeding year by year through 1970 (with a brief final chapter set in 1983).

Second Appeal: Setting

Subjects: 1960s; Book Groups; Brothers; CIA; Classics; Double Agents; Epic Reads; Family Relationships; Friendships; Historical Fiction; Multiple Viewpoints; Vietnam; Vietnam War; YA

Awards: National Book Award; New York Times Notable

Now Try: Johnson is also the author of the novels *Nobody Move, The Name of the World*, and *Already Dead* (as well as the story collection *Jesus' Son*). Tim O'Brien's classics of the Vietnam War, *The Things They Carried* and *Going After Cacciato* (not to mention his novel exploring later effects of the war on its veterans, *In the Lake of the Woods*) might also appeal to these readers, as might Ward Just's *A Dangerous Friend* or Robert Littell's *The Company: A Novel of the CIA*. Other authors who are stylistically daring in their fiction might be suggested to these readers, including Richard Powers (*The Echo Maker, The Time of Our Singing*, and *Plowing the Dark*), Don DeLillo (*Falling Man, Underworld*, and *Libra*), David Gates (*Jernigan, Preston Falls*, and *The Wonders of the Invisible World: Stories*), and William T. Vollmann (who also won the National Book Award, for his novel *Europe Central*) A nonfiction title that combines memoir, travel, and history (as well as the viewpoints of many of his subjects) is Tom Bissell's *The Father of All Things: A Marine, His Son, and the Legacy of Vietnam*.

Jones, Sadie.

🏵 *The Outcast*. **Harper, 2008. 347pp. ISBN 9780061374036.**

As a witness to his mother's accidental death, ten-year-old Lewis Aldridge suffered the shock and guilt of that severe trauma; to make matters worse, his father didn't know how to comfort him, remarried quickly, and sent Lewis off to boarding school, where he embarked on a career of self-mutilation and crime. After committing arson at the age of seventeen and serving two years in prison, he is now set to return to his father's home and community, but the transition will not be an easy one, as not every resident aware of his history is happy about his return.

Subjects: 1950s; Alcoholism; British Authors; Family Relationships; Family Secrets; First Novels; Great Britain; Historical Fiction; Women Authors; Women Writing as Men; Young Men

Awards: Costa First Novel Award

Now Try: Other novels in which accidents and people's choices affect families for years to come might be suggested to these readers, including Kim Barnes's *A Country Called Home*, Jeffrey Eugenides's *The Virgin Suicides*, and Daniel Clay's *Broken*. Another novel of family secrets and homecomings (and by a British author to boot) is Justin Cartwright's *The Promise of Happiness*. Another author who might appeal to Jones's readers is Joyce Carol Oates, whose novels often feature bleak story lines and unflinching considerations of family and community life; they include *My Sister, My Love: The Intimate Story of Skylar Rampike, Them*, and *We Were the Mulvaneys*.

Julavits, Heidi.

🌺 *The Uses of Enchantment*. **Doubleday, 2006. 356pp. ISBN 9780385513234.**

At the age of sixteen, Mary Veal disappeared from the grounds of the Semmering Academy (an all-girls' institution in New England) and went missing for a month, then reappeared, claiming that she couldn't remember anything that had happened. (Suspicions about whether she was kidnapped or was a rather more willing runaway lingered.) Julavits splits the narrative into three stories; short chapters titled "What Might Have Happened" provide a glimpse into how the disappearance might have been caused, while longer chapters relate the parallel stories of Mary's meetings with a psychologist named Dr. Hammer and the 1999 death of her mother Paula, after which she returns home to a rather prickly unwelcome from her two other sisters, Regina and Gaby.

Subjects: 1990s; Book Groups; Family Relationships; Kidnapping; Mothers and Daughters; New England; Private Schools; Psychological Fiction; Runaways; Teenage Girls; Teenagers; Women Authors

Awards: New York Times Notable

Now Try: Julavits is a founding editor of the literary journal *The Believer*, and has written two other novels, *The Mineral Palace* and *The Effect of Living Backwards*. Another novel that features a teen girl's mysterious disappearance is Stewart O'Nan's sobering *Songs for the Missing*; Elizabeth Strout's novel *Amy and Isabelle* features an inappropriate relationship between a young girl and one of her teachers. In Kathe Koja's YA novel *Going Under* a young girl struggles in her relationship with the psychologist meant to help her. Although the reader knows what has happened to the main character throughout Alice Sebold's novel *The Lovely Bones*, it is similar to Julavits's book in that her family is never quite sure what has happened to their missing daughter. The nonfiction account *Live Through This: A Mother's Memoir of Runaway Daughters and Reclaimed Love* by Debra Gwartney, might prove an interesting related read.

Kalpakian, Laura.

🌺 *Delinquent Virgin: Wayward Pieces*. **Graywolf Press. 1999. 264pp. ISBN 9781555972950.**

Kalpakian offers nine short stories, most of which are set in the fictional community of St. Elmo, California, but which vary in the types of main characters in them. In one story, a church's plaster Madonna statue starts to show up in different places in the community, making the priest worry that even his statues have a better feel for the town than he does; in another, an upstanding member of the community, who just delivered the high school's commencement address about the importance of truth, asks another man for a not-so-truthful favor. Irony abounds, but Kalpakian's tone is still gentle.

Subjects: California; Community Life; Humor; Short Stories; Small Press; Women Authors

Awards: ALA Notable

Now Try: Kalpakian has also written the novels *American Cookery*, *The Memoir Club*, and *Caveat*. In Diane Schoemperlen's quietly thoughtful novel *Our Lady of the Lost and Found*, the mother of God also plays a part—by showing up on the doorstep of a middle-aged Canadian woman for a short vacation. Other short story collections published by Minnesota's independent and eclectic Graywolf Press might also appeal, including J. Robert Lennon's *Pieces for the Left Hand*, David Rosenthal and Merce Rodoreda's *My Christina and Other Stories*, and Steve Sterns's *The Wedding Jester*—as might an essay collection such as Ander Monson's *Neck Deep and Other Predicaments* or Charles Baxter's *The Business of Memory*.

Kelman, James.

Kieron Smith, Boy. Harcourt, 2008. 422pp. ISBN 9780151013487.

Kelman's stream-of-consciousness (rendered in a subtle written dialect that makes you hear the regional Scottish accent in your head as you read) narrative is told by Kieron Smith, a boy who faces all the challenges of childhood, which are sometimes underestimated as traumas. Kieron shares as much as he understands about his family's relationships, his favored elder brother Mattie, and the deaths of various family members, as well as the typical tribulations of school, friendships, and adolescence.

Subjects: Coming-of-age; Family Relationships; First Person; Friendships; Glasgow; Scotland; Scottish Authors; Social Class; Young Boys

Now Try: Kelman is also the author of the Man Booker Prize winning novel *How Late It Was, How Late*, as well as the more recent novel *You Have to Be Careful in the Land of the Free* and the story collections *The Good Times* and *Busted Scotch*. Another Scottish author known for his skill with both dialect and dialogue (as well as for his unflinching look at sometimes unpleasant topics) is Irvine Welsh, whose novels *Trainspotting, Glue,* and *Crime* might be suggested to these readers. Another author who can convincingly write from a child's point of view is Roddy Doyle, whose novel *Paddy Clarke Ha Ha Ha* also won the Booker Prize; Mark Haddon's coming-of-age narrative *The Curious Incident of the Dog in the Night-Time* might also appeal, as might David Mitchell's *Black Swan Green*. Although about an Irish childhood and not a Scottish one, Frank McCourt's evocative memoir of a childhood spent in poverty and difficult family relationships, *Angela's Ashes*, might also be suggested.

Kennedy, A. L.

🎗 *Day: A Novel.* Knopf, 2008. 273pp. ISBN 9780307266835.

Kennedy offers a different type of war story in this World War II–era novel that is set five years after Alfie Day's involvement in it. Day, a Royal Air Force tail gunner who also spent time in a German POW camp, is struggling to find a sense of purpose in his life in postwar Britain, and thinks he may find a source of companionship when he signs up to work as an extra in a historical film about the war. Unfortunately, the movie's subject serves only to dredge up his memories of the internment camp where he was imprisoned (stories about which are told in flashback) and to unsettle him further. Kennedy has been lauded for her prose style, and this novel, in addition to its stories told in flashbacks, also features narrative shifts (most notably into the second person) and characters' internal thoughts relayed in italics.

Subjects: Book Groups; British Authors; Flashbacks; Historical Fiction; Movies; Prisoners of War; Women Authors; Women Writing as Men; World War II

Awards: Costa Book of the Year Award; Costa Novel Award

Now Try: Kennedy's other titles include the novels *Paradise* and *Everything You Need*, as well as the story collection *Indelible Acts*. Other novels in which men struggle with the aftereffects of war are Pat Barker's Regeneration Trilogy (*Regeneration, The Eye in the Door,* and *The Ghost Road*) and Tim O'Brien's *In the Lake of* *the Woods*; British author Robert Graves's memoir of his life after fighting in World War I, *Goodbye to All That*, might also appeal to these readers.

Keret, Etgar.

The Girl on the Fridge. **Farrar, Straus & Giroux, 2008. 171pp. ISBN 9780374531058.**

Keret's collection of short stories has been referred to by some critics as an example of "flash fiction"—and most are, indeed, very short pieces. (There are forty-six in this 171-page collection.) Many are comical, some are surreal, and some include horrifying examples of violence that are only too realistic; many of the stories combine all three of those attributes.

Subjects: Humor; Israeli Authors; Jewish American Authors; Quick Reads; Short Stories; YA

Now Try: Keret is also the author of the story collections *The Nimrod Flipout* and *The Bus Driver Who Wanted to Be God and Other Stories*. Aimee Bender is another short story writer whose stories feature highly imaginative elements; her collections include *Willful Creatures* and *The Girl in the Flammable Skirt*. Both Cynthia Ozick (*The Pagan Rabbi, and Other Stories* and *The Shawl: A Story and a Novella*) and Abraham Yehoshua (*The Continuing Silence of a Poet*), like Keret, sometimes include Jewish themes in their short fiction collections.

Kessel, John.

The Baum Plan for Financial Independence. **Small Beer Press, 2008. 315pp. ISBN 9781931520515.**

Kessel's anthology of short stories, many of which have appeared in science fiction magazines, feature a surreal tone and fantastic events; many of the stories are either homages to or reimaginings of other famous literary tales (in one story, Austen's Mary Bennet character meets the doctor Victor Frankenstein).

Subjects: Books and Reading; Fantasy; Humor; Literary Allusions; Science Fiction; Short Stories; Small Press

Now Try: Kessel is better known as a science fiction writer; his novels in that genre are *Corrupting Dr. Nice, Meeting in Infinity*, and *Good News from Outer Space*; he has also written another story collection, *The Pure Product: Stories*. Other short story authors who may appeal to his readers are Kelly Link (*Pretty Monsters, Magic for Beginners*, and *Stranger Things Happen*) and Ray Bradbury (*We'll Always Have Paris: Stories* and *The Cat's Pajamas*). The popular satire of Jane Austen's *Pride and Prejudice*, Seth Grahame-Smith's *Pride and Prejudice and Zombies*, might also make for a fun and literary read-alike, as might the decidedly postmodern humor collection *The McSweeney's Joke Book of Book Jokes* (published by McSweeney's Books).

Khemir, Sabiha.

The Blue Manuscript. **Verso, 2008. 307pp. ISBN 9781844673087.**

A book as beautiful as the Blue Manuscript, handmade thousands of years ago as an Islamic holy book, can never be owned by just one time period. In this novel Khemir weaves together the story of the modern-day archaeologists searching for the book in Egypt with the story of the book's creation and travels in the tenth century. In the present day, her characters, including Zohra, a woman who struggles with her cultural identity as both a Tunisian and an Englishwoman ("my mother the west, my father the east"), form uneasy alliances with one another as they all pursue the relic for different reasons.

Subjects: Academia; Archaeology; Biracial Characters; Books and Reading; Culture Clash; Egypt; Historical Fiction; Islam; Suspense; Women Authors

Now Try: The journey of a similar cultural treasure and antiquity is described in Geraldine Brooks's novel *People of the Book*. Khemir's novel is thoughtful but is rather challenging in format and story; a similar cult favorite nonfiction author who made a career out of reporting on culture clashes, Ryszard Kapuscinski, might also be suggested to these readers (his titles include *The Shadow of the Sun* and *Travels with Herodotus*). Other nonfiction titles on the sometimes vicious and downright criminal activities surrounding the antiquities world might also appeal, such as Herbert Krosney's *The Lost Gospel: The Quest for the Gospel of Judas Iscariot* and Tudor Parfitt's *The Lost Ark of the Covenant*.

Now Consider Nonfiction . . . Literary Travel

Literary travel narratives are characterized by their authors' use of language and prose styling and how they apply it, not only to landscape or character description, but also to rather more existential concerns such as what it means to belong or observe other cultures. These are reflective stories, not written to describe a place or tell the story of a journey, but rather to provoke thoughts about the nature of our regular places in the world, as well as our world's many unique geographies, cultures, and peoples.

Frazier, Ian. *Great Plains*.

Iyer, Pico. *Sun after Dark: Flights into the Foreign*.

Newby, Eric. *Slowly Down the Ganges*.

Raban, Jonathan. *Passage to Juneau: A Sea and Its Meanings*.

Stuever, Hank. *Off Ramp: Adventures and Heartache in the American Elsewhere*.

West, Rebecca. *Black Lamb and Grey Falcon: A Journey through Yugoslavia*.

Winchester, Simon. *The River at the Center of the World: A Journey Up the Yangtze, and Back in Chinese Time*.

Labiner, Norah.

🌿*Miniatures: A Novel*. **Coffee House Press, 2002. 381pp. ISBN 978-1566891363.**

The appeal of Labiner's novel is not so much in the story—young Fern Jacobi, talented but aimless, travels to Ireland and ends up working as a housekeeper for two brothers (and one of their wives, who shares the trio's secrets with Jacobi before she feels confident enough to begin her own writing life)—as it is in the literary allusions made throughout. Her style itself has been described as a tribute "to the prose styles of such literary giants as the Brontë sisters, Proust, and Mary Shelley."

Subjects: Brothers; Family Secrets; First Person; Housecleaners; Ireland; Literary Allusions; Literary Lives; Small Press; Suicide; Travel; Women Authors; Writers and Writing

Awards: ALA Notable

Now Try: Labiner has produced two other novels, one in 1998 (*Our Sometime Sister*) and another in 2009 (*German for Travelers: A Novel in 95 Lessons*). Another novel of family secrets (although darker in tone) is Sebastian Barry's *The Secret Scripture*; A. S. Byatt's literary *The Virgin in the Garden* (the first volume in her <u>Frederica Potter</u> series) might also appeal. Although lighter in tone, Nancy Peacock's nonfiction writing manual, *A Broom of One's Own: Words on Writing, Housecleaning, and Life*, might also appeal to readers who enjoy the parallels between the writing life and one of hard manual labor.

Lazar, Zachary.

Sway: A Novel. **Little, Brown, 2008. 255pp. ISBN 9780316113090.**

Lazar provides a fictional re-creation of the 1960s through a series of interconnected narratives featuring real-life individuals and some of their seminal experiences; included here are re-creations of such cultural zeitgeist moments as film director Kenneth Anger shooting the movie *Scorpio Rising*, Bobby Beausoleil falling under the thrall of the Manson family, and many other familiar episodes from that era.

Subjects: 1960s; Anger, Kenneth; Beausoleil, Bobby; Biographical Fiction; Drug Abuse; Historical Fiction; Interconnected Stories; Manson, Charles; Music and Musicians; Pop Culture

Now Try: Lazar is also the author of the novel *Aaron, Approximately* and the true crime memoir *Evening's Empire: The Story of My Father's Murder*. Other novels that evoke the time period and settings of the 1960s might also appeal, such as Roccie Hill's *Three Minutes on Love*, Peter Carey's *His Illegal Self*, Denis Johnson's *Tree of Smoke*, and Janis Hallowell's *She Was*; although set in the 1980s, Mary Gaitskill's *Veronica* features a similar undertone of a society in flux. Related nonfiction titles might also appeal to these readers, including Mark Kurlansky's history of the period, *1968*, as well as Vincent Bugliosi's true crime classic, *Helter Skelter* (also about the Manson family and the cult following they inspired).

Le Guin, Ursula.

Lavinia. **Harcourt, 2008. 279pp. ISBN 9780151014248.**

In Virgil's epic tale *The Aeneid*, the character Lavinia (Aeneas's second wife) is only described in a few lines, and she never speaks. In Le Guin's novel, Lavinia tells her own story, from her childhood as the royal daughter of King Latinus and Queen Amata, to her mother's insistence on (and her own reluctance about) her marriage to Amata's nephew Turnus, her marriage instead to Aeneas, and the civil war the marriage helps foment.

Subjects: Ancient History; Fantasy; Historical Fiction; Italy; Literary Allusions; Marriage; Rome; Women Authors; YA

Now Try: Le Guin, of course, is a popular and prolific author of fantasy and science fiction novels such as *The Left Hand of Darkness*, *The Dispossessed* (the first book in the <u>Hain</u> series), and *Changing Planes*. Other classical literary retellings might appeal to these readers, including Jo Graham's *Black Ships*, Seamus Heaney's *Beowulf: A New Verse Translation*, and Ciaran Carson's *The Tain*; Stephanie Plowman's *The Road to Sardis*, about the Peloponnesian War, might also be suggested. Other novels in which women find their voices after a lifetime of being suppressed or ignored are Sebastian Barry's *The Secret Scripture* and Sarah Hall's dystopian novel *Daughters of the North*.

Leigh, Julia.

Disquiet. Penguin, 2008. 120pp. ISBN 9780143113508.

Leigh's slim novel evokes exactly the feeling stated in its title. Siblings Marcus and Olivia have both returned to their ancestral home in rural France, where their mother still lives. Olivia (often referred to in the text as simply "the woman") arrives with two young children in tow, fleeing from her abusive husband and their home in Australia. Marcus and his wife Sophie had thought to spend time there after the birth of their first child (who, tragically, dies at birth). Underlying tension and Sophie's inability to let go of the small bundle that is her baby make this is a short but thoroughly sobering read about family and our human frailties.

Subjects: Australian Authors; Brothers and Sisters; Death and Dying; Family Relationships; France; Psychological Fiction; Quick Reads; Women Authors

Now Try: Leigh is also the author of the novel *The Hunter*. Other slim and somewhat disquieting novels that might appeal to these readers are Tim Winton's *Breath* (Winton is also Australian), Ian McEwan's *On Chesil Beach*, and M. J. Hyland's *Carry Me Down*. Ann Hood's memoir *Comfort: A Journey Through Grief*, about the death of her child, might also provide a poignant read-alike for these readers.

Lethem, Jonathan.

Chronic City. Doubleday, 2009. 467pp. ISBN 9780385518635.

Former child star Chase Insteadman is known throughout Manhattan for his role on the television program *Martyr & Pesty*, his aimless current lifestyle, which leaves him the time to be a fixture at the city's biggest social events and dinner parties; and his tragic status as the fiancé of infamous astronaut Janice Trumbull, who is trapped on the International Space Station (which is ringed by mines in space, preventing its residents from leaving orbit themselves). When he meets a strange man named Perkus Tooth, he finds that Tooth's many conspiracy theories aren't all wrong—and some even feature Insteadman himself.

Subjects: Actors and Acting; Friendships; Humor; New York City; Pop Culture

Now Try: Lethem is also the author of another novel set among the boroughs of New York, *Motherless Brooklyn*, as well as the essay collection *The Disappointment Artist*. Two other authors who might appeal to Lethem's fans are Kurt Vonnegut (whose literary science fiction titles *Slaughterhouse-5* and *The Sirens of Titan* might particularly appeal) and Michael Chabon (*The Amazing Adventures of Kavalier and Clay* and *The Yiddish Policeman's Union*).

🪶 *Fortress of Solitude.* Doubleday, 2003. 511pp. ISBN 9780385500692.

Dylan Ebdus and Mingus Rude, boyhood friends despite their different races (in 1970s Brooklyn, race matters), spend their days doing what boys do: getting in trouble, making discoveries, and, in Dylan's case (as he is one of the few whites left in the neighborhood) drawing the attention of the neighborhood bullies. When he and Mingus find a magical ring that allows them to fly, however, they embark on heroic adventures, albeit with mixed results. In the latter half of the novel, the story is told from Dylan's adult perspective, but magic has not forsaken him; he rediscovers the ring and a new power it offers him.

Subjects: 1970s; 1980s; Brooklyn; Classics; Coming-of-age; Magic Realism; New York City; Race Relations; Superheroes

Awards: ALA Notable

Now Try: Lethem likes to bend genre conventions in his novels, which include *Motherless Brooklyn*, as well as the more "science fiction-y" *Gun, with Occasional Music* and *Amnesia Moon*. A similar author who rivals Lethem's imaginative themes is Michael Chabon, whose *The Amazing Adventures of Kavalier and Clay* or *Gentlemen of the Road* might also be suggested; also of interest might be another semi-fantasy about superhero powers, *Superpowers* by David Schwartz. Nelson George's scholarly but still very readable cultural history *Post-Soul Nation: The Explosive, Contradictory, Triumphant, and Tragic 1980s as Experienced by African Americans (Previously Known as Blacks and Before That Negroes)* might also make for an interesting related read.

Lianke, Yan.

Serve the People! **Black Cat, 2007. 217pp. ISBN 9780802170446.**

Lianke's slim but subversive satirical novel, which was originally banned in his homeland of China for its "slander and overflowing depictions of sex," offers the story of Liu Lian, a Chinese army commander's bored wife, and one of the commander's subordinates, Wu Dawang, whom Liu Lian seduces (in a nice twist on the power of Mao's words, her household plaque proclaiming "Serve the People" is the tool she uses to make her needs known to Wu Dawang). Set in the 1960s at the height of Mao Zedong's cultlike popularity, the story centers on the physical encounters and eventually the love between Liu Lian and Wu Dawang, but also manages to say plenty about the control over every aspect of people's lives that Mao sought to exert.

Subjects: 1960s; Books in Translation; China; Chinese Authors; Cultural Revolution; Dark Humor; Mao Zedong; Marriage; Men Writing as Women; Quick Reads; Satire; Small Press

Now Try: This is the first novel by Lianke to be translated into English; hopefully more will follow. Other novels by Chinese authors, particularly those that make the most use of the fewest words, might also be suggested, including those by Ha Jin (*Waiting*, *The Bridegroom: Stories*, and *A Free Life*), Zhu Wen (*I Love Dollars and Other Stories of China*, which was translated, as was this novel, by Julia Lovell), and Ma Jian (*The Noodle Maker* and *Stick out Your Tongue*).

Littell, Jonathan.

The Kindly Ones. **Harper, 2009. 983pp. ISBN 9780061353451.**

The narrator of Littell's epic novel of World War II and the Holocaust, Max Aue, is perhaps the most simultaneously repulsive and magnetic character in Holocaust fiction. A former SS officer who started life over in France by assuming a new identity, at the close of his life as a successful lace manufacturer and family patriarch, he writes his own memoir of the war and its atrocities (including the many in which he participated).

Subjects: Books in Translation; Epic Reads; Explicit Sexuality; First Novels; First Person; France; Germany; Historical Fiction; Holocaust; Unreliable Narrator; Violence; World War II

Now Try: The *Library Journal* review of this novel compared it to such other books about moral dilemmas as Albert Camus's *The Plague*, William Styron's *Sophie's Choice*, Christoph Hein's *Settlement*, and Günter Grass's novels *The Tin Drum* and *Cat and Mouse* (Grass's memoir, *Peeling the Onion*, might also appeal). Ira Levin's classic about former

Nazi officers trying to escape detection while living out their lives is *The Boys from Brazil*; Imre Kertész's much shorter *Detective Story* is another Holocaust novel from the Nazis' point of view. Other massive novels that showcase their authors' literary skills are Roberto Bolaño's *2666*, David Foster Wallace's *Infinite Jest*, and Peter Nadas's *A Book of Memories*.

Livesey, Margot.

The House on Fortune Street. Harper, 2008. 311pp. ISBN 9780061451522.

In this interlocking tale of multiple viewpoints and different time periods, Livesey's four protagonists go about their lives in close proximity to one another, but the overarching story line shows how little they actually know one another. Sean and Abigail live together on the top floor of the house on Fortune Street, while Dara (Abigail's best friend from college) lives downstairs; Dara's father Cameron also makes an appearance in the second part of the book, telling the story of his life and providing glimpses for the reader of why he left Dara when she was a child. The novel is also a literary love letter of sorts; Livesey pays homage to literary classics by borrowing their themes and story lines; authors so imitated include Lewis Carroll (*Alice in Wonderland*), Charlotte Brontë (*Jane Eyre*), and Charles Dickens (*Great Expectations*).

Second Appeal: Character

Subjects: Book Groups; Family Relationships; Great Britain; Homes; Literary Allusions; London; Love Affairs; Multiple Viewpoints; Scottish Authors; Suicide; Women Authors

Now Try: Livesey is also the author of *Criminals, The Missing World, Eva Moves the Furniture,* and *Banishing Verona*. Other novels that include shifting viewpoints and time periods might be offered, including Graham Swift's *Waterland*, Ian McEwan's *Atonement*, and Saher Alam's *The Groom to Have Been* (which the author describes as having been inspired by Edith Wharton's classic *The Age of Innocence*). Books by the classic authors alluded to in Livesey's text (Charlotte Brontë and Charles Dickens, for starters) might be fun read-alikes, as might Elizabeth Strout's Puliter Prize–winning novel of interconnected stories, *Olive Kitteridge*, or Penelope Lively's *Consequences*.

Lopate, Phillip.

Two Marriages. Other Press, 2008. 264pp. ISBN 9781590512982.

In this two-part novella, Lopate examines two very different marriages. The first story, told in diary form, is about Gordon and his Filipino wife Rita, whose motivation for marrying Gordon quickly becomes clear as she starts feverishly bringing members of her extended family (including children and even her husband from her first marriage) to America; the second, told at more of a narrative distance, is about a couple named Eleanor and Frank and their argument about his son.

Subjects: Book Groups; Family Relationships; Marriage; Men's Lives; Quick Reads

Now Try: Before this slim novel; it had been a while since Lopate tried his hand at fiction; his earlier novels *Confessions of Summer* and *The Rug Merchant* were published in 1979 and 1987, respectively. He has recently written several more collections of essays, including *Getting Personal, Against Joie de Vivre*, and the memoir/travelogue *Waterfront: A Walk around Manhattan*. Other novels in which men struggle to come to terms with the women and relationships in their lives are J. M. Coetzee's *Disgrace*, Tim O'Brien's *Tomcat in Love*, and Chang-Rae Lee's somewhat more lighthearted *Aloft*.

Mackey, Nathaniel.

🌳 *Bass Cathedral*. **New Directions, 2008. 183pp. ISBN 9780811217200.**

Lovers of literature and jazz will find much to like in Mackey's freestyle novel in letters, in which the narrator, known only as N., writes about his experience and love of jazz to an unknown recipient. Very much a novel of impressions and riffs, and less a complete narrative, this is the fourth in Mackey's series of novels and continues the epistolary form found in his earlier titles: "Aunt Nancy's bass solo was now clearly something else, a lank, double-jointed duet which, loose and on speaking terms with lateral drift, made its availability or amenability to other voices abundantly clear."

Subjects: African American Authors; Epistolary Fiction; Jazz; Music and Musicians

Awards: New York Times Notable

Now Try: Mackey's work is decidedly free-flowing (much like the jazz music about which he writes, some would argue), although this has been described as the most accessible volume in his ongoing **From a Broken Bottle Traces of Perfume Still Emanate** (volumes one through three were *Bedouin Hornbook, Djbot Baghostus's Run*, and *Atet, A.D.*); a book he coauthored, *Moment's Notice: Jazz in Poetry and Prose*, might also appeal. Another decidedly surreal novel about a jazz musician (don't assume it's a human) is Rafi Zabor's *The Bear Comes Home*. Alex Ross's critically acclaimed nonfiction title about music and its effects on us, *The Rest Is Noise: Listening to the Twentieth Century*, might also be a good related read.

Malouf, David.

🌳 *The Complete Stories*. **Pantheon Books, 2007. 508pp. ISBN 9780375424977.**

Australian author Malouf offers both his published and unpublished short stories in this meaty volume, which features powerful descriptions not only of the always interesting and unique Australian landscape, but also of human connections, misunderstandings, youthful events of significance, friendships, sicknesses and deaths, and everything else in between. The collection is organized in four sections: the previously unpublished group under the heading "Every Move You Make," and the rest previously published as the collections *Dream Stuff, Antipodes*, and *Child's Play*.

Subjects: Australia; Australian Authors; Family Relationships; Love Affairs; Short Stories

Awards: ALA Notable

Now Try: Malouf is a prolific author with whom not enough readers are familiar; his readers might enjoy his novels *Dream Stuff, The Conversations at Curlow Creek, Remembering Babylon, The Great World, Antipodes*, or *Johnno*, as well as his autobiography *12 Edmondstone Street*. Other Australian authors who offer narratives set in Australian landscapes and history might also appeal, including Peter Carey (*The True History of the Kelly Gang* and *Oscar and Lucinda*), Nikki Gemmell (*Alice Springs*), and Tim Winton (*The Turning: New Stories* and *Dirt Music*). Other short story collections by such critically revered authors as Julian Barnes (*The Lemon Table*) and Paul Theroux (*The Collected Stories*) might also appeal.

Mandanipour, Shahriar.

Censoring an Iranian Love Story. **Knopf, 2009. 295pp. ISBN 9780307269782.**
With echoes of the tragic love story of Romeo and Juliet throughout his narrative, Mandanipour tells the story an Iranian author (also named Shahriar Mandanipour) trying to write about two lovers in contemporary Iran (the "story within a story" is told from both the man's and the woman's points of view), but whose work is continually censored by the Iranian government. The characters in the author's story, Sara and Dara, become real themselves as the author describes the former's love of books, the latter's love of movies, and the overwhelming love the two have for each other.

Second Appeal: Character

Subjects: Book Groups; Books in Translation; Censorship; Iran; Literary Allusions; Love Affairs; Men Writing as Women; Multiple Viewpoints

Now Try: Another novel about an unusual love story (which included much more explicit love scenes) that faced real-life censorship is Yan Lianke's *Serve the People!* about China during the height of Mao Zedong's cult of personality. Another novel in which the main character shares a name with the author (similar to this book's "meta" feel) is Mischa Berlinski's *Fieldwork: A Novel.* Rabih Alameddine also tells a story within a story in the novel *The Hakawati.* Nonfiction titles about Iranian society might also appeal to these readers, including Azar Nafisi's popular memoir *Reading Lolita in Tehran* and Marjane Satrapi's graphic novel memoirs *Persepolis* and *Persepolis 2.*

McCarthy, Cormac.

🐾 *No Country for Old Men.* **Knopf, 2005. 309pp. ISBN 9780375406775.**
McCarthy never shies away from violence in his sometimes surreal, often bleak narratives of characters either pursuing their own single-minded purposes or seeking to avoid the dark purposes of others, and this story is no exception. After finding the scene of a Texas border gun battle over drugs, complete with several dead bodies, bricks of heroin, and a case containing more than $2 million, Llewelyn Moss takes the case, although he knows this action will most likely involve unsavory consequences for both him and his new bride. Moss is right; two very different men will follow him, one to protect him and the other to destroy him: lawman Sheriff Bell (whose inner monologue is told in brief chapters throughout the narrative) and a murderous assassin named Chigurh.

Subjects: Book Groups; Classics; Law Enforcement; Movies; Suspense; Texas; Violence; Westerns

Awards: ALA Notable

Now Try: McCarthy's other novels, particularly the equally dark and violent *Blood Meridian* and *The Road,* might be suggested, as might his Border Trilogy, which started with the title *All the Pretty Horses.* Decidedly unromantic Westerns like Pete Dexter's *Deadwood,* Loren Estleman's *The Master Executioner,* and John Nichols's *The Milagro Beanfield War* might appeal, as might the classic true crime narratives *In Cold Blood* by Truman Capote and *Helter Skelter* by Vincent Bugliosi.

🏵 *The Road*. **Knopf, 2006. 241pp. ISBN 9780307265432.**

In this bleak novel of the future, father and son trudge through a postapocalyptic world, pushing a shopping cart with all their possessions, searching for whatever food and provisions they can salvage, avoiding the other horrific and horrifying remnants of humanity (who have largely turned to scavenging other survivors), and following the road to the ocean with vague hopes of salvation. Masterfully contrasting the father's will to survive and to save his son at all costs with the son's questioning of that mentality, McCarthy blends science fiction with philosophy.

Subjects: Apocalypse; Bleak Future; Book Groups; Classics; Family Relationships; Fathers and Sons; Quick Reads; Science Fiction; Survival; Violence

Awards: ALA Notable; Pulitzer Prize

Now Try: McCarthy has long been noted for his ability to combine masterful prose with bleak and violent subject matter; his earlier books, including his Border Trilogy (*All the Pretty Horses, The Crossing,* and *Cities of the Plain*), *Blood Meridian,* and *No Country for Old Men,* might also appeal. Books similar in subject and ominous tone include Richard Matheson's classic *I Am Legend* and Jim Crace's *The Pesthouse.* Authors of science fiction books in the bleak futures subgenre might also be suggested, including Margaret Atwood, Octavia Butler, Aldous Huxley, and Kurt Vonnegut. Although the setting of this novel is not Western, McCarthy is considered a pioneer of the new type of Western genre books that feature bleaker landscapes and stories; books of this type that might appeal to these readers are Pete Dexter's *Deadwood* and Loren D. Estleman's *The Master Executioner.*

McCarthy, Tom.

🏵 *Remainder*. **Vintage, 2005. 308pp. ISBN 9780307278357.**

The reader is always one step behind in this stream-of-consciousness narrative, in which a man who has received an undescribed but memory-damaging injury (from something falling out of the sky) and a large amount of settlement money, goes about his recovery paying to have his memories and imagined visions of his memories reconstructed for him. Events take a darker turn when he abandons his more prosaic memory reenactments in favor of more violent and unpredictable events.

Subjects: Book Groups; British Authors; Dark Humor; First Novels; First Person; Great Britain; London; Violence

Awards: New York Times Notable

Now Try: Other novels in which the narrators know more than they're telling might appeal to these readers, including *Novel about My Wife* (Emily Perkins), *Kings of Infinite Space* (James Hynes), and *Then We Came to the End* (Joshua Ferris). Novels in which the real and surreal blend effortlessly are Steven Hall's *The Raw Shark Texts,* Rivka Galchen's *Atmospheric Disturbances,* and Mark Z. Danielewski's *House of Leaves.* In Richard Powers's *The Echo Maker,* a man also struggles with a traumatic injury that has affected his memory and perception.

McCartney, Alistair.

The End of the World Book. **University of Wisconsin Press, 2008. 306pp. ISBN 9780299226305.**

McCartney combines memoir and fiction in this novel made up of alphabetical entries (early on, the narrator confesses his love for *The World Book Encyclopedia* and its organizational style) on such topics as Abercrombie and Fitch, Death Metal,

Gossip, and Sodomy. The entries vary in length from a sentence to a few pages; all use evocative language, such as that found in the entry for Sunset: "Every day the sun sets on us, all drippy and pink and contemptuous."

Subjects: Australian Authors; Explicit Sexuality; First Novels; Gay Men; GLBTQ; Small Press

Now Try: Lydia Davis's story collections always feature somewhat stylistically daring stories as well and might appeal to these readers; they are *Varieties of Disturbance* and *Samuel Johnson Is Indignant.* McCartney has also contributed to a collection of essays titled *Wonderlands: Good Gay Travel Writing* (edited by Raphael Kadushin).

McEwan, Ian.

🎗 *Atonement.* **Doubleday, 2001. 351pp. ISBN 9780385503952.**

Questions of memory, family dynamics, class distinctions, and the slippery nature of knowledge and memory take the forefront in McEwan's novel of British family life just before and during World War II. Tensions are already high when Briony's family gathers at their home on a sultry summer afternoon: they have recently taken in three young cousins whose parents are going through divorce; daughter of the house Celia is resisting falling in love with Robbie, the son of her family's hired help; and precocious Briony sees much and understands little as she moves among the various family members. After witnessing a scene of passion between Robbie and Celia, she later accuses Robbie of assaulting her cousin, which leads to his incarceration and eventual induction into the army at the height of the war (the horrific battle at Dunkirk is described at length). The novel shifts between settings and time periods, and throughout it poses questions about love, blame, and atonement.

Subjects: British Authors; Classics; Family Relationships; Great Britain; Love Affairs; Multiple Viewpoints; Social Class; Unreliable Narrator; World War II

Awards: ALA Notable; National Book Critics Circle Award

Now Try: McEwan's many novels vary widely in plot and setting, but all share a similar tension of storytelling; they include *The Comfort of Strangers, Black Dogs, On Chesil Beach, Saturday,* and *Amsterdam.* Another convoluted novel of secrets and misunderstandings is Donna Tartt's *The Secret History;* Michael Cox's *The Meaning of Night* (with an unreliable narrator of the most unreliable variety) might also appeal to these readers. In Evelyn Waugh's classic novel *Brideshead Revisited,* the societal effects of the complex British class system is also explored at length. A. S. Byatt's novels of flashbacks, complete with lyrical prose similar to fellow Brit McEwan's, might also appeal, particularly *Possession* and *The Biographer's Tale.*

🎗 *On Chesil Beach.* **Doubleday, 2007. 203pp. ISBN 9780385522403.**

McEwan's slim novel about a traumatic honeymoon spent on the British coast during the 1960s tells the story of a young married couple, both virgins, who struggle with the physical and emotional demands of marriage. The narrative also reflects on the details of their lives in the aftermath of the early days of their marriage.

Subjects: Book Groups; British Authors; Classics; Great Britain; Marriage; Quick Reads; Sexuality; Social Class

Awards: ALA Notable; New York Times Notable

Now Try: McEwan's other shorter novels, including *Black Dogs, Saturday, Enduring Love,* and the more suspenseful *The Comfort of Strangers,* might appeal to these readers, as might his story collections *First Love, Last Rites* and *In Between the Sheets.* McEwan's prose style has also been compared to that of Julian Barnes, whose novels *Talking It Over* and *Staring at the Sun* might be suggested; the vagaries of marriage are also described in Phillip Lopate's novella in two stories, *Two Marriages.* Another prize-winning author, J. M. Coetzee, also has a way of drawing readers into the inner lives of his characters, particularly in such novels as *Life and Times of Michael K., Disgrace,* and *Diary of a Bad Year.*

🎗 *Saturday.* Doubleday, 2005. 289pp. ISBN 9780385511803.

For London neurosurgeon Henry Perowne, February 15, 2003 is anything but ordinary: an early morning plane crash, demonstrations against the war in Iraq, road rage—all spiral into an introspective family dinner that ends back where it all began—first the hospital and finally Henry's bedroom.

Subjects: 9/11; British Authors; Day in the Life; Family Relationships; Great Britain; Health Issues; Huntington's Disease; London; Men's Lives

Awards: ALA Notable

Now Try: McEwan's earlier novel, *Atonement,* tells the story of an upper-middle-class family set in pre– and post–World War II England and also showcases McEwan's gifted use of language. Another beautifully written novel is Michael Ondaatje's *The English Patient,* the story of four survivors living together in a deserted Italian villa at the end of World War II. Other novels that take place over the course of one day are James Joyce's *Ulysses,* Saul Bellow's *Seize the Day,* and Alexander Solzhenitsyn's *A Day in the Life of Ivan Denisovitch.* Although it covers an entire life rather than one day, Paul Harding's slim novel *Tinkers* also provides an in-depth look at one man's life and thoughts. Another author who might appeal to McEwan's readers is the British author Sebastian Faulks, whose novels *Engleby, Human Traces,* and *On Green Dolphin Street* might all be suggested as read-alikes.

Meek, James.

🎗 *The People's Act of Love.* Canongate, 2005. 391pp. ISBN 9781841957302.

The year is 1918, and the setting is frigid Siberia, where revolution, in the form of Bolshevik soldiers, has reached even the tiny village of Yazyk. Then, from the wilderness around the village, a mystic and revolutionary named Samarin emerges and joins the broad mix of humanity already living there: a marooned squad of Czech soldiers, members of a somewhat bizarre but very dedicated Christian sect, and a Russian photographer named Anna Petrovna, who refuses to conform to the villagers' idea of how a woman should act.

Second Appeal: Setting

Subjects: 1910s; Historical Fiction; Love Affairs; Photography; Psychological Fiction; Russia; Soviet Union; War; World History

Awards: ALA Notable

Now Try: Meek is also the author of *We Are Now Beginning Our Descent, Museum of Doubt,* and *Drivetime.* This book is, even in the words of reviewers who loved it, "challenging fiction"; its fans might also be up to other challenging and classic works of literature, including Graham Greene's *The Power and the Glory,* Joseph Conrad's *Heart of Darkness,* and Fyodor Dostoyevsky's *Crime and Punishment* or *The Brothers Karamazov.* Bernard Du Boucheron's *The Voyage of the Short Serpent,* also set in a cold climate and centered on religious issues (although it is set five centuries earlier) might also be suggested. Those readers fascinated by the Russian history and landscape might also be interested in Aleksandr Solzhenitsyn's historical <u>Red Wheel</u> series, comprising *August 1914: The Red Wheel*, *November 1916*, *March 1917*, and *April 1917*.

Melnyczuk, Askold.

The House of Widows: An Oral History. Graywolf Press, 2008. 255pp. ISBN 9781555974916.

Sixteen years after his father Andrew's suicide (which he unfortunately witnessed), James Pak, historian and civil servant in the U.S. Counsel of Public Affairs in Vienna, Austria, sets out to finally understand the causes of his father's death. Following clues that include his father's military uniform, a glass jar, and a letter in a foreign language, he travels throughout the world trying to piece together his father's life and past, the stories of which he relates through flashbacks.

Second Appeal: Story

Subjects: European History; Family Relationships; Family Secrets; Fathers and Sons; Flashbacks; Small Press; Suicide; Travel; Ukraine; War; World War II

Now Try: Melnyczuk is also the author of *Ambassador of the Dead* and *What Is Told*. In Jonathan Safran Foer's novel *Everything Is Illuminated*, the protagonist seeks to understand his past by traveling to meet the woman who saved his grandfather from the Holocaust; a suicide also has long-term repercussions in Dirk Wittenborn's sprawling novel *Pharmakon*. A nonfiction title in which an author tries to understand her father's suicide is Joan Wickersham's *The Suicide Index*; thoughtful nonfiction travel narratives might also be suggested, such as Tom Bissell's *Chasing the Sea: Lost Among the Ghosts of Empire in Central Asia* and Colin Thubron's *In Siberia*.

Menger-Anderson, Kirsten.

Doctor Olaf van Schuler's Brain. Algonquin Books of Chapel Hill, 2008. 290pp. ISBN 9781565125612.

Multiple generations of van Schuler and Steenwycks doctors (starting with their descendants Olaf van Schuler and Adalind Steenwycks in 1660s New Amsterdam, also known as New York City) make appearances in these connected stories. Unflinchingly detailing sometimes gruesome historical medical procedures and learning methods, the author nonetheless considers carefully the cost of human suffering and the motivations of those who undertake to heal others.

Second Appeal: Setting

Subjects: 17th Century; Book Groups; Doctors; First Novels; Health Issues; Historical Fiction; Interconnected Stories; Medicine; Multiple Viewpoints; New York City

Now Try: Other authors who work scientific precepts and language into their novels are Alan Lightman (*The Diagnosis* and *Einstein's Dreams*) and Jim Crace (*Being Dead* and *The Gift of Stones*). Mary Roach provided a blurb for this novel, and her extremely readable nonfiction books might appeal to these readers, including *Stiff: The Curious Lives of Human Cadavers* and *Bonk: The Curious Coupling of Science and Sex.* Also of interest might be character-rich nonfiction medical histories, such as D. T. Max's *The Family That Couldn't Sleep* and Bill Hayes's *The Anatomist: A True Story of Gray's Anatomy*.

Now Consider Nonfiction . . . Literary Science

Literary science titles take as their subjects a variety of biological phenomena and scientific tenets, but their primary appeal lies in their authors' reflective and skillful prose writing styles. These books do not explain new scientific theories or discoveries, but are designed to explore the effects and outcomes of scientific principles more philosophically. They feature leisurely pacing and writing, often described as "poetic" or "lyrical."

Ackerman, Diane. *An Alchemy of Mind.*

Capra, Fritjof. *The Tao of Physics.*

Carson, Rachel. *The Sea Around Us.*

González-Crussi, F. *On Being Born: And Other Difficulties.*

Nuland, Sherwin. *How We Die: Reflections on Life's Final Chapter.*

Quammen, David. *Natural Acts: A Sidelong View of Science and Nature.*

Meno, Joe.

The Great Perhaps. Norton, 2009. 414pp. ISBN 9780393067965.

Each member of the Casper family is distracted: Jonathan, the patriarch, is a paleontologist in search of a giant squid that may or may not still exist; Madeline, his wife, struggles with both her belief in her own work and experiments with animal behavior, as well as the behavior of the rest of her family members; and their teenage daughters Amelia and Thisbe are following the separate paths of political and religious questioning (respectively). The complexity of his characters is echoed in Meno's shifting viewpoints and writing styles; when telling Madeline's story, for example, he offers the reader lists of her discrete thoughts. In the end the family, along with their grandfather Henry, finds they are not quite as far apart as they have assumed.

Subjects: Chicago; Domestic Fiction; Family Relationships; Marriage; Men's Lives; Multiple Viewpoints; Science; Teenagers

Now Try: Meno won the Nelson Algren Literary Award and has also written the novels *Tender as Hellfire, How the Hula Girl Sings, Hairstyles of the Damned,* and *The Boy Detective Fails.* Other novelists who explore modern family dynamics are Justin Cartwright (*The Promise of Happiness* and *Leading the Cheers*), Tom Perrotta (*Little Children* and *The Abstinence Teacher*), Dirk Wittenborn (*Pharmakon*), and Ward Just (*Exiles in the Garden*).

Miles, Jonathan.

🏆 *Dear American Airlines.* Houghton Mifflin, 2008. 180pp. ISBN 9780547054018.

Bennie Ford is trying to make up for a lifetime of mistakes by flying from New York City to LA to attend his estranged daughter Stella's commitment ceremony, when American Airlines intervenes, canceling his flight out of O'Hare, imperiling his chances of making it to the wedding, and prompting one of the longest and most surreal complaint letters (for a full refund of his $392.68 ticket) in the history of literature. The letter comprises the entire novel, in which Bennie ruminates on his childhood, his complex relationships, his current life living with his mother in

New York, and his work as a translator (the Polish novel he's translating makes many appearances in the narrative). Although Bennie is not a completely sympathetic character, he does possess what reviewers have referred to as a "hilarious narcissism."

Subjects: Book Groups; Books and Reading; Dark Humor; Epistolary Fiction; Family Relationships; First Novels; Men's Lives; Quick Reads; Satire; Travel

Awards: New York Times Notable

Now Try: Another strange book in which air travel plays a role is James Meek's *We Are Now Beginning Our Descent*. Another novel in which an older man looks back on his life and a book with which he was intimately involved is Nicole Krauss's *The History of Love*; Rohinton Mistry's *The Scream* features an old man's railings against life and society; and P. F. Kluge's *Gone Tomorrow*, about a retired professor who has been working on a novel for several decades, might also be suggested. Author Elizabeth Gilbert compares Miles to Martin Amis, whose somewhat bleakly humorous novels *The Rachel Papers* and *Success* might be good read-alikes. A nonfiction author who might appeal to fans of Miles's somewhat cranky narrator is Jim Knipfel, whose memoirs *Slackjaw* and *Ruining It for Everybody* somehow combine cynicism and sanguine acceptance.

Millet, Lydia.

How the Dead Dream. Counterpoint, 2008. 244pp. ISBN 9781593761844.

"T." starts his life fascinated with the physical form of money (his passion leads him to store coins in his mouth, just to taste them) and, as he ages, becomes equally as fascinated with making money—a task at which he excels. Although he has spent most of his young life exerting his will on others and remaining aloof from complicated relationships and other assorted messes (in his fraternity, he's the one who never gets drunk), his carefully controlled life begins to break down when his mother comes to live with him (after she is left by his father, who has his own very specific reasons for ending the marriage), and he loses the one woman he's ever truly loved. Soon the only thing that gives him solace is the company of animals, which leads him to break into zoos and eventually to head on his own quest into the wilderness.

Subjects: Animals; California; Death and Dying; Family Relationships; Grief; Los Angeles; Love Affairs; Mothers and Sons; Quick Reads; Small Press; Young Men

Now Try: All of Millet's writing is characterized by her extreme imagination; her earlier novels include *Oh Pure and Radiant Heart*, *Everyone's Pretty*, and *George Bush, Dark Prince of Love*. Other imaginative but surprisingly gentle novels published by the independent publisher Soft Skull Books might also be suggested, such as Jonathan Evison's *All About Lulu*, Shannon Burke's *Black Flies*, or Jonathan Scott Fuqua's *Gone and Back Again*. Alison Bechdel's graphic novel memoir *Fun Home*, in which she explores her complicated relationship with her (for much of his life) closeted father, might also appeal to these readers.

Millhauser, Steven.

🐾 *Dangerous Laughter: Thirteen Stories.* Knopf, 2008. 244pp. ISBN 978-0307267566.

Millhauser's satirical and humorous stories cover such ground as the disappearance of a completely forgettable woman ("The Disappearance of Elaine

Coleman"), a lengthy description of cartoon action and violence ("Cat 'N Mouse"), subversive clubs formed for no other reason than to encourage strenuous laughing ("Dangerous Laughter"), a tower being built from earth to heaven and its impact on those in its shadow ("The Tower") , and an entire town built to replicate a true town so residents can go and visit it and pry into their neighbors' lives ("The Other Town") , among other stories and allegories. Deft with language and thoughtful in scope, Millhauser's stories all explore themes of obsession and subcultures, and will leave readers wondering long after they've finished reading.

Subjects: Community Life; Dark Humor; Satire; Short Stories; Society

Awards: ALA Notable; New York Times Notable

Now Try: Millhauser's other story collections are *The King in the Tree, The Knife Thrower and Other Stories, The Barnum Museum*, and *In the Penny Arcade*; he has also written the novels *Enchanted Night* and *Martin Dressler: The Tale of an American Dreamer*. The feel of these stories is almost like that of retro science and pulp fiction; story collections by such classic speculative fiction authors as Kurt Vonnegut (*Welcome to the Monkey House*), Roald Dahl (*Kiss, Kiss*), and Ray Bradbury (*Classic Stories* and *The October Country*). Another author noted for his skill with language is Aleksandar Hemon; his 2009 story collection *Love and Obstacles* might appeal to Millhauser's fans.

Mistry, Rohinton.

🏹 *Family Matters.* **Knopf, 2002. 431pp. ISBN 9780375403736.**

Regret and unhappiness dog the days of Nariman, an elderly man suffering from Parkinson's disease in 1990s Bombay. Pressured due to religious differences to give up his true love in order to enter into an arranged marriage with a more suitable widow, Nariman now lives with the two children of her former marriage, neither of whom he feels any real connection to. When he must recuperate after an accident and goes to live with his other daughter Roxana and her family in a very crowded apartment, it becomes clear that everyone has challenges to face, and how each of these characters chooses to face them is the true story.

Second Appeal: Setting

Subjects: Arranged Marriages; Bombay; Brothers and Sisters; Canadian Authors; Elderly; Epic Reads; Family Relationships; Friendships; India; Literary Allusions; Love Affairs; Marriage; Stepfamilies

Awards: ALA Notable; James Tait Black Memorial Prize; Kiriyama Pacific Rim Book Prize; Torgi Literary Award

Now Try: Mistry's other novels include *The Scream, Such a Long Journey*, and *A Fine Balance*. Authors whose use of language and style is similar to Mistry are Jhumpa Lahiri (*The Namesake*) and Amitav Ghosh (*The Hungry Tide*). Another novel that came close to winning the number of awards that this one did (if not more) was Edward P. Jones's critically acclaimed historical novel *The Known World*; Kiran Desai's *The Inheritance of Loss* was also a critically popular novel that appealed to a wide range of readers. The plotlines of this novel broadly echo those found in Shakespeare's play *King Lear*; another modern literary retelling of that story is Jane Smiley's *A Thousand Acres*.

Mitchell, David.

🏹 *Cloud Atlas.* **Random House, 2004. 509pp. ISBN 9780375507250.**

Mitchell's novel, described by many as "ambitious," offers multiple story- and timelines, which vary widely in setting and voice; each narrative is begun in the first half of the book and then interrupted at a key juncture, only to be concluded in the second half. The six narratives are set in such divergent times as the nineteenth century, the 1930s, and the 1970s (among others), and the stories are told by characters who work as journalists, composers, and servants (among other jobs).

Second Appeal: Story

Subjects: 1930s; 1950s; 1970s; 19th Century; British Authors; Experimental Fiction; First Person; Historical Fiction; Interconnected Stories; Race Relations

Awards: ALA Notable; New York Times Notable

Now Try: Mitchell's earlier novels, *Number9Dream* and *Ghostwritten*, are similarly adventurous in style; his later novel, *Black Swan Green*, though a more stereotypical coming-of-age novel, also includes imaginative flourishes. Other authors whose daring styles might appeal to Mitchell's fans are Mark Danielewski (*House of Leaves* and *Only Revolutions*), David Foster Wallace (*Infinite Jest* and *The Broom of the System*), and Jonathan Lethem (*Motherless Brooklyn*, *Amnesia Moon*, and *Gun, with Occasional Music*).

Mojtabai, A. G.

All That Road Going. TriQuarterly Books, 2008. 196pp. ISBN 978-0810152007.

In this "anti-road novel," Mojtabai presents the stream-of-consciousness viewpoints of a number of travelers stuck together on a bus going down the highway, as well as the narration of the trip by the bus driver trying in his own way to shepherd his passengers to their destinations safely. In the sometimes first-person wonderings and the conversations among the passengers, the author powerfully depicts individuals engaging in the rootless, constant movement that seems to define much of American culture today.

Subjects: First Person; Multiple Viewpoints; Quick Reads; Road Novels; Small Press; Society; Travel; Women Authors

Now Try: Mojtabai has written a number of other novels, including *Ordinary Time* and *Called Out*, as well as the short story collection *Soon: Tales from Hospices*. Other "road novels" that might appeal to these readers are Roland Merullo's *Breakfast with Buddha*, John Haskell's rather darker *American Purgatorio*, and Jack Kerouac's classics *On the Road* and *The Dharma Bums*; novels featuring international locations and the restless movement of protagonists are Aravind Adiga's *The White Tiger* and Dave Eggers's *You Shall Know Our Velocity*. Nonfiction travelogues might also be suggested, such as Hank Stuever's *Off Ramp: Adventures and Heartache in the American Elsewhere*, Mark Singer's *Somewhere in America*, and Ken McAlpine's *Off Season: Discovering America on Winter's Shore*.

Morgan, C. E.

All the Living. Farrar, Straus & Giroux, 2009. 199pp. ISBN 9780374103620.

When Aloma joins her boyfriend Orren Fenton on the tobacco farm he has inherited from his family, all of whom died in an accident, she knows that she loves him but can't decide if she can give up her dream of studying music and piano to live the challenging life of farming and partnership. This is a slim novel, and the prose is sparse, but that fits the feel of the lovers' relationship: intense but conflicted. Also on display is Aloma's struggle to put aside her own sense of rootlessness (raised first by an aunt and uncle and then in a mission school) and her ambivalence about creating a home with Orren, especially as he buries himself in his own grief.

Subjects: 1980s; Agriculture; Book Groups; Death and Dying; Explicit Sexuality; First Novels; Kentucky; Love Affairs; Quick Reads; Religion; Rural Life; Women Authors

Now Try: Other novels in which women try to assimilate their relationships with their surroundings are Kim Barnes's *A Country Called Home*, Wallace Stegner's classic *Angle of Repose*, Ron Rash's rather darker historical fiction title *Selena*, and Hillary Jordan's *Mudbound: A Novel*. Women's memoirs with self-discovery themes might also appeal, such as Jill Ker Conway's *The Road from Coorain*, Esmerelda Santiago's *The Turkish Lover*, and Mary Karr's *The Liar's Club* and *Cherry*.

Morrison, Toni.

🏵 *Love: A Novel.* **Knopf, 2003. 201pp. ISBN 9780375409448.**

At the heart of Morrison's novel is Bill Cosey, whose charisma and business acumen helped him become a powerful and influential figure in 1940s and 1950s America. Owner of a popular hotel and resort in a largely African American community, Cosey's story is told from the viewpoints of the women who knew and loved him, and from the vantage point of the present day: Cosey has died, and the women telling the story have been brought together to jockey for position and a share in what he left behind in his will.

Second Appeal: Character

Subjects: 1940s; 1950s; African American Authors; African Americans; Book Groups; Community Life; Flashbacks; Hotels; Love Affairs; Marriage; Men's Lives; Women Authors

Awards: ALA Notable; New York Times Notable

Now Try: Morrison's other novels might appeal to these readers, including her classics *The Bluest Eye, Beloved, Paradise*, and *A Mercy*. Another story of African American community life is Colson Whitehead's *Sag Harbor*; another novel about a man's life as told primarily by women is T. C. Boyle's historical novel *The Women* (about Frank Lloyd Wright). Nonfiction biographies of African Americans who refused to compromise in their pursuit of excellence might be powerful read-alikes; these include Geoffrey Ward's *Unforgivable Blackness: The Rise and Fall of Jack Johnson*, David Remnick's *King of the World: Muhammad Ali and the Rise of an American Hero*, and Robert Gordon's *Can't Be Satisfied: The Life and Times of Muddy Waters*.

A Mercy. **Knopf, 2008. 167pp. ISBN 9780307264237.**

Morrison's slim novel combines masterful storytelling with surprisingly quick pacing in this historical story of a young slave girl named Florens, and her acquisition by Dutch trader and farmer Jacob Vaark. Vaark is at first unwilling to accept her as payment for a plantation owner's debt to him, but then decides that she will be a help to his wife, Rebekka, still reeling from multiple miscarriages and the death of their daughter, as well as other servants employed in their household, including a girl named Sorrow and a Native American girl named Lina. All three will respond to Florens in different ways, but the struggle of surviving in the harsh wilderness of the New World will in some ways bind them all together.

Subjects: 17th Century; African American Authors; Book Groups; First Person; Historical Fiction; Marriage; Multiple Viewpoints; New York; Quick Reads; Race Relations; Slavery; Women Authors

Now Try: Morrison's other novels featuring strong bonds (even if they are not always friendly ones) between women might be offered, including *Beloved, Sula,* and *Love.* Other literary historical novels about race relations might also be good related reads; these include Zakes Mda's *The Madonna of Excelsior,* Lawrence Hill's *Any Known Blood* and *Someone Knows My Name,* and Edward P. Jones's *The Known World.* Jeffrey Lent's novel *In the Fall,* set after the Civil War, features a white main character who marries a runaway slave. This novel was also the winner of the 2009 Tournament of Books (held by the Web journal *The Morning News*); other literary novels it just squeaked by to win might appeal to Morrison's readers, including Tom Piazza's *City of Refuge,* Jhumpa Lahiri's *Unaccustomed Earth,* and Hari Kunzru's *My Revolutions.*

Munro, Alice.

🎗 *Runaway: Stories.* Knopf, 2004. 335pp. ISBN 9781400042814.

Munro's eight surprisingly lengthy (but quickly paced) "short" stories all feature strong and thoughtfully drawn women characters at various stages in their lives. In the title story, a woman is encouraged by friends to leave her husband, with mixed results; a cycle of three connected stories showcases a woman's falling in love, how she deals with aging and ill parents, and her daughter's choosing of a lifestyle much different from her own; and in the remaining stories other issues of love, relationships, and mortality all make repeat appearances.

Second Appeal: Story

Subjects: Aging; British Columbia; Canadian Authors; Family Relationships; Love Affairs; Marriage; Short Stories; Women Authors; Women's Fiction

Awards: ALA Notable; New York Times Notable; Scotiabank Giller Prize

Now Try: Munro's other story collections, including *The View from Castle Rock* and *Hateship, Friendship, Courtship, Loveship, Marriage: Stories.* Two other Canadian women authors whose short story collections might be suggested are Carol Shields (*Collected Stories*) and Margaret Atwood (*Dancing Girls* and *Moral Disorder*). Critically lauded Irish author Anne Enright has written the story collection *Yesterday's Weather,* which is similar in feel to Munro's volume. In 2009 Munro won the Man Booker International Prize; previous winners included Ismail Kadaré and Chinua Achebe.

Murakami, Haruki.

🎗 *Blind Willow, Sleeping Woman.* Knopf, 2006. 333pp. ISBN 978-1400044610.

In this collection of twenty-four short stories, Murakami doesn't so much provide discrete narratives as give brief glimpses into Asian culture and time period set pieces. Set primarily in Japan, many explore the mundane details of Murakami's characters' lives as they deal with love, sickness, and other challenges, while others are more surreal in nature.

Subjects: Books in Translation; Japan; Japanese Authors; Magic Realism; Multicultural; Short Stories

Awards: ALA Notable

Now Try: Two of these stories, "Firefly" and "Man-Eating Cats," were eventually adapted by Murakami into the novels *Norwegian Wood* and *Sputnik Sweetheart*, which might also appeal to these readers. Steven Millhauser's somewhat surreal short story collection *Dangerous Laughter: Thirteen Stories* might be a stylistic read-alike, and the short novel *Twenty Fragments of a Ravenous Youth* by Xiaolu Guo (although it is set in China, not Japan) provides an interesting look into modern Asian and youth culture.

🎗 *Kafka on the Shore.* **Knopf, 2005. 436pp. ISBN 9781400043668.**

Fifteen-year-old runaway Kafka Tamura boards a bus from Tokyo to a town he chooses at random, where he immerses himself in both self-directed study in a library and fantasies about the head librarian, Miss Saeki. In a parallel story line that runs much closer to Kafka's than is immediately apparent, an older man named Nakata (who has the ability to speak with cats) also flees his home after a murder upsets his carefully structured life.

Subjects: Books in Translation; Fantasy; Japan; Japanese Authors; Magic Realism; Murder; Teenage Boys; Teenagers

Awards: ALA Notable

Now Try: Murakami's other novels, including his imaginative *Norwegian Wood*, *A Wild Sheep Chase*, and *The Wind-Up Bird Chronicle*, might also appeal to these readers. Other works of mythic reality might also be suggested, including Peter Hoeg's *The Quiet Girl*, John Twelve Hawks's *The Traveler*, Moacyr Scliar's *The Centaur in the Garden* (more a work of magic realism, but still similar), and Mark Ferrari's *The Book of Joby*.

Nelson, Antonya.

Female Trouble: A Collection of Short Stories. **Scribner, 2002. 249pp. ISBN 9780743218719.**

In Nelson's collection of thirteen stories, she weaves tales of characters rebelling against what euphemistically used to be known as "female trouble," in the form of relationships, rape, love affairs, and the sometimes frustrating inconsistency of men.

Subjects: Family Relationships; Love Affairs; Marriage; Rape; Short Stories; Women Authors

Now Try: Nelson is also the author of a story collection that provides the male point of view, *In the Land of Men*, and other short story collections, *Nothing Right*, *Some Fun*, and *Family Terrorists*. Susan Minot's short story collection *Lust and Other Stories*, Alice Munro's *Hateship, Friendship, Courtship, Loveship, Marriage: Stories*, and Lorrie Moore's *Birds of America* might be good stylistic read-alikes for Nelson.

O'Brien, Tim.

🎗 *July, July.* **Houghton Mifflin, 2002. 322pp. ISBN 9780618039692.**

Members of the 1969 graduating class of Darton Hall College reconvene for their thirty-year reunion; the multiple story lines taking place at the reunion are interspersed with the stories of each individual friend and classmate.

Second Appeal: Character

Subjects: 1960s; Class Reunions; Friendships; Midlife Crisis; Minnesota; Multiple Viewpoints

Awards: New York Times Notable

Now Try: O'Brien is also the author of the classics of psychological damage and war *In the Lake of the Woods, Going after Cacciato,* and *The Things They Carried*. Other novels about groups of friends and their relationships are Galt Niederhoffer's *The Romantics* and Eli Gottlieb's *Now You See Him;* other novels in which reunions (sometimes with first loves; sometimes not) play a vital part are Mary Morris's *Acts of God*, Justin Cartwright's *Leading the Cheers*, and Mary Guterson's *We Are All Fine Here*. Janis Hallowell's novel about a 1960s war protestor, *She Was*, also examines events from that time period and how they continue to affect lives even today.

Oe, Kenzaburo.

🎗 *Rouse Up, O Young Men of the New Age.* **Grove Press, 2002. 259pp. ISBN 9780802117106.**

Oe's autobiographical novel explores the relationship between a father and his brain-damaged son (who is nicknamed Eeyore), as well as with the rest of his family. Although politically active, and returning at the very beginning of the novel from a speaking tour on which he spoke out against nuclear weapons, the narrator of the book is rather more involved with the life of his own mind than with the lives of his family members (a common charge against writers). Throughout this surprisingly personal and tender (and beautifully written) novel, the narrator learns why his son was so distressed to see him go on his trip and comes to a greater understanding of and appreciation for his home life (particularly through the reading of William Blake's poetry, which also plays a part in the narrative, and lines from which serve as Oe's chapter headings).

Subjects: Autobiographical Fiction; Books and Reading; Books in Translation; Fathers and Sons; Health Issues; Japan; Japanese Authors; Men's Lives; Mental Health; Political Fiction

Awards: ALA Notable

Now Try: Oe is also the author of the similarly autobiographical novels *A Personal Matter, The Pinch Runner Memorandum,* and *A Quiet Life*. Novels and story collections by the Japanese and Nobel Prize–winning author Yasunari Kawabata might also appeal to these readers; they include *Snow Country, Beauty and Sadness,* and *Palm of the Hand Stories*. Nonfiction memoirs in which authors deal with their health issues and the health issues of loved ones might also be suggested, including Lucy Grealy's *Autobiography of a Face* and Robert McCrum's *My Year Off: Recovering Life After a Stroke*.

Ogawa, Yoko.

The Housekeeper and the Professor. **Picador, 2009. 180pp. ISBN 978-0312427801.**

The Housekeeper (none of the characters in Ogawa's slim novel has a name, with the exception of the Housekeeper's son, who receives the nickname "Root" from the Professor) embarks on a job like none she's ever had before: keeping house for an elderly mathematician and scholar, whose prior head injury has made him unable to remember anything that's happened to him since the accident for longer than eighty minutes. The Professor tries to remember things longer by pinning notes about people and events to his suit, but primarily he spends his days working on obscure mathematical problems in solitude, until his relationship with the Housekeeper and her son

Root (so named by him because his head and short haircut remind the Professor of the square root sign) deepens into a friendship that is all the more real for having to be relearned each day.

Subjects: Book Groups; Books in Translation; Elderly; Friendships; Japan; Japanese Authors; Mathematics; Quick Reads; Women Authors

Now Try: Ogawa is also the author of the novel *The Diving Pool*. Novels by another Japanese author, Kenzaburo Oe, might be suggested, including *An Echo of Heaven* and *A Quiet Life*; Haruki Murakami's story collection, *Blind Woman, Sleeping Willow*, is very similar in tone, as is Anita Desai's short but lyrical novel *Clear Light of Day*. Nonfiction books in which math is described in a literary fashion might be enjoyed by these readers, including John Derbyshire's *Prime Obsession: Bernhard Riemann and the Greatest Unsolved Problem in Mathematics*, Charles Seife's *Zero: The Biography of an Idea*, or David Foster Wallace's *Everything and More*.

Olds, Bruce.

🎗 *Bucking the Tiger*. **Farrar, Straus & Giroux, 2001. 371pp. ISBN 9780374117276.**
Olds reimagines the life of Old West legend Doc Holliday in this novel that reads more like the best of all possible nonfiction accounts, complete with fictional poems, letters, and dialogues attributed to Holliday, as well as news accounts both factual and fabricated. Consumptive, violent, and famous at least partially for the wild company he kept, Holliday's fictional biography reads as wild as the West it's portraying.

Second Appeal: Character

Subjects: Biographical Fiction; Historical Fiction; Holliday, Doc; Literary Allusions; Violence; Westerns

Awards: ALA Notable

Now Try: Olds is the author of a similar biographical novel about John Brown, titled *Raising Holy Hell*. Other unromantic Westerns that may appeal to these readers are Loren Estleman's *Journey of the Dead*, Pete Dexter's *Deadwood*, and Robert Parker's *Gunman's Rhapsody*; other novels about Doc Holliday might be good related reads (Paul West's *O.K.: The Corral, the Earps, and Doc Holliday*) as might nonfiction (Gary Roberts's *Doc Holliday: The Life and Legend*). Another historical novel that combine letters, news accounts, and other "primary sources" is Michael Ondaatje's *The Collected Works of Billy the Kid*.

Ondaatje, Michael.

🎗 *Divisadero*. **Knopf, 2007. 273pp. ISBN 9780307266354.**
At least two stories are told in Ondaatje's novel of multiple viewpoints; in the first story, it is 1970s California, and the sisters Anna and Claire are growing up without a mother on their family's farm. When Anna is caught having sex with her father's hired man, Coop, the beating her father administers to him drives them apart forever. Coop flees the farm, and Anna finds her way to southern France, where she researches a book on a French author named Jean Segura. Her research and the novel she writes then provide the second story of the book, as the stories of Anna's family are left open-ended and Segura's story, from the time of World War I, takes over.

Subjects: 1970s; Adoption; California; Canadian Authors; Family Relationships; First Person; France; Love Affairs; Multiple Viewpoints; Siblings; Sisters; World War I

Awards: Governor General's Literary Awards

Now Try: Ondaatje is the author of four other novels: *Anil's Ghost, The English Patient, In the Skin of a Lion*, and *Coming Through Slaughter*. Other authors with literary styles similar to Ondaatje's might be suggested, including Italo Calvino (*If on a Winter's Night a Traveler*), Nathan Englander (*For the Relief of Unbearable Urges* and *The Ministry of Special Cases*), Ian McEwan (*The Comfort of Strangers, Amsterdam, Saturday*, and *Atonement*), and Heidi Julavits (*The Uses of Enchantment*).

Ozick, Cynthia.

🎗 *Dictation: A Quartet*. Houghton Mifflin, 2008. 179pp. ISBN 978-0547054001.

This slim volume contains four novellas (three previously published), widely divergent in subject but with chutzpah-filled characters who are described with an indulgent eye toward their foibles. In one story she imagines a meeting between the secretaries of the literary masters Henry James and Joseph Conrad; in another (reminiscent of the movie *The Producers*) an actor opens a play only to find it an accidental comedic triumph. The remaining two stories describe the sometimes difficult (but usually worthwhile) examination and forging of family relationships.

Subjects: Dark Humor; Family Relationships; Jewish American Authors; Literary Lives; Quick Reads; Women Authors

Awards: New York Times Notable

Now Try: Ozick writes in a variety of formats and genres; her historical novel *Heir to the Glimmering World* might appeal to these readers, as might her story collection *The Pagan Rabbi, and Other Stories* or her essay collections *The Din in the Head, Quarrel & Quandary*, and *Fame & Folly*. Another imaginative novel about the family (or not) of Henry James is Richard Liebmann-Smith's *The James Boys: A Novel Account of William, Henry, Frank, and Jesse*. Other women authors who are unique stylists and skilled literary craftswomen are A. S. Byatt (*Possession, The Shadow of the Sun*, and her trilogy featuring Frederica Potter, *The Virgin in the Garden, Still Life*, and *Babel Tower*), Iris Murdoch (*Henry and Cato; The Sea, The Sea*; and *Under the Net*), and Joyce Carol Oates (*Blonde, You Must Remember This, Faithless*, and *We Were the Mulvaneys*).

Page, Jeremy.

🎗 *Salt: A Novel*. Viking, 2007. 322pp. ISBN 9780670038688.

In postwar England, in the salt marshes of Norfolk and the Midlands, a German airman falls from the sky one day in 1944; he is taken in by a strange and solitary woman named Goose, who reads fortunes in the clouds. Although she nurses him back to health and becomes pregnant by him, he leaves shortly after their meeting, leaving her to raise her daughter Lil alone. Although Lil also later leaves the marshes, her son Pip, who either cannot or will not talk, returns to his grandmother's home, where eventually his mother Lil and her husband George will follow him. Although the landscape itself is a harsh mistress and will prove dangerous to members of his family, it is Pip's growing infatuation with an older girl named Elsie that will bring about the greatest tragedy of all.

Second Appeal: Setting

Subjects: British Authors; Family Relationships; First Novels; Great Britain; Historical Fiction; Love Affairs; Magic Realism; Mythology; Unreliable Narrator

Now Try: Family members trying to unravel mysteries might consider E. Annie Proulx's *The Shipping News* or Graham Swift's *Waterland* (both of which feature similarly harsh landscapes), while those readers fascinated by the setting and the art of cloud reading might try Gavin Pretor-Pinney's delightful nonfiction *The Cloudspotter's Guide: The Science, History, and Culture of Clouds*. Another fantastic novel, although it is one that is based on a mythological story, is C. S. Lewis's similarly language-driven *Til We Have Faces*.

Paine, Tom.

🌳 *Scar Vegas: And Other Stories.* **Harcourt, 2000. 215pp. ISBN 9780151004898.**

Paine switches voices and subjects readily in these ten very different short stories, from an ex-con attending his sister's wedding in Las Vegas who becomes involved in some serious nastiness while there, to a boatload of Haitian refugees; from a developer razing the forest in the depths of Myanmar, to a cross-dressing Marine officer who decides he can no longer keep his secret. They're not easy stories to read (one reviewer described them as "feral") , but they're not easily forgotten, either.

Subjects: Las Vegas; Nevada; Quick Reads; Short Stories

Awards: ALA Notable; New York Times Notable

Now Try: Paine followed this collection with a novel titled *The Pearl of Kuwait*. Charles Bock's novel *Beautiful Children* shares a high-energy prose style and not-always-pleasant subject matter (as well as the setting of Las Vegas) with Paine's collection. Other short story authors who might be suggested to Paine's readers are Chris Offutt (*Out of the Woods: Stories*), Rick Moody (*Demonology*), and Frederick Busch (*Don't Tell Anyone*); novels by Joe Connelly (*Bringing Out the Dead* and *Crumbtown*) and Shannon Burke (*Black Flies*) might also appeal.

Palahniuk, Chuck.

Pygmy. **Doubleday, 2009. 241pp. ISBN 9780385526340.**

Palahniuk's main character, nicknamed "Pygmy" (but who refers to himself as "agent number 67") is not actually a foreign exchange student who has come to stay with the über-American Cedar family (genial father, fashion-conscious and overly thin mother, two children, each with their own pharmaceutical regimens); he is rather a highly trained foreign operative who has been sent, along with several colleagues, to integrate into American society and complete a terrorist mission. But can he maintain the will to help destroy the culture he works so hard to infiltrate? Written in the form of mission reports, in the dialect of a non-native English speaker, Palahniuk's quickly paced novel features the same high energy his fans have come to expect, but not all readers will be able to make it to the ending through scenes of graphically (lovingly?) described violence.

Subjects: American Midwest; Dark Humor; First Person; Friendships; Pop Culture; Quick Reads; Satire; Society; Violence

Now Try: Palahniuk is no stranger to offering stories that include graphic sexuality and violence, but he completes his satires with punchy writing and compelling characters; readers of this novel might also consider his classic title *Fight Club*, as well as *Choke, Lullaby,*

Haunted, and *Snuff* (about the porn industry). Other novels in which authors blend satire and black humor might appeal, such as Bret Easton Ellis's *American Pscyho*, Tama Janowitz's *Peyton Amberg* and *Slaves of New York*, Clancy Martin's *How to Sell*, and Denis Johnson's *Nobody Move*.

Penney, Stef.

🎗 *The Tenderness of Wolves*. Simon & Schuster, 2006. 371pp. ISBN 978 1416540748.

The full harshness of life in a frigid climate during the nineteenth century is unflinchingly displayed in Penney's historical novel. When her seventeen-year-old son Francis disappears from their small northern Canadian community, his mother (known throughout the story only as Mrs. Ross) becomes both determined and desperate to find him, particularly when Laurent Jammet, a fur-trapping neighbor of theirs, is found murdered and scalped. As Mrs. Ross sets out to discover Francis's whereabouts, she must trust and travel with a half-Indian trapper, William Parker, who himself is under suspicion for the murder of the fur trader.

Subjects: 19th Century; Biracial Characters; British Authors; Canada; First Person; Historical Fiction; Murder; Women Authors

Awards: Costa Book of the Year Award; Costa First Novel Award

Now Try: Other novels that feature characters on a quest (often through harsh landscapes) are Gil Adamson's *The Outlander*, Jim Crace's *The Pesthouse*, and Cormac McCarthy's *The Road*; another novel with a character who has always felt ostracized by his community is Sadie Jones's *The Outcast*. Other titles that have won the Costa First Novel Award might also appeal to these readers, including Catherine O'Flynn's *What Was Lost*, Tash Aw's *The Harmony Silk Factory*, Susan Fletcher's *Eve Green*, and D. B. C. Pierre's *Vernon God Little*.

Perkins, Emily.

Novel about My Wife. Bloomsbury, 2008. 271pp. ISBN 9781596911666.

Perhaps best described as postmodern gothic, Perkins's eerie novel is told in flashback by Tom, who tries to trace his wife Ann's (who, the reader learns almost immediately, is dead) growing paranoia and certainty that she is being stalked by a black man throughout her pregnancy with their son Arlo. As they live in an area of London that has yet to be gentrified, Tom can't be certain his wife isn't telling the truth about her follower, and distracted by his own failing screenwriting career and their finances, it is difficult for him to properly assuage his wife's fears; some of which, in light of events at the climax of the novel, seem to be well founded.

Subjects: Book Groups; British Authors; Family Relationships; First Person; London; Marriage; Pregnancy; Suspense; Women Authors; Women Writing as Men

Now Try: Perkins is also the author of the novel *Leave Before You Go* and the story collection *Not Her Real Name and Other Stories*. Rivka Galchen's *Atmospheric Disturbances*, though even more daring in style and storytelling, likewise includes a married couple who are no longer sure of each other's identities. A book in which the secret of a girl's troubled relationship with her stepbrother provides a similarly suspenseful read is Jonathan Evison's *All About Lulu*.

Petterson, Per.

🖤 *Out Stealing Horses.* **Graywolf Press, 2005. 258pp. ISBN 9781555974701.**

Sixty-seven-year-old Trond retreats to a cabin in the woods and his own solitude after the deaths of his wife and sister; the last person he expects to find living down the road from him is a man he met fifty years earlier when they were both boys caught up in tragic circumstances. His chance meeting with this neighbor, Lars, leads Trond to reflect on the summer they met, his relationship with his father and his father's wartime experiences, and his friendship with another boy, Jon, with whom he spent a morning "stealing horses" (borrowing them, more like). Told partially in flashbacks, and with a moody, wintry atmosphere, this is a novel firmly rooted in Petterson's native Norway.

Subjects: 1940s; Book Groups; Books in Translation; Classics; Death and Dying; Elderly; Fathers and Sons; First Person; Flashbacks; Friendships; Men's Lives; Norway; Small Press; World War II

Awards: New York Times Notable

Now Try: Petterson is the author of two other novels: *To Siberia* and *In the Wake*. Another atmospheric story in which a man looks back on a life-changing event is Tim O'Brien's *In the Lake of the Woods*. The somewhat graphic mysteries of Henning Mankell, set in Sweden and featuring world-weary detective Kurt Wallander, might also appeal; the series starts with *Faceless Killers*, *The Dogs of Riga*, *The White Lioness*, and *The Man Who Smiled*. Petterson is published by the independent publisher Graywolf Press; other novels from that publisher might be suggested, including J. Robert Lennon's *Castle*, George Packer's *Central Square*, and Mary Rockcastle's *Rainy Lake*.

Powers, Richard.

🖤 *The Echo Maker.* **Farrar, Straus & Giroux, 2006. 451pp. ISBN 9780374146351.**

After Mark Schluter is involved in a serious truck accident and recovers from a coma induced by it, he is diagnosed with Capgras syndrome (a rare disorder in which sufferers cannot reconcile their visual and emotional identifications of people they know). He is cared for by his sister Karin, who struggles to understand the syndrome but can't help being hurt by her brother's conviction that she is not his sister but an impostor; to help him, she sends for a neurologist, who is suffering from his own crisis of confidence after the failure of his latest book.

Subjects: Brain; Brothers and Sisters; Family Relationships; Health Issues; Nebraska; Neurology; Rural Life; Siblings

Awards: National Book Award

Now Try: Powers is also the author of the novels *The Time of Our Singing*, *Plowing the Dark*, and *Gain*. Kent Haruf's *The Tie That Binds* is another masterful look at the bonds within families, as are Louise Erdrich's *The Beet Queen* and Jane Urquhart's *The Stone Carvers*. Fiction by Pete Dexter (*The Paperboy*), Russell Banks (*The Sweet Hereafter*), and David Guterson (*East of the Mountains*) might also appeal. The neurologist character in this title is often described as being "like Oliver Sacks"; nonfiction by that author, including *The Man Who Mistook His Wife for a Hat* and *An Anthropologist on Mars*, might also be offered to these readers.

Robinson, Marilynne.

🎀 *Gilead: A Novel.* Farrar, Straus & Giroux, 2004. 247pp. ISBN 978-0374153892.

The year is 1956, and seventy-six-year-old John Ames, a native of Gilead, Iowa, is writing an extended letter to his young son. In failing health, he wants his son to understand who he is (so his son can better understand his roots) and to learn about the difficult relationship between John's own father and grandfather, a pacifist and an abolition activist, respectively, who were different from each other but nonetheless could love each other. Told in languid prose with a nostalgic feel, Robinson's novel also touches on issues of other family relationships and spirituality, and somehow combines her measured pace with a surprising lightness of touch.

Second Appeal: Character

Subjects: 1950s; American Midwest; Book Groups; Classics; Elderly; Epistolary Fiction; Family Relationships; Fathers and Sons; Gentle Reads; Historical Fiction; Iowa; Men's Lives; Spirituality; Women Authors; Women Writing as Men

Awards: ALA Notable, National Book Critics Circle Award; New York Times Notable; Pulitzer Prize

Now Try: Robinson has also written a companion piece to this novel, *Home*, as well as the earlier novel *Housekeeping* and the nonfiction titles *Mother Country* and *The Death of Adam*. Those who enjoy Robinson's measured pacing might consider another book related by a somewhat elderly narrator, Wendell Berry's *Jayber Crow*, or Sara Gruen's popular novel *Water for Elephants*. Anne Lamott's nonfiction titles in which she examines her faith might also be enjoyable related reads; they are *Traveling Mercies*, *Plan B: Further Thoughts on Faith*, and *Grace (Eventually): Thoughts on Faith*.

🎀 *Home.* Farrar, Straus & Giroux, 2008. 325pp. ISBN 9780374299101.

Robinson's companion piece to her Pulitzer Prize winning novel *Gilead* is an interpretation of the biblical parable of the prodigal son, and she tells the story of the Boughton family of Gilead, Iowa, in the 1950s, with attention to domestic details and spiritual overtones. When siblings Jack and Glory Boughton return home to care for their elderly and ailing father, they must recalibrate their own relationships, while their father strives to help his son Jack, whose tempestuous personal life threatens, as always, to upset his family's harmony and Jack's own well-being.

Second Appeal: Character

Subjects: 1950s; American Midwest; Book Groups; Classics; Domestic Fiction; Family Relationships; Fathers and Sons; Historical Fiction; Iowa; Siblings; Spirituality; Women Authors

Awards: New York Times Notable

Now Try: Readers who enjoy this book will probably have already read its prequel, *Gilead*, but they might also consider Robinson's earlier novel, *Housekeeping*. Fans of this rather gentle but not typically sentimental storytelling might also consider such novels as Mary Ann Shaffer and Annie Barrows's *The Guernsey Literary and Potato Peel Society*, Wendell Berry's *Jayber Crow* (or any of his novels set in the fictional town Port William, Kentucky), or Kent Haruf's *Eventide*.

Roth, Philip.

🌳 *Everyman*. **Houghton Mifflin, 2006. 182pp. ISBN 9780618735167.**

Roth's eponymous "everyman" is a successful businessman with two sons (Randy and Lonny), a daughter (Nancy), three ex-wives, and his own variety of health problems. Rather than showing how his character is unique, Roth's narrative plots the trajectory of a life in which all is almost achingly mundane: work, marriage, kids, sickness, death.

Subjects: Classics; Family Relationships; Health Issues; Jewish American Authors; Men's Lives; Quick Reads

Awards: PEN-Faulkner Award

Now Try: Roth is a prolific author; although this book is not part of any series, his Nathan Zuckerman books (starting with *The Ghost Writer* and *Zuckerman Unbound*) might be suggested, as might his memoir *Patrimony*, in which he relates the story of his father's final illness and death. Richard Ford's Frank Bascombe series, starting with the novel *The Sportswriter*, might also appeal to these readers. Essay collections by Phillip Lopate, including *Against Joie de Vivre* and *Getting Personal*, might appeal to these readers, as might Julian Barnes's nonfiction work *Nothing to Be Frightened Of*, which is similar to Roth's allegory more in tone than in subject (Roth's subject is life before death, whereas Barnes ruminates largely on his beliefs about life after death).

Sandor, Marjorie.

🌳 *Portrait of My Mother, Who Posed Nude in Wartime: Stories*. **Sarabande Books, 2003. 213pp. ISBN 9781889330839.**

Sandor offers a collection of ten interconnected stories about the dynamics of an American Jewish family throughout the twentieth century, spending considerable time on the secrets they keep from one another. Also explored in the stories are the family's personalities, their mobility (Grandma Eve lived in Indiana; more recent matriarchs hail from California), their marriages, and their pursuit of love and happiness.

Subjects: Family Relationships; Family Secrets; First Person; Jews and Judaism; Short Stories; Women Authors

Awards: National Jewish Book Award

Now Try: Sandor has written another volume of stories, *A Night of Music*, as well as the essay collection *The Night Gardener*. This volume has been compared to Alice Munro's *The Beggar Maid*; another volume of interconnected stories, Elizabeth Strout's Pulitzer Prize–winning *Olive Kitteridge*, might also be suggested. Another prominent Jewish American author is Cynthia Ozick; her story collections include *Levitation* and *The Pagan Rabbi, and Other Stories*. (Elisa Albert's collection *How This Night Is Different: Stories* might also be of interest.)

Saramago, José.

🌳 *The Cave*. **Harcourt, 2002. 307pp. ISBN 9780151004140.**

Cipriano Algor, the elderly potter at the heart of Saramago's powerful and allegorical novel, succeeds in changing his career from making pots and other vessels to making ceramic dolls, but his success at adapting to the modern world is challenged when he and his family begin to learn the secrets of what really goes on at the "Center," a large complex where he had previously been taking his goods to be sold.

Subjects: Books in Translation; Elderly; Philosophical Fiction; Portuguese Authors; Professions; Quick Reads

Awards: ALA Notable; New York Times Notable

Now Try: Saramago's other imaginative novels might be suggested, including *Death with Interruptions, Seeing, Blindness,* and *The Double.* Jim Crace's novel *The Gift of Stones,* also about individuals plying an ancient craft, might appeal, as might Kazuo Ishiguro's philosophical and literary science fiction novel *Never Let Me Go.* Another author whose style is similar to Saramago's is Paulo Coelho, whose titles *The Alchemist* and *The Fifth Mountain* might be suggested; other titles that might appeal are Naguib Mahfouz's *Arabian Nights and Days,* Julio Cortazar's *Hopscotch,* and Haruki Murakami's *After Dark.*

Scibona, Salvatore.

The End: A Novel. **Graywolf Press, 2008. 297pp. ISBN 9781555974985.**

When Rocco LaGrassa learns that his son has died in a POW camp in Korea, he abruptly ceases believing in God, family, and hard work. His story is told alongside other anecdotes from the lives of fellow community members (events that took place on the same day he learned of his son's death, August 15, 1953).

Subjects: 1950s; American Midwest; Day in the Life; First Novels; Historical Fiction; Immigrants and Immigration; Multiple Viewpoints; Ohio; Small Press

Now Try: Another novel from the Korean War era is Philip Roth's *Indignation;* Richard Bausch's slim novel *Peace* is set during the Vietnam War, but similarly questions the necessity for war. Scibona's novel also features many immigrant characters; other novels with immigrant themes are Rose Tremain's *The Road Home,* Mark Helprin's *Ellis Island and Other Stories,* and Kevin Baker's *Dreamland.* Another novel featuring a close-knit Italian American family is Roland Merullo's *Revere Beach Boulevard.* Immigrant nonfiction memoirs might also be suggested, including Laura Schenone's memoir/cookbook *The Lost Ravioli Recipes of Hoboken* and Diana Abu-Jaber's *The Language of Baklava.*

Sebald, Winfried Georg.

🏵 *Austerlitz.* **Random House, 2001. 298pp. ISBN 9780375504839.**

The narrator of Sebald's novel about history, the Holocaust, and the life of an immigrant is the friend of a man named Jacques Austerlitz, who was sent to Wales as a child to escape the horrors of the concentration camps during World War II. Growing up believing that his Welsh foster parents were his birth parents, Austerlitz only starts on his journey to learn the truth about his parents, Prague Jews who were lost in the war, after he flashes back to a memory of his emigration as a four-year-old.

Subjects: Books in Translation; First Person; German Authors; Great Britain; Holocaust; Jews and Judaism; Prague; World War II

Awards: ALA Notable; National Book Critics Circle Award

Now Try: Sebald is also the author of the acclaimed novels *After Nature, Vertigo, The Rings of Saturn,* and *The Emigrants.* Other novels about the Holocaust that might appeal to these readers are Bernhard Schlink's *The Reader*, Francine Prose's *Guided Tours of Hell*, Markus Zusak's *The Book Thief*, and Elie Wiesel's *Night, Dawn, The Accident*, and *Twilight*.

Sellers, Susan.

Vanessa & Virginia. **Houghton Mifflin Harcourt, 2008. 213pp. ISBN 978-0151014743.**

Sellers tells the story of the relationship between author Virginia Woolf and her sister, the painter Vanessa Bell, in this first-person (told from Vanessa's point of view) narrative. Although the sisters were fierce artistic competitors (even though they were creative in different media), they were even fiercer rivals for the affection of their parents and their beloved brother, Thoby.

Subjects: 19th Century; 20th Century; Bell, Vanessa; Biographical Fiction; Family Relationships; First Novels; First Person; Great Britain; Literary Lives; Quick Reads; Siblings; Sisters; Women Authors; Woolf, Virginia; Writers and Writing

Now Try: Novels by Virginia Woolf might be enjoyed by these readers, including *Mrs. Dalloway*, *To the Lighthouse*, and *Orlando: A Biography* (as well as the nonfiction title *A Room of One's Own*). Michael Cunningham's novel *The Hours*, which also features Virginia Woolf as a character, might be suggested. The scholarly but very readable nonfiction title *Mrs. Woolf and the Servants*, which provides another viewpoint into the domestic life of the sisters, might be a good related read, as might Mary Ann Caws's *Women of Bloomsbury: Virginia, Vanessa, and Carrington*. This novel also features a blurb by Susan Vreeland, whose literary historical novels might also appeal: *Girl in Hyacinth Blue* and *The Passion of Artemisia*.

Setiawan, Erick.

Of Bees and Mist. **Simon & Schuster, 2009. 416pp. ISBN 9781416596240.**

Setiawan's ambitious first novel centers on a young girl named Meridia, growing up in a nameless place and unspecified time, who feels stunted by her loveless home (which is filled, in the best metaphorical fashion, by a cold mist). When she meets and falls in love with the charming Daniel, she is quick to swap her home for his, but soon finds that all is not as it seems in his perfect family, which is led by his strong-minded and strong-willed mother, Eva.

Second Appeal: Character

Subjects: Coming-of-age; Family Relationships; Fantasy; First Novels; Horror; Love Affairs; Magic Realism; Men Writing as Women

Now Try: Although much more grounded in reality, Antonya Nelson's short story collection *Nothing Right* also explores a variety of family relationships and tensions. Fans of magic realism might consider other books that engage in this style, such as Gabriel García Márquez's *One Hundred Years of Solitude*, Isabel Allende's *The House of Spirits*, or Kevin Brockmeier's *The Brief History of the Dead* and *The View from the Seventh Layer*. Other books that blend fantasy and realistic fiction are Margo Lanagan's *Tender Morsels* and Charles de Lint's *The Mystery of Grace*.

Shields, Carol.

Collected Stories. **Fourth Estate, 2004. 593pp. ISBN 9780060762032.**

Although better known as a novelist, Shields also produced numerous and thoughtful short stories about family, love, and community relationships throughout her career. This collection includes fifty-six stories, including the previously unpublished "Segue."

Subjects: Canadian Authors; Short Stories; Women Authors

Now Try: Shields is the author of many popular and critically acclaimed novels, including *The Stone Diaries, Happenstance, Unless,* and *Larry's Party*. Other short story authors who might appeal to Shields's readers are Alice Munro (*Hateship, Friendship, Courtship, Loveship, Marriage: Stories* and *The View from Castle Rock*), Diane Schoemperlen (*Red Plaid Shirt*), Mary Swan (*The Deep and Other Stories*), and Antonya Nelson (*Female Trouble, Nothing Right,* and *The Expendables*). *The Penguin Book of Canadian Short Stories*, edited by Jane Urquhart, might also prove a fun related read.

Shteyngart, Gary.

The Russian Debutante's Handbook. **Riverhead Books, 2002. 452pp. ISBN 9781573222136.**

Twenty-five-year-old Vladimir Girshkin is an unabashed believer in the American dream, and has been ever since he emigrated from Russia as a child. Although he works in a nonprofit immigrant assistance organization, his relationships with his dominatrix girlfriend and another émigré known as the Fan Man (who has connections to the Russian mob in the fictional Republic of Stolovaya) lead him to become involved with the crime scene in the Republic's city of Prava (often referred to as the "Paris of the 90s") , where he shows a talent for fleecing students and tourists.

Subjects: 1990s; Classics; Dark Humor; First Novels; Immigrants and Immigration; Jewish American Authors; Russian Americans; Satire; Young Men

Awards: ALA Notable; National Jewish Book Award; New York Times Notable

Now Try: Shteyngart is also the author of the satirical novel *Absurdistan*. Fans of satirical novels might also consider George Saunders's novels *The Brief and Frightening Reign of Phil* and *CivilWarLand in Bad Decline*, Tova Reich's *My Holocaust* or *The Jewish War*, Rhoda Lerman's *Animal Acts*, Etgar Keret's story collections *The Girl on the Fridge* and *The Nimrod Flipout*, or Torsten Krol's *Callisto*. A more story-driven novel of crime, history, and both of their effects on families and individuals is Josh Bazell's literary thriller *Beat the Reaper*.

Smith, Ali.

The First Person: And Other Stories. **Pantheon Books, 2008. 206pp. ISBN 9780307377715.**

Smith's twelve short stories offer evocative vignettes of love, friendship, and the dialogue of relationships. In an added stylistic twist, most of these stories are also told in the first person, with the exception of two stories (helpfully titled "The third person" and "The second person") .

Subjects: Family Relationships; First Person; Friendships; Literary Lives; Love Affairs; Quick Reads; Scottish Authors; Short Stories; Women Authors

Now Try: Smith is also the author of *The Accidental, Free Love, Other Stories and Other Stories,* and *The Whole Story and Other Stories*. She has also written a spectacular nonfiction love letter to books and the act of reading in her personal history/memoir, *The Book Lover*. Although a bit more experimental in style, Lydia Davis is another short story writer whom Smith's readers might enjoy; her collections are *Samuel Johnson Is Indignant* and *Varieties of Disturbance*.

Strauss, Darin.

More Than It Hurts You. **Dutton, 2008. 401pp. ISBN 9780525950707.**

Josh and Dori Goldin have the perfect life, well provided for by Josh's job in TV ad sales, with a healthy eight-month-old baby named Zack. However, when Dori takes Zack to the emergency room with mysterious symptoms and refuses to let him be tested further, claiming that the hospital staff is incompetent, their perfect world begins to crumble as pediatrician Dr. Darlene Stokes questions whether Dori suffers from Munchausen-by-proxy (a disease in which parents will harm their own children to garner attention). A visit from a social worker and media speculation follow the allegations; also on display are racial issues and tensions, because the Goldins are Jewish and Dr. Stokes is an African American woman.

Second Appeal: Character

Subjects: African Americans; Book Groups; Doctors; Family Relationships; Health Issues; Jews and Judaism; Mass Media; Medicine; Race Relations; Satire; Social Class

Now Try: Strauss is also the author of the critically acclaimed historical novels *Chang and Eng* and *The Real McCoy*. Another satirical novel that might appeal to these readers is Joyce Maynard's classic *To Die For*; other novels in which marriages seem to be slowly unraveling might also be suggested, such as Tom Perrotta's *The Abstinence Teacher* or *Little Children*, Richard Yates's classic *Revolutionary Road*, and Frederick Busch's *Girls: A Novel*. A nonfiction account of families dealing with culture clashes and trying to navigate the health care system is Anne Fadiman's classic *The Spirit Catches You and You Fall Down*; Julie Gregory's memoir *Sickened: The Memoir of a Munchausen by Proxy Childhood* might also be a compelling related read.

Subercaseaux, Elizabeth.

A Week in October. **Other Press, 2008. 208pp. ISBN 9781590512883.**

When Clara Griffin learns she has breast cancer and is dying, she starts recording her thoughts and confessions in a daily diary, which is found and read by her husband Clemente. Told in alternating chapters, first from Clara's point of view and then Clemente's, the reader can never be sure how much of Clara's narrative is true and how much is fantasy (Clemente faces the same uncertainty and can't decide if Clara's notes about sexual fantasies were things she actually acted upon with others; he's also stunned to learn she knows all about his affairs).

Subjects: Adultery; Books in Translation; Cancer; Chilean Authors; Death and Dying; Diary; Marriage; Multiple Viewpoints; Quick Reads; Small Press; Suspense; Women Authors

Now Try: Subercaseaux has also written another novel, *The Song of the Distant Root*. Another novel about a marriage and the wife's death is Emily Perkins's *Novel About My Wife*. As a Chilean author, her style might remind some of another critically acclaimed Chilean female author, Isabel Allende (*The House of the Spirits*, *Daughter of Fortune*, and *Portrait in Sepia*).

Thomas, Michael.

🎗 *Man Gone Down.* **Black Cat, 2007. 431pp. ISBN 9780802170293.**

Going through difficulties with his white wife, the unnamed narrator of Thomas's novel is a thirty-five-year-old black man, struggling with issues of both race and selfhood. Although he desperately misses his three children, he is having trouble putting aside memories of his own childhood, in which his prodigious talent and intelligence helped him excel in Boston schools to which he was bused, but which was also characterized by following in his parents' alcoholic footsteps. Although he takes any jobs he can find, primarily in construction, to help pay for the education and support of his family, the narrator also experiences ambivalence about the life he was living and whether or not he does truly want to return to it.

Subjects: Abuse; African American Authors; African Americans; Alcoholism; Book Groups; Boston; Family Relationships; First Novels; First Person; Flashbacks; Marriage; Men's Lives; New York City; Race Relations

Awards: International IMPAC Dublin Literary Award

Now Try: Issues of race, family life, and community are also addressed in Nathan McCall's (somewhat less subtle novel about gentrification) *Home: A Novel*, as well as his memoir, *Makes Me Wanna Holler: A Young Black Man in America*. Another novel in which a man is rather at a loss for how to fix his marriage is Joseph O'Neill's *Netherland*; Junot Díaz's popular novel *The Brief Wondrous Life of Oscar Wao* might also provide a similar reading experience. Another book about complex relationships within an African American family is Stephen Carter's *The Emperor of Ocean Park*; David Haynes's *Live at Five* might also appeal. Readers interested in nonfiction titles might enjoy James McBride's memoir *The Color of Water* or Danzy Senna's *Where Did You Sleep Last Night?*, both of which are about the authors' parents' interracial marriages.

Tóibín, Colm.

🎗 *The Master: A Novel.* **Scribner, 2004. 338pp. ISBN 9780743250405.**

The inner life of novelist Henry James is revealed in this measured, thoughtful fictional biography, which focuses on James's travels, his work and writing, and his sexuality (the whole truth of which the author alludes to but never resolves, in a nod to James's nineteenth-century culture).

Subjects: 19th Century; Biographical Fiction; Historical Fiction; James, Henry; Victorian; Writers and Writing

Awards: International IMPAC Dublin Literary Award

Now Try: Tóibín's other novels include *Brooklyn: A Novel, The Blackwater Lightship*, and *The Story of the Night*. Richard Liebmann-Smith's imaginative novel *The James Boys: A Novel Account of William, Henry, Frank, and Jesse* might appeal, and the nonfiction titles *A Ring of Conspirators: Henry James and His Literary Circle, 1895–1915* by Miranda Seymour and *The Jameses: A Family Narrative* by R. W. B. Lewis might be good related reads. Other literary historical novels set during the Victorian age in Great Britain include Dan Simmons's thriller *Drood* (about Charles Dickens), Sarah Waters's *Tipping the Velvet* (which also explores issues of sexuality), and Katie Roiphe's *Still She Haunts Me* (about Lewis Carroll).

Trevor, William.

🎗 *Cheating at Canasta: Stories.* Viking, 2007. 231pp. ISBN 9780670018376.

In this collection of twelve short stories, Irish author Trevor displays his skill at describing both characters and landscapes, while also providing perfectly formed (if short) narratives. Trevor has also never been one to shy away from the darker events of the human experience, relating in his tales details of blackmail, adultery, the need for money to survive, and many other events.

Subjects: Family Relationships; Ireland; Irish Authors; Quick Reads; Short Stories

Awards: ALA Notable

Now Try: Trevor is also the author of the story collections *A Bit on the Side, The Hill Bachelors,* and *The Collected Stories,* as well as the novels *The Story of Lucy Gault, Death in Summer,* and *Felicia's Journey.* Another Irish author, whose short story collection, *Yesterday's Weather,* may be of interest to Trevor's readers, is Anne Enright; her novels *The Gathering* and *What Are You Like?* could also be suggested. The novels of Sebastian Barry (another Irish author) are also steeped in the Irish landscape and national character; they include *Annie Dunne, A Long Long Way, The Whereabouts of Eneas McNulty,* and *The Secret Scripture.*

Trudel, Sylvain.

Mercury Under My Tongue. Soft Skull, 2008. 159pp. ISBN 9781933368962.

Seventeen-year-old Frederic Langlois is wise beyond his years; he has been forced to become so, as he is in the hospital facing the end stages of terminal cancer. He spends his days writing letters to family members that he plans to have another resident of his floor mail on the one-year anniversary of his death, but his essential self shines through the poetry he writes and shares only with another cancer sufferer, fifteen-year-old Marilu. In Frederic, Trudel has created a character whom the reader will (sadly) become attached to even in the face of mortality.

Subjects: Books in Translation; Canada; Cancer; Death and Dying; Friendships; Philosophical Fiction; Poetry; Small Press; Teenage Boys; Teenagers; YA

Now Try: Christine Schutt's *All Souls,* which features a teenage girl suffering from cancer, might prove both a stylistic and subject read-alike for this novel; Jim Knipfel's dark memoirs of his own health struggles might also be suggested (*Slackjaw* and *Quitting the Nairobi Trio*). Also of interest might be other Soft Skull Press novels that feature young characters, such as Jonathan Evison's *All About Lulu* or Matthue Roth's *Candy in Action.*

Vapnyar, Lara.

Broccoli and Other Tales of Food and Love. Pantheon Books, 2008. 148pp. ISBN 9780375424878.

In each of Vapnyar's short stories food plays nearly as central a role as human relationships and love. The six stories all feature Russian immigrants (Vapnyar herself emigrated from Russia in 1994) in various stages of their émigré experiences, from the lonely man who saves money to procure the services of a prostitute, to the pair of elderly ladies engaged in a fierce cook-off to attract the attention of a widower; Vapnyar concludes the collection with a section of recipes.

Subjects: Food; Immigrants and Immigration; Multicultural; New York City; Quick Reads; Recipes; Short Stories; Women Authors

Now Try: Vapnyar is also the author of *There Are Jews in My House* and *Memoirs of a Muse: A Novel*. Novels in which food plays an important role may appeal to these readers, including Laura Esquivel's *Like Water for Chocolate*. Rose Tremain's *The Road Home* is another story of modern-day immigration. Food nonfiction, such as Laurie Colwin's *Home Cooking*; *Death by Pad Thai*, collected by Douglas Bauer; or memoirs like Ruth Reichl's *Tender at the Bone, Comfort Me with Apples,* or *Garlic and Sapphires*, might also appeal. Amazon's recommendation, a good one I think, is Anya Ulinich's *Petropolis.*

Vollmann, William.

🎗 *Europe Central.* Viking, 2005. 811pp. ISBN 9780670033928.

Vollmann's mammoth undertaking in this novel was to provide another point of view about the events and stories of World War II, setting his novel in Eastern Europe and telling stories from the viewpoints of such real historical figures as Kathe Kollwitz, Kurt Gerstein, Dmitri Shostakovich, and several military leaders. He does not stick to the purely factual in his storytelling; his characters also include a magically shape-shifting Nazi officer and other Wagnerian embodiments of myth. Although universally lamented for its unwieldy length, many critics found this to be a compelling work of highly researched historical fiction.

Subjects: 1940s, Biographical Fiction, Eastern Europe; Epic Reads; European History; Germany; Historical Fiction; World War II

Awards: National Book Award

Now Try: Vollmann is known for his stylistically challenging novels and his equally avant-garde nonfiction; his novels include the historical novel *Argall* (about Jamestown) and *The Royal Family*; his nonfiction titles include *Rising Up and Rising Down* (a massive study of violence), *Poor People* (which combines text and photography), and the memoir *Riding Toward Everywhere* (about his experiences riding freight trains). Other stylistically daring authors who might appeal to Vollmann's readers are Thomas Pynchon (*Gravity's Rainbow, The Crying of Lot 49,* and *Mason & Dixon*) and David Foster Wallace (*Infinite Jest*).

Wiggins, Marianne.

The Shadow Catcher. Simon & Schuster, 2007. 323pp. ISBN 9780743265201.

Wiggins combines a present-day narrative with fictionalized anecdotes from the life of Edward S. Curtis, a man who was obsessed with photographing Native American communities and life on reservations in the nineteenth and early twentieth centuries. She weaves together the two stories; in the present day, she appears as a character who is trying to sell a movie script, while the historical stories focus on Curtis, his abandonment of his family, and the harshness of life on reservations.

Second Appeal: Setting

Subjects: 19th Century; 20th Century; American History; American Indians; American West; Biographical Fiction; Curtis, Edward S.; Family Relationships; Historical Fiction; Photography; Women Authors

Now Try: Wiggins's other novels include *Evidence of Things Unseen, Almost Heaven, Eveless Eden, John Dollar,* and *Separate Checks*. Another classic nonfiction compilation of text and photographs is Walker Evans and James Agee's *Let Us Now Praise Famous Men*; a more contemporary account of reservation life can be found in Sherman Alexie's novel *Reservation Blues*. A writer whose style is similar to Wiggins's in her attention to the external world is Annie Dillard (*The Living* and *The Maytrees*).

Wolff, Tobias.

🎗 *Our Story Begins: New and Selected Stories.* **Knopf, 2008. 379pp. ISBN 978-1400044597.**

Memoirist and novelist Wolff offers a collection of short stories (thirty-one in all) rich with the everyday details of falling in love, obsession, dealing with uncouth neighbors, challenges at work, and many other human foibles and occurrences. Many of the stories are quite short, from five to ten pages long, and most include well-drawn characters and evocative vignettes.

Subjects: Family Relationships; Love Affairs; Short Stories

Awards: ALA Notable

Now Try: Wolff is a popular memoirist; his nonfiction titles include the classic *This Boy's Life* and the Vietnam War–era *In Pharaoh's Army*. He has also written a novel, *Old School*. He also edits the American Lives series of memoirs from the University of Nebraska Press; titles from that series that might be suggested are Ted Kooser's *Local Wonders*, Floyd Skoot's *In the Shadow of Memory*, and Mimi Schwartz's *Thoughts from a Queen-Sized Bed*. Short stories by authors such as Raymond Carver (*Short Cuts* and *Cathedral*) and Richard Ford (*A Multitude of Sins*) might also be good read-alikes.

Now Consider Nonfiction . . . Essay Collections

Readers who enjoy short story collections and novellas might consider the nonfiction equivalent of short fiction: the short pieces of nonfiction known as essays. Most appealing to these readers might be personal essays, in which authors strive to understand the personal and make it more broadly applicable to the world around them, often relying heavily on their writing skill to do so.

Berry, Wendell. *The Way of Ignorance.*

Chabon, Michael. *Maps and Legends.*

Didion, Joan. *Slouching Towards Bethlehem.*

Franzen, Jonathan. *How to Be Alone.*

Hardwick, Elizabeth. *American Fictions.*

Lopate, Phillip. *Getting Personal.*

Saunders, George. *The Braindead Megaphone.*

Siegel, Lee. *Falling Upwards: Essays in Defense of Imagination.*

Wallace, David Foster. *Consider the Lobster.*

Appendix A

Bridges to Genre Fiction

Adventure

Chupack, Edward. *Silver: My Own Tale as Written by Me with a Goodly Amount of Murder.*

Guterson, David. *The Other.*

Mastras, George. *Fidali's Way.*

Parks, Tim. *Rapids: A Novel.*

Salak, Kira. *The White Mary.*

Thornton, Lawrence. *Sailors on the Inward Sea.*

Fantasy

Barker, Nicola. *Darkmans.*

Brockmeier, Kevin. *The View from the Seventh Layer: Stories.*

Bull, Emma. *Territory.*

Carey, Edward. *Alva & Irva: The Twins Who Saved a City.*

Carson, Ciaran. *The Tain: A New Translation of the Tain bo Cuailnge.*

Díaz, Junot. *The Brief Wondrous Life of Oscar Wao.*

Groff, Lauren. *The Monsters of Templeton.*

Le Guin, Ursula. *Lavinia.*

Millar, Martin. *The Good Fairies of New York.*

Murakami, Haruki. *Kafka on the Shore.*

Gentle Reads

Berry, Wendell. *Andy Catlett: Early Travels.*

Berry, Wendell. *Hannah Coulter.*

Earley, Tony. *The Blue Star.*

Haig, Matt. *The Labrador Pact.*

Logsdon, Gene. *The Last of the Husbandmen.*

Maillard, Keith. *The Clarinet Polka.*

Ogawa, Yoko. *The Housekeeper and the Professor.*

Robinson, Marilynne. *Gilead: A Novel.*

Robinson, Marilynne. *Home: A Novel.*

Shaffer, Mary Ann, and Annie Barrows. *The Guernsey Literary and Potato Peel Pie Society.*

Historical Fiction

Agee, Jonis. *The River Wife: A Novel.*

Antunes, Antonio Lobo. *The Inquisitors' Manual.*

Baker, Kevin. *Strivers Row.*

Barker, Pat. *Life Class.*

Barnes, Julian. *Arthur & George.*

Baruth, Philip. *The Brothers Boswell.*

Benioff, David. *City of Thieves.*

Bloom, Amy. *Away: A Novel.*

Boyle, T. Coraghessan. *The Women: A Novel.*

Brooks, Geraldine. *March.*

Carey, Peter. *The True History of the Kelly Gang.*

Charyn, Jerome. *Johnny One-Eye: A Tale of the American Revolution.*

Cisneros, Sandra. *Caramelo.*

Clarke, Breena. *Stand the Storm.*

Dean, Debra. *The Madonnas of Leningrad.*

Doctorow, E. L. *The March: A Novel.*

Doig, Ivan. *The Eleventh Man.*

Du Boucheron, Bernard. *The Voyage of the Short Serpent.*

Ghosh, Amitov. *Sea of Poppies.*

Gold, Glen David. *Sunnyside.*

Goldman, Francisco. *The Divine Husband.*

Goolrick, Robert. *A Reliable Wife.*

Grenville, Kate. *The Secret River.*

Hill, Lawrence. *Someone Knows My Name.*

Hunt, Samantha. *The Invention of Everything Else.*

Iagnemma, Karl. *The Expeditions: A Novel.*

Jin, Ha. *War Trash.*

Jones, Edward P. *The Known World.*

Jones, Sadie. *The Outcast.*

Kennedy, A. L. *Day: A Novel.*

Kent, Kathleen. *The Heretic's Daughter.*

Kneale, Matthew. *English Passengers.*

Lee, Janice Y. K. *The Piano Teacher.*

Matthiessen, Peter. *Shadow Country.*

McEwan, Ian. *Atonement: A Novel.*

McGraw, Erin. *The Seamstress of Hollywood Boulevard.*

Menger-Anderson, Kirsten. *Doctor Olaf van Schuler's Brain.*

Morrison, Toni. *Love: A Novel.*

Morrison, Toni. *A Mercy.*

Pamuk, Orhan. *My Name Is Red.*

Penney, Stef. *The Tenderness of Wolves.*

Roth, Philip. *The Plot Against America.*

Scibona, Salvatore. *The End: A Novel.*

Scott, Joanna. *Follow Me.*

Scott, Joanna Catherine. *The Road from Chapel Hill.*

See, Lisa. *Shanghai Girls.*

Sellers, Susan. *Vanessa & Virginia.*

Sullivan, Faith. *Gardenias: A Novel.*

Tóibín, Colm. *Brooklyn: A Novel.*

Tóibín, Colm. *The Master: A Novel.*

Unsworth, Barry. *Land of Marvels.*

Urrea, Luis Alberto. *The Hummingbird's Daughter.*

Vollmann, William. *Europe Central.*

Weber, Katharine. *Triangle: A Novel.*

Woodward, Gerard. *August.*

Horror

Adrian, Chris. *A Better Angel: Stories.*

Fonseca, Rubem. *The Taker: And Other Stories.*

Ford, Jeffrey. *The Shadow Year.*

Hynes, James. *Kings of Infinite Space.*

Humor

Bennett, Alan. *The Uncommon Reader.*

Buckley, Christopher. *Supreme Courtship.*

Crandell, Doug. *Hairdos of the Mildly Depressed.*

Davis, Lydia. *Samuel Johnson Is Indignant: Stories.*

DuCornet, Rikki. *The One Marvelous Thing.*

Hamilton, Jane. *Laura Rider's Masterpiece.*

Harrison, Jim. *The English Major.*

Johnson, Denis. *Nobody Move.*

Krol, Torsten. *Callisto: A Novel.*

Merullo, Roland. *American Savior: A Novel of Divine Politics.*

Pierre, D. B. C. *Vernon God Little.*

Shteyngart, Gary. *The Russian Debutante's Handbook.*

Taylor, Billy. *Based On the Movie.*

Mystery and Detection

Chabon, Michael. *The Final Solution: A Story of Detection.*

Ferraris, Zoë. *Finding Nouf.*

Hemon, Alaksandar. *The Lazarus Project.*

Horn, Dara. *The World To Come.*

O'Flynn, Catherine. *What Was Lost.*

Price, Richard. *Lush Life.*

Welsh, Irvine. *Crime.*

Romance

Alam, Saher. *The Groom to Have Been.*

Drayson, Nicholas. *A Guide to the Birds of East Africa.*

Hoffman, Alice. *Skylight Confessions.*

Jaffe, Michael Grant. *Whirlwind: A Novel.*

Jordan, Toni. *Addition.*

Niederhoffer, Galt. *The Romantics.*

Waldman, Ayelet. *Love and Other Impossible Pursuits.*

Science Fiction

Beckett, Bernard. *Genesis: A Novel.*

Bender, Aimee. *Willful Creatures: Stories.*

Crace, Jim. *The Pesthouse: A Novel.*

Galchen, Rivka. *Atmospheric Disturbances.*

Hall, Sarah. *Daughters of the North.*

Ishiguro, Kazuo. *Never Let Me Go.*

Kessel, John. *The Baum Plan for Financial Independence.*

Lethem, Jonathan. *Fortress of Solitude.*

McCarthy, Cormac. *The Road.*

Millhauser, Steven. *Dangerous Laughter: Thirteen Stories.*

Mitchell, David. *The Cloud Atlas.*

Morrow, James. *The Philosopher's Apprentice.*

Winterson, Jeannette. *The Stone Gods.*

Suspense

Barker, Pat. *Double Vision.*

Baxter, Charles. *The Soul Thief.*

Carrell, Jennifer Lee. *Interred with Their Bones.*

Choi, Susan. *A Person of Interest.*

Gottlieb, Eli. *Now You See Him.*

Harris, Joanne. *Gentlemen and Players.*

Khadra, Yasmina. *The Attack.*

Lennon, J. Robert. *Castle: A Novel.*

Martínez, Guillermo. *The Book of Murder.*

Mosley, Walter. *Diablerie: A Novel.*

O'Connor, John. *Star of the Sea.*

Rash, Ron. *Serena: A Novel.*

Ruiz Zafón, Carlos. *The Angel's Game.*

Schwartz, Leslie. *Angels Crest.*

Thrillers

Bazell, Josh. *Beat the Reaper.*

Bennett, Ronan. *Zugzwang: A Novel.*

Morris, Mary McGarry. *The Last Secret.*

Senna, Danzy. *Symptomatic.*

Terrell, Heather. *The Map Thief.*

Western

Adamson, Gil. *The Outlander: A Novel.*

Carlson, Ron. *Five Skies.*

Doig, Ivan. *The Whistling Season.*

Haruf, Kent. *Eventide.*

McCarthy, Cormac. *No Country for Old Men.*

Olds, Bruce. *Bucking the Tiger.*

Olmstead, Robert. *Far Bright Star: A Novel.*

Proulx, Annie. *Fine Just the Way It Is: Wyoming Stories 3.*

Women's Fiction

Anam, Tahmima. *A Golden Age*.

Bacon, Charlotte. *Split Estate*.

Baker, Tiffany. *The Little Giant of Aberdeen County*.

Barry, Brunonia. *The Lace Reader*.

Bates, Judy Fong. *Midnight at the Dragon Café*.

Berg, Elizabeth. *Home Safe*.

Berg, Elizabeth. *We Are All Welcome Here*.

Bohjalian, Chris. *Trans-sister Radio*.

Christensen, Kate. *The Great Man*.

Crouch, Katie. *Girls in Trucks: Stories*.

Dubus, Andre, III. *The Garden of Last Days*.

Enright, Anne. *Yesterday's Weather: Stories*.

Fowler, Karen Joy. *Wit's End*.

Glass, Julia. *I See You Everywhere*.

Haigh, Jennifer. *The Condition: A Novel*.

Harris, Joanne. *The Girl with No Shadow*.

Hendricks, Judith Ryan. *The Laws of Harmony*.

Hosseini, Khaled. *A Thousand Splendid Suns*.

Julavits, Heidi. *The Uses of Enchantment*.

Kallos, Stephanie. *Sing Them Home*.

Kingsolver, Barbara. *Prodigal Summer*.

Kogan, Deborah Copaken. *Between Here and April*.

Lipman, Elinor. *The Family Man*.

Lipman, Elinor. *My Latest Grievance*.

Lively, Penelope. *Consequences: A Novel*.

Livesey, Margo. *The House on Fortune Street*.

Long, Kate. *The Bad Mother's Handbook*.

Mapson, Jo-Ann. *The Owl & Moon Café*.

Messud, Claire. *The Emperor's Children: A Novel*.

Miller, Sue. *The Senator's Wife*.

Morton, Kate. *The Forgotten Garden*.

Munro, Alice. *Runaway: Stories*.

O'Dell, Tawni. *Sister Mine*.

Pupek, Jayne. *Tomato Girl*.

Sittenfeld, Curtis. *American Wife*.

Somerville, Patrick. *The Cradle: A Novel*.

Strauss, Darin. *More Than It Hurts You*.

Tucker, Lisa. *The Promised World*.

Tyler, Anne. *Digging to America*.

Viswanathan, Padma. *The Toss of a Lemon*.

Walbert, Kate. *A Short History of Women*.

Wildgen, Michelle. *You're Not You*.

Appendix B

Book Awards

American Library Association Notable Nonfiction Books

History: www.ala.org/ala/rusa/rusaprotools/rusanotable/notablebooks.htm

Lists of Notable Books: www.ala.org/ala/rusa/rusaprotools/rusanotable/thelists/notablebooks.htm

Each year a twelve-member committee from the CODES (Collection Development and Evaluation Section) of the association selects twenty-five titles each of fiction, poetry, and nonfiction that are "very good, very readable, and at times very important." The Notable Books listings have existed, in various forms, since 1944.

Betty Trask Prize

Information: http://www.societyofauthors.org/prizes-grants-and-awards/prizes-for-fiction-and-non-fiction/the_betty_trask_prize/index.html

Awarded annually by the Society of Authors, a nonprofit organization in the United Kingdom (founded to "protect the right and further the interests of authors,") in the name of a reclusive romance novelist, this prize is given to the best first novel written by a Commonwealth citizen under the age of thirty-five.

The Booker/Man Booker Prize

Home page: http://www.themanbookerprize.com/

List of winners: http://www.themanbookerprize.com/prize/archive

The Booker Prize was founded in 1969 by Booker McConnell, Ltd., and was originally known as the Booker-McConnell Prize. In 2002 the Man Group investment company took over sponsorship of the award, although they retained the "Booker" name and founded the Booker Prize Foundation to administer it. It is awarded each year to recognize the best original full-length novel, written by a citizen of either the Commonwealth of Nations or Ireland.

Costa/Whitbread Award

Information: http://www.costabookawards.com/awards/index.aspx

List of winners: http://www.costabookawards.com/awards/previous_winners_archive.aspx

The Costa Book Awards were first awarded starting in 1971 and were known as the Whitbread Prizes. Since 2006, when the Costa Coffee company took over their sponsorship, they have become known as the Costa Awards. They are given in five categories—First Novel, Novel, Biography, Poetry, and Children's Books—and recognize some of "the most enjoyable books of the year by writers based in the UK and Ireland."

The Giller Prize

Information: http://www.scotiabankgillerprize.ca/

Past winners: http://www.scotiabankgillerprize.ca/past_winners.htm

The Scotiabank Giller Prize is awarded annually for the best novel or collection of short fiction written by a Canadian. It was founded in 1994, and in 2005 Scotiabank took over sponsorship of the award, increasing the prize money to $50,000.

The Governor General's Literary Awards

Information: http://www.canadacouncil.ca/prizes/ggla/default.htm

Awarded annually in seven categories (Fiction, Literary Nonfiction, Poetry, Drama, Children's Literature—text, Children's Literature—illustration, and Translation), these awards are given to recognize the best titles published each year in Canada. They are administered by the Canada Council for the Arts and have been awarded since 1936.

The *Guardian* Fiction Prize/Guardian First Book Award

Information: http://www.guardian.co.uk/books/guardianfirstbookaward

The *Guardian* newspaper has sponsored this award since 1963. It was originally awarded to novels that were published in the United Kingdom (by British or Commonwealth authors), but in 1999 the prize was renamed the Guardian First Book Award and can now be awarded to fiction or nonfiction titles. Winners are chosen by a panel of judges who are assembled by the literary editor of the *Guardian*.

The Hawthornden Prize

Information: http://en.wikipedia.org/wiki/Hawthornden_Prize

The Hawthornden Prize is a British literary award given annually to the "best work of imaginative fiction." Although it is most often given to works of fiction, it has also been awarded to poetry, drama, and nonfiction. It was established in 1919.

The International IMPAC Dublin Literary Award

Information: http://www.impacdublinaward.ie/

List of winners: http://www.impacdublinaward.ie/awardarchive.htm

Cosponsored by the Dublin City Council, the municipal government of Dublin City, and the productivity improvement company IMPAC, this award was founded in 1994 and is open to all novels published in English (or English translation). Each year a panel of judges, many of whom are authors themselves, chooses the winner.

The James Tait Black Memorial Prize

Information: http://websiterepository.ed.ac.uk/explore/people/jamestaitblack/

This prize was founded to honor James Tait Black, a partner in the A & C Black publishing firm, and was first given in 1919. To be eligible books must have originated with a British publisher, and the winners are chosen by the Professor of English Literature at the University of Edinburgh in Scotland.

The Kiriyama Prize/ The Kiriyama Pacific Rim Book Prize

Information: http://www.kiriyamaprize.org/

Although the Web site for the Kiriyama Prize notes, at the time of this writing, that the "prize is being restructured," it has been awarded since 1997 to "recognize outstanding books about the Pacific Rim and South Asia that encourage greater mutual understanding of and among the peoples and nations" of the region.

The LAMBDA Literary Awards

About the Awards: http://www.lambdalit.org/lammy.html

Awards Archives: http://www.lambdalit.org/Lammy/lammy_archives.html

Lambda Literary Awards are given annually (and have been since 1988) in twenty categories and recognize the best works of lesbian, gay, bisexual, and transgender literature.

The *Los Angeles Times* Book Awards

Information: http://www.latimes.com/extras/bookprizes/judging.html

List of winners: www.latimes.com/extras/bookprizes/winners.html

The *Los Angeles Times* has distributed a variety of both fiction and nonfiction awards (including biography, current interests, fiction, first fiction, and young adult literature) annually since 1980.

The Miles Franklin Award

Information: http://www.cultureandrecreation.gov.au/articles/milesfranklin/

First awarded in 1957, the Miles Franklin Award is presented annually to the best "published novel or play portraying Australian life in any of its phases." It was created through a bequest by Australian author Stella Maria Sarah Miles Franklin and is currently administered by the Permanent Trustee Co., Ltd., of Sydney, Australia.

The National Book Award

Information: www.nationalbook.org/history.html

List of winners: www.nationalbook.org/nba2007.html

The National Book Award has been awarded since 1950, but the National Book Foundation, which helps to support its choices, was established in 1989 to "raise the cultural appreciation of great writing in America." Each year it names one award winner based on literary merit in the categories of fiction, nonfiction, and poetry.

The National Book Critics Circle Award

Information: http://www.bookcritics.org/

The National Book Critics Circle was founded in 1974 and currently consists of more than 700 active book reviewers. Its board of directors nominates and selects the winners of its annual award in the categories of fiction, general nonfiction, biography/autobiography, poetry, and criticism.

New York Times Notable Books

2007 List: http://www.nytimes.com/2007/12/02/books/review/notable-books-2007.html?_r=1&oref=slogin

At the end of every year the *New York Times* lists the notable fiction, nonfiction, and poetry books that were published during that year, as culled from favorable reviews in *The New York Times Book Review*. (The link provided goes to the most recent list, for 2008; an Internet search of "new york times notable" and any year will retrieve the annual lists.)

The Orange Prize for Fiction and Award for New Writers

Information: http://www.orangeprize.co.uk/home

The Orange Prize for fiction was established in 1996 to recognize high-quality fiction by women authors (and is judged exclusively by women as well). The Orange Award for New Writers was launched in 2005. The award is administered by Booktrust, a United Kingdom charity for promoting literacy, and is sponsored by Orange, a British broadband company.

The PEN/Faulkner Award for Fiction

Information: http://www.penfaulkner.org/awardforfiction.htm

Administered by the PEN/Faulkner Foundation, this prize is given to "honor the best published works of fiction by American authors." It was founded in 1980 and is currently judged annually by a panel of three judges, who are chosen by the directors of the PEN/Faulkner Foundation.

The Prix Goncourt

Information: http://www.britannica.com/EBchecked/topic/477413/Prix-Goncourt

The Prix Goncourt is one of the most important literary awards in France. It was created in 1903, at the same time that the Académie Goncourt, a literary society (the chief duty of which is to award this prize) was founded. The prize is awarded for works of French prose and is announced annually in November.

The Pulitzer Prizes

History of the Pulitzer Prizes and Awards Archives: www.pulitzer.org

Pulitzer Prizes are awarded annually to "distinguished" works of fiction (and nonfiction) and have been awarded since 1917.

The Sapir Prize

Information: http://en.wikipedia.org/wiki/Sapir_Prize

The Sapir Prize recognizes works of fine literature that are published in Israel. It is administered by Israel's state lottery, and the winner is selected each year by a new panel of judges (and announced during Israel's Hebrew Book Week in June). It was first awarded in 2000.

The Whitbread Award. *See* **Costa/Whitbread Award**

Appendix C

Resources

Internet Resources

Ann Arbor Public Library Books Blog
http://www.aadl.org/catalog/books

The Ann Arbor (Michigan) Books Blog is a surprisingly universal and interesting blog recounting book news and linking to numerous award sites and other book and reading-related news. It is frequently updated.

Atlanta Booklover's Blog Booklover's Toolbox
http://atlantareader.wordpress.com/booklovers-toolbox

The Booklover's Toolbox is a helpful listing of Internet resources subdivided by categories, including links to blogs and Web sites about award winners, best-seller lists, book chats, movies based on books, and reading groups. It is maintained by the staff of the Atlanta-Fulton Public Library's Ponce de Leon branch.

Bookbitch
http://www.bookbitch.com/

Bookbitch is a fiction review site that focuses on genre fiction (although a wide variety of mainstream and literary fiction titles are reviewed here as well) and includes reviews written by a number of dedicated readers. It is maintained by Stacy Alesi (she also provides a generous number of the site's reviews), who contributed a chapter on "Reader's Advisory in the Real World" to Libraries Unlimited's *Nonfiction Reader's Advisory*, edited by Robert Burgin.

BookBrowse
http://www.bookbrowse.com

The BookBrowse site allows readers to browse multiple reviews of current and popular books by genre, setting, time period, theme, and publication date. It also provides resources and reading guides for book clubs.

Booklist

http://www.booklistonline.com

Although the majority of the *Booklist* reviews available on this site can be accessed by subscribers only, this site also offers several books and reading blogs and other features that will be useful to all readers' advisors striving to keep on top of title awareness and book news. It also allows the user to browse the entire current issue of *Booklist* online.

Booklist Center

http://home.comcast.net/~dwtaylor1

The Booklist Center site boasts that it offers the "Web's Largest Collection of Book Lists," and currently at 346 lists in 82 categories, it may deserve that distinction. Readers may browse lists by a wide variety of both fiction and nonfiction categories, such as Biography, Business, Fantasy Fiction, Humor, Speculative Fiction, and Westerns.

Bookninja

http://www.bookninja.com

Canada's premiere books blog, written by poet and author George Murray, offers a plethora of book reviews and news link, as well as timely commentary on the news. Along with Bookslut and Elegant Variation, it is a must-read for any advisor hoping to learn more about mainstream—and particularly literary—authors and titles.

Bookreporter.com

http://www.bookreporter.com

Bookreporter.com is jam-packed with information about books, from award lists to reviews to reading group guides, not to mention a very helpful "Books to Movies" page that discusses the latest movie adaptation news.

Bookslut

http://www.bookslut.com

BookSlut features reviews of both fiction and nonfiction books, updated monthly. The site also has numerous columns about books and interviews with authors, as well as a fantastic and frequently updated book news blog at www.bookslut.com/blog/

Citizen Reader

http://www.citizenreader.com

I'm not a disinterested party in this Web site; at this blog, I review primarily nonfiction books, but lately an equal number of fiction titles have been creeping in. I don't accept either review copies or advertising, so be warned: when I don't like a book, I don't feel compelled to say that I do. My reviews may not be the best in town, but I can promise you they're the most heartfelt. Frequently I also host online book clubs, in which we discuss books in the blog comments, and we also have some great discussions about the nature of reading and who reads what.

Curled Up with a Good Book

http://www.curledup.com

The Curled Up with a Good Book site offers both fiction and nonfiction reviews and comprehensive author interviews. It is also an attractive site that features graphics of each book cover and a 1- to 5-star rating system. Many of the nonfiction books covered are more specific and scholarly ones that aren't often reviewed at other sites.

Dear Reader

http://www.dearreader.com

Dear Reader is a great and personable site at which users can sign up to receive daily excerpts of fiction (and other) titles through e-mail.

The Early Word

http://www.earlyword.com

Featuring "news for collection development and readers advisory librarians," this title-awareness site offers news about forthcoming fiction and nonfiction titles, as well as publishing and book world news and commentary.

The Elegant Variation

http://marksarvas.blogs.com/elegvar/

The Elegant Variation, authored by Mark Sarvas (who has himself written a novel titled *Harry, Revised*), offers all manner of book and entertainment news and links. It also is a great resource for thumbnail reviews of new books.

Elmhurst Public Library (Illinois) booklists

http://www.elmhurst.lib.il.us/booklist

Most of the Elmhurst Public Library lists are fiction only, but some also include nonfiction titles.

Fiction_L

http://www.webrary.org/rs/Flmenu.html

Fiction_L is a listserv devoted to readers' advisory and fiction (although the collective brain is great at answering nonfiction questions as well). The Morton Grove Public Library site (where Fiction_L is archived) also provides booklists periodically culled from the listserv.

Fimoculous

http://www.fimoculous.com

This blog offers multiple thoughts on books (and compiles very helpful "Best of" literary lists at the end of the year), but is even more interesting for its other entertainment news and media links.

Gnooks,

http://gnooks.com

Enter an author you like, and Gnooks will provide a visual map of similar authors, using data provided from its visitors, many of whom must be avid readers, who take the time to fill out quick interest surveys and indicate similar authors they enjoy.

GoodReads
http://www.goodreads.com

GoodReads is another social networking and book site that allows users to add books they own or enjoy to their own "libraries," which they can then share with other friends or display on their own blogs or Web sites. It also lets users find books and "book shelves" that other readers have created, such as "chick lit" and "guilty pleasures," and can be a lot of fun for serendipitous browsing.

Harford County Public Library (Md.) Readers Place
http://www.hcplonline.info/readers/recommendedbooks.html

This nice service provides new fiction and nonfiction reviews, as well as a collection of links to Web sites for book lovers.

IndieBound
http://www.indiebound.org

Previously known as the Book Sense program for independent booksellers, IndieBound provides resources to help readers find such bookstores in their areas, as well as lists of "indie bestsellers" from smaller and independent booksellers nationwide. Also check out their smokin' hot T-shirts, which feature the tagline "Eat, Sleep, Read."

LibraryThing
http://www.librarything.com

LibraryThing is a social networking site that lets users catalog their own book collections, write book reviews, provide the "tags" they think best describe those books, and see what their friends and other members are reading and have read. Even if you don't want to join the site, it can be illuminating to read its users' reviews and to enter a title to see what readers who have catalogued that title also own or have catalogued (as a relational database, it's not perfect; just like Amazon, its simple suggestions can't be relied upon as read-alikes, but they are sometimes illuminating). Another fun tool to use here is the "Unsuggester" (at www.librarything.com/unsuggester), which lets users enter a title and "unsuggests" books that are completely "unsimilar" to it.

The Millions
http://www.themillions.com

The Millions is one of the most venerable litblogs out there and has been publishing online since 2003. It features book reviews, book news, and articles on publishing, reading, and all subjects literary. It is edited by C. Max Magee and hosts an impressive lineup of contributors and feature writers.

Morton Grove Public Library Webrary
http://www.webrary.org/rs/bibmenu.html

As noted in the Fiction_L annotation, this site also features nonfiction booklists created by Morton Grove librarians and Fiction_L contributors.

National Public Radio Books Page

http://www.npr.org/books/

The National Public Radio site offers book recommendations, book reviews, and author information.

New York Times best seller lists

http://www.nytimes.com/pages/books/bestseller/ index.html

This site offers current best seller lists, broken down into categories such as hardcover fiction and nonfiction, paperback trade fiction, and graphic books.

Overbooked

http://www.overbooked.org

Overbooked provides lists of books that have received starred reviews in any or all of the higher profile review publications, including *Library Journal*, *Booklist*, *Publishers Weekly*, and *Kirkus*. Its focus is primarily fiction titles, but it also includes nonfiction booklists.

The Reader's Advisor Online Blog

http://www.readersadvisoronline.com/blog

Although the Reader's Advisor Online is a subscription database based on all of the Libraries Unlimited titles in the Genreflecting and Real Stories series, the blog is freely available and caters to readers' advisors, library staff, and readers alike. Edited by Cynthia Orr, it features weekly lists of fiction and nonfiction best sellers, new titles, and "under the radar" titles, as well as a wide variety of articles about books, publishing trends, and readers' advisory tips and tricks.

Reader's Club Fiction Book Reviews

http://www.plcmc.org/readers_club/category.asp?cat=1

The Reader's Club Web site offers to be "your guide to enjoyable books," and seeks to fulfill that promise by offering one-paragraph reviews of fiction and nonfiction titles. It also provides lists of reading resources, author interviews, and patron-written reviews. The site is maintained by a group of librarians in North Carolina.

Reading Group Choices

http://www.readinggroupchoices.com

Reading Group Guides

http://www.readinggroupguides.com

Both these reading group sites provide numerous and thoughtful questions for book discussions of fiction and nonfiction titles.

The Rumpus

http://therumpus.net/

The Rumpus is an online magazine that is "focused on culture." As such, it offers frequent links to book news, reviews, and other articles of interest to readers and culture (and not just "pop culture," mind) junkies.

Shelfari

http://www.shelfari.com

Shelfari is a social networking site that allows users to build their own libraries (entering books they've read), assign books the tags they want to, and see their friends' libraries and reading lists. If you don't want to join, it also allows you to browse book lists organized according to its users' tags and subjects, as well as those popular books that receive the most positive reviews.

Waterboro Public Library (Maine)

http://www.waterborolibrary.org/bklistnonf.htm

The Waterboro Public Library site offers a collection of both fiction and nonfiction booklists from various libraries.

Subscription Databases

Books and Authors

Fiction/Nonfiction Connection

NoveList

Reader's Advisor Online

Print Resources

Review Journals

Booklist

Bookmarks Magazine

Kirkus Reviews

Library Journal

The London Book Review

The New York Times Book Review

The New York Times Review of Books

Publishers Weekly

Reading about Reading

Adams, Lisa, and John Heath. *Why We Read What We Read: A Delightfully Opinionated Journey Through Contemporary Bestsellers*. Sourcebooks, 2007.

Booker, Christopher. *The Seven Basic Plots: Why We Tell Stories*. Continuum, 2004.

Brottman, Mikita. *The Solitary Vice: Against Reading*. Counterpoint, 2008.

Cyr, Ann-Marie. *Something to Talk About: Creative Booktalking for Adults*. Scarecrow Press, 2006.

Darnton, Robert. *The Case for Books: Past, Present, and Future*. PublicAffairs, 2009.

Edmundson, Mark. *Why Read?* Bloomsbury, 2004.

Forster, E. M. *Aspects of the Novel*. Harcourt, Brace, 1927.

Miller, Laura J. *Reluctant Capitalists: Bookselling and the Culture of Consumption*. University of Chicago Press, 2006.

Rooney, Kathleen. *Reading with Oprah: The Book Club That Changed America*. State University of New York Press, 2004.

Smiley, Jane. *Thirteen Ways of Looking at a Novel*. Knopf, 2005.

Striphas, Theodore G. *The Late Age of Print: Everyday Book Culture from Consumerism to Control*. Columbia University Press, 2009.

Reading Guides

Bosman, Ellen, John P. Bradford, and Robert Ridinger. *Gay, Lesbian, Bisexual, and Transgendered Literature*. Libraries Unlimited, 2008.

Bridges, Karl. *100 Great American Novels You've (Probably) Never Read*. Libraries Unlimited, 2007.

Dawson, Alma, and Connie Van Fleet. *African American Literature: A Guide to Reading Interests*. Libraries Unlimited, 2004.

Drew, Bernard A. *100 Most Popular African American Authors: Biographical Sketches and Bibliographies*. Libraries Unlimited, 2006.

Frolund, Tina. *Genrefied Classics: A Guide to Reading Interests in Classic Literature*. Libraries Unlimited, 2006.

Herald, Diana Tixier, and Wayne Wiegand. *Genreflecting: A Guide to Popular Reading Interests, Sixth Edition*. Libraries Unlimited, 2005.

Hooper, Brad. *Read On . . . Historical Fiction: Reading Lists for Every Taste*. Libraries Unlimited, 2006.

Hooper, Brad. *The Short Story Readers' Advisory: A Guide to the Best*. ALA Editions, 2000.

Johnson, Sarah L. *Historical Fiction: A Guide to the Genre*. Libraries Unlimited, 2005.

Johnson, Sarah L. *Historical Fiction II: A Guide to the Genre*. Libraries Unlimited, 2009.

Martínez, Sara. *Latino Literature: A Guide to Reading Interests*. Libraries Unlimited, 2009.

Pearl, Nancy. *Book Lust*. Sasquatch Books, 2003.

Pearl, Nancy. *More Book Lust*. Sasquatch Books, 2005.

Pearl, Nancy. *Now Read This II: A Guide to Mainstream Fiction, 1900–2001*. Libraries Unlimited, 2002.

Pearl, Nancy, with Martha Knappe and Chris Higashi. *Now Read This: A Guide to Mainstream Fiction, 1978–1998*. Libraries Unlimited, 1999.

Reisner, Rosalind. *Jewish American Literature: A Guide to Reading Interests*. Libraries Unlimited, 2004.

Saricks, Joyce G. *The Readers' Advisory Guide to Genre Fiction, Second Edition*. ALA Editions, 2009.

Smith, Sharron, and Maureen O'Connor. *Canadian Fiction: A Guide to Reading Interests*. Libraries Unlimited, 2005.

Trupe, Alice. *Thematic Guide to Young Adult Literature*. Greenwood, 2006.

Vnuk, Rebecca. *Read On . . . Women's Fiction*. Libraries Unlimited, 2009.

Vnuk, Rebecca. *Women's Fiction Authors: A Research Guide*. Libraries Unlimited, 2009.

Readers' Advisory

Moyer, Jessica E. *Research-Based Readers' Advisory*. ALA Editions, 2008.

Ross, Catherine Sheldrick, Lynne McKechnie, and Paulette M. Rothbauer. *Reading Matters: What the Research Reveals about Reading, Libraries, and Community*. Libraries Unlimited, 2005.

Saricks, Joyce G. *Readers' Advisory Service in the Public Library, Third Edition*. ALA Editions, 2005.

Shearer, Kenneth D., and Robert Burgin. *The Readers' Advisor's Companion*. Libraries Unlimited, 2002.

Appendix D

How to Create a Dynamic Book Club

Nancy Pearl

Book clubs are not a new idea in the United States. The Great Books Reading and Discussion programs have been popular with adult readers since their inception in 1947. What is new is a widespread interest in developing reading communities in a variety of shapes and formats. The Washington Center for the Book at the Seattle Public Library annually presents "If All of Seattle Read the Same Book," during which book groups throughout the Puget Sound area read and discuss the same book, then come together over three days to meet and talk to the author. Interested readers can join in a book discussion group online (a good one is Booktalk.org, at www.booktalk.org). Special interest reading groups online can be found at www.readinggroupsonline.com. Readers may watch Oprah's Book Club on television or participate in National Public Radio's once-a-month Book Club of the Air. There are book groups that meet at public libraries, bookstores, and literary and community centers. Or you can start a book club of your own that meets at the homes of friends and neighbors.

Although many people find that reading is a totally pleasurable solitary activity and have no desire to talk about what they read in a structured setting, the growing popularity of book groups makes it clear many readers find that their appreciation of, pleasure in, and understanding of a book are broadened and deepened through discussion.

Although *Now Read This* and *Now Read This II* (and *Now Read This III*) are not guides to setting up and running a book group (I've included a brief list of such guides at the end of this appendix), they can help in selecting books for your group. Nearly every book included in the *Now Read This* guides is a fine choices for a book discussion, but the ones designated "Book Groups" make for an especially interesting discussion.

That being said, here are some of the more basic issues to keep in mind when you're beginning, or reinvigorating, a book group.

Choosing a Book to Read

Those who have been part of an unsuccessful book group will agree that choosing the right books to discuss is one of the most difficult (and enjoyable) aspects of a successful book club.

There are several issues to keep in mind when you're choosing books for your group. It's important to realize that not every member of a group is going to like every book that's discussed. Book groups are based on the premise that reading likes and dislikes are idiosyncratic. Everyone in a group may read exactly the same book, with identical covers and identical pagination, but in fact, each member is reading a different book. Each person brings to his or her reading of a book a unique history with a unique set of memories and influences. Each person is in a different place in his or her life when reading the book. And all of those differences—as subtle or as obvious as they might be—greatly influence how and why certain people may like or dislike any particular book. Keep in mind that these differences are often what make for an exciting discussion!

People often wonder what makes a book good for a discussion. Although it's true that sometimes a book that one group finds totally stimulating is a total dud for another group, in general there are books that lead to good discussions and books that don't.

I find it helpful to think of book discussions this way: When you're talking about a book, what you're really talking about is everything that the author hasn't said; in effect, all that white space on the printed page. Because of this, books that are plot-driven (that is, most mysteries, Westerns, and romances; some science fiction/fantasy novels; and many mainstream novels) often don't make good choices for discussion. In these books, the author spells out everything for the reader, the plot predicaments are neatly tied up, and character development is subordinate to the story. There's little to say except, "I loved (or hated) the book," or "Wasn't that interesting?"

The best books for discussion are those with three-dimensional characters who are forced to make difficult choices, under difficult situations. Why a character behaved as he or she did is often a fruitful question to raise with the group. For example, in Ward Just's *A Dangerous Friend*, why was Sydney so determined to rescue the captured American pilot? In Graham Greene's *The End of the Affair*, why didn't Sarah leave her husband? In Edith Wharton's *The Age of Innocence*, why, at the end of the novel, does Archer refuse to see Ellen? In Eudora Welty's *The Optimist's Daughter*, why did Judge McKelva marry Fay, a woman as different from his first wife as anyone could be?

Other good choices are books with ambiguous endings, where the outcome of the novel is not crystal clear. There is certainly no general consensus about what happens at the end of Tim O'Brien's *In the Lake of the Woods*, James McManus's *Going to the Sun*, Wallace Stegner's *The Angle of Repose*, James Buchan's *The Persian Bride*, Tim Winton's *The Riders*, and Jon Cohen's *The Man in the Window*.

In addition, books that relate to the readers' own experiences (a mothers-and-daughters group might enjoy discussing Amy Tan's *The Joy Luck Club*) and books that contain controversial ideas are generally good springboards for discussion.

There are also several pairs of books that make good discussions. Although some groups discuss these books in the same meeting, the busy schedules of most book group participants may make it better to read and discuss these in successive months. Good pairs include

- Molly Gloss's *Wild Life* and Robert Michael Pyle's *Where Bigfoot Walks: Crossing the Dark Divide*

- Michael Cunningham's *The Hours* and Virginia Woolf's *Mrs. Dalloway*

- Ward Just's *A Dangerous Friend* and Graham Greene's *The Quiet American*

- E. Annie Proulx's *Close Range*, Kent Haruf's *Plainsong*, and Tim Egan's *Lasso the Wind*—a good triple-header.

A five-month reading blitz, such as on Africa and consisting of Barbara Kingsolver's *The Poisonwood Bible*, Joseph Conrad's *Heart of Darkness*, Ronan Bennett's *The Catastrophist*, Adam Hochchild's *King Leopold's Ghost*, and Ann Jones's *Looking for Lovedu*, is also a way to ensure good discussions, as each month's conversation will build on the books read in the previous months. Mixing nonfiction and fiction together in these groups of books can result in wonderful discussions.

Some books seem to have been written for the benefit of book groups. These are the books that you just can't stop talking about, books that raise so many issues that conversation is nonstop. It's difficult to see how a discussion about Andre Dubus III's *House of Sand and Fog*, Ernest Gaines's *A Lesson Before Dying*, Russell Banks's *The Sweet Hereafter*, Barbara Kingsolver's *The Poisonwood Bible*, or Tim O'Brien's *In the Lake of the Woods* can help but be successful. No duds here, I promise you!

Discussing the Book

Although many groups don't see the necessity for a group leader (either a member of the group or a paid facilitator), my experience has been that someone needs to take responsibility for keeping the discussion flowing and on track and to make sure that everyone who wants to has a chance to offer his or her opinion. One way to make this happen is to designate a leader (perhaps rotating with each meeting) whose job it is to come up with some questions to get the discussion started and keep it going. Another option is for each group member to take the responsibility of coming to the meeting with one discussion question about the book. Some groups find it useful to have the leader also bring information about the author along with reviews or articles about the book.

The Internet has made a huge difference in the ease with which book group members can access information about specific books and authors. Most publishers, as well as other institutions and organizations who regularly create reading group discussion guides, have made them available on their Web sites. Simon & Schuster (www.simonsays.com), HarperCollins (http://www.harpercollins.com/Readers/reading Groups.aspx), and Random House (www.randomhouse.com/vintage/read/) are particularly active in producing reader's guides for their books. Ballantine Books binds in a reader's guide in their most popular book club books.

Although there are questions specific to particular books, there are also some general questions that can be asked about any work of fiction.

- How does the title relate to the book?

- What is the theme of the book?

- Are the characters believable? Did you understand why they behaved as they did?

- Were all the characters equally well developed?

- Consider the structure of the book. Did the author make use of flashbacks? Was the book written in the first person? From multiple points of view? Why did the author choose to present the plot this way?

- Can you imagine an ending other than the one the author wrote?

- What if the book were written from another character's point of view—what would be different, and what would be the same?

Book Group Guides

Some of my favorite guides to book groups are included in the following list. Although there is, of course, some duplication in the discussions of the nuts and bolts of successful book groups, each of these books offers valuable insights and suggestions for choosing books and ensuring positive experiences for everyone in the group.

- Shireen Dodson, *The Mother-Daughter Book Club: How Ten Busy Mothers and Their Daughters Came Together to Talk, Laugh, and Learn Through Their Love of Reading* (HarperPerennial, 1997)

- Elisabeth Ellington, *A Year of Reading: A Month-by-Month Guide to Classics and Crowd-Pleasers for You and Your Book Group* (Sourcebooks, 2002)

- Monique Greenwood, Lynda Johnson, and Tracy Mitchell-Brown, *The Go on Girl! Book Club Guide for Reading Groups* (Hyperion, 1999)

- Rachel Jacobsohn, *The Reading Group Handbook: Everything You Need to Know to Start Your Own Bookclub* (Hyperion, 1998)

- David Laskin and Holly Hughes, *The Reading Group Book* (Plume, 1995)

- Diana Loevy, *The Book Club Companion: A Comprehensive Guide to the Reading Group Experience* (Berkley Trade, 2006)

- Victoria Golden McMains, *The Reader's Choice: 200 Book Club Favorites* (Morrow, 2000)

- Pat Neblett, *Circles of Sisterhood: A Book Discussion Group Guide for Women of Color* (Harlem River Press, 1996)

- Mickey Pearlman, *What to Read: The Essential Guide for Reading Group Members and Other Book Lovers* (HarperPerennial, 1999)

- Rollene Saal, *The New York Public Library Guide to Reading Groups* (Crown, 1995)

- Patrick Sauer, *The Complete Idiot's Guide to Starting a Reading Group* (Alpha Books, 2000)

- Ellen Slezak, *The Book Group Book.* 3rd ed. (Chicago Review Press, 2000)

- Lauren Zina John, *Running Book Group Discussions: A How-to-Do-It Manual* (Neal-Schuman Publishers, 2006)

Author/Title Index

Note: Page numbers in **boldface** indicate main entries.

Aaron, Approximately, 228
Abagnale, Frank, Jr., 18, 155
Abbey, Edward, 166
Abbott, Shirley, **1–2**, 172
Abide with Me, 168, 177
Aboulela, Leila, 99, 140
About a Boy, 34, 140, 160
About Alice, 106
About Grace, 17
About My Sisters, 65, 151
Abstinence Teacher, The, 49, **84**, 106, 137, 148, 167, 173, 200, 238, 256
Absurdistan, 220, 255
Abu-Jaber, Diana, 19, 43, 253
Abundance of Katherines, An, 33, 157
Abyssinian Chronicles, 32
Accident, The, 254
Accidental, The, 255
Accidental Tourist, The, 102, 118
Accidents in the Home, 45, 104, 132
Achebe, Chinua, 222, 243
Acid Row, 95
Ackerman, Diane, 238
Ackroyd, Peter, 42, 121
Across a Hundred Mountains, 42
Across the Wire: Life and Hard Times on the Mexican Border, 42
Act of Faith, 88
Acts of God, 245
Acts of Love on Indigo Road, 2
Adams, Carrie, 93
Adams, Lorraine, 7
Adams, Richard, 171
Adamson, Gil, 21, 69, 86, **194**, 210, 249
Adamson, Joy, 133
Addition, 23, **143–144**
Adiga, Aravind, 34, **47–48**, 119, 129, 241
Admission (Korelitz), 74, 114, 134, 143, **148–149**, 163, 172
Admissions, 65
Adrian, Chris, 75, 81, **194**
Adventures of Augie March, The, 170, 219
Adventures of Huckleberry Finn, The, 116

Adventures of Kavalier and Clay, The, 125
Adventuress, The, 163
Affinity, 94
Affliction, 103
After Dark, 253
After Long Silence, 109
After Nature, 253
After Such Knowledge: Memory, History, and the Legacy of the Holocaust, 109, 219
After the Plague, 110
Against Joie de Vivre, 170, 231, 252
Against the Day, 215
Agarwal, Shilpa, **98**
Age of American Unreason, The, 209
Age of Innocence, The, 98, 231
Age of Iron, The, 103
Age of Shiva, The, **178**
Agee, James, 259
Agee, Jonis, **2**, 140
Aguero Sisters, The, 26, 60
Ahmedi, Farah, 20
Ain't Nobody's Business If I Do, 166
Air, 40, 66
Air Between Us, The, 24
Air We Breathe, The, 42
Aisha, 39
Akpan, Uwem, 26, 222
Alam, Saher, 51, **98**, 119, 231
Alameddine, Rabih, **48**, 233
Albert, Elisa, 99, 128, 252
Alberto, Eliseo, 87
Albion's Story, 21
Albom, Mitch, 18
Alcalá, Kathleen, 13
Alchemist, The, 253
Alchemy of Mind, An, 238
Alentejo Blue, 49
Alexander, Robert, 53, 155
Alexie, Sherman, 5, 200, 260
Alfred and Emily, 38, 103, 105, 216
Algren, Nelson, 123, 219, 220
Ali, Monica, **48–49**, 98, **99**, 116, 119, 140
Ali, Tariq, 83

Alibek, Ken, 53
Alice Springs, 232
Alison, Jane, 108, 191
Alive: The Story of the Andes Survivors, 84
All About Lulu, 57, **126**, 239, 249, 258
All Aunt Hagar's Children, 70, 165
All Creatures Great and Small, 133
All Flesh Is Grass, 28
*All God's Children: Inside the Dark and
     Violent World of Street Families,* 199
All Other Nights, 68
All Over but the Shoutin', 179, 181, 187
All Over Creation, 172
All Quiet on the Orient Express, 212, 214, 222
All Quiet on the Western Front, 28, 105
All Rivers Flow to the Sea, 157
*All Shall Be Well and All Shall Be Well and
     All Manner of Things Shall Be Well,*
     197
All Souls, 99, 184, 258
All That Matters, **12**, 51
All That Road Going, 23, 34, **241**
All the Living, 24, 175, **241–242**
All the Names, 3
All the Pretty Horses, 36, 233, 234
All the Sad Young Literary Men, **128**
Allen, Sarah Addison, 98
Allende, Isabel, 8, 13, 42, 81, 98, 149, 200,
     254, 256
Allingham, Margery, 203
Allison, Karen Hubert, 156
Almost Heaven, 259
Almost No Memory, 206
Almost Perfect Moment, An, 152
Aloft, 7, 117, **151**, 232
Along Came Mary, 156
*Alphabetical Life, An: Living It Up in the
     World of Books,* 138, 214
Already Dead: A California Gothic, 70, 223
Alternadad, 118, 168
Alternatives to Sex, 24
Alva & Irva: The Twins Who Saved a City,
     163, **202–203**
Alvarez, Julia, 3, 13, 42, 60, **99–100**, 103,
     130, 208
Alvarez, Walter, 53
Always Outnumbered, Always Outgunned, 81
Amateur Marriage, The, 112, 120, 153
*Amazing Adventures of Kavalier and Clay,
     The,* 89, 203, 204, 208, 212, 213, 229,
     230
Amazon Extreme, 83

Ambassador of the Dead, 237
Amber Room, The (Berry), 92
*Amber Room, The: The Fate of the World's
     Greatest Lost Treasure,* 68
Amber Spyglass, The, 52
*Ambling into History: The Unlikely Odyssey of
     George W. Bush,* 174
Ambulance Girl, 57
America by Land, 35
*American Chica: Two Worlds, One
     Childhood,* 43, 146
American Cookery, 224
American Fictions, 260
American Nerd: The Story of My People, 160
American Psycho, 82, 176, 249
American Purgatorio, 218, 241
American Savior: A Novel of Divine Politics,
     79
American Wife, 160, 166, **174**
American Woman, 61, 103, 134, 191
Ames, Greg, **2–3**, 107, 128
Ames, Jonathan, 2–3
Amick, Steve, 178
Amidon, Stephen, **49**
Amigoland, 12
Amirrezvani, Anita, 19
Amis, Martin, 90, 239
Amnesia Moon, 230, 241
Among the Missing, 81, 109, 198, 201
Amongst Women, 157
Amsterdam, 4, 166, 174, 190, 197, 235, 247
Amulet, 200
Amulet of Samarkand, The, 52
Amy and Isabelle, 131, 177, 184, 224
Anam, Tahmima, **100**, 129
*Anatomist, The: A True Story of Gray's
     Anatomy,* 237
Anderson, M. T., 61
Anderson, Scott, **195**
Anderson, Sherwood, 14, 170
Anderson-Dargatz, Gail, **3**
Andy Catlett: Early Travels, **9**, 10
Angela's Ashes, 41, 79, 211, 225
Angels, 70
Angels and Demons, 59
Angels Crest, **89**
Angel's Game, The, 78, **87**
Angle of Repose, 24, 86, 187, 218, 242
Angus, Colin, 83, 92
Anil's Ghost, 15, 56, 247
Animal Acts, 255
Animal Dreams, 25, 147

Animal, Vegetable, Miracle: A Year of Food Life, 6, 10, 25, 147
Animals in Translation, 132
Animals Make Us Human, 132
Annie Dunne, 198, 258
Annunciation of Francesa Dunn, The, 134
Another Bullshit Night in Suck City, 86, 127, 168
Ansay, A. Manette, 24, 144, 164
Anshaw, Carol, 120
Answer Is Always Yes, The, 107, **126–127,** 179–180, 199
Antelope Wife, The, 126, 220
Antelope's Strategy, The: Living in Rwanda after the Genocide, 198
Anthills of the Savannah, 222
Anthropologist on Mars, An, 250
Antipodes, 232
Antunes, Antonio Lobo, **3,** 41
Any Human Heart, **109–110**
Any Known Blood, 68, 188, 243
Apex Hides the Hurt, 188
Apologize, Apologize!, 137, **145**
Apologizing to Dogs, 22, 117
April 1917, 237
April & Oliver, 126
Arabian Nights and Days, 253
Arana, Marie, 43, 146
Arax, Mark, 30
Arc of Justice: A Saga of Race, Civil Rights, and Murder in the Jazz Age, 199
Arctic Dreams: Imagination and Desire in a Northern Landscape, 10
Are You Experienced?, 179
Are You Somebody? The Accidental Memoir of a Dublin Woman, 212
Arenas, Reinaldo, 26, 124, 208
Argall, 259
Aridjis, Chloe, **4**
Arlington Park, **117–118,** 144, 148
Armadillo, 110
Armitage, Simon, 60
Armstrong, Heather, 118, 168
Arranged Marriage, 119
Arsonist's Guide to Writers' Homes in New England, An, 49, **61–62**
Art & Lies, 95
Art of Mending, The, 55, 108
Art of Political Murder, The: Who Killed the Bishop?, 87, 130
Art of Racing in the Rain, The, 133
Artemis Fowl, 159

Artemisia, 121, 202
Arthur & George, **105,** 197
Artist of the Floating World, An, 221
As Nature Made Him: The Boy Who Was Raised as a Girl, 55
Ascension, 20
Ashland, 194
Aslam, Nadeem, 20, 34, 99, **100–101,** 141, 145
Assault, The, 115
Astonishing Life of Octavian Nothing, Traitor to the Nation, The, 61
At Home in Mitford, 9
At Home in the World, 120
At Play in the Fields of the Lord, 29
At Weddings and Wakes, 211
Atet, A.D., 232
Atkinson, Kate, 65, 176, 183
Atlas of Unknowns, 119, **142–143,** 173
Atmospheric Disturbances, 125, 128, 211, **215,** 234, 249
Atomic America, 183
Atonement, 130, 153, 174, 197, 231, **235,** 236, 247
Attack, The, **72,** 141, 145
Attenberg, Jami, **101**
Atwood, Margaret, 52, 66, 80, 95, 177, 221, 234, 243
August, **45,** 196
August 1914: The Red Wheel, 237
Austen, Jane, 226
Auster, Paul, **49–50,** 144, **195–196**
Austerlitz, **253–254**
Austin, Mary, 10
Austin, Paul, 194
Autobiography of a Face, 99, 245
Autobiography of a Family Photo, 166
Autobiography of Malcolm X, The, 5, 188
Autobiography of My Mother, The, 222
Averill, Thomas Fox, **4–5**
Aw, Tash, 249
Away (Bloom), 21, 31, 37, 40, 41, **109,** 155, 174
Away (Urquhart), 21, 109, 185
Azzopardi, Trezza, 7

Babel Tower, 113, 247
Baby Tree, The, 31
Bachelor Boys, 179
Back of Beyond, The: Travels to the Wild Places of the Earth, 39, 93
Back Roads, 164

Back When We Were Grownups, 18, 112, 127, 163, 184
Bacon, Charlotte, 81, **101–102**, 108, 111, 122
Bad Behavior, 214
Bad Boy, 85
Bad Dirt, 14, 36
Bad Girl, The, **185**
Bad Girl Creek, 156
Bad Habits: A Love Story, 57
Bad Monkeys, 52, 212
Bad Mother: A Chronicle of Maternal Crimes, Minor Calamities, and Occasional Moments of Grace, 93, 154
Bad Mother's Handbook, The, 132, **153–154**
Baghdad without a Map, 56
Bailey, Blake, 121
Baker, Kevin, **5**, 216, 253
Baker, Tiffany, **102–103**, 115, 144, 168, 169
Baker Towers, 133
Baker's Apprentice, The, 138, 156
Bakopoulos, Dean, 42–43
Baldacci, David, 63
Balkan Express, The: Fragments from the Other Side of the War, 121
Ball, Edward, 32, 70
Bananas: How the United Fruit Company Changed the World, 26
bandele, asha, 130
Banishing Verona, 231
Bank, Melissa, 14, 143
Banks, Iain, 33, 45, 160
Banks, Russell, **103**, 216, 250
Banville, John, 191, **196**, 198
Barakat, Ibtisam, 72
Barber, Charles, 96
Barbery, Muriel, **103–104**, 177, 218
Barker, Nicola, 114, **196–197**, 200
Barker, Pat, 10, 101, **104–105**, 158, 185, 204, 225
Barkley, Charles, 30
Barnes, Jonathan, 131
Barnes, Julian, **105**, **197**, 232, 236, 252
Barnes, Kim, 3, **5–6**, 11, 102, 146, 167, 168, 223, 242
Barnum Museum, The, 240
Barracks, The, 157
Barrett, Andrea, 42
Barrico, Alessandro, **197–198**
Barrowcliff, Mark, 160
Barrows, Annie, 15, **37–38**, 153, 177, 178, 251
Barry, Brunonia, 65, 71, **105–106**, 134, 139, 150

Barry, Sebastian, 33, 181, **198**, 211, 218, 228, 258
Barry, Susan, 53
Barth, John, 61
Barthelme, Frederick, **6–7**, 44, 69, 158, 171, 201, 207
Baruth, Philip, **50**, 76, 82, 105, 113
Based on the Movie, **180**
Bass Cathedral, **232**
Bass, Rick, 11, 17, 35
Bates, Judy Fong, 12, **50–51**, 150, 173
Bauer, Douglas, 259
Bauer, Joan, 43, 104
Baum, Dan, 7, 44
Baum Plan for Financial Independence, The, 198, 201, 211, 216, **226**
Bausch, Richard, **51**, 253
Baxter, Charles, 17, **106–107**, 122, 127, 214, 225
Bay of Angels, The, 112
Bayley, John, 196
Bazell, Josh, **51–52**, 62, 73, 202, 213, 255
Beach, The, 82, 158
Beachcombing for a Shipwrecked God, 117
Beachy, Kyle, 2, 16, **107**, 128, 147, 162
Beah, Ishmael, 20, 116, 222
Beals, Melba Pattillo, 177
Bean Trees, The, 25, 138, 147, 156, 189
Bear Comes Home, The, 232
Beast God Forgot to Invent, The, 22
Beasts of No Nation, **221–222**
Beat the Reaper, **51–52**, 62, 73, 202, 213, 255
Beattie, Ann, 214
Beaufort, **27–28**
Beautiful Blue Death, A, 105
Beautiful Boy: A Father's Journey Through His Son's Meth Addiction, 127
Beautiful Children, 20, 29, 165, **199**, 200, 248
Beautiful Dreamer, 40, 116, **199**
Beauty and Sadness, 245
Because They Wanted To, 75, 214
Bechdel, Alison, 120, 239
Beckett, Bernard, **52**, 80
Bedouin Hornbook, 232
Bedroom Secrets of the Master Chefs, The, 33
Beekeeper's Apprentice, The, 105, 203
Beemer, 77
Beet Queen, The, 126, 250
Beethoven Was One-Sixteenth Black: And Other Stories, **216**
Before Night Falls, 124, 208
Before We Were Free, 100, 208

Before You Know Kindness, 55
Beggar Maid, The, 252
Beginner's Greek, 145, 153
Behind the Scenes at the Museum, 183
Behindlings, 197
Beijing Coma, 217
Being Dead, 62, 194, 237
Bel Canto, 36, 63, 166
Believers (Baxter), 17, 106
Believers, The (Heller), 101, 108, **137**, 141,
        145, 174, 191, 204
Bellow, Saul, 170, 219, 236
Belong to Me, 84, 173
Beloved, 216, 242, 243
Ben Jelloun, Tahar, **7–8**
Bender, Aimee, **198**, 201, 206, 211, 226
Beneath the Clouds and Coconut Leaves, 186
Benedict, Elizabeth, 24
Benioff, David, 19, 28, **53**, 155
Benjamin, David, 35, 183
Bennett, Alan, 38, **53–54**
Bennett, Ronan, **54**
Bennetts, Leslie, 154
Beowulf: A New Verse Translation, 60, 228
Berendt, John, 39
Berg, Elizabeth, **55**, 99, 101, **107–108**, 153
Berger, Joseph, 67
Berlinski, Mischa, **8–9**, 100, 233
Berne, Suzanne, **108**
Bernstein, Harry, 43, 91, 161
Berry, Steve, 92
Berry, Wendell, 2, **9–10**, 17–18, 28, 124, 137,
        157, 251, 260
Beside Still Waters, 91
Best and the Brightest, The, 135
Best of Montana's Short Fiction, The, 14
Better Angel, A: Stories, 75, 81, **194**
Better Homes and Husbands, 2, 11, 154
Between a Rock and a Hard Place, 84
Between Here and April, **72–73**, 88, 138, 144,
        158, 165, 176
Between the Bridge and the River, 33
Beyond, The, 64
*Beyond Bogotá: Diary of a Drug War
        Journalist in Colombia,* 78
Bible Salesman, The, **18**, 62, 117, 155
Big Fish, 48, 94, 218
Big Nap, The, 93
Bigsby, Christopher, 40, 116, **199**
Bill from My Father, The, 127, 181
Biller, Maxim, 162
Billy Bathgate, 209, 216

Bing, Stanley, 58, 62
Bingham, Sallie, **108–109**
Biographer's Tale, The, **113**, 235
*Biohazard: The Chilling True Story of the
        Largest Covert Biological Weapons
        Program in the World,* 53
Birders: Tales of a Tribe, 18
Birds of America, 109, 244
Birds without Wings, **14–15**
Birdsell, Sandra, 15
Birkett, Dea, 93
Birmajer, Marcelo, 125
Birth of Stones, A, 62
Birthday Present, The, 67
Bissell, Tom, 29, 38, 67, 93, 104, 134, 141,
        168, 223, 237
Bit on the Side, A, 211, 258
Black Book, The, 83
Black Brook, 122
Black Cherry Blues, 44
Black Dogs, 235, 236
Black Flies, **57**, 239, 248
Black Girl, White Girl, 81
*Black Lamb and Grey Falcon: A Journey
        Through Yugoslavia,* 8, 227
Black Ships, 57, 228
Black Skin, White Masks, 188
*Black Swan, The: The Impact of the Highly
        Improbable,* 209
Black Swan Green, 27, 33, 122, 154, **160**, 162,
        164, 225, 241
Blackberry Wine, 135
Blackbird: A Childhood Lost and Found, 159
*Blackwater: The Rise of the World's Most
        Powerful Mercenary Army,* 90
Blackwater Lightship, The, 257
Blake, James Carlos, 35
Blankets, 157
Bleachy Haired Honky Bitch, 145, 181
Blind Man Can See How Much I Love You, A,
        109
Blind Man of Seville, The, 86
Blind Submission, 65, 180
Blind Willow, Sleeping Woman, **243–244**, 246
Blindness, 3, 63, 253
*Blink: The Power of Thinking without
        Thinking,* 195
Blonde, 247
Blood Doctor, The, 67
Blood Kin, 41, **63**
Blood Meridian, 197, 210, 233, 234
Blood of Fathers, The, 19

Blood of Victory, 54
Blood-Dark Track, 35
Bloom, Amy, 21, 31, 37, 40, 41, **109**, 155, 174
Bloom, Stephen, 122
Blount, Roy, Jr., 44
Blue Blood, 180
Blue Diary, 139
Blue Eyes, 60
Blue Latitudes, 56
Blue Manuscript, The, **226–227**
Blue Mountain, The, 81
Blue Movie, 82
Blue Nile, The, 16
Blue Star, The, 28, 43, 91, 120, **123–124**
Blue Taxi, The, 26
Bluesman, 123
Bluest Eye, The, 31, 216, 242
Blumenthal, Ralph, 150
Blunt, Giles, 72
Boat, The, **74–75**
Boaz, Amy, **10**
Bob the Gambler, 7
Bock, Charles, 20, 29, 165, **199**, 200, 248
Body Artist, The, 50, 81, 207
Body Surfing, 129, 134, 145
Bohjalian, Chris, **55**
Boice, James, 148, 190, 199, **200**, 205
Bolaño, Roberto, 78, 86, 130, 197, **200**, 202, 208, 231
Bone Black: Memories of Girlhood, 24
Bonesetter's Daughter, The, 48, 109, 146
Bonfire of the Vanities, The, 56
Bonk: The Curious Coupling of Science and Sex, 237
Book Borrower, The, 156
Book Lover, The, 255
Book of Clouds, **4**
Book of Dahlia, The, **99**, 128
Book of Dave, The, 90
Book of Dead Birds, The, 24
Book of Fame, The, 71
Book of Getting Even, The, 118, **179–180**
Book of Illusions, The, 50, **195–196**
Book of Joby, The, 244
Book of Medicines, 220
Book of Memories, A, 231
Book of Murder, The, **78**, 86, 87
Book of Ruth, The, 135
Book of Saladin, The, 83
Book of Salt, The, 34
Book Thief, The, 77, 213, 254

Bookmaker's Daughter, The, 2
Books: A Memoir, 171
Bookseller of Kabul, The, 20, 101, 140–141, 145, 158
Bookshop, The, 17
Boom! Voices of the Sixties, 167
Boomsday, 56
Borderlands: Short Fiction, 35
Borges, Jorge Luis, 149
Born Free: A Lioness of Two Worlds, 133
Born on a Blue Day, 132
Born Standing Up: A Comic's Life, 180, 218
Boswell, James, 50, 113
Boswell's Presumptuous Task: The Making of the Life of Dr. Johnson, 50
Bourdain, Anthony, 49, 180
Bourke, Anthony, 133
Bowden, Mark, 13
Bowe, John, 90
Boy, 67
Boy Detective Fails, The, 238
Boy Who Went Away, The, 66
Boyd, William, **109–110**
Boylan, Jennifer Finney, 55
Boyle, Kevin, 199
Boyle, T. Coraghessan, **110–111**, 113, 153, 167, 189, 242
Boys from Brazil, The, 230–231
Bradbury, Ray, 34, 56, 64, 205, 221, 226, 240
Bradley, Alan, 104
Bragg, Rick, 179, 181, 187
Braindead Megaphone, The, 212, 260
Brainwash: The Secret History of Mind Control, 63, 72
Branch, Taylor, 5
Brandeis, Gayle, 24
Branwell: A Novel of the Brontë Brother, 50
Brass Knuckles, 123
Brave New World, 52, 66
Bray, Libba, 43
Brazzaville Beach, 110
Bread Alone, 138, 156
Break It Down, 156, 206
Breakdown Lane, The, 160
Breakfast of Champions, 73
Breakfast with Buddha, 23, 79, 241
Breaking Lorca, 72
Breath, 34, 44, 113, 126, **189–190**, 200, 229
Breathing Lessons, 106, 135, 184
Breezes, The, 35
Breitweiser, Kristen, 172
Breslin, Jimmy, 52

Brick Lane, 49, 98, **99**, 116, 119, 140
Bridegroom, The: Stories, 39, 230
Brideshead Revisited, 118, 140, 235
Bridge Between Us, A, 191
Bridge of Sighs, **170–171**
Brief and Frightening Reign of Phil, The, 63, 90, 206, 212, 255
Brief History of the Dead, The, 201, 205, 254
Brief Wondrous Life of Oscar Wao, The, 48, 115, 125, 171, 197, 199, **208**, 212, 257
Briggs, Raymond, 184
Bright, Susie, 202
Bright Lights, Big City, 32
Bright Shiny Morning, **20**, 29
Bringing Down the House: The Inside Story of Six MIT Students Who Took Vegas for Millions, 77
Bringing Out the Dead, 13, 57, 248
Brinkman, Kiara, **111**, 136, 157, 213
Brittain, Vera, 105
Broccoli and Other Tales of Food and Love, 182, 220, **258–259**
Brockmeier, Kevin, 5, **201**, 205, 254
Brokaw, Tom, 120, 167
Broken, 200, **204–205**, 210, 223
Broken Cord, The, 152
Broken for You, 144, 184
Broken Paradise, 26
Broken Verses, 99, 134
Bromell, Henry, 140
Brontë, Charlotte, 43, 112, 231
Brooklyn, **40–41**, 156, 181, 257
Brookner, Anita, **111–112**, 118, 153
Brooks, Geraldine, **56**, 70, 92, **112**, 116, 141, 155, 186, 227
Brooks, Max, 210
Brooks, Robin, 59
Broom of One's Own, A: Words on Writing, Housecleaning, and Life, 167, 228
Broom of the System, The, 241
Brother and Sister, 118, **182**, 183
Brotherly Love, 190
Brothers and Keepers, 188
Brothers and Sisters, 166, 177
Brothers Boswell, The, **50**, 76, 82, 105, 133
Brothers Karamazov, The, 236
Brown, Carrie, **112**
Brown, Dan, 59
Brown, Larry, 18
Brown, Rita Mae, 168
Brown, Rosellen, 101
Brownsville: Stories, **12**, 13, 42, 157

Brox, Jane, 6
Brundage, Elizabeth, 182
Bruni, Frank, 174
Brush Country, 36
Bryson, Bill, 124
Buchan, James, 37, 100
Bucking the Tiger, **246**
Buckley, Christopher, **56**, 79, 90
Buffalo Lockjaw, **2–3**, 107, 128
Bufo & Spallanzani, 214
Buford, Bill, 176
Bugliosi, Vincent, 228, 233
Bull, Emma, **57**
Burgess, Anthony, 82
Buried Book, The: The Loss and Rediscovery of the Great Epic of Gilgamesh, 56
Burke, James Lee, 44
Burke, Shannon, **57**, 239, 248
Burn, 57
Burnett, John, 51
Burns, Olive, 25
Burnt Shadows, 99, 100
Burnt Umber, 110
Burroughs, Augusten, 77, 127, 168
Bus Driver Who Wanted to Be God and Other Stories, The, 226
Busch, Frederick, **201**, 248, 256
Bushnell, Candace, 2, **11**, 154
Business of Memory, The, 225
Busted Scotch, 225
Buten, Howard, 132
Butler, Octavia, 95, 234
Butler, Robert Olen, 44, 136, **201–202**
Butt, The: An Exit Strategy, **89–90**
Buzbee, Lewis, 171
Buzzell, Colby, 28
By Night in Chile, 130, 200
By the Lake, **156–157**, 198
By the Lake of Sleeping Children: The Secret Life of the Mexican Border, 42
Byatt, A. S., 56, **113**, 114, 187, 228, 235, 247
Byrne, Janet, 10

Cage, The, 109
Cage Keeper and Other Stories, The, 123
Cahill, Thomas, 15
Caldwell, Ian, 59
Caliban's Shore, 25–26, 82
Caliph's House, The: A Year in Casablanca, 4, 7, 23
Call If You Need Me: The Uncollected Fiction and Other Prose, 5

Callaghan, Barry, 91
Callahan, Tess, 126
Callahan's Crosstime Saloon, 144
Called Out, 241
Calligrapher's Daughter, The, **146**
Callisto, **73**, 255
Calvino, Italo, 149, 247
Calvo, Javier, 200, **202**, 208
Camel Bookmobile, The, 71, 112
Cameron, Peter, 107, 140
Campbell, Bebe Moore, 166, 177
Camus, Albert, 230
Cancer Vixen: A True Story, 99
Candy in Action, 258
Cane River, 115, 164
*Can't Be Satisfied: The Life and Times of
   Muddy Waters,* 121, 242
Can't Wait to Get to Heaven, 94
Cape Ann, The, 178
Capote, Truman, 233
Capra, Fritjof, 238
Captain Alatriste, 92
Captain Kidd, 60
Caputo, Philip, 88
Caracol Beach, 87
Caramelo, **12–13**, 15, 42
Carey, Edward, 163, **202–203**
Carey, Jacqueline, **58**, 175
Carey, Peter, 21, 25, 44, **58**, 73, **113**, 139, 149,
   215, 228, 232
Carlson, Ron, **11–12**
Carrell, Jennifer Lee, **58–59**, 87
Carroll, Jonathan, 122
Carry Me Down, 197, 229
Carrying the Torch, 62
Carson, Ciaran, **59–60**, 228
Carson, Rachel, 238
Carter, Stephen, 257
Carter Beats the Devil, 53, 216
Cartwright, Justin, 68, **113–114**, 197, 204,
   223, 238, 245
Carver, Raymond, 5, 260
Casares, Oscar, **12**, 13, 42, 157
Case Histories, 65, 176, 183
Caspian Rain, **161–162**
Cassandra, Lost, 37
Castillo, Ana, 12, 42, **60**
Castle, 29, **75–76**, 166, 250
*Castle in the Backyard, A: The Dream of a
   House in France,* 135
Cat and Mouse, 230
Catastrophist, The, 54

Catch-22, 53, 73
Catch Me If You Can, 18, 155
Catcher in the Rye, The, 107, 160, 190
Catfish and Mandala, 75
Cathedral, 260
Cather, Willa, 10, 124
Cat's Eye, 66
Cat's Pajamas, The, 226
Caucasia, 91, 122, 166
Cave, The, **252–253**
Caveat, 224
Caws, Mary Ann, 254
Cecchini, Toby, 180
Celebration, 158
Celestial Navigation, 120, 208
Celibate Season, A, 120
Cellist of Sarajevo, The, **20**, 100, 101, 145
Censoring an Iranian Love Story, **233**
Centaur in the Garden, The, 244
Central Square, 250
Ceremony, 220
Cereus Blooms at Night, 160
Certain Age, A, 143
Chabon, Michael, 89, 125, **203–204**, 208, 212,
   213, 216, 229, 230, 260
Chadha, Yogesh, 188
Chaikin, Andrew, 53
Chairman Mao Would Not Be Amused, 217
Chamberlain, Marisha, **114**
Chance, Megan, 71
Chandra, G. S., 150
Chandra, Vikram, 83
Chang and Eng, 76, 256
Chang, Iris, 51, 169
Chang, Leslie T., 217
Changing Planes, 228
Chaon, Dan, 81, 109, 198, 201
Chaplin, Charles, 216
Chapman, Peter, 26
*Character Studies: Encounters with the
   Curiously Obsessed,* 148
Charlie and the Children, 37
Charlie Chaplin and His Times, 216
Charming Billy, 211
Charms for the Easy Life, 81, 178
Charyn, Jerome, **60–61**
Chasing Harry Winston, 74
*Chasing the Sea: Among the Ghosts of Empire
   in Central Asia,* 93, 141, 237
Chater, Veronica, 159
Chatwin, Bruce, 9, 22, 26
Chaviano, Daina, 26

Cheating at Canasta: Stories, 157, 181, 211, **258**
Cheever, John, 136
Cheever: A Life, 121
Chemistry and Other Stories, 86
Cherian, Anne, 98, 119
Cherry, 242
Chessman, Harriet Scott, 15, 121
Chevalier, Tracy, 121
Chez Moi, **16–17**, 135
Chiaverini, Jennifer, 115
Chicago: City on the Make, 219
Child, Julia, 135
Childhood and Other Neighborhoods, 123
Children of Men, 221
Children's Hospital, The, 194
Children's Hour, The, 182
China Dog and Other Tales from a Chinese Laundry, 51
Chinese in America, The: A Narrative History, 51
Chocolat, 16–17, 66, 135
Chocolate War, The, 190, 210
Choi, Susan, **61**, 103, 134, 191
Choke, 82, 248
Choy, Wayson, **12**, 51, 75
Christensen, Kate, 36, 68, 74, 101, 163, 174, 191, **204**
Christensen, Lars Saabye, **114–115**
Christie, Agatha, 42, 203
Chroma, 201
Chronic City, **229**
Chrysalis, The, 92
Chuck Klosterman IV, 147
Chupack, Edward, **61**, 92
Church of Dead Girls, The, 64
Cider House Rules, The, 104, 142
Circling My Mother, 132
Circus in Winter, The, 14
Cisneros, Sandra, **12–13**, 15, 42
Cities of the Plain, 36, 234
Citizen Vince, 204
City, 197
City Boy, 181
City Life: Urban Expectations in a New World, 4
City of Falling Angels, The, 39
City of Glass, 196
City of Refuge, 7, 29, 243
City of Thieves, 19, 28, **53**, 155
City of Your Final Destination, The, 107
Civil Action, A, 90

CivilWarLand in Bad Decline, 85, 255
Clarinet Polka, The, **28–29**
Clark, Martin, 18
Clarke, Austin, 12, 68
Clarke, Breena, 68, **115**
Clarke, Brock, 49, **61–62**
Clarke, Susanna, 57
Classic Stories (Bradbury), 240
Clay, Daniel, 200, **204–205**, 210, 223
Cleage, Pearl, 115
Cleanup, The, 57
Clear, 197
Clear Light of Day, 16, 186, 246
Clearing, The, 194
Cleave, Chris, 78, **115–116**
Cleaver, 78, 83, **166**, 196
Clinch, Jon, 112, **116**
Clock Winder, The, 112, 120, 189
Clockers, 85
Clockwork Orange, A, 82
Close Range, 14, 36
Closed Circle, The, 154
Closing Time, 73
Clothes They Stood Up In, The, 54
Cloud Atlas, The, 63, 160, **240–241**
Cloud Chamber, The, 19
Cloud Forest, The, 9, 30, 88
Cloud Garden, The: A True Story of Adventure, Survival, and Extreme Horticulture, 78
Cloudsplitter, 103
Cloudspotter's Guide, The: The Science, History, and Culture of Clouds, 248
Cloudstreet, 44, 190
Club Dumas, The, 54, 87, 92
Coal Black Horse, 35
Coal Run, 164
Coast of Akron, The, 152
Coast of Chicago, The, 123
Coastliners, 66
Cocker, Mark, 18
Coe, Jonathan, 154, 183, 197, 218
Coelho, Paulo, 253
Coetzee, J. M., 32, 103, 153, **205**, 207, 216, 232, 236
Coffee Trader, The, 25, 50, 83, 87
Cohen, Leah Hager, 153, 175
Cohn, Rachel, 104, 157
Colapinto, John, 55
Cold Mountain, 37, 112, 194, 209
Cold Sassy Tree, 25
Cole, Marjorie Kowalski, 24

Colfer, Eoin, 159
Coll, Steve, 90, 100
Collapse: How Societies Choose to Fail or Succeed, 219
Collected Stories, The (Paley), 156
Collected Stories (Shields), 156, 243, **254–255**
Collected Stories, The (Theroux), 232
Collected Stories, The (Trevor), 258
Collected Works of Billy the Kid, The, 246
Collected Works of T. S. Spivet, The, 125
Collection of Beauties at the Height of Their Popularity, A, 189
Collins, David, **62**, 77
Collins, James, 145, 153
Collins, Paul, 171
Color of Lightning, The, 111, 115, 209
Color of Summer, The, 26
Color of Water, The, 187, 257
Color Purple, The, 31
Colossus, 27, 188
Colour, The, 182
Columbine, 150
Colwin, Laurie, 106, 259
Come to Me, 109
Comfort: A Journey Through Grief, 229
Comfort and Joy, 140
Comfort Me with Apples, 259
Comfort of Strangers, The, 4, 107, 174, 190, 197, 235, 236, 247
Comfortably Numb: How Psychiatry Is Medicating a Nation, 96
Coming Through Slaughter, 247
Commitments, The, 120, 157, 162, 209
Company, The: A Novel of the CIA, 223
Complete Stories, The (Malouf), **232**
Complications: A Surgeon's Notes on an Imperfect Science, 180, 194
Conant, Jennet, 54
Concise Chinese-English Dictionary for Lovers, A, 217
Condition, The, 133–134
Confederacy of Dunces, A, 73, 85, 179, 181
Confederates in the Attic, 56
Confessions of a Fallen Woman, 15
Confessions of a Political Hitman, 79
Confessions of a Prep School Mommy Handler, 74
Confessions of a Tax Collector, 180
Confessions of Max Tivoli, The, 57
Confessions of Nat Turner, The, 70
Confessions of Summer, 231
Confinement, 112

Confusion, The, 61
Conlon, Edward, 180
Connelly, Joe, 12, **13**, 57, 123, 157, 248
Conover, Ted, 176
Conrad, Joseph, 92, 210, 236
Consequences, **152–153**, 231
Consider the Lobster, 260
Conspiracy of Paper, A, 25, 50, 87
Continental Drift, 103
Continuing Silence of a Poet, The, 226
Contrarians, The, 24
Contrary Farmer, The, 28
Conversations at Curlow Creek, The, 232
Conway, Jill Ker, 124, 242
Coomer, Joe, 22, **117**, 179
Coop: A Year of Poultry, Pigs, and Parenting, 6, 137
Cooper, Bernard, 127, 181
Cooper, Dennis, 85
Cooper, Helene, 103, 116
Coraline, 64
Corelli's Mandolin, 15
Cormier, Robert, 190, 210
Cornish, D. M., 61
Coronation Everest, 39
Correcting the Landscape, 24
Corrections, The, 32, **127**, 212
Corrupting Dr. Nice, 226
Cortazar, Julio, 253
Cosmopolis, 207
Cosmopolitan: A Bartender's Life, 180
Country Called Home, A, 3, **5–6**, 11, 102, 146, 167, 168, 223, 242
Country Life, The, 118, 144
Coupland, Douglas, 165
Couples, 136
Cox, Michael, 48, 50, 67, 82, 105, 235
Crace, Jim, **62–63**, 66, 71, 194, 210, 234, 237, 249, 253
Cracking India, 119
Cradle, The, 110, **175**
Crandell, Doug, **117**
Crawfish Mountain, 24, **44**
Crazed, 222
Crime, **94–95**, 131, 225
Crime and Punishment, 236
Crime in the Neighborhood, A, 108
Criminals, 231
Crimson Petal and the White, The, 21, 212
Cross Channel, 105, 197
Crossing, The, 36, 234
Crossing California, 24, **26–27**

Crossing Over, 12, 60
Crossing to Safety, 17
Crossley Baby, The, 58
Crouch, Katie, **13–14**
Crow Lake, 111
Crow Road, The, 33, 45, 160
Cruel Shoes, 218
Cruelest Journey: Six Hundred Miles to Timbuktu, 88
Crumbtown, 12, **13**, 123, 157, 248
Cry of the Peacock, 161
Crying of Lot 49, The, 215, 259
Cuadros, Paul, 12
Cullen, Dave, 150
Cummins, Jeanine, 165
Cunningham, Michael, 36, 111, 130, 153, 254
Cup of Light, A, 34
Cure for Death by Lightning, A, 3
Cure for Grief, The, 137
Cure for Modern Life, The, 183
Curious Earth, A, 45
Curious Incident of the Dog in the Night-Time, The, 111, **131–132**, 133, 160, 213, 225
Cusk, Rachel, 73, 93, **117–118**, 140, 144, 148, 180
Cutting for Sign, 12, 60
Cutting for Stone, 48, 116, 134

D. H. Lawrence: A Biography, 10
Da Vinci Code, The, 59
Dahl, Roald, 67, 214, 240
Dale Loves Sophie to Death, 106
Damascus Gate, 51
Damballah, 188
Damrosch, David, 56
Damrosch, Phoebe, 165
Dance Real Slow, 69
Dancer, 30
Dancing Girls, 243
Dandelion Wine, 64, 205
Dangarembga, Tsitsi, 31
Dangerous Friend, A, 223
Dangerous Joy of Dr. Sex and Other True Stories, The, 135
Dangerous Laughter: Thirteen Stories, 75, 203, **239–240**, 244
Dangerous Woman, A, 80
Danielewski, Mark Z., 234, 241
Dante Club, The, 83
Danticat, Edwidge, 100, 208
Darjeeling, 178

Dark, The, 157
Dark Amongst Women, The, 198
Dark Side, The: The Inside Story of How the War on Terror Turned into a War on American Ideals, 90
Darkmans, 114, **196–197**, 200
Darkness Casts No Shadows, 76
Darling, Lynn, 73
Darling, The, **103**
Dash, Leon, 130
Daswani, Kavita, 99
Daughter, 130
Daughter of Fortune, 13, 200, 256
Daughters of Juarez, The: A True Story of Serial Murder South of the Border, 60
Daughters of the North, **66**, 71, 91–92, 95, 228
Davis, Claire, **14**
Davis, Kathryn, **205**
Davis, Lydia, 156, 201, **206**, 235, 255–256
Dawn (Butler), 95
Dawn (Wiesel), 254
Day, Cathy, 14
Day, 45, **225–226**
Day at the Beach, A, 123, 172
Day in the Life of Ivan Denisovich, A, 236
Day No Pigs Would Die, A, 124
Daydreaming Boy, The, 29
De Bernières, Louis, **14–15**, 44
De Blasi, Marlena, 4
De Botton, Alain, 208
De Haven, Tom, 89
De Kretser, Michelle, 44, **206–207**
de Lint, Charles, 254
De los Santos, Marisa, 84, 93, 173
Dead Fathers Club, The, 133
Deadwood, 233, 234, 246
Deaf Sentence, **153**, 207
Dean, Debra, **15**, 37, 68, 155
Dean, Zoey, 65
Dear American Airlines, **238–239**
Dear Husband: Stories, 81
Dearly Departed, The, 152
Death: A Life, 85
Death by Pad Thai, 259
Death Comes for the Archbishop, 10
Death in Belmont, A, 49
Death in Summer, 258
Death of Adam, The, 251
Death of Vishnu, The, 34, 178
Death with Interruptions, 254
Debt to Pleasure, The, 114

Dedicated Man, A, 67
Deep and Other Stories, The, 255
Defining the Wind: How a 19th Century Admiral Turned Science Into Poetry, 59
Delany, Elizabeth, 115
Delany, Sarah, 115
Delicate Edible Birds, 131
DeLillo, Don, 50, 81, 127, **207**, 223
Delinquent Virgin: Wayward Pieces, **224–225**
Demonology, 248
Denby, David, 208
Denfield, Rene, 199
Deportees and Other Stories, The, **209**, 211
D'Erasmo, Stacey, 102, **207–208**
Derbyshire, John, 246
Dervishes, **22**
Desai, Anita, **16**, 119, 186, 246
Desai, Kiran, 34, 37, 49, 98, **118–119**, 161, 182, 186, 240
Desarthes, Agnes, **16–17**, 135
Deschamps, Héléne, 54
Desert Solitaire: A Season in the Wilderness, 166
Deserter, The, 68
Destiny, 83, 166
Detective Story, 63, **71–72**, 231
Devil in a Blue Dress, 81, 85
Devil in the Details, The, 143, 146
Devil in the White City, The, 58
Devil Wears Prada, The, 74
Dew, Robb Forman, 106
Dewey: The Small-Town Library Cat Who Changed the World, 133
Dexter, Pete, 140, 190, 233, 234, 246, 250
Dharma Bums, The, 241
Diablerie, **81**
Diagnosis, The, 237
Diamond, Jared, 219
Diamonds of the Night, 76
Diary of a Bad Year, **205**, 216, 236
Diary of Anne Frank, The, 38
Díaz, Junot, 48, 115, 125, 171, 197, 199, **208**, 212, 257
Dick, Philip K., 50, 87, 221
Dickens, Charles, 71, 185, 231
Dickey, Eric Jerome, 30
Dictation: A Quartet, 170, **247**
Didion, Joan, 20, 106, 108, 191, 196, 260
Diezmo, The, 35
Digging to America, 18, 150, **184**
Dillard, Annie, 17, 30, 36, 260

Din in the Head, The, 247
Dinner at the Homesick Restaurant, 25, 27, 114, 127, 129, 178, 181
Dirt, 57
Dirt Music, 44, 190, 232
Dirty Diplomacy, 195
Disappointment Artist, The, 229
Discomfort Zone, The, 32
Disgrace, 32, 153, 205, 207, 216, 232, 236
Dispatches, 51, 134–135
Displaced Persons: Growing Up American after the Holocaust, 67
Dispossessed, The, 228
Disquiet, **229**
Disreputable History of Frankie Landau-Banks, The, 152
Distance Between Us, The, 20, 88
Distant Lover, The, 67
Distinguished Guest, The, 127, 160
Disturbances in the Field, 172
Divakaruni, Chitra Banerjee, 98, 99, **119**, 129, 134, 143, 150, 178, 186
Dive from Clausen's Pier, The, 189
Divine Husband, The, **130**
Divine Secrets of the Ya-Ya Sisterhood, The, 14, 129, 156
Diving Pool, The, 246
Divisadero, 15, **246–247**
Djbot Baghostus's Run, 232
Do Not Deny Me: Stories, **180–181**
Doc Holliday: The Life and Legend, 246
Doctor Copernicus, 196
Doctor Olaf von Schuler's Brain, 186, **237**
Doctorow, E. L., 5, 60–61, 111, **209**, 216
Doerr, Anthony, **17**
Dog Who Wouldn't Be, The, 133
Dog Year, A: Twelve Months, Four Dogs, and Me, 133
Dog's Life, A, 133
Dogs of Bedlam Farm, The, 133
Dogs of Riga, The, 250
Dogs of War, The, 195
Doig, Ivan, **17–18**, 29, **119–120**, 124
Dolittle, Sean, 57
Domestic Particulars, 201
Donofrio, Beverly, 120, 154
Donoghue, Emma, **120**
Donohue, Keith, 164
Don't Cry: Stories, 75, 162, 194, 214
Don't Let's Go to the Dogs Tonight: An African Childhood, 22, 38, 127
Don't Tell Anyone, **201**, 248

Dorcas Good: The Diary of a Salem Witch, 71
Dorian: An Imitation, 90
Dorris, Michael, 152
Dostoyevsky, Fyodor, 236
Double, The, 253
Double Bind, The, 55
Double Down, 7
Double Fault, 174
Double Vision, 10, 101, **104**, 158, 185, 204
Dovey, Ceridwen, 41, **63**
Down the Nile: Alone in a Fisherman's Skiff, 129
Downtown: My Manhattan, 2, 4, 27
Downtown Owl, 13, 43, 86, **147**
Doyle, Arthur Conan, 105
Doyle, Roddy, **120**, 157, 162, **209**, 210, 211, 225
Dr. Neruda's Cure for Evil, 191
Drabble, Margaret, 144
Dragoman, György, 205, **210**
Draine, Betsy, 135
Draining the Sea, 29
Drakulic, Slavenka, 10, 63, 90, **121**, 130, 147, 185, 204
Drama City, 85
Drayson, Nicholas, **18**
Dream, The: A Memoir, 43
Dream for When You're Feeling Blue, 55, 153
Dream of the White Village, The: A Novel in Stories, 50
Dream Stuff, 232
Dreaming in Cuban, 6, 26
Dreamland, 5, 253
Dreams from My Father, 122, 124
Dress Your Family in Corduroy and Denim, 181
Dressing Up for the Carnival, 156
Driftless: Photographs from Iowa, 122
Driftless Area, The, 13, 86, **121–122**, 147
Drinking Coffee Elsewhere, 91, **165–166**
Drive Me Crazy, 30
Drivetime, 236
Driving Over Lemons: An Optimist in Andalucia, 4
Drood, 95, 257
Drop City, 111, 113, 167
Drown, 208
Drowning Ruth, 89, 164
Drury, Tom, 13, 86, **121–122**, 127, 147
D'Souza, Tony, **122**
Du Boucheron, Bernard, **210**, 236–237
Du Maurier, Daphne, 61

Dubus, Andre, 73, 78, 89, **122–123**, 131
Duchess of Bloomsbury, The, 38, 54
DuCornet, Rikki, **210–211**
Dumbfounded: Big Money, Big Hair, Big Problems, or Why Having It All Isn't for Sissies, 145
Dunn, Mark, 120
DuPont Circle, **24**, 27, 92, 140, 166, 205
Durable Goods, 108
Durcan, Liam, **63**, 69, 71
Durrow, Heidi, 24
Dusk and Other Stories, 214
Duveen: A Life in Art, 68
Dybek, Stuart, 24, 27, **123**, 220
Dyer, Geoff, 140
Dying Animal, The, 142
Dyke, Tom Hart, 78

Earhart, Rose, 71
Earley, Pete, 54
Earley, Tony, 28, 43, 91, 120, **123–124**
Earling, Debra Magpie, 126
Earthly Possessions, 23
East of the Mountains, 217, 250
Easy Way Out, The, 152
Eat, Pray, Love, 17, 41
Eating Animals, 213
Echo House, 24
Echo Maker, The, 128, 207, 223, 234, **250**
Echoes of the Dance, 182
Eclipse, 196
Eco, Umberto, 83, 87
Ecstasy: Three Tales of Chemical Romance, 95
Eden's Outcasts: The Story of Louisa May Alcott and Her Father, 112
Edgerton, Clyde, **18**, 62, 117, 155
Edith Wharton, 121
Edwards, Kim, 89, 106
Effect of Living Backwards, The, 224
Egan, Jennifer, 32, 94, 131
Eggers, Dave, 20, 111, 127, 222, 241
Ehrenreich, Barbara, 165, 176
Ehrlich, Gretel, 10, 39
84, Charing Cross Road, 38, 54
Einstein's Dreams, 237
Eire, Carlos, 43
Eiseley, Loren, 36
Election, 27, 84, 167
Electric Michelangeo, The, 66
Elegance of the Hedgehog, The, **103–104**, 177, 218

Elegy for Iris, 196
The Eleventh Man, The, 29, **119–120**, 124
Elfish Gene, The: Dungeons, Dragons, and Growing Up Strange, 160
Eliot, Marc, 15, 156
Elizabeth Costello, 205
Ella Minnow Pea, 120
Ellen Foster, 152, 157, 169, 177, 189
Ellington Boulevard, 11, 24, **27**
Elliot, Jason, 39, 93, 101, 140
Elliott, Stephen, 176
Ellis, Bret Easton, 82, 176, 249
Ellis Island and Other Stories, 253
Elroy Nights, 7
Emigrants, The, 253
Emperor of Ocean Park, The, 257
Emperor's Children, The, **32**
Empire Falls, 147, 171
Empire of Ice Cream, The, 64
Enchanted Night, 240
Enchantment of Lily Dahl, The, 141
Enchantress of Florence, The, 215
End, The, **253**
End of California, The, **190**
End of Manners, The, 141, 158
End of the Affair, The, 198
End of the Story, The, 206
End of the World As We Know It, The, 21
End of the World Book, The, **234–235**
End of Vandalism, The, 122
Endless Love, 176
Enduring Love, 236
Enemy Women, 115, 209
Enger, Leif, 19, 86, **124–125**, 126
Enger, Lin, **19**, 125
England, England, 105, 197
Englander, Nathan, **125**, 143, 170, 247
Engleby, 236
English, T. J., 16, 26
English Creek, 119
English Major, The, **22**
English Passengers, 21, **25–26**
English Patient, The, 15, 75, 91, 236, 247
Enright, Anne, 33, 137, 141, 181, 198, **211**, 243, 258
Envy, 108, **136**
Epicure's Lament, The, 204
Erdrich, Louise, 42, **125–126**, 147, 220, 250
Erickson, Carolly, 21–22, 25, 82
Esau, 91

Escape: The True Story of the Only Westerner Ever to Break Out of Thailand's Bangkok Hilton, 78
Esquivel, Laura, 16–17, 42, 259
Essential Charlotte, The, **172**
Estleman, Loren, 233, 234, 246
Ethel and Ernest: A True Story, 184
Eugenides, Jeffrey, 55, 126, 205, 210, **212**, 223
Europa, 83, 166
Europe Central, 223, **259**
Eva Luna, 149
Eva Moves the Furniture, 231
Evans, Polly, 34, 88
Evans, Walker, 259
Eve Green, 249
Eveless Eden, 259
Evening, 15, 151, 173, 214, 218
Evening Is the Whole Day, 48, 119
Evening's Empire: The Story of My Father's Murder, 228
Eventide, 35, 44, **136–137**, 251
Every Tongue Got to Confess, 188
Everybody Loves Somebody, 173
Everyman, 170, **252**
Everyone Worth Knowing, 74
Everyone's Pretty, 57, 239
Everything and More, 246
Everything Bad Is Good for You, 209
Everything Is Illuminated, 127, 149, **212–213**, 219, 237
Everything Ravaged, Everything Burned, **181–182**, 218
Everything That Rises: A Book of Convergences, 206
Everything Will Be All Right, 45, 132
Everything You Know, 102, 137
Everything You Need, 225
Evidence of Things Unseen, 259
Evison, Jonathan, 57, **126**, 239, 249, 258
Excellent Women, 153
Exiles, 88
Exiles in the Garden, 201, 238
Exit Ghost, **169–170**, 205
Expeditions, The, **69**, 142
Expendables, The, 162, 255
Explorers of the New Century, 221
Exposure, 136
Extra Man, The, 2
Extremely Loud and Incredibly Close, 32, 35, 127, **213**

Exuberance: Passion for Life, 195
Eye in the Door, The, 104, 105, 225
Eyre Affair, The, 64

Faber, Michael, 21, 212, 214, 221
Faceless Killers, 250
Factory Girls: From Village to City in a Changing China, 217
Fadiman, Anne, 134, 256
Fagone, Jason, 13
Fahrenheit 451, 56, 221
Fainaru-Wada, Mark, 90
Fair Warning, 136, 202
Faithless, 247
Falcon and the Snowman, The: A True Story of Friendship and Espionage, 54
Fall, 165
Fall of Frost, The, 105
Fall of Troy, The, 42
Fall on Your Knees, 106, 131, 150
Falling Boy, **157**, 183
Falling Man, 50, **207**, 223
Falling on Cedars, 161
Falling Slowly, 112, 153
Falling through the Earth, 29, 158
Falling Upwards: Essays in Defense of Imagination, 260
Fame & Folly, 247
Family Happiness, 106
Family Man, The, **152**, 172
Family Matters, **240**
Family of Spies: The John Walker Spy Ring, 54
Family Terrorists, 244
Family That Couldn't Sleep, 237
Famished Road, 222
Famous Builder, 203
Famous Suicides of the Japanese Empire, **161**, 191
Fanon, Frantz, 188
Fanon, **188**
Fantasy Writer's Assistant, The, 64
Far Bright Star, **35**
Far from the Madding Crowd, 173
Far Reaches, The, 120
Far Tortuga, 29
Farewell, My Subaru: An Epic Adventure in Local Living, 6
Fargo Rock City, 107, 147
Farming of Bones, The, 100, 208
Fast Food Nation, 90
Fast Lane, 168

Fasting, Feasting, 16, 119, 186
Fat Girl, 103
Fatal Shore, The: The Epic of Australia's Founding, 25
Fatelessness, 71
Father of All Things, The: A Marine, His Son, and the Legacy of Vietnam, 29, 38, 104, 134, 168, 223
Fatherland, 87, 204
Fathers and Daughters, 152, 172
Fatsis, Stefan, 176
Faulks, Sebastian, 236
Fay, 18
Fear and Loathing in Las Vegas, 176
Fearless, 191
Fearless Jones, 81
Feast of Love, The, 106, 107, 122
Feast of the Goat, The, 100, 185
Federico, Meg, 108, 132
Feet on the Street: Rambles around New Orleans, 44
Feig, Paul, 160
Feldstein, Peter, 122
Felicia's Journey, 181, 258
Female of the Species, The, 81, 174
Female Trouble: A Collection of Short Stories, 39, 81, 162, 181, **244**, 255
Feminine Mistake, The: Are We Giving Up Too Much?, 154
Fencing Master, The, 54, 83, 92
Ferber, Edna, 30
Ferguson, Craig, 33
Ferrari, Mark, 244
Ferraris, Zoë, 9, **19–20**, 72
Ferrell, Monica, 107, **126–127**, 179–180, 199
Ferris, Joshua, 165, 221, 234
Fessler, Ann, 182
Fever Trail, The: In Search of the Cure for Malaria, 88
Few Green Leaves, A, 153
Fforde, Jasper, 64
Fidali's Way, **78–79**, 83
Fidelity, 10
Field of Stars, 156
Fieldwork, **8–9**, 100, 233
Fierce, 146
Fierce Attachments, 132
Fierce People, 96
Fies, Brian, 99
Fifth Child, The, 216
Fifth Mountain, The, 253
Fig Eater, The, 111

Fight Club, 81, 82, 176, 248
Filter House, 66
Filth, 33
Final Solution, The: A Story of Detection, **203**, 204
Finch, Charles, 105
Finder: A Novel of the Borderlands, 57
Finder, The, 136
Finder, Joseph, 62
Finders Keepers, 13
Finding Caruso, 6
Finding Nouf, 9, **19–20**, 72
Fine, Doug, 6
Fine Balance, A, 186, 240
Fine Just the Way It Is: Wyoming Stories 3, 14, **36**
Fingersmith, 94
Finishing School, The, 190
Finn, 112, **116**
Finnie Walsh, 20
Fiona Range, 80
Fire in the Blood, 15, 38
Firefly Cloak, 169
Firmin: Adventures of a Metropolitan Lowlife, **171**
First Light, 42
First Love, Last Rites, 236
First Man-Made Man, The, 212
First Part Last, The, 130
First Patient, The, 63
First Person and Other Stories, The, 162, **255–256**
Fisk, Robert, 28, 48
Fiskadoro, 70
Fitch, Janet, 80, 150
Fitzgerald, F. Scott, 35–36
Fitzgerald, Penelope, 17
Five Photos of My Wife, 16
Five Quarters of the Orange, 66, 135
Five Skies, **11–12**
Five-Forty-Five to Cannes, The, **22–23**, 177
Fixing My Gaze: A Scientist's Journey into Seeing in Three Dimensions, 53
Flag for Sunrise, A, 51
Flagg, Fannie, 94, 103, 156
Flanagan, Caitlin, 154
Flanagan, Richard, 123
Flanders Panel, The, 54, 78
Flannery: A Life of Flannery O'Connor, 121
Flash Fiction Forward: 80 Very Short Stories, 206
Flaubert, Gustave, 143

Flaubert's Parrot, 105
Flawless Skin of Ugly People, The, 117
Fleming, Thomas, 79
Fletcher, Susan, 249
Flick, Sherrie, 5
Flinn, Kathleen, 17, 135
Floating Brothel, The, 25
Floor of the Sky, The, 5
Florida, 184
Flow My Tears, the Policeman Said, 50
Flower Children, 167
Flower in the Skull, The, 13
Flying, 151
Flynn, Laura, 146, 168
Flynn, Nick, 86, 127, 168
Foden, Giles, 3, 195
Foer, Jonathan Safran, 32, 35, 127, 149, **212–213**, 219, 237
Folding Star, The, 140
Follow Me, **172–173**, 187
Fonseca, Rubem, **213–214**
Fontana, Marian, 172
Fool, 79
Foolscap, 117, 155
For Love of Politics: Inside the Clinton White House, 174
For Matrimonial Purposes, 99
For the Relief of Unbearable Urges, 125, 143, 170, 247
Ford, Jeffrey, **64**
Ford, Richard, 84, 151, 171, 182, 197, 201, **214**, 252, 260
Foreign Correspondent, The, 54
Foreign Student, The, 61
Forever, 31
Forgotten Garden, The, 71, **80–81**, 198
Forster, E. M., 38
Forsyth, Frederick, 195
Fortress of Solitude, **229–230**
Fortunate Age, A, 163
Fortune's Daughter, 139
Found: The Best Lost, Tossed, and Forgotten Items from Around the World, 5
Foundling, The, 61
Four Blondes, 11
Four Corners: A Journey into the Heart of Papua New Guinea, 88
Four Corners of the Sky, The, **154–155**, 172
Fourth Hand, The, 142
Fowler, Karen Joy, 56, **64**
Fowles, John, 94
Fox Evil, 95

Frank Lloyd Wright: A Biography, 111
Frankfurt, Harry G., 209
Franscell, Ron, 165
Frantz Fanon: A Biography, 188
Franzen, Jonathan, 32, **127**, 212, 260
Frazier, Charles, 37, 112, 194, 209
Frazier, Danny Wilcox, 122
Frazier, Ian, 8, 227
Freddy and Fredericka, 209
Free: And Other Stories, 166
Free Life, A, 161, 222, 230
Free Love, 255
Freedomland, 85
Fremont, Helen, 109
French, Tana, 164
Frey, James, **20**, 29
Frey, Stephen, 63
Frida: Biography of Frida Kahlo, 121
Frida Kahlo: Brush of Anguish, 121
Frida's Bed, 10, **121**, 130, 147, 185, 204
Friday Nights, 182
Fried Eggs with Chopsticks, 34, 88
*Fried Green Tomatoes at the Whistle Stop
    Café,* 94, 103, 156
Friedman, Thomas, 48
Friends, Lovers, Chocolate, 18
From Beirut to Jerusalem, 48
From Day to Day, 115
Fromm, Pete, 6
Frucht, Abby, 98, 151
Full Matilda, The, 30
Fuller, Alexandra, 11, 22, 38, 127
Fun Home, 120, 239
Fundamentals of Play, The, 154
Funnies, The, 76
Fuqua, Jonathan Scott, 239
Furst, Alan, 54
Future of Love, The, **1–2**, 172
Future of the Past, The, 219

Gabaldon, Diana, 186
Gaiman, Neil, 64, 159
Gain, 250
Gaines, Ernest J., 112
Gaitskill, Mary, 75, 138, 146, 162, 194, 208,
    214, 228
Galatea 2.2, 52
Galchen, Rivka, 125, 128, 211, **215**, 234, 249
Galloway, Steven, **20**, 100, 101, 145
Gallows View, 67
Gamble, Terry, 145
Game of Shadows, 91

Gandhi: A Life, 188
Ganesan, Indira, 186
Gang That Couldn't Shoot Straight, The, 52
García, Cristina, 26, 60
García Márquez, Gabriel, 149, 200, 218, 254
Garcia's Heart, **63**, 69, 71
Garden of Last Days, The, 73, 89, **122–123**,
    131
Garden Spells, 98
Gardenias, **178**
Gardens of Kyoto, The, 186
Gardner, John, 60
Garland, Alex, 82, 158
Garlic and Sapphires, 259
Gaslin, Glenn, 77
*Gatekeepers, The: Inside the Admissions
    Process of a Premier College,* 149
Gates, David, 182, 223
Gathering, The, 33, 137, 141, 181, 198, **211**,
    258
Gautreaux, Tim, 194
Gawande, Atul, 180, 194
Gazelle, 211
Gelman, Rita Golden, 88
Gemmell, Nikki, 232
Generation Kill, 76
Genesis, **52**, 80
*Genius for Living, A: The Life of Frieda
    Lawrence,* 10
Genova, Alice, **128**
Gentlemen and Players, **66–67**, 135, 137
Gentlemen of the Road, 203, 204, 230
Genuine Reality: A Life of William James, 76
George, Nelson, 230
George Bush, Dark Prince of Love, 239
Georgia O'Keeffe: A Life, 10
Gerhart, Ann, 174
German Bride, The, 31
German for Travelers: A Novel in 95 Lessons,
    228
Gershten, Donna, 24
*Gertrude Bell: Queen of the Desert, Shaper of
    Nations,* 42
Gerzina, Anthony, 116
Gessen, Keith, **128**
Gesture Life, A, 151
Get Shorty, 70, 180
Getting a Life, 114
Getting Personal, 170, 231, 252, 260
Ghosh, Amitav, 56, 88, 98, 100, 122,
    128–129, **215**, 240
Ghost at the Table, A, **108**

Ghost in Love, The, 122
Ghost of John Wayne, and Other Stories, The, 12
Ghost Road, 104, 105, 225
Ghost Soldiers: The Forgotten Epic Story of World War II's Most Dramatic Mission, 75
Ghost Wars, 90
Ghost Writer, The, 87, 142, 170, 205, 252
Ghosts, 196
Ghostwritten, 160, 241
Giant, 30
Giant's House, The: A Romance, 103
Giardina, Denise, 183
Gibb, Camilla, 12
Gibbons, Kaye, 81, 152, 157, 169, 177, 178, 189
Gibson, Gregory, 31
Gibson, Tanya Egan, **64–65**
Gift of Stones, The, 237, 253
Gilbert, Elizabeth, 17, 41, 148, 217
Gilead, 173, 218, **251**
Gillespie, Hollis, 145, 181
Gillison, Samantha, 22
Ginsberg, Debra, **65**, 139, 151, 165, 180
Ginseng Hunter, The, 20, **40**, 75, 146, 199, 222
Girl Cook, 49
Girl from Botany Bay, The, 21–22, 25, 82
Girl in Hyacinth Blue, 121, 254
Girl in the Flammable Skirt, The, 198, 201, 211, 226
Girl in the Glass, The, 64
Girl Named Zippy, A, 124, 146
Girl on the Fridge, The, 198, **226**, 255
Girl Who Fell from the Sky, The, 24
Girl Who Trod on a Loaf, The, 205
Girl with a Pearl Earring, 121
Girl with No Shadow, The, 16–17, 66, **135**
Girl with the Dragon Tattoo, The, 78, 202
Girls (Busch), 201, 256
Girls, The (Lansens), 129, **150–151**, 163, 183, 203
Girls in Trouble, 182
Girls in Trucks: Stories, **13–14**
Girls Like Us: Carole King, Joni Mitchell, and Carly Simon—and the Journey of a Generation, 121
Girls Who Went Away, The, 182
Gladwell, Malcolm, 195
Glamorama, 82
Glass, Julia, 108, 114, 123, **129–130**, 156

Glass Castle, The, 124, 151, 187
Glass of Time, The, 82
Glass Palace, The, 129, 215
Gloria, 28
Glover's Mistake, **74**, 107
Glue, 33, 95, 225
Gob's Grief, 194
God Bless You, Dr. Kevorkian, 73
God Lives in St. Petersburg, 67
God of Small Things, The, 119
Godden, Jon, 102
Goebel, Joey, 66
Goines, Donald, 85
Going after Cacciato, 51, 223, 245
Going Back to Bisbee, 10
Going to the Sun, 83
Going Under, 224
Gold, Glen David, 53, 196, **215–216**
Golden, Arthur, 37
Golden Age, A, **100**, 129
Golden Compass, The, 52
Golden Notebook, The, 216
Goldin, Farideh, 162
Goldman, Francisco, 87, **130**
Goldstein, Naama, 39
Goldstein, Rebecca, 149
Golem's Eye, The, 52
Golems of Gotham, The, 213
Golfing with God, 79
Gone and Back Again, 239
Gone to Soldiers, 120
Gone Tomorrow, 64, 148–149, 153, 170, 216, 239
Gone with the Wind, 37
Gonzalez, Ray, 12
González-Crussi, F., 238
Gooch, Brad, 121
Good Dog, A: The Story of Orson, Who Changed My Life, 133
Good Fairies of New York, The, 4, 32, **158–159**, 171
Good Faith, 175
Good Family, 145
Good in Bed, 143
Good Indian Wife, A, 98, 119
Good Intentions, 16
Good Life, The (McGraw), 31
Good Life, The (McInerney), 2, 32, 35, 123, 172, 207
Good Man of Nanking, The: The Diaries of John Rabe, 169
Good Mother, The, 159

Good News from Outer Space, 226
Good Scent from a Strange Mountain, A, 44
Good Thief, The, 19
Good Times, The, 225
Goodbye, Earl, 156
Goodbye to All That, 226
Goodman, Matthew Aaron, **130**, 189
Goolrick, Robert, **21**, 40, 80, 109, 150, 175
Gopnik, Adam, 93, 184
Gordimer, Nadine, 32, **216**
Gordon, Mary, 132
Gordon, Robert, 121, 242
Gordon-Reed, Annette, 32, 116
Gornick, Vivian, 132
Gottlieb, Eli, 62, **65–66**, 217, 245
Gough, Julian, 40, 74, 146, 148
Gourevitch, Philip, 72
Gowdy, Barbara, 123, 126, **130–131**, 202
Grace (Eventually): Thoughts on Faith, 251
Gracious Plenty, A, 169
Graham, Jo, 57, 228
Grahame-Smith, Seth, 226
Grande, Reyna, 42
Grandin, Temple, 132
Grass, Günter, 230
Grass Dancer, The, 220
Gravedigger's Daughter, 81
Graves, Robert, 226
Graveyard Book, The, 64
Gravity's Rainbow, 215, 259
Gray, Francine du Plessix, 22
Grealy, Lucy, 99, 245
Great American Novel, The, 87
Great and Terrible Beauty, A, 43
Great Apes, 90
Great Expectations, 71, 185
Great Gatsby, The, 35–36
Great Man, The, 36, 68, 74, 101, 163, 191, **204**
Great Perhaps, The, **238**
Great Plains, 8, 227
Great Starvation Equipment, The, 183
Great World, The, 232
Greatest Generation, The, 120
Greatest Generation Speaks, The, 120
Green, John, 33, 66, 157, 190
Green Lantern, The, 60
Green, Sheldon, 110
Greenblatt, Stephen, 59
Greene, Bob, 120
Greene, Graham, 38, 39, 103, 195, 198, 236
Greene, Melissa Faye, 148

Greer, Andrew Sean, 57, 158
Gregory, Julie, 256
Greider, William, 219
Grendel, 60
Grenville, Kate, 2, 9, **21–22**, 44, 68, 81
Grief Observed, A, 191
Grift, The, **65**, 139
Grifters, The, 85
Grimsley, Jim, 140
Groff, Lauren, **131**
Grogan, John, 133
Groom to Have Been, 51, **98**, 119, 231
Groopman, Jerome, 194
Grossman, Austin, 89
Grossman, Dave, 76
Grossman, Edith, 185
Group, The, 163
Gruen, Sara, 9, 91, 94, 151, 160, 173, 251
Guardians, The, 12, 42, **60**
*Guernsey Literary and Potato Peel Pie
    Society, The,* 15, **37–38**, 153, 177, 178,
    251
Guibert, Emmanuel, 101, 104
Guide to the Birds of East Africa, A, **18**
Guided Tours of Hell, 254
Gulag Archipelago, The, 8
Gun Seller, The, 52
Gun, with Occasional Music, 230, 241
Gunman's Rhapsody, 246
Guns, Germs, and Steel, 219
Guo, Xiaolou, 40, **216–217**, 244
Gutcheon, Beth, 98, 160
Guterson, David, 75, 161, **217**, 250
Guterson, Mary, 163, 175, 245
Gwartney, Debra, 120, 224

Hacker, Katharina, **217–218**
Had a Good Time, 44
Haddon, Mark, 111, **131–132**, 133, 154, 160,
    213, 225
Hadley, Tessa, 45, 104, **132**
Hafvenstein, Joel, 78
Hagen, George, 182
Haig, Matt, **132–133**, 207
Haigh, Jennifer, **133–134**
Hairdos of the Mildly Depressed, **117**
Hairstyles of the Damned, 238
Haji, Nafisa, **134**
Hakakian, Roya, 20, 43, 146
Hakawati, The: A Story, **48**, 233
Halberstam, David, 135
Haley, Alex, 5, 188

Half Broke Horses, 25, 103, **186–187**
Half Brother, The, **114–115**
Half Life, 66
Hall, Brian, 105, 112
Hall, Meredith, 173, 182
Hall, Sarah, **66**, 71, 91–92, 95, 228
Hall, Steven, 234
Hallinan, Joseph T., 195
Hallman, J. C., 194
Hallowed Ground: A Walk at Gettysburg, 16
Hallowell, Janis, 61, 73, 113, **134–135**, 167, 228, 245
Hamid, Moshin, 123
Hamill, Pete, 2, 4, 5, 27, 31
Hamilton Case, The, 207
Hamilton, Jane, **135**, 150, 168
Hamilton, Masha, 20, 71, 88, 112
Handbook to Luck, A, 26
Handle with Care, 134
Handler, Daniel, 126
Handling Sin, 117, 155
Handmaid's Tale, The, 52, 66, 80, 85, 221
Hanff, Helene, 2, 38, 54
Hannah Coulter, 2, **9–10**
Hannah, Kristin, 156
Happenstance, 255
Happy Marriage, A, 161, **191**, 196
Harbor, 7
Hard Sell: The Evolution of a Viagra Salesman, 52
Hard Trail to Follow, 36
Harding, Paul, **218**, 236
Hardman, Robert, 54
Hardwick, Elizabeth, 260
Hardy, Thomas, 173
Harmon, Adam, 28
Harmony of the World, 17, 106
Harmony Silk Factory, The, 249
Harr, Jonathan, 90
Harris, Joanne, 16–17, **66–67**, **135**, 137
Harris, Robert, 87, 204
Harrison, Colin, 136
Harrison, Jim, **22**, 69, 166
Harrison, Kathryn, 108, **136**
Harry and Catherine, 201
Harry, Revised, 128
Hart, Matthew, 58
Haruf, Kent, 6, 18, 35, 43–44, 86, 125, **136–137**, 250, 251
Haskell, John, **218**, 241
Haslett, Adam, 75

Hateship, Friendship, Courtship, Loveship, Marriage, 81, 181, 243, 244, 255
Hatzfeld, Jean, 198, 222
Haunted, 82, 249
Haunting Bombay, **98**
Havana Nocturne: How the Mob Owned Cuba—And Then Lost It to the Revolution, 16, 26
The Havana Room, 136
The Have-Nots, **217–218**
Having Our Say: The Delany Sisters' First 100 Years, 115
Havoc, in Its Third Year, 54
Haweswater, 66
Hayes, Bill, 237
Hayes, Billy, 78
Haynes, David, 30, 257
He Drown She in the Sea, **160–161**
Heaney, Seamus, 60, 228
Heart Earth, 120
Heart of Darkness, 92, 210, 236
Heart of the Matter, The, 103
Heartbreaking Work of Staggering Genius, A, 111, 127
Heat, 176
Heat and Dust, 119
Heat Moon, William Least, 17, 36
Heather Blazing, The, 41
Heaven's Prisoners, 44
Hedges, Peter, 122
Hein, Christoph, **67**, 230
Heir to the Glimmering World, 213, 247
Helget, Nicole Lea, 158
Hell, 205
Hellenga, Robert, 18
Heller, Joseph, 53, 73
Heller, Zoë, 91, 101, 102, 108, 126, **137**, 141, 145, 174, 191, 204
Hell's Angels, 176
Helms, Beth, **22**
Help, The, 55, 176, **177**
Helpless, 123, **130–131**
Helprin, Mark, 5, 23, 31, 110, 209, 253
Helter Skelter, 228, 233
Hemingses of Monticello, The: An American Family, 32, 116
Hemon, Aleksandar, 4, **219**, **220**, 240
Hendricks, Judith Ryan, **138**, 156
Hendrickson, Paul, 24, 199
Henkin, Joshua, 66
Henry and Cato, 247

Henry James: The Imagination of Genius, 76
Henry of Atlantic City, 169
Hensher, Philip, 145, 154, 160, 215
Her Fearful Symmetry, 129, 151, **163**, 203
*Here and Nowhere Else: Late Seasons of a
    Farm and Its Family,* 6
*Here at the End of the World We Learn to
    Dance,* 71
Here on Earth, 139
Here We Are in Paradise, 124
Here's Your Hat, What's Your Hurry, 109
Heretic's Daughter, The, **71**, 106
Hermann, Nellie, 137
Hermit's Story, The, 17
Herr, Michael, 51, 134–135
Herrera, Hayden, 121
Herriot, James, 133
Hersey, John, 51
Herson, Joanna, 31
Herzog, 170
Hessler, Peter, 4, 34
Hester, 199
Heti, Sheila, 113
Hewson, David, 54
Hiaasen, Carl, 44
Hickam, Homer, 35, 120, 124, 183
Hicks, Robert, 116
Hidden Assassins, The, 86
Hide and Seek, 95
Hiding Place, The, 7
High Art, 214
High Fidelity, 107, 140, 160
Highest Tide, The, 124
Highsmith, Patricia, 67
Highwire Moon, 42
Hijuelos, Oscar, 5, 26, 60
Hilda and Pearl, 156
Hill, Lawrence, **67–68**, 70, 115, 188, 243
Hill, Roccie, **138**, 228
Hill, Susan, 78, 94
Hill Bachelors, The, 157, 181, 211, 258
Hinden, Michael, 135
Hippolyte's Island, 83
Hirsh, M. E., 145
His Illegal Self, 58, 73, **113**, 228
History of Love, The, 102, **149**, 155, 159, 213,
    239
History of Reading, A, 209
Hitchcock, Jane Stanton, 11
Hochschild, Adam, 26
Hodgson, Barbara, 83
Hodgson, Moira, 22, 102

Hoeg, Peter, 244
Hoffman, Alice, **138–139**, 156, 177–178
Hoffman, Eva, 43, 109, 219
Hogan, Linda, **220**
Hold Love Strong, **130**, 189
Hollinghurst, Alan, 118, **139–140**, 166, 180
Hollington, Kris, 54
Hollywood Dodo, The, 180
Holm, Pamela, 24
Holthe, Tess Uriza, **22–23**, 177
Holy Cow: An Indian Adventure, 4
Holy Fools, 135
Home, 218, **251**, 257
Home Across the Road, 167
Home Cooking, 259
Home Game, 118
*Home Girl: Building a Dream House on a
    Lawless Block,* 7, 27, 30
Home Land, 2, 62
Home on the Field, A, 12
Home Safe, **107–108**
Home School, 175
Home Schooling: Stories, 109
Home Truths, 153
Homes, A. M., 108, 182, 214
*Honeymoon in Tehran: Two Years of Love
    and Danger in Iran,* 161
Hong Kong, 16
Honigsbaum, Mark, 88
Hood, Ann, 229
Hood, 120
hooks, bell, 24
Hope and Other Dangerous Pursuits, 8
*Hope in the Unseen, A: An American Odyssey
    from the Inner City to the Ivy League,*
    188
Hopscotch, 253
Horace Afoot, 169
Horan, Nancy, 111
Horn, Dara, 15, **68**, 114
Hornby, Nick, 34, 107, 120, **140**, 160
Horse Heaven, 175
Horsemen of the Esophagus, 13
Horwitz, Tony, 56
Hospital for Dead Poets, The, 194
Hosseini, Khaled, 20, 99, 100, 101, 116, 134,
    140–141, 143, 145, 161
Hot Zone, The: A Terrifying True Story, 53
Hotel Alleluia, The, 26
Hotel du Lac, 112
Hotel Eden, The, 11
Hotel New Hampshire, The, 142

Houghteling, Sara, 15, **68**
Hour I First Believed, The, 134, **150**
Hours, The, 36, 111, 130, 153, 254
House at Riverton, The, 81, 105
House at Sugar Beach, The: In Search of a Lost African Childhood, 103, 116
House Lights, The, 175
House of Leaves, The, 234, 241
House of Mirth, The, 114
House of Sand and Fog, The, 78, 122–123
House of Sleep, The, 197
House of the Spirits, The, 13, 42, 81, 98, 200, 254, 256
House of Widows, The: An Oral History, 4, **237**
House on Fortune Street, The, 153, 189, **231**
House on Mango Street, The, 13
Housekeeper and the Professor, The, **245–246**
Housekeeping, 251
How Doctors Think, 194
How Elizabeth Barrett Browning Saved My Life, 144, 153
How I Gave My Heart to the Restaurant Business, 156
How It Ended, 182
How Late It Was, How Late, 225
How the Dead Dream, 201, **239**
How the Dead Live, 90
How the Garcia Girls Lost Their Accent, 60
How the Hula Girl Sings, 238
How the Irish Saved Civilization, 15
How This Night Is Different: Stories, 99, 252
How to Be Alone, 127, 260
How to Be Good, 120, 140
How to Buy a Love of Reading, **64–65**
How to Make an American Quilt, 189
How to Make Love Like a Porn Star, 82
How to Sell, **77**, 249
How to Teach Filthy Rich Girls, 65
How to Tell When You're Tired, 11
How We Decide, 195
How We Die: Reflections on Life's Final Chapter, 238
Howarth, David, 115
Howell, Georgina, 42
Hubert's Freaks, 31
Hughes, Robert, 25
Hughes, Ted, 60
Huler, Scott, 59, 176
Hull, Jonathan, 110
Hullabaloo in the Guava Orchard, 98, 119
Human Capital, 49

Human Traces, 236
Hummingbird's Daughter, The, 13, 15, **42**, 86, 130, 147
Hungry Tide, The, 56, 88, 98, 100, 122, **128–129**, 215, 240
Hungry Woman in Paris, 17
Hunt, Samantha, **23**, 144
Hunter, The (Leigh), 229
Hunters, The (Messud), 32
Hunts in Dreams, 122, 127
Hurston, Zora Neale, 188
Huston, Charlie, 52, 202
Hustvedt, Siri, **141**
Huxley, Aldous, 52, 66, 234
Hyde, Catherine, 152
Hyland, M. J., 197, 229
Hynes, James, 110, 131, 205, 215, **221**, 234

I Am a Pencil: A Teacher, His Kids, and Their World of Stories, 18
I Am Charlotte Simmons, 56, 142
I Am Legend, 234
I Am Not Jackson Pollock, 218
I Ask the Impossible, 60
I Know This Much Is True, 134, 150
I Love Dollars and Other Stories of China, 230
I Love You More Than You Know, 2–3
I Sailed with Magellan, 24, 27, **123**, 220
I See You Everywhere, 108, 114, **129**, 130
I Smile Back, 84, 137, 143, **148**, 167
I, the Divine: A Novel in First Chapters, 48
I Think of You: Stories, **39**
I Wouldn't Start from Here: The 21st Century and Where It All Went Wrong, 51
Iagnemma, Karl, **69**, 142
Ice Cream War, An, 110
Ice Museum, The: In Search of the Lost Land of Thule, 144
Idea of Perfection, The, 21
Ideas of Heaven, 38
If Morning Ever Comes, 25, 103, 129
If on a Winter's Night a Traveler, 247
If You Lived Here, I'd Know Your Name, 18
Ignorance, 220
Ignorance of Blood, The, 86–87
Iliad, An, 197
I'll Go to Bed at Noon, 45
I'll Take It, 179
I'm Looking through You: Growing Up Haunted, 55
Imagined London, 4, 8

Imagining Argentina, 92, 125
Immense Journey, The, 36
Impartial Recorder, The, 3
Impressionist, The, 73, 215
In an Antique Land: History in the Guise of a Traveler's Tale, 215
In Between the Sheets, 236
In Case We're Separated, 156
In Cold Blood, 233
In Custody, 16
In God We Trust, All Others Pay Cash, 34–35, 183
In Memory of Junior, 18
In My Father's Name, 30
In Other Rooms, Other Wonders, **34**
In Persuasion Nation, 85
In Pharaoh's Army, 260
In Search of King Solomon's Mines, 88
In Search of Snow, 42
In Siberia, 8, 237
In the Drink, 204
In the Eye of the Sun, 39
In the Fall, 86, 209, 243
In the Family Way, 172
In the Fold, **118**, 140, 180
In the Image, 68
In the Kitchen, **48–49**
In the Lake of the Woods, 28, 134, 223, 225–226, 245, 250
In the Land of Men, 244
In the Name of God, 72
In the Night Season, 51
In the Penny Arcade, 240
In the Shadow of Memory, 260
In the Shadow of No Towers, 172
In the Shadows of the Morning, 88
In the Skin of a Lion, 247
In the Time of the Butterflies, 3, 13, 42, 100, 103, 130, 208
In the Wake, 115, 250
In the Walled City, 165
In the Wilderness: Coming of Age in an Unknown Country, 6
In the Woods, 164
In the Yucatan, 16
Incendiary, 116
Incognegro, 5, 116, 199
Indecision, 128, 218
Indelible Acts, 45, 225
Independence Day, 171, 214
India, 186

Indian Creek Chronicles: A Writer Alone in the Wilderness, 6
Indignation, 87, **170**, 180, 253
Ines of My Soul, 13
Infinite Jest, 197, 208, 231, 241, 259
Information, The, 90
Inglorious, **144–145**
Inheritance, 186
Inheritance of Loss, The, 34, 37, 49, **118–119**, 161, 182, 186, 240
Inn at Lake Devine, The, 152
Inquisitors' Manual, The, **3**, 41
Inside the Sky: Meditations on Flight, 151
Instance of the Fingerpost, An, 59
Instant Love, 101
Intercourse: Stories, 136, **201–202**
Interpretation of Murder, The, 54, 59
Interpreter of Maladies, 39, 149
Interred with Their Bones, **58–59**, 87
Into the Beautiful North, 12, 13, **42–43**, 86
Into the Heart of Borneo, 9
Into the Valley: Marines at Guadalcanal, 51
Into the Wild, 12, 84, 166, 217
Into Thin Air, 84
Intuitionist, The, 188
Invention of Everything Else, The, **23**, 144
Invisible Cities, 149
Invisible Sign of My Own, An, 198, 201, 211
Invisible Wall, The: A Love Story That Broke Barriers, 91, 161
Iodine, 107, **146**
Iona Moon, 6
Irish Game, The: A True Story of Crime and Art, 58
Irregulars, The: Roald Dahl and the British Spy Ring in Wartime Washington, 54
Irving, John, 22, 69, 103, 104, 117, **142**, 151, 171
Isabel's Daughter, 138
Isegawa, Moses, 31–32
Ishiguro, Kazuo, 52, 75, **221**, 253
Island, The, 188
Island of Eternal Love, The, 26
Istanbul: Memories of the City, 15, 83
It Seemed Like a Good Idea at the Time, 22, 102
It Sucked and Then I Cried, 118, 168
Italian Education, An, 166
Italian Fever, 77
Italian Neighbors, 166
Itch, 166

It's a Crime, **58**, 175
It's Superman!, 89
Iweala, Uzodinma, **221–222**
Iyer, Pico, 8, 188, 227

Jackson, Shelley, 66
Jacobs, A. J., 176
Jacoby, Susan, 209
Jade Peony, The, 12, 51, 75
Jaffe, Michael Grant, 7, **69**
James, Henry, 95
James, P. D., 221
James, Tania, 119, **142–143**, 173
*James Boys: A Novel Account of William,
        Henry, Frank and Jesse,* 50, **76**, 247,
        257
Jameses, The: A Family Narrative, 76, 257
Jameson, Jenna, 82
Jamestown, 63, 208
Jamison, Kay Redfield, 195
Jane Austen Book Club, The, 56, 64
Jane Eyre, 43, 112
Janowitz, Tama, 143, 249
Jayber Crow, 2, 10, 17–18, 28, 137, 157, 251
Jazz, 5
Jen, Gish, 161
Jenkins, Peter, 88
Jennings, Kate, 3, 128
Jentz, Terri, 126, 165
Jeremy Thane, 204
Jernigan, 223
Jesse James: Last Rebel of the Civil War, 76
Jesus' Son, 223
Jewel, 164
Jewish War, The, 255
Jhabvala, Ruth Prawer, 119
Jian, Ma, 217, 230
Jiles, Paulette, 111, 115, 209
Jim the Boy, 28, 43, 124
Jin, Ha, 39, 73, 161, **222**, 230
Joe, 18
Joe College, 27, 137, 167
Joern, Pamela Carter, 5
John Dollar, 259
John Henry Days, 188
Johnno, 232
*Johnny One-Eye: A Tale of the American
        Revolution,* **60–61**
Johnson, Angela, 130
Johnson, Deborah, 24
Johnson, Denis, 28, **69–70**, 73, 195, 208, 212,
        218, **222–223**, 228, 249

Johnson, Diane, 129
Johnson, Mat, 5, 116, 199
Johnson, Steven, 209
Jonathan Strange and Mrs. Norrell, 57
Jones, Chris, 53
Jones, Edward P., 68, **70**, 115, 165, 240, 243
Jones, Gayl, 165–166
Jones, Lloyd, 68, **70–71**
Jones, Sadie, **223**, 249
Jordan, Hillary, **24**, 242
Jordan, Toni, 23, **143–144**
Journey from the Land of No, 20, 43, 146
Journey of the Dead, 246
Journey without Maps, 39
Joyce, James, 200, 236
Judge Savage, 166
Julavits, Heidi, 72, **224**, 247
Julie and Romeo, 18
Julie and Romeo Get Lucky, 18
July, Miranda, 162, 182, 206
July, July, **244–245**
July's People, 32
Jump and Other Stories, 32, 216
Jumping the Green, 89
Junger, Sebastian, 49, 84
Junior's Leg, 44
Juno and Juliet, 40, 74, 146, 148
Jury of Her Peers, A, 148
Just, Ward, 24, 201, 223, 238

Kabul, 145
Kabul Beauty School, 141
Kadaré, Ismail, 3, 243
Kaddish for a Child Not Yet Born, 71
Kadushin, Raphael, 235
Kafka on the Shore, **244**
Kafka-Gibbons, Paul, **24**, 27, 92, 140, 166,
        205
Kalish, Mildred Armstrong, 184
Kallos, Stephanie, 25, 103, 108, **144**, 159,
        168, 184
Kalpakian, Laura, **224–225**
Kaplan, Fred, 76
Kapuscinski, Ryszard, 227
Karma and Other Stories, 39
Karon, Jan, 9
Karr, Mary, 127, 158, 169, 214, 242
Katz, Jon, 133
Kavenna, Joanna, **144–145**
Kawabata, Yasunari, 245
Keefer, Janice Kulyk, 71
Keep, The, 32, 94, 131

Keeping Faith, 139
Keith, Sam, 6
Kelly, Elizabeth, 137, **145**
Kelly, Thomas, 57
Kelman, James, **225**
Kelton, Elmer, 18, 30, 35, 36
Kennedy, A. L., 33, 45, **225–226**
Kennedy, Pagan, 135, 211
Kennedy, William P., 216
Kent, Kathleen, **71**, 106
Kept Man, The, **101**
Kerasote, Ted, 133
Keret, Etgar, 198, 206, **226**, 255
Kerouac, Jack, 241
Kertész, Imre, 63, **71–72**, 231
Kessel, John, 198, 201, 211, 216, **226**
Key, Joshua, 68
Khadra, Yasmina, **72**, 101, 140, 141, **145**
Khemir, Sabiha, **226–227**
Kick Me: Adventures in Adolescence, 160
Kidd, Chip, 96
Kidd, Sue Monk, 32, 55, 115, 156, 177
Kieron Smith, Boy, **225**
Killing Ground, The, 9
Killing Jar, The, **33**
Killing Johnny Fry, 81, 176
Killing Yourself to Live, 147
Kim, Eugenia, **146**
Kimmel, Haven, 107, 124, 138, **146**
Kincaid, Jamaica, 222
Kind of Flying, A, 11
Kindly Ones, The, 67, 200, 202, 213, **230–231**
King, Laurie, 105, 203
King in the Tree, The, 202, 240
King Lear, 240
King Leopold's Ghost, 26
King of California, The: J. G. Boswell and the Making of a Secret American Empire, 30
King of the World: Muhammad Ali and the Rise of an American Hero, 242
King's Gold, The, 78, 83
Kings of Infinite Space, 110, 131, 205, 215, **221**, 234
Kingsolver, Barbara, 6, 9, 10, 22, **25**, 88, 100, 138, **147**, 151–152, 156, 189
Kingston, Maxine Hong, 146
Kinky Gazpacho: Life, Love & Spain, 41
Kirchner, Bharti, 178
Kirshenbaum, Binnie, 152
Kiss, The, 136
Kiss, Kiss, 214, 240

Kissing the Virgin's Mouth, 24
Kitchen Boy, The, 53, 155
Kitchen Confidential, 49, 180
Kite Runner, The, 20, 99, 100, 101, 116, **140–141**, 145
Klein, Joe, 79
Klosterman, Chuck, 13, 43, 86, 107, **147**
Kluge, P. F., 64, 148–149, 153, 170, 216, 239
Kneale, Matthew, 21, **25–26**
Knee Deep in Wonder, 115
Knife Thrower and Other Stories, The, 240
Knight, Michael Muhammad, 7
Knipfel, Jim, 52, 117, 145, 239, 258
Knockemstiff, 123
Knots and Crosses, 95
Know Nothing, 9
Knowledge of Hell, 3
Knowles, John, 66, 183, 190
Known World, The, 68, **70**, 115, 240, 243
Koënings, N. S., **26**
Kogan, Deborah Copaken, **72–73**, 88, 104, 138, 144, 158, 165, 176
Koja, Kathe, 224
Konkans, **122**
Koolaids: The Art of War, 48
Kooser, Ted, 260
Koppelman, Amy, 84, 137, 143, **148**, 167
Korelitz, Jean Hanff, 74, 114, 134, 143, **148–149**, 163, 172
Kotlowitz, Alex, 188
Kozol, Jonathan, 90
Kraft, Eric, 151
Krakauer, Jon, 12, 84, 166, 217
Krauss, Nicola, 74
Krauss, Nicole, 102, **149**, 155, 159, 213, 239
Krol, Torsten, **73**, 255
Krosney, Herbert, 56, 227
Kundera, Milan, 174, 220
Kunkel, Benjamin, 128, 218
Kunstler, Howard James, 63, 66, 210, 218
Kunzru, Hari, 61, **73**, 215, 243
Kurlansky, Mark, 59, 167, 228
Kushiel's Chosen, 58
Kushiel's Dart, 58
Kushner, Rachel, **26**

LaBastille, Anne, 6
Labiner, Norah, **227–228**
Labors of the Heart: Stories, **14**
Labrador Pact, The, **132–133**, 207
Lace Reader, The, 65, 71, **105–106**, 134, 139, 150

Lacuna, The, **147**
Ladder of Years, 31, 112, 173, 184
Ladies' Lending Library, The, 71
Ladies' Man, The, 152
Ladies of Grace Adieu and Other Stories, The, 57
Lady in Blue, The, 92
Lahiri, Jhumpa, 39, 75, 98, 99, 102, 119, 134, 140, **149–150**, 160, 209, 240, 243
Laird, Nick, **74**.107
Lakhani, Anisha, **74**
Lalami, Laila, 8
Lamazares, Ivonne, 26
Lamb, Christina, 145
Lamb, Wally, 134, **150**, 179
Lamb: Mystical Gospel According to Biff, Christ's Childhood Pal, 79
Lamb in Love, 112
Laments, The, 182
Lamott, Anne, 251
Lanagan, Margo, 254
Lanchester, John, 114
Land of Green Plums, The, 3
Land of Little Rain, The, 10
Land of Marvels, **41–42**
Landing, **120**
Langer, Adam, 11, 24, **26–27**
Langewiesche, William, 12, 60, 151
Language of Baklava, The, 43, 253
Lansens, Lori, 129, **150–151**, 163, 183, 203
Lansky, Aaron, 155
Lapierre, Alexandra, 121, 202
Lark and Termite, 115, 168, 178
Larry's Party, 255
Larsen, Reif, 125
Larson, Erik, 58
Larsson, Stieg, 78, 202
Lasser, Scott, 161
Last American Man, The, 148, 217
Last Chicken in America, The, 209
Last Chinese Chef, The, **33–34**, 138
Last Evenings on Earth, 200
Last Kabbalist of Lisbon, The, 83
Last King of Scotland, The, 3, 195
Last Life, The, 32
Last Night at the Lobster, **164–165**
Last Night in Montreal, **39–40**, 66
Last Night in Twisted River, **142**
Last Noel, The, 155
Last of the Husbandmen, The, **28**
Last of the Just, The, 149
Last Orders, 124, 179

Last Report on the Miracles at Little No Horse, The, 42
Last Run, The: A True Story of Rescue and Redemption on the Alaskan Seas, 84
Last Secret, The, 78, **80**, 173
Last Supper, The: A Summer in Italy, 118
Last Witchfinder, The, 71, 80
Lauck, Jennifer, 159
Laughlin, Emma, 74
Laura, 19, 43, 136
Laura Rider's Masterpiece, **135**
Laurie, Hugh, 52
Lavinia, **228**
Law of Averages, The, 7, 201
Law of Similars, The, 55
Lawhead, Stephen, 60
Laws of Harmony, The, **138**
Lawson, Mary, 111
Lay of the Land, The, 171, 214
Laying on of Hands, The, 54
Layover, 132, 143, 148
Lazar, Zachary, **228**
Lazarus Project, The, 4, **219**, 220
Le, Nam, **74–75**
Le Divorce, 129
Le Guin, Ursula K., 80, **228**
Leading the Cheers, 114, 238, 245
Leap Year, 140
Learners, The, 96
Leave Before You Go, 249
Leaving Home, **111–112**, 118
Leaving Tanger, **7**, 8
Leavitt, Caroline, 182
LeBlanc, Adrian Nicole, 130, 148
Lecturer's Tale, The, 221
Lee, Chang-Rae, 7, 117, **151**, 232
Lee, Harper, 112, 124, 125, 164, 183, 204
Lee, Hermione, 121
Lee, Janice Y. K., 12, 31, 34, **75**
Leech, Garry, 78
Leeson, Nick, 77
Lefevre, Didier, 101, 104
Leff, Valerie Ann, 2, 11, 154
Leffland, Ella, 178
Left Hand of Darkness, The, 80, 228
Legend of Colton H. Bryant, The, 11
Legend of Sigurd and Gudrun, The, 60
Legs, 216
Lehane, Dennis, 106
Lehrer, Jonah, 195
Leigh, Julia, **229**
Lemercier, Frederic, 101, 104

Lemon Table, The: Stories, 105, **197**, 232
Lemon Tree, The: An Arab, The, a Jew, The, and the Heart of the Middle East, 20, 48
Lende, Heather, 18
Lennon, J. Robert, 29, **75–76**, 166, 224, 250
Lent, Jeffrey, 86, 209, 243
Leonard, Elmore, 70, 180
Leopard Hat, The: A Daughter's Story, 109
Leopold, Aldo, 10
Lerman, Rhoda, 255
Leshem, Ron, **27–28**
Lesley, Craig, **151–152**
Lessing, Doris, 38, 103, 105, 216
Lesson Before Dying, A, 112
Lesy, Michael, 21
Let the Great World Spin, **30–31**
Let the Trumpet Sound: A Life of Martin Luther King, Jr., 188
Let Us Now Praise Famous Men, 259
Lethem, Jonathan, **229–230**, 241
Letter from New York, 2
Letters from a Lost Generation, 105
Letters of Saul Bellow, The, 179
Levin, Ira, 230 231
Levison, Iain, 165, 221
Levitation, 252
Levithan, David, 104, 157
Levy, Adrian, 68
Lewan, Todd, 84
Lewis, C. S., 191, 248
Lewis, Michael, 77, 118
Lewis, R. W. B., 76, 257
Lewycka, Marina, 213
Lianke, Yan, 202, 222, **230**, 233
Liar's Club, The, 127, 158, 169, 214, 242
Liar's Poker, 77
Liberation, 173
Libra, 223
Lieberman, Nancy, 65
Liebmann-Smith, Richard, 50, **76**, 247, 257
Lies of the Saints, 31
Life and Times of Mexico, The, 16, 147
Life and Times of Michael K., 236
Life and Times of the Last Kid Picked, The, 35, 183
Life and Times of the Thunderbolt Kid, The, 124
Life Before Death, 151
Life Class, 10, **104–105**, 185
Life Laid Bare, 198, 222
Life Mask, 120

Life of Samuel Johnson, The, 50, 113
Life of the Skies: Birding at the End of Nature, The, 18
Life Without Water, 138, **167**, 175
Lifeguard, The, 218
Life's Work, A: On Becoming a Mother, 73, 93, 118
Light in the Window, A, 9
Light of Day, The, 179
Light of Falling Stars, The, 76
Lightman, Alan, 237
Like Family: Growing up in Other People's Houses, 158
Like Water for Chocolate, 16–17, 259
Limbo, and Other Places I Have Lived, 41
Lindsey, Robert, 54
Line of Beauty, The, 118, **139–140**, 166, 180
Link, Kelly, 198, 226
Lin-Liu, Jen, 34
Lion Called Christian, A, 133
Lipman, Elinor, 65, **152**, 172
Lipstick Jihad: A Memoir of Growing up Iranian in America and American in Iran, 161
Lipstick Jungle, 11, 154
Lipsyte, Sam, 2, 62, 128
Liquidation, 71
Lisicky, Paul, 203
Liss, David, 25, 50, 83, 87
Litman, Ellen, 209
Littell, Jonathan, 67, 200, 202, 213, **230–231**
Littell, Robert, 223
Little, Benilde, 166
Little Altars Everywhere, 14
Little America, 140
Little Bee, 78, **115–116**
Little Bird of Heaven, 81
Little Children, 49, 84, 118, 137, 143, 148, 158, **167–168**, 173, 200, 238, 256
Little Friend, The, 164
Little Giant of Aberdeen County, The, **102–103**, 115, 144, 168, 169
Little Green Men, 56
Little Heathens, 184
Little Love Story, A, 128
Little Stranger, The, **94**, 98
Little Women (Alcott), 112
Little Women (Weber), 187
Live at Five, 30, 257
Live Through This: A Mother's Memoir of Runaway Daughters and Reclaimed Love, 120, 224

Lively, Penelope, 151, **152–153**, 231
Lives and Times of Bonnie & Clyde, The, 58
Lives of Rocks, The, 17
Livesey, Margot, 153, 189, **231**
Living, The, 30, 260
Living at Nature's Pace, 28
Living to Tell, 114, 194
Lloyd: What Happened, 62
Llywelyn, Morgan, 210
Local Girls, 177–178
Local Wonders, 260
Locked Room, The, 196
Lockhart, E., 152
Lodato, Victor, 125
Lodge, David, **153**, 162, 207
Lodger Shakespeare, The: His Life on Silver Street, 59
Logan's Storm, 44
Logsdon, Gene, **28**
Lolita, 126, 131, 220
London Fields, 90
Lone Surfer of Montana, Kansas, The, 5
Lonely Soldier: The Memoir of an American Soldier in the Israeli Army, 28
Lonely Werewolf Girl, 32
Long, Kate, 132, **153–154**
Long After Midnight at the Nino Bien: A Yanqui's Missteps in Argentina, 4
Long Long Way, A, 198, 258
Long March and in the Clap Shack, The, 222
Long Night of White Chickens, The, 130
Long Way Down, A, 140
Long Way Gon, A: Memoirs of a Boy Soldier, 20, 116, 222
Long Way Round, 83
Longings of Women, The, 174
Long-Legged House, The, 10
Look Me in the Eye: My Life with Asperger's, 132
Looking for Alaska, 33, 66, 157, 190
Looking Good, 29
Loop, The, 22, 117
Loop Group, 180
Loose Woman, 13
Loot, and Other Stories, 216
Lopate, Phillip, 170, 205, **231–232**, 236, 252, 260
Lopez, Barry, 10
López, Josefina, 17
Lord Jim, 92
Losing Everything, 168, 214
Losing Julia, 110

Losing Mum and Pup, 56
Lost Ark of the Covenant, The, 227
Lost Art of Walking, The: History, The, Science, The, Philosophy, The, and Literature of Pedestrianism, The, 8
Lost Dog, The, 44, **206–207**
Lost Geography, 81, 102
Lost Gospel, The: The Quest for the Gospel of Judas Iscariot, 56, 227
Lost in a Good Book, 64
Lost in Mongolia, 83, 93
Lost in the City, 70
Lost in the Forest, **159**, 160
Lost in Translation: A Life in a New Language (Hoffman), 43, 109
Lost in Translation (Mones), 34
Lost Mountain, 44
Lost Nation, 86
Lost Ravioli Recipes of Hoboken, The, 253
Lost, The: Searching for Six of Six Million, 155
Lott, Bret, 164
Love, **242**, 243
Love Enter, 24
Love and Obstacles: Stories, 219, **220**, 240
Love and Other Impossible Pursuits, **93**, 137
Love, Etc., 197
Love Hexagon, The, 179
Love in the Driest Season, 38, 184
Love in the Present Tense, 152
Love in the Time of Cholera, 149
Love Invents Us, 109, 174
Love Is a Mix Tape, 91, 161, 191
Love Medicine, 126
Love of a Good Woman, The, 39, 181
Love or Something Like It, 173, 175
Love Stories in This Town, 123
Love Today: Stories, 162
Love Walked In, 93
Love Wife, The, 161
Love, Work, Children, 27, 154
Lovely Bones, The, 151, 164, 224
Lovely Green Eyes, **76–77**, 210
Loves of Judith, The, 91
Loves That Bind, 185
Loving Frank, 111
Lucky, 73
Lucky in the Corner, 120
Lucky Ones, The, 118
Ludmila's Broken English, 85
Lullaby, 82, 248
Lunch at the Piccadilly, 18, 117

Luncheon of the Boating Party, 121
Lush Life, 70, **85**
Lust and Other Stories, 154, 214, 244
Lustig, Arnost, **76–77**, 210
Lydia Cassatt Reading the Morning Paper,
    121
Lynch, Jim, 124
Lyndon Johnson and the Majorettes, 29
Lynn, Kenneth Schuyler, 216

MacDonald, Ann-Marie, 106, 131, 150
MacDonald, Sam, 107
Macdonald, Sarah, 4
Macey, David, 188
Machete Season, 198, 222
Machine Dreams, 168
Mackey, Nathaniel, **232**
Mackler, Carolyn, 104
Maclean, Norman, 84
MacLeod, Alistair, 12
Macy, Caitlin, **154**
Madame Bovary, 143
Madden, Deirdre, 198
Madonna of Excelsior, The, **31–32**, 243
Madonnas of Leningrad, The, **15**, 37, 68, 155
Magic for Beginners, 198, 226
Magic Hour, 156
Magic Seeds, 73
Magician's Assistant, The, 166
Magus, The, 94
Maheu, Layne, 133
Mahfouz, Naguib, 253
Mahoney, Rosemary, 129
Mail, 120, 144, 152
Maillard, Keith, **28–29**
Mailman, 76
Make Believe, 173
*Makes Me Wanna Holler: A Young Black Man
    in America,* 30, 257
Making It Up, 153
Making Love to the Minor Poets of Chicago,
    24
Malcolm and Juliet, 52
Malcolm X, 5, 188
Malinche, 42
Malone, Michael, 117, **154–155**, 172
Malouf, David, **232**
Mambo Kings Play Songs of Love, The, 5, 60
Man Gone Down, **257**
Man in the Dark, **49–50**
Man in the High Castle, The, 87
Man in the Picture, The, 78, 94

Man of My Dreams, The, 174
*Man on the Moon, A: Voyages of the Apollo
    Astronauts,* 53
Man Walks into a Room, 149
Man Who Created Paradise, The, 28
Man Who Mistook His Wife for a Hat, The,
    215, 250
Man Who Smiled, The, 250
Man Who Tried to Save the World, The, 195
Man with the Golden Arm, The, 123, 219, 220
Mandanipour, Shahriar, **233**
Manguel, Alberto, 209
Manhattan Nocturne, 136
Mankell, Henning, 250
Manrique, Jaime, 41
Manseau, Peter, **155**
Many Aspects of Mobile Home Living, The, 18
Map of Glass, A, **184–185**
Map of Love, The, 39
Map of the World, A, 135, 150
Map Thief, The, **92**
Maps and Legends, 260
Maps for Lost Lovers, 34, 99, 101, 145
Mapson, Jo-Ann, **155–156**
March (Brooks), 56, 70, **112**, 116
March, The (Doctorow), 209, 216
March 1917, 237
Marchetto, Marisa Acocella, 99
Marciano, Francesca, 141, 158
Marcom, Micheline Aharonian, **29**
Markoe, Merrill, 133
Markovits, Benjamin, 152, 172
Marks, Stephen, 79
Marley & Me, 133
Marshall, Paule, 138
Martin, Clancy, **77**, 249
Martin, David Lozell, 168, 214
Martin, Douglas A., 50
Martin, Russell, 195
Martin, Steve, 132, 173, 180, 218
Martin, Valerie, **77–78**, 80
*Martin Dressler: The Tale of an American
    Dreamer,* 240
Martínez, Guillermo, **78**, 86, 87
Martinez, Ruben, 12, 60
Martinique, 188
Mary Reilly, 77
Mason & Dixon, 259
Massacre of the Dreamers, 60
Master, The, 41, 105, 112, 169, 181, **257**
Master Bedroom, The, 45, 104, **132**
Master Butchers' Singing Club, The, 42

Master Executioner, The, 233, 234
Masters, Alexander, 197
Mastras, George, **78–79**, 83
Matheson, Richard, 234
Mathilda Savitch, 125
Matloff, Judith, 7, 27, 30
Matrimony, 66
Matteson, John, 112
Matthiessen, Peter, 9, **29–30**, 88
Mattison, Alice, 41, **156**
Max, D. T., 237
Maxey, James, 89
Maximum City: Bombay Lost and Found, 48, 102
Maxwell, William, 159
Maxxed Out, **62**, 77
Mayer, Jane, 90
Mayes, Frances, 4
Mayle, Peter, 4, 133
Maynard, Joyce, 19, 69, 85, 120, 256
Maytrees, The, 260
McAlpine, Ken, 241
McBride, James, 115, 187, 257
McCaig, Donald, 37
McCall, Nathan, 7, **30**, 257
McCall Smith, Alexander, 18, 56–57, 104
McCann, Colum, **30–31**
McCarthy, Cormac, 36, 52, 62–63, 194, 197, 199, 210, **233–234**, 249
McCarthy, Mary, 124, 163
McCarthy, Pete, 39
McCarthy, Tom, 221, **234**
McCarthy's Bar: A Journey of Discovery in the West of Ireland, 39
McCartney, Alistair, **234–235**
McCauley, Stephen, 24, 152
McClanahan, Ed, 124
McCouch, Hannah, 49
McCourt, Frank, 41, 79, 180, 211, 225
McCourt, Malachy, 211
McCracken, Elizabeth, 103, 109
McCrum, Robert, 128, 245
McDermott, Alice, 211
McEvoy, Dermot, 13, **79**
McEwan, Ian, 4, 107, 130, 153, 166, 174, 179, 190, 196, 197, 229, 231, **235–236**, 247
McGahern, John, **156–157**, 198
McGhee, Alison, **157**, 183
McGrath, Patrick, 48
McGraw, Erin, **31**, 109
McGregor, Ewan, 83
McInerney, Jay, 2, 32, 35, 123, 172, 182, 207

McLain, Paula, **157–158**, 165
McManus, James, 83
McMillan, David, 78
McMurtry, Larry, 72, 171, 180
McNeil, Leggs, 82
McPherson, James, 16
McSweeney's Book of Poets Picking Poets, The, 206
McSweeney's Joke Book of Book Jokes, The, 206, 226
Mda, Zakes, **31–32**, 243
Mean Spirit, 220
Meaning of Night, The, 48, 50, 67, 105, 235
Means of Escape, 88
Measure of Endurance, A: Unlikely Triumph of Steven Sharpe, 148
Medwed, Mameve, 120, 144, 152, 179
Meek, James, **158**, 185, **236–237**, 239
Meely LaBauve, 44
Meeting in Infinity, 226
Mefisto, 196
Mehran, Marsha, 140
Mehta, Suketu, 48, 102
Melnyczuk, Askold, 4, **237**
Meltzer, Brad, 62
Memoir Club, The, 224
Memoir from an Antproof Case, 110
Memoirs of a Geisha, 37
Memoirs of a Muse, 259
Memoranda, 64
Memories of a Catholic Girlhood, 124
Memories of My Melancholy Whores, 218
Memory Keeper's Daughter, 89, 106
Memory of Old Jack, 10
Men and the Girls, 182
Men Giving Money, Women Yelling, 156
Men in Black, 176
Men Who Stare at Goats, The, 63
Menand, Louis, 219
Mendelsohn, Daniel, 155
Mendelson, Cheryl, 2, 11, 27, 30, 118, 154
Menger-Anderson, Kirsten, 186, **237**
Meno, Joe, **238**
Mercury Under My Tongue, 77, 99, 128, 157, **258**
Mercy, A (Morrison), 68, **242–243**
Mercy (Santoro), 88
Merle's Door, 133
Merullo, Roland, 23, **79**, 128, 241, 253
Messiah of Stockholm, The, 213
Messud, Claire, **32**
Mestre-Reed, Ernesto, 26

Metaphysical Club, The: A Story of Ideas in America, 219
Metroland, 105
Metz, Julie, 101
Meyers, Jeffrey, 10
Mezrich, Ben, 77
Michell, John, 59
Microserfs, 165
Middle Ground, The, 144
Middlesex, 55, **212**
Midnight at the Dragon Café, 12, **50–51**, 150, 173
Midnight Express, 78
Midnight's Children, 98, 213
Midwives, 55
Milagro Beanfield War, The, 233
Miles, Jonathan, 82, **238–239**
Milk, Sulphate, and Alby Starvation, 32, 62, 159
Millar, Martin, 4, **32–33**, 62, **158–159**, 160, 164, 171, 190
Miller, Adrienne, 152
Miller, Sue, 127, **159–160**, 166, 173, 174
Millett, Lydia, 57, 201, 205, **239**
Millhauser, Steven, 75, 202, 203, **239–240**, 244
Million Little Pieces, A, 20
Millionaires, The, 62
Mills, Kay, 55, 177, 188
Mills, Magnus, 11, 73, 159, 212, 215, 221
Millstone, The, 144
Milner, E. R., 58
Mimi's Ghost, 83
Minaret, 99, 140
Minatoya, Lydia, 43, 51
Mind-Body Problem, The, 149
Mineral Palace, The, 224
Miniatures, **227–228**
Minimum of Two, 44
Ministry of Special Cases, The, **125**, 143, 170, 247
Minority Report, 221
Minot, Eliza, 159
Minot, Susan, 15, 151, 154, 173, 202, 214, 218, 244
Minotaur, The, 67
Minotaur Takes a Cigarette Break, The, 60
Miracle at Sing Sing, 150
Mirror in the Well, 29
Mishler, William, 148
Missing World, The, 189, 231
Mississippi Sissy, 124, 169

Mister Pip, 68, **70–71**
Mistress of Spices, The, 119, 186
Mistress's Daughter, The, 108, 182, 214
Mistry, Rohinton, 186, 239, **240**
Mitchard, Jacquelyn, 160
Mitchell, David, 27, 33, 63, 122, 154, **160**, 162, 164, 225, **240–241**
Mitchell, Margaret, 37
Moaveni, Azadeh, 161
Moehringer, J. R., 35, 86, 107, 123, 145, 183
Mohawk, 171
Mohr, 67, **168–169**
Mojtabai, H. G., 23, 34, **241**
Moment's Notice: Jazz in Poetry and Prose, 232
Mom's Cancer, 99
Monaghan, Nicola, **33**
Mones, Nicole, **33–34**, 138
Monk, Bathsheba, 14
Monk Swimming, A, 211
Monkey Hunting, 26
Monson, Ander, 225
Monsters of Templeton, The, **131**
Monstrous Regiment of Women, A, 105
Montana 1948, 136
Moo, 149, 175
Moody, Rick, 248
Moon, Elizabeth, 132
Moon Deluxe, 7
Moon Palace, 144
Moon Tiger, 151, 153
Moonlight Hotel, **195**
Moonlight on the Avenue of Faith, 161
Moore, Christopher, 79
Moore, Judith, 103
Moore, Lorrie, 109, 244
Moorehead, Alan, 16
Mootoo, Shani, **160–161**
Moral Disorder, 177, 243
Moral Hazard, 3, 128
More Than It Hurts You, 80, 96, **256**
More Than You Know, 98, 160
Morgan, C. E., 24, 175, **241–242**
Morgan, Jude, 10
Morgantown, 29
Morituri, 72
Morningside Heights, 2, 11, 27, 30, 118, 154
Morpheus, 218
Morris, Errol, 72
Morris, Jan, 16, 39
Morris, Mary, 245
Morris, Mary McGarry, 78, **80**, 173

Morris, Willie, 124
Morrison, Toni, 5, 31, 68, 216, **242–243**
Morrow, James, 52, 71, **80**
Mortenson, Greg, 20, 78–79, 141
Morton, Kate, 71, **80–81**, 105, 198
Mosley, Walter, **81**, 85, 176
Mosquito Coast, The, 100, 158
Moss, Barbara Robinette, 146
Mother Country, 251
Mother Knot, 136
Mother Night, 53
MotherKind, 168
Motherless Brooklyn, 229, 230, 241
Mothers and Sons: Stories, 179, **181**, 211
Mouthful of Air, A, 148
Mover of Bones, The, 5
Moviegoer, The, 107
Mowat, Farley, 133
Mr. and Mrs. Prince, 116
Mr. Paradise, 70
Mr. Potter, 222
Mr. Sebastian and the Negro Magician, **93–94**
Mrs. Dalloway, 114, 214, 254
Mrs. Kimble, 133
Mrs. Woolf and the Servants, 254
Mudbound, **24**, 242
Mueenuddin, Daniyal, **34**
Mueller, Andrew, 51
Muir, John, 10
Mulberry Empire, The, 145, 215
Mulisch, Harry, 115
Müller, Herta, 3
Multitude of Sins, A, 182, 197, 201, **214**, 260
Munro, Alice, 39, 81, 181, **243**, 244, 252, 255
Mura, David, **161**, 191
Murakami, Haruki, **243–244**, 246, 253
Murder in Mesopotamia, 42
Murdoch, Iris, 247
Murray, Craig, 195
Museum of Doubt, 236
Museum of Dr. Moses, The, 81
Music and Silence, 182
Music Lesson, 187
MVP, 200
My Antonia, 124
My Art, My Life, 121
My Autobiography (Chaplin), 216
My Christina and Other Stories, 224
My Cousin Rachel, 61
My Dog Skip, 124
My Dream of You, 212
My Father's Tears and Other Stories, 84

My First Summer in the Sierra, 10
My French Kitchen: A Book of 120 Treasured Recipes, 135
My Friend Leonard, 20
"My Girlfriend Comes to the City and Beats Me Up," 176
My Holocaust, 255
My Invented Country: A Nostalgic Journey Through Chile, 8
My Jim, 116
My Latest Grievance, 65, **152**
My Life as a Fake, 149
My Life as a Man, 170
My Life, Starring Dara Falcon, 214
My Name Is Red, 15, **83**
My Revolutions, 61, **73**, 243
My Sister, My Love: The Intimate Story of Skylar Rampike, 223
My Sister's Keeper, 134
My Son's Story, 32
My Stroke of Insight, 128
My War: Killing Time In Iraq, 28
My Year in France, 135
My Year of Meats, 191
My Year Off: Recovering Life after a Stroke, 128, 245
Myron, Vicki, 133
Mysteries of My Father, 79
Mysteries of Winterthurn, 81
Mystery of Grace, The, 254
Mystic Arts of Erasing All Signs of Death, The, 52, 202
Myth of You and Me, The, 40, 158, 163, 189

Nabokov, Vladimir, 126, 131, 220
Nadas, Peter, 231
Nadelson, Theodore, 76
Nafisi, Azar, 20, 38, 71, 233
Nahai, Gina, **161–162**
Nailah, Anika, 166
Naipaul, V. S., 73
Naked Olympics, The: The True Story of the Ancient Games, 59
Name All the Animals, 111
Name of the Rose, The, 83, 87
Name of the World, The, 223
Names of the Dead, The, 165
Namesake, The, 98, 99, 119, 134, 140, 149, 240
Naming the Spirits, 92
Nanny Diaries, The, 74
Nansen, Odd, 115

Naomi and Ely's No Kiss List, 104, 157
Napoleon and the Chicken Farmer, 71
Nasarina, Tasalima, 100
Nathan Coulter, 2, 137
Native Speaker, 151
Nattel, Lillian, 155
Natural Acts: A Sidelong View of Science and Nature, 238
Natural Order of Things, The, 3
Nature Girl, 44
Nazi Literature in the Americas, 200
Necessary Sins, 73
Neck Deep and Other Predicaments, 225
Nelson, Antonya, 39, 78, 81, 109, 114, **162**, 181, 194, **244**, 254, 255
Nemirovsky, Irene, 15, 38, 91
Neon Rain, 44
Neruda, Pablo, 200
Nervous Conditions, 31
Netherland, 2, 4, 31, 32, **35–36**, 127, 158, 172, 207, 218, 257
Never Cry Wolf, 133
Never Die Alone, 85
Never Let Me Go, 52, **221**, 253
Neverwhere, 159
New City, The, 49
New Confessions, 110
New Life, The, 83
Newby, Eric, 8, 102, 227
Newjack: Guarding Sing Sing, 176
News from Paraguay, The, **41**
News of the World, The, 11
Next of Kin, 182
Nicholas, Lynn, 68
Nicholls, Charles, 59
Nicholls, David, 74, 107, 120, **162**
Nichols, John, 233
Nichols, Peter, 93
Nicholson, Geoff, 8, 180
Nicholson, Joy, 16
Nick and Norah's Infinite Playlist, 157
Nickel and Dimed: On (Not) Getting by in America, 165, 176
Niederhoffer, Galt, 14, 65, **162–163**, 245
Niemi, Mikael, 19, **34–35**
Niffenegger, Audrey, 23, 66, 94, 129, 151, **163**, 174, 186, 203
Night, 254
Night and Hope, 76
Night Garden, The, 24
Night Gardener, The (Pelecanos), 85
Night Gardener, The (Sandor), 252

Night of Music, A, 252
Night Watch, The, 94
Nimrod Flipout, The, 198, 206, 226, 255
Nine, The: Inside the Secret World of the Supreme Court, 57
Nine Lives: Death and Life in New Orleans, 7, 44
Nine Parts of Desire: Hidden World of Islamic Women, 56, 141
Nineteen Minutes, 150
1972: A Novel of Ireland's Unfinished Revolution, 210
1968, 167, 228
No Country for Old Men, 194, **233**, 234
No Great Mischief, 12
No Longer at Ease, 222
No Man's Lands: One Man's Odyssey Through the Odyssey, 176
No One Belongs Here More Than You, 162, 182, 206
No One Gardens Alone: A Life of Elizabeth Lawrence, 112
No. 1 Ladies Detective Agency, The, 18, 56, 104
No True Glory: A Frontline Account of the Battle for Fallujah, 28
No Way To Treat a First Lady, 56
Nobodies: Modern American Slave Labor and the Dark Side of the New Global Economy, 90
Nobody Gets the Girl, 89
Nobody Move, **69–70**, 73, 218, 223, 249
Nobody's Fool, 13, 22, 117, 118, 147, 151, 155, 171
Nobody's Girl, 162
Nobody's Son: Notes from an American Life, 42
Noodle Maker, The, 230
Normal: Transsexual CEOs, Crossdressing Cops, and Hermaphrodites with Attitudes, 109
North, 201
North, Sterling, 124, 133
Northern Clemency, The, 154, 160
Norwegian Wood, 244
Not Her Real Name and Other Stories, 249
Not Quite What I Was Planning: Six-Word Memoirs by Writers Famous and Obscure, 206
Not Yet, 12
Nothing But a Smile, 178
Nothing Is Quite Forgotten in Brooklyn, 41, **156**

Nothing Right: Short Stories, 78, 109, **162,** 244, 254, 255

Nothing to Be Frightened Of, 105, 197, 252

NoVA, 148, 190, 199, **200,** 205

Novel About My Wife, 35, 66, 204, 215, 234, **249,** 256

November 1916, 237

Now You See Him, 62, **65–66,** 217, 245

Now You See It—Stories from Cokesville, PA, 14

Nowhere Man, 219, 220

Nugent, Benjamin, 160

Nuland, Sherwin, 238

Number9Dream, 160, 241

Nursery Crimes, 93

O Beulah Land, 9

O the Clear Moment, 124

Oates, Joyce Carol, 81, 223, 247

Oates, Stephen B., 188

Obama, Barack, 122, 124

Object of My Affection, The, 24

Objects in Mirror Are Closer Than They Appear, 187

O'Brien, Tim, 28, 51, 134, 151, 171, 207, 223, 225–226, 232, **244–245,** 250

Observatory Mansions, 203

Ocean in Iowa, An, 122

O'Connor, John, **82**

October Country, The, 240

O'Dell, Tawni, 108, 129, **163–164**

O'Donnell, Patrick K., 54

Oe, Kenzaburo, **245,** 246

Of Bees and Mist, **254**

Of Men and Their Mothers, 120, 179

O'Faolain, Nuala, 211–212

Off Ramp: Adventures and Heartache in the American Elsewhere, 227, 241

Off Season: Discovering America on Winter's Shore, 241

Officer Friendly and Other Stories, 86

Offutt, Chris, 248

O'Flynn, Catherine, 104, 152, 157, 163, **164,** 165, 176, 202, 213, 249

Ogawa, Yoko, 104, **245–246**

Oh Pure and Radiant Heart, 201, 205, 239

O'Hanlon, Redmond, 9

O.K.: The Corral, the Earps, and Doc Holliday, 246

O'Keeffe, Georgia, 10

Okri, Ben, 222

Old Patagonian Express, The: By Train Through the Americas, 23

Old School, 188, **190,** 260

Olds, Bruce, **246**

Olive Kitteridge, 23, 44, 123, 130, 150, 168, **177–178,** 184, 231, 252

Olmstead, Robert, **35**

Olson, Sigurd, 36

On Beauty, 137, 166

On Being Born: And Other Difficulties, 238

On Bullshit, 209

On Chesil Beach, 179, 196, 197, 229, **235–236**

On Green Dolphin Street, 236

On Killing: The Psychological Cost of Learning to Kill in War and Society, 76

On Mystic Lake, 156

On Purpose, 74

On the Grand Trunk Road, 100

On the Nature of Human Romantic Interaction, **69**

On the Night Plain, 76

On the Road, 241

O'Nan, Stewart, 72–73, 89, 158, **164–165,** 176, 224

Once Removed, **191**

Once Upon a Day, 183

Once Upon a Town: The Miracle of the North Platte Canteen, 120

Ondaatje, Michael, 15, 56, 75, 91, 236, **246–247**

One by One in the Darkness, 198

One Dangerous Lady, 11

One Day in the Life of Ivan Denisovich, 8

One Fifth Avenue, 2, **11,** 154

One Foot in Eden, 86

One Good Turn, 65, 183

One Hundred and One Ways, 191

One Hundred Years of Solitude, 200, 254

One Man's Wilderness: An Alaskan Odyssey, 6

One Marvelous Thing, The, **210–211**

One Vacant Chair, **117,** 179

O'Neill, Joseph, 2, 4, 31, 32, **35–36,** 127, 158, 172, 207, 218, 257

Only Revolutions, 241

Open House, 108

Open Road: The Global Journey of the Fourteenth Dalai Lama, 188

Open Sea, 197

Opening Skinner's Box, 96

Operatives, Spies, and Saboteurs: The Unknown Story of the Men and Women of WWII's OSS, 54

Opium Season: A Year on the Afghan Frontier, 78

Oracle Bones: A Journey Between China's Past and Present, 4

Oracle Night, 50

Oranges Are Not the Only Fruit, 120

Orchard, 43

Orchid Thief, The, 148

Ordinary Genius, **4–5**

Ordinary Seaman, The, 130

Ordinary Time, 241

Ordinary White Boy, The, 62

Oresteia of Aeschylus, The, 60

Origin, 19

Orlando, 254

Orlean, Susan, 148

O'Rourke, P. J., 57

Oryx and Crake, 52, 66, 80, 95, 221

Osborne, Jennifer, 82

Oscar and Lucinda, 21, 58, 113, 139, 215, 232

Other, The, **217**

Other Family, The, 58

Other Hollywood, The: The Uncensored Oral History of the Porn Film Industry, 82

Other Stories and Other Stories, 255

Otto, Whitney, 189

Our Kind, 186

Our Lady of Greenwich Village, 13, **79**

Our Lady of the Forest, 217

Our Lady of the Lost and Found, 79, 224

Our Lives Are the Rivers, 41

Our Sometime Sister, 228

Our Story Begins: New and Selected Stories, 75, 190, **260**

Out of My Skin, **218**

Out of Silence: A Journey into Language, 195

Out of the Woods: Stories, 248

Out Stealing Horses, 19, 34, 69, 115, 126, 141, 142, 217, **250**

Outcast, The, **223**, 249

Outlander, The (Adamson), 21, 69, 86, **194**, 210, 249

Outlander (Gabaldon), 186

Outside Valentine, 58

Outwitting History: The Amazing Adventures of a Man Who Rescued a Million Yiddish Books, 155

Over and Under, 34, 125, **183**, 217

Owl & Moon Cafe, The, **155–156**

Oxford Murders, The, 78

Oxford Project, The, 122

Oxygen Man, The, 190

Ozeki, Ruth, 172, 191

Ozick, Cynthia, 170, 213, 226, **247**, 252

Packer, Ann, 102

Packer, George, 250

Packer, Z. Z., 91, **165–166**

Paddock, Jennifer, 158

Paddy Clarke Ha Ha Ha, 120, 209, 210, 225

Pagan Rabbi, The, and Other Stories, The, 226, 247, 252

Page, Jeremy, 115, **247–248**

Paine, Tom, **248**

Paint It Black, 80

Painted Desert, 7

Pakistani Bride, The, 99

Palace of Illusions, The, 119, 129

Palahniuk, Chuck, 81, **82**, 85, 176, **248–249**

Pale View of the Hills, A, 221

Paley, Grace, 156

Palm of the Hand Stories, 245

Palmer, Michael, 63

Pamuk, Orhan, 15, **83**

Paper Shadows, 12

Paper Towns, 33, 157

Paperboy, The, 140, 190, 250

Paradise, 45, 225, 242

Paradise Alley, 5, 216

Paretsky, Sara, 138

Parfitt, Tudor, 227

Paris Trance: A Romance, 140

Parker, Robert, 246

Parks, Tim, 78, **83**, **166**, 196

Parting the Waters: American in the King Years, 1954-1963, 5

Partisan's Daughter, A, 15

Party of One: Loner's Manifesto, 145

Passage to India, A, 38

Passage to Juneau: A Sea and Its Meanings, 227

Passing for Normal: A Memoir of Compulsion, 144

Passing On, 153

Passion, 10

Passion and Prejudice: A Family Memoir, 109

Passion of Artemisia, The, 254

Passionate Man, A, 182

Pastoralia: Stories, 85, 206

Patchett, Ann, 36, 63, 147, 160, **166**, 189, 214

Pathseeker, 71
Patrimony, 252
Patron Saint of Liars, The, 166
Patterson, Kevin, 83
Paula Spencer, **120**, 209
Peace, **51**, 253
Peace Like a River, 19, 86, **124–125**, 126
Peacock, Nancy, 138, **167**, 175, 228
Pearl, Matthew, 83
Pearl, 199
Pearl Diver, The, 40
Pearl of Kuwait, The, 248
Pears, Iain, 59, 78
Peck, Robert Newton, 124
Pedant in the Kitchen, The, 105
Peel My Love Like an Onion, 60
Peeling the Onion, 230
Pelecanos, George, 85
Pendle, George, 85
Penguin Book of Canadian Short Stories, The, 255
Penney, Stef, **249**
Peony in Love, 31, 75, 173
People of the Book, **56**, 92, 112, 155, 186, 227
People of the Whale, 220
People's Act of Love, The, 158, **236–237**
People's Republic of Desire, The, 217
Percy, Walker, 107
Perez-Reverte, Arturo, 54, 78, 83, 87, 92
Perfect Arrangement, A, 108
Perfect Circle, A, 98
Perfect Elizabeth: A Tale of Two Sisters, The, 172
Perfect Happiness, 153
Perfect Match, 139
Perfect Storm, The, 84
Perfect Wife, The: Life and Choices of Laura Bush, 174
Perfection: A Memoir of Betrayal and Trust, 101
Perkins, Emily, 35, 66, 204, 215, 234, **249**, 256
Perma Red, 126
Perrotta, Tom, 27, 49, **84**, 106, 118, 137, 143, 148, 158, **167–168**, 173, 200, 238, 256
Perrottet, Tony, 59
Perry, Michael, 6, 18, 57, 137, 147
Persepolis, 20, 161, 233
Persepolis II, 161, 233
Persian Bride, The, 37, 100
Person of Interest, A, **61**, 134
Personal Matter, A, 245

Pessl, Marisha, 104
Pesthouse, The, **62–63**, 66, 71, 194, 210, 234, 249
Petropolis, 259
Petroski, Henry, 59
Petterson, Per, 19, 34, 69, 115, 126, 141, 142, 217, **250**
Peyton Amberg, **143**, 249
Pham, Andrew, 75
Phantom Limbs of the Rollow Sisters, The, 117
Pharmakon, 76, **95–96**, 136, 237, 238
Phillips, Jayne Anne, 115, 168, 178
Philosopher's Apprentice, The, 52, **80**
Philosophy Made Simple, 18
Photographer, The: Into War-Torn Afghanistan with Doctors without Borders, 101, 104
Physiogomy, The, 64
Piano Teacher, The, 12, 31, 34, **75**
Piazza, Tom, 7, 29, 243
Picoult, Jodi, 134, 139, 150
Pictures at an Exhibition, 15, **68**
Pieces for the Left Hand, 224
Pieces from Berlin, The, 15
Piercy, Marge, 41, 103, 120, 134, 160, 166, 174
Pierre, D. B. C., **84–85**, 249
Pig Boy's Wicked Bird, 117
Pigeon and a Boy, A, **91**
Pigs in Heaven, 25, 138, 152, 156, 189
Pilgrim at Tinker Creek, 17, 36
Pilot's Wife, The, 134, 138, 139, 174
Pinch Runner Memorandum, The, 245
Pinhook: Finding Wholeness in a Fragmented Land, 10
Pipkin, John, 169
Pity the Nation: Abduction of Lebanon, 28, 48
Place on Earth, A, 2, 9, 124, 137
Place Will Comfort You, The, 39
Plague, The, 230
Plague of Doves, The, **125–126**, 220
Plain Heathen Mischief, 18
Plainsong, 6, 18, 35, 44, 136
Plan B: Further Thoughts on Faith, 251
Playdate with Death, A, 93
Please Don't Come Back from the Moon, 42–43
Pleasure, 30
Pleasure of Eliza Lynch, The, 211
Pleasure of My Company, The, 132, 218
Plot Against America, The, **87**, 170, 204
Plowing the Dark, 223, 250

Plowman, Stephanie, 228
Pocketful of Names, 117
Poe: A Life Cut Short, 121
Poet Mungo, 48
Poetry of Pablo Neruda, The, 200
Poets in Their Youth, 149
Poison, 136
Poisonwood Bible, The, 9, 22, 25, 88, 100,
    138, 147
Polished Hoe, The, 12, 68
Polito, Robert, 121
Pollack, Neal, 118, 168
Pollock, Donald Ray, 123
Polly's Ghost, 98
Pomegranate Soup, 140
Poor People, 259
Popular Music from Vittula, 19, **34–35**
*Population 485: Meeting Your Neighbors One
    Siren at a Time,* 18, **57,** 137, 147
Porcupine Year, The, 42
Porno, 82
Pornographer, The, 157
*Portland Vase, The: Extraordinary Odyssey of
    a Mysterious Roman Treasure,* 59
Portnoy's Complaint, 87, 170
Portrait, The, 78
Portrait in Sepia, 13, 200, 256
*Portrait of My Mother, Who Posed Nude in
    Wartime: Stories,* **252**
Portrait of the Artist as a Young Man, 200
Position, The, 135, 186
Possession, 56, 113, 114, 187, 235, 247
Post-Birthday World, 153, **174**
Post-Soul Nation, 230
Pothen, Moncy, 186
Power, Susan, 220
Power, **220**
Power and the Glory, The, 38, 236
Power Play, 62
PowerBook, The, 95
Powers, Richard, 52, 128, 207, 223, 234, **250**
Practical Magic, 139, 156
Practice of Deceit, The, 24
PrairyErth, 17, 36
Prayer for Owen Meany, A, 22, 69, 103, 104,
    117, 142, 171
Prayer for the Dying, A, 165
Prep, 65, 74, 137, 154, 163, 174
Prestige, The, 94
Preston Falls, 223
Preston, Richard, 53, 176
Pretor-Pinney, Gavin, 248

Pretty Monsters, 226
Price, Jill, 128
Price, Richard, 70, **85**
Pride and Prejudice, 226
Pride and Prejudice and Zombies, 226
Priest, Christopher, 94
Primary Colors, 79
Prime Green: Remembering the Sixties, 167
*Prime Obsession: Bernhard Riemann and the
    Greatest Unsolved Problem in
    Mathematics,* 246
Primitive, The, 49
Prisoner of War, 190
Prisoner's Wife, The, 130
Prisons, 9
Private State, A, 102
Probable Future, The, 139
Prodigal Summer, **25,** 147
Proenneke, Richard, 6
Professor and the Housekeeper, The, 104
Promise of Happiness, The, 68, **113–114,** 197,
    204, 223, 238
Promised World, The, **183**
Prose, Francine, 254
Proulx, E. Annie, 14, **36,** 106, 211, 248
Prozac Nation, 96
Ptolemy's Gate, 52
*Publish or Perish: Three Tales of Tenure and
    Terror,* 221
Pullman, Phillip, 52
Pupck, Jayne, **168**
Pure Product: Stories, The, 226
Pursuit of Alice Thrift, The, 152
Puttermesser Papers, The, 170
Pye, Michael, 15
Pygmy, 85, **248–249**
Pym, Barbara, 153
Pynchon, Thomas, 70, 215, 259

Quammen, David, 238
Quarantine, 62
Quarrel & Quandary, 247
Queen of Dreams, 143, 178
Queen of Hearts, 91
Question of Attraction, A, 74, 107, 120, **162**
Question of Bruno, The, 219, 220
Quick, Matthew, 144–145, 152
Quiet American, The, 38, 103, 195
Quiet Girl, The, 244
Quiet Life, A, 245
Quindlen, Anna, 4, 8
Quitting the Nairobi Trio, 258

Raban, Jonathan, 227
Rabbit Factory, The, 18
Rabbit, Run, 84, 136, 151, 170
Rabe, John, 169
Rachel Papers, The, 239
Radulescu, Dominica, **36–37**
Rag and Bone: A Journey Among the World's Holy Dead, 155
Ragtime, 61, 111, 209, 216
Raiders, The: Sons of Texas, 35
Rain Before It Falls, The, 218
Rainlight, 157
Rainy Lake, 250
Raising Blaze, 65
Raising Holy Hell, 246
Rall, Ted, 101
Ralston, Aron, 84
Rand, Ayn, 208
Randall, Alice, 116
Random Family: Love, Drugs, Trouble, and Coming-of-age in the Bronx, 130, 148
Range of Motion, 101
Rankin, Ian, 95
Rape of Europa, The, 68
Rape of Nanking, The, 169
Raphael Affair, The, 78
Rapids, **83**, 166
Rapture, 202
Rapture of Canaan, The, 6, 169
Rascal, 124, 133
Rash, Ron, **85–86**, 187, 194, 242
Rats: Observations on the History and Habitat of the City's Most Unwanted Inhabitants, 59
Ravelstein, 170
Raw Shark Texts, The, 234
Rawles, Nancy, 116
Ray, Janisse, 10
Ray, Jeanne, 18
Ray in Reverse, 94
Read, Piers Paul, 84
Reader, The, 190, 254
Reading Lolita in Tehran, 20, 38, 71, 233
Real McCoy, The, 76, 256
Realuyo, Bino, 140
Rebecca, 61
Rebel Angels, 43
Recipe for Bees, A, 3
Reconsidering Happiness, 5
Red April, 9, **86–87**, 185, 197–198
Red Car: Stories, **108–109**
Red Clay, Blue Cadillac, 155

Red Dog, 15, 44
Red Letters, 161
Red Plaid Shirt, 255
Reddi, Rishi, 39
Redemption Falls, 82
Reece, Erik, 44
Rees, Sian, 25
Referred Pain, 172
Regeneration, 104, 105, 185, 225
Rehearsal, The, 189
Reich, Tova, 255
Reichl, Ruth, 17, 259
Reidy, Jamie, 52
Relative Stranger, A, 107
Reliable Wife, A, **21**, 40, 80, 109, 150, 175
Relin, David Oliver, 20, 78–79, 141
Remainder, 221, **234**
Remains of the Day, The, 221
Remarque, Erich Maria, 28, 105, 222
Remembering, 9
Remembering Babylon, 232
Remnick, David, 242
Rendell, Ruth, 61, 67
Republic of East L.A.: Stories, The, 12
Rescue Missions, 201
Reservation Blues, 260
Reserve, 103, 216
Resistance, 87
Rest Is Noise, the: Listening to the Twentieth Century, 232
Restoration, 182
Restraint of Beasts, The, 11, 73, 159, 212, 221
Return of the Caravels, The, 3
Returning to Earth, 22
Reuss, Frederick, 67, **168–169**
Revere Beach Boulevard, 253
Revolutionary Road, 148, 167, 256
Reynolds, April, 115
Reynolds, Sheri, 6, **169**
Rhett Butler's People, 37
Rhodes, David, 159
Rhys, Jean, 112
Rich Man's Table, The, 176
Richer Dust, A, **10**
Riding in Cars with Boys, 120, 154
Riding Toward Everywhere, 259
Ring of Conspirators, A: Henry James and His Literary Circle, 1895-1915, 257
Rings of Saturn, 253
Rios, Julian, 185
Rip in Heaven, A: A Memoir of Murder and Its Aftermath, 165

Rising Up and Rising Down, 259
Risk Pool, The, 155
Riven Rock, 111
River at the Center of the World, The: A Journey up the Yangtze, and Back in Chinese Time, 8, 227
River, Cross My Heart, 115
River Dogs, 35
River Midnight, The, 155
River Song, 151
River Town: Two Years on the Yangtze, 34
River Wife, The, **2**
Rivera, Diego, 121
Roach, Mary, 237
Road, Cristy, 57
Road, The, 52, 63, 194, 199, 210, 233, **234**, 249
Road Dogs, 70
Road from Chapel Hill, The, **37**
Road Home, The, 7, 37, 49, **182**, 209, 253, 259
Road to Esmerelda, The, 16
Road to Fez, The, 7
Road to Sardis, The, 228
Road to Wellville, The, 111
Roberts, Adam, 195
Roberts, Gary, 246
Robinson, Lewis, 49, **86**, 89
Robinson, Marilynne, 173, 218, **251**
Robinson, Peter, 67
Robinson, Roxana, 10
Robinson, Spider, 144
Robison, John Elder, 132
Rock Island Line, 159
Rockabye: From Wild to Child, 168
Rockcastle, Mary, 250
Rocket Boys, 35, 124, 183
Rodoreda, Merce, 224
Rodriguez, Deborah, 141
Rodriguez, Luis, 12
Rodriguez, Teresa, 60
Rogue Trader, 77
Roiphe, Katie, 257
Romantic, The (Gowdy), 126, 131
Romantics, The (Niederhoffer), 14, 65, **162–163**, 245
Roncagliolo, Santiago, 9, **86–87**, 185, 197–198
Ronson, Jon, 63
Road from Coorain, The, 124, 242
Room of One's Own, A, 254
Room with a View, A, 38

Rope Walk, The, **112**
Rosa Lee, 130
Rosario, Nelly, 208
Roscoe, 216
Rose Grower, The, 207
Rose Variations, The, **114**
Rosen, Jonathan, 18
Rosenbaum, Thane, 213
Rosenfeld, Lucinda, 3
Rosenthal, David, 224
Rose's Garden, 112
Rosnay, Tatiana de, 176
Ross, Alex, 232
Rost, Peter, 52
Roth, Matthue, 258
Roth, Philip, **87**, 142, **169–170**, 180, 204, 205, **252**, 253
Rothbart, Davy, 5
Rothschild, Matthew, 145
Rotters' Club, The, 154, 183, 197
Rounds, 201
Rouse, Wade, 74
Rouse Up, O Young Men of the New Age, **245**
Roy, Arundhati, 119
Roy, Lucinda, 26
Royal Family, The, 259
Rubenfeld, Jed, 54, 59
Ruby in Her Navel, 41
Rudnick, Paul, 179
Ruff, Matt, 52, 106, 110, 139, 212
Rufus, Anneli, 145
Rug Merchant, The, 231
Ruining It for Everybody, 117, 145, 239
Ruiz Zafón, Carlos, 78, **87**
Rule of Four, The, 59
Rules of Engagement, The, 112, 153
Rules of the Road, 43, 104
Rules of the Wild, 158
Rumors of Peace, 178
Run, 160, **166**
Runaway: Stories, 181, **243**
Runaway Quilt, The, 115
Runemarks, 67
Running, 29
Running with Scissors, 127, 168
Rush Home Road, 151
Rushdie, Salman, 98, 213, 215
Russian Debutante's Handbook, The, 48, 77, 219, 220, **255**
Russländer, The, 15
Russo, Richard, 13, 22, 106, 117, 118, 147, 148, 151, 153, 155, **170–171**, 207

Rybczynski, Witold, 4
Ryman, Geoff, 40, 66

S: A Novel about the Balkans, 121
Sabatini, Rafael, 61
Sabbathday River, The, 148
Sabbath's Theater, 142, 170
Sacks, Oliver, 215, 250
Sacred Country, 182
Sacred Games, 83
Sacred Hunger, 41
Sacred Night, The, 7, 8
Safelight, 57
Safer, 57
Sag Harbor, **187–188**, 242
Sailing the Wine Dark Sea, 15
Sailors on the Inward Sea, **92**
Saint Maybe, 40, 107, 116, 118, 129, 184
Saints at the River, 86
Salak, Kira, 9, 26, **88**, 129
Salesman, The, 82
Salinger, J. D., 107, 160, 190
Salt (D'Erasmo), 208
Salt (Page), 115, **247–248**
Salt: A World History, 59
Salter, James, 214
Samarasan, Preeta, 48, 119
Samaritan, 70, 85
Samartin, Cecelia, 26
Samson, Ian, 3
Samuel Johnson Is Indignant, 201, **206**, 234, 256
Sand Castle, The, 168
Sand Child, The, 7, 8
Sand County Almanac, A, 10
Sanders, Scott Russell, 17, 36
Sandhogs, 57
Sandman, The: Preludes and Nocturnes, 159
Sandor, Marjorie, **252**
Sandpiper, 39
Santiago, Esmerelda, 242
Santoro, Lara, 88
Sarah's Key, 176
Saramago, José, 3, 63, **252–253**
Sari of the Gods, 150
Sarvas, Mark, 128
Saskiad, The, 112
Satanic Verses, The, 213
Satrapi, Marjane, 20, 161, 233
Saturday, 179, 197, 235, **236**, 247
Saul and Patsy, **106**, 107, 122

Saunders, George, 63, 85, 90, 206, 212, 255, 260
Saunders, Kate, 179
Savage, Sam, **171**
Savage Art: A Biography of Jim Thompson, 121
Savage Detectives, The, 130, 200, 208
Saving Agnes, 118
Saving the World, 13, **99–100**
Say When, 55
Say You're One of Them, 26, 222
Sayers, Dorothy, 203
Sayrafiezadah, Said, 161–162
Scahill, Jeremy, 90
Scapegoat, The, 9
Scar Vegas: And Other Stories, **248**
Schaffert, Timothy, 117
Scheme for Full Employment, The, 159
Schenone, Laura, 253
Schimmel, Betty, 91
Schlink, Bernhard, 190, 254
Schlosser, Eric, 90
Schmais, Libby, **172**
Schoemperlen, Diane, 79, 224, 255
Schooled, **74**
Schulman, Audrey, 109
Schulman, Helen, 123, 172
Schutt, Christine, 99, 184, 258
Schwartz, David, **88–89**, 230
Schwartz, Leslie, **89**
Schwartz, Lynne Sharon, 32, 172
Schwartz, Mimi, 260
Schwartz-Bart, André, 149
Schwarz, Christina, 89, 164
Scibona, Salvatore, **253**
Scientific Romance, A, 50
Scliar, Moacyr, 244
Scotia Widows, The, 164
Scott, Joanna, **172–173**, 187
Scott, Joanna Catherine, **37**
Scott, Martin, 32–33, 159
Scott-Clark, Catherine, 68
Scream, The, 239, 240
Sea, The, 191, **196**, 198
Sea Around Us, The, 238
Sea Change: Alone Across the Atlantic in a Wooden Boat, 93
Sea of Poppies, 129, **215**
Sea, the Sea, The, 247
Seal Wife, The, 136
Seamstress of Hollywood Boulevard, The, **31**, 109, 173

Searching for Caleb, 40, 65, 112, 184, 189
Searching for the Secret River, 21
Searls, Damion, 211
Seas, The, 23
Seashore Year, A, 208
Season for the Dead, A, 54
Season of the Rainbirds, 101
Season of the Snake, 14
Sebald, Winfried Georg, **253–254**
Sebold, Alice, 73, 151, 164, 224
Second Death of Unica Aveyano, The, 26
Second Honeymoon, 118, 182
Second Marriage, 158
Second Nature, 139
Secrest, Meryle, 68, 111
Secret Agent, The, 92
Secret Diary of a Call Girl, The, 180
Secret History, The, 67, 94, 107, 127, 163, 235
Secret Life of Bees, The, 32, 55, 115, 156, 177
Secret River, The, 2, 9, **21–22**, 44, 68, 81
Secret Scripture, The, 33, 181, **198**, 211, 218, 228, 258
Secret Supper, The, 92
Secret Word, A, 158
Secrets of the Tsil Café, 5
Security, **49**
Sedaris, David, 181
See, Lisa, 31, 51, 75, 119, 143, 146, **173**
See You in a Hundred Years: Four Seasons in Forgotten America, 6
Seeing, 3, 253
Seeing Mona Naked, 5
Seeking Rapture, 136
Seierstad, Åsne, 20, 101, 140–141, 145, 158
Seife, Charles, 246
Seifer, Marc, 23, 143
Seize the Day, 236
Self, Will, **89–90**
Sellers, Susan, 50, 76, 105, **254**
Sellevision, 77
Semple, Maria, **173**, 175
Senator's Wife, The, **159–160**, 166, 173, 174
Senna, Danzy, 74, **90–91**, 122, 166, 257
Separate Checks, 259
Separate Peace, A, 66, 183, 190
Septembers of Shiraz, The, 161
Serena, **85–86**, 187, 194, 242
Sernovitz, Gary, 24
Serpent in Paradise, 93
Serve the People!, 202, 222, **230**, 233

Serve the People: A Stir-Fried Journey Through China, 34
Service Included: Four-Star Secrets of an Eavesdropping Waiter, 165
Sessums, Kevin, 124, 169
Set This House in Order, 106, 110, 139, 212
Setiawan, Erick, **254**
Setterfield, Diane, 131, 187, 220
Settle, Mary Lee, 9, 158
Settlement, **67**, 230
Setton, Ruth Knafo, 7
Seven Days in the Art World, 68, 114
Seven Sisters, The, 144
Severance, 202
Seville Communion, The, 92
Sewing Circles of Heart, The: A Personal Voyage through Afghanistan, 145
Sex and the City, 11
Sex, Drugs, and Cocoa Puffs: A Low Culture Manifesto, 147
Sex Wars, 41
Sexing the Cherry, 95
Seymour, Miranda, 257
Shadow Baby, 157
Shadow Catcher, The, **259–260**
Shadow Country, **29–30**
Shadow Lines, The, 215
Shadow of the Sun, The, 227, 247
Shadow of the Wind, The, 87
Shadow Year, The, **64**
Shaffer, Mary Ann, 15, **37–38**, 153, 177, 178, 251
Shah, Tahir, 4, 7, 23, 88
Shakespeare, William, 240
Shalev, Meir, **91**
Shambling Towards Hiroshima, 80
Shame, 100
Shame of the Nation: Restoration of Apartheid Schooling in America, The, 90
Shamrock Tea, 60
Shamsie, Kamila, 99, 100, 134
Shanghai Girls, 51, 75, 119, 143, 146, **173**
Shape of Snakes, The, 95
Sharmila's Book, 178
Sharpe, Matthew, 63, 126, 208
Sharper Your Knife the Less You Cry, The, 17, 135
Shaw, Deirdre, 173, 175
Shawl, Denise, 66
Shawl, The: A Story and a Novella, 226
She Got up off the Couch, 146

She Was, 61, 73, 113, **134–135**, 167, 228, 245
Sheers, Owen, 87
Sheff, David, 127
Sheffield, Rob, 91, 161, 191
Shell Collector, The, **17**
Shelter, 168
Shelton, Richard, 10
Shepherd, Jean, 34–35, 183
Sherrill, Steven, 60
She's Come Undone, 150, 179
She's Not There: A Life in Two Genders, 55
Shields, Carol, 113, 120, 131, 156, 165, 185, 243, **254–255**
Shields, Jody, 111
Shigekuni, Julie, 191
Shipping News, The, 106, 211, 248
Shiva Dancing, 178
Shopgirl, 173, 218
Shorris, Earl, 16, 147
Short Cuts, 5, 260
Short History of a Prince, The, 135
Short History of Tractors in Ukrainian, A, 213
Short History of Women, A, **186**
Shout Down the Moon, 183
Shreve, Anita, 129, 134, 138, 139, 145, 174
Shreve, Susan Richards, **91–92**
Shriver, Lionel, 150, 153, **174**
Shroud, 196
Shteyngart, Gary, 48, 77, 219, 220, **255**
Shutter Island, 106
Shutterbabe, 72, 104, 138
Sick Girl, 99
Sick Puppy, 44
Sickened: Memoir of a Munchausen by Proxy Childhood, 256
Sides, Hampton, 75
Sidhwa, Bapsi, 99, 119
Siegel, Lee, 260
Sierra, Javier, 92
Signal, The, 11
Silber, Joan, 26, **38**
Silk, 197
Silko, Leslie Marmon, 220
Silver Linings Playbook, The, 145, 152
Silver: My Own Tale as Written by Me with a Goodly Amount of Murder, **61**, 92
Silverstein, Amy, 99
Simmons, Dan, 95, 257
Simon, Linda, 76
Simple Genius, 63
Simple Habana Melody, A: (From When the World Was Good), 26

Simple Plan, A, 73, 86
Simpson, Eileen, 149
Simpson, Helen, 114
Since the Layoffs, 165, 221
Sing Them Home, 25, 103, 108, **144**, 159, 168, 184
Singer, Katie, 109
Singer, Mark, 148, 241
Singing and Dancing Daughters of God, The, 117
Singing Wilderness, The, 36
Sir Gawain and the Green Knight, 60
Sirens of Baghdad, The, 72
Sirens of Titan, The, 229
Sisman, Adam, 50
Sister Mine, 108, 129, **163–164**
Sister of My Heart, 98, 119, 134, 143, 178
Sisters Antipodes, The, 108, 191
Sittenfeld, Curtis, 65, 74, 137, 154, 160, 163, 166, **174**
Sixpence House, 171
Size of the World, 26, **38**
Skateaway, 69
Skinny Dip, 44
Skoot, Floyd, 260
Sky Below, The, **207–208**
Sky Fisherman, The, 151
Sky, the Stars, the Wilderness, The, 11
Skylight Confessions, **138–139**
Slackjaw, 52, 117, 145, 239, 258
Slam, 160
Slammerkin, 120
Slatalla, Michelle, 2, 10, 187
Slater, Lauren, 96
Slaughterhouse-5, 95, 229
Slaves in the Family, 32, 70
Slaves of New York, 143, 249
Sleeping Father, 126
Slide, The, 2, 16, **107**, 128, 147, 162
Slouching Towards Bethlehem, 260
Slow Air of Ewan McPherson, The, 5
Slow Man, 205
Slowly Down the Ganges, 8, 102, 227
Slowness, 174
Small Crimes in an Age of Abundance, 25
Small World: An Academic Romance, 162
Smiley, Jane, 30, 58, 149, **174–175**, 240
Smith, Ali, 162, **255–256**
Smith, Alison, 111
Smith, Joanna Rakoff, 163
Smith, Sally Bedell, 174
Smith, Scott, 73, 86

Smith, Zadie, 81, 98, 137, 166
Snapper, The, 120, 157, 209
Snark: A Polemic in Seven Fits, 208
Snow, 15, 83
Snow Angels, 165
Snow Country, 245
Snow Falling on Cedars, 75, 217
Snow Flower and the Secret Fan, 146, 173
Snow in August, 5, 31
Snow Leopard, The, 30
Snuff, **82**, 176, 249
So Brave, Young and Handsome, 19, 125
So Far from God, 60
So Long, See You Tomorrow, 159
Social Crimes, 11
"Socialism Is Great!": A Worker's Memoir of the New China, 217
Sofer, Dalia, 161
Solace of Leaving Early, The, 146
Solace of Open Spaces, The, 10
Solar Storms, 220
Soldier of the Great War, A, 209
Solomon, Deborah, 121, 208
Solzhenitsyn, Aleksandr, 8, 236, 237
Some Fun, 244
Some Great Thing, 68
Some Ruin Must Fall, 212
Some Things That Stay, 189
Somebody Else's Daughter, 182
Someday this Pain Will Be Useful to You, 140
Somehow Form a Family, 124
Someone Knows My Name, **67–68**, 70, 115, 188, 243
Someone Not Really Her Mother, 15
Somerville, Patrick, 110, **175**
Something for the Pain: One Doctor's Account of Life and Death in the ER, 194
Something Like Beautiful, 130
Something Out There: Stories, 216
Something Rising (Light and Swift), 146
Something Wicked This Way Comes, 34, 64, 205
Sometimes You See It Coming, 5
Somewhere in America, 241
Somnambulist, The, 131
Son of the Circus, A, 69
Song Before It Is Sung, The, 114
Song of Brooklyn: An Oral History of America's Favorite Borough, 15, 156
Song of Solomon, 216
Song of the Crow, 133

Song of the Distant Root, The, 256
Song of the Water Saints, 208
Song Reader, The, 183
Song Yet Sung, 115
Songlines, 9, 22, 26
Songs for the Butcher's Daughter, **155**
Songs for the Missing, 72–73, 89, 158, 164, **165**, 176, 224
Songs in Ordinary Time, 80
Songs of the Kings, The, 41
Songs Without Words, 102
Sons of Mississippi: A Story of Race and Its Legacy, 24, 199
Sons of Texas, 30
Soon I Will Be Invincible, 89
Soon: Tales from Hospices, 241
Sophie's Choice, 77, 116, 230
Sorrows of an American, The, **141**
Sot-Weed Factor, The, 61
Soueif, Ahdaf, **39**
Soul Thief, The, **106–107**, 127, 214
Sound of Us, The, **189**
South, The, 41
South of Resurrection, 2
Southern, Terry, 82
Spark, Muriel, 190
Sparks, Nicholas, 184
Spechler, Diana, 72, 158, 164, **175–176**
Special Topics in Calamity Physics, 104
Speckled Monster: A Historical Tale of Battling Smallpox, The, 59
Speed, John, 186
Speed of Dark, The, 132
Speed of Light, 11
Spell, The, 140
Spencer, Scott, 82, **176**
Spider, 48
Spiegelman, Art, 172
Spies of Warsaw, The, 54
Spirit Catches You and You Fall Down, The, 134, 256
Split Estate, **101–102**, 108, 111
Spoiled: Stories, **154**
Spooner, 190
Sportswriter, The, 84, 151, 171, 197, 214, 252
Spot of Bother, A, 132, 154
Spragg, Mark, 6
Sputnik Sweetheart, 244
Spyglass: An Autobiography, 54
St. John Mandel, Emily, **39–40**, 66
Stain, The, 211
Stand the Storm, 68, **115**

Standard Operating Procedure, 72
Standing in the Rainbow, 94
Star of the Sea, **82**
Stardust, 159
Staring at the Sun, 236
State by State, 22
Status Anxiety, 208
Stay Here with Me, 35
Steep Approach to Garbadale, The, 45
Stegner, Wallace, 17, 24, 86, 187, 218, 242
Steiker, Valerie, 109
Stein, Garth, 133
Steinbeck, John, 22
Steinberg, Jacques, 149
Stephenson, Neal, 61
Stepmother, The, 93
Stern, Jane, 57
Sterns, Steve, 224
Stevenson, Robert Louis, 61, 92
Stewart, Chris, 4
Stewart, Leah, 40, 158, 163, 189
Stewart, Sean, 98
Stick out Your Tongue, 230
Stiff: Curious Lives of Human Cadavers, 237
Stiles, T. J., 76
Still Alice, **128**
Still Life, 113, 247
Still She Haunts Me, 257
Stille, Alexander, 219
Stockett, Kathryn, 55, 176, **177**
Stolen Child, The, 164
Stone, Robert, 51, 167
Stone Carvers, The, 21, 69, 91, 185, 250
Stone Diaries, The, 185, 255
Stone Gods, The, **95**
Stone's Fall, 78
Stories of Richard Bausch, The, 51
Stories of Vladimir Nabokov, The, 220
Storm Riders, **151–152**
Storming Heaven, 183
Story of a Marriage, The, 158
Story of Edgar Sawtelle, The, 19, 21, 86, 106, 125, 133, 144, 150, 168
Story of Lucy Gault, The, 258
Story of My Life, The, The: An Afghan Girl on the Other Side of the Sky, The, 20
Story of the Night, The, 257
Story Sisters, The, **139**
Straight Man, 22, 106, 117, 148, 151, 153, 171, 207
Straight, Susan, 42
Strange Piece of Paradise, 126, 165

Stranger Things Happen, 198, 226
Strauss, Darin, 76, 80, 96, **256**
Streatfeild, Dominic, 63, 72
Street Players, 85
Strivers Row, **5**, 216
Strong Motion, 127
Stroud, Jonathan, 52
Strout, Elizabeth, 23, 44, 123, 130, 131, 150, 168, **177–178**, 184, 224, 231, 252
Stuart, 197
Stuck: Why We Can't (or Won't) Move On, 145
Student of Living Things, A, **91–92**
Stuever, Hank, 227, 241
Stuffed: Adventures of a Restaurant Family, 49
Stupidest Angel, The, 79
Styron, William, 70, 77, 116, 222, 230
Subercaseaux, Elizabeth, 151, **256**
Subject Steve, The, 2, 62, 128
Subtle Knife, The, 52
Success, 239
Successor, The, 3, 63
Such a Long Journey, 240
Sugar Island, The, 26
Suicide Index, The: Putting My Father's Death in Order, 102, 237
Suite Francaise, 15, 38, 91
Sula, 243
Sullivan, Faith, **178**
Sullivan, Robert, 59
Summer of Ordinary Ways, The, 158
Sun After Dark: Flights into the Foreign, 8, 227
Sunday Philosophy Club, The, 18, 56–57, 104
Sunday's Silence, 161
Sundown, Yellow Moon, 19, 28, **43–44**, 66, 136
Sunley, Christina, 106, 134
Sunnyside, 196, **215–216**
Superpowers, **88–89**, 230
Superstud: Or, How I Became a 24-Year-Old Virgin, 160
Supreme Courtship, **56**, 79
Suri, Manil, 34, **178**
Susannah Morrow, 71
Suskind, Ron, 188
Sutcliffe, William, 77, 160, **178–179**
Suzy, Led Zeppelin, and Me, **32–33**, 159, 160, 164, 190
Swallow the Ocean, 146, 168
Swallows of Kabul, The, 72, 101, 140, **145**
Swan, Mary, 255

Swann, 113
Swann, Maxine, 167
Sway, **228**
Sweet Far Thing, The, 43
Sweet Hell Inside, The, 70
Sweet Hereafter, The, 103, 250
Sweet In-Between, The, **169**
Sweetness at the Bottom of the Pie, The, 104
Sweetness in the Belly, 12
Swift as Desire, 42
Swift, Graham, 124, **179**, 190, 231, 248
Swimming-Pool Library, The, 140
Swope, Sam, 18
Symptomatic, 74, **90–91**

T. Rex and the Crater of Doom, 53
Tademy, Lalita, 115, 164
Tain, The: A New Translation of the Tain bo Cuailnge, **59–60**, 228
Taker, The: And Other Stories, **213–214**
Taking the Wall, 2
Talarigo, Jeff, 20, **40**, 75, 146, 199, 222
Taleb, Nicholas Nassim, 209
Talented Mr. Ripley, The, 67
Tales from the Blue Archives, 92
Tales from the Perilous Realm, 60
Tales of a Female Nomad, 88
Tales Out of School, 179
Taliesin, 60
Talk Before Sleep, 99, 108
Talk Talk, **110**, 113, 153, 189
Talking It Over, 236
Talking to High Monks in the Snow: An Asian American Odyssey, 43, 51
Tammet, Daniel, 132
Tan, Amy, 48, 109, 146
Tango Player, The, 67
Tao of Physics, The, 238
Taqwacores, The, 7
Tartt, Donna, 67, 94, 107, 127, 163, 164, 235
Tasting the Sky: A Palestinian Childhood, 72
Taxonomy of Barnacles, A, 65, 163
Taylor, Benjamin, 118, **179–180**
Taylor, Billy, **180**
Taylor, Jill Bolte, 128
Taylor, Stephen, 25–26, 82
Tea, 102
Teacher Man, 41, 180
Tears of the Giraffe, 18
Telex from Cuba, **26**
Templar Legacy, The, 92
Temple Dancer, The, 186

Temporary, The, 118
Ten Days in the Hills, 58, **174–175**
Tender as Hellfire, 238
Tender at the Bone, 17, 259
Tender Bar, The, 35, 86, 107, 123, 145, 183
Tender Mercies, 101
Tender Morsels, 254
Tenderness of Wolves, The, **249**
Ten-Year Nap, The, 186
Terrell, Heather, **92**
Territory, **57**
Terrorist, The, 84
Tesla: Man Out of Time, 143
Tess of the D'urbervilles, 173
Testament of Youth, 105
Thank You for Smoking, 56, 90
Thanksgiving Night, 51
Tharps, Lori, 41
That Distant Land: The Collected Stories of Wendell Berry, 9, 10, 17
That Old Ace in the Hole, 36
That Old Cape Magic, **171**
Theft, 44, 58, 113
Theft: Stories, **26**
Their Eyes Were Watching God, 188
Them: A Memoir of Parents, 22
Them (McCall), 7, **30**
Them (Oates), 223
Then She Found Me, 152
Then We Came to the End, 165, 221, 234
Therapy, 153
There Are Jews in My House, 259
There Are No Children Here, 188
There Is No Me Without You, 148
There Is Room for You, **102**, 122
Theriault, Reg, 11
Theroux, Paul, 23, 100, 158, 232
These High, Green Hills, 9
They Came Like Swallows, 159
They Whisper, 202
They Would Never Hurt a Fly, 63, 90, 121
Thicker than Water, 136
The Thin Place, The, **205**
Things Fall Apart, 222
Things That Fall From the Sky, 5, 201
Things They Carried, The, 28, 223, 245
Things We Do for Love, The, 156
Thinking in Pictures, 132
Thinks, 153
Third Angel, The, 139
Third Child, The, 160, 166
Third Secret, The, 92

Thirst, 49
13 Steps Down, 61
Thirteenth Tale, The, 131, 187, 220
This Blinding Absence of Light, 7, **8**
This Boy's Life, 124, 179, 181, 190, 260
This Cold Heaven: Seven Seasons in Greenland, 39
This House of Sky, 119–120
This Is the Life, 35
This Little Light of Mine: The Life of Fannie Lou Hamer, 55, 177, 188
This Must Be the Place, 4
This One Is Mine, **173**, 175
This Side of Brightness, 30
Thomas, Michael, **257**
Thompson, Craig, 157
Thompson, Hunter, 176
Thompson, Jean, **180–181**
Thompson, Jim, 85
Thon, Melanie Rae, 6
Thoreau, Henry David, 36
Thornton, Lawrence, **92**, 125
Thornton, Sarah, 68, 114
Thoughts from a Queen-Sized Bed, 260
Thousand Acres, A, 30, 175, 240
Thousand Days in Tuscany, A: A Bittersweet Adventure, 4
Thousand Splendid Suns, A, 101, 134, 140, **141**, 143, 161
Thraxas, 32–33, 159
Three Apples Fell from Heaven, 29
Three Cups of Tea, 20, 79, 141
Three Incestuous Sisters, The, 163
Three Junes, **129–130**, 156
Three Minutes on Love, **138**, 228
Three Musketeers, 125
Three to See the King, 215
Three Weeks with My Brother, 184
Three Women, 174
Through the Children's Gate: A Home in New York, 93, 184
Through the Safety Net, 106
Throw Like a Girl, 181
Thubron, Colin, 8, 237
Ticket to Ride, A, **157–158**, 165
Ticknor, 113
Tie That Binds, The, 6, 18, 44, 86, 125, 136, 250
Tiger Claw, 186
Til We Have Faces, 248
Timbuktu, 50
Time It Never Rained, The, 18, 36

Time of Our Singing, The, 207, 223, 250
Time Travelers Strictly Cash, 144
Time Traveler's Wife, The, 23, 66, 94, 163, 174, 186
Tin Drum, The, 230
Tin-Can Tree, The, 111, 137
Tinkers, **218**, 236
Tinti, Hannah, 19
Tiny One, The, 159
Tipping Point, The, 195
Tipping the Velvet, 94, 257
'Tis, 41, 79
To a Fault, 74
To Afghanistan and Back, 101
To Die For, 69, 85, 256
To Hell with All That: Loving and Loathing Our Inner Housewife, 154
To Kill a Mockingbird, 112, 124, 125, 164, 183, 204
To See You Again: A True Story of Love in a Time of War, 91
To Siberia, 250
To the Lighthouse, 254
Tóibín, Colm, **40–41**, 105, 112, 156, 169, 179, **181**, 211, **257**
Tolan, Sandy, 20, 48
Tolkien, J. R. R., 60, 208
Tom Sawyer, 116
Tomato Girl, **168**
Tomcat in Love, 151, 171, 207, 232
Tomorrow, **179**
Too Far from Home: A Story of Life and Death in Space, 53
Toobin, Jeffrey, 57
Toole, John Kennedy, 73, 85, 179, 181
Tooth and Claw, 110
Tooth and Nail, 95
Toothpick, The: Technology and Culture, 59
Tortilla Curtain, The, 110
Torture the Artist, 66
Toss of a Lemon, The, 48, 98, 146, **185–186**
Toughest Indian in the World, The, 5, 200
Tourmaline, 173
Tower, Wells, **181–182**, 218
Towing Jehovah, 80
Town Beyond the Wall, The, 71–72
Town on Beaver Creek: Story of a Lost Kentucky Community, The, 2, 10, 187
Tracks, 220
Trading Up, 11
Traig, Jennifer, 143, 146
Trail of Heart's Blood Wherever We Go, A, 35

Trailer Trashed, 145, 181
Train Go Sorry, 153
Train Home, The, 91
Train to Trieste, **36–37**
Trained to Kill, 76
Trainspotting, 33, 82, 95, 199, 225
Transgressions, 109
Transgressors, The, 85
Transmission, 73
Trans-sister Radio, **55**
Traveler, The, 244
Traveling Mercies, 251
Travels in the Scriptorium, 50
Travels with Charley, 22
Travels with Herodotus, 227
Treasure Island, 61, 92
Treasures in Heaven, 13
Tree of Smoke, 28, 70, 195, 208, 212,
    222–223, 228
Tremain, Rose, 7, 37, 49, **182**, 190, 209, 253,
    259
Trespass, **77–78**, 80
Trevor, William, 157, 181, 211, **258**
Triage, 195
Triangle, **187**
Triangle: Fire That Changed America, 187
Triangular Road, 138
Tricking of Freya, The, 106, 134
Trillin, Calvin, 106
Trollope, Joanna, 118, **182**, 183
Trouble (Christensen), 174, 204
Trouble (Somerville), 175
Troublesome Offspring of Cardinal Guzman,
    The. 15
Truck: A Love Story, 137
Trudel, Sylvain, 77, 99, 128, 157, **258**
True History of the Kelly Gang, The. 21, 25,
    58, 113, 232
True North, 22, 69, 166
Trump: Art of the Deal, 62
Truong, Monique, 34
Trussoni, Danielle, 29, 158
Truth & Beauty: A Friendship, 214
Truth about Celia, The. 201
Tuck, Lily, **41**
Tucker, Lisa, **183**
Tucker, Neely, 38, 184
Tucker, Todd, 34, 125, **183**, 217
Tuesdays with Morrie, 18
Turkish Lover, The. 242
Turn of the Screw, The. 95
Turnaround, The. 85

Turning Japanese, 161
Turning, The: New Stories, **44**, 190, 232
Turtle Valley, **3**
Twain, Mark, 116
12 Edmondstone Street, 232
Twelve Hawks, John, 244
Twelve Times Blessed, 160
25th Hour, The, 53
Twenty Fragments of a Ravenous Youth, 40,
    216–217, 244
Twenty-One: Selected Streets, 201
Twenty-Seventh City, The, 127
2666, 78, 86, 130, 197, **200**, 202, 208, 231
Twilight (Wiesel), 254
Two Cities, 188
Two Girls, Fat and Thin, 214
Two Marriages, 170, 205, **231–232**, 236
Two Under the Indian Sun, 102
Tyler, Anne, 18, 23, 25, 27, 31, 40, 65, 102,
    103, 106, 107, 111, 112, 114, 116, 118,
    120, 127, 129, 135, 137, 149–150, 153,
    163, 173, 178, 181, **184**, 189, 208

Ugly Man, 85
Ulinich, Anya, 259
Ulysses, 200, 236
Umbrella Country, The. 140
Unaccustomed Earth, 39, 75, 98, 102, 119,
    134, **149–150**, 160, 209, 243
Unbearable Lightness of Being, The. 174, 220
Uncivilized Beasts and Shameless Hellions, 51
Uncommon Reader, The. 38, **53–54**
Unconsoled, The, 221
Under the Net, 247
Under the Skin, 212, 221
Under the Tuscan Sun, 4
Underpainter, The, 110, 185
Understudy, The, 162
Underworld, 207, 223
Undiscovered Country (Enger), **19**, 125
Undiscovered Country (Gillison), 22
Undue Influence, 112
Unexpected Light, An: Travels in Afghanistan,
    39, 93, 101, 140
Unfinished Life, An, 6
Unfinished Season, An, 201
Unforgivable Blackness: Rise and Fall of Jack
    Johnson, 242
Union Street, 104
Unknown Errors of Our Lives, The, 119, 150
Unknown Terrorist, The, 123
Unless, 131, 165, 255

Unquiet Earth, The, 183
Unsettling of America, The, 10, 28
Unsworth, Barry, **41–42**
Until I Find You, **142**
Untouchable, The, 196
Up High in the Trees, **111**, 136, 157, 213
Updike, John, 84, 136, 151, 170
Urban Hermit, The: A Memoir, 107
Urquhart, Jane, 21, 69, 91, 109, 110, **184–185**, 250, 255
Urrea, Luis Alberto, 12, 13, 15, **42–43**, 86, 130, 147
Used World, The, 138, 146
Uses of Enchantment, The, 72, **224**, 247
Utopia Parkway: Life and Work of Joseph Cornell, 121, 208
Utterly Monkey, 74

V, 215
Van, 120, 157, 209
Vanessa and Virginia, 50, 76, 105, **254**
Vanilla Bright Like Eminem: Stories, **212**, 214
Vanished Hands, The, 86
Vapnyar, Lara, 182, 220, **258–259**
Vargas Llosa, Mario, 100, **185**
Varieties of Disturbance, 156, 201, **206**, 234, 256
Vast Emotions and Imperfect Thoughts, 214
Vegan Virgin Valentine, 104
Vehta, Med, 161
Verghese, Abraham, 48, 116, 134
Vernon God Little, **84–85**, 249
Veronica, 138, 146, 208, **214**, 228
Versailles, 205
Vertigo, 253
Vida, 103, 134
View from Castle Rock, The, 39, 243, 255
View from the Seventh Layer, The, 5, **201**, 254
Villa of Mysteries, The, 54
Vine, Barbara, 67
Vine of Desire, The, 99, **119**, 143, 178
Vinegar Hill, 24, 144, 164
Violence, 51
Virgin in the Garden, The, 112, 228, 247
Virgin Suicides, The, 126, 205, 210, 212, 223
Visible Spirits, 190
Visiting Physician, The, 91
Viswanathan, Padma, 48, 98, 146, **185–186**
Vivian, Robert, 5
Volk, Patricia, 49
Vollmann, William T., 223, **259**
Von Drehle, David, 187

Vonnegut, Kurt, 53, 66, 73, 95, 229, 234, 240
Vows: Story of a Priest, a Nun, and Their Son, 155
Voyage of the Narwhal, The, 42
Voyage of the Short Serpent, The, **210**, 236–237
Vreeland, Susan, 121, 202, 254

Waiter Rant, 165
Waiting for Snow in Havana: Confessions of a Cuban Boy, 43
Waiting for the Apocalypse: A Memoir of Faith and Family, 159
Waiting (Jin), 73, 161, 222, 230
Waiting: True Confessions of a Waitress, 65, 165, 180
Wake-Up Call: Political Education of a 9/11 Widow, 172
Waking the Dead, 176
Walbert, Kate, **186**
Walden, 36
Waldman, Ayelet, **93**, 137, 154
Walk Across America, A, 88
Walk on the Wild Side, A, 123, 220
Walker, Alice, 31
Walking Across Egypt, 18, 117
Walking in Circles Before Lying Down, 133
Walking Tour, The, 205
Wallace, Daniel, 48, **93–94**, 218
Wallace, David Foster, 197, 208, 231, 241, 246, 259, 260
Walls, Jeannette, 25, 103, 124, 151, **186–187**
Walter, Jess, 204, 207
Walters, Minette, 95
Wanda Hickey's Night of Golden Memories, 183
Wang, Annie, 217
Wapshot Chronicles, The, 136
War Babies, 201
War for the Oaks, 57
War Trash, **222**
Ward, Amanda Eyre, 123
Ward, Geoffrey, 242
Ward, Liza, 58
Ward, Logan, 6
Warriors Don't Cry, 177
Was It Beautiful?, 157
Washington Story, The: A Novel in Five Spheres, 27
Wasted Vigil, The, 20, **100–101**, 141
Wasties, The, 169
Watch With Me, 10
Watch Your Mouth, 126

Water Dogs, 49, **86**, 89

Water for Elephants, 9, 91, 94, 151, 160, 173, 251

Water in Between, The: A Journey at Sea, 83

Waterfront: A Walk around Manhattan, 231

Waterland, 179, 190, 231, 248

Watermelon King, The, 94

Water-Method Man, The, 151

Water's Lovely, The, 61

Waters, Sarah, **94**, 98, 257

Watership Down, 171

Waterworks, The, 5, 209, 216

Watson, Larry, 19, 28, **43–44**, 66, 136

Waugh, Evelyn, 118, 140, 235

Waveland, **6–7**, 44, 69, 171, 207

Way I Found Her, The, 182, 190

Way of Ignorance, The, 260

Way to Paradise, The, 185

Way We Were, The, 182

Ways of Dying, 31

We Are All Fine Here, 163, 175, 245

We Are All Welcome Here, **55**

We Are Now Beginning Our Descent, **158**, 185, 236, 239

We Die Alone: A World War II Epic of Escape and Endurance, 115

We Need to Talk about Kevin, 150, 174

We So Seldom Look on Love, 131, 202

We Were the Mulvaneys, 223, 247

Webb, Charles, 175

Weber, Katharine, **187**

Wedding Jester, The, 224

Wedding Song: Memoirs of an Iranian Jewish Woman, 162

Week in October, A, 151, **256**

Weight of Dreams, The, 2, 140

Weiner, Jennifer, 143

Weis, Margaret, 208

Weisberger, Lauren, 74

Welcome to the Departure Lounge: Adventures in Mothering Mother, 108, 132

Welcome to the Monkey House, 66, 240

We'll Always Have Paris: Stories, 226

Weller, Sheila, 121

Wells, Ken, 24, **44**

Wells, Rebecca, 14, 129, 156

Wellsprings, 185

Welsh, Irvine, 33, 82, **94–95**, 131, 199, 225

Wen, Zhu, 230

Werris, Wendy, 138, 214

Weschler, Lawrence, 206

Wesley, Valerie Wilson, 166

West, Bing, 28

West, Paul, 246

West, Rebecca, 8, 227

West of the West: Dreamers, Believers, Builders, and Killers in the Golden State, 30

Wharton, Edith, 98, 114, 231

What Are You Like?, 211, 258

What Can I Do When Everything's on Fire, 3

What I Loved, 141

What Is the What, 20, 222

What Is Told, 237

What Looks Like Crazy on an Ordinary Day, 115

What Was Lost, 104, 152, 157, 163, **164**, 165, 176, 202, 213, 249

What Was She Thinking?: Notes on a Scandal, 91, 126, **137**

What We Were Doing and Where We Were Going, 211

What We Won't Do, 62

Whatever Makes You Happy, 77, 160, **178–179**

What's Going On: Personal Essays, 30

When I Was Five I Killed Myself, 132

When Madeline Was Young, 168

When Skateboards Will Be Free, 162

When the Nines Roll Over, and Other Stories, 53

When the World Was Steady, 32

When We Were Orphans, 75, 221

When We Were Romans, 25

When Will There Be Good News?, 65

When You Are Engulfed in Flames, 181

Where Did You Sleep Last Night? A Personal History, 91, 257

Where I Was From, 20

Where She Went, 186

Where the Body Meets Memory, 161

Where the Elephants Dance, 23

Where the Sea Used to Be, 11, 17

Where You Once Belonged, 44, 136

Whereabouts of Eneas McNulty, 181, 198, 258

While I Was Gone, 159

Whirlwind, 7, **69**

Whiskey Rebels, The, 25, 50

Whistleblower, The: Confessions of a Healthcare Hitman, 52

Whistling Season, The, **17–18**, 119

White Crosses, 43, 136

White King, The, 205, **210**

White Lioness, The, 250

White Mary, The, 9, 26, **88**, 129
White Nile, The, 16
White Noise, 50, 127, 207
White Oleander, 80, 150
White Rat: Short Stories, 165–166
White Rose, The, 148
White Teeth, 81, 98, 137, 166
White Tiger, The, 34, **47–48**, 119, 129, 241
Whitehead, Colson, 27, **187–188**, 242
Whiteman, 122
Who by Fire, 72, 158, 164, **175–176**
Who Do You Love, 181
*Who Will Tell the People: Betrayal of
    American Democracy,* 219
Who Wrote Shakespeare?, 59
Whole Story and Other Stories, The, 255
Whole World Over, The, 123, 129, 130, 156
Wholeness of a Broken Heart, The, 109
Whore Banquets, 25
Whoreson, 85
Who's Afraid of a Large Black Man?, 30
Why She Went Home, 3
Why We Make Mistakes, 195
Wickersham, Joan, 102, 237
Wide Open, 197
Wide Sargasso Sea, 112
Wideman, John Edgar, **188**
Widow of the South, The, 116
Widow's Walk: A Memoir of 9/11, 172
Wiesel, Elie, 71–72, 254
Wife, The, 135, 186
Wiggins, Marianne, **259–260**
Wild Blue Yonder, 181
Wild Nights, 81
Wild Sheep Chase, A, 244
*Wild Trees, The: A Story of Passion and
    Daring,* 176
Wildgen, Michelle, **188–189**
Wilensky, Amy, 143–144
Will in the World, 59
Willenbrock, 67
Willett, Marcia, 182
Willful Creatures: Stories, **198**, 201, 206, 211,
    226
Williams, Lance, 90
Willing, 82, **176**
Willis, Sarah, **189**
Wilson, Emily Herring, 112
Wilson, Robert, 86–87
Winchester, Simon, 8, 227
Wind Done Gone, The, 116
Winder, Paul, 78

Windley, Carol, 109
Wind-Up Bird Chronicle, The, 244
Winesburg, Ohio, 14, 170
Winger, Anna, 4
Winter, Brian, 4
Winter Range, 14
Winterkill, 151
Winter's Tale, 5, 23, 31, 209
Winterson, Jeannette, **95**, 120
Winton, Tim, 34, **44**, 113, 126, **189–190**, 200,
    229, 232
Wisconsin Death Trip, 21
Wish You Were Here, 165
Wishbones, The, 167
Witches of Eastwick, The, 136
Without a Map, 173, 182
Without Blood, **197–198**
Wit's End, **64**
Wittenborn, Dirk, 76, **95–96**, 136, 237, 238
Wives and Lovers, 51
Wizard: Life and Times of Nikola Tesla, 23,
    143
Wolf Dreams, 72
Wolfe, Tom, 56, 142
Wolff, Tobias, 75, 124, 179, 181, 188, **190**,
    260
Wolitzer, Meg, 135, 186
*Wolves, Jackals, and Foxes: Assassins Who
    Changed History,* 54
Woman in Berlin, A, 77
*Woman Warrior: Memoirs of a Girlhood
    among Ghosts,* 146
Woman Who Can't Forget, The, 128
Woman Who Walked Into Doors, The, 209
Woman Who Walked on Water, The, 41
Woman Who Watches Over the World, The,
    220
Women, The, **110–111**, 242
*Women of Bloomsbury: Virginia, Vanessa,
    and Carrington,* 254
Wonder Spot, The, 14, 143
Wonderful World, 200, **202**, 208
Wonderlands: Good Gay Travel Writing, 235
Wonders of the Invisible World, The, 182, 223
Wonga Coup, The, 195
Wood, Michael, 186
Woodburner, 169
Woodson, Jacqueline, 166
Woodswoman, 6
Woodward, Gerard, **45**, 196
Woolf, Rebecca, 168
Woolf, Virginia, 114, 214, 254

Word "Desire, The," 211
Word Freak, 176
Working Stiff's Manifesto, A, 165, 221
World According to Garp, The, 22, 117, 142, 171
World and Other Places, The, 95
World Below, The, 160
World Lost, A, 2, 9, 10
World Made By Hand, 63, 66, 210, 218
World Made Straight, The, 86
World to Come, The, 15, **68**, 114
World War Z, 210
World's End, 111
Wreck of the Medusa, The: The Most Famous Sea Disaster of the Nineteenth Century, 82
Wretched of the Earth, The, 188
Wright, Evan, 76
Wright, Ronald, 50
Writing from the Center, 17, 36
Writing in an Age of Silence, 138
Writing on My Forehead, The, **134**
Writing on the Wall, The, 32, **172**
Wroblewski, David, 19, 21, 86, 106, 125, 133, 144, 150, 168
Wurtzel, Elizabeth, 96

X President, The: A Novel of the Cigarette Wars, 50

Yancey, Richard, 180
Yarbrough, Steve, **190**
Yates, Richard, 148, 167, 256
Yeadon, David, 39, 93
Year in Provence, A, 4
Year of Living Biblically, The, 176
Year of Magical Thinking, The, 106, 108, 191, 196

Year of Pleasures, The, 55
Year of Wonders, 56, 112
Year That Follows, The, 161
Year with the Queen, A, 54
Yehoshua, Abraham, 226
Yellow Moon Dog, 72
Yellow Raft, The, 152
Yellow-Lighted Bookshop, The, 171
Yesterday's Weather: Stories, 181, **211–212**, 243, 258
Yglesias, Rafael, 161, **191**, 196
Yiddish Policemen's Union, The, 125, **203–204**, 212, 213, 216, 229
Yo!, 60
Yoshikawa, Mako, **191**
You Are Not a Stranger Here, 75
You Have to Be Careful in the Land of the Free, 225
You Look Nice Today, 58, 62
You Must Remember This, 247
You Remind Me of Me, 201
You Shall Know Our Velocity, 20, 241
Young Fundamentalist, The, 123
Young Men and Fire, 84
You're Not You, **188–189**

Zabor, Rafi, 232
Zamora, Martha, 121
Zeidner, Lisa, 132, 143, 148
Zero, The, 204, 207
Zero: The Biography of an Idea, 246
Zhang, Lijia, 217
Zigzag Way, The, **16**
Zimler, Richard, 83
Zoli, 30
Zuckerman Unbound, 252
Zugzwang, **54**
Zusak, Markus, 77, 213, 254

Subject Index

In this index, centuries and other dates are listed in numerical order, before the letter groupings.

8th Century
  *The Tain: A New Translation of the Tain bo
      Cuailnge*, 59–60
9/11
  Double Vision, 104
  The Emperor's Children, 32
  Exit Ghost, 169–170
  Extremely Loud and Incredibly Close, 213
  Falling Man, 207
  The Future of Love, 1
  The Garden of Last Days, 122–123
  The Groom to Have Been, 98
  The Have-Nots, 217–218
  Man in the Dark, 49–50
  Netherland, 35–36
  Saturday, 236
  The Wasted Vigil, 100–101
  The Writing on the Wall, 172
15th Century
  The Map Thief, 92
  The Voyage of the Short Serpent, 210
16th Century
  My Name Is Red, 83
17th Century
  Doctor Olaf van Schuler's Brain, 237
  The Heretic's Daughter, 71
  A Mercy, 242–243
18th Century
  The Brothers Boswell, 50
  *Johnny One-Eye: A Tale of the American
      Revolution*, 60–61
  The Known World, 70
19th Century
  Cloud Atlas, 240–241
  The Divine Husband, 130
  English Passengers, 25–26
  Everything Is Illuminated, 212–213
  The Expeditions, 69
  The Hummingbird's Daughter, 42
  *The James Boys: A Novel Account of Four
      Desperate Brothers*, 76
  The Known World, 70
  The March, 209

  The Master, 257
  The News from Paraguay, 41
  The River Wife, 2
  The Road from Chapel Hill, 37
  Sailors on the Inward Sea, 92
  Saving the World, 99–100
  Sea of Poppies, 215
  The Secret River, 21–22
  The Shadow Catcher, 259–260
  Shadow Country, 29–30
  *Silver: My Own Tale as Written by Me with
      a Goodly Amount of Murder*, 61
  Stand the Storm, 115
  Star of the Sea, 82
  The Tenderness of Wolves, 249
  Territory, 57
  The True History of the Kelly Gang, 58
  Vanessa & Virginia, 254
20th Century
  American Wife, 174
  Any Human Heart, 109–110
  The Bad Girl, 185
  The Calligrapher's Daughter, 146
  Caramelo, 12–13
  Frida's Bed, 121
  The Inquisitors' Manual, 3
  The Lacuna, 147
  Last Night in Twisted River, 142
  Sailors on the Inward Sea, 92
  The Shadow Catcher, 259–260
  Songs for the Butcher's Daughter, 155
  A Thousand Splendid Suns, 141
  Vanessa & Virginia, 254
  The Women, 110–111
1900s
  The Outlander, 194
  A Reliable Wife, 21
  The Seamstress of Hollywood Boulevard,
      31
  The Whistling Season, 17–18
1910s
  Far Bright Star, 35
  Land of Marvels, 41–42

1910s (*Cont.*)
   Life Class, 104–105
   The People's Act of Love, 236–237
   Sunnyside, 215–216
   Triangle, 187
   Zugzwang, 54
1920s
   The Angel's Game, 87
   Away, 109
   The Book of Illusions, 195–196
   Middlesex, 212
   A Richer Dust, 10
   The Seamstress of Hollywood Boulevard,
      31
   Serena, 85–86
1930s
   Cloud Atlas, 240–241
   Mohr, 168–169
   The River Wife, 2
   Shanghai Girls, 173
1940s
   Andy Catlett: Early Travels, 9
   The Blue Star, 123–124
   City of Thieves, 53
   Consequences, 152–153
   The Eleventh Man, 119–120
   Europe Central, 259
   The Final Solution: A Story of Detection,
      203
   Follow Me, 172–173
   Gardenias, 178
   *The Guernsey Literary and Potato Peel Pie
      Society*, 37–38
   Hannah Coulter, 9–10
   The Invention of Everything Else, 23
   The Little Stranger, 94
   Love, 242
   Mudbound, 24
   Out Stealing Horses, 250
   The Piano Teacher, 75
   A Pigeon and a Boy, 91
   The Plot Against America, 87
   Strivers Row, 5
1950s
   August, 45
   The Bad Girl, 185
   The Bible Salesman, 18
   Brooklyn, 40–41
   Cloud Atlas, 240–241
   The End, 253
   Gilead, 251
   Home, 251

   Lark and Termite, 168
   Last Night in Twisted River, 142
   Love, 242
   Midnight at the Dragon Café, 50–51
   Mr. Sebastian and the Negro Magician,
      93–94
   The Outcast, 223
   Pharmakon, 95–96
   The Piano Teacher, 75
   War Trash, 222
   The Whistling Season, 17–18
1960s
   The Age of Shiva, 178
   August, 45
   The Clarinet Polka, 28–29
   *Firmin: Adventures of a Metropolitan
      Lowlife*, 171
   Haunting Bombay, 98
   The Help, 177
   His Illegal Self, 113
   July, July, 244–245
   Life Without Water, 167
   The Little Giant of Aberdeen County,
      102–103
   Old School, 190
   Peace Like a River, 124–125
   Popular Music from Vittula, 34–35
   A Richer Dust, 10
   Serve the People!, 230
   The Shadow Year, 64
   Sundown, Yellow Moon, 43–44
   Sway, 228
   Three Minutes on Love, 138
   Tomorrow, 179
   Tree of Smoke, 222–223
   We Are Welcome Here, 55
1970s
   The Book of Getting Even, 179–180
   Breath, 189–190
   Cloud Atlas, 240–241
   The Condition, 133–134
   Crossing California, 26–27
   The Darling, 103
   Dervishes, 22
   Divisadero, 246–247
   Fortress of Solitude, 229–230
   A Golden Age, 100
   His Illegal Self, 113
   The Kite Runner, 140–141
   Konkans, 122
   Leaving Home, 111–112
   Let the Great World Spin, 30–31

The Little Giant of Aberdeen County,
    102–103
Middlesex, 212
The Ministry of Special Cases, 125
My Latest Grievance, 152
The Other, 217
Over and Under, 183
Popular Music from Vittula, 34–35
The Rose Variations, 114
She Was, 134–135
The Soul Thief, 106–107
Suzy, Led Zeppelin, and Me, 32–33
This Blinding Absence of Light, 8
A Ticket to Ride, 157–158
Train to Trieste, 36–37
1980s
All about Lulu, 126
All the Living, 241–242
Black Swan Green, 160
Crossing California, 26–27
The Darling, 103
Downtown Owl, 147
Fortress of Solitude, 229–230
How to Sell, 77
The Inheritance of Loss, 118–119
The Line of Beauty, 139–140
Nothing Is Quite Forgotten in Brooklyn, 156
A Question of Attraction, 162
Sag Harbor, 187–188
The White King, 210
1990s
All about Lulu, 126
The Answer Is Always Yes, 126–127
Beaufort, 27–28
The Biographer's Tale, 113
Black Flies, 57
The Cellist of Sarajevo, 20
Mister Pip, 70–71
The Russian Debutante's Handbook, 255
There Is Room for You, 102
Tomorrow, 179
The Uses of Enchantment, 224

Abuse
Castle, 75–76
Crime, 94–95
The Gathering, 211
The Have-Nots, 217–218
The Lace Reader, 105–106
Man Gone Down, 257
Over and Under, 183
The Sound of Us, 189

Storm Riders, 151–152
A Thousand Splendid Suns, 141
The Turning: New Stories, 44
Academia
Admission, 148–149
The Blue Manuscript, 226–227
Deaf Sentence, 153
Famous Suicides of the Japanese Empire,
    161
Indignation, 170
The Lost Dog, 206–207
My Latest Grievance, 152
A Person of Interest, 61
A Question of Attraction, 162
The Romantics, 162–163
The Rose Variations, 114
The Senator's Wife, 159–160
The Soul Thief, 106–107
That Old Cape Magic, 171
You're Not You, 188–189
Accidents
Falling Boy, 157
The Five-Forty-Five to Cannes, 22–23
Frida's Bed, 121
Last Night in Twisted River, 142
Actors and Acting
Chronic City, 229
Snuff, 82
Until I Find You, 142
Adoption. *See also* Family Relationships
Brother and Sister, 182
The Cradle, 175
Digging to America, 184
Divisadero, 246–247
The Girls, 150–151
Run, 166
Storm Riders, 151–152
Adultery. *See also* Marriage
The Believers, 137
Brick Lane, 99
Cleaver, 166
Diablerie, 81
The End of California, 190
Envy, 136
Falling Man, 207
The Future of Love, 1
I Smile Back, 148
The Last Secret, 80
Little Children, 167–168
Lost in the Forest, 159
Love and Other Impossible Pursuits, 93
A Multitude of Sins, 214

Adultery (*Cont.*)
  My Latest Grievance, 152
  A Person of Interest, 61
  Peyton Amberg, 143
  The Senator's Wife, 159–160
  Sing Them Home, 144
  Skylight Confessions, 138–139
  This One Is Mine, 173
  Tomato Girl, 168
  A Week in October, 256
  The Women, 110–111
  You're Not You, 188–189
Adventure
  Cleaver, 166
  English Passengers, 25–26
  Fidali's Way, 78–79
  The Four Corners of the Sky, 154–155
  Rapids, 83
  Sailors on the Inward Sea, 92
  *Silver: My Own Tale as Written by Me with
      a Goodly Amount of Murder,* 61
  The Voyage of the Short Serpent, 210
Afghanistan
  The Kite Runner, 140–141
  The Swallows of Kabul, 145
  A Thousand Splendid Suns, 141
  The Wasted Vigil, 100–101
  We Are Now Beginning Our Descent, 158
Africa
  Beasts of No Nation, 221–222
  The Darling, 103
  A Guide to the Birds of East Africa, 18
  Little Bee, 115–116
  Theft: Stories, 26
African American Authors
  Bass Cathedral, 232
  Diablerie, 81
  Drinking Coffee Elsewhere, 165–166
  Fanon, 188
  The Known World, 70
  Love, 242
  Man Gone Down, 257
  A Mercy, 242–243
  Sag Harbor, 187–188
  Stand the Storm, 115
  Them, 30
African Americans
  Drinking Coffee Elsewhere, 165–166
  The Help, 177
  Hold Love Strong, 130
  Love, 242
  Man Gone Down, 257

  More Than It Hurts You, 256
  Sag Harbor, 187–188
  Someone Knows My Name, 67–68
  Stand the Storm, 115
  Them, 30
  We Are Welcome Here, 55
Aging
  Any Human Heart, 109–110
  Runaway: Stories, 243
Agriculture
  All the Living, 241–242
  Daughters of the North, 66
  In the Fold, 118
  The Ginseng Hunter, 40
  The Last of the Husbandmen, 28
  Mudbound, 24
AIDS
  Hold Love Strong, 130
  The Rope Walk, 112
  Saving the World, 99–100
  Veronica, 214
ALA Notable (award)
  Alva & Irva: The Twins Who Saved a City,
      202–203
  *An Arsonist's Guide to Writers' Homes in
      New England,* 61–62
  Atmospheric Disturbances, 215
  Atonement, 235
  The Attack, 72
  Austerlitz, 253–254
  Away, 109
  Beasts of No Nation, 221–222
  Beautiful Dreamer, 199
  Birds without Wings, 14–15
  Black Swan Green, 160
  Blind Willow, Sleeping Woman, 243–244
  The Book of Illusions, 195–196
  Bucking the Tiger, 246
  The Cave, 252–253
  Cheating at Canasta: Stories, 258
  City of Thieves, 53
  Cloud Atlas, 240–241
  The Complete Stories (Malouf), 232
  The Corrections, 127
  *The Curious Incident of the Dog in the
      Night-Time,* 131–132
  Dangerous Laughter: Stories, 239–240
  Delinquent Virgin: Wayward Pieces,
      224–225
  Don't Tell Anyone: Fiction, 201
  Drinking Coffee Elsewhere, 165–166
  English Passengers, 25–26

Family Matters, 240
Finn, 116
Firmin: Adventures of a Metropolitan Lowlife, 171
The Five-Forty-Five to Cannes, 22–23
Fortress of Solitude, 229–230
Gilead, 251
The Ginseng Hunter, 40
The Girls, 150–151
The Hakawati: A Story, 48
The Half Brother, 114–115
The Hummingbird's Daughter, 42
The Hungry Tide, 128–129
The Inheritance of Loss, 118–119
The Inquisitors' Manual, 3
I Sailed with Magellan, 123
Kafka on the Shore, 244
The Kite Runner, 140–141
The Known World, 70
By the Lake, 156–157
The Lemon Table: Stories, 197
Little Children, 167–168
Love, 242
Lovely Green Eyes, 76–77
The Madonna of Excelsior, 31–32
Midnight at the Dragon Café, 50–51
Miniatures, 227–228
The Ministry of Special Cases, 125
Mister Pip, 70–71
Never Let Me Go, 221
No Country for Old Men, 233
Old School, 190
Olive Kitteridge, 177–178
On Chesil Beach, 235–236
Our Story Begins: New and Selected Stories, 260
Peace, 51
The People's Act of Love, 236–237
The Pesthouse, 62–63
The Plot Against America, 87
Popular Music from Vittula, 34–35
The Road, 234
Rouse Up, O Young Men of the New Age, 245–246
Runaway: Stories, 243
The Russian Debutante's Handbook, 255
Samuel Johnson Is Indignant: Stories, 206
Saturday, 236
Scar Vegas: And Other Stories, 248
The Secret River, 21–22
The Shell Collector, 17
Star of the Sea, 82

The Swallows of Kabul, 145
The True History of the Kelly Gang, 58
Unaccustomed Earth, 149–150
Veronica, 214
The Wasted Vigil, 100–101
The Whistling Season, 17–18
Alaska
  Away, 109
  The Yiddish Policeman's Union, 203–204
Alcoholism. *See also* Drug Abuse
  The Age of Shiva, 178
  Angels Crest, 89
  Diablerie, 81
  The Gathering, 211
  Konkans, 122
  Man Gone Down, 257
  Mothers and Sons: Stories, 181
  The Outcast, 223
  Paula Spencer, 120
  The Shadow Year, 64
Alex Award
  Black Swan Green, 160
  City of Thieves, 53
  Drinking Coffee Elsewhere, 165–166
  Finding Nouf, 19–20
  The Kite Runner, 140–141
  Midnight at the Dragon Café, 50–51
  Mister Pip, 70–71
  Mudbound, 24
  Never Let Me Go, 221
  Over and Under, 183
  Peace Like a River, 124–125
  The Whistling Season, 17–18
Algeria
  Fanon, 188
Alternate Histories
  The Plot Against America, 87
  The Yiddish Policeman's Union, 203–204
Alternate Realities
  Man in the Dark, 49–50
Alzheimer's Disease
  Buffalo Lockjaw, 2–3
  A Map of Glass, 184–185
  Still Alice, 128
American History
  Bright Shiny Morning, 20
  The Shadow Catcher, 259–260
  Strivers Row, 5
American Indians
  The Blue Star, 123–124
  The Shadow Catcher, 259–260
  Storm Riders, 151–152

American Midwest
  The Corrections, 127
  Downtown Owl, 147
  The Driftless Area, 121–122
  The End, 253
  Gilead, 251
  Home, 251
  Indignation, 170
  The Last of the Husbandmen, 28
  Laura Rider's Masterpiece, 135
  Ordinary Genius, 4–5
  Over and Under, 183
  Pygmy, 248–249
  Saul and Patsy, 106
  The Slide, 107
  The Sound of Us, 189
  A Ticket to Ride, 157–158
  You're Not You, 188–189
American Revolution
  *Johnny One-Eye: A Tale of the American
    Revolution,* 60–61
  Someone Knows My Name, 67–68
American South
  Beautiful Dreamer, 199
  The Bible Salesman, 18
  The Blue Star, 123–124
  Crawfish Mountain, 44
  The End of California, 190
  Finn, 116
  The Four Corners of the Sky, 154–155
  Girls in Trucks: Stories, 13–14
  Hairdos of the Mildly Depressed, 117
  The Help, 177
  The Known World, 70
  The March, 209
  Mr. Sebastian and the Negro Magician,
    93–94
  The River Wife, 2
  The Sweet In-Between, 169
  Tomato Girl, 168
  Waveland, 6–7
American West
  Eventide, 136–137
  Fine Just the Way It Is: Wyoming Stories 3,
    36
  Half Broke Horses, 186–187
  Iodine, 146
  *The James Boys: A Novel Account of Four
    Desperate Brothers,* 76
  Labors of the Heart: Stories, 14
  The Shadow Catcher, 259–260
  Territory, 57

Amnesia
  Last Night in Montreal, 39–40
Anarchists
  The Lazarus Project, 219
Ancient History
  Lavinia, 228
Anger, Kenneth
  Sway, 228
Animals
  Ellington Boulevard, 27
  *Firmin: Adventures of a Metropolitan
    Lowlife,* 171
  In the Fold, 118
  A Guide to the Birds of East Africa, 18
  How the Dead Dream, 239
  The Hungry Tide, 128–129
  The Invention of Everything Else, 23
  Iodine, 146
  Kings of Infinite Space, 221
  The Labrador Pact, 132–133
  The Lost Dog, 206–207
  A Pigeon and a Boy, 91
  Power, 220
  Prodigal Summer, 25
  *The Tain: A New Translation of the Tain bo
    Cuailnge,* 59–60
  The Thin Place, 205
  Water Dogs, 86
Anthropology
  Fieldwork, 8–9
Anti-Semitism
  Away, 109
  The Plot Against America, 87
Apartheid
  The Madonna of Excelsior, 31–32
Apocalypse
  The Pesthouse, 62–63
  The Road, 234
Appalachians
  Prodigal Summer, 25
Arab Authors
  I Think of You: Stories, 39
Arab–Israeli Conflict
  The Attack, 72
Archaeology
  The Blue Manuscript, 226–227
  Land of Marvels, 41–42
Architects and Architecture
  Skylight Confessions, 138–139
  Waveland, 6–7
  The Women, 110–111
Argentina
  The Ministry of Special Cases, 125

Argentinean Authors
  The Book of Murder, 78
Arizona
  Territory, 57
Arranged Marriages. *See also* Marriage
  Brick Lane, 99
  Family Matters, 240
  The Groom to Have Been, 98
  A Thousand Splendid Suns, 141
Arson
  *An Arsonist's Guide to Writers' Homes in
      New England,* 61–62
Art and Artists
  Any Human Heart, 109–110
  Atlas of Unknowns, 142–143
  Double Vision, 104
  Frida's Bed, 121
  Glover's Mistake, 74
  The Great Man, 204
  I See You Everywhere, 129
  The Kept Man, 101
  The Lacuna, 147
  Life Class, 104–105
  The Madonna of Excelsior, 31–32
  The Madonnas of Leningrad, 15
  A Map of Glass, 184–185
  The Map Thief, 92
  My Name Is Red, 83
  One Vacant Chair, 117
  Pictures at an Exhibition, 68
  The Post-Birthday World, 174
  The Promise of Happiness, 113–114
  A Richer Dust, 10
  The Sky Below, 207–208
  The World To Come, 68
Artificial Intelligence
  Genesis, 52
Asian American Authors
  Aloft, 151
  Once Removed, 191
Asian Americans
  Famous Suicides of the Japanese Empire, 161
  Once Removed, 191
Asian Canadian Authors
  The Groom to Have Been, 98
Asperger's Syndrome
  Up High in the Trees, 111
Astrology
  The Toss of a Lemon, 185–186
Atlanta
  Them, 30

Atrocities
  Lovely Green Eyes, 76–77
Australia
  Addition, 143–144
  Breath, 189–190
  The Complete Stories (Malouf), 232
  Diary of a Bad Year, 205
  The Forgotten Garden, 80–81
  His Illegal Self, 113
  The Lost Dog, 206–207
  The Secret River, 21–22
  The True History of the Kelly Gang, 58
  The Turning: New Stories, 44
Australian Authors
  Addition, 143–144
  The Boat, 74–75
  Breath, 189–190
  The Complete Stories (Malouf), 232
  Disquiet, 229
  The End of the World Book, 234–235
  The Forgotten Garden, 80–81
  His Illegal Self, 113
  The Lost Dog, 206–207
  March, 112
  The Secret River, 21–22
  The True History of the Kelly Gang, 58
  The Turning: New Stories, 44
Vernon God Little, 84–85
Autism
  *The Curious Incident of the Dog in the
      Night-Time,* 131–132
Autobiographical Fiction
  Diary of a Bad Year, 205
  Rouse Up, O Young Men of the New Age,
      245–246

Balmis, Francisco Xavier de
  Saving the World, 99–100
Baltimore
  Digging to America, 184
  Songs for the Butcher's Daughter, 155
Bangladesh
  A Golden Age, 100
Bangladeshi Authors
  A Golden Age, 100
Barcelona
  The Angel's Game, 87
  People of the Book, 56
  Wonderful World, 202
Beausoleil, Bobby
  Sway, 228

Beijing
  The Last Chinese Chef, 33–34
  Twenty Fragments of a Ravenous Youth,
    216–217
Beirut
  The Hakawati: A Story, 48
Bell, Vanessa
  Vanessa & Virginia, 254
Bellwether Prize for Fiction
  Mudbound, 24
Berlin
  Book of Clouds, 4
Biographical Fiction
  Any Human Heart, 109–110
  Arthur & George, 105
  The Biographer's Tale, 113
  The Brothers Boswell, 50
  Bucking the Tiger, 246
  The Darling, 103
  The Divine Husband, 130
  Europe Central, 259
  Fanon, 188
  Frida's Bed, 121
  The Heretic's Daughter, 71
  The Hummingbird's Daughter, 42
  The Inquisitors' Manual, 3
  The Invention of Everything Else, 23
  The James Boys: A Novel Account of Four
    Desperate Brothers, 76
  Johnny One-Eye: A Tale of the American
    Revolution, 60–61
  The Lacuna, 147
  Let the Great World Spin, 30–31
  The March, 209
  The Master, 257
  Mohr, 168–169
  The News from Paraguay, 41
  Pictures at an Exhibition, 68
  The Plot Against America, 87
  Sailors on the Inward Sea, 92
  Saving the World, 99–100
  The Shadow Catcher, 259–260
  Shadow Country, 29–30
  Strivers Row, 5
  Sunnyside, 215–216
  Sway, 228
  Telex from Cuba, 26
  Territory, 57
  The True History of the Kelly Gang, 58
  Vanessa & Virginia, 254
  The Women, 110–111
  The World To Come, 68

Biology
  The Hungry Tide, 128–129
  Prodigal Summer, 25
  The Shell Collector, 17
Bipolar Disease
  The Five-Forty-Five to Cannes, 22–23
Biracial Characters
  The Blue Manuscript, 226–227
  The Blue Star, 123–124
  Helpless, 130–131
  Konkans, 122
  The Madonna of Excelsior, 31–32
  The Plague of Doves, 125–126
  The Rope Walk, 112
  Symptomatic, 90–91
  The Tenderness of Wolves, 249
Birds
  A Guide to the Birds of East Africa, 18
  The Invention of Everything Else, 23
  A Pigeon and a Boy, 91
Bleak Future
  Daughters of the North, 66
  The Road, 234
  The Stone Gods, 95
Blizzards
  Downtown Owl, 147
Bombay
  The Age of Shiva, 178
  Family Matters, 240
  Haunting Bombay, 98
Book Groups
  Admission, 148–149
  The Age of Shiva, 178
  All the Living, 241–242
  American Wife, 174
  The Angel's Game, 87
  The Answer Is Always Yes, 126–127
  Any Human Heart, 109–110
  Atmospheric Disturbances, 215
  The Attack, 72
  Away, 109
  Beautiful Children, 199
  Into the Beautiful North, 42–43
  The Believers, 137
  Birds without Wings, 14–15
  Black Flies, 57
  The Blue Star, 123–124
  The Book of Dahlia, 99
  Breath, 189–190
  Brick Lane, 99
  Bridge of Sighs, 170–171
  The Brief Wondrous Life of Oscar Wao, 208

Brother and Sister, 182
The Brothers Boswell, 50
The Butt: An Exit Strategy, 89–90
The Calligrapher's Daughter, 146
Caramelo, 12–13
Caspian Rain, 161–162
Censoring an Iranian Love Story, 233
The Condition, 133–134
The Corrections, 127
A Country Called Home, 5–6
Crime, 94–95
Crossing California, 26–27
Day, 225–226
Dear American Airlines, 238–239
Digging to America, 184
Doctor Olaf van Schuler's Brain, 237
Double Vision, 104
Downtown Owl, 147
Draining the Sea, 29
The Driftless Area, 121–122
DuPont Circle, 24
The Elegance of the Hedgehog, 103–104
Ellington Boulevard, 27
English Passengers, 25–26
Everything Is Illuminated, 212–213
Extremely Loud and Incredibly Close, 213
Fieldwork, 8–9
Finn, 116
Firmin: Adventures of a Metropolitan
    Lowlife, 171
Follow Me, 172–173
Frida's Bed, 121
The Gathering, 211
A Ghost at the Table, 108
Gilead, 251
The Ginseng Hunter, 40
The Girls, 150–151
A Golden Age, 100
The Groom to Have Been, 98
The Guernsey Literary and Potato Peel Pie
    Society, 37–38
The Hakawati: A Story, 48
Half Broke Horses, 186–187
Haunting Bombay, 98
The History of Love, 149
Home, 251
Home Safe, 107–108
The Housekeeper and the Professor,
    245–246
The House on Fortune Street, 231
How to Sell, 77

The Hungry Tide, 128–129
I See You Everywhere, 129
The Inheritance of Loss, 118–119
Interred with Their Bones, 58–59
Iodine, 146
It's a Crime, 58
The James Boys: A Novel Account of Four
    Desperate Brothers, 76
Johnny One-Eye: A Tale of the American
    Revolution, 60–61
The Kite Runner, 140–141
The Known World, 70
Konkans, 122
The Labrador Pact, 132–133
The Lace Reader, 105–106
The Lacuna, 147
The Last Chinese Chef, 33–34
Last Night at the Lobster, 164–165
Laura Rider's Masterpiece, 135
The Laws of Harmony, 138
The Lazarus Project, 219
Let the Great World Spin, 30–31
Life Class, 104–105
Life Without Water, 167
The Line of Beauty, 139–140
Little Bee, 115–116
The Little Giant of Aberdeen County,
    102–103
Lost in the Forest, 159
Love, 242
Lovely Green Eyes, 76–77
The Madonnas of Leningrad, 15
Man Gone Down, 257
A Map of Glass, 184–185
The March, 209
The Master Bedroom, 132
A Mercy, 242–243
Middlesex, 212
The Ministry of Special Cases, 125
Mister Pip, 70–71
The Monsters of Templeton, 131
More Than It Hurts You, 256
Mr. Sebastian and the Negro Magician,
    93–94
Mudbound, 24
My Name Is Red, 83
No Country for Old Men, 233
Nothing Is Quite Forgotten in Brooklyn,
    156
Novel about My Wife, 249
Now You See Him, 65–66

Book Groups (*Cont.*)

Olive Kitteridge, 177–178

On Chesil Beach, 235–236

Out Stealing Horses, 250

Over and Under, 183

The Owl & Moon Café, 155–156

Peace, 51

People of the Book, 56

The Pesthouse, 62–63

The Philosopher's Apprentice, 80

The Plague of Doves, 125–126

The Plot Against America, 87

Prodigal Summer, 25

The Promised World, 183

A Reliable Wife, 21

Remainder, 234

The Road, 234

The Road Home, 182

The Rope Walk, 112

The Rose Variations, 114

Run, 166

Sag Harbor, 187–188

Sea of Poppies, 215

The Secret River, 21–22

The Senator's Wife, 159–160

Serena, 85–86

Shanghai Girls, 173

She Was, 134–135

Sing Them Home, 144

Sister Mine, 163–164

The Size of the World, 38

Someone Knows My Name, 67–68

Songs for the Missing, 165

The Sorrows of an American, 141

The Soul Thief, 106–107

The Sound of Us, 189

Stand the Storm, 115

Star of the Sea, 82

Still Alice, 128

Strivers Row, 5

Sunnyside, 215–216

The Swallows of Kabul, 145

The Sweet In-Between, 169

Talk Talk, 110

Telex from Cuba, 26

Ten Days in the Hills, 174–175

Theft: Stories, 26

Them, 30

There Is Room for You, 102

A Thousand Splendid Suns, 141

Three Junes, 128–129

Tinkers, 218

Tomato Girl, 168

The Toss of a Lemon, 185–186

Train to Trieste, 36–37

Trans-sister Radio, 55

Tree of Smoke, 222–223

Triangle, 187

Twenty Fragments of a Ravenous Youth, 216–217

Two Marriages, 231–232

Unaccustomed Earth, 149–150

The Uncommon Reader, 53–54

Undiscovered Country, 19

The Uses of Enchantment, 224

Veronica, 214

The View from the Seventh Layer, 201

The Vine of Desire, 119

The Wasted Vigil, 100–101

Water Dogs, 86

Who by Fire, 175–176

The Women, 110–111

The Writing on the Wall, 172

The Yiddish Policeman's Union, 203–204

Books and Reading

2666, 200

The Angel's Game, 87

The Baum Plan for Financial Independence, 226

The Blue Manuscript, 226–227

Dear American Airlines, 238–239

Firmin: Adventures of a Metropolitan Lowlife, 171

The Guernsey Literary and Potato Peel Pie Society, 37–38

The History of Love, 149

How to Buy a Love of Reading, 64–65

Mister Pip, 70–71

People of the Book, 56

The Rope Walk, 112

Rouse Up, O Young Men of the New Age, 245–246

Songs for the Butcher's Daughter, 155

The Uncommon Reader, 53–54

The View from the Seventh Layer, 201

Wit's End, 64

Books in Translation

2666, 200

The Angel's Game, 87

The Attack, 72

Austerlitz, 253–254

The Bad Girl, 185

Beaufort, 27–28

Blind Willow, Sleeping Woman, 243–244

The Book of Murder, 78
The Cave, 252–253
Censoring an Iranian Love Story, 233
Chez Moi, 16–17
Detective Story, 71–72
The Elegance of the Hedgehog, 103–104
Frida's Bed, 121
The Half Brother, 114–115
The Have-Nots, 217–218
The Housekeeper and the Professor, 245–246
The Inquisitors' Manual, 3
Kafka on the Shore, 244
The Kindly Ones, 230–231
Leaving Tangier, 7
Lovely Green Eyes, 76–77
Mercury Under My Tongue, 258
My Name Is Red, 83
Out Stealing Horses, 250
A Pigeon and a Boy, 91
Popular Music from Vittula, 34–35
Red April, 86–87
Rouse Up, O Young Men of the New Age, 245–246
Serve the People!, 230
Settlement, 67
The Tain: A New Translation of the Tain bo Cuailnge, 59–60
The Taker: And Other Stories, 213–214
This Blinding Absence of Light, 8
Twenty Fragments of a Ravenous Youth, 216–217
The Voyage of the Short Serpent, 210
A Week in October, 256
The White King, 210
Without Blood, 197–198
Wonderful World, 202
Bosnia
    People of the Book, 56
Boston
    Firmin: Adventures of a Metropolitan Lowlife, 171
    Last Night in Twisted River, 142
    Man Gone Down, 257
    My Latest Grievance, 152
    Run, 166
Boswell, James
    The Brothers Boswell, 50
Brain
    The Echo Maker, 250
    Garcia's Heart, 63
    Hairdos of the Mildly Depressed, 117
    Still Alice, 128

Brazil
    The Taker: And Other Stories, 213–214
Brazilian Authors
    The Taker: And Other Stories, 213–214
Brett, Dorothy
    A Richer Dust, 10
British Authors
    Alva & Irva: The Twins Who Saved a City, 202–203
    Any Human Heart, 109–110
    Arlington Park, 117–118
    Arthur & George, 105
    Atonement, 235
    August, 45
    The Bad Mother's Handbook, 153–154
    The Believers, 137
    The Biographer's Tale, 113
    Black Swan Green, 160
    Broken, 204–205
    Brother and Sister, 182
    The Bull: An Exit Strategy, 89–90
    Cleaver, 166
    Cloud Atlas, 240–241
    Consequences, 152–153
    The Curious Incident of the Dog in the Night-Time, 131–132
    Darkmans, 196–197
    Daughters of the North, 66
    Day, 225–226
    Deaf Sentence, 153
    Double Vision, 104
    English Passengers, 25–26
    Gentlemen and Players, 66–67
    The Girl with No Shadow, 135
    A Guide to the Birds of East Africa, 18
    In the Fold, 118
    In the Kitchen, 48–49
    Inglorious, 144–145
    The Killing Jar, 33
    The Labrador Pact, 132–133
    Land of Marvels, 41–42
    Leaving Home, 111–112
    The Lemon Table: Stories, 197
    Life Class, 104–105
    The Line of Beauty, 139–140
    Little Bee, 115–116
    A Long Way Down, 140
    The Master Bedroom, 132
    My Revolutions, 73
    Never Let Me Go, 221
    Novel about My Wife, 249
    On Chesil Beach, 235–236

British Authors (*Cont.*)
  The Outcast, 223
  The Post-Birthday World, 174
  The Promise of Happiness, 113–114
  A Question of Attraction, 162
  Rapids, 83
  Remainder, 234
  The Road Home, 182
  Salt, 247–248
  Saturday, 236
  The Stone Gods, 95
  Suzy, Led Zeppelin, and Me, 32–33
  The Tenderness of Wolves, 249
  Tomorrow, 179
  The Uncommon Reader, 53–54
  What Was Lost, 164
  *What Was She Thinking? Notes On a
    Scandal*, 137
  Whatever Makes You Happy, 178–179
British Columbia
  Runaway: Stories, 243
  Turtle Valley, 3
British History
  *The Guernsey Literary and Potato Peel Pie
    Society*, 37–38
Brooklyn
  Brooklyn, 40–41
  Fortress of Solitude, 229–230
  The Kept Man, 101
  Last Night in Montreal, 39–40
  Nothing Is Quite Forgotten in Brooklyn,
    156
Brothers. *See also* Family Relationships;
    Siblings
  Apologize, Apologize!, 145
  Hairdos of the Mildly Depressed, 117
  The Half Brother, 114–115
  How to Sell, 77
  Miniatures, 227–228
  Peace Like a River, 124–125
  Sag Harbor, 187–188
  Three Junes, 128–129
  Tree of Smoke, 222–223
  Water Dogs, 86
Brothers and Sisters. *See also* Family
    Relationships; Siblings
  Brother and Sister, 182
  Buffalo Lockjaw, 2–3
  The Clarinet Polka, 28–29
  The Corrections, 127
  Disquiet, 229
  The Echo Maker, 250

Family Matters, 240
A Golden Age, 100
The Killing Jar, 33
Lark and Termite, 168
Leaving Tangier, 7
Middlesex, 212
The Promised World, 183
Sing Them Home, 144
Skylight Confessions, 138–139
The Sorrows of an American, 141
A Student of Living Things, 91–92
The Whistling Season, 17–18
Who by Fire, 175–176
The World To Come, 68
Buenos Aires
  The Book of Murder, 78
  The Ministry of Special Cases, 125
Bush, George W.
  Callisto, 73
Business
  How to Sell, 77
  It's a Crime, 58
  Maxxed Out, 62
  The White Tiger, 47–48

Calcutta
  Sea of Poppies, 215
California
  Angels Crest, 89
  Based on the Movie, 180
  The Book of Dahlia, 99
  Bright Shiny Morning, 20
  Delinquent Virgin: Wayward Pieces,
    224–225
  Divisadero, 246–247
  Draining the Sea, 29
  The End of California, 190
  Gardenias, 178
  The Grift, 65
  How the Dead Dream, 239
  Lost in the Forest, 159
  Nobody Move, 69–70
  Out of My Skin, 218
  The Owl & Moon Café, 155–156
  The Seamstress of Hollywood Boulevard, 31
  Sunnyside, 215–216
  Talk Talk, 110
  Ten Days in the Hills, 174–175
  Three Minutes on Love, 138
  The Vine of Desire, 119
  Wit's End, 64
  The Writing on My Forehead, 134

Canada
    All That Matters, 12
    Garcia's Heart, 63
    The Girls, 150–151
    The Groom to Have Been, 98
    He Drown She in the Sea, 160–161
    Helpless, 130–131
    How to Sell, 77
    Landing, 120
    Last Night in Montreal, 39–40
    Last Night in Twisted River, 142
    A Map of Glass, 184–185
    Mercury Under My Tongue, 258
    Midnight at the Dragon Café, 50–51
    The Outlander, 194
    The Tenderness of Wolves, 249
    Turtle Valley, 3
Canadian Authors
    All That Matters, 12
    Atmospheric Disturbances, 215
    The Cellist of Sarajevo, 20
    Collected Stories (Shields), 254–255
    Divisadero, 246–247
    Family Matters, 240
    Garcia's Heart, 63
    He Drown She in the Sea, 160–161
    Helpless, 130–131
    Last Night in Montreal, 39–40
    A Map of Glass, 184–185
    Midnight at the Dragon Café, 50–51
    The Outlander, 194
    Runaway: Stories, 243
    Someone Knows My Name, 67–68
    The Toss of a Lemon, 185–186
    Turtle Valley, 3
Cancer
    The Book of Dahlia, 99
    A Happy Marriage, 191
    Mercury Under My Tongue, 258
    The Owl & Moon Café, 155–156
    The Sea, 196
    The Sky Below, 207–208
    A Week in October, 256
Cannes
    The Five-Forty-Five to Cannes, 22–23
Cannibalism
    Kings of Infinite Space, 221
    The Voyage of the Short Serpent, 210
Cape Cod
    That Old Cape Magic, 171
Caribbean
    He Drown She in the Sea, 160–161

Castro, Fidel
    Telex from Cuba, 26
Catholic Church. *See also* Religion
    Konkans, 122
    Our Lady of Greenwich Village, 79
    The Secret Scripture, 198
    The Voyage of the Short Serpent, 210
Cats
    Kings of Infinite Space, 221
Censorship
    Censoring an Iranian Love Story, 233
Central America
    Saving the World, 99–100
Chagall, Marc
    The World To Come, 68
Channel Islands
    *The Guernsey Literary and Potato Peel Pie
        Society*, 37–38
Chaplin, Charlie
    Sunnyside, 215–216
Chess
    Zugzwang, 54
Chicago
    Crossing California, 26–27
    Famous Suicides of the Japanese Empire,
        161
    The Great Perhaps, 238
    I Sailed with Magellan, 123
    Konkans, 122
    The Lazarus Project, 219
    Love and Obstacles: Stories, 220
    Train to Trieste, 36–37
Child Soldiers
    Beasts of No Nation, 221–222
Childbirth
    The Cradle, 175
Child's Point of View
    Beasts of No Nation, 221–222
    A Better Angel: Stories, 194
    Extremely Loud and Incredibly Close, 213
    Peace Like a River, 124–125
    Up High in the Trees, 111
    The White King, 210
Chilean Authors
    A Week in October, 256
China
    The Ginseng Hunter, 40
    The Last Chinese Chef, 33–34
    Mohr, 168–169
    Serve the People!, 230
    Twenty Fragments of a Ravenous Youth,
        216–217

Chinese American Authors
   War Trash, 222
Chinese Authors
   Serve the People!, 230
   Twenty Fragments of a Ravenous Youth,
      216–217
   War Trash, 222
Chocolate
   The Girl with No Shadow, 135
Christina Stead Prize for Fiction
   The Lost Dog, 206–207
   The Turning: New Stories, 44
CIA
   Tree of Smoke, 222–223
Circus
   Mr. Sebastian and the Negro Magician, 93–94
Civil Rights
   The Help, 177
Civil War
   The Known World, 70
   March, 112
   The March, 209
   The Road from Chapel Hill, 37
   Stand the Storm, 115
Clairvoyance
   The Lace Reader, 105–106
Class Reunions
   July, July, 244–245
Classics
   2666, 200
   Atonement, 235
   Away, 109
   Brick Lane, 99
   The Brief Wondrous Life of Oscar Wao,
      208
   Brooklyn, 40–41
   Caramelo, 12–13
   City of Thieves, 53
   The Corrections, 127
   *The Curious Incident of the Dog in the
      Night-Time*, 131–132
   Digging to America, 184
   Everyman, 252
   Everything Is Illuminated, 212–213
   Exit Ghost, 169–170
   Extremely Loud and Incredibly Close, 213
   Falling Man, 207
   Fortress of Solitude, 229–230
   Gilead, 251
   *The Guernsey Literary and Potato Peel Pie
      Society*, 37–38
   The History of Love, 149

   Home, 251
   The Hummingbird's Daughter, 42
   Indignation, 170
   The Inheritance of Loss, 118–119
   The Kite Runner, 140–141
   The Known World, 70
   Little Children, 167–168
   March, 112
   Middlesex, 212
   Midnight at the Dragon Café, 50–51
   My Name Is Red, 83
   Netherland, 35–36
   No Country for Old Men, 233
   Olive Kitteridge, 177–178
   On Chesil Beach, 235–236
   Out Stealing Horses, 250
   Peace Like a River, 124–125
   People of the Book, 56
   The Plague of Doves, 125–126
   The Plot Against America, 87
   Prodigal Summer, 25
   The Road, 234
   The Russian Debutante's Handbook, 255
   Shadow Country, 29–30
   Strivers Row, 5
   Tree of Smoke, 222–223
   The True History of the Kelly Gang, 58
   Unaccustomed Earth, 149–150
   The Uncommon Reader, 53–54
   The Yiddish Policeman's Union, 203–204
Cleveland
   The Sound of Us, 189
Cloning
   The Philosopher's Apprentice, 80
College Life
   The Soul Thief, 106–107
Colonialism
   English Passengers, 25–26
   Land of Marvels, 41–42
   Mister Pip, 70–71
Colorado
   Eventide, 136–137
   The Hour I First Believed, 150
   She Was, 134–135
Columbine High School
   The Hour I First Believed, 150
Coma Patients
   The Kept Man, 101
Comic Books
   Beautiful Children, 199
Coming-of-Age
   Admission, 148–149

All about Lulu, 126
All the Sad Young Literary Men, 128
Andy Catlett: Early Travels, 9
The Answer Is Always Yes, 126–127
Apologize, Apologize!, 145
Beaufort, 27–28
Black Swan Green, 160
The Blue Star, 123–124
Breath, 189–190
Broken, 204–205
City of Thieves, 53
The Clarinet Polka, 28–29
A Country Called Home, 5–6
Crossing California, 26–27
The Curious Incident of the Dog in the Night-Time, 131–132
The Driftless Area, 121–122
Drinking Coffee Elsewhere, 165–166
The Elegance of the Hedgehog, 103–104
Eventide, 136–137
The Expeditions, 69
Falling Boy, 157
Famous Suicides of the Japanese Empire, 161
Finn, 116
Fortress of Solitude, 229–230
Girls in Trucks: Stories, 13–14
Hold Love Strong, 130
How to Buy a Love of Reading, 64–65
How to Sell, 77
I Sailed with Magellan, 123
In the Fold, 118
Indignation, 170
Kieron Smith, Boy, 225
The Killing Jar, 33
The Kite Runner, 140–141
The Lacuna, 147
Lark and Termite, 168
The Last of the Husbandmen, 28
The Line of Beauty, 139–140
Mister Pip, 70–71
Never Let Me Go, 221
Of Bees and Mist, 254
Old School, 190
Over and Under, 183
Peace Like a River, 124–125
The Plague of Doves, 125–126
Power, 220
A Question of Attraction, 162
The Rope Walk, 112
Sag Harbor, 187–188
The Sky Below, 207–208

The Slide, 107
Sundown, Yellow Moon, 43–44
Suzy, Led Zeppelin, and Me, 32–33
The Sweet In-Between, 169
Telex from Cuba, 26
Three Minutes on Love, 138
A Ticket to Ride, 157–158
Twenty Fragments of a Ravenous Youth, 216–217
Unaccustomed Earth, 149–150
Undiscovered Country, 19
Vernon God Little, 84–85
We Are Welcome Here, 55
What Was Lost, 164
The Whistling Season, 17–18
The White King, 210
You're Not You, 188 189
The Zigzag Way, 16
Commonwealth Writers' Prize
    A Golden Age, 100
    Mister Pip, 70–71
    Someone Knows My Name, 67–68
    The True History of the Kelly Gang, 58
Communes
    The Laws of Harmony, 138
    Life Without Water, 167
Communism
    The Ginseng Hunter, 40
    Train to Trieste, 36–37
    War Trash, 222
Community Life
    The Abstinence Teacher, 84
    Andy Catlett: Early Travels, 9
    Broken, 204–205
    Brownsville: Stories, 12
    By the Lake, 156–157
    Crumbtown, 13
    Dangerous Laughter: Stories, 239–240
    Delinquent Virgin: Wayward Pieces, 224–225
    Downtown Owl, 147
    The End of California, 190
    Eventide, 136–137
    The Guernsey Literary and Potato Peel Pie Society, 37–38
    A Guide to the Birds of East Africa, 18
    Hannah Coulter, 9–10
    The Last of the Husbandmen, 28
    The Laws of Harmony, 138
    Little Children, 167–168
    The Little Giant of Aberdeen County, 102–103

Community Life (*Cont.*)
  Love, 242
  Olive Kitteridge, 177–178
  The Pesthouse, 62–63
  Popular Music from Vittula, 34–35
  Sag Harbor, 187–188
  Saul and Patsy, 106
  Security, 49
  Settlement, 67
  The Shadow Year, 64
  Sing Them Home, 144
  Them, 30
  The Thin Place, 205
  Trans-sister Radio, 55
  The Whistling Season, 17–18
Con Artists
  The Four Corners of the Sky, 154–155
Connecticut
  The Hour I First Believed, 150
  Last Night at the Lobster, 164–165
  Skylight Confessions, 138–139
Conrad, Joseph
  Sailors on the Inward Sea, 92
Cornwall
  The Forgotten Garden, 80–81
Corporations
  Telex from Cuba, 26
Corruption
  Crawfish Mountain, 44
  The Darling, 103
  The Inquisitors' Manual, 3
  It's a Crime, 58
  Our Lady of Greenwich Village, 79
  Schooled, 74
Costa Book of the Year Award
  Day, 225–226
  The Secret Scripture, 198
  The Tenderness of Wolves, 249
Costa First Novel Award
  The Outcast, 223
  The Tenderness of Wolves, 249
  Vernon God Little, 84–85
  What Was Lost, 164
Costa Novel Award
  Day, 225–226
  English Passengers, 25–26
  The Secret Scripture, 198
Coups
  Blood Kin, 63
Cricket
  Netherland, 35–36

Crime
  The Angel's Game, 87
  The Bible Salesman, 18
  Callisto, 73
  Crumbtown, 13
  Diablerie, 81
  Fidali's Way, 78–79
  The Last Secret, 80
  Lush Life, 85
  The Outlander, 194
  Security, 49
  The True History of the Kelly Gang, 58
  The White Tiger, 47–48
  Without Blood, 197–198
  The World To Come, 68
Croatian Authors
  Frida's Bed, 121
Cuba
  Telex from Cuba, 26
Cultural Revolution
  Serve the People!, 230
Culture Clash
  All That Matters, 12
  Arthur & George, 105
  The Blue Manuscript, 226–227
  Brick Lane, 99
  Dervishes, 22
  Diary of a Bad Year, 205
  Fidali's Way, 78–79
  Fieldwork, 8–9
  The Groom to Have Been, 98
  The Hungry Tide, 128–129
  I Think of You: Stories, 39
  The Kite Runner, 140–141
  Konkans, 122
  Midnight at the Dragon Café, 50–51
  Moonlight Hotel, 195
  The Piano Teacher, 75
  Power, 220
  Saving the World, 99–100
  The Secret River, 21–22
  There Is Room for You, 102
  Unaccustomed Earth, 149–150
  The Zigzag Way, 16
Curtis, Edward S.
  The Shadow Catcher, 259–260
Czech Authors
  Lovely Green Eyes, 76–77

Dark Humor. *See also* Humor
  All about Lulu, 126

Arlington Park, 117 118
Beat the Reaper, 51–52
A Better Angel: Stories, 194
Broken, 204–205
The Butt: An Exit Strategy, 89–90
Callisto, 73
The Corrections, 127
Crumbtown, 13
Dangerous Laughter: Stories, 239–240
Darkmans, 196–197
Dear American Airlines, 238–239
The Deportees and Other Stories, 209
Dictation: A Quartet, 247
The Driftless Area, 121–122
Inglorious, 144–145
Kings of Infinite Space, 221
A Long Way Down, 140
Love and Obstacles: Stories, 220
The Master Bedroom, 132
Paula Spencer, 120
Pygmy, 248–249
Remainder, 234
The Russian Debutante's Handbook, 255
Serve the People!, 230
The Taker: And Other Stories, 213–214
Until I Find You, 142
Vanilla Bright Like Eminem: Stories, 212
Vernon God Little, 84–85
The Voyage of the Short Serpent, 210
The White Tiger, 47–48
Dark Magic
    Territory, 57
Day in the Life
    Arlington Park, 117–118
    Beat the Reaper, 51–52
    The End, 253
    A Long Way Down, 140
    Saturday, 236
    Tomorrow, 179
Deafness
    Caspian Rain, 161–162
    Deaf Sentence, 153
    The Sound of Us, 189
    Talk Talk, 110
Death and Dying
    2666, 200
    All the Living, 241–242
    Apologize, Apologize!, 145
    The Believers, 137
    A Better Angel: Stories, 194
    Between Here and April, 72–73
    The Book of Dahlia, 99

The Book of Illusions, 195–196
Breath, 189–190
Brooklyn, 40–41
The Cellist of Sarajevo, 20
A Country Called Home, 5–6
Disquiet, 229
The Driftless Area, 121–122
The Eleventh Man, 119–120
The Essential Charlotte, 172
Extremely Loud and Incredibly Close, 213
The Five-Forty-Five to Cannes, 22–23
Five Skies, 11–12
The Future of Love, 1
The Gathering, 211
The Hakawati: A Story, 48
A Happy Marriage, 191
Hold Love Strong, 130
Home Safe, 107–108
How the Dead Dream, 239
I See You Everywhere, 129
The Labrador Pact, 132–133
The Last Chinese Chef, 33–34
The Laws of Harmony, 138
The Little Giant of Aberdeen County,
    102–103
Lost in the Forest, 159
Love and Other Impossible Pursuits, 93
Lovely Green Eyes, 76–77
Man in the Dark, 49–50
A Map of Glass, 184–185
Mercury Under My Tongue, 258
One Vacant Chair, 117
Out Stealing Horses, 250
The Pesthouse, 62–63
The Rope Walk, 112
Run, 166
The Sea, 196
Skylight Confessions, 138–139
The Sorrows of an American, 141
Split Estate, 101–102
A Student of Living Things, 91–92
There Is Room for You, 102
Tinkers, 218
Triangle, 187
Undiscovered Country, 19
Up High in the Trees, 111
Veronica, 214
A Week in October, 256
Without Blood, 197–198
The Writing on the Wall, 172
Denver
    She Was, 134–135

Devil
   Mr. Sebastian and the Negro Magician,
      93–94
Diary
   Any Human Heart, 109–110
   Beaufort, 27–28
   Deaf Sentence, 153
   Diary of a Bad Year, 205
   The Heretic's Daughter, 71
   The River Wife, 2
   Songs for the Butcher's Daughter, 155
   A Week in October, 256
Dictators
   The Inquisitors' Manual, 3
   The News from Paraguay, 41
Diplomats and Diplomacy
   Moonlight Hotel, 195
Disabilities
   Caspian Rain, 161–162
   Falling Boy, 157
   Hairdos of the Mildly Depressed, 117
   Lark and Termite, 168
   The Sound of Us, 189
   Talk Talk, 110
   Turtle Valley, 3
   You're Not You, 188–189
Doctors
   The Attack, 72
   Beat the Reaper, 51–52
   Doctor Olaf van Schuler's Brain, 237
   The End of California, 190
   Garcia's Heart, 63
   The Little Giant of Aberdeen County,
      102–103
   The Little Stranger, 94
   Mohr, 168–169
   More Than It Hurts You, 256
   The Secret Scripture, 198
Dogs
   Ellington Boulevard, 27
   Iodine, 146
   The Labrador Pact, 132–133
   The Lost Dog, 206–207
   The Thin Place, 205
Domestic Fiction
   Aloft, 151
   American Wife, 174
   Andy Catlett: Early Travels, 9
   Arlington Park, 117–118
   August, 45
   Brick Lane, 99
   Brother and Sister, 182

The Condition, 133–134
The Corrections, 127
Digging to America, 184
Don't Tell Anyone: Fiction, 201
Eventide, 136–137
The Great Perhaps, 238
The Help, 177
Home, 251
Home Safe, 107–108
The Hour I First Believed, 150
In the Fold, 118
The Little Giant of Aberdeen County,
   102–103
Lost in the Forest, 159
Love and Other Impossible Pursuits, 93
Midnight at the Dragon Café, 50–51
Mudbound, 24
Olive Kitteridge, 177–178
The Owl & Moon Café, 155–156
Paula Spencer, 120
The Road from Chapel Hill, 37
Saul and Patsy, 106
The Senator's Wife, 159–160
Split Estate, 101–102
This One Is Mine, 173
Unaccustomed Earth, 149–150
The Vine of Desire, 119
Who by Fire, 175–176
Yesterday's Weather: Stories, 211–212
Dominican American Authors
   The Brief Wondrous Life of Oscar Wao,
      208
Dominican Authors
   Saving the World, 99–100
Dominican Republic
   The Brief Wondrous Life of Oscar Wao,
      208
   Saving the World, 99–100
Double Agents
   Tree of Smoke, 222–223
Doyle, Arthur Conan
   Arthur & George, 105
Drug Abuse. *See also* Alcoholism
   The Answer Is Always Yes, 126–127
   Crime, 94–95
   Darkmans, 196–197
   How to Buy a Love of Reading, 64–65
   How to Sell, 77
   I Smile Back, 148
   The Killing Jar, 33
   Paula Spencer, 120
   Sway, 228

Dysfunctional Families. *See also* Family
     Relationships
     All about Lulu, 126
     Apologize, Apologize!, 145
     Beautiful Children, 199
     The Corrections, 127
     A Ghost at the Table, 108
     Hairdos of the Mildly Depressed, 117
     The Lace Reader, 105–106
     Life Without Water, 167
     The Monsters of Templeton, 131
     Nothing Right: Short Stories, 162
     NoVA, 200
     Paula Spencer, 120
     Skylight Confessions, 138–139
     Split Estate, 101–102
     The Sweet In-Between, 169
Dystopia
     Daughters of the North, 66
     Genesis, 52
     The Pesthouse, 62–63
     The Philosopher's Apprentice, 80

Earp, Wyatt
     Territory, 57
Eastern Europe
     Europe Central, 259
     The Lazarus Project, 219
     The Road Home, 182
Education
     The Abstinence Teacher, 84
     Admission, 148–149
     Gentlemen and Players, 66–67
     How to Buy a Love of Reading, 64–65
     Mister Pip, 70–71
     Old School, 190
     Sag Harbor, 187–188
     Saul and Patsy, 106
     Schooled, 74
     Vernon God Little, 84–85
     *What Was She Thinking? Notes On a
          Scandal,* 137
     The Whistling Season, 17–18
Egypt
     The Blue Manuscript, 226–227
     I Think of You: Stories, 39
El Salvador
     Apologize, Apologize!, 145
Elderly
     Andy Catlett: Early Travels, 9
     The Bad Mother's Handbook, 153–154
     Buffalo Lockjaw, 2–3

     The Cave, 252–253
     The Darling, 103
     Deaf Sentence, 153
     Everything Is Illuminated, 212–213
     Family Matters, 240
     Follow Me, 172–173
     Gilead, 251
     The Great Man, 204
     Hannah Coulter, 9–10
     The Housekeeper and the Professor,
          245–246
     The Madonnas of Leningrad, 15
     Man in the Dark, 49–50
     The Master Bedroom, 132
     One Vacant Chair, 117
     Out Stealing Horses, 250
     Songs for the Butcher's Daughter, 155
     The Thin Place, 205
     Tinkers, 218
     Triangle, 187
     Turtle Valley, 3
     Without Blood, 197–198
Elizabeth II
     The Uncommon Reader, 53–54
Environmental Writing
     Crawfish Mountain, 44
     The Hungry Tide, 128–129
     The Other, 217
     The Outlander, 194
     Power, 220
     The Shell Collector, 17
Epic Reads
     2666, 200
     Any Human Heart, 109–110
     Beautiful Children, 199
     Birds without Wings, 14–15
     The Corrections, 127
     Darkmans, 196–197
     Europe Central, 259
     Family Matters, 240
     The Forgotten Garden, 80–81
     The Hakawati: A Story, 48
     The Half Brother, 114–115
     The Hour I First Believed, 150
     The Kindly Ones, 230–231
     Shadow Country, 29–30
     The Toss of a Lemon, 185–186
     Tree of Smoke, 222–223
     Until I Find You, 142
     Wonderful World, 202
Epilepsy
     Tinkers, 218

Epistolary Fiction
  Bass Cathedral, 232
  Dear American Airlines, 238–239
  Gilead, 251
  *The Guernsey Literary and Potato Peel Pie
      Society,* 37–38
  The Heretic's Daughter, 71
  Inglorious, 144–145
  Landing, 120
  The White Tiger, 47–48
Erotica
  Intercourse: Stories, 201–202
Espionage
  Peace, 51
European History
  Europe Central, 259
  The Half Brother, 114–115
  The House of Widows: An Oral History,
      237
Expatriates
  Bridge of Sighs, 170–171
  Leaving Tangier, 7
  We Are Now Beginning Our Descent, 158
Experimental Fiction
  Cloud Atlas, 240–241
  Extremely Loud and Incredibly Close, 213
Explicit Sexuality
  All the Living, 241–242
  Breath, 189–190
  Crime, 94–95
  Diablerie, 81
  Draining the Sea, 29
  The End of California, 190
  The End of the World Book, 234–235
  Envy, 136
  I Smile Back, 148
  Intercourse: Stories, 201–202
  The Kindly Ones, 230–231
  Laura Rider's Masterpiece, 135
  Leaving Tangier, 7
  The Line of Beauty, 139–140
  Lovely Green Eyes, 76–77
  Peyton Amberg, 143
  A Reliable Wife, 21
  Snuff, 82
  The Stone Gods, 95
  Ten Days in the Hills, 174–175
  Until I Find You, 142
  Veronica, 214
  *What Was She Thinking? Notes On a
      Scandal,* 137
  Willing, 176

Exploration
  English Passengers, 25–26

Fairies
  The Good Fairies of New York, 158–159
Fairy Tales
  The Forgotten Garden, 80–81
Family Relationships. *See also* Family
      Secrets; Parenting
  The Age of Shiva, 178
  All about Lulu, 126
  All That Matters, 12
  Aloft, 151
  Alva & Irva: The Twins Who Saved a City,
      202–203
  Andy Catlett: Early Travels, 9
  Apologize, Apologize!, 145
  *An Arsonist's Guide to Writers' Homes in
      New England,* 61–62
  Atlas of Unknowns, 142–143
  Atonement, 235
  August, 45
  The Bad Mother's Handbook, 153–154
  The Believers, 137
  Between Here and April, 72–73
  Birds without Wings, 14–15
  Black Swan Green, 160
  The Blue Star, 123–124
  The Boat, 74–75
  The Book of Dahlia, 99
  The Book of Getting Even, 179–180
  Bridge of Sighs, 170–171
  The Brief Wondrous Life of Oscar Wao,
      208
  Bright Shiny Morning, 20
  Broken, 204–205
  Brother and Sister, 182
  Buffalo Lockjaw, 2–3
  The Butt: An Exit Strategy, 89–90
  The Calligrapher's Daughter, 146
  Caramelo, 12–13
  Caspian Rain, 161–162
  Castle, 75–76
  Cheating at Canasta: Stories, 258
  The Clarinet Polka, 28–29
  Cleaver, 166
  The Complete Stories (Malouf), 232
  The Condition, 133–134
  The Corrections, 127
  A Country Called Home, 5–6
  The Cradle, 175
  Crawfish Mountain, 44

The Curious Incident of the Dog in the Night-Time, 131–132
Darkmans, 196–197
Dear American Airlines, 238–239
Dear Husband: Stories, 81
Dervishes, 22
Dictation: A Quartet, 247
Digging to America, 184
Disquiet, 229
Divisadero, 246–247
Do Not Deny Me: Stories, 180–181
Don't Tell Anyone: Fiction, 201
Downtown Owl, 147
DuPont Circle, 24
The Echo Maker, 250
The Emperor's Children, 32
The End of California, 190
Envy, 136
The Essential Charlotte, 172
Eventide, 136–137
Everyman, 252
Everything Ravaged, Everything Burned, 181–182
The Expeditions, 69
Extremely Loud and Incredibly Close, 213
Falling Man, 207
The Family Man, 152
Family Matters, 240
Famous Suicides of the Japanese Empire, 161
Female Trouble: A Collection of Short Stories, 244
Finding Nouf, 19–20
Finn, 116
The First Person: And Other Stories, 255–256
Follow Me, 172–173
The Four Corners of the Sky, 154–155
Frida's Bed, 121
The Future of Love, 1
Gardenias, 178
The Garden of Last Days, 122–123
The Gathering, 211
A Ghost at the Table, 108
Gilead, 251
The Girls, 150–151
A Golden Age, 100
The Great Man, 204
The Great Perhaps, 238
The Groom to Have Been, 98
The Guardians, 60
A Guide to the Birds of East Africa, 18

Hairdos of the Mildly Depressed, 117
The Hakawati: A Story, 48
Half Broke Horses, 186–187
The Half Brother, 114–115
A Happy Marriage, 191
Haunting Bombay, 98
Her Fearful Symmetry, 163
The Heretic's Daughter, 71
His Illegal Self, 113
Hold Love Strong, 130
Home, 251
Home Safe, 107–108
The House of Widows: An Oral History, 237
The House on Fortune Street, 231
How the Dead Dream, 239
How to Sell, 77
The Hummingbird's Daughter, 42
I Sailed with Magellan, 123
I See You Everywhere, 129
In the Fold, 118
Indignation, 170
The Inheritance of Loss, 118–119
The Inquisitors' Manual, 3
It's a Crime, 58
Kieron Smith, Boy, 225
Konkans, 122
The Labrador Pact, 132–133
The Lace Reader, 105–106
Lark and Termite, 168
Last Night in Montreal, 39–40
The Laws of Harmony, 138
Leaving Home, 111–112
Leaving Tangier, 7
The Lemon Table: Stories, 197
Life Without Water, 167
The Line of Beauty, 139–140
Little Bee, 115–116
Little Children, 167–168
The Little Giant of Aberdeen County, 102–103
The Little Stranger, 94
Lost in the Forest, 159
Love and Other Impossible Pursuits, 93
The Madonna of Excelsior, 31–32
Man Gone Down, 257
Man in the Dark, 49–50
The Master Bedroom, 132
Midnight at the Dragon Café, 50–51
The Ministry of Special Cases, 125
Mohr, 168–169
More Than It Hurts You, 256

Family Relationships (*Cont.*)
   Mothers and Sons: Stories, 181
   Mr. Sebastian and the Negro Magician,
      93–94
   Mudbound, 24
   A Multitude of Sins, 214
   My Latest Grievance, 152
   My Revolutions, 73
   Netherland, 35–36
   Nothing Is Quite Forgotten in Brooklyn, 156
   Nothing Right: Short Stories, 162
   NoVA, 200
   Novel about My Wife, 249
   Of Bees and Mist, 254
   Olive Kitteridge, 177–178
   Once Removed, 191
   The One Marvelous Thing, 210–211
   One Vacant Chair, 117
   Ordinary Genius, 4–5
   *Our Story Begins: New and Selected
      Stories*, 260
   The Outcast, 223
   The Outlander, 194
   The Owl & Moon Café, 155–156
   Paula Spencer, 120
   Peace Like a River, 124–125
   Pharmakon, 95–96
   The Plague of Doves, 125–126
   *Portrait of My Mother, Who Posed Nude in
      Wartime: Stories*, 252
   Prodigal Summer, 25
   The Promised World, 183
   The Promise of Happiness, 113–114
   Red April, 86–87
   A Reliable Wife, 21
   The River Wife, 2
   The Road, 234
   The Road from Chapel Hill, 37
   The Rope Walk, 112
   Run, 166
   Runaway: Stories, 243
   Salt, 247–248
   Saturday, 236
   The Sea, 196
   The Secret River, 21–22
   The Secret Scripture, 198
   Security, 49
   The Shadow Catcher, 259–260
   Shadow Country, 29–30
   The Shadow Year, 64
   She Was, 134–135
   The Shell Collector, 17

Sing Them Home, 144
Sister Mine, 163–164
The Size of the World, 38
The Sky Below, 207–208
Skylight Confessions, 138–139
The Slide, 107
Songs for the Missing, 165
The Sorrows of an American, 141
Split Estate, 101–102
Stand the Storm, 115
Still Alice, 128
Storm Riders, 151–152
The Story Sisters, 139
A Student of Living Things, 91–92
Sundown, Yellow Moon, 43–44
The Sweet In-Between, 169
That Old Cape Magic, 171
Theft: Stories, 26
There Is Room for You, 102
This One Is Mine, 173
Three Junes, 128–129
Three Minutes on Love, 138
A Ticket to Ride, 157–158
Tinkers, 218
Tomato Girl, 168
The Toss of a Lemon, 185–186
Tree of Smoke, 222–223
Trespass, 77–78
Triangle, 187
The Turning: New Stories, 44
Turtle Valley, 3
Two Marriages, 231–232
Unaccustomed Earth, 149–150
Undiscovered Country, 19
Until I Find You, 142
Up High in the Trees, 111
The Uses of Enchantment, 224
Vanessa & Virginia, 254
Veronica, 214
The Vine of Desire, 119
The Wasted Vigil, 100–101
Water Dogs, 86
We Are Welcome Here, 55
Whatever Makes You Happy, 178–179
What Was Lost, 164
The Whistling Season, 17–18
The White Tiger, 47–48
Who by Fire, 175–176
Wonderful World, 202
The World to Come, 68
The Writing on My Forehead, 134
Yesterday's Weather: Stories, 211–212

Family Secrets. *See also* Family Relationships
  The Believers, 137
  The Cradle, 175
  *The Curious Incident of the Dog in the
      Night-Time*, 131–132
  Envy, 136
  Famous Suicides of the Japanese Empire,
      161
  Follow Me, 172–173
  The Forgotten Garden, 80–81
  A Ghost at the Table, 108
  Haunting Bombay, 98
  Her Fearful Symmetry, 163
  Home Safe, 107–108
  The Hour I First Believed, 150
  The House of Widows: An Oral History,
      237
  In the Fold, 118
  The Kept Man, 101
  The Lace Reader, 105–106
  Last Night in Montreal, 39–40
  The Last Secret, 80
  Midnight at the Dragon Café, 50–51
  Miniatures, 227–228
  The Monsters of Templeton, 131
  Nothing Is Quite Forgotten in Brooklyn,
      156
  Now You See Him, 65–66
  Once Removed, 191
  The Outcast, 223
  *Portrait of My Mother, Who Posed Nude in
      Wartime: Stories*, 252
  The Promised World, 183
  The Promise of Happiness, 113–114
  The Seamstress of Hollywood Boulevard,
      31
  The Secret Scripture, 198
  Serena, 85–86
  Shadow Country, 29–30
  Shanghai Girls, 173
  She Was, 134–135
  Sister Mine, 163–164
  The Sorrows of an American, 141
  The Story Sisters, 139
  There Is Room for You, 102
  Tomorrow, 179
  Triangle, 187
  Turtle Valley, 3
  Who by Fire, 175–176
  Wit's End, 64
  The Writing on My Forehead, 134
  The Writing on the Wall, 172

Fanon, Frantz
  Fanon, 188
Fantasy
  Alva & Irva: The Twins Who Saved a City,
      202–203
  *The Baum Plan for Financial
      Independence*, 226
  Darkmans, 196–197
  *Firmin: Adventures of a Metropolitan
      Lowlife*, 171
  The Good Fairies of New York, 158–159
  Kafka on the Shore, 244
  Lavinia, 228
  The Monsters of Templeton, 131
  Of Bees and Mist, 254
  Territory, 57
  Vanilla Bright Like Eminem: Stories, 212
  Willful Creatures: Stories, 198
Farming. *See* Agriculture
Fathers and Daughters. *See also* Family
      Relationships
  Broken, 204–205
  A Country Called Home, 5–6
  The Essential Charlotte, 172
  The Family Man, 152
  The Four Corners of the Sky, 154–155
  A Ghost at the Table, 108
  I Smile Back, 148
  Into the Beautiful North, 42–43
  March, 112
  A Person of Interest, 61
  The Rope Walk, 112
  Tomato Girl, 168
Fathers and Sons. *See also* Family
      Relationships
  Angels Crest, 89
  Cleaver, 166
  *The Curious Incident of the Dog in the
      Night-Time*, 131–132
  Darkmans, 196–197
  DuPont Circle, 24
  The Expeditions, 69
  Famous Suicides of the Japanese Empire,
      161
  Finn, 116
  Gilead, 251
  The History of Love, 149
  Home, 251
  The House of Widows: An Oral History,
      237
  The Kite Runner, 140–141
  Last Night in Twisted River, 142

Fathers and Sons (*Cont.*)
  The Ministry of Special Cases, 125
  Out Stealing Horses, 250
  Pharmakon, 95–96
  A Reliable Wife, 21
  The Road, 234
  Rouse Up, O Young Men of the New Age,
      245–246
  Run, 166
  Storm Riders, 151–152
  Three Junes, 128–129
  Three Minutes on Love, 138
  Tinkers, 218
  Up High in the Trees, 111
Feminism
  Between Here and April, 72–73
  Daughters of the North, 66
  The Stone Gods, 95
Finance
  Maxxed Out, 62
First Novels
  Addition, 143–144
  All about Lulu, 126
  All the Living, 241–242
  All the Sad Young Literary Men, 128
  The Answer Is Always Yes, 126–127
  Apologize, Apologize!, 145
  Atlas of Unknowns, 142–143
  Atmospheric Disturbances, 215
  August, 45
  Based on the Movie, 180
  Beat the Reaper, 51–52
  Beaufort, 27–28
  Beautiful Children, 199
  Between Here and April, 72–73
  Book of Clouds, 4
  The Book of Dahlia, 99
  Bright Shiny Morning, 20
  Broken, 204–205
  The Calligrapher's Daughter, 146
  Dear American Airlines, 238–239
  Dervishes, 22
  Doctor Olaf van Schuler's Brain, 237
  Downtown Owl, 147
  The End, 253
  The End of the World Book, 234–235
  Famous Suicides of the Japanese Empire,
      161
  Fidali's Way, 78–79
  Fieldwork, 8–9
  Finn, 116

*Firmin: Adventures of a Metropolitan
    Lowlife*, 171
The Future of Love, 1
Garcia's Heart, 63
A Golden Age, 100
The Groom to Have Been, 98
The Half Brother, 114–115
Haunting Bombay, 98
The Help, 177
The Heretic's Daughter, 71
Hold Love Strong, 130
How to Buy a Love of Reading, 64–65
In Other Rooms, Other Wonders, 34
Inglorious, 144–145
Interred with Their Bones, 58–59
The Kept Man, 101
The Killing Jar, 33
The Kindly Ones, 230–231
The Kite Runner, 140–141
The Lace Reader, 105–106
Last Night in Montreal, 39–40
The Little Giant of Aberdeen County,
    102–103
The Madonnas of Leningrad, 15
Man Gone Down, 257
Midnight at the Dragon Café, 50–51
The Monsters of Templeton, 131
Mudbound, 24
Of Bees and Mist, 254
Our Lady of Greenwich Village, 79
The Outcast, 223
The Outlander, 194
Over and Under, 183
Peace Like a River, 124–125
The Piano Teacher, 75
Pictures at an Exhibition, 68
A Question of Attraction, 162
Remainder, 234
A Richer Dust, 10
The Rose Variations, 114
The Russian Debutante's Handbook, 255
Salt, 247–248
Schooled, 74
*Silver: My Own Tale as Written by Me with
    a Goodly Amount of Murder*, 61
The Slide, 107
Still Alice, 128
Telex from Cuba, 26
This One Is Mine, 173
Three Minutes on Love, 138
A Ticket to Ride, 157–158

Tinkers, 218
Tomato Girl, 168
The Toss of a Lemon, 185–186
Train to Trieste, 36–37
Undiscovered Country, 19
Up High in the Trees, 111
Vanessa & Virginia, 254
Vernon God Little, 84–85
What Was Lost, 164
The White King, 210
The White Tiger, 47–48
Who by Fire, 175–176
The Writing on My Forehead, 134
You're Not You, 188–189
First Person
    Addition, 143–144
    The Age of Shiva, 178
    All about Lulu, 126
    All That Road Going, 241
    Aloft, 151
    Alva & Irva: The Twins Who Saved a City,
        202–203
    American Wife, 174
    An Arsonist's Guide to Writers' Homes in
        New England, 61–62
    Any Human Heart, 109–110
    Atmospheric Disturbances, 215
    Austerlitz, 253–254
    Beat the Reaper, 51–52
    Beaufort, 27–28
    Beautiful Dreamer, 199
    Black Swan Green, 160
    Blood Kin, 63
    Book of Clouds, 4
    The Book of Murder, 78
    Bridge of Sighs, 170–171
    The Calligrapher's Daughter, 146
    Callisto, 73
    Castle, 75–76
    Chez Moi, 16–17
    City of Thieves, 53
    Cloud Atlas, 240–241
    The Darling, 103
    Dervishes, 22
    Detective Story, 71–72
    Divisadero, 246–247
    Exit Ghost, 169–170
    Extremely Loud and Incredibly Close, 213
    Famous Suicides of the Japanese Empire, 161
    Fieldwork, 8–9

The First Person: And Other Stories, 255–256
The Gathering, 211
Gentlemen and Players, 66–67
A Ghost at the Table, 108
The Ginseng Hunter, 40
The Girls, 150–151
The Guardians, 60
Hannah Coulter, 9–10
The History of Love, 149
The Hour I First Believed, 150
How to Sell, 77
I Sailed with Magellan, 123
In the Fold, 118
Indignation, 170
Johnny One-Eye: A Tale of the American
    Revolution, 60–61
The Kept Man, 101
Kieron Smith, Boy, 225
The Killing Jar, 33
The Kindly Ones, 230–231
The Kite Runner, 140–141
Konkans, 122
Lark and Termite, 168
The Laws of Harmony, 138
Little Bee, 115–116
The Little Giant of Aberdeen County, 102–103
Love and Other Impossible Pursuits, 93
Man Gone Down, 257
Man in the Dark, 49–50
March, 112
Maxxed Out, 62
A Mercy, 242–243
Middlesex, 212
Midnight at the Dragon Café, 50–51
Miniatures, 227–228
Mister Pip, 70–71
Mudbound, 24
My Latest Grievance, 152
Netherland, 35–36
Never Let Me Go, 221
Novel about My Wife, 249
Now You See Him, 65–66
Old School, 190
Out of My Skin, 218
Out Stealing Horses, 250
Peace Like a River, 124–125
The Philosopher's Apprentice, 80
Pictures at an Exhibition, 68
Portrait of My Mother, Who Posed Nude in
    Wartime: Stories, 252

First Person (*Cont.*)
  Pygmy, 248–249
  A Question of Attraction, 162
  A Reliable Wife, 21
  Remainder, 234
  A Richer Dust, 10
  Sag Harbor, 187–188
  The Sea, 196
  The Seamstress of Hollywood Boulevard,
      31
  The Shadow Year, 64
  *Silver: My Own Tale as Written by Me with
      a Goodly Amount of Murder*, 61
  Sister Mine, 163–164
  The Size of the World, 38
  The Sky Below, 207–208
  The Slide, 107
  Songs for the Butcher's Daughter, 155
  The Soul Thief, 106–107
  The Sound of Us, 189
  A Student of Living Things, 91–92
  Sundown, Yellow Moon, 43–44
  Suzy, Led Zeppelin, and Me, 32–33
  The Sweet In-Between, 169
  Symptomatic, 90–91
  The Tenderness of Wolves, 249
  There Is Room for You, 102
  This Blinding Absence of Light, 8
  Three Minutes on Love, 138
  A Ticket to Ride, 157–158
  Tomato Girl, 168
  Tomorrow, 179
  Trans-sister Radio, 55
  The True History of the Kelly Gang, 58
  Turtle Valley, 3
  Undiscovered Country, 19
  Up High in the Trees, 111
  Vanessa & Virginia, 254
  Vernon God Little, 84–85
  Veronica, 214
  War Trash, 222
  *What Was She Thinking? Notes On a
      Scandal*, 137
  Whirlwind, 69
  The Whistling Season, 17–18
  The White Tiger, 47–48
  The Writing on My Forehead, 134
  You're Not You, 188–189
Flashbacks
  Admission, 148–149
  The Attack, 72
  The Book of Dahlia, 99

Bridge of Sighs, 170–171
Day, 225–226
Draining the Sea, 29
Everything Is Illuminated, 212–213
Famous Suicides of the Japanese Empire,
    161
Fieldwork, 8–9
The Gathering, 211
The Ginseng Hunter, 40
The Groom to Have Been, 98
A Happy Marriage, 191
He Drown She in the Sea, 160–161
The House of Widows: An Oral History,
    237
Last Night in Montreal, 39–40
Love, 242
Man Gone Down, 257
A Map of Glass, 184–185
NoVA, 200
Now You See Him, 65–66
The Other, 217
Out Stealing Horses, 250
Peyton Amberg, 143
The Piano Teacher, 75
The Sea, 196
She Was, 134–135
There Is Room for You, 102
The True History of the Kelly Gang, 58
Florida
  Crime, 94–95
  The Garden of Last Days, 122–123
  The Grift, 65
  Power, 220
  Shadow Country, 29–30
Flying
  Aloft, 151
Food
  *Broccoli and Other Tales of Food and
      Love*, 258–259
  Chez Moi, 16–17
  The Girl with No Shadow, 135
  In the Kitchen, 48–49
  The Last Chinese Chef, 33–34
Footnotes
  The Brief Wondrous Life of Oscar Wao,
      208
Fortune Telling
  The Grift, 65
Foster Children
  The Sound of Us, 189
France
  Chez Moi, 16–17

Disquiet, 229
Divisadero, 246–247
The Elegance of the Hedgehog, 103–104
Fanon, 188
The Five-Forty-Five to Cannes, 22–23
The Girl with No Shadow, 135
The Kindly Ones, 230–231
Leaving Home, 111–112
Red Car, 108–109
Fraud
  The Grift, 65
  It's a Crime, 58
  Talk Talk, 110
French Authors
  Leaving Tangier, 7
  The Voyage of the Short Serpent, 210
Friendships
  The Abstinence Teacher, 84
  Admission, 148–149
  All the Sad Young Literary Men, 128
  The Answer Is Always Yes, 126–127
  Arthur & George, 105
  Beat the Reaper, 51–52
  Beautiful Children, 199
  Black Flies, 51
  The Blue Star, 123–124
  Book of Clouds, 4
  Breath, 189–190
  Bridge of Sighs, 170–171
  By the Lake, 156–157
  Chez Moi, 16–17
  Chronic City, 229
  City of Thieves, 53
  Crime, 94–95
  Crossing California, 26–27
  Crumbtown, 13
  Darkmans, 196–197
  The Darling, 103
  Dervishes, 22
  Diary of a Bad Year, 205
  Digging to America, 184
  Double Vision, 104
  Downtown Owl, 147
  The Driftless Area, 121–122
  The Elegance of the Hedgehog, 103–104
  The Eleventh Man, 119–120
  The Emperor's Children, 32
  Eventide, 136–137
  Falling Boy, 157
  Family Matters, 240
  Fidali's Way, 78–79

The First Person: And Other Stories, 255–256
Five Skies, 11–12
The Future of Love, 1
Garcia's Heart, 63
Girls in Trucks: Stories, 13–14
The Great Man, 204
The Guardians, 60
He Drown She in the Sea, 160–161
The Help, 177
Home Safe, 107–108
The Housekeeper and the Professor, 245–246
How to Buy a Love of Reading, 64–65
The Hummingbird's Daughter, 42
In the Fold, 118
Inglorious, 144–145
Into the Beautiful North, 42–43
July, July, 244–245
The Kept Man, 101
Kieron Smith, Boy, 225
The Kite Runner, 140–141
Landing, 120
Last Night at the Lobster, 164–165
Last Night in Twisted River, 142
The Last of the Husbandmen, 28
Leaving Home, 111–112
Life Class, 104–105
The Line of Beauty, 139–140
The Little Giant of Aberdeen County, 102–103
A Long Way Down, 140
Lush Life, 85
Mercury Under My Tongue, 258
Mr. Sebastian and the Negro Magician, 93–94
Netherland, 35–36
Never Let Me Go, 221
Nothing Is Quite Forgotten in Brooklyn, 156
Now You See Him, 65–66
One Fifth Avenue, 11
The Other, 217
Out Stealing Horses, 250
Over and Under, 183
Peace, 51
Power, 220
Pygmy, 248–249
A Question of Attraction, 162
Rapids, 83
A Richer Dust, 10

Friendships (*Cont.*)
  The Road Home, 182
  The Romantics, 162–163
  The Rope Walk, 112
  The Rose Variations, 114
  The Senator's Wife, 159–160
  She Was, 134–135
  The Slide, 107
  The Soul Thief, 106–107
  Spoiled: Stories, 154
  Sundown, Yellow Moon, 43–44
  Superpowers, 88–89
  Suzy, Led Zeppelin, and Me, 32–33
  Symptomatic, 90–91
  Them, 30
  The Thin Place, 205
  A Thousand Splendid Suns, 141
  A Ticket to Ride, 157–158
  Tree of Smoke, 222–223
  Up High in the Trees, 111
  Veronica, 214
  What Was Lost, 164
  *What Was She Thinking? Notes On a
    Scandal,* 137
  Wit's End, 64
  Wonderful World, 202
  You're Not You, 188–189
Fugitives
  His Illegal Self, 113

Gamblers and Gambling
  Nobody Move, 69–70
Gardening
  Leaving Home, 111–112
Gay Men
  The Book of Getting Even, 179–180
  DuPont Circle, 24
  The Emperor's Children, 32
  The End of the World Book, 234–235
  The Family Man, 152
  Into the Beautiful North, 42–43
  Leaving Tangier, 7
  The Line of Beauty, 139–140
  She Was, 134–135
  The Sky Below, 207–208
  Three Junes, 128–129
  The Uncommon Reader, 53–54
  Whatever Makes You Happy, 178–179
Genetics
  Never Let Me Go, 221
Gentle Reads
  Andy Catlett: Early Travels, 9

  The Blue Star, 123–124
  The Eleventh Man, 119–120
  Gilead, 251
  *The Guernsey Literary and Potato Peel Pie
    Society,* 37–38
  A Guide to the Birds of East Africa, 18
  Hannah Coulter, 9–10
  One Vacant Chair, 117
  The Whistling Season, 17–18
Georgia
  Hairdos of the Mildly Depressed, 117
  Them, 30
German Authors
  Austerlitz, 253–254
  The Have-Nots, 217–218
Germany
  Book of Clouds, 4
  Europe Central, 259
  The Kindly Ones, 230–231
  Lovely Green Eyes, 76–77
  Mohr, 168–169
  Settlement, 67
Ghosts
  Haunting Bombay, 98
  Her Fearful Symmetry, 163
  Kings of Infinite Space, 221
  The Little Stranger, 94
Glasgow
  Kieron Smith, Boy, 225
  Suzy, Led Zeppelin, and Me, 32–33
GLBTQ
  Angels Crest, 89
  The Book of Getting Even, 179–180
  DuPont Circle, 24
  The Emperor's Children, 32
  The End of the World Book, 234–235
  The Family Man, 152
  Into the Beautiful North, 42–43
  Landing, 120
  Leaving Tangier, 7
  The Line of Beauty, 139–140
  The Rose Variations, 114
  She Was, 134–135
  The Sky Below, 207–208
  The Stone Gods, 95
  Three Junes, 128–129
  The Uncommon Reader, 53–54
  WhateverMakes You Happy, 178–179
Godmothers
  Wit's End, 64
Government
  Crawfish Mountain, 44

Supreme Courtship, 56–57
Grandfathers. *See also* Family Relationships
 Everything Is Illuminated, 212–213
 The Inheritance of Loss, 118–119
 The Plague of Doves, 125–126
Grandmothers. *See also* Family Relationships
 Caramelo, 12–13
 Everything Is Illuminated, 212–213
 Extremely Loud and Incredibly Close, 213
 Follow Me, 172–173
 Haunting Bombay, 98
 His Illegal Self, 113
 Hold Love Strong, 130
Graphic Novels
 The One Marvelous Thing, 210–211
Great Britain
 Arlington Park, 117–118
 Arthur & George, 105
 Atonement, 235
 August, 45
 Austerlitz, 253–254
 The Bad Mother's Handbook, 153–154
 Black Swan Green, 160
 Brick Lane, 99
 Broken, 204–205
 Brother and Sister, 182
 The Brothers Boswell, 50
 Consequences, 152–153
 *The Curious Incident of the Dog in the
  Night-Time*, 131–132
 Daughters of the North, 66
 Double Vision, 104
 The Final Solution: A Story of Detection,
  203
 In the Fold, 118
 The Forgotten Garden, 80–81
 Gentlemen and Players, 66–67
 Glover's Mistake, 74
 *The Guernsey Literary and Potato Peel Pie
  Society*, 37–38
 Her Fearful Symmetry, 163
 The House on Fortune Street, 231
 In the Kitchen, 48–49
 Inglorious, 144–145
 Interred with Their Bones, 58–59
 The Killing Jar, 33
 The Labrador Pact, 132–133
 The Lemon Table: Stories, 197
 Life Class, 104–105
 Little Bee, 115–116
 The Little Stranger, 94
 A Long Way Down, 140

 The Master Bedroom, 132
 My Revolutions, 73
 On Chesil Beach, 235–236
 The Outcast, 223
 The Post-Birthday World, 174
 A Question of Attraction, 162
 Remainder, 234
 A Richer Dust, 10
 The Road Home, 182
 Salt, 247–248
 Saturday, 236
 A Short History of Women, 186
 The Uncommon Reader, 53–54
 Vanessa & Virginia, 254
 We Are Now Beginning Our Descent, 158
 What Was Lost, 164
 Whatever Makes You Happy, 178–179
Greece
 Three Junes, 128–129
Grief
 A Better Angel: Stories, 194
 The Book of Illusions, 195–196
 Extremely Loud and Incredibly Close, 213
 The Five-Forty-Five to Cannes, 22–23
 How the Dead Dream, 239
 Lost in the Forest, 159
 The Sorrows of an American, 141
 The Sound of Us, 189
 Up High in the Trees, 111
 The Wasted Vigil, 100–101
 The Writing on the Wall, 172
Guatemala
 The Divine Husband, 130
 Draining the Sea, 29
Guernsey
 *The Guernsey Literary and Potato Peel Pie
  Society*, 37–38

Harlem
 Black Flies, 57
 Strivers Row, 5
Haunted Houses
 The Little Stranger, 94
Hawthornden Prize
 Darkmans, 196–197
 The Promise of Happiness, 113–114
Health Issues. *See also* Medicine
 A Better Angel: Stories, 194
 The Book of Dahlia, 99
 The Condition, 133–134
 Doctor Olaf van Schuler's Brain, 237
 The Echo Maker, 250

Health Issues (*Cont.*)
   Everyman, 252
   Exit Ghost, 169–170
   Friday's Bed, 121
   The Girls, 150–151
   Hairdos of the Mildly Depressed, 117
   The Hummingbird's Daughter, 42
   The Kept Man, 101
   The Little Stranger, 94
   More Than It Hurts You, 256
   Never Let Me Go, 221
   The Owl & Moon Café, 155–156
   The Pesthouse, 62–63
   Pharmakon, 95–96
   Rouse Up, O Young Men of the New Age,
      245–246
   Saturday, 236
   The Sky Below, 207–208
   Still Alice, 128
   Veronica, 214
   We Are Welcome Here, 55
   You're Not You, 188–189
Hermaphrodites
   Middlesex, 212
Hindus
   The Age of Shiva, 178
Historical Fiction
   The Age of Shiva, 178
   All That Matters, 12
   Andy Catlett: Early Travels, 9
   Arthur & George, 105
   Away, 109
   The Bad Girl, 185
   The Bible Salesman, 18
   Birds without Wings, 14–15
   The Blue Manuscript, 226–227
   Brooklyn, 40–41
   The Brothers Boswell, 50
   Bucking the Tiger, 246
   The Calligrapher's Daughter, 146
   Caramelo, 12–13
   The Cellist of Sarajevo, 20
   City of Thieves, 53
   Cloud Atlas, 240–241
   Consequences, 152–153
   The Darling, 103
   Day, 225–226
   The Divine Husband, 130
   Doctor Olaf van Schuler's Brain, 237
   The Eleventh Man, 119–120
   The End, 253
   English Passengers, 25–26

Europe Central, 259
The Expeditions, 69
Far Bright Star, 35
The Final Solution: A Story of Detection,
   203
Follow Me, 172–173
The Forgotten Garden, 80–81
Gardenias, 178
Gilead, 251
A Golden Age, 100
The Guernsey Literary and Potato Peel Pie
   Society, 37–38
Half Broke Horses, 186–187
The Half Brother, 114–115
Haunting Bombay, 98
The Help, 177
The Heretic's Daughter, 71
Home, 251
The Hummingbird's Daughter, 42
The Inquisitors' Manual, 3
Intercourse: Stories, 201–202
The Invention of Everything Else, 23
The James Boys: A Novel Account of Four
   Desperate Brothers, 76
Johnny One-Eye: A Tale of the American
   Revolution, 60–61
The Kindly Ones, 230–231
The Known World, 70
The Lacuna, 147
Land of Marvels, 41–42
Lark and Termite, 168
Last Night in Twisted River, 142
Lavinia, 228
Let the Great World Spin, 30–31
Life Class, 104–105
The Little Stranger, 94
Lovely Green Eyes, 76–77
The Madonnas of Leningrad, 15
The Map Thief, 92
March, 112
The March, 209
The Master, 257
A Mercy, 242–243
Middlesex, 212
Midnight at the Dragon Café, 50–51
Mohr, 168–169
Mudbound, 24
My Name Is Red, 83
The News from Paraguay, 41
The Outcast, 223
The Outlander, 194
Peace, 51

People of the Book, 56
The People's Act of Love, 236–237
The Piano Teacher, 75
Pictures at an Exhibition, 68
A Pigeon and a Boy, 91
The Plague of Doves, 125–126
The Plot Against America, 87
A Reliable Wife, 21
The River Wife, 2
The Road from Chapel Hill, 37
Sailors on the Inward Sea, 92
Salt, 247–248
Saving the World, 99–100
The Seamstress of Hollywood Boulevard, 31
Sea of Poppies, 215
The Secret River, 21–22
The Secret Scripture, 198
Serena, 85–86
The Shadow Catcher, 259–260
Shadow Country, 29–30
Shanghai Girls, 173
She Was, 134–135
A Short History of Women, 186
Silver: My Own Tale as Written by Me with a Goodly Amount of Murder, 61
The Size of the World, 38
Someone Knows My Name, 67–68
Songs for the Butcher's Daughter, 155
Stand the Storm, 115
Star of the Sea, 82
Strivers Row, 5
Sundown, Yellow Moon, 43–44
Sunnyside, 215–216
Sway, 228
Telex from Cuba, 26
The Tenderness of Wolves, 249
Territory, 57
This Blinding Absence of Light, 8
Tinkers, 218
Train to Trieste, 36–37
Tree of Smoke, 222–223
Triangle, 187
The True History of the Kelly Gang, 58
The Voyage of the Short Serpent, 210
War Trash, 222
The Whistling Season, 17–18
The Women, 110–111
The World To Come, 68
Zugzwang, 54
Holliday, Doc
Bucking the Tiger, 246
Territory, 57

Hollywood
The Seamstress of Hollywood Boulevard, 31
Sunnyside, 215–216
Ten Days in the Hills, 174–175
Holocaust
Austerlitz, 253–254
Everything Is Illuminated, 212–213
Extremely Loud and Incredibly Close, 213
The Final Solution: A Story of Detection, 203
The Kindly Ones, 230–231
Lovely Green Eyes, 76–77
Homes
Ellington Boulevard, 27
The English Major, 22
The House on Fortune Street, 231
One Fifth Avenue, 11
Them, 30
Honduras
Garcia's Heart, 63
Hong Kong
The Piano Teacher, 75
Horror
Of Bees and Mist, 254
The Little Stranger, 94
Hospitals
A Better Angel: Stories, 194
Hostages
Blood Kin, 63
Hotels
The Elegance of the Hedgehog, 103–104
Love, 242
Housecleaners
Miniatures, 227–228
Humor. *See also* Dark Humor; Satire
Aloft, 151
American Savior: A Novel of Divine Politics, 79
An Arsonist's Guide to Writers' Homes in New England, 61–62
The Bad Mother's Handbook, 153–154
Based on the Movie, 180
The Baum Plan for Financial Independence, 226
The Bible Salesman, 18
Black Swan Green, 160
Bridge of Sighs, 170–171
Brownsville: Stories, 12
Chronic City, 229
The Curious Incident of the Dog in the Night-Time, 131–132

Humor (*Cont.*)
>   *Deaf Sentence,* 153
>   *Delinquent Virgin: Wayward Pieces,* 224–225
>   *Do Not Deny Me: Stories,* 180–181
>   *Downtown Owl,* 147
>   *The Elegance of the Hedgehog,* 103–104
>   *The English Major,* 22
>   *Everything Ravaged, Everything Burned,*
>   181–182
>   *The Family Man,* 152
>   *Firmin: Adventures of a Metropolitan*
>   *Lowlife,* 171
>   *In the Fold,* 118

>   *The Four Corners of the Sky,* 154–155
>   *The Girl on the Fridge,* 226
>   *The Good Fairies of New York,* 158–159
>   *The Guernsey Literary and Potato Peel Pie*
>   *Society,* 37–38
>   *A Guide to the Birds of East Africa,* 18
>   *Hairdos of the Mildly Depressed,* 117
>   *It's a Crime,* 58
>   *Johnny One-Eye: A Tale of the American*
>   *Revolution,* 60–61
>   *Landing,* 120
>   *Last Night at the Lobster,* 164–165
>   *Laura Rider's Masterpiece,* 135
>   *A Multitude of Sins,* 214
>   *My Latest Grievance,* 152
>   *The One Marvelous Thing,* 210–211
>   *One Vacant Chair,* 117
>   *Out of My Skin,* 218
>   *Paula Spencer,* 120
>   *The Philosopher's Apprentice,* 80
>   *Popular Music from Vittula,* 34–35
>   *A Question of Attraction,* 162
>   *Samuel Johnson Is Indignant: Stories,* 206
>   *Saul and Patsy,* 106
>   *Schooled,* 74
>   *The Slide,* 107
>   *Superpowers,* 88–89
>   *Supreme Courtship,* 56–57
>   *Suzy, Led Zeppelin, and Me,* 32–33
>   *That Old Cape Magic,* 171
>   *This One Is Mine,* 173
>   *The Uncommon Reader,* 53–54
>   *Varieties of Disturbance: Stories,* 206
>   *Waveland,* 6–7
>   *WhateverMakes You Happy,* 178–179
>   *Whirlwind,* 69
>   *Willful Creatures: Stories,* 198
>   *Willing,* 176
>   *Wit's End,* 64

Hungarian Authors
>   *Detective Story,* 71–72
Huntington's Disease
>   *Saturday,* 236
Hurricane Katrina
>   *Waveland,* 6–7
Hurricanes
>   *Whirlwind,* 69

Iceland
>   *The Voyage of the Short Serpent,* 210
>   *Willing,* 176
Idaho
>   *A Country Called Home,* 5–6
>   *Five Skies,* 11–12
>   *Labors of the Heart: Stories,* 14
Identity Theft
>   *Talk Talk,* 110
Illinois
>   *Home Safe,* 107–108
>   *Into the Beautiful North,* 42–43
>   *A Ticket to Ride,* 157–158
Immigrants and Immigration
>   *All That Matters,* 12
>   *All the Sad Young Literary Men,* 128
>   *Away,* 109
>   *Brick Lane,* 99
>   *Broccoli and Other Tales of Food and*
>   *Love,* 258–259
>   *Brooklyn,* 40–41
>   *Brownsville: Stories,* 12
>   *The Deportees and Other Stories,* 209
>   *Digging to America,* 184
>   *Draining the Sea,* 29
>   *The End,* 253
>   *The Groom to Have Been,* 98
>   *The Guardians,* 60
>   *The History of Love,* 149
>   *In the Kitchen,* 48–49
>   *The Inheritance of Loss,* 118–119
>   *Konkans,* 122
>   *The Lazarus Project,* 219
>   *Leaving Tangier,* 7
>   *Let the Great World Spin,* 30–31
>   *Little Bee,* 115–116
>   *Love and Obstacles: Stories,* 220
>   *The Madonnas of Leningrad,* 15
>   *Middlesex,* 212
>   *Midnight at the Dragon Café,* 50–51
>   *The Ministry of Special Cases,* 125
>   *Netherland,* 35–36
>   *The Road Home,* 182

The Russian Debutante's Handbook, 255
The Secret River, 21–22
Shanghai Girls, 173
A Short History of Women, 186
Songs for the Butcher's Daughter, 155
Star of the Sea, 82
Trespass, 77–78
Unaccustomed Earth, 149–150
The Vine of Desire, 119
The Writing on My Forehead, 134
Incest
    Middlesex, 212
India
    The Age of Shiva, 178
    Atlas of Unknowns, 142–143
    Family Matters, 240
    Fiduli's Way, 78–79
    Haunting Bombay, 98
    The Hungry Tide, 128–129
    The Inheritance of Loss, 118–119
    Konkans, 122
    Sea of Poppies, 215
    There Is Room for You, 102
    The Toss of a Lemon, 185–186
    Unaccustomed Earth, 149–150
    The White Tiger, 47–48
Indiana
    Iodine, 146
    Over and Under, 183
Indian American Authors
    The Age of Shiva, 178
Indian Authors
    The Age of Shiva, 178
    Haunting Bombay, 98
    The Hungry Tide, 128–129
    The Inheritance of Loss, 118–119
    Sea of Poppies, 215
    The Toss of a Lemon, 185–186
    The Vine of Desire, 119
    The White Tiger, 47–48
    The Zigzag Way, 16
Inquisition
    People of the Book, 56
Interconnected Stories. *See also* Short Stories
    Bright Shiny Morning, 20
    By the Lake, 156–157
    Cloud Atlas, 240–241
    Consequences, 152–153
    Doctor Olaf van Schuler's Brain, 237
    The Have-Nots, 217–218
    I Sailed with Magellan, 123
    In Other Rooms, Other Wonders, 34

Olive Kitteridge, 177–178
A Short History of Women, 186
The Size of the World, 38
Sway, 228
Three Junes, 128–129
The Turning: New Stories, 44
Unaccustomed Earth, 149–150
International IMPAC Dublin Literary Award
    The Known World, 70
    Man Gone Down, 257
    The Master, 257
    My Name Is Red, 83
Internment Camps
    Famous Suicides of the Japanese Empire, 161
Interracial Families
    Run, 166
Interracial Relationships
    Symptomatic, 90–91
Iowa
    The Driftless Area, 121–122
    Gilead, 251
    Home, 251
Iran
    Caspian Rain, 161–162
    Censoring an Iranian Love Story, 233
Iran Hostage Crisis
    Crossing California, 26–27
Iranian Americans
    Digging to America, 184
Iraq War (2003)
    Man in the Dark, 49–50
    Ten Days in the Hills, 174–175
Ireland
    Brooklyn, 40–41
    By the Lake, 156–157
    Cheating at Canasta: Stories, 258
    The Deportees and Other Stories, 209
    The Gathering, 211
    Landing, 120
    Miniatures, 227–228
    Mothers and Sons: Stories, 181
    Paula Spencer, 120
    The Sea, 196
    The Secret Scripture, 198
    Star of the Sea, 82
    The Tain: A New Translation of the Tain bo Cuailnge, 59–60
Irish Authors
    Brooklyn, 40–41
    Cheating at Canasta: Stories, 258
    The Deportees and Other Stories, 209

Irish Authors (*Cont.*)
    The Gathering, 211
    Glover's Mistake, 74
    By the Lake, 156–157
    Landing, 120
    Let the Great World Spin, 30–31
    Mothers and Sons: Stories, 181
    Paula Spencer, 120
    The Sea, 196
    The Secret Scripture, 198
    Star of the Sea, 82
    The Tain: A New Translation of the Tain bo Cuailnge, 59–60
    Yesterday's Weather: Stories, 211–212
    Zugzwang, 54
Islam
    The Blue Manuscript, 226–227
    Finding Nouf, 19–20
    The Groom to Have Been, 98
    Leaving Tangier, 7
    My Name Is Red, 83
    The Swallows of Kabul, 145
    The Wasted Vigil, 100–101
    The Writing on My Forehead, 134
Islamic Revolution
    Caspian Rain, 161–162
Israel, 72
    Beaufort, 27–28
    A Pigeon and a Boy, 91
Israeli Authors
    The Girl on the Fridge, 226
Italian Authors
    Without Blood, 197–198
Italy
    Bridge of Sighs, 170–171
    Lavinia, 228
    Peace, 51
    Trespass, 77–78

James, Frank
    The James Boys: A Novel Account of Four Desperate Brothers, 76
James, Henry
    The James Boys: A Novel Account of Four Desperate Brothers, 76
    The Master, 257
James, Jesse
    The James Boys: A Novel Account of Four Desperate Brothers, 76
James, William
    The James Boys: A Novel Account of Four Desperate Brothers, 76

James Tait Black Memorial Prize
    Family Matters, 240
Japan
    Blind Willow, Sleeping Woman, 243–244
    The Housekeeper and the Professor, 245–246
    Kafka on the Shore, 244
    Mohr, 168–169
    Rouse Up, O Young Men of the New Age, 245–246
Japanese American Authors
    Famous Suicides of the Japanese Empire, 161
    Once Removed, 191
Japanese Americans
    Famous Suicides of the Japanese Empire, 161
    Once Removed, 191
Japanese Authors
    Blind Willow, Sleeping Woman, 243–244
    The Housekeeper and the Professor, 245–246
    Kafka on the Shore, 244
    Never Let Me Go, 221
    Rouse Up, O Young Men of the New Age, 245–246
Jazz
    Bass Cathedral, 232
Jesus
    American Savior: A Novel of Divine Politics, 79
Jewish American Authors
    The Book of Dahlia, 99
    Dictation: A Quartet, 247
    Everyman, 252
    Everything Is Illuminated, 212–213
    Exit Ghost, 169–170
    Extremely Loud and Incredibly Close, 213
    The Final Solution: A Story of Detection, 203
    The Girl on the Fridge, 226
    Indignation, 170
    The Ministry of Special Cases, 125
    The Plot Against America, 87
    The Russian Debutante's Handbook, 255
    The World To Come, 68
    The Yiddish Policeman's Union, 203–204
Jews and Judaism
    All the Sad Young Literary Men, 128
    Austerlitz, 253–254
    Away, 109
    Beat the Reaper, 51–52

The Believers, 137
The Book of Dahlia, 99
The Book of Getting Even, 179–180
Caspian Rain, 161–162
Crossing California, 26–27
Everything Is Illuminated, 212–213
The Final Solution: A Story of Detection, 203
The History of Love, 149
Indignation, 170
The Lazarus Project, 219
The Ministry of Special Cases, 125
Mohr, 168–169
More Than It Hurts You, 256
Once Removed, 191
People of the Book, 56
Pictures at an Exhibition, 68
*Portrait of My Mother, Who Posed Nude in
     Wartime: Stories,* 252
The Romantics, 162–163
Saul and Patsy, 106
Songs for the Butcher's Daughter, 155
Triangle, 187
Who by Fire, 175–176
The Yiddish Policeman's Union, 203–204
Zugzwang, 54
Johnson, Samuel
    The Brothers Boswell, 50
Journalism
    American Savior: A Novel of Divine Politics, 79
    Cleaver, 166
    The Emperor's Children, 32
    The Help, 177
    Maxxed Out, 62
    We Are Now Beginning Our Descent, 158
    The White Mary, 88
Juarez
    2666, 200
Judges
    DuPont Circle, 24
    Supreme Courtship, 56–57

Kahlo, Frida
    Friday's Bed, 121
    The Lacuna, 147
Kansas
    Callisto, 73
    Ordinary Genius, 4–5
    The Seamstress of Hollywood Boulevard, 31
Kashmir
    Fidali's Way, 78–79
Kelly, Ned
    The True History of the Kelly Gang, 58

Kentucky
    All the Living, 241–242
    Andy Catlett: Early Travels, 9
    Hannah Coulter, 9–10
Kenya
    A Guide to the Birds of East Africa, 18
Kidnapping
    Angels Crest, 89
    Beautiful Children, 199
    The Garden of Last Days, 122–123
    Helpless, 130–131
    His Illegal Self, 113
    Last Night in Montreal, 39–40
    Songs for the Missing, 165
    The Uses of Enchantment, 224
    What Was Lost, 164
    Who by Fire, 175–176
Kiriyama Pacific Rim Book Prize
    Family Matters, 240
    Mister Pip, 70–71
Korea
    The Calligrapher's Daughter, 146
    War Trash, 222
Korean Americans
    A Person of Interest, 61
Korean War
    Indignation, 170
    Lark and Termite, 168
    War Trash, 222

Labor History
    Over and Under, 183
    Triangle, 187
Las Vegas
    Beautiful Children, 199
    Scar Vegas: And Other Stories, 248
Latin America
    Detective Story, 71–72
    The Divine Husband, 130
    Red April, 86–87
Latino Authors
    Saving the World, 99–100
Law and Lawyers
    The Believers, 137
    The Butt: An Exit Strategy, 89–90
    DuPont Circle, 24
    Power, 220
    Supreme Courtship, 56–57
Law Enforcement
    Beautiful Dreamer, 199
    Crime, 94–95
    Lush Life, 85

Law Enforcement (*Cont.*)
  No Country for Old Men, 233
  Power, 220
  The Yiddish Policeman's Union, 203–204
Lawrence, D. H.
  A Richer Dust, 10
Lebanon
  Beaufort, 27–28
  The Hakawati: A Story, 48
Legends
  *The Tain: A New Translation of the Tain bo
    Cuailnge,* 59–60
Leningrad
  City of Thieves, 53
  The Madonnas of Leningrad, 15
Lesbians
  Angels Crest, 89
  Landing, 120
Liberia
  The Darling, 103
Lindbergh, Charles
  The Plot Against America, 87
Linguistics
  Deaf Sentence, 153
Literary Allusions
  Arthur & George, 105
  *The Baum Plan for Financial
    Independence,* 226
  The Brief Wondrous Life of Oscar Wao, 208
  Broken, 204–205
  Bucking the Tiger, 246
  Censoring an Iranian Love Story, 233
  Family Matters, 240
  The Final Solution: A Story of Detection, 203
  Finn, 116
  The Groom to Have Been, 98
  The House on Fortune Street, 231
  Intercourse: Stories, 201–202
  *The James Boys: A Novel Account of Four
    Desperate Brothers,* 76
  Lavinia, 228
  March, 112
  Miniatures, 227–228
  Mister Pip, 70–71
  Peyton Amberg, 143
  *Silver: My Own Tale as Written by Me with
    a Goodly Amount of Murder,* 61
  Undiscovered Country, 19
Literary Lives. *See also* Writers and Writing
  2666, 200
  *An Arsonist's Guide to Writers' Homes in
    New England,* 61–62

  The Angel's Game, 87
  The Book of Murder, 78
  The Brothers Boswell, 50
  Dictation: A Quartet, 247
  Exit Ghost, 169–170
  The First Person: And Other Stories,
    255–256
  Home Safe, 107–108
  How to Buy a Love of Reading, 64–65
  The Lazarus Project, 219
  Maxxed Out, 62
  Miniatures, 227–228
  Out of My Skin, 218
  Sailors on the Inward Sea, 92
  Saving the World, 99–100
  Vanessa & Virginia, 254
  Wit's End, 64
London
  The Brothers Boswell, 50
  Consequences, 152–153
  Glover's Mistake, 74
  The Have-Nots, 217–218
  Her Fearful Symmetry, 163
  The House on Fortune Street, 231
  Inglorious, 144–145
  Interred with Their Bones, 58–59
  In the Kitchen, 48–49
  Novel about My Wife, 249
  The Post-Birthday World, 174
  Remainder, 234
  Saturday, 236
  The Uncommon Reader, 53–54
  We Are Now Beginning Our Descent, 158
Long Island
  Aloft, 151
  The Shadow Year, 64
Lopez, Francisco Solano
  The News from Paraguay, 41
Los Angeles
  Bright Shiny Morning, 20
  Draining the Sea, 29
  How the Dead Dream, 239
  Out of My Skin, 218
  Shanghai Girls, 173
  Ten Days in the Hills, 174–175
  This One Is Mine, 173
  The Writing on My Forehead, 134
Louisiana
  Crawfish Mountain, 44
Love Affairs
  Addition, 143–144
  Admission, 148–149

All about Lulu, 126
All the Living, 241–242
The Angel's Game, 87
Any Human Heart, 109–110
Atonement, 235
Away, 109
The Bad Girl, 185
Beat the Reaper, 51–52
Of Bees and Mist, 254
The Believers, 137
The Blue Star, 123–124
Book of Clouds, 4
The Book of Illusions, 195–196
Breath, 189–190
Bright Shiny Morning, 20
Brooklyn, 40–41
The Calligrapher's Daughter, 146
Censoring an Iranian Love Story, 233
The Complete Stories (Malouf), 232
The Condition, 133–134
Crawfish Mountain, 44
The Divine Husband, 130
Divisadero, 246–247
Don't Tell Anyone: Fiction, 201
Double Vision, 104
The Driftless Area, 121–122
The Eleventh Man, 119–120
Ellington Boulevard, 27
The Emperor's Children, 32
The Essential Charlotte, 172
Exit Ghost, 169–170
The Family Man, 152
Family Matters, 240
*Female Trouble: A Collection of Short
        Stories,* 244
Fidali's Way, 78–79
Fieldwork, 8–9
Finding Nouf, 19–20
The First Person: And Other Stories,
        255–256
Follow Me, 172–173
Friday's Bed, 121
The Future of Love, 1
The Ginseng Hunter, 40
Glover's Mistake, 74
The Great Man, 204
The Grift, 65
The Groom to Have Been, 98
*The Guernsey Literary and Potato Peel Pie
        Society,* 37–38
A Guide to the Birds of East Africa, 18
A Happy Marriage, 191

He Drown She in the Sea, 160–161
Her Fearful Symmetry, 163
The House on Fortune Street, 231
How the Dead Dream, 239
How to Sell, 77
The Hungry Tide, 128–129
In Other Rooms, Other Wonders, 34
In the Kitchen, 48–49
Inglorious, 144–145
Intercourse: Stories, 201–202
The Invention of Everything Else, 23
Iodine, 146
*Johnny One-Eye: A Tale of the American
        Revolution,* 60–61
The Killing Jar, 33
Landing, 120
The Last Chinese Chef, 33–34
Last Night at the Lobster, 164–165
Last Night in Montreal, 39–40
Laura Rider's Masterpiece, 135
Life Class, 104–105
Life Without Water, 167
The Little Stranger, 94
The Lost Dog, 206–207
Love, 242
The Master Bedroom, 132
A Multitude of Sins, 214
My Name Is Red, 83
The News from Paraguay, 41
Nobody Move, 69–70
Now You See Him, 65–66
*Our Story Begins: New and Selected
        Stories,* 260
Out of My Skin, 218
The People's Act of Love, 236–237
The Pesthouse, 62–63
The Piano Teacher, 75
Pictures at an Exhibition, 68
A Pigeon and a Boy, 91
The Post-Birthday World, 174
Prodigal Summer, 25
A Question of Attraction, 162
Red Car, 108–109
A Reliable Wife, 21
A Richer Dust, 10
The Road from Chapel Hill, 37
The Romantics, 162–163
The Rose Variations, 114
Runaway: Stories, 243
Salt, 247–248
The Secret Scripture, 198
Serena, 85–86

Love Affairs (*Cont.*)
   The Size of the World, 38
   The Sky Below, 207–208
   Skylight Confessions, 138–139
   The Sorrows of an American, 141
   The Soul Thief, 106–107
   Sundown, Yellow Moon, 43–44
   Suzy, Led Zeppelin, and Me, 32–33
   Ten Days in the Hills, 174–175
   Territory, 57
   This One Is Mine, 173
   Three Minutes on Love, 138
   Train to Trieste, 36–37
   Trans-sister Radio, 55
   Trespass, 77–78
   Triangle, 187
   Turtle Valley, 3
   Twenty Fragments of a Ravenous Youth,
      216–217
   The Wasted Vigil, 100–101
   We Are Now Beginning Our Descent, 158
   What Was Lost, 164
   Whatever Makes You Happy, 178–179
   Whirlwind, 69
   The White Mary, 88
   The Women, 110–111
   The Writing on the Wall, 172
   The Zigzag Way, 16
Lynch, Ella
   The News from Paraguay, 41

Magic and Magicians
   Mr. Sebastian and the Negro Magician,
      93–94
Magic Realism
   Alva & Irva: The Twins Who Saved a City,
      202–203
   The Angel's Game, 87
   Of Bees and Mist, 254
   Blind Willow, Sleeping Woman, 243–244
   Darkmans, 196–197
   The Divine Husband, 130
   Everything Is Illuminated, 212–213
   Firmin: Adventures of a Metropolitan
      Lowlife, 171
   Fortress of Solitude, 229–230
   The Hakawati: A Story, 48
   Haunting Bombay, 98
   Kafka on the Shore, 244
   Man in the Dark, 49–50
   The One Marvelous Thing, 210–211
   Ordinary Genius, 4–5

   Salt, 247–248
   The Sky Below, 207–208
   The Story Sisters, 139
   The Thin Place, 205
   The View from the Seventh Layer, 201
Maine
   Olive Kitteridge, 177–178
   The Romantics, 162–163
   Water Dogs, 86
Malcolm X
   Strivers Row, 5
Man Booker Prize
   The Gathering, 211
   The Inheritance of Loss, 118–119
   The Line of Beauty, 139–140
   The Sea, 196
   The True History of the Kelly Gang, 58
   Vernon God Little, 84–85
   The White Tiger, 47–48
Manson, Charles
   Sway, 228
Mao Zedong
   Serve the People!, 230
Marriage. *See also* Arranged Marriages
   The Abstinence Teacher, 84
   The Age of Shiva, 178
   All the Sad Young Literary Men, 128
   American Wife, 174
   Arlington Park, 117–118
   Atmospheric Disturbances, 215
   The Attack, 72
   Based on the Movie, 180
   Beautiful Children, 199
   The Believers, 137
   Between Here and April, 72–73
   Blood Kin, 63
   Breath, 189–190
   Brick Lane, 99
   Bridge of Sighs, 170–171
   Brother and Sister, 182
   Brownsville: Stories, 12
   The Condition, 133–134
   A Country Called Home, 5–6
   Deaf Sentence, 153
   Dervishes, 22
   Do Not Deny Me: Stories, 180–181
   Don't Tell Anyone: Fiction, 201
   Double Vision, 104
   DuPont Circle, 24
   The End of California, 190
   The English Major, 22
   Envy, 136

Falling Man, 207
The Family Man, 152
Family Matters, 240
Female Trouble: A Collection of Short Stories, 244
The Five-Forty-Five to Cannes, 22–23
Friday's Bed, 121
The Future of Love, 1
A Ghost at the Table, 108
The Great Man, 204
The Great Perhaps, 238
The Groom to Have Been, 98
Half Broke Horses, 186–187
A Happy Marriage, 191
The Have-Nots, 217–218
He Drown She in the Sea, 160–161
Home Safe, 107–108
The Hour I First Believed, 150
I Smile Back, 148
In the Fold, 118
Intercourse: Stories, 201–202
The Kept Man, 101
Konkans, 122
Land of Marvels, 41–42
The Last Chinese Chef, 33–34
Laura Rider's Masterpiece, 135
Lavinia, 228
Life Without Water, 167
Little Bee, 115–116
Little Children, 167–168
Love, 242
Love and Other Impossible Pursuits, 93
The Madonnas of Leningrad, 15
Man Gone Down, 257
Maxxed Out, 62
A Mercy, 242–243
Mudbound, 24
A Multitude of Sins, 214
Netherland, 35–36
Novel about My Wife, 249
Now You See Him, 65–66
On Chesil Beach, 235–236
Once Removed, 191
The One Marvelous Thing, 210–211
Peyton Amberg, 143
The Piano Teacher, 75
The Post-Birthday World, 174
The Promise of Happiness, 113–114
A Reliable Wife, 21
The River Wife, 2
Runaway: Stories, 243
Saul and Patsy, 106

The Sea, 196
The Senator's Wife, 159–160
Serena, 85–86
Serve the People!, 230
Skylight Confessions, 138–139
Storm Riders, 151–152
Ten Days in the Hills, 174–175
That Old Cape Magic, 171
There Is Room for You, 102
This One Is Mine, 173
A Thousand Splendid Suns, 141
Three Junes, 128–129
Tomorrow, 179
Trespass, 77–78
The Turning: New Stories, 44
Turtle Valley, 3
Two Marriages, 231–232
Unaccustomed Earth, 149–150
Up High in the Trees, 111
The Vine of Desire, 119
Waveland, 6–7
A Week in October, 256
The Women, 110–111
Yesterday's Weather: Stories, 211–212
You're Not You, 188–189
Martha's Vineyard
    Apologize, Apologize!, 145
Martin, Steve
    Out of My Skin, 218
Martinique
    Fanon, 188
Maryland
    Digging to America, 184
Massachusetts
    The Heretic's Daughter, 71
    The Lace Reader, 105–106
    Run, 166
    Security, 49
    That Old Cape Magic, 171
    Up High in the Trees, 111
Mass Media
    American Savior: A Novel of Divine Politics, 79
    The Emperor's Children, 32
    More Than It Hurts You, 256
    Whirlwind, 69
Mathematics
    Addition, 143–144
    The Book of Getting Even, 179–180
    The Housekeeper and the Professor, 245–246
    A Person of Interest, 61

Medicine. *See also* Health Issues
   Beat the Reaper, 51–52
   Black Flies, 57
   The Condition, 133–134
   Doctor Olaf van Schuler's Brain, 237
   More Than It Hurts You, 256
   Never Let Me Go, 221
   Pharmakon, 95–96
   Saving the World, 99–100
   Still Alice, 128
Men Writing as Women. *See also* Women
     Writing as Men
   The Age of Shiva, 178
   Into the Beautiful North, 42–43
   Of Bees and Mist, 254
   Brooklyn, 40–41
   Censoring an Iranian Love Story, 233
   The Darling, 103
   The Four Corners of the Sky, 154–155
   The Garden of Last Days, 122–123
   Genesis, 52
   Hannah Coulter, 9–10
   The Hummingbird's Daughter, 42
   The Hungry Tide, 128–129
   Little Bee, 115–116
   Little Children, 167–168
   Middlesex, 212
   Mister Pip, 70–71
   Never Let Me Go, 221
   One Vacant Chair, 117
   Paula Spencer, 120
   A Reliable Wife, 21
   The Secret Scripture, 198
   Serena, 85–86
   Serve the People!, 230
   Someone Knows My Name, 67–68
   A Thousand Splendid Suns, 141
   Tomorrow, 179
   Trans-sister Radio, 55
   The Women, 110–111
Men's Lives
   The Abstinence Teacher, 84
   All the Sad Young Literary Men, 128
   Aloft, 151
   Andy Catlett: Early Travels, 9
   Any Human Heart, 109–110
   *An Arsonist's Guide to Writers' Homes in
     New England,* 61–62
   Based on the Movie, 180
   The Bible Salesman, 18
   The Blue Star, 123–124
   The Book of Illusions, 195–196

Bridge of Sighs, 170–171
Brownsville: Stories, 12
By the Lake, 156–157
Castle, 75–76
The Clarinet Polka, 28–29
Cleaver, 166
Crawfish Mountain, 44
Crumbtown, 13
Deaf Sentence, 153
Dear American Airlines, 238–239
Diary of a Bad Year, 205
The Driftless Area, 121–122
DuPont Circle, 24
The Eleventh Man, 119–120
Ellington Boulevard, 27
The English Major, 22
Envy, 136
Eventide, 136–137
Everyman, 252
Exit Ghost, 169–170
Falling Man, 207
Famous Suicides of the Japanese Empire,
   161
Fidali's Way, 78–79
Five Skies, 11–12
Gilead, 251
The Ginseng Hunter, 40
Glover's Mistake, 74
The Great Perhaps, 238
The Groom to Have Been, 98
A Guide to the Birds of East Africa, 18
Hairdos of the Mildly Depressed, 117
A Happy Marriage, 191
The Hour I First Believed, 150
How to Sell, 77
In Other Rooms, Other Wonders, 34
In the Fold, 118
The Kite Runner, 140–141
Konkans, 122
Last Night at the Lobster, 164–165
Last Night in Twisted River, 142
The Last of the Husbandmen, 28
The Line of Beauty, 139–140
Love, 242
Man Gone Down, 257
March, 112
Maxxed Out, 62
Moonlight hotel, 195
Mothers and Sons: Stories, 181
My Revolutions, 73
Netherland, 35–36
Now You See Him, 65–66

The Other, 217
Our Lady of Greenwich Village, 79
Out of My Skin, 218
Out Stealing Horses, 250
A Question of Attraction, 162
Rapids, 83
Rouse Up, O Young Men of the New Age,
   245–246
Saturday, 236
Shadow Country, 29–30
The Slide, 107
Songs for the Butcher's Daughter, 155
Storm Riders, 151–152
Sundown, Yellow Moon, 43–44
Sunnyside, 215–216
The Swallows of Kabul, 145
That Old Cape Magic, 171
Them, 30
Two Marriages, 231–232
Until I Find You, 142
Waveland, 6–7
We Are Now Beginning Our Descent, 158
Whirlwind, 69
The Whistling Season, 17–18
Willing, 176
The Yiddish Policeman's Union, 203–204
Mental Health
   Addiction, 143–144
   The Brothers Boswell, 50
   The Five-Forty-Five to Cannes, 22–23
   Iodine, 146
   Pharmakon, 95–96
   Rouse Up, O Young Men of the New Age,
      245–246
   The Secret Scripture, 198
   The Soul Thief, 106–107
   Storm Riders, 151–152
   Tomato Girl, 168
Mesopotamia
   Land of Marvels, 41–42
Meteorology
   Whirlwind, 69
Mexican Authors
   Into the Beautiful North, 42–43
   The Hummingbird's Daughter, 42
Mexico
   2666, 200
   Brownsville: Stories, 12
   Caramelo, 12–13
   Far Bright Star, 35
   Friday's Bed, 121
   The Guardians, 60

   The Hummingbird's Daughter, 42
   Into the Beautiful North, 42–43
   The Lacuna, 147
   The Sky Below, 207–208
   The Zigzag Way, 16
Michigan
   The Expeditions, 69
   Middlesex, 212
   Saul and Patsy, 106
Middle East, 72
   The Hakawati: A Story, 48
   I Think of You: Stories, 39
   Moonlight hotel, 195
   The Swallows of Kabul, 145
Midlife Crisis
   Bridge of Sighs, 170–171
   Cleaver, 166
   The English Major, 22
   Envy, 136
   I Smile Back, 148
   July, July, 244–245
   Laura Rider's Masterpiece, 135
   The Master Bedroom, 132
   Rapids, 83
   That Old Cape Magic, 171
   We Are Now Beginning Our Descent, 158
   Willing, 176
Midwest. *See* American Midwest
Military
   Beaufort, 27–28
   Callisto, 73
   Castle, 75–76
   The March, 209
Minnesota
   Falling Boy, 157
   July, July, 244–245
   Peace Like a River, 124–125
   The Rose Variations, 114
   The Sorrows of an American, 141
   Undiscovered Country, 19
Mississippi
   The End of California, 190
   Finn, 116
   The Help, 177
   Mudbound, 24
   Waveland, 6–7
   We Are Welcome Here, 55
Missouri
   The River Wife, 2
   The Slide, 107
Mohr, Max
   Mohr, 168–169

Monsters
    The Monsters of Templeton, 131
Montana
    The Eleventh Man, 119–120
    Labors of the Heart: Stories, 14
    The Whistling Season, 17–18
Montreal
    Garcia's Heart, 63
    Last Night in Montreal, 39–40
Morocco
    Leaving Tangier, 7
    This Blinding Absence of Light, 8
Mothers and Daughters. *See also* Family
        Relationships
    Admission, 148–149
    The Bad Mother's Handbook, 153–154
    Between Here and April, 72–73
    The Calligrapher's Daughter, 146
    Caspian Rain, 161–162
    The Cradle, 175
    Dervishes, 22
    Eventide, 136–137
    The Forgotten Garden, 80–81
    Gardenias, 178
    The Girl with No Shadow, 135
    Home Safe, 107–108
    The Lace Reader, 105–106
    The Laws of Harmony, 138
    Leaving Home, 111–112
    Life Without Water, 167
    The Master Bedroom, 132
    Nothing Is Quite Forgotten in Brooklyn,
        156
    The Owl & Moon Café, 155–156
    The Seamstress of Hollywood Boulevard,
        31
    The Sound of Us, 189
    The Story Sisters, 139
    There Is Room for You, 102
    The Uses of Enchantment, 224
    We Are Welcome Here, 55
    The Writing on My Forehead, 134
Mothers and Sons. *See also* Family
        Relationships
    The Age of Shiva, 178
    Buffalo Lockjaw, 2–3
    How the Dead Dream, 239
    The Lost Dog, 206–207
    Mothers and Sons: Stories, 181
    Red April, 86–87
    The Sky Below, 207–208
    Stand the Storm, 115

    Tomorrow, 179
    Until I Find You, 142
    WhateverMakes You Happy, 178–179
Mountains
    Five Skies, 11–12
Movies
    Based on the Movie, 180
    The Book of Illusions, 195–196
    Day, 225–226
    No Country for Old Men, 233
    The Seamstress of Hollywood Boulevard,
        31
    Snuff, 82
    Sunnyside, 215–216
    Ten Days in the Hills, 174–175
    Twenty Fragments of a Ravenous Youth,
        216–217
Multicultural
    The Age of Shiva, 178
    All That Matters, 12
    Atlas of Unknowns, 142–143
    The Attack, 72
    Birds without Wings, 14–15
    Blind Willow, Sleeping Woman, 243–244
    The Boat, 74–75
    Brick Lane, 99
    *Broccoli and Other Tales of Food and
        Love*, 258–259
    The Calligrapher's Daughter, 146
    Caspian Rain, 161–162
    The Cellist of Sarajevo, 20
    Dervishes, 22
    Fieldwork, 8–9
    Finding Nouf, 19–20
    The Ginseng Hunter, 40
    A Golden Age, 100
    The Groom to Have Been, 98
    The Hakawati: A Story, 48
    Haunting Bombay, 98
    He Drown She in the Sea, 160–161
    The Hungry Tide, 128–129
    The Inheritance of Loss, 118–119
    I Think of You: Stories, 39
    In Other Rooms, Other Wonders, 34
    The Kite Runner, 140–141
    Konkans, 122
    Little Bee, 115–116
    The Madonna of Excelsior, 31–32
    The Ministry of Special Cases, 125
    The Piano Teacher, 75
    The Plague of Doves, 125–126
    The Road Home, 182

Sea of Poppies, 215
Settlement, 67
Shanghai Girls, 173
The Size of the World, 38
The Swallows of Kabul, 145
Theft: Stories, 26
The Toss of a Lemon, 185–186
Train to Trieste, 36–37
Twenty Fragments of a Ravenous Youth,
    216–217
Unaccustomed Earth, 149–150
The Wasted Vigil, 100–101
The White Mary, 88
The White Tiger, 47–48
The Writing on My Forehead, 134
Multigenerational Fiction
    All That Matters, 12
    The Bad Mother's Handbook, 153–154
    Caramelo, 12–13
    Consequences, 152–153
    Eventide, 136–137
    Everything Is Illuminated, 212–213
    Follow Me, 172–173
    The Forgotten Garden, 80–81
    Gardenias, 178
    A Ghost at the Table, 108
    The History of Love, 149
    Hold Love Strong, 130
    The Inheritance of Loss, 118–119
    My Latest Grievance, 152
    The Owl & Moon Café, 155–156
    The Plague of Doves, 125–126
    Prodigal Summer, 25
    The River Wife, 2
    A Short History of Women, 186
    There Is Room for You, 102
    Three Junes, 128–129
    The Toss of a Lemon, 185–186
    Turtle Valley, 3
Multiple Viewpoints
    All That Road Going, 241
    Arlington Park, 117–118
    Arthur & George, 105
    Atonement, 235
    The Bad Mother's Handbook, 153–154
    Beautiful Dreamer, 199
    Birds without Wings, 14–15
    Blood Kin, 63
    Bridge of Sighs, 170–171
    The Brief Wondrous Life of Oscar Wao,
        208
    Bright Shiny Morning, 20

The Cellist of Sarajevo, 20
Censoring an Iranian Love Story, 233
The Condition, 133–134
The Cradle, 175
Crossing California, 26–27
Dervishes, 22
Divisadero, 246–247
Doctor Olaf van Schuler's Brain, 237
Downtown Owl, 147
Ellington Boulevard, 27
The End, 253
Everything Is Illuminated, 212–213
The Expeditions, 69
Follow Me, 172–173
The Forgotten Garden, 80–81
The Future of Love, 1
Gentlemen and Players, 66–67
The Ginseng Hunter, 40
The Great Man, 204
The Great Perhaps, 238
The Guardians, 60
Helpless, 130–131
Her Fearful Symmetry, 163
The History of Love, 149
The House on Fortune Street, 231
I See You Everywhere, 129
It's a Crime, 58
July, July, 244–245
Lark and Termite, 168
Last Night in Montreal, 39–40
Leaving Tangier, 7
Little Bee, 115–116
A Long Way Down, 140
Lost in the Forest, 159
A Mercy, 242–243
Mr. Sebastian and the Negro Magician,
    93–94
Mudbound, 24
My Name Is Red, 83
The News from Paraguay, 41
NoVA, 200
Olive Kitteridge, 177–178
The Owl & Moon Café, 155–156
People of the Book, 56
The Plague of Doves, 125–126
Prodigal Summer, 25
The Promised World, 183
Saving the World, 99–100
Security, 49
Settlement, 67
She Was, 134–135
A Short History of Women, 186

Multiple Viewpoints (*Cont.*)
   Skylight Confessions, 138–139
   Snuff, 82
   Songs for the Missing, 165
   Split Estate, 101–102
   The Story Sisters, 139
   Strivers Row, 5
   Sunnyside, 215–216
   Superpowers, 88–89
   Talk Talk, 110
   Telex from Cuba, 26
   The Thin Place, 205
   A Ticket to Ride, 157–158
   Trans-sister Radio, 55
   Tree of Smoke, 222–223
   The Wasted Vigil, 100–101
   A Week in October, 256
   WhateverMakes You Happy, 178–179
   What Was Lost, 164
   Who by Fire, 175–176
   The Women, 110–111
Murder
   *An Arsonist's Guide to Writers' Homes in
      New England*, 61–62
   The Butt: An Exit Strategy, 89–90
   Callisto, 73
   Detective Story, 71–72
   Draining the Sea, 29
   Fidali's Way, 78–79
   Finding Nouf, 19–20
   In the Kitchen, 48–49
   Interred with Their Bones, 58–59
   Kafka on the Shore, 244
   Lush Life, 85
   Maxxed Out, 62
   Now You See Him, 65–66
   The Outlander, 194
   A Person of Interest, 61
   Red April, 86–87
   Shadow Country, 29–30
   The Shadow Year, 64
   Star of the Sea, 82
   Sundown, Yellow Moon, 43–44
   The Taker: And Other Stories, 213–214
   The Tenderness of Wolves, 249
   The True History of the Kelly Gang, 58
   Undiscovered Country, 19
   The White Tiger, 47–48
   Without Blood, 197–198
   The Yiddish Policeman's Union, 203–204
   Zugzwang, 54

Music and Musicians
   The Answer Is Always Yes, 126–127
   Bass Cathedral, 232
   The Cellist of Sarajevo, 20
   The Clarinet Polka, 28–29
   Ellington Boulevard, 27
   The Good Fairies of New York, 158–159
   Mothers and Sons: Stories, 181
   The Piano Teacher, 75
   The Rose Variations, 114
   Suzy, Led Zeppelin, and Me, 32–33
   Sway, 228
   This One Is Mine, 173
   Three Minutes on Love, 138
Mystery
   Arthur & George, 105
   The Final Solution: A Story of Detection,
      203
   Gentlemen and Players, 66–67
   It's a Crime, 58
   The Labrador Pact, 132–133
   Red April, 86–87
   Sundown, Yellow Moon, 43–44
   Wit's End, 64
   The Yiddish Policeman's Union, 203–204
Mythology
   Salt, 247–248
   *The Tain: A New Translation of the Tain bo
      Cuailnge*, 59–60

National Book Award
   The Corrections, 127
   The Echo Maker, 250
   Europe Central, 259
   The Known World, 70
   The News from Paraguay, 41
   Shadow Country, 29–30
   Three Junes, 128–129
   Tree of Smoke, 222–223
   Veronica, 214
National Book Critics Circle Award
   2666, 200
   Atonement, 235
   Austerlitz, 253–254
   The Brief Wondrous Life of Oscar Wao,
      208
   Gilead, 251
   The Inheritance of Loss, 118–119
   The Known World, 70
   The March, 209
   The Pesthouse, 62–63

National Jewish Book Award
  Everything Is Illuminated, 212–213
  The Final Solution: A Story of Detection,
    203
  A Pigeon and a Boy, 91
  Portrait of My Mother, Who Posed Nude in
    Wartime: Stories, 252
  The Russian Debutante's Handbook, 255
  Songs for the Butcher's Daughter, 155
  The World To Come, 68
Native American Authors
  The Plague of Doves, 125–126
  Power, 220
Native Americans
  The Plague of Doves, 125–126
  Power, 220
Natural Disasters
  Daughters of the North, 66
  Sing Them Home, 144
  Turtle Valley, 3
Nebraska
  The Echo Maker, 250
  Sing Them Home, 144
Neurology
  The Echo Maker, 250
  Garcia's Heart, 63
Neuroscience
  Still Alice, 128
Nevada
  Scar Vegas: And Other Stories, 248
New England
  Admission, 148–149
  The Expeditions, 69
  Last Night at the Lobster, 164–165
  Old School, 190
  Olive Kitteridge, 177–178
  Tinkers, 218
  Until I Find You, 142
  The Uses of Enchantment, 224
New Hampshire
  Last Night in Twisted River, 142
New Jersey
  Admission, 148–149
  The Plot Against America, 87
New Mexico
  Far Bright Star, 35
  The Laws of Harmony, 138
  A Richer Dust, 10
New Orleans
  The Book of Getting Even, 179–180
New South Wales
  The Secret River, 21–22

New York
  Bridge of Sighs, 170–171
  Buffalo Lockjaw, 2–3
  Castle, 75–76
  A Mercy, 242–243
  The Monsters of Templeton, 131
  Sag Harbor, 187–188
  Trespass, 77–78
New York City
  The Answer Is Always Yes, 126–127
  Atlas of Unknowns, 142–143
  Away, 109
  Beat the Reaper, 51–52
  The Believers, 137
  Black Flies, 57
  Broccoli and Other Tales of Food and
    Love, 258–259
  Brooklyn, 40–41
  Chronic City, 229
  Diablerie, 81
  The Divine Husband, 130
  Doctor Olaf van Schuler's Brain, 237
  Ellington Boulevard, 27
  The Emperor's Children, 32
  The Essential Charlotte, 172
  Exit Ghost, 169–170
  Extremely Loud and Incredibly Close, 213
  Falling Man, 207
  The Family Man, 152
  Fortress of Solitude, 229–230
  The Future of Love, 1
  Girls in Trucks: Stories, 13–14
  The Good Fairies of New York, 158 159
  The Groom to Have Been, 98
  His Illegal Self, 113
  The History of Love, 149
  Hold Love Strong, 130
  The Inheritance of Loss, 118–119
  The Invention of Everything Else, 23
  Johnny One-Eye: A Tale of the American
    Revolution, 60–61
  The Kept Man, 101
  Last Night in Montreal, 39–40
  Let the Great World Spin, 30–31
  Lush Life, 85
  Man Gone Down, 257
  Maxxed Out, 62
  Netherland, 35–36
  Nothing Is Quite Forgotten in Brooklyn,
    156
  One Fifth Avenue, 11
  Our Lady of Greenwich Village, 79

New York City (*Cont.*)
  Sag Harbor, 187–188
  Schooled, 74
  The Sky Below, 207–208
  Skylight Confessions, 138–139
  Split Estate, 101–102
  Spoiled: Stories, 154
  Strivers Row, 5
  Symptomatic, 90–91
  Three Junes, 128–129
  Triangle, 187
  Veronica, 214
  The Writing on the Wall, 172
New York Times Notable
  2666, 200
  The Abstinence Teacher, 84
  American Wife, 174
  Atmospheric Disturbances, 215
  The Bad Girl, 185
  Bass Cathedral, 232
  Beasts of No Nation, 221–222
  Beautiful Children, 199
  A Better Angel: Stories, 194
  The Biographer's Tale, 113
  Black Flies, 57
  Black Swan Green, 160
  The Blue Star, 123–124
  The Boat, 74–75
  The Book of Illusions, 195–196
  Breath, 189–190
  Bridge of Sighs, 170–171
  The Brief Wondrous Life of Oscar Wao,
      208
  The Cave, 252–253
  Cloud Atlas, 240–241
  Dangerous Laughter: Stories, 239–240
  Dear American Airlines, 238–239
  Diary of a Bad Year, 205
  Dictation: A Quartet, 247
  Digging to America, 184
  Don't Tell Anyone: Fiction, 201
  Drinking Coffee Elsewhere, 165–166
  The Emperor's Children, 32
  The English Major, 22
  English Passengers, 25–26
  Envy, 136
  Exit Ghost, 169–170
  Fanon, 188
  Fine Just the Way It Is: Wyoming Stories 3, 36
  The Gathering, 211
  Gilead, 251
  His Illegal Self, 113
  Home, 251
  Indignation, 170
  The Inheritance of Loss, 118–119
  The Inquisitors' Manual, 3
  July, July, 244–245
  By the Lake, 156–157
  The Lazarus Project, 219
  Life Class, 104–105
  The Line of Beauty, 139–140
  Little Children, 167–168
  Love, 242
  Lush Life, 85
  The March, 209
  My Revolutions, 73
  Never Let Me Go, 221
  On Chesil Beach, 235–236
  Out Stealing Horses, 250
  The Plot Against America, 87
  Remainder, 234
  The Road Home, 182
  Runaway: Stories, 243
  The Russian Debutante's Handbook, 255
  Scar Vegas: And Other Stories, 248
  The Sea, 196
  The Shell Collector, 17
  Star of the Sea, 82
  Telex from Cuba, 26
  Tree of Smoke, 222–223
  Unaccustomed Earth, 149–150
  The Uses of Enchantment, 224
  Varieties of Disturbance: Stories, 206
  Vernon God Little, 84–85
  War Trash, 222
  Yesterday's Weather: Stories, 211–212
New Zealand Authors
  Mister Pip, 70–71
Noir
  Lush Life, 85
  Nobody Move, 69–70
North Carolina
  The Bible Salesman, 18
  The Road from Chapel Hill, 37
  Whirlwind, 69
North Dakota
  Downtown Owl, 147
  The Plague of Doves, 125–126
  Sundown, Yellow Moon, 43–44
North Korea
  The Ginseng Hunter, 40
Norway
  The Half Brother, 114–115
  Out Stealing Horses, 250

Willing, 176
Norwegian Authors
　The Half Brother, 114–115
Nova Scotia
　Someone Knows My Name, 67–68
Nursing Homes
　Buffalo Lockjaw, 2–3

Obesity
　The Little Giant of Aberdeen County, 102–103
　One Vacant Chair, 117
Ocean
　English Passengers, 25–26
　Sailors on the Inward Sea, 92
　Sea of Poppies, 215
　*Silver: My Own Tale as Written by Me with
　　a Goodly Amount of Murder,* 61
　Star of the Sea, 82
Ohio
　The End, 253
　Indignation, 170
　The Last of the Husbandmen, 28
　Songs for the Missing, 165
　The Sound of Us, 189
Oil
　Crawfish Mountain, 44
Ojibwas
　The Plague of Doves, 125–126
Oliveira Salazar, Antonio de
　The Inquisitors' Manual, 3
Ontario
　The Girls, 150–151
Opium
　Sea of Poppies, 215
Orange Prize
　The Road Home, 182
Oregon
　Storm Riders, 151–152
Organized Crime
　Beat the Reaper, 51–52
　Wonderful World, 202
Oslo
　Willing, 176
Ottoman Empire
　My Name Is Red, 83

Pacific Northwest
　Storm Riders, 151–152
Pakistan
　Brick Lane, 99
　Fidali's Way, 78–79
　In Other Rooms, Other Wonders, 34

The Writing on My Forehead, 134
Pakistani Authors
　In Other Rooms, Other Wonders, 34
　The Wasted Vigil, 100–101
Palestinians
　The Attack, 72
Papua New Guinea
　The White Mary, 88
Paraguay
　The News from Paraguay, 41
Parenting. *See also* Family Relationships
　The Abstinence Teacher, 84
　The Age of Shiva, 178
　Angels Crest, 89
　Arlington Park, 117–118
　The Bad Mother's Handbook, 153–154
　Beautiful Children, 199
　Between Here and April, 72–73
　Brother and Sister, 182
　The Cradle, 175
　The Garden of Last Days, 122–123
　Little Bee, 115–116
　Little Children, 167–168
　Love and Other Impossible Pursuits, 93
　My Latest Grievance, 152
　Nothing Right: Short Stories, 162
　Run, 166
　The Senator's Wife, 159–160
　Songs for the Missing, 165
　Tomorrow, 179
　The Writing on My Forehead, 134
　The Writing on the Wall, 172
Paris
　Chez Moi, 16–17
　The Girl with No Shadow, 135
　Leaving Home, 111–112
　Pictures at an Exhibition, 68
Parkinson's Disease
　The Corrections, 127
　A Ghost at the Table, 108
Pedophilia
　Crime, 94–95
　Helpless, 130–131
PEN-Faulkner Award
　Everyman, 252
　The Great Man, 204
　The March, 209
　Netherland, 35–36
　War Trash, 222
Pennsylvania
　Follow Me, 172–173
　Sister Mine, 163–164

Peru
  The Bad Girl, 185
  Red April, 86–87
Peruvian Authors
  The Bad Girl, 185
Pharmacology
  Pharmakon, 95–96
Philosophical Fiction
  The Cave, 252–253
  Genesis, 52
  Mercury Under My Tongue, 258
  The Philosopher's Apprentice, 80
Photography
  The People's Act of Love, 236–237
  The Shadow Catcher, 259–260
  Three Minutes on Love, 138
Pilots
  The Four Corners of the Sky, 154–155
Pirates
  *Silver: My Own Tale as Written by Me with
    a Goodly Amount of Murder,* 61
Poetry
  Mercury Under My Tongue, 258
Poland
  Songs for the Butcher's Daughter, 155
Polio
  We Are Welcome Here, 55
Political Fiction
  The Age of Shiva, 178
  *American Savior: A Novel of Divine
    Politics,* 79
  American Wife, 174
  *Beethoven Was One-Sixteenth Black: And
    Other Stories,* 216
  Blood Kin, 63
  Crawfish Mountain, 44
  The Darling, 103
  Detective Story, 71–72
  The Divine Husband, 130
  Draining the Sea, 29
  Fanon, 188
  Garcia's Heart, 63
  The Inheritance of Loss, 118–119
  The Inquisitors' Manual, 3
  The Line of Beauty, 139–140
  Moonlight hotel, 195
  My Revolutions, 73
  The News from Paraguay, 41
  Our Lady of Greenwich Village, 79
  The Plot Against America, 87
  Red April, 86–87

Rouse Up, O Young Men of the New Age,
    245–246
Run, 166
The Senator's Wife, 159–160
She Was, 134–135
A Student of Living Things, 91–92
Supreme Courtship, 56–57
The Swallows of Kabul, 145
The White King, 210
Zugzwang, 54
Pop Culture
  Chronic City, 229
  Pygmy, 248–249
  Sway, 228
  Wonderful World, 202
Pornography
  Snuff, 82
Portugal
  The Inquisitors' Manual, 3
Portuguese Authors
  The Cave, 252–253
  The Inquisitors' Manual, 3
Poverty
  Half Broke Horses, 186–187
  Hold Love Strong, 130
  Strivers Row, 5
Prague
  Austerlitz, 253–254
Prep Schools
  Old School, 190
Presidents
  American Wife, 174
Priests
  The Secret Scripture, 198
Prisoners of War
  Day, 225–226
  War Trash, 222
Prisons
  The Hour I First Believed, 150
  The Promise of Happiness, 113–114
  This Blinding Absence of Light, 8
  War Trash, 222
Private Schools
  The Uses of Enchantment, 224
Profanity
  The Book of Dahlia, 99
  NoVA, 200
  Peace, 51
  Vernon God Little, 84–85
Professions
  Based on the Movie, 180

The Cave, 252–253
Five Skies, 11–12
Kings of Infinite Space, 221
The Seamstress of Hollywood Boulevard, 31
Twenty Fragments of a Ravenous Youth, 216–217
Prostitution
   Draining the Sea, 29
   Johnny One-Eye: A Tale of the American Revolution, 60–61
   Lovely Green Eyes, 76–77
   Willing, 176
Psychics
   The Grift, 65
Psychological Fiction
   2666, 200
   An Arsonist's Guide to Writers' Homes in New England, 61–62
   Angels Crest, 89
   The Answer Is Always Yes, 126–127
   Atmospheric Disturbances, 215
   The Attack, 72
   Beasts of No Nation, 221–222
   Blood Kin, 63
   The Book of Illusions, 195–196
   The Book of Murder, 78
   The Brothers Boswell, 50
   Castle, 75–76
   Cleaver, 166
   Disquiet, 229
   Double Vision, 104
   Envy, 136
   Finding Nouf, 19–20
   Gentlemen and Players, 66–67
   A Ghost at the Table, 108
   Haunting Bombay, 98
   His Illegal Self, 113
   Iodine, 146
   Kings of Infinite Space, 221
   The Lace Reader, 105–106
   The Last Secret, 80
   The Little Stranger, 94
   A Map of Glass, 184–185
   Never Let Me Go, 221
   Peace, 51
   The People's Act of Love, 236–237
   The Pesthouse, 62–63
   Pharmakon, 95–96
   Red April, 86–87
   Sailors on the Inward Sea, 92
   Security, 49

Serena, 85–86
The Shadow Year, 64
The Sorrows of an American, 141
The Soul Thief, 106–107
Still Alice, 128
The Story Sisters, 139
Symptomatic, 90–91
This Blinding Absence of Light, 8
Tinkers, 218
The Uses of Enchantment, 224
Vanilla Bright Like Eminem: Stories, 212
Water Dogs, 86
The White Mary, 88
Wonderful World, 202
Zugzwang, 54
Pulitzer Prize
   The Brief Wondrous Life of Oscar Wao, 208
   Gilead, 251
   The Known World, 70
   Middlesex, 212
   Olive Kitteridge, 177–178
   The Road, 234

Quebec
   Last Night in Montreal, 39–40
Quick Reads
   Addition, 143–144
   All That Road Going, 241
   All the Living, 241–242
   Andy Catlett: Early Travels, 9
   The Attack, 72
   Beasts of No Nation, 221–222
   Beat the Reaper, 51–52
   Beautiful Dreamer, 199
   Black Flies, 57
   Blood Kin, 63
   The Book of Getting Even, 179–180
   The Book of Murder, 78
   Breath, 189–190
   Broccoli and Other Tales of Food and Love, 258–259
   The Cave, 252–253
   The Cellist of Sarajevo, 20
   Cheating at Canasta: Stories, 258
   The Cradle, 175
   The Curious Incident of the Dog in the Night-Time, 131–132
   Dear American Airlines, 238–239
   Dear Husband: Stories, 81
   Detective Story, 71–72
   Diary of a Bad Year, 205

Quick Reads (*Cont.*)

Dictation: A Quartet, 247
Disquiet, 229
Do Not Deny Me: Stories, 180–181
Double Vision, 104
The Driftless Area, 121–122
The English Major, 22
The Essential Charlotte, 172
Everyman, 252
Everything Ravaged, Everything Burned, 181–182
Falling Boy, 157
Far Bright Star, 35
The Final Solution: A Story of Detection, 203
Fine Just the Way It Is: Wyoming Stories 3, 36
Firmin: Adventures of a Metropolitan Lowlife, 171
The First Person: And Other Stories, 255–256
Five Skies, 11–12
Friday's Bed, 121
Genesis, 52
The Ginseng Hunter, 40
The Girl on the Fridge, 226
The Good Fairies of New York, 158–159
The Guernsey Literary and Potato Peel Pie Society, 37–38
A Guide to the Birds of East Africa, 18
Hairdos of the Mildly Depressed, 117
Hannah Coulter, 9–10
Home Safe, 107–108
The Housekeeper and the Professor, 245–246
How the Dead Dream, 239
I Smile Back, 148
In Other Rooms, Other Wonders, 34
Indignation, 170
Iodine, 146
It's a Crime, 58
Labors of the Heart: Stories, 14
The Last Chinese Chef, 33–34
Last Night at the Lobster, 164–165
Laura Rider's Masterpiece, 135
The Lemon Table: Stories, 197
Life Without Water, 167
Little Bee, 115–116
Love and Obstacles: Stories, 220
The Madonnas of Leningrad, 15
Man in the Dark, 49–50
The Map Thief, 92

A Mercy, 242–243
Mr. Sebastian and the Negro Magician, 93–94
My Latest Grievance, 152
Nobody Move, 69–70
Old School, 190
On Chesil Beach, 235–236
The One Marvelous Thing, 210–211
Ordinary Genius, 4–5
Out of My Skin, 218
Peace, 51
The Plot Against America, 87
Popular Music from Vittula, 34–35
Power, 220
Pygmy, 248–249
Red Car, 108–109
The Road, 234
Scar Vegas: And Other Stories, 248
Serve the People!, 230
The Shell Collector, 17
Silver: My Own Tale as Written by Me with a Goodly Amount of Murder, 61
Skylight Confessions, 138–139
Snuff, 82
Spoiled: Stories, 154
The Stone Gods, 95
Superpowers, 88–89
Supreme Courtship, 56–57
Suzy, Led Zeppelin, and Me, 32–33
The Swallows of Kabul, 145
The Taker: And Other Stories, 213–214
That Old Cape Magic, 171
The Thin Place, 205
Tinkers, 218
Twenty Fragments of a Ravenous Youth, 216–217
Two Marriages, 231–232
The Uncommon Reader, 53–54
Vanessa & Virginia, 254
The View from the Seventh Layer, 201
Water Dogs, 86
Waveland, 6–7
A Week in October, 256
WhateverMakes You Happy, 178–179
What Was She Thinking? Notes On a Scandal, 137
The White Tiger, 47–48
Willful Creatures: Stories, 198
Without Blood, 197–198
The Zigzag Way, 16

Quilting

Stand the Storm, 115

Race Relations
    Andy Catlett: Early Travels, 9
    Beethoven Was One-Sixteenth Black: And
        Other Stories, 216
    Cloud Atlas, 240–241
    The Darling, 103
    The Deportees and Other Stories, 209
    Drinking Coffee Elsewhere, 165–166
    Fanon, 188
    Finn, 116
    Fortress of Solitude, 229–230
    The Help, 177
    The Known World, 70
    Konkans, 122
    The Madonna of Excelsior, 31–32
    Man Gone Down, 257
    March, 112
    A Mercy, 242–243
    More Than It Hurts You, 256
    Mudbound, 24
    The Road from Chapel Hill, 37
    Sag Harbor, 187–188
    Stand the Storm, 115
    Strivers Row, 5
    Them, 30
    We Are Welcome Here, 55
Racism
    Arthur & George, 105
    Beautiful Dreamer, 199
    Drinking Coffee Elsewhere, 165–166
    He Drown She in the Sea, 160–161
    Strivers Row, 5
Rape
    Female Trouble: A Collection of Short
        Stories, 244
    The Half Brother, 114–115
    The Soul Thief, 106–107
Rats
    Firmin: Adventures of a Metropolitan
        Lowlife, 171
Recipes
    Broccoli and Other Tales of Food and
        Love, 258–259
Refugees
    The Boat, 74–75
    The History of Love, 149
    Settlement, 67
Religion
    The Abstinence Teacher, 84
    All the Living, 241–242
    American Savior: A Novel of Divine
        Politics, 79

    The Bible Salesman, 18
    A Country Called Home, 5–6
    Drinking Coffee Elsewhere, 165–166
    Fieldwork, 8–9
    The Hummingbird's Daughter, 42
    Konkans, 122
    Our Lady of Greenwich Village, 79
    Songs for the Butcher's Daughter, 155
    The Swallows of Kabul, 145
    The Voyage of the Short Serpent, 210
Restaurants
    Chez Moi, 16–17
    In the Kitchen, 48–49
    The Inheritance of Loss, 118–119
    Last Night at the Lobster, 164–165
    Midnight at the Dragon Café, 50–51
    The Owl & Moon Café, 155–156
Retail
    How to Sell, 77
    Last Night at the Lobster, 164–165
    What Was Lost, 164
Revenge
    Serena, 85–86
Reykjavik
    Willing, 176
Riots
    Strivers Row, 5
Rivera, Diego
    The Lacuna, 147
Rivers
    Rapids, 83
Road Novels
    All That Road Going, 241
    The Bible Salesman, 18
    The English Major, 22
Romance
    Addition, 143–144
    The Essential Charlotte, 172
    The Romantics, 162–163
Romania
    Train to Trieste, 36–37
    The White King, 210
Rome
    Lavinia, 228
Royalty
    The Uncommon Reader, 53–54
Runaways
    Beautiful Children, 199
    The Uses of Enchantment, 224
Rural Life. *See also* Small-town Life
    All the Living, 241–242
    Andy Catlett: Early Travels, 9

Rural Life (*Cont.*)
August, 45
A Country Called Home, 5–6
The Echo Maker, 250
Hannah Coulter, 9–10
In the Fold, 118
The Last of the Husbandmen, 28
Mudbound, 24
Russia
Away, 109
City of Thieves, 53
The Madonnas of Leningrad, 15
The People's Act of Love, 236–237
Zugzwang, 54
Russian Americans
The Russian Debutante's Handbook, 255

S. Mariella Gable Prize
One Vacant Chair, 117
Salem
The Heretic's Daughter, 71
The Lace Reader, 105–106
San Francisco
Three Minutes on Love, 138
Veronica, 214
Sarajevo
The Cellist of Sarajevo, 20
Satire. *See also* Humor
American Savior: A Novel of Divine Politics, 79
Any Human Heart, 109–110
The Biographer's Tale, 113
The Butt: An Exit Strategy, 89–90
Callisto, 73
Cleaver, 166
Crumbtown, 13
Dangerous Laughter: Stories, 239–240
Dear American Airlines, 238–239
How to Sell, 77
Intercourse: Stories, 201–202
It's a Crime, 58
Laura Rider's Masterpiece, 135
Man in the Dark, 49–50
Maxxed Out, 62
Moonlight hotel, 195
More Than It Hurts You, 256
The One Marvelous Thing, 210–211
Our Lady of Greenwich Village, 79
Peyton Amberg, 143
Pygmy, 248–249
The Russian Debutante's Handbook, 255
Samuel Johnson Is Indignant: Stories, 206

Security, 49
Serve the People!, 230
Supreme Courtship, 56–57
Ten Days in the Hills, 174–175
This One Is Mine, 173
Varieties of Disturbance: Stories, 206
Vernon God Little, 84–85
Whirlwind, 69
Willful Creatures: Stories, 198
Willing, 176
Saudi Arabia
Finding Nouf, 19–20
School Shootings
The Hour I First Believed, 150
Science
Genesis, 52
The Great Perhaps, 238
The Hungry Tide, 128–129
Science Fiction
The Baum Plan for Financial Independence, 226
Daughters of the North, 66
Genesis, 52
Kings of Infinite Space, 221
Man in the Dark, 49–50
Never Let Me Go, 221
The Philosopher's Apprentice, 80
The Road, 234
The Stone Gods, 95
Scotiabank Giller Prize
Runaway: Stories, 243
Scotland
Kieron Smith, Boy, 225
One Vacant Chair, 117
Suzy, Led Zeppelin, and Me, 32–33
Three Junes, 128–129
Scottish Authors
Crime, 94–95
The First Person: And Other Stories, 255–256
The Good Fairies of New York, 158–159
The House on Fortune Street, 231
Kieron Smith, Boy, 225
Suzy, Led Zeppelin, and Me, 32–33
Seamstresses
The Seamstress of Hollywood Boulevard, 31
Seattle
Away, 109
Sendales y Gómez, Doña Isabel
Saving the World, 99–100
Serial Killers
A Person of Interest, 61
The Shadow Year, 64

Seville
   People of the Book, 56
Sewing
   Stand the Storm, 115
Sex Offenders
   Little Children, 167–168
Sexual Abuse. *See also* Abuse
   The Gathering, 211
   The Story Sisters, 139
Sexuality
   Lost in the Forest, 159
   On Chesil Beach, 235–236
   The Sweet In-Between, 169
   Trans-sister Radio, 55
Shakespeare, William
   Interred with Their Bones, 58–59
   Undiscovered Country, 19
Sherman, William Tecumseh
   The March, 209
Short Stories. *See also* Interconnected Stories
   *The Baum Plan for Financial
      Independence,* 226
   *Beethoven Was One-Sixteenth Black: And
      Other Stories,* 216
   A Better Angel: Stories, 194
   Blind Willow, Sleeping Woman, 243–244
   The Boat, 74–75
   *Broccoli and Other Tales of Food and
      Love,* 258–259
   Brownsville: Stories, 12
   Cheating at Canasta: Stories, 258
   Collected Stories (Shields), 254–255
   The Complete Stories (Malouf), 232
   Dangerous Laughter: Stories, 239–240
   Dear Husband: Stories, 81
   Delinquent Virgin: Wayward Pieces,
      224–225
   The Deportees and Other Stories, 209
   Do Not Deny Me: Stories, 180–181
   Don't Tell Anyone: Fiction, 201
   Drinking Coffee Elsewhere, 165–166
   Everything Ravaged, Everything Burned,
      181–182
   *Female Trouble: A Collection of Short
      Stories,* 244
   Fine Just the Way It Is: Wyoming Stories 3,
      36
   The First Person: And Other Stories,
      255–256
   The Five-Forty-Five to Cannes, 22–23
   The Girl on the Fridge, 226
   Intercourse: Stories, 201–202

I Sailed with Magellan, 123
I Think of You: Stories, 39
In Other Rooms, Other Wonders, 34
Labors of the Heart: Stories, 14
The Lemon Table: Stories, 197
Love and Obstacles: Stories, 220
Mothers and Sons: Stories, 181
A Multitude of Sins, 214
Nothing Right: Short Stories, 162
The One Marvelous Thing, 210–211
Ordinary Genius, 4–5
*Our Story Begins: New and Selected
   Stories,* 260
Popular Music from Vittula, 34–35
*Portrait of My Mother, Who Posed Nude in
   Wartime: Stories,* 252
Red Car, 108–109
Runaway: Stories, 243
Samuel Johnson Is Indignant: Stories, 206
Scar Vegas: And Other Stories, 248
The Shell Collector, 17
Spoiled: Stories, 154
Theft: Stories, 26
The Turning: New Stories, 44
Unaccustomed Earth, 149–150
Vanilla Bright Like Eminem: Stories, 212
Varieties of Disturbance: Stories, 206
The View from the Seventh Layer, 201
Willful Creatures: Stories, 198
Yesterday's Weather: Stories, 211–212
Siamese Twins
   The Girls, 150–151
Siblings. *See also* Family Relationships
   Alva & Irva: The Twins Who Saved a City,
      202–203
   Apologize, Apologize!, 145
   Atlas of Unknowns, 142–143
   The Believers, 137
   Broken, 204–205
   Brother and Sister, 182
   Buffalo Lockjaw, 2–3
   The Clarinet Polka, 28–29
   The Condition, 133–134
   The Corrections, 127
   Divisadero, 246–247
   The Echo Maker, 250
   Envy, 136
   The Gathering, 211
   The Girls, 150–151
   A Golden Age, 100
   The Half Brother, 114–115
   Her Fearful Symmetry, 163

Siblings (*Cont.*)
  Home, 251
  How to Sell, 77
  I See You Everywhere, 129
  The Killing Jar, 33
  Lark and Termite, 168
  Leaving Tangier, 7
  The Little Giant of Aberdeen County,
      102–103
  Once Removed, 191
  Peace Like a River, 124–125
  The Promised World, 183
  The Promise of Happiness, 113–114
  The Rope Walk, 112
  Sag Harbor, 187–188
  The Shadow Year, 64
  Shanghai Girls, 173
  Sing Them Home, 144
  Sister Mine, 163–164
  Songs for the Missing, 165
  The Story Sisters, 139
  A Student of Living Things, 91–92
  This One Is Mine, 173
  Vanessa & Virginia, 254
  The World To Come, 68
  The Writing on My Forehead, 134
  The Writing on the Wall, 172
Sierra Leone
  Someone Knows My Name, 67–68
Silver, Long John
  Silver: My Own Tale as Written by Me with
      a Goodly Amount of Murder, 61
Single Mothers
  Helpless, 130–131
  Lost in the Forest, 159
Sisters. *See also* Family Relationships;
    Siblings
  Alva & Irva: The Twins Who Saved a City,
      202–203
  Atlas of Unknowns, 142–143
  Broken, 204–205
  Brooklyn, 40–41
  Divisadero, 246–247
  The Girls, 150–151
  Her Fearful Symmetry, 163
  I See You Everywhere, 129
  The Little Giant of Aberdeen County,
      102–103
  Shanghai Girls, 173
  Sister Mine, 163–164
  Songs for the Missing, 165
  The Story Sisters, 139

  Vanessa & Virginia, 254
  The Writing on My Forehead, 134
  The Writing on the Wall, 172
Slavery
  The Known World, 70
  A Mercy, 242–243
  The Road from Chapel Hill, 37
  Someone Knows My Name, 67–68
  Stand the Storm, 115
Small Press
  All about Lulu, 126
  All That Road Going, 241
  The Baum Plan for Financial
      Independence, 226
  Black Flies, 57
  The Book of Getting Even, 179–180
  Castle, 75–76
  Delinquent Virgin: Wayward Pieces,
      224–225
  The End, 253
  The End of the World Book, 234–235
  Famous Suicides of the Japanese Empire,
      161
  Firmin: Adventures of a Metropolitan
      Lowlife, 171
  Gardenias, 178
  The Good Fairies of New York, 158–159
  The House of Widows: An Oral History,
      237
  How the Dead Dream, 239
  I Smile Back, 148
  Last Night in Montreal, 39–40
  The Last of the Husbandmen, 28
  Mercury Under My Tongue, 258
  Miniatures, 227–228
  Mohr, 168–169
  One Vacant Chair, 117
  Out Stealing Horses, 250
  A Richer Dust, 10
  Samuel Johnson Is Indignant: Stories, 206
  Serve the People!, 230
  Three Minutes on Love, 138
  Tinkers, 218
  A Week in October, 256
Small-town Life. *See also* Rural Life
  American Wife, 174
  Bridge of Sighs, 170–171
  By the Lake, 156–157
  The Clarinet Polka, 28–29
  A Country Called Home, 5–6
  Downtown Owl, 147
  The End of California, 190

Eventide, 136–137
Labors of the Heart: Stories, 14
The Little Giant of Aberdeen County,
    102–103
Midnight at the Dragon Café, 50–51
Popular Music from Vittula, 34–35
The Rope Walk, 112
Saul and Patsy, 106
Security, 49
Sing Them Home, 144
The Thin Place, 205
Smuggling
    Into the Beautiful North, 42–43
Social Class
    Atonement, 235
    Brownsville: Stories, 12
    Crossing California, 26–27
    Detective Story, 71–72
    The Elegance of the Hedgehog, 103–104
    He Drown She in the Sea, 160–161
    The Hungry Tide, 128–129
    Kieron Smith, Boy, 225
    Konkans, 122
    The Line of Beauty, 139–140
    Lush Life, 85
    More Than It Hurts You, 256
    On Chesil Beach, 235–236
    One Fifth Avenue, 11
    Paula Spencer, 120
    Spoiled: Stories, 154
Society
    All That Road Going, 241
    Dangerous Laughter: Stories, 239–240
    Daughters of the North, 66
    Dear Husband: Stories, 81
    Don't Tell Anyone: Fiction, 201
    Nothing Right: Short Stories, 162
    Pygmy, 248–249
    The Taker: And Other Stories, 213–214
    Twenty Fragments of a Ravenous Youth,
        216–217
    Vanilla Bright Like Eminem: Stories, 212
    The Women, 110–111
South. *See* American South
South Africa
    *Beethoven Was One-Sixteenth Black: And
        Other Stories*, 216
    The Madonna of Excelsior, 31–32
South African Authors
    *Beethoven Was One-Sixteenth Black: And
        Other Stories*, 216
    Diary of a Bad Year, 205

The Madonna of Excelsior, 31–32
South America
    The Taker: And Other Stories, 213–214
South Asia
    A Golden Age, 100
South Carolina
    Serena, 85–86
    Someone Knows My Name, 67–68
Southern Authors
    Red Car, 108–109
    The Sweet In-Between, 169
    Waveland, 6–7
Soviet Union
    The People's Act of Love, 236–237
Spain
    The Angel's Game, 87
    Leaving Tangier, 7
    Wonderful World, 202
Spanish Authors
    Wonderful World, 202
Spirituality. *See also* Religion
    Gilead, 251
    Home, 251
Sports
    The Eleventh Man, 119–120
    The Post-Birthday World, 174
Stepfamilies
    All That Matters, 12
    Family Matters, 240
    Love and Other Impossible Pursuits, 93
    Once Removed, 191
Storms
    Angels Crest, 89
Strokes
    Turtle Valley, 3
Suburbia
    The Abstinence Teacher, 84
    Arlington Park, 117–118
    Beautiful Children, 199
    Broken, 204–205
    I Smile Back, 148
    Little Children, 167–168
    NoVA, 200
    Now You See Him, 65–66
Suicide
    Famous Suicides of the Japanese Empire,
        161
    The Gathering, 211
    Between Here and April, 72–73
    The House of Widows: An Oral History,
        237
    The House on Fortune Street, 231

Suicide (Cont.)
  I See You Everywhere, 129
  A Long Way Down, 140
  Miniatures, 227–228
  NoVA, 200
  Now You See Him, 65–66
  Pharmakon, 95–96
  The Promised World, 183
  Saul and Patsy, 106
  Split Estate, 101–102
Superheroes
  Falling Boy, 157
  Fortress of Solitude, 229–230
  Superpowers, 88–89
Surfing
  Breath, 189–190
Survival
  Fidali's Way, 78–79
  Rapids, 83
  The Road, 234
  This Blinding Absence of Light, 8
Suspense
  Angels Crest, 89
  The Angel's Game, 87
  Beat the Reaper, 51–52
  Beautiful Dreamer, 199
  Blood Kin, 63
  The Blue Manuscript, 226–227
  The Book of Murder, 78
  The Brothers Boswell, 50
  Castle, 75–76
  Crime, 94–95
  Diablerie, 81
  Double Vision, 104
  The End of California, 190
  Fieldwork, 8–9
  Finding Nouf, 19–20
  Garcia's Heart, 63
  The Garden of Last Days, 122–123
  Gentlemen and Players, 66–67
  Helpless, 130–131
  Between Here and April, 72–73
  His Illegal Self, 113
  Interred with Their Bones, 58–59
  Iodine, 146
  The Lace Reader, 105–106
  Land of Marvels, 41–42
  The Last Secret, 80
  Lush Life, 85
  The Map Thief, 92
  Maxxed Out, 62
  The Monsters of Templeton, 131

  My Revolutions, 73
  No Country for Old Men, 233
  Novel about My Wife, 249
  Now You See Him, 65–66
  The Other, 217
  A Person of Interest, 61
  The Pesthouse, 62–63
  Rapids, 83
  A Reliable Wife, 21
  Serena, 85–86
  Settlement, 67
  The Shadow Year, 64
  She Was, 134–135
  The Soul Thief, 106–107
  Star of the Sea, 82
  A Student of Living Things, 91–92
  Symptomatic, 90–91
  Talk Talk, 110
  Trespass, 77–78
  Undiscovered Country, 19
  Water Dogs, 86
  A Week in October, 256
  Zugzwang, 54
Sweden
  Popular Music from Vittula, 34–35

Taliban
  The Swallows of Kabul, 145
  The Wasted Vigil, 100–101
Tasmania
  English Passengers, 25–26
Taylor, Charles
  The Darling, 103
Teachers
  The Abstinence Teacher, 84
  Saul and Patsy, 106
  *What Was She Thinking? Notes On a
    Scandal*, 137
  The Whistling Season, 17–18
Technology
  Genesis, 52
Teenage Boys. *See also* Teenagers
  All about Lulu, 126
  The Answer Is Always Yes, 126–127
  Beautiful Children, 199
  Black Swan Green, 160
  Breath, 189–190
  City of Thieves, 53
  *The Curious Incident of the Dog in the
    Night-Time*, 131–132
  Downtown Owl, 147
  The Guardians, 60

Indignation, 170
Kafka on the Shore, 244
The Master Bedroom, 132
Mercury Under My Tongue, 258
Old School, 190
Over and Under, 183
Popular Music from Vittula, 34–35
Sag Harbor, 187–188
Sundown, Yellow Moon, 43–44
The Turning: New Stories, 44
Vernon God Little, 84–85
*What Was She Thinking? Notes On a
    Scandal*, 137
Teenage Girls. *See also* Teenagers
All about Lulu, 126
The Bad Mother's Handbook, 153–154
Broken, 204–205
Dervishes, 22
The Elegance of the Hedgehog, 103–104
Everything Ravaged, Everything Burned,
    181–182
A Ghost at the Table, 108
The History of Love, 149
How to Buy a Love of Reading, 64–65
Into the Beautiful North, 42–43
Lost in the Forest, 159
Lovely Green Eyes, 76–77
Middlesex, 212
My Latest Grievance, 152
Power, 220
Songs for the Missing, 165
Split Estate, 101–102
The Sweet In-Between, 169
A Ticket to Ride, 157–158
The Uses of Enchantment, 224
Veronica, 214
Teenagers
All about Lulu, 126
The Answer Is Always Yes, 126–127
The Bad Mother's Handbook, 153–154
Beautiful Children, 199
Black Swan Green, 160
Breath, 189–190
Broken, 204–205
City of Thieves, 53
Crossing California, 26–27
*The Curious Incident of the Dog in the
    Night-Time*, 131–132
Downtown Owl, 147
The Elegance of the Hedgehog, 103–104
Everything Ravaged, Everything Burned,
    181–182

Falling Boy, 157
A Ghost at the Table, 108
The Great Perhaps, 238
The Guardians, 60
The History of Love, 149
How to Buy a Love of Reading, 64–65
Into the Beautiful North, 42–43
Kafka on the Shore, 244
The Killing Jar, 33
A Long Way Down, 140
Lost in the Forest, 159
Lovely Green Eyes, 76–77
Lush Life, 85
The Master Bedroom, 132
Mercury Under My Tongue, 258
Middlesex, 212
Mister Pip, 70–71
My Latest Grievance, 152
NoVA, 200
Old School, 190
Over and Under, 183
Popular Music from Vittula, 34–35
Power, 220
Rapids, 83
Sag Harbor, 187–188
Schooled, 74
Songs for the Missing, 165
Split Estate, 101–102
Sundown, Yellow Moon, 43–44
The Sweet In-Between, 169
A Ticket to Ride, 157–158
Tomorrow, 179
The Turning: New Stories, 44
The Uses of Enchantment, 224
Vernon God Little, 84–85
Veronica, 214
*What Was She Thinking? Notes On a
    Scandal*, 137
Television
Whirlwind, 69
Tennessee
Beautiful Dreamer, 199
Terrorism
The Attack, 72
Beaufort, 27–28
Falling Man, 207
The Garden of Last Days, 122–123
My Revolutions, 73
A Student of Living Things, 91–92
Tesla, Nikola
Addition, 143–144
The Invention of Everything Else, 23

Texas
    Based on the Movie, 180
    Brownsville: Stories, 12
    How to Sell, 77
    No Country for Old Men, 233
    One Vacant Chair, 117
    Vernon God Little, 84–85
Thailand
    Fieldwork, 8–9
Theater
    Interred with Their Bones, 58–59
Theft
    Talk Talk, 110
Time Travel
    The Invention of Everything Else, 23
Torgi Literary Award
    Family Matters, 240
Tornadoes
    Sing Them Home, 144
Toronto
    Helpless, 130–131
    Last Night in Twisted River, 142
Torture
    Detective Story, 71–72
    Draining the Sea, 29
    Garcia's Heart, 63
Travel
    All That Road Going, 241
    Any Human Heart, 109–110
    The Bad Girl, 185
    Book of Clouds, 4
    The Cradle, 175
    Dear American Airlines, 238–239
    Dervishes, 22
    The English Major, 22
    English Passengers, 25–26
    Fidali's Way, 78–79
    Fieldwork, 8–9
    The Five-Forty-Five to Cannes, 22–23
    The House of Widows: An Oral History,
        237
    The Hungry Tide, 128–129
    Interred with Their Bones, 58–59
    The Last Chinese Chef, 33–34
    Miniatures, 227–228
    One Vacant Chair, 117
    Peyton Amberg, 143
    Rapids, 83
    Silver: My Own Tale as Written by Me with
        a Goodly Amount of Murder, 61
    The Size of the World, 38

    Talk Talk, 110
    There Is Room for You, 102
    Until I Find You, 142
    We Are Now Beginning Our Descent, 158
    The White Mary, 88
    Willing, 176
Trials
    The Butt: An Exit Strategy, 89–90
    The Heretic's Daughter, 71
    Power, 220
Trillium Book Award
    Helpless, 130–131
Trotsky, Leon
    The Lacuna, 147
Turkey
    Birds without Wings, 14–15
    Dervishes, 22
    My Name Is Red, 83
Twain, Mark
    Finn, 116
Twins. *See also* Siblings
    The Girls, 150–151
    Her Fearful Symmetry, 163

Ukraine
    The House of Widows: An Oral History, 237
Unions
    Over and Under, 183
Unreliable Narrator
    The Angel's Game, 87
    Atmospheric Disturbances, 215
    Atonement, 235
    Beat the Reaper, 51–52
    The Book of Murder, 78
    The Brothers Boswell, 50
    Caramelo, 12–13
    The Darling, 103
    Glover's Mistake, 74
    In the Kitchen, 48–49
    Iodine, 146
    The Kindly Ones, 230–231
    The Lace Reader, 105–106
    A Reliable Wife, 21
    Salt, 247–248
    Settlement, 67
    Silver: My Own Tale as Written by Me with
        a Goodly Amount of Murder, 61
    Sundown, Yellow Moon, 43–44
    What Was She Thinking? Notes On a
        Scandal, 137
    The White Tiger, 47–48

Vancouver
  All That Matters, 12
Venice
  People of the Book, 56
Vermont
  The Book of Illusions, 195–196
  I See You Everywhere, 129
  Last Night in Twisted River, 142
  Man in the Dark, 49–50
  The Rope Walk, 112
  Saving the World, 99–100
  Trans-sister Radio, 55
Victorian
  Arthur & George, 105
  The Master, 257
  A Richer Dust, 10
Vienna
  People of the Book, 56
Vietnam
  Tree of Smoke, 222–223
Vietnam War
  The Boat, 74–75
  The Clarinet Polka, 28–29
  Let the Great World Spin, 30–31
  Life Without Water, 167
  My Revolutions, 73
  She Was, 134–135
  Tree of Smoke, 222–223
Villa, Pancho
  Far Bright Star, 35
Violence
  Beasts of No Nation, 221–222
  Beaufort, 27–28
  Beautiful Dreamer, 199
  Black Flies, 57
  Broken, 204–205
  Bucking the Tiger, 246
  Dear Husband: Stories, 81
  Double Vision, 104
  Draining the Sea, 29
  Far Bright Star, 35
  Fidali's Way, 78–79
  A Golden Age, 100
  The Have-Nots, 217–218
  The Killing Jar, 33
  The Kindly Ones, 230–231
  Mister Pip, 70–71
  Nobody Move, 69–70
  No Country for Old Men, 233
  Peace, 51
  A Person of Interest, 61

Pygmy, 248–249
Remainder, 234
The Road, 234
The Secret River, 21–22
Star of the Sea, 82
The Taker: And Other Stories, 213–214
The Voyage of the Short Serpent, 210
The White King, 210
The White Mary, 88
Without Blood, 197–198
Virginia
  The Known World, 70
  NoVA, 200
  The Sweet In-Between, 169

Wales
  August, 45
  The Master Bedroom, 132
War
  Beasts of No Nation, 221–222
  Birds without Wings, 14–15
  Castle, 75–76
  The Cellist of Sarajevo, 20
  Detective Story, 71–72
  Double Vision, 104
  Draining the Sea, 29
  Fanon, 188
  Far Bright Star, 35
  Fidali's Way, 78–79
  Garcia's Heart, 63
  A Golden Age, 100
  The House of Widows: An Oral History, 237
  Johnny One-Eye: A Tale of the American Revolution, 60–61
  The Kite Runner, 140–141
  Life Class, 104–105
  Man in the Dark, 49–50
  March, 112
  The Ministry of Special Cases, 125
  Mister Pip, 70–71
  Moonlight hotel, 195
  The People's Act of Love, 236–237
  The Piano Teacher, 75
  A Pigeon and a Boy, 91
  The Size of the World, 38
  The Tain: A New Translation of the Tain bo Cuailnge, 59–60
  A Thousand Splendid Suns, 141
  The Wasted Vigil, 100–101
  We Are Now Beginning Our Descent, 158
  Without Blood, 197–198

Washington
    Labors of the Heart: Stories, 14
    The Other, 217
Washington, D.C.
    DuPont Circle, 24
    Stand the Storm, 115
    A Student of Living Things, 91–92
    Supreme Courtship, 56–57
Weather
    Angels Crest, 89
    Downtown Owl, 147
    A Map of Glass, 184–185
    Sing Them Home, 144
West. *See* American West
West Virginia
    The Clarinet Polka, 28–29
    Lark and Termite, 168
Westerns
    Bucking the Tiger, 246
    Far Bright Star, 35
    Fine Just the Way It Is: Wyoming Stories 3,
        36
    *The James Boys: A Novel Account of Four
        Desperate Brothers*, 76
    No Country for Old Men, 233
    Territory, 57
    The Whistling Season, 17–18
Whitbread Award. *See also* Costa Novel
        Award
    *The Curious Incident of the Dog in the
        Night-Time*, 131–132
Widowers
    Aloft, 151
    Digging to America, 184
    A Guide to the Birds of East Africa, 18
    The Sea, 196
Widows
    Digging to America, 184
    A Golden Age, 100
    A Guide to the Birds of East Africa, 18
    Hannah Coulter, 9–10
    Home Safe, 107–108
    Lost in the Forest, 159
    The Outlander, 194
    Paula Spencer, 120
Wilderness
    The Outlander, 194
Wisconsin
    American Wife, 174
    The Cradle, 175
    Laura Rider's Masterpiece, 135
    A Reliable Wife, 21

    Superpowers, 88–89
    The Women, 110–111
    You're Not You, 188–189
Witchcraft
    The Heretic's Daughter, 71
Women Authors
    Addition, 143–144
    Admission, 148–149
    All That Road Going, 241
    All the Living, 241–242
    American Wife, 174
    Angels Crest, 89
    The Answer Is Always Yes, 126–127
    Apologize, Apologize!, 145
    Arlington Park, 117–118
    Atlas of Unknowns, 142–143
    Atmospheric Disturbances, 215
    Away, 109
    The Bad Mother's Handbook, 153–154
    *Beethoven Was One-Sixteenth Black: And
        Other Stories*, 216
    The Believers, 137
    Between Here and April, 72–73
    The Biographer's Tale, 113
    Blood Kin, 63
    The Blue Manuscript, 226–227
    Book of Clouds, 4
    The Book of Dahlia, 99
    Brick Lane, 99
    *Broccoli and Other Tales of Food and
        Love*, 258–259
    Brother and Sister, 182
    The Calligrapher's Daughter, 146
    Caramelo, 12–13
    Caspian Rain, 161–162
    Chez Moi, 16–17
    Collected Stories (Shields), 254–255
    The Condition, 133–134
    Consequences, 152–153
    A Country Called Home, 5–6
    Darkmans, 196–197
    Daughters of the North, 66
    Day, 225–226
    Dear Husband: Stories, 81
    Delinquent Virgin: Wayward Pieces,
        224–225
    Dervishes, 22
    Dictation: A Quartet, 247
    Digging to America, 184
    Disquiet, 229
    Do Not Deny Me: Stories, 180–181
    Double Vision, 104

Draining the Sea, 29
Drinking Coffee Elsewhere, 165–166
The Elegance of the Hedgehog, 103–104
The Emperor's Children, 32
Envy, 136
The Essential Charlotte, 172
Falling Boy, 157
The Family Man, 152
Female Trouble: A Collection of Short Stories, 244
Finding Nouf, 19–20
Fine Just the Way It Is: Wyoming Stories 3, 36
The First Person: And Other Stories, 255–256
The Five-Forty-Five to Cannes, 22–23
Follow Me, 172–173
The Forgotten Garden, 80–81
Friday's Bed, 121
The Future of Love, 1
Gardenias, 178
The Gathering, 211
Gentlemen and Players, 66–67
A Ghost at the Table, 108
Gilead, 251
The Girl with No Shadow, 135
The Girls, 150–151
Girls in Trucks: Stories, 13–14
A Golden Age, 100
The Great Man, 204
The Grift, 65
The Guardians, 60
The Guernsey Literary and Potato Peel Pie Society, 37–38
Half Broke Horses, 186–187
Haunting Bombay, 98
He Drown She in the Sea, 160–161
The Help, 177
Helpless, 130–131
The Heretic's Daughter, 71
Her Fearful Symmetry, 163
Home, 251
Home Safe, 107–108
The Housekeeper and the Professor, 245–246
The House on Fortune Street, 231
How to Buy a Love of Reading, 64–65
I See You Everywhere, 129
I Smile Back, 148
I Think of You: Stories, 39
In the Fold, 118
In the Kitchen, 48–49

Inglorious, 144–145
The Inheritance of Loss, 118–119
Interred with Their Bones, 58–59
The Invention of Everything Else, 23
Iodine, 146
It's a Crime, 58
The Kept Man, 101
The Killing Jar, 33
Labors of the Heart: Stories, 14
The Lace Reader, 105–106
The Lacuna, 147
Landing, 120
Lark and Termite, 168
The Last Chinese Chef, 33–34
Last Night in Montreal, 39–40
The Last Secret, 80
Laura Rider's Masterpiece, 135
Lavinia, 228
The Laws of Harmony, 138
Leaving Home, 111–112
Life Class, 104–105
Life Without Water, 167
The Little Giant of Aberdeen County, 102–103
The Lost Dog, 206–207
Lost in the Forest, 159
Love, 242
Love and Other Impossible Pursuits, 93
The Madonnas of Leningrad, 15
A Map of Glass, 184–185
The Map Thief, 92
March, 112
The Master Bedroom, 132
A Mercy, 242–243
Miniatures, 227–228
The Monsters of Templeton, 131
Mudbound, 24
My Latest Grievance, 152
The News from Paraguay, 41
Nothing Is Quite Forgotten in Brooklyn, 156
Nothing Right: Short Stories, 162
Novel about My Wife, 249
Olive Kitteridge, 177–178
Once Removed, 191
One Fifth Avenue, 11
The One Marvelous Thing, 210–211
The Outcast, 223
The Outlander, 194
The Owl & Moon Café, 155–156
People of the Book, 56
A Person of Interest, 61

Women Authors (*Cont.*)
Peyton Amberg, 143
The Piano Teacher, 75
The Plague of Doves, 125–126
*Portrait of My Mother, Who Posed Nude in
    Wartime: Stories*, 252
The Post-Birthday World, 174
Power, 220
Prodigal Summer, 25
The Promised World, 183
Red Car, 108–109
A Richer Dust, 10
The River Wife, 2
The Road from Chapel Hill, 37
The Road Home, 182
The Romantics, 162–163
The Rope Walk, 112
The Rose Variations, 114
Run, 166
Runaway: Stories, 243
Samuel Johnson Is Indignant: Stories, 206
Saving the World, 99–100
Schooled, 74
The Seamstress of Hollywood Boulevard,
    31
The Secret River, 21–22
The Senator's Wife, 159–160
The Shadow Catcher, 259–260
Shanghai Girls, 173
She Was, 134–135
A Short History of Women, 186
Sing Them Home, 144
Sister Mine, 163–164
The Size of the World, 38
The Sky Below, 207–208
Skylight Confessions, 138–139
The Sorrows of an American, 141
The Sound of Us, 189
Split Estate, 101–102
Spoiled: Stories, 154
Stand the Storm, 115
Still Alice, 128
The Stone Gods, 95
The Story Sisters, 139
A Student of Living Things, 91–92
The Sweet In-Between, 169
Symptomatic, 90–91
Telex from Cuba, 26
Ten Days in the Hills, 174–175
The Tenderness of Wolves, 249
Territory, 57
Theft: Stories, 26

There Is Room for You, 102
This One Is Mine, 173
Three Junes, 128–129
Three Minutes on Love, 138
A Ticket to Ride, 157–158
Tomato Girl, 168
The Toss of a Lemon, 185–186
Train to Trieste, 36–37
Trespass, 77–78
Triangle, 187
Turtle Valley, 3
Twenty Fragments of a Ravenous Youth,
    216–217
Unaccustomed Earth, 149–150
Up High in the Trees, 111
The Uses of Enchantment, 224
Vanessa & Virginia, 254
Varieties of Disturbance: Stories, 206
Veronica, 214
The Vine of Desire, 119
We Are Welcome Here, 55
A Week in October, 256
What Was Lost, 164
*What Was She Thinking? Notes On a
    Scandal*, 137
The White Mary, 88
Who by Fire, 175–176
Willful Creatures: Stories, 198
Wit's End, 64
The World To Come, 68
The Writing on My Forehead, 134
The Writing on the Wall, 172
Yesterday's Weather: Stories, 211–212
You're Not You, 188–189
The Zigzag Way, 16
Women Writing as Men. *See also* Men
    Writing as Women
Angels Crest, 89
The Answer Is Always Yes, 126–127
Apologize, Apologize!, 145
Day, 225–226
Draining the Sea, 29
Envy, 136
Gentlemen and Players, 66–67
Gilead, 251
    In the Fold, 118

In the Kitchen, 48–49
The Lacuna, 147
March, 112
Novel about My Wife, 249
The Outcast, 223
Pictures at an Exhibition, 68

The Road Home, 182
Run, 166
The Secret River, 21–22
Trespass, 77–78
Women's Fiction
   Addition, 143–144
   American Wife, 174
   Away, 109
   Brick Lane, 99
   Brother and Sister, 182
   The Condition, 133–134
   Dervishes, 22
   Digging to America, 184
   The Essential Charlotte, 172
   The Future of Love, 1
   Gardenias, 178
   Girls in Trucks: Stories, 13–14
   The Girl with No Shadow, 135
   Haunting Bombay, 98
   The Help, 177
   Between Here and April, 72–73
   Home Safe, 107–108
   I See You Everywhere, 129
   I Think of You: Stories, 39
   The Lace Reader, 105–106
   Lark and Termite, 168
   The Laws of Harmony, 138
   The Little Giant of Aberdeen County,
      102–103
   Lost in the Forest, 159
   Love and Other Impossible Pursuits, 93
   Nothing Is Quite Forgotten in Brooklyn,
      156
   Olive Kitteridge, 177–178
   The Owl & Moon Café, 155–156
   Prodigal Summer, 25
   The Promised World, 183
   Runaway: Stories, 243
   The Seamstress of Hollywood Boulevard,
      31
   The Senator's Wife, 159–160
   Shanghai Girls, 173
   A Short History of Women, 186
   Sing Them Home, 144
   Sister Mine, 163–164
   Skylight Confessions, 138–139
   Spoiled: Stories, 154
   Still Alice, 128
   The Story Sisters, 139
   Ten Days in the Hills, 174–175
   There Is Room for You, 102
   A Thousand Splendid Suns, 141

Three Junes, 128–129
The Toss of a Lemon, 185–186
The Vine of Desire, 119
The Writing on the Wall, 172
You're Not You, 188–189
Woolf, Virginia
   Vanessa & Virginia, 254
Work Relationships
   Based on the Movie, 180
   Black Flies, 57
   Book of Clouds, 4
   Chez Moi, 16–17
   Five Skies, 11–12
   In the Kitchen, 48–49
   Inglorious, 144–145
   Kings of Infinite Space, 221
   Last Night at the Lobster, 164–165
   The Yiddish Policeman's Union, 203–204
World History
   Any Human Heart, 109–110
   The People's Act of Love, 236–237
World War I
   Divisadero, 246–247
   Life Class, 104–105
   Sailors on the Inward Sea, 92
   Sunnyside, 215–216
World War II
   All That Matters, 12
   Atonement, 235
   Austerlitz, 253–254
   The Blue Star, 123–124
   The Calligrapher's Daughter, 146
   City of Thieves, 53
   Consequences, 152–153
   Day, 225–226
   The Eleventh Man, 119–120
   Europe Central, 259
   Famous Suicides of the Japanese Empire,
      161
   Gardenias, 178
   *The Guernsey Literary and Potato Peel Pie
      Society*, 37–38
   The Half Brother, 114–115
   The House of Widows: An Oral History,
      237
   The Kindly Ones, 230–231
   The Lacuna, 147
   Lovely Green Eyes, 76–77
   The Madonnas of Leningrad, 15
   Mohr, 168–169
   Out Stealing Horses, 250
   Peace, 51

World War II (*Cont.*)
   The Piano Teacher, 75
   Pictures at an Exhibition, 68
   The Plot Against America, 87
   Settlement, 67
Wright, Frank LLoyd
   The Women, 110–111
Writers and Writing
   All the Sad Young Literary Men, 128
   The Angel's Game, 87
   Any Human Heart, 109–110
   The Biographer's Tale, 113
   The Brothers Boswell, 50
   Exit Ghost, 169–170
   A Ghost at the Table, 108
   The History of Love, 149
   Home Safe, 107–108
   The Lacuna, 147
   Last Night in Twisted River, 142
   Laura Rider's Masterpiece, 135
   The Master, 257
   Maxxed Out, 62
   Miniatures, 227–228
   Old School, 190
   A Richer Dust, 10
   Sailors on the Inward Sea, 92
   Saving the World, 99–100
   Vanessa & Virginia, 254
   Willing, 176
   Wit's End, 64
Wyoming
   Fine Just the Way It Is: Wyoming Stories 3,
      36
   Split Estate, 101–102

YA
   All about Lulu, 126
   The Angel's Game, 87
   The Answer Is Always Yes, 126–127
   The Bible Salesman, 18
   Black Swan Green, 160
   The Book of Murder, 78
   The Brief Wondrous Life of Oscar Wao,
      208
   Caramelo, 12–13
   City of Thieves, 53
   Crossing California, 26–27
   *The Curious Incident of the Dog in the
      Night-Time,* 131–132
   Daughters of the North, 66
   The Elegance of the Hedgehog, 103–104
   Falling Boy, 157

Finding Nouf, 19–20
Genesis, 52
The Girl on the Fridge, 226
The Good Fairies of New York, 158–159
The Heretic's Daughter, 71
How to Buy a Love of Reading, 64–65
Into the Beautiful North, 42–43
*Johnny One-Eye: A Tale of the American
    Revolution,* 60–61
Lavinia, 228
Mercury Under My Tongue, 258
Mister Pip, 70–71
Mudbound, 24
Never Let Me Go, 221
Over and Under, 183
Peace Like a River, 124–125
The Philosopher's Apprentice, 80
Power, 220
*Silver: My Own Tale as Written by Me with
    a Goodly Amount of Murder,* 61
Superpowers, 88–89
Suzy, Led Zeppelin, and Me, 32–33
Tree of Smoke, 222–223
Undiscovered Country, 19
Young Boys
   His Illegal Self, 113
   Kieron Smith, Boy, 225
Young Girls
   Caramelo, 12–13
Young Men
   All the Sad Young Literary Men, 128
   The Answer Is Always Yes, 126–127
   Beaufort, 27–28
   The Biographer's Tale, 113
   The Blue Star, 123–124
   The Book of Getting Even, 179–180
   The Brief Wondrous Life of Oscar Wao,
      208
   Buffalo Lockjaw, 2–3
   The Clarinet Polka, 28–29
   Downtown Owl, 147
   The Driftless Area, 121–122
   Fieldwork, 8–9
   Hold Love Strong, 130
   How the Dead Dream, 239
   How to Sell, 77
   Indignation, 170
   The Last of the Husbandmen, 28
   The Line of Beauty, 139–140
   Lush Life, 85
   The Outcast, 223
   The Philosopher's Apprentice, 80

A Question of Attraction, 162
The Russian Debutante's Handbook, 255
The Slide, 107
Songs for the Butcher's Daughter, 155
Superpowers, 88–89
Suzy, Led Zeppelin, and Me, 32–33
Trespass, 77–78
Water Dogs, 86
WhateverMakes You Happy, 178–179

Young Women
  Book of Clouds, 4
  The Essential Charlotte, 172
  Girls in Trucks: Stories, 13–14
  The Monsters of Templeton, 131
  Superpowers, 88–89
  You're Not You, 188–189
  The Zigzag Way, 16
Yugoslavia
  The Cellist of Sarajevo, 20

About the Authors

Nancy Pearl speaks about the pleasures of reading to library and community groups throughout the world and comments on books regularly on NPR's *Morning Edition*, as well as public radio stations in Tulsa, Seattle, Minneapolis, and Milwaukee. In addition to *Now Read This* and *Now Read This II*, she's the author of *Book Crush: For Kids and Teens: Recommended Reading for Every Mood, Moment, and Interest*; *Book Lust: Recommended Reading for Every Mood, Moment, and Reason*; *More Book Lust: 1,000 New Reading Recommendations for Every Mood, Moment, and Reason*, and the forthcoming *Book Lust to Go*, all published by Sasquatch Books. In 2004 she was awarded the Women's National Book Association Award, given to "a living American woman who . . . has done meritorious work in the world of books beyond the duties or responsibilities of her profession or occupation." In 1998 *Library Journal* named her Fiction Reviewer of the Year. She is the model for the Librarian Action Figure. On her monthly television show, *Book Lust with Nancy Pearl*, she has interviewed authors as diverse as E. L. Doctorow, Ann Patchett, and Terry Pratchett.

Sarah Statz Cords has worked for the Madison Public Library and the University of Wisconsin-Madison Engineering Library in Wisconsin. She is the author of *Public Speaking Handbook for Librarians and Information Professionals* (McFarland), *The Real Story: A Guide to Nonfiction Reading Interests* (Libraries Unlimited), and *The Inside Scoop: A Guide to Nonfiction Investigative Writing and Exposés* (Libraries Unlimited). She has taught on the reading interests of adults at the University of Wisconsin-Madison, is an associate editor for the Reader's Advisor Online, reviews books for *Library Journal*, and writes primarily nonfiction book reviews and hosts online book groups at her Web site, Citizen Reader (citizenreader.com). After working with her, she is more starstruck than ever by Nancy Pearl.